ESKIA

Education

African Humanism & Culture

Social Consciousness

Literary Appreciation

Es'kia Mphahlele

Kwela Books
in association with
Stainbank & Associates

The Es'kia Mphahlele Project, of which this book is a part,
is a concept created, researched, developed and managed by
Stainbank & Associates (Pty) Ltd.

This initiative was made possible by Eskom.

www.eskiaonline.com

Stainbank & Associates (Pty) Ltd
and The Es'kia Institute
Private Bag X63, Rivonia, Johannesburg 2128

Kwela Books, P.O. Box 6525, Roggebaai, Cape Town 8012

Cover photograph by Siphiwe Mlambi
Cover design by Stainbank & Associates (Pty) Ltd
Title Es'kia ™ by Mike Stainbank
Typography by Abdul Amien
Set in Berkeley Old Style
Printed and bound by CTP Book Printers, Parow, Cape Town,
South Africa
First edition, first printing 2002

ISBN 0-7957-0151-9 (hardcover)
ISBN 0-7957-0152-7 (softcover)

Dedication

Humbly dedicated to all writers, students, cultural workers, teachers and nation builders who may, I trust, savour these thoughts and draw from what import they derive the inspiration for the tasks of the moment and the years ahead.

A NOTE OF THANKS

I thank my friend Mike Stainbank of Stainbank & Associates, publisher, who immediately took up my casual suggestion that I would be happy to see my papers in print. Thanks for his unremitting drive in planning and executing this project. Thanks to my friends who willingly accepted our request that they form an editorial panel: James Ogude, Sam Raditlhalo, Ndavhe Ramakuela, Marcus Ramogale, Peter Thuynsma – all of them academics. Thanks also to Phaswane Mpe who researched some of the references for listing in the final stages of production.

The editors gave up their time to examine the material before them, and in progressive stages selected the best in order of first, second, and third preference for this book. Thanks also to Rebecca, who journeyed with me in and out of exile, bearing with my scholastic and literary obsessions as a wife and companion. Thanks to all who have enriched my life in many ways in the past sixty years, making me recognise culture as a communally lived and shared identity. I thank my beloved, lifelong friend, the late Khabi Mngoma (Professor of Music), for the influence he had on me as a cultural activist and creator of music, for his warmth, generosity, love of life, his friendship and unique loyalty. Even in his absence from our midst, the memory of him continues to sanctify the pursuit of those truths about our cultural being which, with our intellect and activism, we explored together. Thanks also to Peter Thuynsma, whose love and companionship and intellectual enrichment I have always drawn on in our quest for those other profound truths out of which education is woven, stitch after stitch upon stitch.

A special word of gratitude goes to Eskom for their generous sponsorship, and to Reuel Khoza and Thulani Gcabashe in its top executive ranks for their encouragement, which gave this project its impetus. Thanks also to Premier Mgoako Ramatlhodi and the people of the Limpopo Province for their contribution to the launch.

ES'KIA MPHAHLELE

A NOTE TO THE READER

Citations

As a number of the papers in this book were not intended for publication – some were not even intended for circulation in hard copy – full citation details were not always included, as would be usual in academic writing. The reader will find, then, that some passages and excerpts from poems appear without page numbers, although names of authors and years of publication have, whenever possible, been provided. For publication details, the reader must go the Selected Bibliography. Here, where certain information could not be located, the following have been used to indicate this: *nd* = date of publication missing; *np* = place of publication missing; or simply, *publication details could not be located*.

Because of the impossibility of tracking everything down, there are one or two passages and poetry excerpts the accuracy of which (wording and/or line breaks) could not be double-checked. We regret this, and trust that the reader will appreciate the difficulty of our task.

For our research, we relied on Professor Es'kia Mphahlele's personal library in Lebowakgomo, the Es'kia Mphahlele Centre for African Studies at the University of Venda for Science and Technology, and the libraries of the University of the Witwatersrand in Johannesburg. We are grateful to Professor Mphahlele and the library staff in the two academic institutions for their assistance.

Gender Sensitivity

Social consciousness will often overtake literary conventions. Consider that many of these essays were written in a period preceding gender sensitivity, as reflected in the use of masculine pronouns, 'man' and 'mankind' instead of more inclusive words. The editorial team acknowledges that such language is inappropriate and may be found offensive. However, the decision was taken to retain the original text; this was felt to be more authentic than retroactively 'fixing' the language according to our current understanding and awareness of the issues.

THE EDITORIAL PANEL

CONTENTS

FOREWORD

The dictum that people of exceptional intellectual, creative and spiritual power are twenty-five or even fifty years ahead of their time rings true for Emeritus Professor Es'kia Mphahlele, especially when one considers his long, illustrious and even exacting contribution to the human family in Africa and the world at large.

This foreword to his anthology of critical essays is really more a humble eulogy to the man, Es'kia; to his beautiful, gifted wife and faithful partner, Rebecca; and to the Mphahlele dynasty, which includes ordinary women, men and young folk who drank (and still drink), in different times and ways, from the inexhaustible well of this great, compassionate being called Es'kia.

Scholar, literary luminary, iconoclast, social activist, folk hero, cultural and artistic icon and humanist to the nth degree, Es'kia Mphahlele continues to exemplify that prophetic *honnête homme* quality of essence and vision that characterised the lives of America's legendary Sojourner Truth and the eminent W E B DuBois, author, thinker and harbinger. Luminaries such as Kwegyir Aggrey (1874-1927), Sol T Plaatje (1874-1932) and Archibald Jordan (1906-1968) should also be counted in the list of heroes who in some ways also cast their aura on Es'kia's journey towards fulfilment.

And although Mphahlele's life as scholar, educationist, author, and cultural and social activist was imbued with the endearing and enduring qualities of those radiant thinkers, he was also his own man – asserting vigorously, but humbly, his deep passion and quest for personal independence, for freedom of expression, and even for the exultation of his self over the impediments and traps of race and religion. A self that was burnished in the foundries of alienation and exile; a self that yearned to live in a free and caring world, among free and caring people.

Like so many of his scholarly contemporaries of darker hue, Mphahlele, for all his learning and vision, was not immune to the evils of racists, who relegated both scholar and serf to the level of half-being because of the colour of their skins. Mphahlele and his family could not endure such subservience and binding humiliation, and chose exile in the full knowledge that the same idiosyncrasies waited for them abroad. It is a long time gone, and many painful memories have since flowed under the bridge of time.

The respected compilers of this lucid and expansive anthology of Mphahlele's critical essays tell us succinctly that they want to 'introduce readers to Mphahlele the scholar' – a mission superbly achieved, and a perspective of him I always knew existed.

However, unlike the compilers, I did not enjoy the boon of his direct academic tutelage; mine was a furtive admiration through the distant windows of the Mphahlele classroom in exile, full of fanciful conjecture. On his return to his native land, I was blessed to drink from his fountain. I committed myself to joining his growing flock, feeding on the store of his vast knowledge and experience, drinking from the sap of his charitable spirit, secure in the guidance of his wisdom. I have since been a seeker among thousands, emulating the shepherd-teacher and taking his rod and staff to continue the Mphahlele legacy of *Ubuntu, Botho.*

His family home in Limpopo has become a sanctuary and source of replenishment for literary and scholarly research and cultural exchange. Es'kia the sagacious scholar, social and cultural activist, caring one, humanist, compelling orator, sage, has always marched side by side with Es'kia the questioning social rebel. And like in all such great and compassionate seers, there resides in him – through his works, his thoughts and deeds – a finding, prophetic voice, filled with truth and love, ready to rebuke when called upon, for all those who care to listen.

DON MATTERA

INTRODUCTION

This project began with Es'kia Mphahlele inviting five of us – James Ogude, Marcus Ramogale, Sam Raditlhalo, Ndavhe Ramakuela and Peter Thuynsma – to edit and compile a collection of his critical writings. Each of us was assigned some twenty-five essays, from which to select ten. A month later we had made our selections and we met once again, this time to justify our choices and to consider the contours of the publication. From long hours of debate there emerged four categories which construct veritable facets of Es'kia Mphahlele, the socio-literary critic: Education, African Humanism, Social Consciousness and Literary Appreciation.

We had not only set out to select a healthy handful of essays, we had also set ourselves an unusual task. We had each passed through Es'kia Mphahlele's tutelage, and we had developed a driving desire to share something of our experience of his classroom warmth, his ever-curious intellect, his deep concern for humankind, and his ingenious turn of phrase (he recently equated an attempt to solve an impossible puzzle with 'trying to kiss one's elbow'!)

Many a reader (and re-reader) will engage Mphahlele's theories. Several will find it difficult to relate the opinions to their earlier contexts. Some will disagree, perhaps even disagree vehemently, but through all these intellectual processes Mphahlele will continue to shape our consciousness as he has for the better part of his eighty-odd years of life.

Quite uniquely, his teaching has never been confined or constrained to the four walls of a class- or lecture room.

At the back of this book is an overview of Mphahlele's prowess as a prolific creative writer. From this, it might not be obvious that he is also highly regarded as a practising literary and cultural commentator. It is therefore the business of this volume to introduce readers to Mphahlele the scholar. Our focus here is to select benchmark works from the many stand-alone essays and public addresses. Some of the work included in this volume has often found its way into larger collections, magazines or in academic journals – but the majority of articles collected here have not seen publication.

We must reiterate the need to see Mphahlele's work in its larger context. So, before we look at the essays in this volume, let's first take a quick glance at his published academic essays, which have been presented in three collections.

His thesis for the Master of Arts degree in 1957 was awarded cum laude, and was expanded and published in 1962 as *The African Image*.[1] (A revised edition was issued twelve years later under the same title.) The candid approach with which he examines the many facets of race gives the work remarkable authority, and the relaxed exploration is also a formal version of his search for a definition of self. He does not aim at anything entirely objective but represents, instead, the options and attitudes that determine possible choices. In doing so he mirrors the image of the black man and the personality behind the image. His view of the francophone African philosophy, Negritude, provoked important debates at the time it became a particular socio-cultural concern, leading to major redefinitions. In essence, he confronted an aspect of black pride and pronounced it inadequate.

In *The African Image* he is free of the demands of fiction, but Mphahlele does not cut loose from his characteristic stance: he insists on the personal dimension. Here is yet another search for his true communal value – for the validity of his black personality.

Voices in the Whirlwind and Other Essays[2] appeared in 1972, during his second residence in Colorado. (Retitled here as *My Destiny is Tied to Africa.*) The title essay, the first of six, works through a personal definition of poetry and its meaning. His approach, characteristically, is that of a teacher, and he mentions some of his classroom techniques in teaching poetry appreciation. His premise is that poetry is a state of mind, and he goes on to view African and African-American poetry in relation to Western thought vis-à-vis Christopher Caudwell, Lawrence Lerner and I A Richards's respective theories of literary function and aesthetics. The third essay, *Implications of Color Identity in Pan-Africanism*, was the only one to be published for the first time in this collection. In it he looks at the possibilities for unifying blacks and again touches on Negritude. But any optimism that this collection of essays may have engendered is more or less smothered in the closing lines of its last essay, *Censorship in Africa*, which captures the depths of his disillusionment with the entire South African social fabric:

> *While the Bantu writer is afraid of the written law of censorship, because he is naturally afraid of arrest, detention, and banning, the Afrikaner writer is afraid of both the written law and the sanctions of the tribe, which operate deep down in the subconscious.*

Apart from these two collections, there is the vast number of Mphahlele's critical articles and public addresses scattered about in major journals – and of course a large number have been left unpublished. Most were penned in exile, and exile is a prominent theme. But there are also countless lectures, both major and minor, and a host of journalistic exercises. These are all listed in a comprehensive, if not exhaustive, bibliography published in 1989 by the South African *National English Literary Museum (NELM)* and updated in 2000.

The works that we have collected in this volume attempt to complete the profile of this prolific writer-commentator and provide readers with a startlingly prophetic voice, despite the burden of exile in some cases; in others there is the strident voice that celebrates a new political freedom, or a voice that, with trepidation, anticipates the educational needs of a fledgling democracy. Threadbare and hackneyed as it seemed during the early stages, we found ourselves reluctant to let go of the working title for this collection: *Es'kia – the Time is Now!* It captured the essence and the thrust of what we were about: to appreciate the very texture of his intellectual frustrations, and to revel in the sheer pertinence and appropriateness of what our teacher had said long ago. His time is as much now as it was then.

The selected articles display a daring intellect and a deeply insightful mind, expressed in a richly idiomatic eloquence that all five of us drooled over as students and continue to imbibe today. We have grouped the articles into four categories: Education, African Humanism & Culture, Social Consciousness and Literary Appreciation. Let's look briefly at the salience of each:

TRANS. TO ACCL

and he does so loudly and resound-
ly inimitable, with a dilating voice
ttle when he reads lines from a dirge.
on an eager audience. So too is the
congregation of community workers.
ce is Mphahlele the teacher – a vital
ls the works that are collected in this
ust full throat, and all the while the
hat this is not an imposed series of
es ideas, touches, rubs, caresses all
pes away the veneer for a peek at the

category. These essays explore, indict
g a critical look at the potential of the
kei, or slapping the University of the
ngness to evolve into a truly African
ngratulatory, and are based on a firm
to that of the apartheid State or
ed in history and proclaim a simple
the appropriate education, they will
e of a society.
vs on transforming society. Here he
tion – education for a whole person.
ith as much conviction as he does at
asily from Socrates to Christianity, as
v democracy such as South Africa. Or,
to the Commission on Education in
voicing concerns that are as pertinent
nya shrugging off its colonial yoke.
tive teaching. It is imperative that the
 and as compellingly as possible.

Mphahlele the teacher draws on his own varied canvas of experience. As in his litera-ture, *the dialogue of two selves* is a pervasive metaphor as he grapples with the past and the present. Writing that began by addressing the oppressor, in present times engages more immediately constructive principles and purposes of learning. So it is not at all out of place to have healthy draughts of poetry illustrating educational notions. If personal experience is critical mass here, then it is as representative of the experience of a people – not that of a private individual. And, if it is the collective experience of a people that is vital to Mphahlele's teachings, then it is culture and way of life that is the paramount illustrator.

African Humanism & Culture

To champion an aspect of culture presupposes a philosophical foundation; for Mphahlele it is African Humanism – a more realistic, more practical interpretation of the contentious Negritude of the early 1960s. Mphahlele was a fiery provocateur of Senghor's romantic vision of what constituted 'African', and he wrote bristling counter-arguments at the time. But not simply to contend for the sake of contention, Mphahlele hewed a concept of what is African and of what Africans should expect of themselves as Africans, in his subscription to African Humanism.

Although not as prolific in his publications on humanism as he is on other topics, this section is inextricably linked to both the preceding category of Education and to the Social Consciousness category that follows. Here the history of a continent becomes crit-ical and indeed a mainstay. The *Ubuntu* proclamation that 'I am because we are' is his inevitable starting point, and the titles of the essays are self-evident, ranging from *The Fabric of African Culture* to *Your History Demands Your Heartbeat*.

The thinking in this section on African Humanism is radical. Mphahlele's distrust of organised religion is palpable, and Christianity's coercion in the name of evangelism bears the brunt of his scorn. Yet there is again the dialogue of two selves, between the expediency of West and the indigenous wisdom of Africa. He negotiates the rejection of the individualist principle and reasserts the development of the full human potential in community service.

Social Consciousness

Earlier in this introduction I said that the four categories which form the framework for this volume sketch a veritable profile of Mphahlele the scholar. By this I also meant to include Mphahlele the person, for in this section we see Mphahlele the activist at work. Whether he is to be seen as a political activist or a cultural activist is not for us to deter-mine here. Amusingly, he once said that his body itches from all the labels that have been stuck on him over the years. Perhaps we must be content to regard Es'kia Mphahlele as an activist whose intellectual prowess we can savour.

The works we placed in this section brim and bristle with energy and vigour. Here Mphahlele the teacher and the philosopher have come to play out their convictions. Here the nation builder (*Towards a Definition of Nation Building*) and the sceptic (*What's New in the New South Africa*) write side by side quite comfortably!

These articles accommodate the Mphahlele who bemoans the erosion of traditional family values and morals, kinship and welfare. Here an essay splays open the dilemma the Mphahlele family faced in returning to South Africa after a twenty-year exile: a period of displacement and efforts to stave off alienation in which the four Mphahlele children not only adapted to exile soil, but also adopted the foreign host. *Portrait of a Man in a Glasshouse* is a compelling autobiographical piece in which Mphahlele scours his soul to rationalise his return to ancestral land.

Beyond the personal wrangling, there are the public speeches. One piece extols the potential impact of the Council for Black Education and Research on educational and social development; another is an intense exploration of what we need to deconstruct the colonial paradigm (*From Dependence to Interdependence: Towards Nation Building*). Other articles define what we need to build a nation (*Towards a Definition of Nation Building*), scrutinise the *Black Family in Transition*, and go *In search of an African Middle Class*. But this section is not all theory: his speech at the opening of an exhibition of Gerard Sekoto's paintings is a fine synthesis of Mphahlele the scholar and the teacher. He uses Sekoto's life to illustrate the pain of exile and the hope that simmers beneath the façades exiles oblige themselves to wear.

Literary Appreciation

Unsurprisingly, Mphahlele is most prolific when he considers aspects of literature. An early lesson each of the editors must surely acknowledge under Mphahlele's tutelage is that *literature for the sake of literature* was simply anathema. Did he then propose a utilitarian literature? No. He preferred a literature, i.e. a system of storytelling, of lyricism, of dramatic enactment, that uses an aesthetic to develop and empower the human mind. Literature has to have a social function.

And so the reader will find Mphahlele the teacher most palpable in this section. Here the titles happily sport the poetic: *Prometheus in Chains, Prodigals, Exiles and Homecomings, African Literature: A Dialogue of Two Selves*. The younger reader (whom we dearly hope to attract) must, however, be cautioned not to balk at the figurative qualities of these titles. These essays are intellectual exercises with immensely practical lessons in history and political sensibility, and hold suggestions for the artist in thought and craft. He tackles profound literary issues, as in *The African Critic*, where he outlines his concept of aesthetics in African arts and decries the African continent's appropriation of European-oriented theories of art. He argues for a situation where the artist and the critic listen to one another to produce an aesthetic that will address contemporary issues and answer contemporary questions.

Of particular interest is *My Destiny is Tied to Africa*. It became the title essay of his second collection of criticism, but grew out of a vigorous published dialogue with a fellow critic, Addison Gayle. This dialogue became something of a precursor to the much more public discourse between Ali Mazrui and Wole Soyinka on the Internet. Here is a robust response to Gayle's criticism that he, Mphahlele, leans too much to the West. Mphahlele snaps back by reaffirming his connection with and his indebtedness to Africa as an African.

Other essays in this section are less vitriolic (although vitriolic is not an apt description for the assertiveness in *My Destiny is Tied to Africa*). In his *Notes on the Role of the Writer at the Present Time: Comments and Projections* he deftly argues that every writer is a product of her/his own time, and that their thoughts and feelings can be shaped by events and moments of world history that impact on people as a world community.

This introduction began by labelling Es'kia Mphahlele a teacher, and we suggested that it is the teacher in Mphahlele that must be square and clear in the reader's mind as he or she works through this volume. In the seminal essay *Why I Teach My Discipline* the need for such a backdrop is most clear. Here he contends that he chose to teach English as a career because in West Africa it became a medium of self-realisation for the elite; in South Africa it gave the proletariat a political and economic tool. In the USA his students were less oriented towards savouring the texture of the idiom than they were in exploring the genesis of ideas – there was less sensitivity to the texture of emotions. Yet across these contrasting experiences, English promotes communication across diverse cultural and ethnic boundaries, and helps us discover ourselves through a medium that combines an African sensibility with a foreign mode of expression. It allows understanding of the meeting point between imitation and innovation.

The reader has the choice of coming to this collection of articles, essays and public addresses ahead of reading Es'kia Mphahlele, the creative artist. If so, then we hope that the reader take from this collection an insight into one of the most fertile intellects in South Africa, and is able to apply the workings of this intellect to the richness of the imagination in Mphahlele's fiction and poetry. Should the reader approach this collection after becoming acquainted with the creative Mphahlele, then these works will undoubtedly inform the artistic process as much as it will further enrich and satisfy the experience of the novels, short stories and poetry. Whichever way around, satisfaction is guaranteed.

THE EDITORIAL PANEL

---

1. *The African Image* (London: Faber & Faber, 1962; rev. ed. 1974).

2. *Voices in the Whirlwind and Other Essays* (New York: Hill and Wang, 1972). References are to this edition.

EDUCATION

Alternative Institutions of Education for Africans in South Africa – 1990

Synopsis by Marcus Ramogale

This article was first published in February 1990 in the Harvard Educational Review *(60.1). February 1990 is a significant date in South African history, for on the second day of the month F W de Klerk, the then State President of South Africa, announced the freeing of political prisoners (including Nelson Mandela) and the unbanning of the African National Congress, the Pan Africanist Congress, the South African Communist Party, and other banned political organizations, thus starting a process that culminated in the creation of a non-racial democratic dispensation in 1994. This article articulates some of Mphahlele's views on education in the apartheid South Africa of the 1980s, prior to the events of 1990 and of subsequent years.*

In apartheid South Africa, education was an important instrument of control. The inferior Bantu Education provided to blacks was one of the instruments of subjugation used by the white minority. In order to counteract the demeaning and limiting effects of state-controlled education, some educationists and anti-apartheid activists argued, especially in the 1980s, in favour of alternative education for blacks. In this article, Mphahlele explains what was meant by alternative education then, and he describes some of the alternative educational activities and programmes that black people were involved in. He defines alternative education as 'any form of education that is alternative to that which is provided, planned, and controlled by a political authority'. Alternative education then 'supplemented' formal state-controlled education and did not lead to state-determined examinations and qualifications. It did not seek to replace state-controlled education, but rather sought to provide alternative learning programmes 'outside the conventional school, college, or university curricula, pedagogy and examinations'. The learning options provided in alternative institutions were used alongside official curricula to offer pupils and students alternative, enriching and liberating perspectives. As Mphahlele explains, because alternative institutions expressed 'independent thinking and a sense of deprivation', they were invariably seen as subversive by the authorities.

W|hen one hears the term 'alternative education', the question: 'alternative to what?' naturally follows. In my mind, alternative education is any form of education that is alternative to that which is provided, planned and controlled by a political authority – whether on a local or a national level. Alternative education presents options that can be utilized alternatively or concurrently with public schools as time requires and opportunity dictates.

In order to appreciate the many forms of alternative education in South Africa, it is first necessary to understand the political, economic and cultural situation of Africans in South Africa. Education for Africans reflects the gross inequality linked to the policy of apartheid, which places Africans at the bottom of the social ladder. The results of apartheid policies in education are many. The educational system is segregated, with separate schools and school systems for each racial group (Africans, coloureds, Indians and whites). Schools for blacks (which include all the non-white racial groups) are run on very limited funds, have limited facilities, and use a curriculum that perpetuates the racist policies of apartheid.

The poor situation of State-sponsored education for blacks in South Africa makes the need for alternative educational institutions crucial. At present the State conducts no external programmes for literacy and basic mathematics. Self-help organizations have stepped in to undertake these services that the government has been unwilling to assume. Such alternative structures include the L M Foundation for Literacy, affiliated with the Council for Black Education and Research; Read, Educate and Develop (READ) in Johannesburg and preschools in the major townships.

In this article I will discuss my views about alternative education in South Africa and present some examples of current alternative educational institutions. I will present a vision of how alternative education in this country can draw from 'the souls of people' and shed light on what education can and ought to be for our people.

What Is Alternative Education?

Alternative education can supplement, rather than replace, formal education, providing options that can be utilized along with, or in place of, state-controlled educational institutions. For example, alternative education programmes can provide adults with skills they missed during their school-age years. Programmes that prepare adults to enter a trade or profession, such as bookkeeping, fit this type of education. Such programmes do not require certificates or diplomas.

Alternative education in the South African context must be distinguished from *informal* education, which occurs in such groups as the scout and guides movement, recreational centres, and women's prayer groups. Informal education is incidental and not tightly structured. *Alternative* education, on the contrary, is well structured, and has a seriousness of purpose: a sense of its ability to contribute to the progress of the nation. It is alternative because it happens outside the conventional school, college or university curricula, pedagogy and examinations, and not because of its lack of structure or its subject matter. It develops its own particular form, which addresses the needs of the community and its environment, without the need to prepare the participants for examinations.

Similarly, alternative education must be distinguished from supplementary or continuing education. For example, the government may provide night classes for senior high school courses, which are held outside of formal schooling. But while these programmes utilize alternative *places* and *times* of schooling, they cannot be considered alternative education because they offer formal school subjects for state examinations. They are better described as supplementary or continuing education. This same distinction applies to the new inner-city schools that have mushroomed in response to the urgent cry of thousands who want to pass examinations but have been alienated by state schools, to Saturday schools that offer children additional tutoring in their weak subjects, and to correspondence schools.

One example of alternative education is independent schools, which provide an alternative learning environment because they are interracial. The Sagewood School in Johannesburg, for instance, provides a curriculum for pre-school through Standard 8 (Grade 10) that is based on integrated studies. In Standards 9 and 10 (Grades 11 and 12), the pupils are taken through the official matriculation syllabus to prepare them for their examinations. Sagewood's students have been found to be much readier, both intellectually and emotionally, for university studies than students in mainstream schools.

But the independent schools also have an inherent shortcoming, in that they represent a microcosm of South African society in the quality and kind of cultural assimilation to which blacks are subjected. The onus is on blacks, rather than on their white counterparts, to adapt to and assimilate the cultural values of white South Africa. Blacks have to remember that they are expected to succeed in a white-dominated society, whose rules often negate the highest human values. A richer and more stimulating curriculum is needed in schools, which would help students deal with their own environment, know themselves more deeply, and comprehend the problems of race, colour, and ethnicity in a painfully fragmented country. The curriculum thus needs to be radically changed in content and focus, which in turn calls for a different pedagogy.

Alternative Education and the Political Situation in South Africa

In highly developed societies, when State structures are judged to be inadequate in form or content, philosophically misdirected, or pedagogically unsound – and there is no way of changing or modifying them from within – persons with vision often set up alternative structures. This happens because official structures tend to be set like concrete, becoming rigid and impervious to new or different ideas.

But South Africa is not an open democracy, nor is it highly developed. At least five-sixths of its population live in poverty and bondage. As long as the South African government has vested interests in racial and ethnic fragmentation, alternative programmes and structures of education will not be sanctioned, whether through a central or local authority, black or white. Unfortunately, where open societies might see constructive and legitimate innovations, the South African government sees rebellion.

Indeed, the government is openly hostile to black leaders who are pressing for radical change in education. And since alternative institutions express independent thinking and a sense of deprivation, the authorities see them as resistant to 'law and order'. It is really a matter of: 'If you resist you're damned but you're damned if you don't.'

But alternative education is not per se anti-government, either in fact or in spirit. We are not proposing that our children stop attending school within the State system. However, the State is not doing us a favour by building schools and financing education. The amount of money we pay in direct and indirect taxation ought to earn us a bigger harvest in services. At the same time, schoolchildren and teenagers should have access to institutions that offer alternative programmes for their particular needs. Such programmes enrich participants and give a deeper meaning to knowledge, and at the same time help students select the grain from the chaff in formal schooling.

A particularly urgent task for alternative education is to meet the educational needs of the thousands of students who, since the 1976 student boycotts against inadequate education, have either dropped out of formal schooling or have been thrown out due to their involvement in the boycotts. Our task of educating drop-outs and children who have been frustrated by police harassment and virtually forced out of school takes on an even greater urgency when we consider that the child who was thrown out by the system in 1976 at age ten is now twenty-three, a young adult. And the one who left school at sixteen is now twenty-nine. Some students were thrown into the cruel labour market before they were mentally and emotionally ready for it.

The providers of alternative education need not entertain the ambition of ever influencing the State education system to incorporate their programmes. The South African ruling class believes that innovation is equivalent to opposition – which it does not allow. Because of their political supremacy and economic prosperity, whites in South Africa have gone on blissfully, reproducing their own kind, generation after generation. The awakening of a small white constituency to the immorality of apartheid is not necessarily going to make black people political allies, on the strength of a mutual commitment. Blacks need some time to outlive the effects of an education that bolsters white political and economic supremacy and privilege. Black people still have to engage in sustained political resistance.

Student revolts of the 1960s and 1970s in various parts of the world compelled many educators to examine the often inhumane authority of professors and administrators. In Africa, South America and Asia, university students still have cause to fight the despotism and power of political tyranny, which has stripped citizens of most basic freedoms and rights. State control of education is not innately destructive. But when a governing elite is despotic and tyrannizes citizens, with education and the media in its hands to abuse, citizens get hurt or destroyed. A humanistic national morality fails to evolve, because morality is determined by a small, nervous ruling class, insecure despite the military and police power it has accumulated.

Education is a product of culture. It expresses the culture and helps to define and redefine it. The cultural purpose of an education system rightly belongs in a statement about its philosophical foundations. It is time black people (Africans, Asians and coloureds) saw themselves as *Africans* in more than a geographical sense. The three racial groups that constitute us have all been violated by Europe. Our commitment to the African landscape goes deeper because we have a spiritual bond to it, having suffered for it. In time, the whites will have to outgrow their sense of superiority and merge with the African soil – with the humanism of Africa – if they want to earn the designation 'African'.

In the meantime, a 'New Education' must cut across the dividing lines that have fragmented and alienated our communities from one another and from our African roots. Present-day realities, including the physical and social separation of black communities, make it imperative that we tackle the problem piecemeal in the initial stages of the struggle for change, in our separate regions. We must not wait until political unity is realized. This is a period of transition, during which we should be translating our ideas and hopes for unity into educational policies and practices. Somehow, we should develop a common cultural purpose in our alternative structures. We should not shirk the responsibility, however arduous, of interpreting history, environmental studies, and civics for our students so that they comprehend and appreciate the beginnings of our respective cultures; where we all are at present; what kind of culture we want to shape. In the process, we shall be learning the give-and-take ethic as an actual social process. To have experience of cultures meeting and merging in one's own personal life is essential; only from this point of self-knowledge – built on the strength of one's own traditional beginnings and one's capacity to adapt to other cultures – can we work out a multi-dimensional culture. No longer should the oppressed be bullied into adapting to another culture simply because it wields overwhelming economic and political power.

Our politicians must realize that teachers, students and communities should no longer be exploited for ideological conversion that serves sectional interests. Both the new teacher and the new student, who already exist in our midst (inside and outside the school system), should be seen as part of the process of becoming. The conventional black teacher, who is commonly regarded as a stooge, is just one of the victims.

Teachers must be acknowledged as members of the community, not outside of and against it. Teaching is not the only civil service. Teachers cannot be expected to become banner-flying political activists without risking dismissal. We must allow them to do a *good* job among their students and leave liberation politics to those best qualified to lead. Because 'politics' in South Africa is all-pervading, the teacher can, with the aid of political leaders and the rest of the community, decide wisely what level of politics calls for his or her active engagement. It is partly because teachers have been scared for too long – especially since the resignation of over three hundred teachers in 1977 for political reasons – that education has become a weapon for rallying mass support, one that is used by proponents both of the ideologies against the Establishment and of those backing it.

Students also need to be counselled to re-evaluate their politics and place them in perspective. Teacher, student, and community should no longer be punished for affiliation to this or that political faction, which by definition is a tragically divisive policy. Education and the arts have the potential to unify us and should be our common front. Already, warring political factions entrenched along the education front purport to challenge the institutions of the Establishment. It will be a long time before the wounds heal. Teacher, student, and parent will eventually understand that although education dares not ignore political aspirations, a system of education must address problems that are not readily solved by political confrontation. Education opens options and enables us to sort out short-term and long-term political solutions. It is gratifying to observe the interventions of community groups who understand this. They meet quietly, without any fanfare and sloganeering, and discuss strategies.

The Council for Black Education and Research

I was part of a group of African educators who in 1980 founded the Council for Black Education and Research, now based at Funda Centre in Soweto. In essence we started with this question: what should we do to revolutionize education when centralized State structures resist any change in educational content, such as producing non-racist textbooks? This and other questions have been hanging in the air since Black Consciousness first jolted the minds of our people in the early 1970s and entered the arena of ideas. Premised on black pride and self-reliance, Black Consciousness found articulation in community projects and educational programmes such as the Council.

The Council made a modest beginning in alternative education, without dissuading children from attending formal school. Soon after its founding it adopted an adult education project in Gugulethu, Cape Town, which became the Western Cape Branch of the Council. The project has been attracting young people from eighteen to thirty for the past eight years. The Council provides educational programmes for youth who have left school and for adults who have missed schooling opportunities earlier in their lives, all of whom are literate. We cannot afford to let them disappear into anonymity simply because we do not yet have a back-up system of economic improvement. To educate the public the Council also publishes research papers, including some written lectures, in its journal, *The Capricorn Papers*.

The Council's primary alternative programme consists of an average of four seven-week sessions in a year. Each block of seven weeks is devoted to a theme, on which seven lecture topics are based. Lecturers are specialists in education, sociology, anthropology and economics. An entirely academic approach is discouraged. Lecturers are requested to relate their material to the concrete realities of the participants' lives as they are at present, have been in the past, and should or shouldn't be in the future. Themes also cut across ethnic and urban-rural boundaries.

One topic that is constantly discussed and debated is the division between urban and rural blacks in South Africa today. Since the South African government designated rural areas as Bantustans and 'homelands', urban blacks in South Africa have developed contempt for rural communities. Education is needed to correct this attitude, and the Council has been actively involved in this effort. The popularity of this topic illustrates the social relevance of the Council's themes, since topics are of no use for alternative education if they are merely academic exercises.

While the Council has drawn upon the scholarship of both blacks and whites, its lecturers are mainly blacks, since the Council's aim is to develop black leadership. Topics presented in lectures have come from political studies, sociology, the labour movement, religious studies, law, literature, the performing arts, midwifery, family planning, African history, human geography and education. Thus, the Council has sponsored lectures on such themes as: 'Know Your Country: South Africa'; 'Know Your Continent: Africa'; 'Know Your Environment'; 'Family Life'; 'Growing up in South Africa' (which included one African and one white youth as speakers); 'Black Consciousness'; 'Know Your Civics'; 'The Arts and Their Social Environment'; 'Leadership'; and 'The Ascent of Man', a television series produced by Tadeusz Bronowski for the British Broadcasting Company (BBC).

The founders of the Council for Black Education and Research realized from the beginning that alternative education would have to depart radically from conventional state-run education in its core curriculum and principles. They decided that integrated studies would be its rationale as well as its vehicle. Integrated studies, rather than 'subject teaching' – in which subjects are taught as unrelated to one another – develop a mind that discerns the totality of experience. Integrated studies, therefore, constitute the heart of alternative education, keeping teacher and student constantly in touch with their physical and human environments.

The Council bases its education on what students know about their own environments. Officials of the Council for Black Education and Research then give students the socio-historical context of their environment, and highlight political and economic issues that have a bearing on it, as well as the cause-and-effect relationships that shape it. Unfortunately, we have discovered that although young people may know about their own communities and environments, the State schools have not developed an aptitude to look for connections among the various features of the landscape they know so well. They generally lack the deeper awareness that comes with practising a habit of mind that is formed in the process of establishing relationships among concepts, patterns of behaviour, personalities and so on. In our case, the youth should be inspired, urged, and taught to discern the relationship between their condition of urbanization or rural life and their underprivileged situations; between the lack of jobs and the total dependence on white employment deriving from the traditional policy that says that blacks must be 'educated' to be employed by whites; between the lack of vital services in the townships and rural areas due to a scarcity of artisans such as plumbers, carpenters, electricians, skilled builders and entrepreneurs, and the excessive dependence on industry for employment; and the interrelationships between all these sets of factors. This forum raises questions that we believe our children ought to consider. We have to travel the road of ideas, information and communication in order to experience the awakening of our consciousness, the deepening of our awareness and an expansion of horizons.

The mental processes we are trying to promote in our learners also engage the emotions, through self-knowledge and concern for our fellow human beings. Indeed, the teaching of humanities and sciences must constantly influence real-life attitudes and values, for these facts of life involve them individually and collectively. At the primary level, we have to promote and cherish a concern for all humans as the basis for the liberation of our people. When we know who we are as South Africans and where we are going, which we hope will lead to a clear sense of our relationship with the rest of Africa – real and ideal – we can move toward universal humanism. Eventually we must arrive at a point where we can feel confident that we count in the international forum, where the interdependence of nations is also, through struggle, emerging.

Alternative Education and the Arts

The arts have been served by alternative institutions primarily because the State has never been interested in using schooling to promote creativity. Union Artists pioneered teaching the performing arts in the 1950s and promoted the African Music and Drama Association – based at Dorkay House, Johannesburg – which flourished in the 1960s and early 1970s. Dr. Khabi Mngoma, a maverick who is a veteran in music education in a learning environment he created, has been the most influential figure in this tradition. Hundreds of music students have passed through his hands in his forty years of teaching music outside the conventional schooling system. Some fruits of his labour of love have been the Ionian Choir and the Symphony Orchestra.

The Arts Centre at Funda Centre, Johannesburg, where theatre, music, graphic and plastic arts, and photography are taught, is a modest but vibrant provider of alternative education. So is Funda Centre's Adult Education wing. But even before Union Artists, the Eoan Group in Cape Town was producing singers and dancers of admirable quality. Between the formation of United Artists and the Funda Centre, the Federated Union of Black Artists (Fuba) emerged. Under poet and novelist Sipho Sepamla's direction, Fuba has been teaching fine art, music, dance and theatre. As it enters its second decade, Fuba is experimenting with alternative forms of accreditation for the arts at high school level.

Alternative Education and the Universities

When I advocated, in a graduation address at the University of the Witwatersrand in 1981, that the university establish a community college in one of the urban areas, the idea was allowed to evaporate as soon as it had been aired. I had hoped that such a college would become a vital centre of cultural activity and academic and technical training, accessible to a large number of people in the Witwatersrand-Pretoria-Vaal area who wanted either to attend a two-year college programme, or to continue for another two years in a fully-fledged university for a full degree. I had envisioned it as the kind of multi-purpose establishment the Council for Black Education and Research initially dreamed of.

Ironically, the faculty members who resisted the idea of a satellite campus were young white 'radicals' or liberals with pseudo-leftist leanings. They argued that their university's major responsibility should be to admit more blacks instead of establishing a 'separatist' school, which would only promote the State policy of racial segregation. The implication in this mental block was: 'Come into our university, black folks, you're welcome. But know that you come in on our terms, you take what we teach you… We wish you success at the end of the pipeline… We offer you an education you cannot refuse; it is highly respected in the free world by the highest European standards…' To my dismay, I have often found that many white radicals tend to be more dogmatic than the oppressed. They have nothing to lose, whereas the oppressed have to select options that are not likely to compromise their cause irredeemably.

Then Vista University stepped in, alas! Vista University was established five years ago by the apartheid government. It is neither a community college nor a liberal one.

It became an institution to upgrade teachers from African urban populations who do not have university degrees. It is headquartered in Pretoria with branch campuses in urban centres and offers fully-fledged degree programmes. Can we blame those who attend Vista University in the absence of any other option?

Universities in other parts of Africa, such as Ghana, Ibadan (Nigeria), Makerere (Uganda), and Tanzania, have moved away from the British 'elitist' model and have developed extension services or 'outreach' programmes for the benefit of their local communities. Such African extension services have gradually promoted cultural projects such as theatre, dance, music and poetry readings. By contrast, South African institutions – including public school buildings – are deplorably under-used, once formal teaching hours end. The situation is made more serious by the fact that the Universities of the North, Zululand and Fort Hare were established to serve ethnic interests symbolized by the 'homelands', and have remained outside the mainstream of intellectual life and activity, which flourish best in more densely populated, cosmopolitan areas.

What matters here is not so much that these universities were established in largely rural areas, but that, because of landlessness (that is, small areas, most of which are dry and not productive), the territory each inhabits is sparsely populated and uni-ethnic. To make matters worse, each has been left to raise its own revenues. Administrators and the majority of the faculty in all the rural universities either never had the initiative to broaden the disciplines that are taught or have lost it. There is little connection between academic studies and the environment of the institutions. For example, in the teaching of history, the histories of the surrounding territories could be researched and recorded, from both written and oral sources. Geography could include the distribution and habitation of land, the relationship between drought-prone zones and the spread of population, and water conservation. Biological studies could examine local animal and human life. Instead, the universities have stood aloof from the rural poverty that surrounds them. They are like a single candle flickering in a distant village, calling the lonely traveller to come, while the hope that he will ever arrive gradually diminishes. Thus, if there is to be any hope of developing alternative educational institutions in rural areas, we must focus on utilizing the public schools, perhaps at night and on weekends, since the universities are not willing to help.

Several universities in Africa north of the Limpopo have a department of extra-mural studies or an institute for public education, offering studies not included in the standard curriculum. Such departments even admit candidates who are below university level, thus reaching out to the general population to provide continuing education for those who are literate enough to extend themselves. These institutions have become centres of cultural activity, theatre and dance, music, storytelling, oral poetry, readings from written works, oral history, and plastic and graphic arts.

Education and Community

It is my belief that education must liberate students from the political and economic forces that subjugate our people, and from the low self-esteem and self-hate that oppression inculcates in many of its victims. Education should equip people to break down imposed barriers to self-fulfilment and self-realization. Self-realization can only be valid, however, if the needs of one's community are served by it.

In order for education to achieve this purpose, a reordering of some of its principles is needed. Some of the age-old tenets of educational philosophy – such as the development of mind, body, and spirit – may still be valid. But a radical philosophy of education has to redefine the processes and terms so that fundamental age-old principles can be realized at the concrete level in collective purpose and action. The individual should no longer be the sole focus of teaching, but must also be trained to think and act as a servant of the community. In other words, we need a philosophy of education that will account for the social evils that confront us and empower us to deal with them.

Rabindranath Tagore (1861-1941), the Bengali poet and humanist, points out in his writings that our moral faculty is the means by which we know that life is not made up of disconnected moments – discontinuous and without purpose. This moral sense and purpose, Tagore explains, gives us the power to realize that the self has continuity in time, enabling us to discern that the self extends beyond itself and is not restricted to one's own self.

Contrary to Tagore's view of humanity, the type of education that most Africans first experienced did not focus on the self in relation to community. This education, provided by the missionaries to our continent, served mainly as the bait for capturing African souls to offer up to God. The missionaries taught obedience to political authority, discouraged revolution, and concentrated on saving the individual soul. It was assumed that the individual's salvation would rub off on the community. Missionaries were thus blind to group attitudes developing among whites that were fed by vicious racism and apartheid. Men such as the Anglican Trevor Huddleston, who has challenged the State continually since the 1950s, are relative newcomers in missionary education. The Catholic Bishop Hurley of Natal is another example of the new missionary. He also has continually crossed swords with the apartheid government.

Let us recognize the vigour of the pioneers of missionary education, if only because no government in South Africa was building schools for black people. Missionary education, which lasted until the government took control of the schools in the 1950s, varied in its religious thrust according to denominational divisions. It provided space for students to create their own learning environment, and a starting point from which several of us continued to re-educate ourselves and explore the outer reaches of self-development in relation to the community. The more progressive among the alumni of mission schools were able to use that same education to rethink the narrowness of the church-going religion the scripture lessons had pumped into them.

Indeed, the national efforts in independent Africa toward improving education display the seriousness with which we regard this undertaking. In reality, the history of education in Africa does not go far back; our children are very attentive in schools, and we are not yet bored. The disillusionment our children do feel stems from political, economic, and racial factors; their hope in education is great. In spite of all the mismanagement we see around us on the continent, people still place great value on education.

But does education of itself resolve unjust social, economic, and political conditions? No. Yet education, when it includes self-knowledge and a comprehensive awareness of one's environment – its history, geography, sociology, and ecology – increases one's moral strength to confront one's conditions. It can also make options visible that were previously imperceptible or unthinkable.

Where else can the ideals I have discussed in this article be pursued today, except in alternative institutions? Call them what you will – alternative structures, centres for adult education, community colleges, continuing education, institutes for public education, extension studies, centres for non-formal education – these liberal learning environments go a long way towards developing cultural selfhood and self-esteem among participants. They keep us in touch with ourselves so that we take charge of our environment and cultural direction. We can find ourselves happening to events, instead of always responding to events happening to us.

The Disinherited Imagination and the University's Mission Towards its Restoration – April 1993

Synopsis by Ndavhe Ramakuela

Any useful approach to liberating a nation will entail empowering its youth to feel that they, too, can make a meaningful contribution to social development. This is an underlying message in this address to the University of the North, which draws heavily on Mphahlele's views on African Humanism. Mphahlele feels that education in South Africa, particularly in universities, has lost relevance, and that products of such institutions have lost their dignity and pride. The main problem here, he argues, is their over-reliance on Western thought or, even more damaging, their hostility towards anything that encourages or forces them to think critically. He encourages present-day students to move away from the widespread tradition of seeking butts of blame and criticism most or all the time. He advises them rather to look deep within themselves to develop a consciousness that will be a foundation for future generations – consciousness that is rooted in African philosophy and independent thinking. The main idea is that of developing self-reliance on the part of students. But this goal cannot be achieved if universities continue to uphold weak standards which do not probe students' intellect, or which do not bear any relevance to the communities they serve. He makes an example of a curriculum that is examination-driven, and that ends up insinuating – in students' thinking – that their only goal is to pass exams. Mphahlele advocates an interdisciplinary approach in curriculum design; that curriculum should also be able to transform students' attitudes and perceptions of themselves and their respective communities.

M aster of Ceremonies, the Vice-Chancellor and the Deputies, staff and students, it is once more a great pleasure for me to address you as the general community of this university. Let me say right away how honoured my wife and I feel to be given such a welcome. It is for me yet another renewal time. Like Tennyson's Ulysses: 'I cannot rest from travel; I will drink / Life to the lees,' always following knowledge 'like a sinking star'.

I have been asking myself uneasy questions lately, since accepting the invitation last year to become an Honorary Professor with the English department as my base. Uppermost is the question of why I accepted an invitation, as flattering as it is to me, to enter a house that is not at ease with itself; a house divided; a house that seems to be forever smouldering, ready for any form of unpredictable internal combustion; a house that never had a will of its own, native to its inhabitants and their aspirations; a house that has lived too long – oh so long – under the shadow of political tyranny and its brood of gremlins in the form of security police, censorship, informers, tribalists in white gloves, starched underwear, Pretoria's Law and Order and its local ministers and messengers of death. The North and its four sister ethnic universities have been engaged to one degree or another in a thirty years' war against its own destiny: trying to be a university by every means possible that must frustrate any such achievement. At first we blamed, and justly so, Afrikaner ideology and its major extension, Christian National Education. A fundamentalist approach to mind control which, because of its religious pretensions, commands overwhelming credibility.

When black vice-chancellors stepped in and nothing changed for the better, we realized that, like aliens in science fiction, they were but Law and Order mutants in academic robes. When younger intellectuals moved in, such as Professor Jakes Gerwel and later Professor Chabani Manganyi, we all breathed a sigh of relief. If you can imagine people looking up, eyes searching for that ancient sign amid the stars they hope will presage a bright and spectacular event, you will appreciate the grand wish that attended the ascendancy of these two men to top executive positions. Imagine, too, the slight tremor of the heart that says this might not be real, that we cannot possibly be so blessed. For haven't intrigue, whispers in the dark, treachery, become a way of life in our midst? Particularly here in the North the going has been bumpy for too long, with one upheaval following closely in the wake of the one before, until the link between cause and effect has ceased to exist.

That splendid event was not to be at the University of the North, in a province where, historically, Boer nationalism has been more abrasive, stultifying and intensely disabling than elsewhere. The universities of Durban-Westville and the Western Cape have certainly been better able to contain conflicts than have Zululand, Fort Hare or ourselves. One cannot but deduce that because Asians and coloureds have long enjoyed preferential treatment from the Nationalist regime, the staff and students at those two institutions have been able to stabilize their learning environments sooner and longer, and have achieved a higher incentive to tutor and to learn. But, in addition, we have compounded our own problems and remained ripe for intrigue and treachery from among our own ranks. Almost as if, because black people have become accustomed to hardships for centuries, we have collectively lost our sense of proportion, our ability to distinguish between the norm and the dysfunctional – just as a ghetto family gets used to living with a door banging about on one hinge, until it ceases to be a source of irritation. I hope to point out some of these problems as I proceed.

Here is a hypothetical student – call him X – whose views about the ideal university create a composite picture we are accustomed to. I quote:

> *I believe in the idea of a university that insists on the highest morals. I mean good Christian behaviour that promotes humility, especially among scholars and among those who lead. I want a university that can proclaim aloud and unabashed that it stands for excellence, requiring the study of disciplines whose worth has been tested by unimpeachable scholarship. I'm looking for a university that does not tolerate sloppiness, poor achievement, nor condones low performance symbols. Not for me is an institution where students are always quibbling over the grade a lecturer has given. If they take grades to be the final deciding factor for their future, why don't they work harder for them? Who's standing in their way? Give me a university where there are no marches and other demonstrations continually disrupting academic progress, where a serene learning environment can be created and serious studies can be undertaken.*
>
> *I want a university that is free of threats and intimidations from either students or staff. Look at the mess our ethnic universities have become in the thirty years they have been in existence. Look at Durban-Westville, where demonstrations and boycotts are few and far between. Obviously Asians are driven by a seriousness of purpose, almost as if they were agreed on a common code. We only need to return to the old standards by which lecturer and administrator were accorded their individual traditional status and respect, and students were real scholars.*

Whether we like it or not, we the subject race are – like X – carriers of a disinherited imagination. This is what I mean: to think of standards as good because they are established by the white man and his traditions. 'Universal excellence' refers to the white world and pretends that we are included simply because we the people of colour also inhabit this planet. When we adopt standards alien to our own considered ideals, we inevitably come up with X's half-baked concepts and half-truths in which he is begging the question all the way.

A choir – I shall decline to say from where – came to a teachers' function in Johannesburg one evening two weeks ago. One of its items was an African lullaby. The melody was enchanting, the 'unsung melody' not so sweet. For dramatic effect, each of the women – some twenty or so – had brought on stage a white doll in her arms! Images clashed in my mind, criss-crossing into a tangle, and left me bewildered. The disinherited imagination, alas. The conqueror's world and imagination have stripped the indigenous world of its own myths, poetry, dreams and reveries.

A francophone West African writer, Cheikh Hamidou Kane, in a novel translated into English as *Ambiguous Adventure*, portrays a chief's sister advising a young man that he go to the white man's school to learn how to govern without being right. Against the counsel of other prominent persons, she urges that the people should absorb Western ways and thought, even if they have to sacrifice their indigenous lifeways. Something needs to be destroyed to give place to the new, she argues. This is in colonial Senegal, and she would not have been able to predict the day when her sons and grandchildren, in a manner of speaking educated in Western style, would want to reclaim the imagination she would be happy to see disinherited. Kane wants to explore the ambiguity of our assimilation into the West alternating with efforts to free ourselves from it. It is a pathetic delusion to pretend that our sole task – even in South Africa where the onslaught on the African personality was all but total – is to learn to live with a disinherited imagination.

Time after time I witness certain groups among our people virtually dance themselves into a frenzy at the altar of some non-racial god, while the white scholar researches almost every area of African life and writes volumes about it. And we're still dancing ... Someone is sure to ask: 'But don't you believe in non-racialism?' To which my reply is: 'I unequivocally do, but we rejected the term 'non-white' once because of its negative connotation. I can't see myself running around celebrating my non-some-thingness instead of my somethingness: the fact of being African. No, we have been victims of white dishonesty for too long for us to be indulging in non-racial wet dreams, let alone any degree of orgasmic satisfaction at the sound of words such as 'forgiveness', 'reconciliation', 'New South Africa' – even before the other race has earned these tender mercies.

Furthermore, blacks themselves must take charge of this non-racial process, rather than be programmed into it by members of a race that has conducted the affairs of this country and its institutions on the foundations of racism. If we don't take charge of this phase of our black-white relations, where lasting positive interracial attitudes must be worked out, then we shall never, ever resolve the personality conflicts that characterize the ambiguous and often confused back-and-forth traffic of the disinherited imagination. I repeat: we must provide the ideas. Which presupposes that we must train ourselves to think, to produce ideas that can refine our emotions and vice versa, that can inform our growth and direct it well. I insist that the university and like institutions are at the centre of this process. This is where we have to learn to unmask ourselves of what some scholars call a 'false consciousness'.

Because of the white man's conquest, our imagination has accepted the Western model of the university as the appropriate one for purposes of survival. So with other institutions such as religion, technology and so on. Furthermore, power in all its aspects lies in the hands of the white world, with Japan as a new affiliate. The dark-skinned peoples of the world are in charge of nothing that matters in global terms. I am most impressed by the group of African religious thinkers who are developing Black Theology and Contextual Theology. They are urging believers to take a fresh look at orthodox Christianity so as to reconstruct a theology based on their socio-political context. They are striving for new definitions of the African reality in theological terms. What is left for the theologians is to integrate what they have rediscovered in indigenous African thought and belief so that they become functional beyond the dusty shelves of the archives. For, ultimately, to reclaim the imagination that can with its own momentum bounce off our ancient myths against new realities in search of answers demands of us that we forge new definitions, doesn't it? Redefinitions and revaluations in any society that seeks to renew itself come and go in never-ending cycles. And I can't see the university not becoming one of the fora where these can be debated.

A genuine programme of non-racialism, in which we Africans must play a major role, tapping the best minds among other population groups, must eventually lead to the Africanisation of our institutions of learning. This goes beyond simply filling our schools and colleges with majority blacks. It means revolutionizing the whole range of our curricula, giving them a new direction, a humanistic thrust distinct from the tyranny of didactic approaches that have choked up all the channels of education.

I have lived long enough to observe that democratic government does not per se immediately regard education and its curricula as a top priority. The Nationalist Party, as custodians of white rule properly elected by white voters, has taught us that much. The education of the master race has only been superior to ours at the level of technology and the sciences. For the rest the party has little to show for its leadership. Indeed, it is not uncommon to go through democratic procedures to elect a parliament of fools, idiots and morons, in that order of ascendancy. People never fail to believe that once the political kingdom has been attained, other activities that define a culture – such as education, social welfare, health and the arts – will fall neatly into place. A truly false belief. For every democracy is a gamble, even if its antithesis is too frightening to contemplate.

In the meantime, what do we have? An examination-driven curriculum that excludes a lot that would be meaningful for a developmental approach to education. And yet it is loaded with generations of debris coming from disciplines that only have tradition to justify them – like a polluted river on its predictable journey towards the sea. It is also a curriculum that locks both lecturer and student into a desperate, often unhappy relationship – the former constantly mindful of the attention the student demands. Short lecture periods instead of the normal fifty minutes reduces the status of a university or college to that of a high school. What else can the lecturer do but merely deliver one lecture after another in traditional didactic fashion – facts, facts, facts – rendering student responses well-nigh impossible? Carefully monitored, independent study can break this dreary cycle, with more group tutoring being conducted, and single meetings with the lecturer for consultation. That 'teach me, teach me, teach me' demand that comes from the student with a silent, menacing persistence has got to give way to sanity if we are ever going to promote the transformation of our tertiary institutions.

An exam-driven curriculum leaves little room for interdisciplinary or integrated studies. We can, while we reshape the curriculum, arrange special symposia – some of which must be mandatory for students to attend according to the core discipline they opt for. Credit should be given for active participation in a given number the student attends, without sacrificing scholastic depth. Extension services are imperative, in the form of programmes involving immediate and relatively distant communities.

There needs to be a standing commission on every campus that will initiate and monitor curriculum development. If there are several such commissions, one per campus, a joint resource can develop which will bring together scholars, including visiting educationalists from abroad. But we must take the lead in the latter kind of consultation. A university such as this, I hope, will regard curriculum changes as central to its transformation planning. Such a curriculum commission should naturally include academic staff and students, the latter chosen not merely for political reasons, but for their disposition for independent and free inquiry, and for their interest and enthusiasm concerning the topic. All must be prepared to read widely to establish a cultural context that will illuminate their task and the subject of their inquiry.

We have seen some white universities develop in this country where academics and students are regimented into thinking and feeling alike. They share the same neuroses, the same pathological responses to the presence of blacks, the same ideological squint and so on. Now, alas, we have been turning our own tertiary institutions into something approximating ideological nurseries, where one group can supersede the will of the non-believer, the dissident. There is a nameless but rampant neurosis that is sweeping through our campuses, where the majority of us are unhappy about something and cannot tolerate anybody who wants to be an achiever – even while we secretly admire him or her. We symbolically assassinate the achiever, the hero, by wishing that history bury their names. We even throw stones at intellectuals, considering them 'elitist'.

We fail to realize that there is a difference between being one of an elite and being elitist. The former, 'elite', is an objective statement of fact, referring to one of a relatively small number of the most highly capable and knowledgeable personnel in a specific area of life. 'Elitist' refers to an attitude in a member of the elite. He believes that, being one of the special few, it is right and proper that he should be treated in a special way, because he so deserves. Thus to belong to an elite is a healthy status, unless one day there is unrelenting pressure from a consensus that wants to remove all specialists from society permanently. At the risk of having stones, shoes, dirty underwear, hats, caps, books hurled at me, I cannot but say how dismayed I am to observe this suicidal streak that says: 'Come, let's fail together, because if you succeed we'll alienate you...' Such a threat turns failure into a cult, a fetish.

This suicidal streak points to the violent dissociation that exists between ourselves as staff and students and the institution that contains us, but which we don't really inhabit in the profound sense of the word. To create a cult of failure (as students) and inefficiency (as lecturers) is to negate any attachment we might have wanted to forge with the institution. If such an institution was created for the express purpose of seeing it fail then we owe it to ourselves, for our own sanity and self-love, to turn it around and make it work for us. But not until we snap out of the demotivating malaise that is so rampant, not until we look inwards and locate the thing that poisons our academic life, can we recreate the university; nor are we going to rid it of the ghosts of the past, or exorcise today's demons of civil strife and petty jealousies on our campuses.

Finally, I am looking forward to a university developing which will allow plenty of space for the growth and development of ideas. Ideas that contribute to intellectual growth, in a social climate where the intellect is under siege even in the community of the oppressed (and has become a word of abuse), must be part of the transformation of the North. We have to create groups, cells, where we can debate and exchange ideas on vital issues, and become a think tank from which strategies can be drawn, even segments of policy. We need to loosen up, shake off the hang-ups we may harbour about ideas we do not like because of our political affiliations. We often cherish the hang-ups because if we examined any contending claims our darling myths would be shattered or modified. And if we have no ideas we can call our own in the place of ad hoc myths we see dissolving right before our eyes, we become desperate – like a drug addict who cannot obtain a fix, his only crutch.

I have not said anything about admission procedures, the perennial problem on every black campus that cannot afford at this stage to apply the traditional requirements concerning Matric. Academic support programmes are not the final solution: they are an ad hoc method of meeting a crisis. I am convinced that we should establish community colleges, and have a Sixth Form attached to high schools. South Africa has always resisted the idea of a Sixth Form. The American style of community college has a two-year programme, which provides for those who want a two-year diploma for employment purposes, and also for those who will want a transfer to an established university after the two years. Entry can be arranged at the second or third year, depending on one's grades. Such colleges are day schools for the most part. They ease the entry of the slower student into tertiary studies and admission procedures are relaxed. Community colleges have recently become a subject of great interest among educationalists and non-governmental organizations.

It seems obvious to me that the resolution of unwieldy numbers will ultimately depend on how we confront the problem of poor high school grades, as well as the age-old one arising from parents' desire to fulfil their own dreams in their children, thus sending them to university even when they are not such scholastic material. Here again the community college is good sifting ground, allowing a choice of careers during the two years, with the help of intensive and continuous counselling.

Let me sum up by way of highlighting the issues I have raised. What I say about the North applies also to Fort Hare and Zululand, which I have observed more closely than Durban-Westville and the Western Cape. We shall have to ask some hard questions, of which I list those that I think are the most crucial:

1. Where are we going to draw the line between activism against a racist regime on the one hand, and on the other, against a democratically elected regime backed by a genuine national constitution – if the latter either won't listen to our grievances and demands or drags its feet in responding to them?

2. To amplify (1), by what structures do we cross the transitional bridge from a culture of uncompromising, militant resistance orchestrated by acts of sabotage, to a culture of dissent orchestrated by constitutional procedures towards institutional consensus? For now, if a university is going to function, should we not be creating for it at least a stabilized environment to contain conflict? We see all around us instances of behaviour among our people that show the mental and emotional scars of generations upon generations of oppression and dispossession: in our artistic and literary creations, with their never-ending refrain about what's been and being done to us; in our unwillingness – except among a small band of pioneers – to create our own standards and structures of non-formal education and welfare care centres, because we believe the State owes us incalculable reparations; in our unending insistence that the State should create a single ministry of education conceived and staffed by civil servants, and should give us more textbooks (many of them either outdated or plain rotten at the racist core). Meanwhile we do little or nothing to work out educational, social and economic theory to influence a new content for the physical structures we are shouting for. No. The eternal theme – of the victim who hollers from the depths of a pit for the tyrant to lower a ladder for him – just won't do. We still have to make that transition in our minds from the status of bleeding victim to that of the proactive initiator who knows just what changes he wants.

3. Where do we draw the line between petty grievances that are for *now*, and the prime grievances that affect our future careers and the university's perceived values? In other words, between mashed potatoes that seem to have been blended in a liquid called 'demoralizer' on the one hand, and on the other, a curriculum that is unimaginative and therefore does not elevate nor stimulate?

4. Where do we draw the line between self-defeating acts of vandalism and littering, and civilized acts of protest?

5. How far can, or dare, we push the slogans 'Admit one, admit all' and 'Pass one, pass all'? Are we hearing the ominous sounds of defeat, self-hate, low morale and despair, the drums and cymbals that usher in the omnipotent god of failure?

6. Do we perhaps need a consolidated 'Code of Conduct', drafted by the Students' Representative Council and academic and administrative personnel, and ratified by a two-thirds majority of the joint sitting of the university community? Such a code can explore and establish some moral centre, some moral standard we must all feel accountable to on campus. I offer this strategy for what it is worth, without prejudice to any person or group of persons in the university, as one way that

may contribute to the process of stabilizing the university environment. Such a Code might include matters relating to:

    i. theft of library books;

    ii. misdemeanours on campus such as arson, rape and other forms of physical violence, vandalism, plagiarism, etc.;

    iii. use of premises for a purpose outside the normally accepted one;

    iv. cohabiting of male and female in dorms not prescribed for such companionship, however noble and peaceful;

    v. the sale and possession of liquor and drugs on the grounds, outside (in the case of liquor) the campus bar;

    vi. freedom of inquiry and expression;

    vii. religious freedom;

    viii. academic freedom;

    ix. differences of opinion between the supervisor of a dissertation and its author, leading to a deadlock;

    x. procedures of appeal to higher academic committees in the same discipline;

    xi. procedures that make it possible for students to lay complaints against a lecturer's academic performance or general conduct in the lecture venue, thus pre-empting the summary dismissal of such a lecturer by students and avoiding chaos, embarrassment and acrimony all round;

    xii. procedures that make it possible for a lecturer to lay a complaint against a student/s for any act he/she perceives to be misconduct or negligence related to the lecturer's area of study;

    xiii. discipline.

The issues that I have raised require drastic rethinking of the possible features of a transformed university. I am also certain that you are embarking on a variety of new strategies to meet the new challenges of a university in transition. Nothing here is original, and I must confess that replaying these thoughts was also my way of trying to attain clarity for my own sake. I know that you are exercising your minds about this transformation, and will have even enacted some of the strategies I intimate. The negative features I have pointed out are meant to suggest the positive ones that I think should take their place in the hierarchy of our priorities. I am not the dreamer I was ten years ago, let alone in the years preceding that. But then I'm not supposed to be the fool I was either. Realism chews up the edges of one's idealism, but so be it. You have frightening and daunting odds against you as staff, administration and students, and I can only wish you the greatest success in your endeavours. I feel most privileged and willing to be part of the process.

Concerning the uneasy questions I hinted at at the beginning of this presentation, I should state my reason for having accepted the invitation to come here as an Honorary Professor. This is a house whose beauty lies largely in the humanity that inhabits it. Firstly, no African in his right mind can afford the luxury of prophesying doom for any segment of his/her society. There is a fund of goodness here, in spite of all the stench and muck that characterizes all humanity on this planet. Secondly, I am a thoroughgoing humanist and therefore an idealist. So I have come here armed with an intellect, a heart, an irrepressible passion for teaching and a stubborn persistence. I believe the roles of teacher and student should ideally be interchangeable. You learn from me and vice versa, at different times, in changing situations.

To my student audience I should in all humility like to convey the following message: that stabilizing a learning environment, so that we may study and teach without the irritations that hold us hostage today, is a process we've got to resolve *now*. It is a sad day when we can find it in ourselves to banish a lecturer from class; it is equally sad when lecturers can stay away from classes, however firm may be the belief on each side that justice is in its favour. The name for such a state of affairs is *disorder* bordering on anarchy. The long-term problems are various and more complex, and the mistake we all make is to think that before we can sit down to the task we have enrolled at this university for, the politics have to be resolved. I use the word *politics* here in its broadest and native sense: power relationships. In this sense we find power play in the family and every other institution: who has authority to do what? Never mind what the laws or rules or regulations stipulate. The power game lies in the efforts we make to redefine what the rules lay down.

There are no takeovers in education, and attempts to place people in high positions in an institution of learning in order to create a presence for sectarian-political interests is obscene. The Broederbond and the Nationalist Party did just this. We only need to look at the pathetic products of their universities and colleges to realize the extent of the brain damage that has been wrought. The power struggle in institutions normally goes through many cycles of evolution, until it becomes either irrelevant or something of no consequence in relation to an academic programme and achievement. You have three or four years in a junior degree or an Honours programme. There is little you can do to rush a course of evolution in that time, in the hope that you can arrive at a point of absolute equilibrium and then settle down to school work. Work hard to stabilize your learning environment. Yes, that is of paramount importance. Be contented to contribute so much and no more to the evolutionary process.

I offer this advice also because I have observed that a lot of heat, anger, acrimony, passion, sense of righteous outrage, obsessive sense of mission, even partisan hate are generated in campus activism. These emotional states, repeated time after time, often lead to burnout and take the joy and adventure out of university life.

Some people may very well say I'm talking drivel, or else charge that I'm a pacifist, a reactionary. Especially in these times when it is fashionable to be 'relevant'; even to be recklessly or suicidally relevant. No doubt, too, some students may regard campus activism as psychologically satisfying and a training ground for future leadership. So be it: I accept the latter factor. Indeed it was South Korean students who ran the head of State out of his position a few years ago. But the historical circumstances are different here. Poverty, hunger, functional and cultural illiteracy, a rotten educational system, lack of technical and trade skills and other evil fruits of apartheid are always with us. Ultimately it is a matter of how you budget your time and energies, even when you think that you are destined to be a political leader and must therefore be preparing yourself.

My last piece of counsel has to do with the fact that education should not be perceived as a straight, horizontal line. Rather, we should think of it as a number of moments revolving in endless cycles, with not a single moment ever being the same twice. Hence the exhilarating adventure that education is.

Educating the Imagination – 1993

Synopsis by Peter Thuynsma

In this essay, premised so typically by glancing over his shoulder at his child-hood, Mphahlele explores how he has used his personal experiences to nurture a fervent and disciplined imagination:

'Thomas Hardy says character is fate. It has been my fate to be a teacher and writer. The imagination is my regular beat as it is also the workshop of my mind; the territory of ideas, knowledge, thought and emotion is my hunting ground.'

He appreciates the rough and tumble of his terrorized childhood because:

'Nature led me along its own rugged and smooth paths according to its integrated curriculum.'

'I have been recounting this in order to place the development of the imagination in a proper perspective, i.e. as a social process and as a promi-nent feature in the natural growth of the individual.'

And he moves towards a conscious and critical synthesis:

'I only wish that the West could begin to re-educate itself towards a conscious synthesis; and that "the other" could assimilate and synthesize on its own terms, not those of the master race.'

And:

'... in situations of political conflict and violence we can rescue the imagination, at least for an interim period, from the kind of programming that compels us to repeat ourselves.'

'Educators are faced with the daunting task of setting up structures in which the intellect must find a humanistic environment to regain its right to learn, to attain the farthest reaches of the imagination possible.'

I wish to make this presentation largely narrative rather than argument and theo-retical analysis. I hope I can recount some of my personal experiences without any tone of vanity; so I ask that you please accept these comments merely as observations. Ideally, this essay will help clarify certain things in my own mind relating to the training of the imagination. I can only generalize about the process of the imagination in other writers; about my own I would like to think I am on surer ground.

Thomas Hardy says character is fate. It has been my fate to be a teacher and writer. The imagination is my regular beat as it is also the workshop of my mind; the territory of ideas, knowledge, thought and emotion is my hunting ground. To use another metaphor: I have grown up alternately grappling with hard and almost intractable concepts, and then relaxing to make a pole-vault leap into the realm of the imagination. Yet the concepts keep trailing behind me, as it were, keeping me in con-tact with the real, concrete world – like a kite a person keeps on a string no matter how high it flies, feeding it more line and still more.

I come from a country where for virtually two centuries the people of colour have, as a deliberate policy, been denied the freedom of association, assembly, thought, inquiry and self-expression. For this reason I have constantly treasured and savoured every moment when I could snatch any one of these freedoms. We are still reeling from the nightmare life has been for the majority population – the oppressed and dispossessed. The wounds are still too raw for us even to begin to appreciate the loosening up of some of the racist laws, if they even merit that. Especially because fundamental inequalities still exist: economic, social and political structures – some of them centuries old – still stare us in the face. This, in spite of the fact that the present government possesses the absolute instruments for the immediate dissolution of white supremacy without our assistance, even before we start talking.

I spent the earlier part of my childhood in a pastoral environment as a boy tending cattle and goats. I was, during those seven years, a pupil of nature. It was only in later years that I realized what schooling nature had put me through. I learned even as a seven-year-old that I should monitor a goat or cow giving birth, carry the small kids home at sunset, track down lost animals. I learned to hunt rock rabbits in the moon-light, and to carry wood from the wilds for making the communal fire, where we the boys would listen to the men tell stories. The fascination words have always had for me is an echo of the music of language that registered on my ears in those days, as it con-jured up a strange world for me. A strange world recreated out of familiar things, events and people. The line between the natural and the supernatural often became blurred.

In those days – as I came to discover later – I was thrown upon myself, so that I could contemplate and feel and imagine. There was plenty of time to do this. The darknesses, the silences, the sounds of day and night, the open vastness, landscapes teeming with daylight, shimmering distances of subtropical heat, savannah lying low and biding its time under the winter spell – all these and others provided for me a good training ground from which to launch the odyssey of the imagination.

But this was not to be the journey of typical modern Western man or woman alienated by industrialization and urbanization, an allegory of innocence lost and never to be regained. Those folk tales taught the social relationships and family allegiances that informed a morality we associate with African humanism: *I am because you are, you are because we are*. Quite unlike the odyssey of the intellect that became a cult in earlier Western humanism since the Renaissance, our humanism is essentially spiritual. African humanism recognizes the Vital Force or the Supreme Being at the centre of, and integrating, human, animal and plant life and the inanimate elements of the universe. It is a simple faith free of the tyranny of theology and intellectual argument. This is the measure of the imagination's investment in the power of oral expression.

Since our encounter with Europe, we the colonized communities of the world have been the ones to shoulder the task of synthesizing the West and 'ourselves'. The West has always felt superior and culturally self-sufficient, with no need to learn anything from anybody else. The fierce drive of the intellect buttressed by economic advancement has reinforced that sense of supremacy, even more today than ever before.

This is where the imagination's task lies in child-raising in Africa, Asia and their diasporas today. Right at the crossroads of two main streams of consciousness: the Western, which has pushed the science of manipulating the material world and the environment to the outer frontiers of possibility; and 'the other', which holds on for dear life to that great and splendid pursuit of enduring spiritual values rooted in social relationships, in the integrated personality. I am not in the least suggesting that 'the other' has a monopoly on transcendental wisdom and intuition. I only wish that the West could begin to re-educate itself towards a conscious synthesis; and that 'the other' could assimilate and synthesize on its own terms – not those of the master race.

I had hoped to avoid argument and rather stay with the narrative approach; perhaps my very style of presentation proves the point about synthesis!

The unfolding of the collective imagination through folklore, proverbs and allegory was something we took for granted, without grasping its spiritual dimensions. All I knew was that my imagination was constantly at work. Nature led me along its own rugged and smooth paths according to its integrated curriculum. I imagined that I could, by singing a ditty that said repeatedly: 'Cloud do not blind the sun, waste away, cloud stay out of the sun's way', cause it to dissolve into the blue. It did. I believed that the power of the spoken word had done it! I spoke aloud to trees and other inanimate things. I imagined that I heard them respond. This kind of education, observe, was a way of growing up, of living, rather than a conscious preparation for later life – which we are often told is the overall aim of formal schooling.

My recurring dreams, ever since my mother removed us from the rural area to an African ghetto outside Pretoria, have to this day revolved around my early rural childhood experiences: the cruel and the benign.

By the time Mother came to fetch us, urban ghettos were mushrooming all around as a result of industrial expansion. The white man badly needed labour, but the influx of Africans had to be contained by means of the 'pass' system, which not only checked migrations from the rural areas but also herded us into ghettos. Segregation, apartheid, euphemistically called 'separate development', was the underlying ideology.

Our people had long been forbidden to own land even outside the so-called white areas. Millions of people woke up one day soon after the Land Act of 1913 without any land of their own. They had to leave their sharecropper shacks in droves and were forced into rural ghettos referred to as 'homelands'. The land set aside for the Africans to buy consisted of smallholdings, often with poor water supply and poor soil. Those who had been living there for centuries could only do so because the land was unsuitable for white farming.

Poverty, together with its companion malnutrition, stalked the rural areas. Landlessness became a permanent condition. Even when the land laws are repealed, Africans will not be able to afford to buy land; nor do they possess any farming skills. The drift to the towns seems irreversible for now.

What has happened to the oral tradition in the poverty-stricken countryside? Until the 1930s, people grew the food they ate. Today they buy their food from the nearby store – in small, miserable, absurdly overpriced quantities.

In most rural areas, women still carry firewood from the bush, and water on their heads from the river or communal pump. This used to be a way of growing up for an adolescent girl; a rite of passage, just as it was for her male counterpart to go hunting or to till the soil. Today they carry wood and water for sheer harrowing survival.

Yesterday: ploughing time, the first spring rains, time of harvesting brought out of the people rituals that replayed their poetry, song and dance. Today: no land, no ploughing or harvesting, no rituals, no poetry. Older men and women who can still recite praise songs are dying out. They have no heirs left. We are carriers of a disinherited mind. Time has been dislocated. What poetry exists is woven out of urban life and the political predicament. Or it comes through in work songs of the city.

I have been recounting this in order to place the development of the imagination in a proper perspective, i.e. as a social process and as a prominent feature in the natural growth of the individual.

When I came to live in the urban areas at the age of twelve, survival dramatized itself in other and harsher ways. The poverty, the muck and the stench of slum conditions filled every day and night of our lives. Above all, we had to try to survive white racism and its police force. In the villages one rarely saw a white person. When one did appear, we watched him from the security of the bushes.

I felt an inner compulsion to improve my education. At thirteen I was at a level in school equivalent to the American 4th Grade. Because I tended cattle and goats in the country, my schooling had been erratic out there. In my new setting, I read every scrap of paper I picked up. There were no newsstands in the ghettoes in the 1930s. I relied on neighbours to give me newspapers, no matter how old, to read. My mother's employers in white suburbia gave me their old magazines and books to read – from white girls' and boys' adventures to 'love and romance', that kind of stuff.

By a stroke of luck my hunting expeditions yielded, from a pile of discarded books, Cervantes's *Don Quixote*. I still cannot forget the thrill of discovery I experienced reading Cervantes.

As I went on to mission high school and later to a mission teacher-training institution, both of which had libraries, the unending quest led me through progressively better reading. From guzzling chunks and chunks of printed matter – ripe, raw and rotten – I moved to the higher plane of discriminating reading habits. Books were my refuges in living and social conditions that were created expressly to frustrate our progress and self-realization.

Being an irrepressible moviegoer, I revelled in the silent films of the day. I saw the movie industry change to talkies. My imagination was taking on experiences that were totally different from rural life.

Urban poverty and slum life presented challenges of another order. Whites kicked or pushed us off sidewalks. Most train coaches, entrances into stations, the platforms and waiting rooms were out of bounds for us. Police raids, roadblocks and curfews were an organic part of our lives.

The rural and urban zones of my being are locked in a never-ending dialogue. They constitute a landscape of my being on which is enacted a story that has no ending. As far as my limited understanding goes, it has no beginning either. Maybe one is always at the starting point.

After tracing my origins like this, I can only be reinforced in my belief that poetry is always with us. Every one of us experiences poetic states of mind at one time or another – even those least endowed with thinking powers. I think this is what John Locke and Wordsworth were trying to tell us about our experiencing of the physical world. A field of daffodils, a lake, a breeze, a cloud – their associations all combine to create a totality of experience we call poetry. It is poetry as a state of mind.

A woman is sitting by the roadside, suckling a baby. A commonplace scene so typical in the developing world. A flight of birds is enacting a ballet-like scene up there against the blue. Carefree, far away from human concerns. Far away from trucks and other vehicles that chew up the road and leave clouds of dust in their wake. The woman waits and endures, as do so many other women of the world: waiting and enduring. Like the trees she's sitting under. Massive concrete inhabitants of the city behind me heave themselves up into space, as if they were jostling for attention.

The poetic essence of the above lies in the relationships the mind intuits between the disparate elements one is contemplating. When the mind and sensory perceptions recreate new or familiar relationships, perceiving things as an organic whole, a poetic state of mind results. And so we realize poetry is a way of perceiving.

I took to writing short fiction in the 1950s while reading Nikolai Gogol, Chekhov, Tolstoy, Pushkin, Faulkner, Richard Wright, Langston Hughes, Zora Neale Hurston, Lorraine Hausbury, James Baldwin, Hemingway, Sherwood Anderson, John Steinbeck, Margaret Walker, Kingsley Amis, Mulk Raj Anand, Rabindranath Tagore and others.

Soon after I left South Africa in 1957 to teach in Nigeria, I became acquainted with West African writers. Among them were Wole Soyinka, poets Christopher Okigbo, J P Clarke, Efua Sutherland, Kofi Awoonor and Kwesi Brew, and novelists Chinua Achebe, Cyprian Ekwensi and Ama Ata Aidoo. I had left a literary renaissance in my native country to enter that of West Africa.

This array, I venture to suggest, should indicate the literary culture that rubs off on one, stimulating the imagination in a person destined to be a writer. I say this because it seems that one who is not destined to become a writer may read profusely for intellectual and emotional enrichment, yet never be driven to tap his or her own imagination for the creation of literature. No value judgement intended, just a fact. There was almost a kind of inevitability with which I fell in love with the well-told story and found myself playing at storytelling. There is also something about language that bewitches me. I hang on words and expressions I hear when I converse with people or hear them address a public. My imagination becomes highly activated, constantly at white heat.

What do these disparate features ask of each other to create a poetic image? Possibly nothing. But there is that inner compulsion for the imagination to create a picture that will harmonize them, to establish the rhythm that lies in the relationships between phenomena. Evidently the imagination cannot bear disorder. Poetry is always there. What we need to do is pluck it from the tree. Recreate it. Refine it as we do any sophisticated thing – writing it or speaking it, expressing vigorous feelings with vigorous words.

I seem to be answering the question: where and how did it all begin? Surely, in order to educate the imagination, the creative person has to learn how to deal with the world of things, events, people; open up all the pores of the body, bombard the sense organs until they cannot help but register impressions that press against them, and must try to make meaning out of them. We are forever seeking meanings in the world around us, because these meanings in the external world help us discover the meanings of ourselves at every stage of our growth. To train the imagination is also to train the emotions. I feel what I think; I think what I feel.

So while I say the world is here around us to educate the imagination in each of us, I am also saying that we have to apply our sense organs and our faculty to project ourselves into the world around us, to intuit its meanings.

We can be wrong-headed in our interpretation of this world, but if we don't falsify our feelings, if we don't go for cheap thrills, if we don't live by borrowed feelings, if we are faithful to our feelings all round, then we can extract meanings that do justice to the thing, event, the people we experience. We can learn to discriminate between what increases and elevates us and the dross that lowers the quality of the imagination.

There are political and social upheavals among the poorer nations of the world today. The artist responds to such predicaments as to others, through his own kind of sensibility – the use of the written word or of body movement or sculpture or song, as well as through the activism society demands of him.

The intensity of the upheavals comes and goes in waves and in cycles. The 1960s saw in the United States an activist intensity that polarized your racial and ethnic communities. At such times there seems to the artist to be nothing – but *nothing* – as important, as sacred, as freedom. Writers become completely absorbed in this predicament, which in turn almost swallows us up. We begin to programme the imagination, to channel it so that it serve our ideals, our vision of what we perceive as a glorious future.

In the process we pump energy into our diction, and more and still more until we imagine that words themselves are like missiles. We invest words with the mystical power that can bring ramparts tumbling down. We speak with the tongues of prophets, priests, gurus. We invoke the presence of our ancestors, especially the spirits of our heroes. We often imitate oratory in our drama and poetry. Poetry becomes theatre. If the poetry and drama of the black world have anything in common, it is this aptitude to recapture the resonance of oratory. At its best, oratory is also a form of poetry. In this regard, there are close correspondences between African-Americans and blacks in South Africa.

I feel constrained at this point to say something that is quite unpopular in my country. We are at that stage in our history when we lose all patience with those who do not embrace our own tactics toward liberation. We would like all people to think alike, speak and act alike. Some groups even kill for their beliefs. This is the point I want to put across for what it is worth: that in situations of political conflict and violence we can rescue the imagination, at least for an interim period, from the kind of programming that compels us to repeat ourselves. Even if we acknowledge that writers often repeat themselves, we must surely realize that there is a certain kind of repetitiousness that spells stagnation. The imagination begins to atrophy. For this is when we live on borrowed passion, heroics, certitudes. The imagination may well retreat a bit at this point, reorganize itself, sharpen focus and restore the fullness of its landscape. The imagination then becomes our sanctuary.

One of the ways of salvaging the imagination, I suggest, is through this very method of recapturing with the written word the power of incantation, of oral delivery, of the ancient inner magic of language as metaphor. Another way is to provide as full a context for protest as possible, if protest there must be. Myth-making and context lend resonance to our creations. The myth is that never-ending story of life: children are still being born, women still wait and endure, men still betray one another, we still dream both idle and meaningful dreams ... and we must keep trying to negotiate the meeting point between art and history: an effort that is itself the enduring purpose of life.

Gwendolyn Brooks has said in a foreword to an anthology of poetry compiled by Langston Hughes (1971):

> At the present time, poets who happen also to be Negroes are twice tried. They have to write poetry, and they have to remember that they are Negroes. Often they wish that they could solve the Negro question once and for all, and go on from such success to the composition of textured sonnets or buoyant villanelles about the transience of a raindrop, or the gold-stuff of the sun. They are likely to find significances in those subjects not instantly obvious to their fairer fellows. The raindrop may seem to them to represent racial tears – and those might seem, indeed, other than transient. The golden sun might remind them that they are burning.

During the 1950s when a crop of writers, including myself, emerged around the *Drum* magazine in Johannesburg, I wrote bitter stories. I choked on the stuff and the heartburn it was releasing. The bitterness left me emotionally drained. I knew that I could not sustain the anger without doing myself harm. I went into exile, to teach in Nigeria. With my exit came my release. Even though I continued to write mainly about the life I had left behind, I had the freedom to learn to tame my bitterness with language. Words hammered out on the anvil of life itself, words lifted out of the fire of imagination and reordered into the shape of poetic truths.

It may often appear that the poet in an environment of political conflict and tyranny simply revels in predicting doom for the oppressor. But anger hurts badly. It can be corrosive if sustained and we do not tame it with words. Take the scene, for instance, that the imagination recreates in the poem, *The Beginning of a Long Poem on Why I Burned the City*, by Lawrence Benford, an African-American writer. His metaphor is awe-inspiring:

> – *And I grew up!*
> *Like a wild beast awaking*
> *To find his mate eaten*
> *In one second I grew up*
> *With the fires that flamed*
> *In my soul. Fires that burned*

– Holes in the soft spots of my heart.
(So as not to bleed to death)
They were plugged with lead
And I went off to college
With a Gasoline can
(from The New Black Poetry)

Violence and political tyranny are universal experiences. The artist refines emotions by taming them with the use of language, whether they be painful or joyful, whether they celebrate or draw our attention to human agony. Africa is writhing with the pain of civil strife today, with tyranny, with famine, with genocide. It is raw pain waiting for the artist to tame and refine with language.

Although I felt discontented and restless in the last three of my nine years in the United States, just raring to return home, I realized more than ever before that I had come a long way from my small village and slum beginnings. During my twenty years' exile I had enjoyed the freedom to move in and learn from a diversity of cultures – here, in Africa, in Europe.

I have learned, too, that even in open democracies, such as there are in America and Western Europe, there are pockets of bigoted morality that operates under the banner of Christianity; the same as we are witnessing in some Islamic states. This often places the imagination in a state of siege. Indeed, it has become impossible to talk meaningfully about the imagination without reference to culture, its breeding ground: belief, ideology, education, values and so on. The dilemma is compounded by the diversity of moral standards in the world determined by religious beliefs. For instance, the dominant Islamic states will decide that the imagination that fathered Salman Rushdie's *The Satanic Verses* is an insult to God, the ultimate abomination calling for the ultimate penalty.

Bigots will continue to thrive: a price we have to pay for the democratic ideal. This promises us the right to be what we will and still ensure that we do not claim any right to violate another human being – physically, or by blackmail, or by setting up barricades around our freedom to be.

I have been talking about the imagination that comes into play when I write fiction and poetry, even literary journalism. I am aware, however, that over decades now scientists have endeavoured to relate their specialized studies to morality. They have, much to their credit, expanded the frontiers that have for long defined the concepts yielded by the imagination. Conservation of the environment, the moral questions to which medical practice is now compelled to seek answers – these are but two of several areas where we are witnessing the humanizing of the scientific imagination.

'Bantu Education', as it came to be called, is a product of Afrikaner nationalism and apartheid ideology. It was designed in the early 1950s to provide the kind of schooling for Africans that would enslave the mind. Before 1953, when Bantu Education became law, curricula and syllabi were the same for black and white, but facilities were separate and unequal. The new curricula and syllabi compelled teachers to instruct their children on how to *be* inferior and *feel* inferior.

The rationale was to lower the quality of education for the Africans so that we do not aspire to pastures set aside for whites. The State insisted on mother-tongue instruction from elementary through high school, knowing full well that English text-books were not going to be translated in due time or ever. This would also counter political activism, because the Mandelas, the Sobukwes and fellow activists had been educated in the earlier system of schooling. The frontiers of the imagination would be thus limited, because ideas that come with education were blocked.

The battle is on. The mind is straining at the chains in order to break them. The children of high-school age are still angry. Their kind of anger readily finds expression through the destruction of school property – something tangible, destructible, some-thing that symbolizes white authority.

Educators are faced with the daunting task of setting up structures in which the intellect must find a humanistic environment to regain its right to learn, to attain the farthest reaches of the imagination possible.

Finally, the beauty of this adventure is that the imagination does not wait for the day when we shall have rid ourselves of tyranny. It overarches history and may get there long before the event. As Albert Camus implies in his essay on art as rebellion, the imagination reorganizes reality where there was chaos before. The artist is rebelling against disorder. Now, I leave you this dirge by the South African poet, Don Mattera, which relates the bulldozing of the last houses of Sophiatown, particularly his own home, in 1960. There is disorder here in the very act of tyranny; there is injustice. The language of the dirge subdues the passion of anger, distilling it so that we, the readers, share the memory of that devastating event:

The Day They Came for our House ... (Sophiatown, 1962)

The sun stood still
in the sullen wintry sky
a witness
to the impending destruction.

Armed with bulldozers
they came
to do a job nothing more
just hired killers.

We gave way
there was nothing we could do
although the bitterness stung in us,
in the place we knew to be part of us
and in the earth around,

We stood.

Slow, painfully slow
clumsy crushers crawled
over the firm pillars into the rooms
that held us
and the roof that covered our heads,

We stood.
Dust clouded our vision
We held back our tears
It was over in minutes,

Done.

Education as a Process of Growth – 1982

Synopsis by Marcus Ramogale

This graduation address at the University of Cape Town on 7 December 1982 was presented under the title: 'Address to Diploma and Certificate Recipients at the University of Cape Town'. In it we meet Mphahlele the consummate, highly sought-after public speaker. In this speech, he looks at the interplay between education and politics in what was apartheid South Africa.

Mphahlele proposes to see education as 'a process of growth, a coming into being, into awareness of self and environment.' If education entails 'awareness', then the educated, including the University of Cape Town's graduates, ought to realize that racially segregated South Africa is 'a sick society.' This awareness, Mphahlele suggests, will help undermine the racial barriers put in place by apartheid planners. He then goes on to talk about the non-racial ideal of the 1950s, 'when the African-Indian-Coloured Congress movement and the white Congress of Democrats tried to appeal to reason and compassion.' The black leadership then, influenced by the liberal and rational principles of 19th-century England, was convinced that white South Africa would be amenable to logical argument. Disappointment and 'traumatic bewilderment' came when the apartheid state responded ferociously. Because of this, Mphahlele suggests, the principle of non-racialism has become hollow for some black people. Given this situation, what role should education play in uniting a divided society? For Mphahlele, concrete structures and processes – including increased admission of black students into liberal institutions of higher learning, accompanied by the recruitment of a black faculty – should be put in place to achieve this. White liberal institutions should concentrate on this instead of being preoccupied with 'conserving standards of western civilization.' The Cape Town graduates, Mphahlele concludes, should 'ponder the quality and depth of ... [their] awareness ... in relation to these irksome issues.'

It is interesting to note that the issues Mphahlele raised in this speech, in particular increased access to white institutions by black students and the recruitment of a black faculty, are now part of the Ministry of Education's higher education plan in post-apartheid South Africa.

L et us for a moment think of education as process rather than as subjects, disciplines, training programmes neatly packaged into curricula and syllabi, all given endorsement and authority through exams, certificates, diplomas and so on. Education as a process of growth, a coming into being, into awareness of self and environment, a cultural process.

I wonder at what stage, for instance, white children become aware that they are in a school that excludes blacks, in as much as they see blacks for the first time as domestic workers, farm labourers, delivery men and so on. Racial mixing in a few private schools and in the so-called open universities like the University of Cape Town is still too tentative, self-conscious, too loaded against the pathetically small numbers of blacks, to serve as a clear index to the quality of interaction that takes place.

Let us consider the deeper levels of awareness, where we begin to contemplate the brutal consequences of our segregated lives; where we should begin to explore ways of dealing with both the consequences and the roots of our malady. For, beneath the glitter and the neon lights and the oft-celebrated splendour of this country's industrial and economic prosperity for those whose colour is 'right', ours is a sick society: one racial segment sicker than the other, one ideological tribe the sickest of the lot. More important and highly placed people than I have repeatedly sounded warnings about the disastrous implications for our future inherent in institutionalised racism and violence, in the conceit of power. I need not replay those warnings; they have been mounting in urgency and in apocalyptic stridency since the turbulent decade of the 1950s. The question that keeps knocking at the window of my consciousness is whether education as cultural process will ultimately undermine or reinforce the barriers that have been fixed and are still being forged between whole communities.

I passionately shared the idealism of the 1950s, when the African-Indian-Coloured Congress movement and the white Congress of Democrats tried to appeal to reason and compassion from the platform of non-racialism. Most of the black leadership had studied at Fort Hare and a smaller number at the English-language universities. They had, like so many other African nationalists north of the Zambezi who were leading their movements towards freedom from colonial rule, assimilated the libertarian ideas of 19th-century England and the notion of the paramountcy of Reason – as articulated by John Stuart Mill, Jeremy Bentham, William Cobbett and so on. As idealists, we had no doubt that the white people of this country shared the libertarian traditions of Europe, as they themselves never ceased to remind us that they were custodians of a civilization two thousand years old. So much of British literature, so much of what we were taught in mission institutions, so much of what we read in the press, drummed into our heads that democracy was a Christian virtue. And because whites proclaimed their Christian faith so loudly and told us that to be Christian was to be civilized and vice versa, it just didn't make any sense when, instead of reason and compassion, hell was let loose when we shouted, 'Freedom in our time!'

That idealism was violently shaken by the Bantu Education Act (1953) as well, and the removal of Sophiatown attended by military convoys. But it was blown to bits by the Treason Trial (1956-61), by Sharpeville (1960), by the Rivonia Trial, by the banning of the political movement. And then the tortuous road to exile. June 1976 merely confirmed the cruelty of the time.

The memory of these incidents was rudely jolted again when I read an article by Edward Norman in *The Times Literary Supplement* (28 October, 1982) entitled 'Is Democracy really Christian?' Mr. Norman restates the traditional teaching of the churches concerning democracy. Such teaching associates it with 'individual judgment of each citizen,' even while democracy operates through consensus. Mr. Norman sees democracy as merely a device whereby a governing elite and its opponents bring to the masses ideas they have formulated in order for constituencies to endorse their claims to power. He sees the contending parties all arguing within a received constitutional framework, so that what is actually at issue is each party's programme. A democracy could easily operate within the framework of a wrong-headed ideology and promote it. The consensus could also be wrong-headed: the majority is not always right. East-European socialisms are also entitled to call themselves democracies, according to their own understanding of the ethical nature of collectivism in the relationship between state and the masses.

Mr. Norman ultimately concedes that democracy is a plausible 'filter of competing human enthusiasms,' without the moral claims Christianity makes for it. Our own idealism of the 1950s, on the other hand, was rooted in the received moralistic assumptions attaching to democracy. Compassion being at the very centre of African humanism, you can imagine our traumatic bewilderment in response to the ferocity of the State machine once it got into motion against the forces of opposition. Another harsh lesson, closely related to this mistaken notion of democracy, was our observation of how easy it is for the Western world to draw a neat and clear line between, on the one hand, church morality that passes for Christian conscience and moral action, and on the other, political practice. Each of these, we noticed, has its own ethics, whatever campaigning rhetoric may tell us about South Africa being a Christian country.

In the midst of these experiences, reinforced by more arrests, detentions and other related travails, blacks today speak apologetically about non-racialism. The African National Congress in exile still talks non-racialism, but in a way one chews bubblegum that has lost its taste. The distinction the press popularly claims exists between 'Black Consciousness groups' and 'non-racialism groups' is too facile and falsifies our political reality. The question remains: are black leaders in the near or distant future going to be the ones to set up bridges as an exercise in interracial coexistence?

Another question: what should education's role be in a fragmented society denied the cohesion required for it to realize itself? We have got to believe that while education sets up discontents, divine or otherwise, it also reconciles; it synthesizes. But it is not enough to believe this. It is after all but an axiom. Women and men of education should be planning and executing structures whose declared objective will be to provide a base for this axiom to be realized.

I'm not at all persuaded, in spite of declarations of intent and belief from liberal institutions of higher learning, that they have reached the limit of their capacity in admitting blacks or creating extension services for them. Much more remains to be done than the present token gestures to deal with the problems of the student's impoverished background once he or she has been admitted. Black faculty should be recruited. It is a disgrace that in spite of overtures to the principals of the liberal universities, virtually nothing has been done for the 1,500 students Fort Hare refused to readmit last October. Why has academic life become so emasculated in this country? I keep asking myself.

But then, the failure on the part of liberal universities to act more resolutely on the whole crisis of tertiary education for blacks is typical of the general petrified mood of white liberals and radicals. They have become immobilized by the sheer ferocity and might of the political authority. And so they turn around in circles and make pleasant noises about black rule; education for an African future; black-white ratio of 50:50 in the white universities; bridging courses and academic support for the poor student in a white school/university; academic standards, and so on, while seeming to promise shelter for the 'deserving' few out of the millions around clamouring for higher education. South Africa is a country choking on the authoritarian morality of church and society that largely suppresses the humanistic conscience. And yet a small band of black church leaders have been influencing synod decisions, and to a considerable extent liberalizing the open white church establishment. There has been no corresponding process in liberal universities.

It could be argued that universities, being heavily State-funded, function within prescribed limits. And yet there exists today at least a fund of philanthropic goodwill among industrialists quite unprecedented in our history, and universities could tap this for bigger extension programmes in black areas. As one of those by-products of the experiment in racial and cultural interaction, philanthropy, it ought to be hinted, cannot be considered to have fully benefited an underprivileged people until it actively promotes the birth and nurturing of creative and enterprising black leadership in the target area of sponsorship.

The only hope there is for white universities to be truly liberalized is for them to admit many more black students and staff as *conscious* policy, as an *ethical imperative*. As a complementary measure, the universities must increase their extension programmes in town and country. For this an inter-university committee must be established outside the Committee of Principals, which has become an arena for faction fights

White institutions have been traditionally preoccupied with conserving 'standards' of Western civilization and/or a tribal culture. Outside of institutions, blacks and whites have been preoccupied with surviving each other, with whites dictating the terms and the rules of the game all the way. Splendid opportunities for interracial, cross-cultural living and discourse have been lost.

Says Professor NC Mangangi:

> *When we write, paint, sing and dance primarily to conserve culture, we kill something ... the hodgepodge that is education in our country today is not futuristic enough. It is so intimately tied up with our outmoded ideas about race and our conservationist approach to culture and identity that it hardly is a preparation for the kind of Southern Africa that is emerging on the historical horizon.*

Even as I congratulate you all here on the attainment of diplomas and certificates, I cannot help but ask you to ponder the quality and depth of your awareness, your growth, in relation to these irksome issues. I offer no brilliant answers. I merely want to share my musings with you. You are products of an education system, as we all are in this country, in the management of which a political authority is hell-bent on monitoring all the way our intellectual and moral growth, on bottling and canning human minds with desperate quasi-scientific preservatives. We hardly know the joys of the humanistic intellectual enterprise in the collective sense of that phrase. The challenge before you is to re-educate and liberate yourself. Keep pushing, and may the adventure you have embarked upon yield the best you could wish for yourself and your immediate humanity.

Education as Community Development – 1990

Synopsis by Peter Thuynsma

An alternative title, or even a subtitle, for this public address/essay could be a splendidly contentious 'Transforming Society' – for this is really what Es'kia Mphahlele's fervent intellect advocates.

In essence, he examines the purpose and appropriateness of education for both black and white South Africans alike, and he asks why education has distanced itself from well-reasoned cultural goals and from the whole purpose of living. He is pessimistic about the prospects for success of the existing education system in South Africa's new-found democracy, unless it discovers new and extended goals. He also wonders:

'....why education has never consciously served the purpose of cultivating the whole person, who once upon a time gave us a glimpse of the subterranean stream where fears, discontents, motivations lurk, where our self-esteem alternates between heroism and self-devaluation?'

Here is a graceful and critically comparative tableau of selected educational systems and educational philosophies, ranging from Socrates to Christianity, and the consequent texture of citizenship they bred. Mphahlele identifies the salient educational needs in a new democracy as: education for participatory citizenship, self-driven learning, exploratory research, and both socialization and counter-socialization. He suggests that there is a need to study social phenomena with an open mind. Then quite urgently he advocates an education that will allow us to engage actively and even change our environment; to break the continuum that has traditionally required us to fit in with the physical and human environment.

Ultimately, this erudite discussion proposes a community development that is appropriate to the cultural, political and economic goals of a community (both local and national). It insists that the process forms an organic continuum from pre-school to adult education – involving the active participation of both formal and non-formal learning agencies along the way – to ensure a natural and ongoing growth in awareness of one's total environment. This can only lead to a greater awareness of one's rights and responsibilities within micro and macro human landscapes.

In his conclusion, Mphahlele makes fairly copious mention of types of com-

munity education programmes, the most promonent perhaps being the Council for Black Education and Research, a Soweto-based non-governmental organisation (NGO) that he founded on his return from his twenty-year exile. That bold initiative bears clear testament to the hands-on actuality that underscores the authority with which Es'kia Mphahlele can address the complexities and tensions inherent in the concept of community education.

I t is almost impossible not to repeat oneself in any discussion of education – especially because it is perhaps the most talked-about subject next to the price of potatoes! One keeps coming back to a road one recognizes as familiar because we have travelled it before, and done so several times too. The political seasons may come and go – transforming the landscape where the years of plenty and of scarcity and illness will alternate, perhaps even drag on to remind us of our mortality. Yet the questions concerning education – the arguments, the grievances, the pleadings, the demands, the actions of defiance and so on – will remain; they will keep coming back to plague us. And so the roads cross and crisscross, bend, climb up and down. We are always at the starting point.

I should like, before getting to my central theme, to give a brief recital of my thoughts on being asked to be a consultant for the 'revival' of a mission secondary school that used to be in Johannesburg. It died in 1956 with the enforcement of the Group Areas Act. The name shall remain unannounced, as the idea needs to be pushed further still towards a concrete realization. The statement I made to the Executive Committee of the alumni organization that conceived the revival is as follows:

The principle of building a new interracial school is wholly acceptable. The old St X students' sentiments, inspired by the zeal of the founding fathers and reinforced by the memories we cherish of the happy learning environment that school provided – these are unimpeachable. The project is more than worth undertaking: it is an imperative.

We cannot switch the clock back to the historical circumstances in which the church mission in England came to establish the school. Mission-school education, State-aided or not, was the predominant system available to Africans from the 19th century into the decade of World War Two. It was in the 1940s that day high schools emerged in urban townships. From as far back as the early 1920s, however, secular community schools were established in various parts of rural South Africa. The money for these ventures came from village communities and local authorities.

The present time requires not only the drive to build new structures, but also the vision of, and passion for, social content with a philosophical base to make the structures meaningful for community development. The vision will inform the curricula, i.e. what is to be taught, in relation to what, to what purpose, in what order and with what emphases. We must, therefore, outgrow the very beginnings that gave so many of us a launching platform, so to speak. We mustn't be bogged down by the idyllic picture we may still have of a self-contained, quiet mission station with students enjoying a sheltered book or vocational education – imported – with native teachers enjoying sheltered, if dedicated, employment.

The phrase 'community development' is crucial for me. It means that a school should no longer be content to be like a light flickering in the dark. The school's curriculum should make it imperative for pupils to contribute to their environment, which is also its human setting.

To transfer curricula of formal schooling bodily, the curricula that we have inherited from tradition, will simply continue to impoverish mind and spirit. For that is where we are today.

We should forthwith set up a Committee on Studies. This will investigate curricula and certification and propose the direction to be taken in both these and related issues. The members of this committee should of necessity be educationalists.

There should be a post-secondary two-year lap preparatory for university, college, or technical or any other post-secondary career – even a job that requires no more than elementary literacy.

Since writing the above I have been applying my mind to education as community development in preparation for such a process; education as growth and a way of life. An American educationalist wrote in 1942:

Many schools are like islands set apart from the mainland of life by a deep moat of convention and tradition.

Across this moat there is a drawbridge which is lowered at certain periods during the day in order that the part-time inhabitants may cross over to the island in the morning and back to the mainland at night.

Why do these young people go out to the island? They go there in order to learn how to live on the mainland. (Carr, 1942, cited in Cook, 1977:1)

This is sadly the case in most countries of the world today – almost fifty years later – and a matter of great concern in all of them. Something of cataclysmic dimensions has happened to the goals of education since the times of Georgias (c480-380 BC), Pythagoras (c490-c421 BC), Socrates (c470-399 BC) and Plato (427-347 BC). The Christian introduction of a new spiritual dimension of the human personality, followed by the European industrial revolution, influenced the direction education was to take, while at the same time complicating it.

Socrates shared the scepticism of the Sophists; but he did not share their unquestioning trust in traditional morality. He saw his role as a teacher, as a liberator of pupils' minds from confusion and dogma. He believed strongly that the mind could discover the truth about the physical world and its human life. This would help it to recognize the truth once discovered, especially concerning good. Inquiry would dispel the confusion.

Plato developed Socrates' ideas further. He observed and recognized in the individual the power to reason, a desire for the good life and the ability to use reason to decide what is good for these appetites. Plato believed in the power of education as a tool for reform in the individual and in the state.

The Greeks, no doubt, saw education as a way of ensuring conformity. To this extent they carried over the more ancient, spontaneous assimilation and transmission of the community's lifestyles, customs and mores from generation to generation. The use of reason for the pursuit of education was for the Greeks the right of an elite. They entrusted a certain class with the right to teach. Plato would insist on a system of universal, compulsory public education. Reason distinguished Greek and Roman education from its spontaneous forms.

Then Christianity came. Its pristine morality was replaced, often even corrupted, by the theologies and morality devised by church denominations. The rise of nationalism and industrialization in Europe, 19th-century notions of race, the problems of economic and social welfare, of political freedom, the role of education in relation to these and other events and issues – they all combined to complicate further the concept of morality and civilization at large.

Something became unhinged, and the disassociation that occurred is suggested in the quotation from Carr cited above. To carry the metaphor further: there are too many doors hanging on one hinge and banging about in the wind. The good life, i.e. economic advancement, has assumed centre-stage. Today it is regarded as old-fashioned, reactionary, unpopular to suggest other values that have at least equal claim to our commitment. 'People want jobs!' the cynics shout. 'Give us jobs!'

Educational planning and practice have disengaged to a large extent from morality, from cultural ideals in general, from the ideals of personhood, and from the highest aspirations of the community, both locally and nationally. I think Europe, followed by North America, became so affluent that the values of education came to be perceived and articulated in materialistic terms, with the accent on open markets. Managers, entrepreneurs and technocrats were needed to run the huge and ever-expanding industrial machine. Education was planned with this goal uppermost in the scale of values held by the relevant government authorities. 'Manpower needs' defines for them the human condition. Alas!

Now we realize that we have to grope our way back to beginnings: not to the concept of education for the few chosen ones, but to the time when the lofty ideals of thinkers such as Cardinal John Newman (England, 1801-1890), John Dewey (United States, 1859-1952), and Rabindranath Tagore (India, 1861-1941) echoed endearingly in the corridors of learning. Newman was a passionate advocate of a liberal education – to counterbalance the 19th-century notions of utility as the basis of the enterprise called education. John Dewey was committed to the democratic ideal in education. Tagore emphasized self-knowledge and human relations, deriving from profound spiritual experience, as part of the educational ideal. Furthermore, Dewey, as a reformer, wanted education to be related to students' interests, to free it from recapitulation of human experience – i.e. the routine recital of facts, figures and opinions. He insisted on the 'continuous reconstruction of experience'.

It is not in categorical rejection of utility and material welfare that these thinkers, and others like them, upheld these and other profound values. Rather they remind us that the whole person needs to be educated or cultivated, if you will.

Let me first try to redefine the problem and the progressive thinking that attempts to confront it. I shall do this by restating it in the form of general assumptions that I believe we can agree upon:

1. We are striving to educate for full citizenship based on democratic government.
2. A democratic society places reason and the people's ability to think for themselves high on the list of its faculties in relation to a liberal education. Faith in reason, too, is a basic prerequisite for developing a democracy. *Developing* is the operative word here, for education must be seen as a process of that very development. It is not the ultimate landing-point the education venture is meant to ferry us to that should fulfil us, but the venture itself as exploration.
3. Too much education today is didactic: an expository recital of what the teacher regards as items of truth. This is especially so in the social sciences. The teacher tries to simplify truth as if one and only one view were correct – often the one that is hallowed by the text that purports to deliver it. We need instead to expose the student to diverse and contrasting interpretations. Students must be trained to think for themselves, to explore issues and phenomena for themselves. *They must eventually free themselves from the tyranny of the text*.
4. We all go through a process of socialization in our childhood and youth. This means that we learn the traditions, customs, rules and lifestyles of our society, from the local community to the larger mass called the *nation*. We do so as if there were no other society, no other sets of values. This is as it should be. One can say this without pretending that race and apartheid in South Africa hasn't put us all, black and white, through a process of socialization based on false values, aspirations, moral standards and religion determined by the dominant economic and political culture. There is, however, also a process an American educationist calls 'counter-socialization'. This is a way in which we outgrow socialization. We strike out on our own, independently of society, even while we are of it. This way the student is able to expand mentally, spiritually, emotionally, morally.

5. Social studies as a discipline is the most relevant part of a liberal education in the training of citizens in the highest ideals of democracy. This has its contradictions. While we want to train people to think for themselves, to face contending opinions, we have at the same time to educate for nationhood, which demands constructive consensus and positive conformity. Herein lie the tensions that only reason and faith in reason can resolve. Democracy and citizenship, civics, should be an integral part of social studies in the curriculum right from primary school. It requires more intelligent planning than we observe in the present system. We also need better texts.

6. It is in social studies that indoctrination grows rank and can become uncontrollable. It can become more successful than the teacher ever dreamed of, but it may also swing back against him. Publishers are implicated in this, as Shirley H Engle and Anna S Ochoa note:

   Textbook publishers, driven by the necessity to sell books and afraid of self-appointed censors, contribute to indoctrination by either omitting or watering down the coverage of any topic that occasions controversy. (1988)

   Mere exposition of facts passes on 'inert ideas' – i.e. ideas that merely float in the mind without being applied concretely, or tested, or even grouped in new combinations. 'What use is the idea?' is a question that should constantly concern us.

7. The teacher needs additional resources to back up his class texts. These will promote in the student a habit of mind that demands a study of social phenomena with an open mind. This is at the same time a way of encouraging' teachers to improve their public image in the community, as well as their own self-esteem which could not be lower than it is today.

I thought to catalogue the above irrefutable (to my view) assumptions so that we keep reminding ourselves of them as we explore education as community development. In 1982 Mrs Rebecca Mphahlele founded a child development centre in Lebowakgomo, fifty kilometres south-east of Pietersburg. This is a growing town, semi-rural, but which will never revert to an entirely rural status. Malnutrition is rife here. Most of the heads of families are away for at least a month at a time as migrant workers on the Reef and in Pretoria. Consequently mothers carry the whole weight of the parenting process.

Decisions have to be made. The child's education for its present is just as crucial as it is for its future. In other words, the demands of the child's environment which education should match are here and now. The education should empower the child to change the environment. It is, after all, an environment we found when we were locked up in the reserves, ever since the Land Act of 1913. We have constantly tried to bale out of these rural catchments called 'reserves', for we never had the political or material resources to do more than merely survive the environment. Result: stagnation. But the same can be said of the urban ghettos. We have merely been taught to fit into, rather than to transform, the urban environment.

If we had had the choice, we would have had a fighting chance to evolve an educational system that would empower us to change our human and the physical environments. So much for a didactic education and the expository teaching it demands. It also makes teaching a cushy job, doesn't it? But God forbid, that's not why I love it!

I mention Mrs Mphahlele's project because it promises a nucleus for a bigger experiment in education as community development. There is a pre-school division, which offers an opportunity for adult training in parenting skills, nutrition and the development of vegetable gardening for domestic consumption and for marketing. Education here becomes an involvement in life, an organic part of growth.

Another side of the coin in the transformation of an environment presents a Palestinian, Muni Fasheh of East Jerusalem, who recounts in a journal his experiences in community education. He speaks of the existing education among his people as an agent of hegemony, and proposes an alternative model of community education:

> I believe that most graduates of the formal education system within the Palestinian community are like the Israeli hen: their survival depends on external support, and their values are based on artificial, induced, or symbolic qualities. Such graduates live on a special mixture of courses and curricula that are 'scientifically and rationally' planned and prepared for them by experts, mainly from abroad. Further, such graduates are in general alienated from their environment and are mostly blind or insensitive to its basic problems and needs. When the surrounding conditions change, or when real world situations must be dealt with, such graduates become confused: the 'correct' answers and ready solutions they learned in the schools and universities suddenly become useless and meaningless. (Harvard Educational Review, 1989:19)

Echoes of home! Observe that this Palestinian educator does not conceive of any distinction between education *as* community development and education *for* community development. What pupils and students learn and study should ideally be a way of *perceiving* one's community and developing awareness of its nature, its environment and needs.

'Community development' should imply 'in the interests of...' The curriculum must be seen to fit into the cultural, political and economic goals of the community, local and national. Education *as* community development can take place from pre-school, through high school and later in a community dominated by adults. Adult learning requires a core curriculum rather than a mere replication of what goes on in formal school. Adults have their own needs to respond to, which is to answer questions about adult roles – e.g. their roles as citizens, as members of labour unions and political organizations, in parenting, in conservation of the environment, in burial and other benefit societies, community child care, insurance of life and property, consumer boycotts, family planning and so on.

This is the kind of community-based education in which the people and the teacher, rather than the State, create their own curriculum. Socialization carries over smoothly into the phase of counter-socialization that community-based education provides. For here the authoritarian and didactic approach, no matter how notoriously successful it may have been in formal school, is sure to be resented. And rightly so.

This habit of mind we call 'awareness' should stand us in good stead even when we change location – no matter how many times. Again, what pupils and students learn should ideally start to refine the process of developing into adulthood, in the place of what prevails today. The actual situation is that education is one process, formal, and growing up is another, casual. Parenting is also casual, depending very much on that old-time assimilation of customs that are passed on from generation to generation. After a wholesome formal education it should ideally be a natural process to move on to adult education.

A Chilean, Salomon Magendzo, discusses in the same journal the distinction between the State's formal education and 'popular education', or community-based education. We keep coming back to that concept of *transformation of society* through education, by both the better-off and the poor.

South Africa is very much like Chile in its centrally planned education. Industry has adopted the State's criteria and credentials. Consequently, in order to survive one has to go through State-sponsored and State-certificated schooling. There are hardly any alternatives. We hear echoes of home when we read Magendzo:

> *Ever since its inception, the educational system has had as its primary function the training of people for productive activity. At the same time, since it has its roots in middle-class values, the political system has turned education into its favoured instrument for promoting the ideology of social mobility, and in the process has saturated the schools with the ideology of these middle-class values.* (Harvard Educational Review, 1989:49)

The author continues to point out that the monolithic curriculum creates the illusion of equal opportunity; diversity is thus disregarded. Thus urban, semi-rural and rural communities are treated alike by a uniform teaching practice. Such a centralized system in Chile imposes the dominant culture on everybody. Magendzo further states:

> *The goals of popular education are based on the idea of building a participating and democratic society. In this sense, popular education is opposed to 'education for all' of the kind that has been imposed on all communities by the national elites. Instead, popular*

education requires an educational methodology that radically calls into question the authoritarian practices and the mechanical transmission of knowledge characteristic of traditional pedagogy. It stresses dialogue, group learning, and values the participant's experience as the foundation for further learning and knowledge. The educator is considered a facilitator of a collective educational process, someone who is able to question critically different perceptions of reality and custom, and to contribute to the formulation of new knowledge that addresses the problems of poor communities and the actions those communities want to undertake. (ibid.)

Something tells me that the clamour for a single department or ministry of education and integration of schools, however justified and perhaps motivated by sane aspirations, eventually only changes one kind of bureaucracy for another. We only get one massive institution in exchange for several relatively simple ones.

We are not anywhere near discussing what is missing deep down there in the curriculum, in our teaching practices, in the examination questions that are set, and in our cultural goals. We seem to be scared to get down to these fundamentals of a sound education system informed by democratic ideals and re-examine them. We are not asking ourselves where the relative emphases went wrong. Why has education, equally for black and white, distanced itself from well-reasoned cultural goals and the whole purpose of living? Why has it not discovered new or extended cultural goals? Why has education never consciously served the purpose of cultivating the whole person, who once upon a time gave us a glimpse of the subterranean stream where fears, discontents and motivations lurk, where our self-esteem alternates between heroism and self-devaluation?

Isn't it due to our fragmented consciousness that we have either created or allowed curricula that cannot bridge the extensive gap between rural sensibilities on the one hand and urban consciousness on the other? An organic sense of life is impossible as long as we are educated to deal only with knowledge packaged for its present autonomous departments, be they institutional or internalised in us. Even as I ask these questions I am aware that education not only sets up discontents but can also resolve them, even reconcile them. Also, I am aware that these questions may not have anything to do with the price of potatoes. But they raise for me more enduring issues – beyond the present crisis.

It must make our hearts bleed to see our rural communities isolated out there to sink or swim in their soul-battering poverty. Where is the kind of education that can help us to tame and change our environment instead of simply adapting to it? Our hearts must bleed even more to realize that education cannot in its present form raise our consciousness towards a unified sensibility as rural and urban communities.

As Dr Ken Hartshorne says in his Etheridge Commemoration Lecture, we do not need special education for rural areas. It wouldn't work, because people move to and fro between cities, towns and villages:

> ...*rural areas must be re-defined to include a much greater and effective component of adult, non-formal education, based on motivation, participation and mobilisation of the local people. As far as formal schooling is concerned the first step is to reduce the obvious inequalities that exist in the rural areas.* (17 May, 1989)

Apropos of consciousness, let me quote from an interview with an African-American involved in community development in Boston, USA, Mel King. It is said that 'his passion is transformation, finding ways to support human development, learning for life ...'

> *The system can't run faster than our minds. You can raise consciousness faster than the system. It's faster than a speeding bullet, if you would. There's nothing faster. I really believe that this consciousness-raising is where it is, and that no matter what's going on out there today we can be aware of and process some things that we need to be about. If we are not conscious about the dynamics of the relationships that exist then we won't even know what's happening with other institutions or the community that's off and running.*
>
> *Here is where the consciousness raising has to involve youth directly in the analysis of those issues they are facing daily. Issues such as: why are people unemployed? Why has the school budget been cut? Who makes those decisions? Why are people like them more employed or unemployed than other people? What is the impact of drugs and crime on them and their communities? Who benefits and who loses? What are responsible ways of dealing with their sexuality? What leads children to have children? What are the routes that they can travel to be all they can be? What are the opportunities? What are the deterrents? What are the strategies that must be developed and worked on? Do they have a vision of what would make themselves, their communities, and the world work?* (Harvard Educational Review, 1990:510)

I think that we shall forever need institutions of non-formal education designed for young and older adults. These are two major interest groups that a community-based education is intended to mobilize. The reason we shall need these is the very fact that we are trapped within walls we seldom talk about: part of the hidden curriculum.

I don't know who in particular draws up curricula and syllabi in this country. Very few people will tell you. We educators can only deduce from the curricula and slant of textbooks in the social sciences. A lot of damage has been done to the thinking capacities of students who have been through such texts and had to prove what they have committed to memory. The slant is ideological, based on the author's narrow upbringing and schooling, and fundamentalist conceptions of the human being and the destiny of men, women and children. This will continue until the team designing the curricula is radically reconstituted.

This radical reconstitution of the team is the first priority. The same alternative institutions will still be required to take care of those segments of the community the State has neglected for a long time, and others only the community can be sensible of. No community should be static and entrust to the State *all* the educational planning. Nor would there be much progress if it were possible for the State to provide everything. There are programmes it would be incapable of conducting. The State is not always, if ever, going to respond to the changes felt by the community from time to time. It is these changes in the people's wants and priorities that require a flexible core curriculum. The community ought then to organize a volunteer teachers' corps as one of its self-help development projects.

Even the developed democracies, where the State is relatively better equipped and more sophisticated, have alternative education centres. In several cases the local government comes up with financial assistance for these projects without demanding even a small measure of control.

The American National Community School Education Association defined community education as:

> ...a comprehensive and dynamic approach to public education:

> It is a philosophy that pervades all segments of education programming and directs the thrust of each of them towards the needs of the community... It affects all children, youth and adults directly or it helps to create an atmosphere and environment in which (everybody) find security and self-confidence, thus enabling them to grow and mature in a community which sees its schools as an integral part of community life. (NCSEA, 1968:6).

I have already suggested, although not in so many words, that we have been dumped in urban and rural localities as black communities. We have had neither the material nor political resources to create an education that could empower us to take charge of our community organization. For all the calamities, stresses, grievances and political upheavals that throw us all into some arena, we are still strangers to one another and to our environments. Because of the very nature of the issues that bring us together, we bring anger and nervous crisis-motivated energies to meetings, marches and rallies; we are even afraid of one another, lest we be accused of betrayal of the community if we express dissent on certain strategies that enjoy a 'quick-fix', ad hoc consensus.

On the other hand, political consciousness has been raised to the point where community education has now at least a physically and socially mobilized constituency to give it meaning. Welfare groups of a self-help nature have also emerged in our communities, women being in the leadership of most of them. These groups take care of orphans, the aged, the physically and mentally handicapped, pre-school education, child welfare, victims of alcoholic and drug abuse and so on. Resources and trained personnel are so thinly distributed that these welfare groups are few and far between.

Adult education and after-school childcare and education are sadly lacking. State schools have in most cases not been willing to make premises available for any activity outside their own night high schools, and these in venues that are few and far between. South Africa has the most disgracefully underused educational and welfare centres in the Third World, where school premises are in use night and day, weekends and vacation times – for lifelong learning and enrichment. In other countries public facilities are potentially available twenty-four hours of the day, seven days a week, fifty-two weeks of the year for facilitators of community effort. The community may be a township divided into neighbourhoods for effective operation.

The 'community education process' identifies a problem that needs solving in community life. The problem involves members of the community in public forums, committees, task forces and so on. Large numbers of individuals representing segments of the community become actively involved. Community educators are facilitators and leaders trained in the process of problem-solving projects.

They organize classes where individuals can develop skills, attitudes and knowledge needed for self-development and community welfare. The community educators and other leaders identify one problem at a time through a systematic needs-assessment process. Priorities are established and goals set for the most critical of these. Major constraints are also identified and efforts are made to resolve them. It becomes a matter of bringing the school to the community in more than just the physical sense of its presence; in this sense, the community, too, comes to the school. This is the case both for the schools that develop the child and those that develop the adult, young and old. It is in this effort that the relationship between learning for the job market and learning for living comes fully into play and finds a point of reconciliation.

The Council for Black Education and Research at Funda Centre in Greater Soweto is an institution the present speaker directs. He was among its founders in 1980, at a time when it was felt that we needed a leadership in matters of education. A leadership that would speak from a position of enlightened authority instead of always reacting to Government policy.

The Council's programme of non-formal education attracts young people from the level of senior high school through college, and generally people of ages 18 – 35. The lectures are based on themes, planned on the basis of seven Saturday mornings per theme. There are four such 'blocks' of seven weeks in the year. The topics change from year to year. Examples of themes: Know Your Continent – Africa; Know Your Country – South Africa; Family Life; Leadership; Your Environment; Labour Movements and Organization; Social Work and the Politics of Dispossession; Education; Know Your

Civics; the Arts and Social Reconstruction; Learning for the Job Market and Learning for Living; and so on. The topics for each theme are interdisciplinary, bringing together geography, history, the sciences, literature, the visual and performing arts, government, political studies, sociology, economics, medicine and nursing. Lecturers on different topics are urged not to be abstract and academic in their presentations. Where they *have* to use technical terms they must explain as much as possible. We consciously treat a theme in a way that gives it social significance because it touches the lives of the participants. Discussion is encouraged, even during a lecture.

We have discovered that such integrated studies promote in participants the habit of mind that establishes relationships between issues, events and phenomena, and thus a sense of organic unity in knowledge. Knowledge becomes an act of knowing when it can give an account of itself in the changing of attitudes and the process of independent inquiry. We have observed over the years the progress of student teachers that have attended our lectures for two to three years. There has been a remarkable transformation in their personalities: they are highly articulate; they bring to any topic a seriousness of purpose, independent thinking, and mature judgments and evaluation. Those participants who belong to trade unions or are workers in any class – artisans, administrators, professionals and so on – report that our inter-disciplinary lectures have opened their minds and their attitudes towards the work they like and towards their fellow-employees.

The Council is extending its programme of integrated studies into Greater Soweto as a pilot project involving kids who have been thrown out of the system or have dropped out. Their ages range between approximately fourteen and sixteen. At this stage in the Council's work, many other members of the community will be invited to monitor the operation of the two pilot centres – the Y.W.C.A in Dube and Ipelegeng centre in Jabavu – each containing three classes.

The Council has a branch in Cape Town and another in Pretoria engaged in other forms of community teaching and learning, e.g. home crafts, as well as interdisciplinary lectures. Two more are coming up in Northern Transvaal and Natal. We are also engaged in seven research projects in black communities – i.e. family counselling, student counselling, aptitude testing, the effects of financial aid on community projects, the after-effects of influx control, present-day home ownership and residence and interracial attitudes in integrated schools. Research fellows are working on these projects for their higher degrees.

I mention the work of the Council for Black Education and Research merely to indicate humble beginnings in community education and education as community development. These beginnings have the potential to grow countrywide into something much bigger than us. The variety of community programmes such an institution could undertake from region to region is incalculable.

Call it adult, continuing, alternative or community education or child development, this enterprise provides ample opportunities for structures and strategies in education that the State could not possibly conceive or be capable of conducting. Especially in a plural society such as South Africa, it is the people – who live their education in whatever group history has assigned them to – who must conduct it. To conduct an education is by turns to create it, to help us heave ourselves up and take that heroic step that leads us into the rites of passage from the sheltered workshop of socialization. From then on we are on our own – in a sense, in the realm of counter-socialization. Here we think for ourselves as individuals in the context of community.

We have a brutal history to learn from, if this ever teaches anybody. I am referring here to Christian National Education, which went into labour and gave birth to an illegitimate, deformed creature called Bantu Education. The monstrous folly in CNE was that it kept its children much too long in the cradle, where dummies and nap-kins were changed as many times as the mother was inspired to reinforce her social-ization strategies, e.g. through Sunday school, church, veld school, school proper, college, university, public rallies, brotherhood cults and so on. Inspiration was backed up by an inner compulsion born of the same process of socialization.

And so we have here a rather undignified image of grey-haired men and women with dummies in their mouths. Some try to speak an adult language without spitting out the dummy, others can only manage to grunt and gargle words of a kind. A few – God bless them – leapt out of that cradle with a sudden, fierce discovery that the sun had risen twelve hours before and they must catch up on the odyssey that is counter-socialization. May Providence have mercy on them!

From Knowledge to Education – 1989

Synopsis by Ndavhe Ramakuela

The main argument of this article is that the development of schools helps communities to discover themselves. The address was delivered at Bankuna High School in Nkowankowa, near Tzaneen. Bankuna, like Orlando High, is one of the prestigious high schools in the Northern Province (now Limpopo Province), which during the 1980s attracted students from as far as Soweto. It produced good students who now occupy strategic positions in government and the private sector.

Mphahlele emphasises here the need to develop the learner's potential, particularly to make them reach a level of maturity and independence where they can think and develop things for themselves. Mphahlele reiterates the idea that knowledge is power, that if people have the right kind of education they will eventually be able to build the moral fibre of their society outside the confinement of forced religious activities.

Mphahlele appreciates the invitation to a high school and looks at it as a development, particularly at a time when the country is ravaged by violence. Schools should become agents of moral and intellectual upliftment, and he encourages Bankuna to be a beacon of hope in this regard.

You have done me proud to invite me to celebrate with you your first quarter of a century in the life of Bankuna. The festival is all the more justifiable when there is so much death around, when we have become cannibals who laugh and cheer or stand immobilized while cities are burning, while school buildings are being razed to the ground, or stripped to the floor by petty thieves. Personalities, people, institutions and the dreams and ideals that inspired their origins and growth – their ashes lie there, a cold reminder of how oppressed people can hate themselves. For it must take extraordinary and blood-chilling self-hate and low self-esteem for a community to rip to pieces Orlando High School, brick by brick by rafter – picking its bones as it were, the way vultures and crows do to their prey. Today only the hollowness of what were classrooms echoes uselessly the voices of students and teachers and the business they were engaged in. Bankuna is also fortunate to be living, when Bantu Education has been chewing up the very fabric of a people's culture with the mindless relentlessness of termites, especially since 1953.

It takes courage, vision and a fiery sense of purpose and mission to establish a school or another institution that is intended to serve a whole community. This last clause flows from my passionate belief that a school should by its very nature, as an expression of a community's ideals and hopes, be an activist establishment. An activist is a person who urges and strives for social action in any community, whether such action is strictly political or concerns social change in a broader sense. A school that does not become an agent for community development becomes a mere venue for a club. Our thanks to you, Mr D Z J Mtebule, Sir, for having been fired by such a sense of mission that would yield a centre of enlightenment like Bankuna.

There is a pattern to all of this. Here in rural Northern Transvaal are hundreds of schools built out of the lean savings of our deprived people in their own communities. Then the political authority steps in to pay the teachers, monitor its existence and supply books. This is proof of how for centuries we have used our poor financial resources and labour to build where the government refuses to provide. So Bankuna stands as one of many living monuments, every brick of which represents our sweat and our labour of love. The structure tells the story of our burning yearning for learning, and our collective will to survive our miserable conditions. In Bankuna miserable conditions have been transformed into a driving creative force and purpose.

These living monuments fill our rural landscape across this country; they also remind us of many a hero and heroine, sung and unsung, who obeyed a divine call to build a school or inspire one to be created. I am not aware if our researchers for a senior degree in education have ever recorded the labours of these heroes in order to immortalize them. Their life histories would tell us volumes about the minds, personalities, drive, consuming passion, unflagging stubbornness of will, and compassion that they were gifted with. We would also see ourselves as communities through the histories – how we responded from decade to decade, generation to generation, to such leadership. For a good deal of history nowadays is drawn from what the researcher is told by the older people.

The joys of being a dedicated teacher far outstrip the agonies of the profession. Put in another way, the agonies give a deeper meaning to the joys. For to know our sorrow is to know our joy.

On an occasion such as today's, memories flood the mind and heart of those either too young or too old to forget: faces of the old students and teachers, some of whom may be here today; faces of students and teachers who have passed on to the Great Beyond; faces of rebels who were, or are, forever setting your consciousness on fire – for better or worse; faces of the spineless, belly-crawling stooges who betrayed both themselves and those who trusted them; faces of the faithful and loyal; the face of that loud student or teacher who bragged about conquests over girls he had lost or about brains and courage he never had. Yes, you the pioneer remember those moments, now so embarrassing, when you failed those loyal to you. At the same time you recall those moments, now so heart-warming and revitalizing, when you performed heroic deeds for your staff or students.

I am talking here of the profit and loss one experiences as a leader of people in any institution, in the whole arena of human relationships. For ultimately it comes down to that, doesn't it? Relationships in which a good leader develops the aptitude to balance personal desires and perceptions against the demands of his office, his authority. Much of this authority, I must add, has everything to do with accountability to the public. But it is, as we know only too well, a public that is fragmented into social and political constituencies. To know what hat to put on for which constituency, one must draw from the wisdom of the ages and adapt those lessons to present-day conditions.

There are two thoughts I should like to leave today with you, i.e. the staff and students of Bankuna as well as the parents and the rest of the community from which the school draws its students. One is that we should grasp and appreciate the distinction between schooling or knowledge and education. Schooling is a process or programme we go through in an institution. This could be a school with walls or one without walls such as a correspondence college, a prison or media-transmitted instruction. Normally, schooling comes with the gathering of knowledge, also called information at its most basic. One listens, reads and is informed in the process of knowledge gathering. Going to school or possessing knowledge does not of itself make an educated person. Most of what processes knowledge towards an education depends on the inner personality of the student in relation to his environment. The personality has to conquer the environment by taming it and using it to go beyond that point of survival. I speak of 'conquer' and 'survival' because the environment, whether rural or urban, is not of our making. We were placed in it by white governments, and from time to time the ground was removed from under our feet, so that we have always been strangers to our environment in the spiritual sense of the term.

Because the learner has to be taught to use his inner resources in taming the environment, genuine education must be learner-centred rather than a platform from which the teacher exercises his or her authority, often with the instruments of pain. Most of our 'education' today is in this kind of school – a centre of control rather than education. And I sing loud praises to all those who survived it and became bigger human beings in the open university of life.

Knowledge properly absorbed expands the mind, proportionate to the volume of the information. But we have to do something with the knowledge for it to be an agent of education. We have to constantly test its worth, subject it to thorough scrutiny and opposition. This assumes that school or college or university and community provide access to knowledge, and a climate for free independent inquiry and freedom of expression both among teachers and students. For goodness's sake, let us listen to our students and do something about their discontents. For they are telling us that they are hurting.

By testing our knowledge against conflicting evidence, by weighing its worth in relation to the demands for knowledge from our environment – immediate and less immediate – we can use that knowledge to help us understand, nay, comprehend, and deal with our environment (human, social and physical). At this stage, knowledge has not only become an act of knowing, instead of a ready-packaged article in a super-market; it has also become a tool for enriching our lives and giving them purpose. When knowledge thus becomes an organic part of the personality, we then know what we want to know and should know; the reasons why we want to and should know it; and how we want to and should know it. Knowledge at this profound level is not only part of the personality, but it also defines and expresses it. Education has begun to happen.

It now remains for society to experience several cycles of this process, this act of knowing. There will then be an accumulation of knowledge of various kinds and communal uses. From such uses we consolidate, urge and redefine our religious beliefs and practices. A culture, a tradition, has taken root. Because we have been colonized these past three hundred years, and are still colonized – being consumers rather than makers, designers or planners or originators – we have lived through several cycles of knowledge selected for us by our white rulers for their own purposes. We have for generations been buying knowledge which we then had to take to a repair shop. Those of us who are not equipped with the sense of inadequacy that takes us to the repair workshop collapse on the wayside, becoming a home for chickens before we die; or else we walk about like robots or zombies, remote-controlled by the master-race. Only the self-educated, who survived their primary school beginnings by the skin of their teeth, have been able to create options for themselves. Indeed, the education of the oppressed is nothing if it does not stimulate its participants to create options for themselves. For options that already exist when we leave the shelter of school life look like real or fictional bodies in outer space. They were not meant to be inhabited by people of our race and colour.

Inasmuch as culture cannot afford to be static, knowledge also moves in a pro-gressive line, leading us to new discoveries all the time. We must see to it, though, that with the growth and deepening of knowledge, we also develop our moral sense. The nuclear bomb, nerve gas and other devices of mass killing are a product of knowl-edge that shoved aside all moral responsibility that teaches the sanctity of life. Our moral sense exists in the faculty to know that life is not made up of fragments, unre-lated to one another; there is continuity in life and we owe one another as humans our own lives, even though the debt can never be paid in full. This is what education must attain, when we have it.

The second thought I beg to leave with you is that the greatest token of gratitude, the greatest tribute, we can pay to the founders of our institutions of learning is to strive to preserve them and develop them into better and still better centres of education. A proper educational institution by definition revitalizes its immediate community and the larger society. Because, on the strength of what I have argued earlier concerning knowledge, real education only takes place when it represents the needs of the community. That is, only an educated community can know what is good education. Through outreach programmes, teachers and students can educate the community so that it can eventually articulate its needs.

May Bankuna never fall like Orlando High and its contemporaries. May it live to see better and more prosperous years, when there shall be peace and plenty for all who work for them and have the opportunity to do so. May Bankuna become part of that process of becoming which is the essence of education. May Bankuna increasingly express *us* who inhabit and surround it, in the spirit of the New Education that is straining to be born.

Growing up in South Africa – 1955

Synopsis by Peter Thuynsma

In this essay, Mphahlele traces the politico-educational influences that are inevitable in the life of a child in 1980s apartheid South Africa. Seamlessly and eloquently he also sprints through selected alleyways of his own childhood to reconcile the apparent theory with reality, as well as to develop the authority with which he later analyses the country's piteous education system.

However damning his description of the inadequacies of the national, racially skewed learning system – and however palpable and pained his political perspective is – his intention remains a professional concern. The South African child will, despite tremendous obstacles, emerge from the system with knowledge of life's experiences, but without the ability to apply the knowledge through disciplined, coherent life skills.

In an eminently readable prose style, a style which fuses critical comment with story-telling narrative, Mphahlele then masks his pride and delineates the development of the Council for Black Education and Research – which Mphahlele founded in Johannesburg and which, at one time, had branches in Pretoria and Cape Town. This essay does not extol the community development angles of such community-based organizations, but here he advocates the rich curriculum for a humanistic learning environment.

B y the age of six an urban African child has already become acquainted with police terror, the arm of the law and State violence. The child's parents may both be detained for political offences, real or imagined. The father alone or mother alone may be in detention. Detention without trial is for an indefinite period – it has lasted three years in some cases, after which the detainees have been released without any charge.

Since 1976, however, children up to sixteen years of age have not been mere spectators. They have been collected in the classrooms and at their homes by the police, with military backup constantly patrolling the streets. The children, several of them between ten and fourteen, have been kept in cells occupied by long-term adult prisoners. The year 1984 marked the mass boycotts of municipal house rentals. The aftermath of that event was the treason trial of a batch of activists who had done nothing more than demonstrate peacefully in the streets. Their long sentences are on appeal. (In the same period of upheavals, four men and a woman were sentenced to hang for the violent death of a village councillor and the gutting of his house and shop. Their sentences were commuted to terms of imprisonment.) A child growing up today in South Africa, even though a non-participant, witnessing these gross injustices against his peer group and his seniors, must often wonder what growing up is preparing him for. But he is also aware how painfully vulnerable a black childhood is at all times.

The evil of political tyranny that surrounds the growing child is overwhelming. There is a valiant group of white and black lawyers who are always ready to take on cases of detention involving a person of any age. But they work against a relentless, unforgiving system of detentions, especially when no charges are laid. Often the police refuse to disclose any information about the place of detention. Last February (1984), a group monitoring detentions was banned because of its public revelations of child abuse by the State and the ugly psychological effects of such treatment. One might ask, what has happened to the so-called civilized standards South African whites are supposed to be the torchbearers of?

No white school has ever been raided by police and army in the whole history of South Africa. Since the schoolchildren's revolt of 1976 against the imposition of Afrikaans as the medium of instruction for certain subjects, and the massacre that followed of over five hundred unarmed children by the police, school campuses were never going to be the same again. It has come to the point where teachers are often afraid for their own safety in the classroom. A teacher can be ordered by the student leadership to stop a class in progress for a meeting to be held to discuss students' grievances and related strategies. The teacher is regarded as a symbol of authority and an agent of government and police who have laid a siege on education – literally and figuratively.

The imposition of Afrikaans as a medium of instruction was intended by the state to relegate English to a minor status, being traditionally the teaching language after the first four years of a child's school life. On the other hand, Afrikaans is hated by blacks because it is the language of political despotism. Yet the language issue was only the flashpoint in conditions of overcrowded housing and transport, poor public sanitation, slum living, urban and rural poverty, the overall poverty of the curricula, the prohibitive labour market for teachers. The mood of anger and frustration had been building up, compounded by low levels of school achievement and an increasing drop-out rate, ever since separate and low-grade curricula were introduced for Africans in 1953. What was set in motion then was education for slavery. In explicit terms, speeches by white legislators in parliament justified a lower system of education by urging that we, Africans, should not be educated to entertain expectations that could be not fulfilled, because we would want to enter pastures where we could not compete with the white man. Perversely true, because those pastures had already been pegged – with a security fence around them as it were.

Before 1953 the African child, though in segregated schools situated in segregated residential areas, was taught according to the same curricula as those for white schools. It could never be a question of separate and equal, since we had hardly any libraries and science laboratories except in some boarding institutions. White schools, on the contrary, were well equipped. But the relatively high and elevating content of education I went through, and later taught, provided a springboard from which those who had it in them could leap to greater heights through self-assertion and achievement. These schools were then administered by the missionary churches who had built them. In 1953, all the schools – except those that could support themselves financially – were taken over entirely by the State. Some of the Roman Catholic schools were self-supporting and had the option of retaining control, while being at the same time compelled to administer the poor curricula for accreditation.

In the early 1980s, a government commission recommended parity in educational content for blacks and whites, and one government department of education instead of the present five racial divisions. It was also recommended that wherever communities desired it, no matter how ethnically separated we may be, there should be integrated schooling. The government rejected these proposals, but permitted private white schools to admit limited numbers of blacks.

I have thus far sketched the life of a child growing up in the 1980s. A child who must be constantly aware that he is being policed by both black and white. He grows up to feel the muscle of white authority at an early age. There was a time when, as with Palestinian children and youth, the sight of an armed white man touched off an impotent anger, which children could only express by throwing rocks at their tormentors. What follows can easily be imagined. Today, South African children are learning that rock-slinging can be self-defeating. Still, the psychological effects all this has on children breeds the kind of person who is unlikely ever to respect the law. He can only fear and hate it. What kind of life lies before these children of wrath when they will need to behave as full-grown citizens in a future South Africa? They have been highly politicised, which colours every issue that confronts them. One is bound to ask: will this be the norm for every growing child as of today? Certainly, as long as the South African system persists, where the schoolchild holds centre stage, it will become a rite of passage to land in the hands of police and be tortured; one that every child will feel compelled to experience.

Let me explain the process of growing up in South Africa with an autobiographical sketch. When I lived in the rural areas from the ages of five to twelve, I attended formal school irregularly, as I had to take livestock out to pasture and spend the whole day with wild nature. During the ploughing and harvesting seasons, I did not attend school at all. I stumbled along through Standard 3, which amounts to five years from the entry age of seven.

We grew our own food, as the villagers still had small plots of land allotted to them by the local authority. We also fed abundantly on wild fruits. Wild nature was largely my teacher during those Depression years. I developed a sense of direction, of distances, of heights and depths. I had to exercise responsibility over the newly born goats and calves, and carry the kids home. My sensory perception became acute – smell, sight, touch, taste, hearing and body balance. Standing on top of a mountain gave me perception. One's instincts also became sharp. They stood me in good stead when I had to track lost animals.

Even in those days the land had begun to shrink and lose its productive value. For most of the able-bodied young people were leaving rural life for migrant labour contracts at the mines and in industry, the latter being open and requiring no contracts. But once in an urban area one had to carry a pass, which restricted one's movements.

My own mother was by turns a domestic worker and seamstress in Pretoria, some two hundred and fifty miles away. For lack of manpower the land deteriorated fast, with only women and children left scratching the surface of the soil to eke out a living. The last of the livestock any family might have possessed was sold for food and clothing. There was a big logo on the front wall of a white man's store on the edge of the village (the only store for miles), advertising mining labour. Men came here for recruitment, the white man acting as an agent. Each year about Christmas-time the men came home. The law did not permit migrant workers, least of all those at the mines, to take their families with them. They lived in single-sex hostels on the mine compounds. Domestics mostly lived on their employers' premises, where they were not allowed to keep a family. In the early years of the migrant labour system, the money sent to the family by the worker helped buy seeds and food commodities they did not grow. In time, as the land became still less productive owing to inadequate care, the women stopped even attempting to cultivate anything. As the only materials for fuel were wood and dry cow dung, the land was further stripped of its life-giving energy by deforestation and cow-dung gathering.

Meanwhile the white man's land flourished under the care of African labour tenants. They were permitted to put up mud-and-timber shacks with grass thatching on the land. The reserves, as the rural villages were called, were becoming overpopulated. According to earlier land laws, especially the Land Act of 1913 and the Trust Lands Law of 1936, the boundaries of the rural reservations were fixed. Land was not to change hands between blacks and whites; the whites owned eighty-seven percent of the total landmass of South Africa. The thirteen percent prescribed then for Africans has not yet been attained.

In 1931 my mother came to fetch us to live with her in the location – as ghettos were called then – near Pretoria. Having left for the rural areas when I was barely conscious of who or what I was, noisy, slummy ghetto life was going to be a totally different experience from that of the open spaces under open skies. A dual sensibility developed in me that was to influence my responses to a diversity of experiences in my adult life. Yet my most vivid sense of place derives more from my ghetto life: the stench, the rocky streets, the tin-and-timber shacks we lived in, the continuous din and buzzing, the pall of coal smoke that hung in the air: not smoke from chimneys but from open braziers. The recurring theme of most of my dreams, however, is my rural experience – at once harsh, rugged and idyllic.

Our domestic life went to ruins when the attempt to restore harmony between a brutal father and a caring, gentle mother died like a stream that runs into desert sand. Father abandoned the home. Mother went back to domestic work, leaving us with grandmother and my aunt. She lived in the employer's yard and visited on certain weekends. My brother, sister and I attended regular school for the first time when I was twelve.

I had to fetch laundry by bicycle from white suburbia before school on Monday mornings for my folks to wash, and return it Friday afternoons after school. What American children do today outside school for spending money, we had to perform to supplement the family income. This was the reason for the Saturday trips to the market, to carry vegetables on a go-cart for whites in the suburbs; and going to the golf course to caddie. We clambered up garbage dumps to scratch for burnt-out coal for use as fuel in tin braziers, which was the common way of cooking and heating in the ghettoes. We raided Indian hawkers' backyards to salvage overripe bananas and tomatoes for the family.

We had to stay out of the white man's way on the sidewalks. Especially when a group of them, no matter how tender in age, walked abreast, as was their custom. We lived in perpetual fear of the white man. He knew it and gloried in it. Fights between us and white boys were most uncommon as we lived separate lives in segregated areas.

Back in the rural areas we rarely saw a white man. He was a curiosity, something to be looked at through the bushes where a lot of us would be skulking away. In the city he was too much with us, mostly in the form of the police. We got to know the white man as an agent of fear and pain, before we had any idea of him as a human being.

Our parents brewed sorghum beer to sell to men who came to the house. The income accruing from this and from the laundry, supplemented by what my mother earned as a domestic worker or as a seamstress, made up the sum total of the house-keeping income. Most wages earned by Africans were below the poverty datum line – lower than those for whites, Indians and the so-called coloureds.

Pretoria was one of the 19th-century catchments of the Great Trek migration of the Boers from the Cape in the south. It was the centre of fierce and unrelenting Boer-British conflict, since England was the colonial master from 1806, after Holland had lost a war that was fought in Europe. The African thus had two colonial masters: one purely as a historical fact – descendants of Dutch traders-become-settlers (first called Boers, then Afrikaners); and the other as a fact of international colonial law – the British. We felt the Boer's presence most acutely in the rural areas as farm workers, and in our constant encounters with the newly-arrived urban Boer. He was for the most part the failed farmer and constituted the new phenomenon of the poor urban white. In order to solve the problem of the poor illiterate white, the government instituted the so-called Civilized Labour Policy. This was intended to place poor whites in departments of manual work such as supervision of African workers on the railway, road and bridge construction projects. The latter were reserved for white artisans. Other jobs reserved for poor whites were cleaning government buildings, where they could enjoy a little respectability. In short, this policy lent a respectable exterior to manual work *because* it was being performed by whites, but which was previously considered low and dirty enough for the Africans and the Indians. The so-called coloureds were concentrated mostly in the Cape Peninsula – on the wine farms, some in city factories. We thus became the target for the wrath of poor whites within the city, mostly Boers.

All our energies were dissipated in the sheer day-to-day survival which included avoidance of physical confrontation with whites. This fear easily turned into hate inside me. But a residual fear continued at the same time to orchestrate the hate when I became more and more aware in my teens that we were residentially segregated from whites, that they possessed all good things while we lived in penury because of our race and colour. Indeed, I felt poverty crawl all over me like some palpably evil slime. All over downtown Pretoria were monuments of the white man's supremacy: separate entrances and exits in and out of public buildings, the railway station and so on. City parks were forbidden ground for blacks. Separate days were set to visit the zoo; on Sundays there were separate visiting times for blacks and whites. In my wild imagi-nation I even fancied that the caged baboons and monkeys could tell apart the pink-and-pale from the dark visiting days. All places of entertainment in the city were out of bounds for blacks – a common pattern countrywide.

Political protest was for adults, we believed. It is they who in the 1920s assembled on the city's sidewalks in defiance of the law preserving such places for whites only. It was a contingent of men, organized by the African National Congress in Pretoria, who boarded second-class coaches of a train in defiance of the law that restricted us to the third-class coaches. Both these events opened up the sidewalks for everybody. Extra second-class train coaches were hitched on for blacks only, i.e. Africans, Indians and coloureds together.

I worked hard in school to make up for the lost years when I lived in the rural areas. The survival game in the ghetto was different from the demands of rural life. Whereas we had to survive natural disasters that characterized rural life – such as famine, destructive locust swarms, drought, excessive rains and so on – ghetto life was preoccupied with food, shelter and the pass laws that regulated and restricted our mobility from town to town. Every African male from sixteen upward had to carry a pass and show it to any policeman, any white man, who demanded it.

After 1948, when the present ruling party took over government, what had been social custom was written into the Statute Book: separate amenities, separate ethnic grouping and residential areas – not only for whites, coloureds, Asians and Africans, but also for African-language groups. Each ethnic or language group had its own schools and residential areas. There were separate education curricula, ministries and departments of education for the whites, Indians, coloureds and Africans. Racial discrimination became a more legislated process than ever before, so that the judicial system itself became politicised. For instance, judges had to administer mandatory convictions of political offenders. This means that the courts, lower and higher, have increasingly been manned by individuals who sympathize with the government on most political issues. As a direct outcome of the dual administration of justice affecting whites as against people of colour, the Lawyers for Human Rights was formed, reinforcing the Centre for Legal Research, founded earlier. Both consist mostly of liberal-minded whites who handle political cases affecting mostly blacks.

These are recent events which I felt needed narrating in order to show some developments that make 1948 a significant watershed. It is also to indicate some of the ways in which the judicial system – the central pillar of apartheid – has been corrupted. Children from ten years of age have most dramatically become victims of this corrupted process since the unrest on school campuses began in 1976.

Let me backtrack to my teenage years. It is easy for one to slip into the facile tendency to invest the state of poverty with the quality of a necessary rite of passage. Then one can declare self-righteously: 'I've paid my dues.' It is no such luxury for black people in South Africa or for any other community in the world. It is a fact of life that exists as a result of a combination of factors, internal and external, chief of which is lack of political power to redress this monopoly of economic resources by a minority population.

But as I became conscious of the visible differences between black and white entrenched in the legal system and the Constitution, I invested all my efforts in surviving – together with my mother, aunt and grandmother, brother, sister and uncles. There were no newspaper stands in the ghettoes. We had no money to buy the newspaper in the city. But certain people I knew brought home the evening paper after work, and those who walked to the city to buy the Sunday paper were happy for me to collect them after they were done with them. I read nearly every piece of printed matter I collected or picked up in the street. I read until it hurt (for years now I have continued to advise my students: 'Read, read, read until it hurts.') I collected old magazines from my mother's workplace in the suburbs. Libraries in the ghettoes were unheard of and the city library was closed to us. A number of white suburban ladies came and dumped used books in our community centre. There were no bookshelves to speak of, so when you wanted to read a book you rummaged through the miscellaneous heap on the floor. A shot in the dark, as you didn't even know what kind of book you wanted. No such guidance was given in class. That would have been a merely academic gesture anyhow.

Schooling was not free, but my mother managed from her meagre earnings to send me to a boarding secondary school after I had come out top over pupils from all the schools of the region. This was an added inspiration for her. With a first class pass in junior high, I obtained a scholarship from a missionary institution for teacher training. So many of us who could not afford senior high school were constantly nagged by the fear that we would not be able to proceed to college, for lack of money. The government offered no scholarships for blacks. So we went to train as primary school teachers or nurses, the former a two-year course, the latter a four-year programme. While teaching elementary school, we upgraded our high school education by private correspondence studies. This entitled us to teach in high schools. But one soon realized that for senior high school subjects it equipped one better to possess a university degree. So we pursued degree studies by correspondence with the University of South Africa. It was multiracial, but we held racially separated graduation ceremonies! (Today it is fully integrated.) This is the route I took, while raising a family, until I obtained the MA degree in English and Psychology. By then I had begun to publish short fiction in one of the only two picture magazines being published by whites in the 1950s for circulation among blacks.

There was one university college for blacks only – Fort Hare College, now a full-fledged university. It was founded in 1916 by the Scottish Church. Most of its graduates later became political activists and went through the whole gamut of treason trials, bannings, labelling as communists, sabotage trials, imprisonment on Robben Island, the gallows, house arrests and so on. Not that the missionaries taught or inspired political rebellion. On the contrary, they preached patience, obedience to authority, and respect for the laws of the country. Yet they invested a lot in formal education of a reasonably decent standard. This provided a launching pad for us to be able to improve our academic and professional standing on our own.

The inferior education of today, exclusively planned for blacks – especially Africans – does not equip its clients with the will and capacity for self-education after the attainment of a certificate. Thus the children, aware of their own demoralizing shortcomings, have become angry with themselves and with the system they cannot grasp nor intellectually contain. We are witnessing today a high and increasing dropout rate in schools, defiance of teachers by pupils, and destruction of school property. If Bantu Education has sharpened the children's political awareness, it has also crippled a whole generation to the extent of not knowing how to correct the ignorance and the imbalances this has led to. This is ultimately the main difference between the products of Bantu Education as a stultifying process, and the pre-1953 system as a springboard for greater heights. Man for man, woman for woman, the older teachers, nurses, doctors – few though they may be in numbers – are made of sterner stuff than their counterparts who came out of the later institution.

children are similarly ignorant of urban concerns. But the rural child has ambitions, felt or latent, of one day cutting loose and following the crowds who are drawn to the neon lights. The urban child grows up knowing that the government has succeeded in isolating rural communities by giving them phoney self-rule, which is at best a form of local government. Among the youth, the thinking is that those rural communities out there got what they asked for, i.e. the status of homeland and self-rule. Far from the truth! The State's policy of consolidating the ancient ethnic enclaves is intended to fragment South Africa so that each homeland sooner or later attains self-rule and becomes a 'nation state'. The people were given no choice. The oft-repeated statement by members of government that South Africa is a multinational state can easily be traced back to this habit of equating language and ethnic unit with nation. Then the white population can be conceived as a nation (predominantly Afrikaans) and not a minority group within the total population.

During the years of unrest and harassment on school campuses, a myth took shape that perceived rural schools as a more sedate learning environment. So urban parents sent their children to those schools. True enough, there is a greater seriousness and singleness of purpose in rural schools, although they are poorly equipped; but upheavals and rebellions have come to feature almost as frequently on rural campuses as on urban ones. The State is not in the least prepared to listen to the children's grievances and demands. It relies on the iron-fist 'solution'.

Comparing myself as a boy with the youth of today, certain ironies and paradoxes emerge. We were poorer in my day than children are today. We were always scrounging for food, whereas today's student by and large has spending money for food during school break. The children dress better than we did. Patched trousers are a rarity today. Yet junk food, which is what school children feed on, was not as prevalent in my day as it is today. There were fewer distractions back then. We tended to create our own entertainment instead of what music cassettes, radio and deafening explosive music concerts provide as external sources today. Again, today's student activist is always sure of a plate of food when he returns from a late night meeting or from a day of harrowing encounters with the law.

The primary point of difference, however, is that education had not yet become politicised in my time. It had not yet occurred to the ruling class that it could turn education into an instrument of ideological control. It was at junior high boarding school and at teacher-training college, that my political consciousness gradually took shape. I took part in political debates. The atmosphere created by World War Two added another dimension to our debates and discussions on campuses. I became more ready to stand up to whites than ever before – among the teaching community and in the streets. Reading press reports about the war opened our minds. Knowledge of other atrocities and authoritarian regimes created a historical context for us in which we could understand our plight as South Africans. The lessons of history were coming home to us.

I think that early in a person's life his or her social environment, in combination with his inner resources and character, creates in him or her a disposition to inquire, search, yearn to discover, respond acutely to events and circumstances; and to probe relationships between events, people, ideas, phenomena and so on. All over the world the child is exceeding the adults' traditional expectations of what it should know and not know at certain levels of its growth. But the South African child who grows up on the dark side of the colour and racial divide lives about eighteen years in a space of about ten. At fifteen he is much more mature than his white counterpart. But it is a desperate maturity, which is often a severe handicap in his formal schooling. He is angry, afraid, recklessly daring, because he is under siege: police and military surveillance is forever with him. And the educational system was never designed to be a tool to make self-emancipation possible. It was intended to enslave him, incapacitate him. He possesses knowledge from life's experiences, but has not the ability to mobilize them into a coherent, disciplined force that will illuminate meanings.

For this reason some of us have established institutions that should provide a healthier – because humanistic – learning environment; a superior – because it is richer – curriculum. We need funding to enable us to recruit available teachers and to rent premises in the townships, to procure books for a bookmobile that will supply reading materials at all the centres. We know we shall be running the gauntlet by exposing ourselves to banning by the State. But I am confident we can get by if we do not overtly incite rebellion against the State. We already have an infrastructure, which we established in 1980, for alternative education programmes. Our slogan says: 'Knowledge for Growth, Power, Nationhood'. We study, among other things, social institutions, including political strategies, family life, leadership. We teach for living rather than for examinations. For if our children get to know their physical and human environment intimately, they will get a better grasp of the issues that come with the area of study. To teach them to think is also to help them to develop the intelligence and resilience to confront our social, economic and political problems. There are several other institutions of alternative learning, and our Council for Black Education and Research is only one of them. But it is the only one that brings together children who have been thrown out of the system during political upheavals or have dropped out in a state of frustration.

Child-raising among black South Africans goes against all the traditional patterns we have come to associate with the civilized world. Although several of these time-honoured patterns have been and are being challenged elsewhere, the general principles remain valid: parental love, care and a good home for the child; a home and social climate which will promote the best in the child, including creativity and the skill and art of self-expression; responses from the family that are elevating for both parent and child; developing in the child a sense of his social role as it ought to be acted out.

In South Africa even these principles are being violated and frustrated by the political authority. Juvenile delinquency and all its concomitants will stay with us for a long, long time to come. In South Africa correctional institutions and strategies are motivated largely by the desire for revenge. And revenge breeds revenge. Because South Africa is not a member of the United Nations Children's Fund, as a result of its history of apartheid, no appeal from us for funding to salvage what we can from the damaged lives of black children has received any positive response. For only governments may deal with an international organization such as UNICEF.

I have come full circle, it would seem. Having survived the traumas of my own turbulent childhood by some miracle, and having obeyed the inner compulsion to become a teacher, I'm once more back in the world of children. Children whose lives have run into an ambush, and who are crying out to be rescued.

Challenges of Changing Educational Systems[1] – 1964

Synopsis Ndavhe Ramakuela

Although originally written for the Kenyan government, the implications of this article cut across Africa – or any country that is in the process of self-emancipation. Here there is no going back to stories/narrative as a mode of exploration or exposition, as one would find in other pieces. Mphahlele goes straight to the point: the discussion of self-determination and how that can be achieved. He argues that the government will have to enforce a cultural awakening; that, even as the government talks about non-racialism, it should know what it is up against; that the African worldview should be given prominence.

'It is pathetic to see African children in multiracial nursery schools in Nairobi being taught tales about dukes, princes, kings, castles and so on – things that belong in Europe – and being subjected to illustration material that recalls a European way of life.'

The same challenges that faced Kenya in the 1960s are what South Africa still battles with today: how education can be changed to suit a new context; how education can bring about a new African child. That children should be exposed to their own cultures first, is Mphahlele's argument.

Mphahlele encourages the government to look at the teaching of art, music, theatre and dancing, literature and language. He reminds the government that Africa has artistic and cultural traditions to be proud of, and that there can be no excuse for tormenting the African child with European traditions when he or she is not yet ripe to make mental and emotional links, and thus engage with other traditions fruitfully.

Before we determine the course of cultural development and its place in the educational system of Kenya, we might consider the physical, social and economic realities that the government of Kenya will have to reckon with.

Kenya may like to create a non-racial society or a multiracial society. 'Multiracial' refers to the mere physical composition of a society, no matter in what proportions: a plural society in other words, in which three races can live side by side for a century

---

1 This paper was originally entitled "Memorandum to the Commission on Education in Kenya", May 1964.

and remain in separate compartments, retain their respective identities. In a multira-cial society, the various racial groups may very well continue each in its own culture, so that there never grows a national culture in which everyone shares (without feel-ing that he is outside it). 'Non-racial' refers to attitudes. It means that in a non-racial community, races should strive towards a stage where there will be no regard for race, where people will merge and the question of minorities will become irrelevant. The corollary is inter-marriage (yes, it is as serious as that!).

We have to admit that everywhere in Africa the African has always been the one to take something from European culture, and never the other way round. Neither has the Indian made his culture available or accessible to the European or the African; nor has he adopted (as a group) European and African ways of life. History suggests that for a long time to come Indians outside India will continue to represent a cultural island. I don't know how the government will want to reconcile this (if ever) with the policy of integration. The problem of religious practice can probably best be settled by making the integrated school secular, so as to leave the after-school time for sepa-rate or joint religious rituals. The question of Friday for Muslims will have to be resolved. One hopes that future generations, if not ours, will be mature – liberated – enough to allow for economical teaching in the place of the traditional 'scripture' les-son on the school timetable. For a start, special tutors can be brought in who are knowledgeable about, at least, Islam, African Religion, Christianity, Hinduism and Buddhism. Integrated religious studies are called for in this scenario.

Will Europeans ever adopt any proportion of African culture, having so far ignored it except as a subject of study? It is difficult to imagine it, but it is not impossible. Undoubtedly, traditionally white schools have always looked outward and prepared their children for a way of life that has nothing to do with their immediate environ-ment, outside the earning of a livelihood.

The above-mentioned points may suggest that schools can only be *physically* inte-grated, never *culturally*. I would not presume to predict for certain. But we have to start *somewhere*. The point to begin must be African culture, which, in the long view, must mean a harmonisation and reconciliation of tribal cultures. European influences in fact bring about a neo-African culture, as we can see throughout this continent. It can hardly be expected that a people who have always had to yield ground and adopt European culture can be contented with political independence without cultural inde-pendence. The first campaign, then, is to repair the damage that the missionaries – through their schools and churches – have done to the African confidence by con-demning his way of life as totally heathen and fit for firewood.

It means, therefore, that our education has to be given a strong African bias. It is pathetic to see African children in multiracial nursery schools in Nairobi being taught tales about dukes, princes, kings, castles and so on – things that belong in Europe – and being subjected to illustration material that recalls a European way of life. It is pathetic, too, to see African children being drilled in European ballet dancing in certain places, instead of the traditional dances of their people. All this means that the African is being integrated on the European's own terms; this in turn means that the African has to *aspire* to the European's cultural world. This is a country where the African has political power but not the economic power to sustain it. While striving to break down economic barriers to total integration (token integration as it exists at present is a mockery), the Government has to insist that African folklore should be taught right from the nursery school stage. It will enrich the European child's mind as well and give it a truly African setting to identify itself with. For the sake of the African's self-realisation and self-recognition, he and his children need to be helped to relate to their immediate environment – to the music, art, theatre and literature that speak their language. Let them be exposed to the media of their own culture, so that they can better decide how many European ways to adopt, how many to reject – always from a position of strength, of self-knowledge, of self-confidence. It is not as if I were suggesting that the African needs to excavate an archaeological site in order to dig out the fossils of African culture. It is still a living culture, which can be seen in its continuity in the hinterland as it were: the traditional dances, crafts, music and so on still live on.

We should assume that urban Africans here have not yet decided to be fully urbanised to the point of being committed to town living. While this is an advantage in the sense that they still retain a close link with rural culture, it is also a disadvantage because it delays the process of sophistication and of detribalisation that is necessary for urban culture to evolve. In South Africa, for instance, there is a virile urban culture that has emerged in spite of conditions that reject the African. This is because a process of urbanisation has taken in four million Africans over the last two centuries; they have become committed to city life, with nothing to go back to in rural areas. The Government's policy of apartheid and the Bantustans is a conscious effort to break the back of a nationalism that has evolved over the last fifty years, during which period tribal divisions have become negligible. And yet this urban culture is decidedly African in character and idiom. We should assume further that more industries are going to crop up in the towns of Kenya which will absorb more workers, and that this factor – coupled with the very important one of good housing that is required – will help townspeople to accept the fact of urbanization and its assumptions. It is the function of the social worker and the educator to steady the minds of a people in the process of becoming urbanized, so as to help them contain the shock that town life brings with it and to avoid most of the social maladies that it creates all over the world.

I see all this being done by bringing traditional idioms of culture to the city, even as we use modern mass media as the vehicles to maintain the link between the rural and urban streams of consciousness. The town folk should actually be involved inside and outside schools and community centres in these traditional cultural activities. I can see, for instance, community development leaders organizing adult dance clubs in the towns as well as in the rural areas. While the twist, the rock-'n-roll and the cha-cha-cha should not be discouraged, we should bring home to townfolk that a person only *loses* himself in these dance idioms; in traditional dancing he restrains his ego in the interests of group performance and *expresses* himself this way. The emotional experience traditional dancing provides runs, and should run, deeper than in the imported 'canned' idioms. East African guitar music is a popular idiom and should be encouraged so that it can develop a distinctive East African character.

Recommendations

1. Art

The teaching of art should be intensified in the institutions of lower education. This requires more teachers who can teach art. Vacation art courses can be organized jointly by the Education Ministry and the Department of Extramural Studies for teachers who are inclined towards art. Another and more economical method would be to ask the Fine Arts department of the University College to cut down the time for the diploma to two years (after H.S.C.) to enable the production of as many art teachers as possible. Four years in a department of Fine Arts is utter wastage, and is not even necessary for those who want to paint or sculpt rather than teach. The teachers can conduct quarterly art workshops in various schools. In such workshops a teacher spends a week in a school guiding the interested pupils in the use of local materials, pencil and brush. He has to repeat this at intervals so as to keep track of what the pupils are doing.

2. Music

Here we need a programme in which batches of teachers will be brought to a central place and spend three months at a time learning full-time, so as to go back and teach. In the teaching of pupils themselves – and the training of teachers – African folk songs and oral storytelling should be used extensively, drawn from various tribes so as to promote the cause of a *national* culture. Centres can be set up in various parts of the country. Incentives can be used to encourage more teachers to take this course by recognizing the extra qualification it involves for teaching service.

3. Theatre and dancing

Simple plays adapting folk tales for the stage and sketches of day-to-day life should be the starting point. I should discourage the acting of Shakespeare in secondary schools because this is invariable done in order to help pupils answer exam questions on Shakespeare, and it encourages the feeling of snobbery among those who act.

There are several African plays that can be acted. Scenes can be acted in Swahili from the comprehensible Shakespeare plays like *Merchant of Venice, Julius Caesar* and *Macbeth*. Traditional music and dance should as much as possible be incorporated into African drama.

4. Literature

English masters in secondary schools should be encouraged to form writers' clubs among the pupils so as to stimulate creative writing. These should be in the upper forms of secondary school. The syllabus for English secondary school should leave room for compulsory reading and study of African writing, which is quite abundant already. This will help alleviate the agony children have to go through, learning something they can never identify with. Pupils in the upper forms should be made to realize that they are capable of becoming writers even before they reach university.

At this point I may mention in parenthesis that the literature syllabus in African fiction is generally out of touch with reality. While African fiction, drama and poetry should be set for the secondary school exams, literature of the British Isles should also be taught – but it should be 20th-century literature, which is relevant to the modern student's experience. The student should be made to read the prose version of Shakespeare plays and not touch the original dramatic texts until he is in the Sixth Form. And here he should not be made to study the 'problem plays'. He should be given the simpler ones like *The Merchant of Venice, Romeo and Juliet, Julius Caesar, Anthony and Cleopatra*. It is rather unfair to expect a pupil to understand Shakespeare before he has had something like four to five years' contact with English poetry. Experience has shown that in secondary school pupils merely memorise facts and criticism from books and reproduce them in the exams. This ruins a pupil's literary tastes for life. Dr Graham Hough of Cambridge University has said as much about English students recently; how much truer it must be about African students. The literature of the periods before the 20th century should only begin to be tackled from the Sixth Form upwards.

Edinburgh University has recently introduced into its syllabus a course on the Commonwealth novel – from Britain, Africa, India, Malaysia, New Zealand and the West Indies. This is a very good way of making the study of literature a pleasure rather than pain, and relieves the student of the burden of things like Anglo-Saxon, Milton, etc.

5. Language

Although some people choose to write creatively in English, there are several others (and more should be encouraged) who will choose Swahili. This means a crash programme for the training of teachers who will teach Swahili right from the primary levels upwards. The Ministry of Education should employ Swahili experts *now* to devise a short, speedy practical system of learning the language so as to put teachers through it in two months at the most. The French have perfected the audio-visual method, through which I went in Paris. Four hours a day of listening and repeating and recording (without writing) gives one a through grounding in French in six weeks, enough to enable one to speak the language. Thereafter one is left to oneself, and reading and writing comes very easily. Some such system, or a modification of it, can produce a considerable number of Swahili speakers and teachers in a few years, and thus exploit the language as a more valuable instrument of nation building and literary activity.

Finally, may I say that Chemchemi Cultural Centre is most willing to work together with the Government, through the Ministry of Education, towards the creation of the society envisaged by the right-thinking people of Kenya; to help our people restore equilibrium in their way of life by providing activities whereby they will be involved at various levels in living African culture and adapt it to a changing society. Already Chemchemi is in contact with all the secondary schools in Kenya and encouraging them to form 'writers' clubs', which I shall address on African literature and creative writing as and when I am invited. Through our monthly newsletter they are kept informed about the cultural problem we are all engaged in tackling.

The Burden of History and the University's Role in the Recreating of its Community and its Environment – 1995

Synopsis by James Ogude

In this most eloquent and passionate graduation address at the University of the Witwatersrand, Mphahlele confronts the underbelly of South Africa's higher education and brings to the surface in a most candid manner the real causes of the crisis that bedevils tertiary institutions in this country. Delivered during one of the most critical and tumultuous moments in South African higher education's history, the speech challenges South African intellectuals – particularly our white compatriots – to confront the burden of our history.

Part of the crisis, the address argues, has to do with an uncritical adherence to tradition or 'set habits and formulae of operation' in white tertiary institutions. This mindset, rooted in white supremacist ideology, whether of liberal humanist or fundamentalist leaning, tends to undermine any attempts to negotiate a healthy relationship between students, staff and administration. The other baggage has to do with a whole history of oppression and tyranny that students and some staff carry with them. What this has bred is bad faith and a strong sense of alienation among blacks. Indeed, the negative image of the black self that educational institutions instil has reduced blacks to perpetual victims, who can hardly galvanise their energies towards positive action.

To address this crippling legacy, South Africans will have to engage with the perverted morality that underpins the white man's education – to which many blacks cling in the hope that it will deliver the coveted white power and material world to them. The real challenge lies in how this moral dilemma can be reversed to re-invigorate black self-reliance and affirmation of selfhood. The problem is also how to reverse the negative self-image internalised by many blacks, and to repudiate of the inflated self-image of white South Africans.

Mphahlele feels quite strongly that the gradual swelling of black student numbers in historically white universities such as Wits affords us the opportunity to turn transformation into a learning experience, in which full human rights and democracy can find genuine articulation beyond the mechanics of governance and representation. Transforming the curriculum beyond academic programmes to encompass the total environment, or what Mphahlele calls the life-space of the students, is at the core of all these ideas.

The address challenges our white educators to immerse themselves in what is African by merging with its human and physical landscape, and rejecting their intellectual complacency and false security. The urgent project is for the white institutions to create the space that would allow for the rise of non-racialism out of multiracialism – to forge a genuine intercultural enterprise. The burden of history then, the address concludes, is how to make the giant leap – like Soyinka's men of Ogun – from those values that divide us to those that unite and celebrate our humanity. This, Mphahlele avers, is a task in national engineering and in the restoration of a broken community that calls for a compelling, creative imagination beyond the colour line.

M r Chancellor, Vice-Chancellor, Members of Council, Graduates and Members of the Wits Community at large, Ladies and Gentlemen, thank you for your heart-warming citation. I do not promise any words of wisdom, plain or prophetic; I can promise only what seems to make contextual sense – only what sounds to me like good sense. The basis of genuine prophecy is poetry and a poetic sensibility, plus the ecstasy of its revelation in transcendental terms. The days of prophecy are gone; today our minds are pathetically fragmented, worse than what city life spawns. And all we succeed in producing are lyrics about our social reality, and apocalyptic statements from time to time about some public catastrophe.

Graduation is a good time to take stock of the cumulative realization of all our energies for mentors, students and the rest of the campus. May I congratulate the graduates, many of whom, I'm sure, will be taking a deep breath to heave themselves up for the next stretch of the highway towards their respective careers.

In the heat and crush, push and shove, urgency, preoccupations, panic and heart-burn of the times, it is easy to lose sight of the essence of the dramatic events and issues that have come to the forefront of our consciousness these days around tertiary institutions. We are also afraid of coming to terms with the burden of our history, which bedevils the education crisis we are in. This crisis, we observe, brings out the ugliest in us as academics, students, workers and administrators, and often belies the best we can bring to the hammer and anvil on which we are currently trying to reshape the present into the future.

The historically White universities have a particular tradition, a history going back no less than seventy years, an articulated ideology – whether tentatively humanistic or as fundamentalist as a steam engine mindlessly in love with its own tracks. All with set habits and formulae of operation. Yet all were founded on the basis of white supremacy, often in the guise of trusteeship. I want to believe that the search is on for bold alternatives, leading towards the resolution of the maladjustments that define our freedom time.

What so painfully blurs matters is the whole baggage we naturally bring with us to a discussion of any issue or grievance between students, staff and administration.

The baggage on the administration's side contains precepts, minuted precedents, assumptions, formulae, dogmatic assertions of academic excellence, budgetary dos and don'ts, and a residual strain of racism. This strain is all the more mischievous because it eludes explicit particularization, while it undermines the verbalized high moral ground an institution's leaders have been trying to maintain in the last two decades or so. I acknowledge the high levels of performance in the natural sciences. It is the social sciences and humanities, where attitudinal positions and social consciousness and interaction take centre stage, that demand of us to lay the Eurocentric ghost.

On the other side of a turbulent campus life, staff or students (or both) bring with their grievances a whole history of oppression and the tyranny that has sustained it. Some of it internalised, some articulated. In all this we sense from time to time the unspoken belief, justified or not, that no concessions can be enough to lay to rest their sense of injustice. Each side thinks it senses bad faith in the other. Soon, tempers are on fire.

Few people would condone the ugly consequences of bad faith, real or imagined. But on both sides we simply have to acknowledge that we still have to outlive generations of silent endurance developing into resistance, then into rebellion, leading to exile abroad and at home; each phase with its attendant pain.

Ever since the beginnings of the Black Consciousness Movement in the early 1970s, which also renewed our awareness of the Pan-African ideal, blacks – especially the Africans – have been questioning the assumptions of the culture that brought the white man to his status of supremacy. Likewise, we have been asking questions about our own identity, e.g. the ease with which we assimilated the white man's education in the hope of grabbing the power we had come to believe was built into that culture. We should wrench this power from white hands, we believed, without even bothering about its morality.

Consciousness of identity, or the search for the latter, is rooted in what an African American critic and scholar refers to as the *frontier*. To black America, he says, 'frontier is an alien word; for in essence, all frontiers established by the white psyche have been closed to the black man.' True of our case as well. Our present-day conflicts go much deeper than physical violence to humans and landscape. The dark shadows in our nightmares define a conscious life in our separate worlds. Blacks and whites cherish divergent dreams, subconscious longings, beliefs; folk traditions and the collective unconscious; and notions of heroism, self-worth, and institutional loyalty, especially in venues we only physically inhabit. Our sense of being differs from that of Western man.

With devastating clarity we realized what strangers we were and still are to our own environment. Nor have we ever owned the means with which to reshape the environment we inhabit, to appropriate it in the metaphysical as well as the physical sense. And the education we have been subjected to before – but even worse after – 1953 led us to fashion false dreams based on a false morality, a false home to be socialized into. Hence the unfortunate emotions we invest in our image of ourselves as perpetual victims, an image that ironically demotivates where it should galvanize us into positive action.

The present lull in the Black Consciousness exhortations towards self-reliance and the affirmation of a black selfhood may suggest to some that all of us have settled for political and economic advancement without any heed of the intellectual and spiritual alternatives we can evolve. But movements driven by a passionate intensity have a way of coming and going in cycles, as long as the historical conditions make it necessary.

Perhaps while we try all ways possible to stabilize campus life, we should constantly remind ourselves that one of the major positive things about the gradually increasing black student presence on historically white campuses is that it can have a liberalising and liberating impact on the institution as a whole: an education that carries a price, too. These campuses simply have to rewrite the rules, review old procedures and protocols, exorcise traditional reflexes that go centuries deep and stretch beyond the frontiers of the intellect and its problem-solving capacity.

We have to allow this very transformation process to be a learning experience, a growing together, and a way of realizing the full meaning of human rights and democracy as a way of life rather than simply the mechanics of government and representation. All this can be promoted by a revitalization, reorientation and enrichment of formal school organization and educational content, plus non-formal education.

I am told the Academic Support programme at Wits had to change from being merely what its designation tells us. It has had in addition to attend to its student's environmental comfort: residences and other accommodation. Which is as it should be. There is on the other side of the hill a higher plane, from which Gestalt psychologists and educationalists view the environment. It is relevant to our learning situation in this country. American psychologist Kurt Lewin tells us that individuals behave according to how they conceptualise their 'life space': both individual and his environment, plus all those influences that have a bearing on his behaviour – his image of himself, his beliefs. He may or may not be aware of these factors; some are real, some not. Life space is not an area with geographic dimensions, but is the total environment as a subjective reality. Learning, in Lewin's terms, effects change in one's perception of life space. All this implies the following, among other things, in relation to the promotion of the democratic ideal: students have distinct notions of their life space and unique perceptions of their social world; any constituency on campus, young and adult, can come forward at decision-making with both rational and irrational solutions driven by emotion, intuition and impulse. Hence our insistence on an enduring connection between school subject and the students' lives. With an ever-deepening self-knowledge that is an accumulation of the above experiences, we can learn to rid ourselves on all sides of cant, posturing, the rhetoric of self-justification

81

and superstition. By superstition I refer to that in us that habitually sets generalization above fact.

We know that there is no public morality across racial lines that we can appeal to. Furthermore, just too many white compatriots are ambivalent about the need for them to *earn* the name 'African'. These factors have led to fragmentation of responsibility. Africanism goes much deeper than the fact of being on this continent, or being a member of a political organization designated 'African'. This can be a good time and place to take up the challenge, to begin the journey towards merging with the African human and physical landscape. This, after all, is how multiracialism can rise to non-racialism, which goes concurrently with the intercultural enterprise, before the latter totally refines and supersedes it.

We cannot, of course, ignore the fact that a number of black Africans themselves have to tap the collective memory for all the things we need to know about the essence of being African. For we have assimilated half-baked Western thought and beliefs, which have uprooted us, left us directionless and chasing rainbows. No further to go because the whites' system clipped our wings, and the road back to our ancestors, our original mentors, is pretty dark and untraceable. Only their voices reach us faintly, now and again, when elderly folk remember aloud. We have thus developed according to the white man's image of us, his expectations of us. This is a dilemma we the black Africans can best resolve ourselves, without the white man's tutelage, which we know only too well as the letdown of the centuries.

Having been born into privilege, most of our white compatriots have been socialized into the belief that they were destined always to lead by virtue of being an extension of western civilization. Positions of leadership were going to be theirs for the taking, by standards set by themselves to measure both their own performance and that of blacks. In too many of them this has induced an extravagant sense of security, and an unwillingness to apply their minds to intercultural issues at the deepest levels possible. It is the blacks who have always had to assimilate and struggle to find some equilibrium for survival. It won't do simply to intellectualise the life of the African, if you do not *feel* the essence of being one. I mean the way in which you can activate your physical senses and intuitive self, tune into and register the movements of the sea of African humanity and its inner mysteries. It also confirms the realization that the way to exploring the universal does not bypass humanity but finds the axe, the plough, the sense of being and other equipment right here in the concourse of humanity. The black man is every bit in that concourse, also as an explorer – a more experienced one. He will not accept tokenism for long. Already he is kicking doors everywhere to open them.

The essence of being limply here is also tied up with the urgent need to go beyond merely reshaping structures, important as that is. Throughout the country transformation and curriculum content is a talking point. We demand that the new curriculum speak to our multicultural aspirations, our social and physical reality, to the interconnectedness between local, continent-wide, and global concerns. We must know our Africa well. It is encouraging to hear Professor W Makgoba, Deputy Vice-Chancellor for academic affairs, express sentiments that can inspire a reshaping of our universities to express an African reality, if I may be allowed to paraphrase and amplify. In this context I interpret 'African' in the profoundest sense of that life space with which learner and institution are bonded, the focus here being at the primary level the essence of Africa. I imply in the life-space theory the organic whole that true education seeks to develop, the divergent perceptions it seeks to harmonize. We should thus be talking here of re-education, re-socialization, re-orientation and a radically transformed learning environment determined by the demands of this organic whole.

Blacks are themselves still trying to overcome their own inner conflicts. Just one example: we stand in a love-hate relationship with ethnicity and the ghetto. From this history we have inherited the habit of mind that says: 'The law was not made to protect me but to exterminate me; if not, to dispossess me, humiliate me.' The rankling, soul-twisting question in us swings between how to make the giant leap from this habit of mind into the new realm of democratic responsibility and, at the other pole, who will atone, among all this host of people who are getting away with all that their legalized evil has made of me.

This is the burden of our history we cannot afford to ignore – even as we struggle to reconcile conflicts – while we apply our mental energies to the transformation of the curriculum, to nation building. Nation building is every step of the way a healing process for which an institution should enlist the intellectual forces of both black and white. It is a way of learning how to outlive our ancient tribalisms, chiefdoms, federalist hang-ups, and all those tribalists that stomp around in TV face-the-nation masks and suits, mouthing off the rhetoric of enclaves for themselves where cultural self-determination and autonomy (white or black) is expected to be acted out. A rhetoric that shows how deep down the neurosis of fear filters: fear of oneself, the fear of genuine liberty.

Finally, I think we need to restore the creative imagination to its proper role. We should not confine the term to the individual and the arts. In strategic planning, too, for instance, and in computer wizardry the creative imagination enjoys full play. Collective imaginations in decision-making should be able to produce imaginative answers when the various elements have been reorganized into a coherent whole – much as the writer works on a poem. The imagination, as Shelley tells us, has the capacity to deal with facts and calculating processes to image that which we know.

The Rightful Place of African Culture in Education – 1982

Synopsis by Ndavhe Ramakuela

In this piece Mphahlele answers the question: Is it possible to incorporate African culture into our educational systems? Put differently, how can Africans liberate themselves from the many years of religious and political colonialism?

The article begins by outlining the kind of conquest Africans were subjected to. Since colonialism, he states, Africans never had the opportunity to shape and develop their own visions and define their needs and desires. As a result of this deprivation, with or without their resistance, culture – including their religions – was suppressed by the colonial powers. Yet other oppressed people have been proactive even in the face of their oppressors. Mphahlele cites the example of Afrikaners facing British rule. Bantu education contributed substantially to the deprivation of Africans; it took away from them the will and ability to be independent thinkers, as well as opportunities whereby they could become self-reliant and independent.

Mphahlele is concerned that, even after the revolution of 1976, education for Africans is not geared towards lifelong learning. This is a time for the community to intervene, starting first by re-examining the role of teachers – in the process making them feel proud about their jobs, encouraging them to be more creative, and particularly supporting them in their endeavours to explore their own cultures with the learners. At some stage the community is also asked to give direction to the teachers, to share with them aspects of their cultures that may be useful in their teaching.

1. The teaching of African culture will not be complete if it is not interlinked with other educational systems and events worldwide. Mphahlele also warns that the transition to multiracialism should be treated carefully.
2. A number of issues also emerge from this article: interdisciplinary teaching, 'outcome-based education' and modularisation are what Mphahlele seems to be advocating.
3. He also advocates that education should be a natural process, linked to the social and natural environments, and to the lived experiences of learners.

But these are only thoughts and ideals that may be lost sight of if there are no establishments or institutions whose primary task is to advocate African-centred cultural practices, teaching and learning environments.

I

How did our education come to where it is? The British imposed their own system of education on the Boers and Africans – the latter through mission schools and training – when they ruled the Cape Colony from 1795 to 1802 and from 1806 to about 1901.

When the Boers won the peace in 1902 – and then after the Union of South Africa was formed in 1910 – whites continued to operate a system of education they had inherited from British rule. All they did was give it a white South African content. In other words, South African history, geography, religious studies (termed scripture) and the language of the Afrikaner enjoyed emphasis among the things that were taught. The examination system, promotion by examination from class to class up to school-leaving certificate or matriculation, the number of subjects and their grouping all bore the British stamp in the early days. Even later, in spite of certain changes that gave birth to the Joint Matriculation Board, to a first three-year degree structure and to an examining body set up under a specific law, the British influence lingered.

As a conquered people, Africans had to learn what whites had planned for themselves. As we had separate schools from whites, ours was called 'Native Education'. We wrote the same public examinations – final primary school, junior certificate and matric – but were made to stay longer in primary and secondary school than whites.

Our schools were all church-controlled. They were called 'State-aided' schools, as the government paid the teachers and gave some financial grants to meet the cost of buildings, basic teaching materials and furniture. Several white churches also built schools for whites under a more or less similar system of financing, with white schools being funded on a higher scale.

The role of the church and its influence in both black and white schools, let alone in the administration of education, confirmed the white man's claim that South Africa was a 'Christian country'. The Indians were allowed to teach their own religious content – Islamic or Muslim religion, Hindu, and so on – in their own schools. The Jews established private schools; the so-called coloured people ran their schools like whites. Teachers' salaries in Indian and coloured schools were considerably higher than those in African schools for similar qualifications, even though they were still lower than those for whites. It was not uncommon, however few such cases were in proportion to our population, for black Africans who could 'pass' to move into coloured schools for better salaries – just as was happening in industry and in everyday life, if an African wanted to cheat the pass laws. 'Pass-carrying natives' became a category of people who were paid low wages and could not go on strike, mine workers included, according to an urban act.

Christian missionaries, whose schools Africans attended, tried everything they could to 'cleanse' us of our traditional beliefs and ways. They believed that Christianity held the only answer to the Ultimate Truth about God and humankind. They merely tolerated Islam and Hinduism, because there was an ancient literature that was written about these faiths. They did not care to know what ancient African religion was. Because we have no printed scriptures – and Europeans do not believe a faith exists unless it can be read – our faith was dismissed as a road to darkness, as a belief in magic. We thus came to realize that we had been conquered both on the battlefield where men fight to kill or subdue, and on the other battlefield, where the soul struggles for self-realization, self-knowledge, self-emancipation. In the mission school there was no inch given for the deviant, the person who differs from the herd, for the traditionalist who believed in God but did not consider Christ as his saviour or medium through which to reach God.

But we all know that where the soul, the human spirit of man, is concerned, conquest is never complete, even when political conquest is absolute. People may be afraid to cry out in protest or ask questions when they are in an institution like school. They may even allow themselves to be baptized and confirmed in a particular denomination. But the human soul still refuses to be regimented, still remains unpredictable. See how many change from one denomination to another, how many break away from 'established churches' (i.e. those set up by whites).

Once outside, the soul listens more and more intently to voices that echo a traditional past which, stubbornly, persists in the mind of modern humankind. Because tradition and the present live side by side in our condition. Indeed, it is the condition of all colonized humans. Despite all appearances, the Afrikaner also has two personalities: the one that asserts Afrikanerdom as a political creed with religious overtones, and the one that has to cope with the demands of Western colonial civilization, which he flaunts before us as a badge of respectability when it suits him. The fact that he worships the God of Western man can be confusing, because he holds on to a political creed that the West would like to believe is a thing of the past, something it has itself evolved from or is ashamed of.

South African education, for both white and black, is authoritarian, precisely because it is inspired by political dominance as well as by a religion that considers itself to hold the Ultimate Truth. It is a religion that never stops to doubt, to question itself, because it regards itself as the Absolute Way. An authoritarian education, by definition, imposes authority, rules and regulations, standards and discipline as conceived by those who make policy at the top. At no time in our history have we ever been consulted by authority in the process of educational planning. Because our education all over the country is planned along the rigid lines that came from the British tradition, and was then reinforced by the Calvinistic view of human nature as basically prone to evil and in need of salvation, it produces people who are not supposed to question their own religious values.

The structure of our education offers a restricted number of subjects, leaving little room for the person who wants to pursue a career that requires a broad base. Because of their position of economic and political privilege, whites can break out from this cocoon when they have left high school. And yet, because they do not have the freedom of association with people of another race, the privilege that allows them to break out is still limited. They will thus remain mentally and spiritually imprisoned in their own kind of ghetto existence.

When Bantu Education broke upon us in 1953, we were already experiencing an extension of an authoritarian system. The authority tinkered with the curriculum and the syllabus in order to lower the quality of education for us; it imposed mother-tongue instruction right through high school. This last item has since been discontinued. But it has left an indelible mark on the classroom performance of our children, on their morale and that of the teacher. We can observe the pitiable degree to which they fail to articulate ideas either in English or their mother-tongue, or to make the connections across the curriculum that enrich education and indeed mark a person as *educated*.

The two architects of Bantu Education, Dr H F Verwoerd and his secretary Dr W Eiselen – both now deceased – distrusted missionary education. They were convinced that the missionaries, especially those of English stock, were teaching us to rebel against political authority; that they were giving us an education unrelated to the ordained position of the white man as boss, and the inferior position the African was destined to hold for all time. Thus, in the view of Verwoerd and Eiselen, the missionaries were instilling into us expectations that would never be fulfilled in white society – because white rule had already decided we were to be educated to serve its interests. They concocted the idea of 'Bantu culture', by which the content of our education was to be determined. By 'Bantu culture' they really meant 'tribal customs'. We, on the other hand, never recognized tribal culture. We believe in African culture that cuts across artificial boundaries. African culture has roots going down several centuries deep. No one can wish it away, unless we ourselves deny it. At the deepest spiritual level African culture unifies the whole continent. Of course missionary schooling was unrelated to our life as an African people living in a white-ruled part of the continent – but not in the way Verwoerd wanted to represent it. A highly-educated man like him (he had a doctoral degree in psychology from a German university) must have known this, but he decided to twist the facts.

Certainly, the students who formed the Youth League of the African National Congress at Fort Hare in 1949 (a year after the National Party came into power) wanted the ANC to take on a more militant nationalist character in the place of a body whose 'old guard' leadership continually protested by delegation and telegram sent to Cabinet ministers. The students were products of missionary schooling. But they became rebellious *in spite* of the mission school, where we were summarily expelled if we revolted against *any* authority; where disobedience against authority was regarded as unchristian; where biblical ethics could never be challenged. The saving grace of mission schooling was that there were good teachers who inspired students to read widely and debate issues, and the learning environment on campus was healthy and open. Teacher-student relations were generally wholesome.

What is the situation today, twenty-five years after Bantu Education has been in force? As far as the connectedness (or lack of it) between what is taught and what our lives demand as an oppressed people is concerned, we are still at the zero mark. This education has nothing to do with the pupils' and teachers' living conditions: overcrowded housing, backyard rooming, back-alley abortions, lack of room to do one's homework, lack of land to grow food, the changing rural landscape, migrant labour, single-sex hostels, overcrowded schools, poor library facilities (or utter lack of them), separatist religious sects, joblessness, disease, poverty, ignorance and so on. This is the teachers' world, and the pupils', too.

Education does not strengthen the pupil to enable him to understand the life he goes back to outside the walls of the school. If the subject content allows it, the teacher should continually establish correspondences between what is taught and the life of our people. Knowledge gives power – power to understand and also to resolve life problems.

The imposition of Afrikaans as a medium of instruction in 1976 was only a small item in the whole catalogue of deeply felt injustices. A primary factor was despair in the pupil: his progressive loss of power to deal with his impoverished, uninspiring environment. His classroom performance was deteriorating in quality because of the drop in the teacher's morale and the loss of study and communication skills over some years. So what was school worth to him? The less teachers, parents and government were inclined to listen to him, the more inarticulate and violent the student became.

Although the appalling loss of life in 1976-77 has had the effects of deterring open and collective boycotts and street demonstrations, and it would appear that the students have settled for hard work towards the attainment of an education, the overpowering examination motive is still with us. What we are really seeing is a frantic preoccupation with the 'magic' needed to pass examinations. The content of what is taught is still as remote from life as ever. How to waylay the examiner – that is what school is all about. The passing of examinations as the prime motivation has begun to give an account of itself at university. One can hear and feel the rumblings of discontent among the students here, often expressed in terms of other complaints or grievances; all amount to a dissatisfaction with authoritarianism.

What role has African culture in a system of which we are not planners, and which conducts examinations requiring knowledge outside the range of that culture?

We need to restore and strengthen the teacher's morale and self-esteem by encouraging him to re-educate himself, to upgrade his academic standing. It has been the tendency so far, because of our confused sense of political priorities, to antagonize the teacher; to make him feel he/she is a traitor by staying on and not resigning. Even while we want our children taught, we join the parents and students in berating the teacher.

The teacher needs us to reconfirm his conviction that he is wanted; that for this, if for nothing else, it is worth his efforts to upgrade himself so as to give more of himself/herself in the school. Teachers should work harder to inform themselves about African culture as one of the elements of self-knowledge that will strengthen them and give them a sense of direction. Even while they try to satisfy the requirements of public exams, they can enrich the content of their teaching. Teachers who do not know anything but vague bits and pieces of their own origins, the traditional culture their people were coming out of when they were colonized; teachers who do not know what happened to them and their people when they were colonized; teachers who never question the beliefs white people have pumped into them, and therefore never ask where the people's present culture is leading to – such teachers are of little use to us; especially at a time when we need a more passionate sense of commitment to survive the present education system.

In spite of what we have said about the authoritarian system of our education, which is run by circulars, proclamations, rules and regulations that come from the highest authority, we can still devise ways of enriching our education.

We need to study African culture as it was in the beginning and what has happened to it: how it has been drowned in parts by the aggressive culture of the Western world, and how it has survived in one form or another. African culture has not been static, or preserved in a bottle like a chemical waiting to be analysed. It has been changing, yielding to new ways, partially disappearing, coming up again, adapting. If well informed about African culture and its spiritual values, we shall be better equipped to know what we are educating for. The current teacher's objective – what we are educating for – has never been queried, or debated, because we have taken it for granted that the white man's objective is ours. After all he planned our education, we think, and his purpose must be ours. He has always drummed it into our heads that he is civilizing us, uplifting us, equipping us to work in his industries and teach our people to prepare them for a similar role. In other words, we have been educated for another person's purpose, to fit into his scheme of things, not for our purpose. We have never been permitted to conceive and develop our own purpose. A knowledge of African culture – of who we are, what we have been, what we want to be – should equip us to understand better what is at stake; what we are being educated, and educating, for.

Examples of what we are teaching have to come from our own lives. For instance, we are great users of coal as fuel. Most whites use electricity for cooking and heating purposes. An urban township that is covered with a blanket of smoke from coal stoves is nothing like a white suburb. Right here examples are going to conflict, if the teacher is talking about coal as a mineral. Also, coal mining involves migrant labour, which concerns African workers and not white workers. Miners' unions are separate too for black and white. Hardly any class lesson is complete if references are not made to real life experience, which in turn constitutes the social context. Blacks and whites live separate lives, so the social context for each will be peculiar to his lifestyle.

Principals and superintendents have to organize the school timetable in such a way that the subjects taught can be seen as interrelated. History, geography, social studies, civics, religious knowledge, language and literature, the biological sciences and the physical sciences need to be taught in relation to one another. For example, gold and coal are more than mere 'products' of South Africa. These minerals involve recruitment of labour, migrant labour. The metal we don't see (gold) brings riches to South Africa without our knowing it; we benefit little from it. Recruitment of labour is mostly in the rural areas and in the territories adjacent to South Africa. They are underdeveloped, and have little or no local employment outside the professions like teaching, nursing, medicine and the civil service. Blacks use coal as fuel; its dangers as fuel can be seen in the incidence of death as a result of carbon monoxide poisoning. We need to know the chemistry of coal. The price of coal has been soaring in the last number of years, which affects blacks mostly. And yet coal is exported in great quantities. Coal as fuel in contrast to electricity. Coal as a source of petroleum products, the story of Sasol – oil from coal.

These are only a few examples of how products of a country can come alive in the classroom and cease to be merely another dead mineral. There is a human story involved in each. Thus geography, economics, sociology, history (e.g. the development of the steam-engine, where coal is concerned) come together in interdisciplinary teaching. Gold has been known to be a 'precious and widely coveted mineral for centuries'. Man has killed for it, slaved for it, conquered for it. And yet gold is not seen by anybody that doesn't mine or process it. Once a week, the principal should arrange for such knowledge to be made available to the higher primary and secondary school pupil. There should be a line-up of teachers who will successively lecture to combined classes on a topic which they will have researched.

Likewise, crops will be related to human life, to economics, to social life (e.g. maize and the lack of nutrition in processed maize meal; sugar, energy, disease and so on). Religious knowledge will be related to our traditional morality, e.g. respect for the aged, for our parents – no matter how wrong we may think they are. It will be related to our need to aspire to great heights, to reach out to the larger universe; to the need to understand fully the obstacles that stand in our way, and to attain a sense of common decency and communal life.

The point in all of this is to establish subject learning in the classroom as a gateway to a broader knowledge of ourselves. It is also to encourage the habit of inquiry in the student, the habit of research, independent thinking; in short, positive curiosity.

Traditional African belief establishes a unity in the universe. Everything is related to something else. Nothing stands as an autonomous entity. School knowledge and activity should reinforce our need for one another, our traditional need to congregate in places, to move towards other people. Knowledge and activity should reconfirm our traditional compassion and love of life for its own sake, our impulse to share. Although we shall of necessity teach according to a syllabus leading to final examinations, we must also educate for nationhood – which goes beyond the exam room. For this our learners need to be informed about ethnic groupings, historical migrations, chiefdoms and kingdoms; how wars, conquests and their opposites have brought us to where we are. We all have to learn that the primary enemy of nationhood is negative ethnicity – tribalism.

The arts should be a vital feature of our education. If the timetable does not allow for this, teachers must be prepared to run extramural groups, discussions and art activities: painting, drawing, carving, handicrafts, music and music appreciation, and book discussions (or literary clubs). African culture should be the basis for these activities. African literature (continent-wide) should be read and discussed, the teacher giving the lead and training the participants to lead. It is in such extramural activities where informal learning takes place. It is a healthy learning environment where the teacher will get to know the pupil as a human being rather than as a person who must always take orders, as in a classroom relationship.

Culture is nothing static, as we emphasized before. Introducing African culture into our learning is also a way of creating an awareness of culture in a state of change and continuity. There are surviving aspects of our culture that should be promoted. Education should convey that knowledge of our origins and of our present will help us decide which features or elements of culture should be revived or kept alive, and which rejected. We have for generations talked about these choices but never really consciously planned anything towards such a synthesis.

The enlargement of both the teacher's and the pupil's mind will give us something of value to hold on to. It will stabilize us, inasmuch as we shall be enriched. A deeper knowledge of ourselves as a people with an ancient culture is bound to strengthen us and enhance our self-esteem against the forces that threaten to diminish us.

We must by all means have teachers, doctors, nurses, lawyers, technicians, artisans, machine operators, accountants, bookkeepers, secretaries, business managers and businessmen and so on to fulfil the demands of modern life. But we must also have direction. African culture can give us the values that will point the way. Leading from this is the whole moral base of our education. Without African culture to inform us and against which to judge a national morality in the making, without knowing what parts of it to use for our wellbeing, we are doomed. Because of the destruction of so much of our traditional selves we have come to despise ourselves, and to hold our fellow Africans in the rural areas in low esteem. Self-contempt will be our death.

In later school life children are assaulted with Shakespeare, Milton, Tennyson, Keats; and without previous knowledge of African writers and artists, their contempt for themselves and others of their race increases to an intolerable degree.

If we know the Supreme Being and the unity of the universe our forefathers believed in, if we know intimately the social relationships they valued so much, religious knowledge or studies should liberate our minds. We need to free ourselves from the state of mind in which we see ourselves as grovelling sinners, in which we constantly despise ourselves because we do not recognize God in ourselves. A Sesotho saying goes (in paraphrase): 'Boteng bya motho ke Modimong.' The inner self of a person is where God resides.

Finally, this whole discussion means that we shall have to overcome the shame of being Africans and of embracing our highest traditions. We need not fear that by restoring our traditional dignity we shall be promoting Bantustans and 'separate development'. It will be impossible to promote these ideas because they are not *our* concepts, they were not created by us. African culture cuts across separating boundaries. The urban child must be taught rural life, and the rural child urban life. If we believe that the mind refuses to be encamped, then we must also believe that education as a carrier of culture will give the mind the power to push out beyond the fence that wants to limit our growth as a people.

II

And we must spare some thought for our institutions. An institution is an establishment or organization created to promote some public object or function. Institutionalised religion is the kind that finds expression through institutions or organizations such as churches, and through priests. It is also called 'organized religion'. This is to distinguish it from religion that is all belief, without church or any other ritual (routine practice in which a group of people or individuals participate). There is, of course, hardly a religion that does not contain ritual; the mere fact that it is a religion means it is organized, it is an institution, it has a ritual. Religion should be largely a spiritual experience, rather than institutional; otherwise the institution easily corrupts the religion.

To institutionalise certain objectives or certain theories, therefore, is to establish an organization that will give them expression. There may or there may not be a building for an institution.

Think of the 1820 (British) settlers' society, the Federasie van Afrikaanse Kultuurverenigings (Federation of Afrikaans Cultural organizations), the Islamic organizations, the Zionist movements, the Jewish Board of Deputies. Think of charitable organizations like the Child Welfare Society, the Society for the Care of the Blind, organizations or clubs that collect membership fees for burial or household purposes and so on. Think of political movements, trade unions. All these are institutions that seek to preserve and give expression to certain beliefs through programmes; they consist of members who think generally alike, who find a common home in them.

What national cultural organizations do Africans have? Hardly any. There are political organizations, trade unions, local cultural clubs, yes. Of course the national political organizations that are now banned did express a political culture that had an African style. But the promotion of culture at a spiritual level was not the purpose for which those institutions were formed. We do have the Council for Black Education and Research, which is national, as is the Educational Opportunities Committee in the South African Council of Churches. But their functions, although national in size, are specialized; they only incidentally embrace a cultural purpose or direction, to the extent that education and religion are elements of culture.

1. Extramural activities

Extramural studies and activities: for these the teacher must have a renewed sense of commitment to cultural development. He should devote at least one day in the week for cultural activity after school. By cultural activity we do not include scouting, wayfaring or any other form or recreation. The scout and wayfarer movements are the products of colonialism. We are thinking of music (choral and other forms), music appreciation, painting, drawing, sculpture, clay modelling; book or literary clubs in which African literature will be studied and discussed. A writers' club in which students interested in creative writing and journalism will meet and read their own scripts, and to which available published writers (including journalists) will be invited to talk about their work. A debating or discussion club where more meaningful live social issues will be discussed (not, for instance, useless topics like 'polygamy versus one wife one man', or 'the merits and demerits of education'. They are stale topics and of no use for the development of the mind).

We are talking about creative, not recreational, activities. By music we don't mean exclusively singing, except when this is important for music appreciation. A record player and/or tape recorder is essential for this activity. If schools can spend as much money as they are doing on long trips for sport and other forms of entertainment, they should be able to invest money in art materials, stereo equipment, records; in reference books that the Education Department does not provide.

In extramural activities we as teachers can get to know more about the people we teach than we do in the classroom. Pupils and students learn more about the teacher than in the classroom. We are in touch with the real person, in a relaxed atmosphere, unafraid of authority. We get to know each other's real thoughts and feelings – teacher and pupil. We express ourselves more freely.

So the arts and other creative activities, being themselves forms of *self-expression*, are bound to release the students' energies and train them in communication skills, in independent thinking. But this can only happen if the content of these modes of expression is informed by African culture. The subject matter must be relevant to the students' lives. On the other hand, students learning to write should not be led to think that merely to document real experience, or write about and depict suffering, or debate topics that deal with the participants' experience, will take us forward. The students should push towards a discovery of the meaning of their lives, however partial or transitory. The truth cannot be arrived at in an afternoon or evening. We work towards the truth. In working towards the truth, we are also searching for the African self.

2. Community development

The student should be taught to understand that the school is not a monastery. Parent-teachers' associations should be established. Through them the school will realize its true role. It will be a way in which the school can be involved in community development. Through adult education conducted in the schools in the evenings, parents can – if they participate – learn more about what their children are being taught at school. This means that adult education should be more than a programme leading to national examinations or for literacy. It should grapple with social problems.

There should be courses that can focus the immediate attention of adults on community problems. We need an enlightened adult population. Courses may be taught, for instance, on the parents' role in the enrichment of their neighbourhood school; taking care of the pre-school child; taking care of the adolescent; sex education; nutrition; teacher-parent relationships; culture and its place in the home and the school; starting and managing a community project; community leadership; the parent's role in career guidance and so on.

3. Enrichment of the syllabus

The teacher who has a sense of challenge and commitment will spend more time on his homework than is the case today. He will expose his students to a wide range of reference. He will research his topics for each day. If he is continually probing African culture, he will incorporate it into his teaching by always making 'reference' to the culture of his and the student's milieu, i.e. human environment. He will reach back to the community continually so that his subject, and the topics within this, will be taught *in context* – the one the student is most intimately familiar with. He will use press cuttings abundantly, and encourage his students to read these on the classroom wall. The press represents culture as it is lived.

The principal should structure a timetable for teachers to take turns in a once-a-week lecture on a topic that requires an interdisciplinary approach. Each of the topics will be planned in such a way that the teacher in charge in a particular week will need to arm himself with encyclopaedic knowledge from various disciplines. The subject of coal is but a single item among several that require interdisciplinary instruction.

In the individual classroom subjects, the teacher should continually send his students out to research information in the community. In Standard 7 they should already be grappling with material that they receive from members of the community. An exercise can be presented by the teacher in language work, in geography, in history, in health science and in other branches of social studies, that requires community-based research on a small scale. For instance: where the community's water comes from; how many clinics there are in a community; how many patients are served per day in each clinic; how the community spends its leisure time; the kind of landscape a township stands on; what drainage system prevails; other features determined by landscape; human relationships in homes that have television.

Throughout, it should be impressed on the students' minds that education should be related to real life, should bring the learner into intimate contact with his environment This way the student will be better equipped to deal intelligently with the examination while being educated to understand his living conditions and to cope with them. All this relates in turn to culture, urban or rural or semi-rural or semi-urban.

Why all this emphasis on culture? Culture includes education, which is – put in the simplest terms – the learning process in which the mind, the body and the spirit grow up and mature. It helps us to master our environment and live creative lives. Education is a carrier of culture while it is itself part of culture.

At various times in the Afro-American's history, he has had to scream out his consciousness of self as a black man surrounded by white American culture, and whose community is about a quarter of the total population. The whites could suck him in entirely if he let them, and if white racism did not stand in the way of total absorption. 'I'm black and I'm proud' and 'I'm American but I'm also African', we have heard the African American declare time and again. The voice has continued to echo across two decades since the 1960s. The blacks pushed the campaign for the civil rights struggle still further, compelling the American to concede them more constitutional rights and opportunities for self-advancement. Without any power worth talking about (that depends on numbers or weaponry), the black man had to rely on his cultural consciousness, on his sense of self-worth, to make the white man take notice and recognize him as a distinct race, even while he is an American. In this sense, the black man has fought every inch of the way, supported by the moral force of his ethnic presence and of his black consciousness. He has won a number of victories, which has given him energy for more action.

African culture can provide this moral force if we listen to voices that echo the wisdom of our ancestors. Knowing who we are, where we have come from, and what has happened to us as a result of the formidable political and economic forces that determine our lives, will help us map out our cultural destiny. This whole process, given a sense of purpose through organized activity, can help us to survive the cruelty of the times. Shall we accept the challenge?

If we accept the challenge, we must work for a cultural renaissance, or revival, or renewal. It is time we talked among ourselves, even while we direct protests, demands, pleas, to white political authority. It is time we did some soul searching and asked what is wrong with ourselves, and how we can survive. But we need to do better than merely survive. We should know what our strengths are, and how we can channel them towards national fulfilment.

Once again, African culture is not a museum specimen. It is a dynamic feature of our lives. By 'dynamic' we mean not static, having motive force, being active, potent, energetic, having influence. Because it is active, it assimilates – i.e. adopts – while it can also resist. We have thus to keep redefining it at each stage. Only *we* who live the culture can define it meaningfully. Only *we* should be the ones to decide what African culture should do in the face of modern technology, what the latter should do to it. We must accept wholesome, enriching change, but we must determine the size and extent of the change. True enough, while other people run our lives – while we are mere pawns in their political economic and social schemes – we may fail to take charge of our cultural life. But we must insist that we still have a fighting chance to decolonise our minds, to liberate them – so that we may be able to determine the *quality* of that other liberation with the moral strength deriving from the freedom of the mind, of the spirit.

Thoughts on the Place of Literature in English Within the Context of Enlightened Pedagogy – 1994

Synopsis by Marcus Ramogale

Mphahlele wrote this paper in August 1994, a few months into the new post-apartheid South Africa. In it he looks at the apartheid past and at the present as he makes suggestions for the future with respect to literary studies.

In this piece, we meet Mphahlele the teacher as he mulls over the role and place of literature in a progressive educational system. He starts by looking at the role played by vernacular literatures in what was apartheid South Africa. He finds that these literatures never became 'an intellectual resource' and that they failed to develop the 'emotional depth' one expects to find in good writing. The reason was that the apartheid state's emphasis on separate linguistic, cultural and social development was not about development but control; it was a divide and rule strategy. Another reason was that the dynamism of vernacular writing was hindered by the fact that the literature was written solely for school-children. With virtually no literature for an adult readership there was, as a consequence, no culture of reading among black people outside the classroom. The non-participation of blacks in the book industry helped to make matters worse.

With regard to literature written in English, a language Mphahlele sees as an enabler of national unity and consciousness, he finds the situation different. He finds the traditional English literary canon 'pretty heavy' for many students and teachers in South African schools. This is something that has scared many of them from English studies. The new provinces, he hopes, will prescribe African writing in the high schools in order to make literary studies relevant for students and teachers. Also, 'it is reasonable that we shift the emphasis on the great canon in order… to listen to other voices: literatures that invite us into the inner mysteries of their respective cultures.' In South African universities the literary situation is slightly better, Mphahlele says. He finds gratifying the teaching of African literature in South African universities and the presence of 'an appreciable core of academics' who are familiar with African writing. For Mphahlele, literature is not just a 'discipline' but also has a social function as 'an act of culture, an act of self-knowledge.'

The last section of the paper looks at some aspects of literary pedagogy from Mphahlele's own teaching experience. For Mphahlele the teacher, teaching and reading literature is a form of 'adventure.' This is the attitude he has sought to develop in his students in his forty years of teaching English at university.

For better or worse, our native languages have enjoyed or suffered emphasis in the name of 'separate development' and the squinted Eiselen-Verwoerd view of what they called 'Bantu culture'. The emphasis has not been matched by their actual capacity to produce literatures that could enrich them. Their potential capacity is quite a different thing. Since 1953 the use of indigenous languages at school in this country has been an overtly political issue.

The master race has also sought to take charge of the flow and spread of ideas by keeping the lid firmly down on intellectual growth. Largely for this reason, and for lack of a share in the business of book production, very little vernacular literature has become an intellectual resource – or even developed the emotional depth we have come to expect in good writing. Little or nothing has emerged with the resonances of Mofolo's *Chaka* (1925), *Moeti wa Bochabela* (1906-7), William Wellington Gqoba's allegory, *Discussion Between the Christian and the Pagan*, AC Jordan's *Ingqumbo Yeminyanya* (1940) or BW Vilakazi's poetry, *Inkondlo ka Zulu* (1935), or Mqhayi's works. By the same token, the territories of Lesotho and Botswana, with independent presses, have done much better.

I do not mean to belittle the adult literature that has appeared in the last few years, nor what has been done for the school readership. But adult attitudes towards the mother-tongue have been shaped by the politics of education and the economics of publishing and book marketing. The vernacular school readers, because of the politics of their publishers, have not in the last fifty years sown the seed of an enduring love for the language and its ideas that would extend into one's adult years. I'm talking about a love – if the book is enriching – that reaches back to the spoken language for the reader to recognize its heightened use in print.

It is a new trend that publishers are trying to encourage writing in African languages for levels of readership where adult concerns take centre stage. If this trend pays off in the long run in the interests of the reading public, we may yet see a number of titles translated from one language to another. This will reinforce a reading culture that we talk so much about and yet do very little to begin to develop. Those who have the money resist the cultural ideas of any but those who have no radical opinion and plans to offer. It is also a comfortable thought for them to believe that what we propose is really the State's responsibility. Those who do have ideas for radical but feasible projects neither have capital nor even people who can believe enough in them to support their proposals to financial institutions.

Although I speak of translations, we should bear in mind that they are a thankless job in material terms. It will still require subsidisation from the State to make it worthwhile for a person to undertake the task. This does not in any way guarantee publication either, as publishers constantly watch market trends. If business incidentally promotes culture, of which education is a part, they are all the happier – but this goal does not feature highly in the order of priorities among run-of-the-mill book producers. But for a country that wants to make sure that every language deserves attention in print, one of the ways to counter the evils of ethnicity will have to be access into ideas across ethnic boundaries via translations.

We cannot overemphasize the need for a language to develop a literature for its own survival. This must range from popular marketplace literature to the more enduring, highbrow poetry, narratives, expositions and literary journalism. Nor can literature flourish in the cultural conditions of present-day South Africa, where there is hardly any discourse among blacks around specific books of local and general interest. Secondly, intellectual activity among whites is inbred, elitist and fragmented. We need to engage in the exchange of ideas, which in turn will feed into our literatures – even while we develop ideas that derive from the world of books in languages that we can comprehend. We shall have to jack ourselves up, we blacks, who have for a long time shied away from any free play of ideas. We need to develop greater self-confidence where corporate intellectual activity is so thinly spread and sporadic. We shall have to free ourselves from the long-established syndrome of dependence, of total reliance on white leadership.

We must use the existing infrastructure in publishing enterprises under white control that are willing to create partnerships with us. This way we should be able to rethink and change our priorities vis-à-vis language distribution, target audiences, and dissemination of the literature we produce. We shall also need a literature that invites the reader to experience a wider range of emotional and intellectual responses. Outlets for the sale of books will have to move to high-density areas, even outside the industrial and commercial city centres. Monopolies such as CNA and Exclusive Books, where only the few haves can afford to buy reading material, will have to give way to companies that are willing to invest in the cultivation of reading habits among our people.

In the meantime, while we are reorganizing our cultural and economic priorities as I've suggested above, I'm still the classroom practitioner. I'm here to teach English. Whatever its status will eventually be, it will still offer itself as a medium of ideas – especially through the printed word. We may have to decide on the relative degrees of mastery of the language we dare to expect and insist on as policy. I do not rightly know. What I'm sure of is that language is thought and we think in a particular language. Shoddy writing or speech in any language reflects lazy or disorganized thinking and should be a source of concern to us. Teachers and students or pupils should be able to work out difficulties in the use of language. This requires a good working relationship between the two sides instead of constant competition, conscious or unwitting, for the sympathies of State and the public.

The teacher/lecturer faces, every day, dismayingly huge numbers of students. Until we are reasonably funded to employ more teachers for controlled student numbers, we shall have to devise strategies for making the personal contact the teacher requires with students. We have not yet seriously considered such strategies, because we have been scared of taking unpopular decisions. And not without reason either, given the stark, cold fact that a corrupt government has been in charge of us all these years. In addition, the political bosses of yesterday, plus an influential academic establishment, have long resisted the concept of the community or junior college – or even the Sixth Form. Such institutions can ease the student into tertiary education and also afford him/her time to consider career options after two years of junior college. As things stand, we head straight for academic institutions meant specifically for book learning.

We shall have to abandon or modify the traditional type of final examinations, even after things have been normalized. At present they test nothing more than assimilated bits of textbook knowledge that say nothing about life in the real world, nor contribute anything to our intellectual life. We keep flogging questions about content and methodology arising from textbooks and lectures without ever realizing that we are seeking answers on impossible terms, namely the continued delivery of didactic pedagogy for no other reason than that the system is hallowed by tradition.

We still believe, as our forebears did – may blessings and peace be upon them – that engineered obstacles in the learning process are necessary because they are challenging, or for positive ends. We lack the courage to explore new avenues, new humanistic modes of operation. Even those intellectuals whose counsel the State condescends to invite eventually come to conclusions that derive from their own socialization in the ethic of racial divisions: a dead-end of tradition. The State publishes report after report to endorse false or half-baked theories and formulae.

The teaching of English has everything to do with this larger context of our education. No new theories about the multilingual, multiracial society are going to rescue the teaching of English from the present mess, which results partly from the hocus-pocus industry now thriving under the name of 'English as a Second Language', and in part from the poor qualifications of many of our teachers for the subject.

In order to deal with multilingual and multiracial issues, we simply have to burn down the ideological Bastille that has held us hostage all these years. For Verwoerd and Eiselen did not invent educational ideology. It was there long before 1950, but on the hidden agenda of white rule. We have to explore human relationships across the artificial barriers white rule has created over the centuries. What we used to take for granted in these relationships must now come under microscopic examination and be evaluated empirically, beyond mere academic interest. This is only one aspect of reconstruction.

Formal education remains the primary prerequisite in the making of a writer, in any language. It seems to me that the language one emerges with from high school as one's primary medium of expression – among one's peers in daily life, at work, in post-secondary studies, at home – this common denominator will prove to be the mainstay in a person's effort to deal with ideas, to utilize, articulate and communicate them.

Questions

1. Do we intend to programme people to be multilingual, and at the same time to master a language – like English – which is international and through which ideas largely come to us, at least for now?
2. Do we foresee a day when our native languages will carry us through tertiary education as the media of instruction? Before that 'far-off divine event', are we going to exploit English to the fullest extent for purposes of mobilizing ideas, in the same way it became, like French and Portuguese, an agent of anti-colonial nationalism?
3. If that future day dawns, shall we be so competent in the construction and articulation of ideas in each one of the nine native languages? (This is important if writers deriving from a sound education insist on using the mother tongue. Lesotho, Swaziland and Botswana are sufficiently homogeneous countries to create an incentive to construct ideas in the respective ethnic languages. This is fertile soil for vernacular literature to germinate and grow, feeding on surrounding ideas and helping to conceptualise new issues, new strategies for existence and self-realization. And yet none have abandoned English.)
4. Whichever way the politics of language usage are going to interact and determine this aspect of our cultural life, we shall still be faced with the stark fact that our level of English usage is alarmingly low, even at college and university. Are there any real pedagogical reasons for changing from the scheme we have followed for generations: mother-tongue instruction in sub-standard A and B through to Standard 3; English as a subject from Standard 3, and as a medium of instruction from Standards 3 or 4 on? We have not witnessed any deviance, psychological, social or otherwise, as a result. I cannot rightly ignore the cogent argument for the claims of the other ten languages. Neither can they themselves rightly ignore the historical role of English in the moulding of a nationalist consciousness against colonialism throughout our continent. One does not have to be an anglophile to acknowledge this. Have we really resolved the problem of ancient tribalisms that today are resurfacing? There is a lot of talk today about which ethnic language is spoken by most Africans. The hierarchy of political leadership has long displayed aspirations to separatism and ethnic supremacy.

The teaching-learning environment will improve. For this we obviously need new-thinking, dedicated teachers/lecturers, reasonable numbers of teachers and students to make it possible for sound pedagogy to be conducted, and healthier student-teacher relationships. One also believes that the larger socio-political and economic forces will be under control, and that our society will attain much greater active confidence in itself and its future.

English Literature

Chaucer, Shakespeare, Milton, Dryden, Pope, Joseph Addison, Samuel Johnson, Samuel Richardson, the Brontës, George Eliot, Jane Austen, Virginia Woolf, Wordsworth, Byron, Shelley, Keats, Dickens, Tennyson, Thomas Hardy, Matthew Arnold, TS Eliot, and relative newcomers Steinbeck, Pound, and Faulkner are all found on the staple menu for English literary studies – or groupings of one kind or another of the authors whom tradition has canonized. The above literary canon is pretty heavy and has scared away many students, teachers and lecturers from English literature, especially those who are not surrounded by constant discourse on English literature in sitting rooms, on campuses, in the media, and so on.

In South African universities African writers, especially the locals, are thrown into the curriculum – although somewhat apologetically. It is gratifying to observe that there is an appreciable core of academics who are highly knowledgeable about African literatures in English and French and other areas of African studies. We hope that the provinces will prescribe African writing in the high schools, something which the old provincial administrations resisted for the most part. At the University of the Witwatersrand, a division of African Literature has existed since 1983; it has now become a substantive department. The core study is based on African, African-American and Caribbean literatures, originally in English, French and Portuguese, in translation. There is ample room for cross-references between the literatures under study.

In academia, very often we resist any suggestion to juxtapose literary works we have been schooled by tradition to regard as less than 'great' with those of the 'Great Tradition' listed above. We suspect that if we accommodate alternative titles, we are lowering our esteem for the canon. It really should not come down to an either/or resolution – as if the two sets of literature were staking contending claims. We adopt this attitude because we are used to reading and teaching literature as a *discipline*, an academic study. We ignore the fact that literature is an act of culture, an act of self-knowledge and an act of language. It is a social act as much as it is a literary set of events or moments: a process, while at the same time we read its products. Now that English has touched so many nations in the world, who are also producing literatures in it, it is only reasonable that we shift the emphasis from the great canon in order to listen more profitably to other voices. Literatures that invite us into the inner mysteries of their respective cultures: Africa and its American-Caribbean diaspora, Asia and so on.

Anthony Easthope, Professor of English and Cultural Studies at Manchester

Metropolitan University, wrote an article recently in *Literature Matters No 14* (published by the British Council) entitled 'The Death of Literature'. He reminds us that the subject English Literature, 'with the assumptions and methods associated with it, was really only invented during the 1930s as a result of work (in modern literary criticism – my parentheses) mainly by William Empson and I.A. Richards.' This, he explains, came about 'on the basis of a silent opposition between the canon of Great Literature and its other, popular culture.'

In this view, Easthope continues, literature is crafted, imaginative and elevating. You have to read it closely and respond as a thinking individual. The other side of the coin shows us popular literature (song, radio, film, television). This is a collective; it is no strain on the imagination to read and respond to; it is even anti-life in the view of those who prefer highbrow literature. You can enjoy this popular art instinctively, whereas you need a reasonably high education and special training to gain entry into the meaning of the elevated literary product.

The common claim among the elite who are capable of reading and talking about such literature is that it is great because it explores and heightens certain 'imperishable Truths about human nature'. In this view, its greatness assigns to it a place above the familiar (meaning also, in my deduction, mundane or ordinary) plane of living. The claim goes further, to insist that a great work 'will stay great, because it is always read slightly differently each time.'

Professor Easthope persuasively suggests a way out: study the traditional canonical texts alongside products of popular culture, 'one political, one academic.' It is 'more democratic' this way. Also, study will have to be more objective, asking us to prejudge texts to distinguish them from others. By 'objective' Easthope must be implying non-arbitrary, not bullied by the critical canon. Ironically, it follows that to refuse to stay exclusively within the canon is to be subjective; only it is a subjectivity that does not bear the stamp of literary authority.

I am sure that Easthope interprets 'popular culture' to be the way of life *that is actually made by people for themselves*, i.e. *those* we *do not normally count among an elite*. The phrase should not, as it did in its much earlier English usages, imply inferior as seen by the upper, 'cultivated' classes – or something created among them to curry favour or power with the masses. Let's admit that the 'common people' have their own artistic creations, their own poetry. One may even add that cultural products created by an artist outside the lower masses, but which have an appeal among them, are more self-conscious than what the masses themselves might compose.

'Cultural studies' is what Easthope proposes as a solution to the problem of reconciling the 'great books' with the 'everyperson books'. Ngugi wa Thiong'o, Kenyan writer, introduced to the University of Nairobi a number of years ago the Department of Literature to replace the antique Department of English. A number of African, European, American and Asian literatures in English are studied, not only British.

Both this and the Manchester innovation make sense to me. Such a department must then reflect literatures in English as an open lively concourse of cultures, responding to multilingual, national, gender and class needs, and so on.

The Texts

Throughout my forty years of teaching English at university, I have invariably asked my students to avoid choking up their essays with abundant quotations and footnotes. I insisted on knowing what *they* as individual students felt and thought about a literary item: what such literature did to and for them. Whether it did or did not do anything, I wanted to know the reasons for such sentiment. I advised that they read critical texts to help them reconstruct the intellectual history related to the literature, a context of ideas as part of culture. This would enlighten them more about the text.

In other words, I like to see if the student writing a paper has grasped the contents of the critical reference text he is using to illuminate the main text, enough to be able to paraphrase and condense the material for the purpose. He or she can still acknowledge his or her source of reference in the body of the essay. I suspect that the academic who credits students for chunks of quotations that are little more than show is himself simply too lazy to pursue the writer's own effort at self-articulation.

Just as several teachers and students prefer chewing the sawdust that comes from literary texts in the form of study notes and summaries of plots to the labour of reading the original works, there are many who read criticism even before the original book – if they even start it. The study of literature becomes the bane of their student days. They bring no sense of adventure to the reading of literature, because it is treated by most like a cadaver lying on the pathologist's table.

I would not prescribe Shakespeare for today's matriculation students, except those whose proficiency in English allow it. Nor would I be keen to teach his plays in the State schools. It's excruciating for both teacher and students, for obvious reasons. Some of the independent schools may have a fighting chance in tackling the bard. For Standard 9 through 10, I should prescribe about twenty items of modern poetry; one modern play longer than one act; a volume of African short stories – about thirty; and three to four 20th-century novels, preferably one British and two to three African. If we are keen to teach language through literature as well as in other ways, it seems only fair to have students read what their cultural experience can help them penetrate, and whose language is lucid for their own stage of education. Options can be built into this list, so that native speakers of English may select what they think is more challenging if they so wish. Non-native speakers would not be prevented from exercising this kind of option.

Thoughts on Intellectual Freedom – 1988

Synopsis by Sam Raditlhalo

Eight years prior to this address, Es'kia Mphahlele, while addressing another group of graduates at the University of the Witwatersrand (see 'Landmarks of Literary History in South Africa' in Literary Appreciation), charged the institution with refusing to evolve into an African University. He returns to this theme in a different guise when delivering this address to the class of 1988. This time the emphasis is on the individual growing up in a fragmented society and the burden of moral accountability; the challenge of being African in the profoundest sense. This address adopts a two-pronged approach: it highlights the shortcomings of a liberal institution that instills a disturbing societal conformity and conservatism in the students, while appealing to the students to strike out on their own. He reminds the students: 'Seldom are we disposed to assert freedom from the tyranny of the tribe, be it an economic, ideological, religious or social circle'. If the students are to be truly free, Es'kia urges them to free themselves of coercion, co-option and the sanctions of the tribe – something the university did not deem fit to inculcate or encourage. The purpose of the address becomes apparent when Es'kia explores the myriad ways in which African peoples have had to struggle with assimilation, rejection and attempting a synthesis between their selves and Western culture. He calls on the students to attempt the same process in reverse: to be willing to understand the essence of being African beyond the simple fact of a geographic identity. What is called for from the graduates is to embark on the adventure towards an integrated personality.

It baffles reason that government should have been conceived, constituted and shaped by those who are proud to call themselves citizens, patriots to boot – and yet should empower itself to turn against them and suppress them with all the weaponry imaginable: the same weaponry purchased and manufactured with public money.

After a number of busy years, institutional violence develops a life of its own, its own ethic operating by its own logic. Its own momentum in the never-ending cycle of birth and death. Only it destroys what it seeks to protect. There is practically nothing the citizens can do to resist effectively the institution that savages them, or to check its prosecution – retribution cycle. The master race calls it democracy. Officials dress it up and put it on a carnival or commemoration float to wave and smile at the wretched and impotent spectators. Tomorrow democracy – or this brand of it – will sign decree upon decree demanding that heads shall roll: democracy turned executioner.

One of the most remarkable skills of the enlightened intellect is its ability to withdraw without disengaging and vice versa. The intellect feels constrained to pause and contemplate, to encompass disparate elements of experience, to analyze and synthesize, to assert its own organic view of life; the intellect becomes even more sharply aware of its own nature in the context of history that shapes it and is shaped by it. More than this, it intuits the pervasive and all-encompassing process of the human spirit we call civilization even while it serves as the latter's agent.

It is the midnight hour or daybreak. The braying and roar and shrieks and baying of politicians who run our lives have receded, the rhetoric renewing its venom for yet more onslaughts. I find myself contemplating this process called intellectual or academic freedom. The former relates more to an individual condition; academic freedom to a collective or communal condition or process. They cannot be mutually exclusive.

Freedom, we are told by scholars, is a moral and a social concept. It refers to the absence of coercion or constraint by another person or institution. In its more popular sense, freedom suggests a release from a condition, deriving from European liberalism and individualism. One must be free to choose one's goals or actions, to choose between available alternatives, unrestrained by the will of another person or institution – even when one is prevented by natural or social conditions, or lack of means to act as one has chosen, e.g. under conditions of poverty.

Bertrand Russell defined freedom in general as the 'absence of obstacles for the realization of one's desires.' This is begging the question. For the definition assumes that one's desires necessarily express the 'free' agent's inner character. Not so. Ours is a fishbowl existence in this country; the white man's being rather like a huge asylum without visible fences.

By all the means available, the political authority has overtly and covertly programmed our individual and collective desires. It has blacked out alternative avenues of knowledge and manipulated our school systems to serve its own purposes of control rather than encourage the unqualified emancipation of its citizens. Furthermore, it has injected into the process of education an ideological element whose overruling motive is conformity with the State's own perception of what we must be schooled to do.

Our morality is determined by the State, whether it be the morality of white trusteeship or the survival morality of the black man. If Bantu Education is like a flea market managed by civil servants who themselves have come to accept the inferiority of the state's greasy, patched-up wares, the white man's education is a Hyperama planned and run by civil servants who strut about in paper hats touting their tinsel and plastic wares. Conformity is at the heart of this whole bazaar. I take off my hat to those who have managed to strike out into academic pursuits that express their own personalities instead of the primitive tribal myths they were nurtured on.

The State has mapped out neat little areas which must appear unfenced, un-policed, accessible. The State may often appear shy of intrusion when it knows that its judicial, legal and education systems have been set to regulate the quantity and flow of the water through canals it has carved out. Thus, beside the written decrees and proclamations to permit this, control and prohibit that, there are indirect controls to negate, neutralize or conceal alternative choices.

To be real, then, freedom of the intellect must also make alternative choices known and understood, in addition to the absence of coercion. Literacy and education increase our options and help us create some, as well as increasing our capacity to decide between them. Otherwise freedom counts for little or nothing, except as an agent of anarchy or stagnation, or the conformity we associate with police-dog docility. I am also implying here that the decrease or increase of State subsidisation is only one aspect of the whole debate about academic freedom. So is the presence or absence of police terror on the campuses, or the decision about who shall be allowed to lecture on campus as a visitor. Freedom of the individual intellect is embattled in other ways, ways that have to do with the content of university education: what the student is taught, the stuff lecturers are made of.

Seldom are we disposed to assert freedom from the tyranny of the tribe, be it an economic, ideological, religious or social group. We have been educated to believe that we are more secure within our respective sects. We only need to follow a formula or code, however antiquated or alien to life on this continent. Conformity makes life easier. All too often the percussion instruments – the drums, the whistles, the cymbals, the tambourines – drown the voices and the melody. At the end of the year they proclaim our triumphs over books, lecturers and examiners.

We have no national morality in a fragmented South Africa. Rather, we have sec-tional codes of morality. Tribal or sectional morality is loudmouthed, desperate – such as that of the neo-Nazis and the thousands who agree with them but are not bold enough to proclaim their creed on the open forum.

For this reason, the burden of moral accountability to oneself is so much greater – almost unbearable. Ultimately, you have only yourself to answer to. The freedom of choice is yours. Most of you here come from a class that wields power of one kind and another. You have thus alternatives through which to counter negative or self-immobilizing conformity.

The irony is that although a university or college education should free you from the sausage machine, or help you to neutralize its effects, there is a most disturbing institutional conformity and conservatism that lies heavy in the belly of every South African university and college.

They respond to political crises, to the minions of the law that stampede across the campuses in routine fashion. Their main ammunition is their verbal assertion of academic freedom. This is a statement of fact and not meant to dismiss the universities' process of resistance.

I am still underscoring the conformity with which we respond to the juggernaut of tyranny. I also want to underscore the Eurocentric survivals of the renaissance in South African universities, which will not let go in order for us to evolve institutions that are truly African. In other words, South African universities are trying to survive on contradictory terms. In addition to this, there are lecturers in these universities who are still slaves of conformity in the things they teach and the methods they use. They drag their souls behind them across the campus and from one lecture theatre to another, reciting stale lectures with a kind of liturgical inevitability.

Back to the individual intellect. Assume that you spend your first twenty to thirty years totally or partially under the care of parents and institutions – all hell-bent to mould you in their own images so that you conform to the so-called 'traditional South African way of life'. Now is the time for you to sort out the junk from true learning. Just as important as the black man's struggle for political and economic power is the struggle for the white man's soul – on all fronts of the ideological spectrum and by as many constituencies. That struggle calls for your own independent judgement. You can, on the other hand, take the easy way out and go along with the blinkered herd.

You do not have much time left to take the other road, to turn around and re-orientate yourself. Free yourself of coercion, co-option and the sanctions of the tribe. I could not express it in other than apocalyptic terms – that time is running out.

I like to think that this is the least a university education should have done to and for you: that you should now, more than ever before, be able to work out your priorities regarding the areas and ways of conformity; to sort out humanistic conformity from pathological and compulsive affiliation to dead-end causes. Now is the time to explore the ways and means of becoming African in the profoundest sense of the word, i.e. beyond the simple fact of geographic identity.

In other words, depending on the population group you have been assigned to, you have to question the freedoms you have always taken for granted on your side of the racial divide. There is more to this than simply joining the picket lines and street marches and political movements traditionally associated with the black man's causes; more to it than simply carrying a banner and echoing the freedom cry. It is a matter of confronting self, examining self and evaluating it in a historical context. You have to study Africa in all its aspects. Become immersed in its cultural history and life.

The devotee of a jealous God may boast freedom of worship and yet never exercise that freedom in questioning his inherited faith: what John Stuart Mill would call the 'despotism of custom'. It amounts to a mechanical faith that merely recycles man's transgressions, remorse and absolution.

The subjugated peoples of this continent have, since the days of slavery and colonialism, grappled with the processes of assimilation, rejection and synthesis of Western culture and the African personality. The white man, from his position of supremacy, has never considered African thought and belief and life-ways worthy of assimilation or even comprehension. The burden of synthesis has always lain on the African's shoulders, because he has had to survive an aggressive and self-righteous civilization.

Your education should also promote a synthesis between your Western heritage and African values that are both humanistic and accessible. The first lesson is humility and willingness to understand the essence of being African. Casually mixing with blacks is not nearly enough. The journey I am proposing for you calls for emotional and intellectual involvement, a lesson in humanistic coexistence at its deepest levels.

I wish to conclude by congratulating all the graduates and wishing you success in your future endeavours, especially in the adventure towards an integrated personality.

AFRICAN
HUMANISM
& CULTURE

Africa in Exile – 2000

Synopsis by Ndavhe Ramakuela

We have here a picture of exile as an Africa-wide concern. In this paper Mphahlele broadens our understanding of the concept of exile by showing how it affects the individual as a whole – politically, artistically and psychologically. Perhaps one of its highlights is its intimation that, even after political independence in their respective countries, many people remain very much in exile in their homes. Artistically, writers are unable to reach down to their creative springs – either because they are displaced, or because they cannot look deep inside themselves to see what there is to love about their own culture. Displacement and alienation are particularly acute for artists who are unable to return to their original home. When the spirit has not teamed up with the locale to produce a lasting peace with the environment, exile becomes a daily process that manifests itself in many forms. Mphahlele goes further to illustrate that for writers this kind of exile is revealed through images borrowed largely from the West. Despite the paper's general tone, its closing remarks give the impression that, after all the troubles and misgivings, there is something to gain in exile – an opportunity to engage in introspection and thus understand oneself; a process towards rediscovery of one's cultural heritage.

These words come from a poem in a collection published by the late Arthur Nortjé in 1973:

The isolation of exile is a gutted
warehouse at the back of pleasure streets:

I peer through the skull's black windows
wondering what can credibly save me

Origins trouble the voyager much, those roots
that have sipped the waters of another continent
I suffer the radiation burns of silence;
it is not cosmic immensity or catastrophe
that terrifies me:
it is solitude that mutilates

One of the brilliant lights on the landscape of South African poetry, Nortjé was born in Oudtshoorn and died in Oxford in 1970 at the age of twenty-eight, victim of a fatal drug trip.

In the *New York Times* Edward Said, the Palestinian scholar and thinker, called exile 'the unhealable rift forced between a human being and a native place.' Another writer called it a 'ghetto of the mind'. These experiences show that exile cannot be an ideal state for a person to live in. Said knows the condition of exile from inside, having lived outside his homeland most of his life. Yet the Israeli-Palestinian conflict and the wars and other confrontations it has generated have constantly exercised Said's mind since the 1980s. From his example and that of others, it is clear that the intellect's engagement with human affairs blunts much of the edge of exile. It is an unconscious process of survival. But even for the diehard ideologue, flung out by his homeland's savage politics as an activist, there comes a time when exile becomes unbearable in the mind and in the mechanics of living.

There are periods when, as an exile, time seems to reel off in perceptibly slow motion. Then there are times when the clock of your life seems to tick faster; its con-veyer belt seems afterwards to have slipped unnoticeably fast from under your feet. All in all, time seems to contract on you; you live more intensely than ever before. There is so much to learn, in structured and informal ways, that was forbidden you back home; you chew and gulp down life in big chunks, hungry for more and more knowledge.

Exiles. The numbers keep growing. Every political upheaval in Africa yields yet another crop of exiles. I saw it happen in the twenty years I was an exile. I met them in Africa, in Europe, in North America. One of our earliest exiles was Alfred Hutchinson. He jumped bail during the Treason Trial in 1957 and fled the country, eventually landing in Ghana.

In 1958, when I had just left South Africa and was teaching in Nigeria, it was generally believed that white-ruled Southern Africa was the only part of the conti-nent that could qualify for the kind of violence that throws people out into exile. Those were the high political times immediately after Ghana's independence, during which the French colonies – with the exception of Guinea (West Africa) – were negotiating Charles de Gaulle's offer of independence in two years' time. The im-pending release of Jomo Kenyatta of Kenya from prison was being hotly debated in Africa and London. Those were the days when the then Prime Minister H. F. Verwoerd in South Africa and Sir Roy Wellensky of the Federation of Rhodesia and Nyasaland were issuing threats all around against their dissident African subjects. Wellensky was proclaiming African nationalism as so much poppycock. Verwoerd had a treason trial on, in which one hundred and fifty-six members of the Congress Alliance and affiliated trade unions were in the dock for allegedly attempting to overthrow the government by violence.

In December 1958, Kwame Nkrumah, head of the newly-independent Ghana, called the All-African Peoples Conference, which was mostly attended by representatives of resistance movements still operating in colonial countries. Ethiopia was conspicuously absent. I made my first acquaintance with activists who were later to be presidents – and who then, like Nkrumah, were violently toppled and found themselves looking for asylum in friendly states. I met men like Patrice Lumumba, who was later to be assassinated in the Congo – a murder orchestrated by America's CIA. Then there was Kenneth Kaunda, the top man of his liberation movement. He was the natural first president of Zambia, but where is he now?

Five years into exile, at forty-three (in 1962), I was employed as director of African Programmes by the Paris-based International Association for Cultural Freedom. I made a tour of African states to survey their cultural institutions. By then, countries like Malawi, Uganda, Kenya and Tanzania were a year or two into independence. President Banda and some of his party associates were rebuking South African refugees and exiles for not returning home 'to fight the whites'. His party's newspaper attacked refugees for being 'cowards'.

These, together with the Nigerian experience, were some of the most engaging years of our exile. I lapped up whatever there was to learn in volumes, chunks, feeling free in a way no words can phrase. I remember vividly how high my spirits were, vicariously filled with pride on viewing especially the whole theatrical setting and regalia of strong, self-confident Nigerians, Ghanaians, Senegalese, Malians, and so on, under the rising sun of their glorious arrival in the international community.

Sharpeville exploded on March 20, 1960. We were in Nigeria then, in that northern spring. We listened to the BBC news with a childhood friend who had just fled from South Africa and was preparing to proceed to the coast to take a teaching job. He and his family would not return home until the mid-1980s. We both suddenly broke into a litany of sorts about the tremors we knew filled the hearts of our compatriots in and outside this country. I felt a twinge of guilt for not being back home, as if our presence would have made any difference. The vanity of man.

With the subsequent banning of the African National Congress and the Pan-Africanist Congress, and the arrest and/or dismissal of several teachers for their attempted resistance to 'Bantu' and coloured education, more South Africans left the country. They took various and tortuous routes that cut through Botswana, the Rhodesias, East Africa, and thence either to Ethiopia or Zaire. Some of them – assisted by scholarships from international organizations like the African American Institute and other American organizations, the United Nations, Scandinavian governments, the British Anti-Apartheid Movement, the Germans and Russians – proceeded to receptive countries for higher studies. We must regard the treason trialists and other activists who were sent to Robben Island and other mainland prisons as exiles of the time.

As an indication of the pattern that was emerging – national upheavals – Kwame Nkrumah needed only to visit Peking, in an attempt to mediate in the Indo-Chinese conflict, for a military coup to happen in Ghana. He sought asylum in Guinea. Then the Nigerian deluge broke out in 1966, followed by the Biafran war of secession. Milton Obote of Uganda had to flee the wrath of a military junta to become an exile in Tanzania, whose President Julius Nyerere had earlier driven Obote's enemies out. Already a few intellectuals had left Uganda to get away from Obote's dictatorship. Exiles, still more exiles, were to be found in African states. Nyerere's Tanzania, Nkrumah's Ghana, Banda's Malawi, Kenyatta's Kenya, Touré's Guinea, North Africa, Ethiopia, Sudan, the Central African Republic, Zaire – all these were to see their sons and daughters join the South Africans, the Angolans and the Mozambiquans in African and Western capitals.

Almost overnight after independence, I witnessed the tragic unfolding of the imperial theme, as Shakespeare would have dramatized it. News filled the air of treachery, assassination, palace rebellions, preventive detention, government corruption, neo-colonial plots to subvert independence, public executions involving rebels, individual members of the parliamentary opposition being liquidated and so on. Each time the bell tolls the death of one person, several refugees spill across frontiers. Intellectuals who are frustrated because the existing neo-colonial structures of education resist new ideas are leaving to seek intellectual freedom in other cultures.

And the clock ticked off the hours, days, months, years. You were not getting any younger. The first year or two you were learning to come to terms with your condition of exile. Learning to adjust to the new environment; learning to work out your priorities: what you want and must do towards the realisation of your aspirations, towards self-realisation. A profession? A trade? Politician? Soldier? You realised that you were on trial, a trial in which you had either to answer to yourself or to the demands of a military/political mission. The first few years were full of excitement. If ever you passionately needed to make the right choices, this was the paramount time. Especially when the excitement wore off. The pragmatist in you had to replace the romantic. You realised that the old assumptions you came out of your native land with were crumbling inside you. All the assumptions that you might find the rest of Africa unsophisticated and slow-moving because it was not driven by racist oppression – all these evaporated. Men I met as cabinet ministers in newly independent states were exiles three years later. The same Malawians who had earlier reviled exiles from Southern Africa had fled to Tanzania, where I found them when my job took me there a few years later.

Savagely repressive regimes stay in power relatively long in Africa. Violent authoritarian rule, the lack of political sophistication and strong, rigid ethnic loyalties are among the factors responsible for this. Such regimes will stay for a long time, especially if they sustain their levels of repression at somewhere between a state of utter chaos and lack of will to govern, and the type of atrocities Uganda's Idi Amin and Nigeria's Abacha wreaked. And so exiles from countries where there is even a semblance of 'benevolent dictatorship' remain outside the longest.

It is interesting to ponder the unevenness of tyranny that the apartheid government here was able to juggle with so competently. The 'Bantu homelands' were only one of the techniques that worked so well for the white leaders. But of course even such tricks cancel out in the final equation. The 1950s and 1970s were enough to set the stage for bigger upheavals before the most bruising decade – the 1980s – broke upon us. The 1976 Soweto revolt was a clear signal.

You are a refugee today. As soon as you find asylum in a country disposed to grant it, you are an exile. Indeed, mentally you already consider yourself one as soon as you cross the border of your country of refuge – to the extent that you are conscious of what you are fleeing from and where you are heading to seek such a country.

The Statute of the Office of the United Nations High Commissioner for Refugees defines a refugee in an international context. The Statute goes back to 1950, but was ratified by only some states. On September 4, 1967, a Protocol took effect that was added to the Convention to cover the status of refugees. So, more countries became signatories to the Protocol in addition to those who were responsible for the 1950 Convention Agreement.

In his book *The Anatomy of Exile* (1972), Paul Tabori asks us to consider the following points of definition, arrived at after testing an initially tentative definition against the sentiment of several exiles:

1. An exile is a person who is compelled to leave his homeland – though the forces that send him on his way may be political, economic, or purely psychological. It does not make an essential difference whether he is expelled by physical force or whether he makes the decision to leave without such immediate pressure.
2. The status of the exile, both material and psychological, is a dynamic one. It changes from exile to emigrant or emigrant to exile. These changes can be the result both of circumstances altering his homeland and of the assimilation process in his new country. An essential element in this process is the attitude of the exile to the circumstances prevailing in his homeland that are bound to influence him psychologically.
3. The contribution of the exile can be determined by his efforts at assimilation, his desire to become accepted and by the assets (spiritual and intellectual) he brings with him. That is, he might acquire skills and knowledge in the country of reception that enable him to make such a contribution, or he might cling to his original national and spiritual identity – which makes such a contribution more valuable and more acceptable.
4. The exile may leave with the full determination to return; this resolve is likely to

weaken and fade in direct proportion to the length of absence. It is exceptional that it survives more than one generation.

5. However eager for assimilation, the exile will always retain an often subconscious interest in and affection for his homeland. (He may be watching the Olympic Games and cheer with equal enthusiasm the representatives of his native country and those of his adopted country.)

6. The contribution of the exile to his new country is always likely to be greater than his influence still felt in the land of his birth. His successes abroad are likely to be envied and derided.

There are some variants of his categories, as Tabori readily admits. One can readily think of the following:

1. Essentially, African exiles have left owing to immediate pressure, or out of frustration in the practice of a profession. The frustration may be rooted in considerations of material welfare or spiritual self-fulfilment, or both.

2. The attitude of the exile to the 'circumstances prevailing in his homeland' that influence him psychologically varies from person to person – with the possible exception of exiles who leave as a group, bound together by an ideology. Even then, the longer the group stays outside, the greater the likelihood of separation as the members find avenues for their professional fulfilment separate from one another.

3. Where exiles come as refugees and are accommodated in camps according to their affiliation with exiled political parties, the longer they have been away the greater the likelihood of internal fighting, splinter factions and even, in extreme cases, killings. This happened to MPLA (Popular Movement for the Liberation of Angola), Frelimo (Liberation Front of Mozambique), Zapu and Zanu (Zimbabwe African People's Union and African National Union), and South Africa's PAC (Pan-Africanist Congress) and ANC (African National Congress).

4. In countries that provide camps, there may be professionals – teachers, lawyers, doctors, writers – who share a common nationality with the freedom fighters. These professionals are employed by the country of reception under conditions that make assimilation and an immigrant status impossible. Relations between the two groups of exiles are commonly uneasy. The intellectual most often resigns himself to his personal academic pursuits. Even in relation to the political leadership from his own country, he is gradually made to feel irrelevant because he is no longer (if he ever was) regarded as a freedom fighter.

5. By and large, because of the shortage of jobs in African countries and the propensity of these countries to take care of their own first, Europe – including Britain – and North America have become the main areas of political asylum.

6. There are exiles who return home even if the political situation they left behind may not have changed for the better. The reasons for this are mainly psychological.

7. I would venture to say that there are only a negligible number of African intellectuals who would assert, as so many European exiles do, that they left because of
their countries' backwardness and philistinism, the latter being a concern of artists.

8. Of a singular kind, one imagines, is the loneliness of the ruler or members of
the ruling class who had to flee the retribution that awaits them after a 'people's
revolution' – and for whose blood the masses cry out. They have to go into hiding
wherever they can find asylum. They are kept on sufferance, euphemistically
called 'humanitarian grounds', by the host government. This view, of course,
assumes that such people have a high degree of sensitivity and intellect. Even
when the host government sympathizes with their cause, owing to its own homegrown tyranny toward the masses, 'it can never be like home'. And power is sweet:
to lose it is to forfeit your whole purpose for living. Amin (Uganda) and Jean-Bédel
Bokassa (Central African Republic) are among this last category.

And the years roll by. Each day that dawns moves you in some direction; marking time
on one spot is out of the question for most. Move anyhow! You're not getting any
younger: a reality you cannot conceal from yourself.

The mechanics of living may very well be taken care of for the exile who contributes his skills to his host country. The exiles who live in camps, too, may want for
little in material welfare. They may all be provided for by the UN Commission for
Refugees, and travel freely on UN documents. But ultimately, it is the individual who
is left with the burden of exile as a condition of the mind. He has to face himself and
try to resolve this condition. This is especially so among intellectuals. There is a point
beyond which the camp leader – the leader of an organisation or the commander in
the barracks, where military training is conducted for refugees or freedom fighters –
can never reach the individual in his charge.

Beyond this is the exile's private world, a personality loaded with contradictions,
riddled with guilty feelings concerning the people who need his services back home.
You may perhaps be one in a cluster of exiles in the same city or district thrown
together by a common fear, common hopes. Two insecure persons cannot room
together with ease. So you feed on one another's miseries and insecurity. You attend
the same parties. Several of these parties are embassy or consulate functions. You
move in with a sense of belonging; you have an international status. You are being
noticed by the segment of the international community closest to you. Being there
makes you a 'legitimate' exile, and exile justifies your being there. Who of your political enemies back home would dare cross that threshold to be graciously received by
the ambassador and his wife, and still maintain his poise? Who would sail in and
assert a cosmopolitan presence? Who?

You are thrown together in a house and memory takes you all back home.
Anecdotes are reeled off. You seek out the daily newspapers and look for news about

home. You analyse it to a meaningless point. When, when, when will that glorious day come – the return?

'The government's running scared – there's a split in the ruling party. Hear me tell you boys, it's not long before we march back in.'

'Strong people scared – that's the kind that become even more brutal, sadistic.'

'They say my ma's very ill.'

'Hey, my sister just got married – I should've been there. Me and my sister were close.'

'The ancestors will be with you, you've been in touch with your ma all these years. Think of Kotsi. Remember he didn't know his ma was dead till six years after her burial.'

'Guess who's in the city, fellows?'

'Ya?'

'Chief.'

'What's so new about that? He's often here.'

'Don't be dumb – the rebels, of course! The gang of eight, man. That's why he's here.'

'Discipline. Some people don't know we've got to stick together in exile.'

'Either you're a nationalist or you're not – no revisionist mumbo-jumbo in that department. They've got to be disciplined.'

'Yes, but what if there's dictatorship in the movement? Why should we take that kind of manure from one another when we don't want the whites pissing on us?'

'You want to join the gang?'

'No, but I just can't stand this any longer!'

'Where would the movement be if we allowed every fat mouth from the rank and file to tell the leaders how to run it? Democracy's a luxury in a freedom movement in exile.'

'And don't you be talking subversion, my friend. You forget you're still under a cloud until you're cleared.'

'You think I care about being called an informer?'

'You damn well should care – I would.'

'Try me – hey, the world's big, man, call me an informer, persecute me for it. I'll move elsewhere. Would still be better than moulding and collecting cobwebs in our brains like we're doing here in a walkie-talkie organization.'

'You've no right to speak like that about the Front.'

'What'll you do – assassinate me? What a laugh. I'm not assassination material anyhow, there are real mean ones in other countries. The Front is bored because it hasn't got a strategy for the grand return – you know, with blazing guns. That's why we chew each other's arses off, even gun each down.'

'Shut up!'

The words keep coming: sad words, barbed words, venomous words. And the lonely ones keep coming back for more hurt. Suspicion, the guilt, borrowed bravery and stamina, the impotent anger, the vicarious exasperation touched off by events back home. You hear among your compatriots theories about the home situation that will prove later to be quite irrelevant – a home situation that is progressively receding into the hazier areas of memory. You live with that haunting sense of loss and lack of a cultural context that can be intimately felt. And all these negative thoughts and images rush into the vortex of your person, expand and bubble into a poisonous yeast that can be soul-mutilating.

And when the major freedom movements of Angola (MPLA), Mozambique and Zimbabwe shot their way back home, when Obote returned to Kampala – for better or worse – those left in exile looked on with a mixture of pride, hope, envy and immo-bilising exasperation. And again, some decided to abdicate, stand away for a while; tried to better their own educational standing. Several could be found teaching in schools and universities in various parts of the world. For, besides teaching, what other escape route or refuge could there be for exiles?

I always felt fortunate to have my wife and kids around me, so we had each other. Bringing them up in Africa – Nigeria, Kenya, Zambia – and then France was no prob-lem as our children were still small. They became teenagers in the United States. We were constantly competing with their peer groups in our efforts to instil the values we were nurtured in back home. Even then, we were constantly trying to modify our ideas about those values so as not to appear to the kids to be overly rigid in our style of discipline. Being back now for the last twenty three years, we have come to be woefully aware that we won only a small part of the battle for their soul, lost most of it. Now they are men; they can in any case exercise their own judgment regarding themselves and their own children. All four sons are still in the United States. More than even on home ground, the lesson that registered poignantly on us when in exile is that there are no absolutes in this process of rearing children. A cliché? Certainly, but one that pops up in different guises and renews itself from one generation to the next, one millennium to the next.

There are millions of families of all nationalities who have experienced the same gains and losses in bringing up their children in exile. There is a whole complex tangle in parent-child relationships that defies any simplistic, orthodox assumptions, any social formula. I have not yet met an exile who didn't feel cheated to some extent by history, by being forced to leave home. You struggle every step of the way to find a method of neutralising or slowing down and compensating for the ill effects of root-lessness in young ones. We grew older in exile even as we looked after our children, whose ages were not diminishing either. We always felt strong in our sense of ancestral roots and presence, so we were saved much of the agony for ourselves. For the children, pain, dismay and bewilderment alternated with the joyful days when sheer blood ties – the primordial sense of family and love – kept us going, surviving and recreating the values we felt were adequate.

Some of us have returned home after an absence of fifteen to twenty years. My own case history as an exile goes back to 6 September, 1957. I have come to know that exile for the writer, or the artist in general, has psychological complexities that only the individual can try to delineate for himself or herself – and for others who may care to listen. During a social upheaval, a writer often feels an inner compulsion to give a share of his time to a cause as a social animal rather than as an artist. It seems perfectly natural to make such a distinction when you are on your own home ground. But in exile you seem to have been thrown onto your own ego centre, so that to hurt the writer is to hurt the whole person. Put in another way, you seem to be living in a rented glasshouse. Vulnerable. You can see clearly only when the rain is gone or when there is no mist. You pray that the lease holds until – who knows? If even possible, full or partial involvement in practical concerns of your host country is not easy.

You and your family press upon one another. There is an extraordinary degree of interdependence among you all, until the children begin to socialize and move in and out of the family circle. For a while you let go, and even if you don't like their peer group – who are acting out another culture or subculture – you feel the relief is worth it. You hope that you can manage the peer influence. In reality, you never fully grasp its influence sufficiently to be able to control or forestall it. It is pressure that eventually seems to live its own life, disembodied, harshly or subtly menacing for family relations. Before you know it, both your children and their peers have grown up and gone on to other enterprises or are trapped in the teenage daze.

As a writer, you seem more than ever before to be watching closely the rise and fall of the dial – whatever it is – that you use for measuring the intensity and pressure of experience. You are overly conscious. You are too aware of your mental growth, as if you were contemplating a personality moving in front of your eyes. As if it wouldn't surprise you to have to monitor your own funeral. You seem to be curled up and listening to the juices flow inside you, to every beat of your heart, every pulse in your veins. You think you can even detect the malfunctioning of some part of you that is going to burst into pain. You seem incapable of responding to real life experience with the ordinary instruments endowed on every person, because something compels you to judge an experience as if it demanded a literary interpretation – one that has to be sifted through your artist's sensibility and replayed in a verbal medium.

While I absorbed the African environment outside South Africa and felt at home in cultures that were so similar in essentials to my own, I consciously and unconsciously resisted assimilation into the local setting throughout my nine years in the United States. I was scared of the commitment that would hold me and make return to South Africa more and more difficult. Neither my wife nor I had any such fear as exiles in Africa. I was again thinking of the implications such commitment would have for my writing. One step further into the American setting, I feared, would throw me out of the definition of exile. Unless I could sustain an arbitrary definition to assert a non-emigré status, I would be living at least half a lie.

Much has also to do with the circumstances of one's leaving a home country. I did so because I was banned from teaching, having campaigned against the inferior education the authorities were imposing on black Africans. I would have continued to teach even in a system I loathed, because I was sure that that very act would give me a purpose – that thing for which one lives when one wants to create beauty out of chaos and make sense of it. Let the imponderables fall where they might – like the events of 1976, in which schoolchildren revolted against the same inferior system of education – I would be guided by my instinct as a teacher in what to do.

I left on a South African passport, which I abandoned two years after my exit, because it was endorsed only for my initial destination – Nigeria. We registered as subjects of the United Kingdom and Colonies (Nigeria being a colony then), which facilitated travel for me and my family to any place in the world that was accessible. But my wife and I knew we would one day want to return. We lived nine years in West, East and Central Africa, two years in France and nine years in the United States. For the last five, my wife and I kept feeling that we were irrelevant outside Africa. To whom was I teaching the literatures of Africa, its diaspora and the West? Should I not be where black literatures are organized and taught as a functional and organic part of African development; located, therefore, where there is a living cultural forum for them – on their own native soil? Shouldn't I be spending the rest of my life contributing to this development of the African consciousness, in whichever constituency is accessible?

I had come into an American tradition that had started long ago, and could not grasp the American's cultural goals. I saw them as too fragmented for me to feel part of a unified purpose beyond physical survival and mastery of technical skills. I have always wanted to teach in a community whose cultural goals and aspirations I could comprehend, because education is for me an agent of culture, even while it is culture itself. And culture for me is, as the word suggests, a way of growing up, of increasing oneself, a community's way of realising itself. I could only identify intellectually and emotionally with the black American's condition, but could not in any tangible, particular way feel his history. To be actively and meaningfully involved in a people's concerns and political struggle as a genuine participant, you should feel its history. On the contrary, I kept feeling that that river was passing me by; its complexity defied the oversimplification contained in the assertion, *I am black* or phrases such as *the melting pot* – as some Americans say wistfully. And one thing we should not tolerate as a people is intellectual dishonesty, faked involvement that has only repeated slogans to subsist on.

I would be fifty-eight come December of 1977, while Rebecca had turned fifty-seven the previous August. Twenty years older than when I left in September 1957. Steve Biko, initiator and leader of the Black Consciousness Movement, had just died from a savage assault by prison officials. A frozen, brooding, searing silence reigned in the country. I felt my accumulated knowledge and experience had a good chance of entering the realm of wisdom. I felt much less impetuous in my judgment of events;

by the same token I felt more circumspect. My intellect had been enriched and refined by the African and African American experience, not to mention my own teaching projects. There were still charred vehicles and brick structures in Soweto to show partly what 16 June, 1976 had developed into. But, of course, we came to learn of the mayhem the State police had released upon the children, driving several of them into exile, where we had just been. We learned of the secret mass burials of corpses by the police.

I had come back in September 1976 for a preliminary visit, the first after nineteen years as we had been forbidden earlier to re-enter. We returned to find most things had changed for the worse. The black townships had grown immense – Soweto for instance. The problem of re-entry began when we were told that we had lost our urban residential 'rights'. First, I was unanimously appointed to the Chair and professorship of English at the University of the North, still a 'Bantu' institution. But the then Rector, with the authority of the then Minister of Bantu Education – a certain Cruywagen – vetoed the decision. The officials in Bantu Administration gave us the run-around, with all the arrogance of a system raging mad, hell-bent on controlling the 'Bantu'; fencing us in, so to speak, with hounds one could imagine to have fangs of steel. When the University of the Witwatersrand employed us in 1979, lawyers discovered that professionals were excluded from that section of the Urban Act. It took five years, from 1977, for us to have our citizenship restored.

When we were in the United States we got to learn that an academic can, if he likes, lose himself in intellectual pursuits – move only in the university community and be insulated from the rest of the larger humanity out there: safe, cosy, contented. I didn't want that to happen to me, so my self-respect hung on the frail thread of long distance commitment. I also realised that the longer we were away from South Africa, the angrier, the more outraged I felt against the plight of the black Africans – out of sheer impotence. In a sense, my homecoming was another way of dealing with impotent anger. It was also a way of extricating myself from twenty years of the compromise that exile itself is. Indeed, exile had become for me a 'ghetto of the mind'. At fifty-eight, we were happy to feel still capable of working – for a living and in projects for community development.

We left our sons, then grown men; and a daughter, at twenty-seven, the second in line – who, to our unspeakable grief, was to die fifteen years later, still in the United States. They would, in their own good time, decide what to do, in a country that offered many more opportunities than South Africa. Also, the change in education and lifestyle would be more than they could negotiate, having sucked on the roots of other cultures. This, we realise with a terrible pang of regret, is for us the final compromise. Their loss of the benefits of an African sense of being is something they cannot feel, as it is unknown to them. But, considering Africa's current social, economic and political disempowerment, one can still buy some time for adjusting decisions towards some point of equilibrium.

The question that will always haunt us is whether our exile actually reaped for us gains that our offspring can also enjoy. But then we tell ourselves that in any case they would have to make their own decisions. What Soyinka calls the 'tyranny of blood', and what I in other respects call the tyranny of place, are truths that resist debate, full stop! There is this about exile: there is an age below which it yields tremendous benefits to the individual ego, and there is an age beyond which the local setting can make impossible demands on one's commitment. But always we are humbly aware that we know volumes more about ourselves – the limits of what we can achieve and what is within our capacity.

My wife and I often observed the lifestyle of elderly people in the United States. They seemed so insecure, so vulnerable; more so than we had witnessed in Africa. Movies often showed elderly folk cooped up – whether single or as couples – in apartment buildings, living in fear. We began to fear that as we grew older, we too would be trapped in this kind of life until we would have lost the will to leave. We would have to sell our house and move into an apartment. We might not find a place that could accommodate my library, which had grown over the years in exile. Would the social security and university pension incomes maintain us? Our children were already champing at the bit, raring to be gone at the age of eighteen. The US still seemed to us the best country for them to take their chances in, to find jobs. There are 'opportunity schools' where adults and younger citizens go, for free or a nominal fee, for self-improvement – the opposite of South Africa with its rigid paper and curricular requirements. For us, the best thing would be to move back home, we decided. The children had tacitly declared their 'independence', American style.

The epilogue to this has been our sad revelation, on our return, concerning elderly folk in South Africa. Their welfare is pathetic. In addition, the young prey on them, often appropriating their lean pension money, or else silently blackmailing them into supporting them as grandchildren or sons and daughters who are jobless. Old-age homes, which did not exist among blacks before we left – because of extended family care – are becoming a common feature. Township/shanty-town life is constantly threatening for the elderly: rape; burglaries; violent assaults often leading to murder; appropriation of pension money by the bully of the household, wrenched from the old people to the accompaniment of threats of death. Rural life is no freer from these traumatic changes.

Another aspect of our homecoming is that it concludes for me a cycle in the life of a writer. Like all the other writers in South Africa, I felt the pressures of censorship acutely. The real sense of community that I feel now helps me understand the nature of my audience better, which must help define the functions of literature at the grassroots level. In more ways than one I can deal with something tangible, something real, rather than the shadows and echoes that haunted me in exile – the recurrent dream about people coming after me because they believed I had something of value, which I knew I didn't possess.

African Humanism and the Corporate World – 1994

Synopsis by Sam Raditlhalo

After the enigma of the 27 April 1994 elections, African Humanism – Botho, Ubuntu, Vumunhu, Vhuthu – was the buzzword in business circles, and it was appropriated by everyone in blatant 're-positioning' manoeuvres. In July of that year, Mphahlele entered the discussion on this vital part of the South African social fabric in a way that is unmistakably Mphahlelesque. A position paper by Reuel Khoza – 'African Humanism: A Discussion Paper' – is the impetus for this article by Mphahlele. It is striking that what Khoza writes is so closely tied in to Mphahlele's concept of African Humanism. Key aspects of the talk resonate with South African corporate culture, and what the managers of companies and corporations can do to avoid the pitfalls of Eurocentric approaches to management. The African's organic view of the universe cannot sustain itself in this world of cut-throat economics and politics. While Africans tend to create a world made up of people, the corporatist worldview surely does violence to such a perspective; this is what Khoza's paper sought to obviate. Mphahlele teases out the practical implications of the discussion paper while clarifying exactly what African Humanism is. He discusses African Humanism as two levels of behaviour in a human context – as a state of mind and as a purposeful act of knowing. African Humanism seems to have been abandoned without any effort to learn from it and adapt it to today's changing business world, despite Mphahlele's efforts. 'Reckless Individualism' in a globalising environment cannot be reconciled with what Mphahlele believes is at the heart of our humanity.

I

African Humanism – *Ubuntu, Botho, Vumunhu, Vhuthu* – is a belief that:

1. Human life, of which the person and personalised social units to which he/she belongs are the sole, sacred receptacles, is central to the universe.
2. The violation of this life by any means is an outrage to the ancestors, to the natural order, and the Supreme Being; to the life force, or – as the Belgian cleric-

philosopher Placide Tempels translates it – the 'vital force'. African Humanism is based on religious thought and belief in this force. To account for a number of rituals and other practices, Africans say that their purpose is to acquire life, strength, or vital force; to live strongly. We pray that the force shall continue to drive our lives into posterity.

3. 'Force' should be taken to refer to being. To *be* underscores the value of life.

4. There are other realities beyond the phenomena we perceive through our physical senses, an essence which only intuition and inspiration can interpret to us – either directly or through the agency of 'those who know' ('bo-reatseba' in Sesotho – we who know). This phrase refers to the traditional healer, diviner, elder-sage, the myth-making poet. 'Know' here is more than a cognitive act.

5. This accounts for the African's organic world view (holism) that does not break life down into the physical, the psychic and the spiritual-moral. The Supreme Being is present in all things, living and physically inanimate, creating an integrated whole; all the components of the universe are interrelated.

6. The ancestors are spirits of our relations and, in the national or community sense, leaders who once walked this earth and knew the pain and joy of living. They are our intercessors for access to the Supreme Being. Death is but a passage from this world into the happy land of the ancestors. We are traditionally optimistic/idealistic about our after-death condition – as against the Christian idea of heaven and hell, sin and damnation, salvation and alienation.

7. African Humanism also rests on the social manifestation of the organic view: the value we place on social relationships and the sacredness of life for life's sake, rather than as a running battle between body and spirit, at the end of which the latter hopes for rewards in the after-life.

8. To do another human being wrong or, in the extreme case, to kill or maim or cripple him/her is to do violence to the best in you. Society requires or hopes for restitution of some kind for such an act.

9. The African loves to create a world of people, rather than, as is the trend in Western society, live a secluded life, feeling alienation and a compulsion for external sources of joy.

10. We tend to look at life as a cyclical process by which the flux of time causes events we experience and sweeps them in their pre-ordained direction. They then come round again, but in another guise; they are never the same twice.

11. The traditional desire is *to be* rather than to conquer other souls, as Christian proselytization has endeavoured to do for centuries, in an even more intensive and sustained manner than Islam. This desire stems from the humanistic respect for other people's beliefs. It also underscores the fact of African Humanism being the life we create, the religious experience that we cherish, rather than mechanical temple-going faith.

12. In such a social order, individualism becomes an alien condition. It has brought into our midst a whole baggage of drives, compulsions, urges, neuroses and ambitions for things that are not enduring. It merely fulfils our acquisitive instincts.

Reuel Khoza (*African Humanism – A Discussion Paper*) writes:

> *Man's nature, his wants, and his capacities are to a great extent the product of society and its institutions. His most effective behaviour is usually through groups and organizations... These units by turns often promote and frustrate individualistic ideals.*

He further states that in the context of *Ubuntu* 'man' can only be identified in relation to other human beings. The common saying is: 'I am because you are, you are because we are'.

II

Here I discuss strategies towards a possible realization of humanistic relationships and leadership in politics, economics and business.

Let us, for the sake of convenience, consider African Humanism on two planes: (a) as a state of mind, a consciousness, a way of perceiving; and (b) as a social order, a possible option for a way of life based on (a), and a purposeful act of knowing and of behaving in a human context. These are really two aspects of an indivisible concept of thought and belief.

We have to accept that no fast-food formula is possible in a country just emerging from a nightmare of cultural-racial fragmentation. Aspect (a) requires information, education (formal and informal), lectures and study-discussion groups, seminars, etc. Difficulty may arise where, as is so common among academics, we lack leadership that can steer such an information programme with the knowledge of African culture and history from pre-colonial times through to the present. What may also aggravate things is the scepticism even in knowledgeable academic circles concerning these themes and the validity and relevance of African Humanism. But the difficulties are not absolute nor insurmountable.

A person with knowledge can be asked to organize and administer the programme, slotting in the believers wherever we need to integrate the areas of knowledge into a pointed inquiry into the role of African Humanism, given the information groups have.

Africans in this country, especially urbanized Africans, are confused about matters of culture. They are often unwilling to participate in such discussions, lest they lower their self-esteem as sworn enemies of tribal cultures of Verwoerd's invention. Against this, the advantage is that there is a collective memory, or collective unconscious, among blacks. Without being able to articulate the concept, the working class can, at the cognitive level, tune into African Humanism.

Black Consciousness, before it became institutionalized into a political camp, helped students, artists, writers and social activists to appreciate at least the dynamics of African Humanism. Black Consciousness endures, albeit in a truncated or dislocated form. Although all constituencies – economic (including trade unions), social, political, business, educative, etc. – need this programme, I would urge immediate action in the business world.

Another reason for a programme is that we should open a forum where 'African Humanism in the business world' can be debated. From time to time, workshops can be held or 'occasional' papers published. Summaries can be produced in the vernacular languages. I would insist, in accordance with what I have learned over more than twenty years of adult education at the literate level, that the papers be in simple English. Technical concepts must all be simplified, if they have to appear. Close intimate groups and sessions are in the long run more effective than mass get-togethers, where scholars and political ideologues usually strike a pose for the gallery.

The following are some suggested topics for debate:

Leadership, Hospitality, Campaign for Service Quality

This is an area that can be discussed among existing groups, such as NAFCOC (National African Chamber of Commerce), BMF (Black Management Forum), Chambers of Commerce and Industry, etc. Again, this requires papers and other forms of information on African Humanism and leadership in business and commerce. This is to offer the basics about the topic in order to make access possible to the theme of African life and thought. Once more, I cannot see us discussing meaningfully as long as people at large are in the dark. Fortunately, there is abundant published information on the topic, much of which can be simplified. In addition, at every turn when existing formations meet, not in large theatrical gatherings but in intimate groupings, it should be possible to leave an additional slot for our theme.

Generally, we associate African Humanism – as this essay demonstrates – with a pre-technological time (in the Western sense) of myth and human warmth. In other words, with pastoral life. All the more reason that we should meet in groups and discuss ways in which we can apply the wisdom of a past but surviving age to the present.

We would need to negotiate the tricky bend of expressing the poetic image of common human decency to the corporate world. That Reuel Khoza has accomplished part of this deserves commendation.

When I get into a shop in our town – entirely African – and observe rudeness from a young assistant on the other side of the counter, against myself or someone else, I immediately deliver a loud rebuke: 'What has happened to the manners you have been brought up with?' If the other person is an adult, I say: 'What has happened to us that we should have lost our hospitality?' Notice the switch to the plural 'us', 'we', 'our'. But I wouldn't think of saying this to an adult in a white store in Pietersburg, because I assume I would be speaking on a different wavelength. Perhaps we may then resort to an information campaign to push the idea of hospitality and good manners.

I am now thinking that Khoza's idea of a community concept of business is the best, because it purports to create a different human environment for greater possibilities. The implication is that the old environment is intractable, and so he injects human warmth into an otherwise cold, rigid operation and relationship.

Reuel Khoza

1. 'Corporate culture.... in South Africa today is very Eurocentric.' He cites as an example the decision-making process that is informed by power relations rather than consensus. Negotiations are all too often determined by us-and-them perceptions.
2. He would urge that a 'conducive environment' be created on the ground in order to promote optimal functioning of strategy, organizational structure, systems, financial controls, etc.
3. (i) An overall concept of business in South Africa, he points out, is required to 'take account of the traditions and culture of the African participants in commerce and industry.'

   (ii) The community concept entails perceiving 'the business organization as a community to which the individual' belongs. A member by choice, rather than one with a fixed legal contract.' Required for such a community: 'close interpersonal relationships and group interactions held together by a feeling [awkwardly expressed, here] of security and harmony' among all members. Faithful membership of the community.

   (iii) The community concept in business is based essentially on humanistic and humane principles, but it must also prevail in the whole outlook on methods and practices. Rules and regulations are necessary but only to facilitate interpersonal relations.

   (iv) Approachable management is important.

   (v) Free flow of information in the business community is desirable.

Implications of the Community Concept of Management

1. Managerial reality is socially and culturally determined. The community concept provides 'a sound basis for team learning' to counter the Eurocentric habit of mind

that is hung up on the demand of individual excellence. This spawns 'reckless individualism' in South African corporations.

2. A community concept of management can help develop 'a greater sense of oneness' in the corporation. This will counter the older view that sees only an 'adversarial relationship between managers and the managed' in preference to consensus.

3. 'Social responsibility programmes should be more natural' in business management, within the idea of an establishment that is like a community. The spirit of communalism is thus consolidated.

Khoza concludes with the following:

> An eclectic culture is needed that recognizes that Europe and other countries will continue to contribute to the expertise that exists in business and economic developments. At the same time we must accept that a lot can be learned significantly in the process evolving South African strategies for dealing with the world of work.

Elsewhere Khoza emphasizes the fact of synthesis. He gives a gentle nudge to remind us of the difficulties that characterize South Africa's political economy – its multiracial, multi-cultural, ethnic constitution, with ancient conflicts, prejudices and clashing ideologies. The concept of community in business has these to confront. All the greater must be the distance between many of the corporations and that ideal of an industrial harmony capable of high productivity. It's a daunting challenge.

A Personal View:

There is a lot of talking and didactic lecturing in this country across racial lines. Somewhere focus becomes diffused. Furthermore, we talk mostly when we are negotiating terms and are preoccupied with the them-and-us relationship, with scoring debating points. We need to talk frankly, aiming to:

1. arrive at an understanding of the problems faced by African Humanism;
2. appreciate clearly what happened to all the races in this country as a result of the deprivation and dispossession of the majority population;
3. consider and estimate the profit and loss in the black-white encounter;
4. initiate a forum of ideas where a conscious programme can be arrived at of education, information, workshops, seminars, etc., so that we learn to listen to one another rather than to the buzzwords, banner words and so on that whip all around us;
5. publish and disseminate the ideas in various forms and languages;

6. focus on the worlds of business, commerce and work for an introduction of the above new concepts;
7. recover from the violence African Humanism has suffered; often we ourselves being the agents of the resulting confusion of human values.

Images from the oral tradition

A Song

The dog is great among dogs,
Yet he serves man.
The woman is great among women,
Yet she waits upon her children.

The hunter is great among hunters,
Yet he serves the village.
Singer and dancer are great among entertainers,
Yet they sing and dance for king and servants.

The soldier is great among soldiers,
Yet he serves the nation.
The ruler is great among rulers,
Yet he serves his people.

Idiomatic sayings

It is for wisdom that people travel together.
Two crocodiles, having a common stomach, nevertheless fight over the food. [If people cannot work in harmony when they have common interests, chaos results.]
The strength of the crocodile is the water. [His real helpers are his own kin.]
Go round this way, there is no hunting; go round that way, there is no game. [When men go hunting, they have to agree to go one way together, otherwise they won't catch anything.]
When you move, do not destroy your abode; you may go back to it one day. The only place where one does not return is the mother's womb. Likewise, do not pollute the well after drinking.
When you are visiting, ask for the hoe and make your way to the field.
Yours is only what you have eaten. [You can only be sure of the food you have eaten: you have no absolute possession of anything else. Said of one who was wealthy yesterday and today has been reduced to poverty.]

The heart of a human being is a sea. [It is never fully contented: like the sea where all the rivers empty themselves without ever filling it.]

Collective labour

This is associated with the custom of sharing. When a man was an invalid, the villagers went to work his field. We get together to thatch a family's roof. The communal spirit – sense of community, the compulsion to gravitate towards people – is the attribute that has proved to be the most resilient. With the disruption of family and community life by migrant labour, landlessness and other economic forces, we observe survivals of the communal soul in various new forms of social structures. Obviously these formations exist as support systems: stokvels, burial societies, sports clubs, the church, associations that create their own rituals, etc. The exercise of compassion is an organic part of the community spirit.

Notes towards an Introduction to African Humanism: A Personal Inquiry – 1992

Synopsis by Peter Thuynsma

One of the most appealing traits in Mphahlele's scholarship is how often one's readings of his critical writings intersect with his penchant for utilizing his own life experiences in his work. It is often a pervasive feature, not merely as a backdrop but as an authentic illustration and a vehicle to convey a lesson. When present, Mphahlele the person is palpable – as is the gravitas of Mphahlele the teacher.

These 'Notes' blend the man and the teacher through a rather unique approach, and as we wade into the discussion we must remember that this is in essence a discussion on the development of a peoples' social and political structures and moral being. Despite such a weighty subject, Mphahlele approaches it in the manner of a fireside chat, utterly confident in his subject and its value; as he says, most invitingly:

'Let me sweep out some fallen leaves and twigs in my yard before I let you in for chit-chat about African humanism.'

Here Mphahlele sketches the contours of his thinking on humanism, and has the scholarly temerity to present a cutting dichotomy at the onset: 'I believe, am prepared to doubt and still I will believe'; while he premises his conversation on the poignant truth that human life as the center of the scheme of things brings with it not only the native intellect but its spiritual or religious essence.

The essay then deftly winds its way through the conjectures on the origins of African Humanism and tests these against the two best-advertised religions, Islam and Christianity. But the path also sweeps the reader through the contending views on Negritude and enumerates five key values, viz. the belief in a Supreme Being; family and social relationships; moral conduct; the deep desire for peace; and the art of healing.

The conversation then harnesses literature to personalize, as it were, these principles at work in a human – albeit a fictional – social landscape; examples are drawn from Achebe and Awonoor's work. Then, in an intricate yet lucid approach, Mphahlele entertains the critical thought of Donatus Nwoga's essay entitled: The Chi, Individualism and Igbo Religion. Mphahlele concludes this discussion following a veritable path through the salient features of African Humanism with this question:

'Are we taking charge of the synthesis between the best and enduring values from both sides of the cultural encounter, or are we merely drifting and leaving it to fate?'

And, with a burst of optimism:

'I am sure we can count on universities and other institutions of the world interested in Africa to serve as facilitating centres.'

An inquiry into African Humanism is, in my case, a search for my own soul. We are all aware of how Westernised we have become; establishing our African identity has become an imperative – even if we have to create a myth. A myth gives its native community a sense of spiritual unity. A myth is an act of faith: it confers a 'sociological status', as Malinowski would put it, 'which demands precedent'. It validates or sanctions a moral code.

Furthermore, myth promotes harmony between humans and nature in a triumphant, inviolable, pantheistic union that negates death. We are impoverished if we remain forever untouched by the compelling poetry intrinsic to myth, to allegory, to symbolism. Nor does it matter that we are not all black Africans – as there are also North African Arabs. The fact that we are that part of Africa, especially south of the Sahara, that displays features suggesting a unity of its cultures confers upon us the right to claim an identity that distinguishes us and the African diaspora from other cultural clusters.

And so I'm setting out my thoughts armed with abundant faith and some native intelligence – both monitored by the artist in me, self-tutored in the empirical approach to reality. In other words: I believe, am prepared to doubt and still I will believe.

We might trace Western humanism to ancient Greece and Rome. But it had to find a revival in the Renaissance, which translated it into the fine arts, literature, music, ideas, scientific advancement, exploration and legal systems. At some point in its development, dissociation occurred between the Renaissance intelligence and the moral content of humanity. Especially in the world of science, exploration and commerce. This intelligence, often going under the name of 'reason', seemed unstoppable. It spawned invasions and conquest of territory. It made it possible for explorers such as Christopher Columbus to savage the natives of the Caribbean and elsewhere, and for the slave trade to flourish. More recently, it resulted in two world wars and Hitler's perversions, followed shortly by the bomb that destroyed Hiroshima and Nagasaki. The humanism of Europe became an intensely intellectual adventure.

Those who came to institutionalise themselves as humanists distrusted religion and belief in the supernatural. True enough, Christianity and Islam could claim some form of humanism – the latter even more than the former, several of whose white constituencies have remained racially exclusive – even racist – to this day. Islam has always been all-inclusive. On the contrary, we cannot separate African humanism from African thought and belief, including religion. The black African, about whom I shall be talking in particular, cherishes a world view that perceives an organic universe: a dichotomy between the realms of the intellect and spiritual experience would be untenable, even inconceivable. Human life as the centre of the scheme of things brings with it not only the native intellect but also its spiritual or religious essence.

Senegalese Cheikh Anta Diop's notion of the Egyptian origins of African civilization is most persuasive. He argues that after the Sahara had dried up, by 7000 BC – and the virtual liquidation of the Nile cultures by Egypt's successive conquerors – the Negroes had to adapt to a new life in the hinterland. This was not as demanding as the Nile environment. In the latter, agricultural occupations had made imperative the development of mathematics and other sciences; for irrigation schemes as well as for the architecture that produced the pyramids. Here in the hinterland it was, Diop tells us, that the Africans settled down to develop their social and political structures and moral being, in the absence of a material civilization. They were isolated, because of the closure of the Mediterranean routes during Egypt's occupation, which had brought to an end a ten-thousand-year civilization; and there was an absence of the busy material culture the Nile valley had shaped. These major factors reinforced the will to develop a profound sense of being.

Let me sweep out some fallen leaves and twigs in my yard before I let you in for chit-chat about African Humanism. I ask you not to be bored with this personal anecdote. It has a lot to do with the long-standing but unorganised debate whether African Humanism exists or not. Rolled around it are questions about culture. So many of us are in a hurry to make a success in a world dominated by western civilization that we have hardly any time to take stock of where we come from, and whether we have chosen the right direction to move in. A discussion of African Humanism is a question of culture, of anthropology, by which I mean simply what we do, how and why.

In 1963 I organized a conference of writers and academics under the auspices of the International Congress for Cultural Freedom in Paris, to discuss the need for African Literature to be part of the university curriculum in Africa south of the Sahara.

We then came under heavy attack by an African American brother in terms that made Anglophone Africans appear reactionary for being enemies of the Negritude movement. Our brother's belligerent tone got my back up, as I was personally singled out. He had bluntly advocated that for the French-language side of the curriculum, universities should select works that had been inspired by and conveyed the message of Negritude clearly. I had countered by saying that there was good writing in French that carried no such message, or in which it was only peripheral. Especially fiction that, by its very nature, defied categories. It couldn't sustain a programmed stance or fighting talk and still pretend to be fiction; not the way talkative verse can attain a momentary poise of credibility when spoken in a captivating voice. Then came the attack from our brother.

The next day I returned to the conference with a statement that said, among other things:

> What would be the point of moaning about 'our traditional culture', much of which has been knocked about as a result of military conquest, economic and industrial activity, the migrant labour system which destroys communal and family life, the removal of whole communities from place to place by government decree, the conscious efforts of old-fashioned missionaries, etc.? To fight a rearguard action by trying to revive pure traditional culture (among large populations in urban townships, on white people's farms, in impoverished rural areas) as an effort to break down the present structures, would be unrealistic.

The sociological information about South Africa in this passage is true. Some ten years later I realized that I was in fact attacking the romanticism of Negritude as an artistic canon. Senghor made it appear that, because you were Negro, this was the way to express reality. Negritude was more style than theme, he had said. My view was a negation of a Negritude programme, and still is. And I know that of all the Negritude poets of his time, Léopold Sédar Senghor was the greatest exponent of cultural synthesis – something he actually displayed in the fusion of style and content in his poetry. His poetry spoke greater truth than his activist prose. By the end of that decade, when I had digested my West African experiences, I had become wiser. As I was later to say in *Afrika My Music*, Nigeria restored Africa to me. Negritude had then become acceptable to me as a social concept, minus the romanticism, which also includes the image of Africa as an innocent continent – the antithesis of the violent Western world. It became acceptable to me as an Africanist consciousness.

Let me enumerate the prominent features of African Humanism:

1. *We believe in the Supreme Being.* But because we are closest to our ancestors, we have reverence for them. They are our intercessors. They know the pain and joy of living, so they are our main point of reference in our relation to the immediate world around us. The Supreme Being is a poetic conception whose presence we take for granted, but which exists as an all-pervading vital force in the mountains, rivers, valleys, and the plant and animal kingdoms. African oral poetry is also witness to these forces, to this interconnectedness of human, animal, plant, inanimate environments and the cosmos. At the centre is human life, which merges with its environment even while deriving nourishment from it. Ancestors are an extension of our earthly life, so death is nothing to be feared. Every family

has its own ancestors, but there are also communal ancestors who live in the unconscious memory. We join the happy realm of our immediate ancestors when we die. If we die in old age we ourselves become ancestors. We love life for its own sake and death is but a passage from one form of life to another. This sacred bond between our ancestors and us can be ritualised: e.g. we bury the woman's after-birth in the yard so that the wheel of regeneration is kept spinning. When we slaughter a beast, whether we come to the ancestors as communicants or as supplicants, blood, fire and water become time after time the medium for our interconnectedness as humans. At the primary level we are responsible for our relationships. At the level at which we feel powerless because a violent rupture is threatening in our relationships or has occurred, we call others in the extended and immediate family so that we talk and try to mend things, or prevent the flood bursting into the home, as we say.

2. *Family and social relationships.* This is one of the strongest pillars on which human-ism rests: *I am because you are; we are because you are.* The complex pattern of social relationships, which has endured for centuries and keeps surfacing in different forms after being truncated by the money economy, migrant labour, loss of land, and the creation of white urban areas – these relationships are another pillar of African humanism. Whatever happens, human life must survive as a collective or communal force.

3. *Moral conduct.* For the human being to survive this world, and upon death rejoin his ancestors, he endeavours to maintain harmony with all the forces that he per-ceives – physically, emotionally and intellectually. Which means that one has per-petually to attempt to maintain a natural order in which there is a balance with a variety of forces – placating some and beseeching others – but ideally seeking to survive triumphantly. A sense of wrongdoing can be atoned for by speaking to the person wronged through an intermediary. One doesn't take the easy way of seek-ing absolution from the Supreme Being through the ancestors first, saying: 'The Great Benevolent Being has forgiven me, therefore you also must.' Wrongdoing is not conceived, as it is in the West, in theological terms, as the abstraction called *sin.* Your character is determined or shaped by being morally upright and being at peace with the ancestors and other humans. Purification rites are essential in the moulding of character. To fortify ourselves against evil forces that threaten to lead us astray, or bring epidemics and other disasters, specific purifications rites must be conducted by custodians of these inner mysteries of our culture. Always the human self in the midst of others. We are traditionally great talkers, find comfort in talking to other people, and also want others to know that they can unburden themselves by talking to us.

4. Hunger for immortality and the desire to be at peace with the divine forces and fellow-humans make *religion* imperative. Religion should be a spiritual experience

in which we search for the Highest Reality beyond our physical being. Our oral poetry is our way of communicating with the divine forces, for poetry is a way of perceiving, a way of seeking to touch the Highest Reality beneath the surface of things. Rabindranath Tagore, Bengali poet and humanist, tells us that infinitude, which I equate with the Highest Reality without bypassing basic reality, should not be thought of as a straight line stretching out into the mists of some limitless unknowable realm. Rather it is a series of revolving moments in which we keep reconnecting with other people – without beginning, without end. No single moment is ever the same twice, but the general pattern goes on revolving. This is how African Humanism, at its most sublime, is meant to perpetuate itself from generation to generation, with the full knowledge that replicas are merely accidents.

5. *The art of healing*. An extension of that connection between the human being and nature as a vital force is revealed in the approach of the traditional doctor to his or her patient. He first enquires of the patient if he and his family members get along. Any bitter quarrels? He wants to establish if the illness may have something to do with the psychological health of the patient, without engaging in any elaborate rationalizations. He knows that it is futile trying to heal the body if the spirit is troubled. The medicine he dispenses is organic: an animal or vegetable product. He invokes the presence of his ancestors and that of the patient to strengthen the healing medium. The power of the spoken word is right there in the healing process, in the poetic incantation. The doctor keeps in very close contact with the patient so that the process is not impersonal. Human life is at the centre of his concern.

6. There is at work here also what the African American thinker Leonard Barrett calls *Soul Force*, in relation to the blacks across the Atlantic. His point is that African Americans survived two hundred years of slavery through the power derived from the Soul Force – an African heritage. This implies that whatever the African may endure as victim of slavery or colonialism or white racism, it was but a moment in the interminable revolutions of human relationships – the fact of infinitude. This amounts to total reliance on individual and collective resilience.

African Humanism is not a proselytising way of life. It has never sought to colonize anybody, a trait that has been common in the two most advertised religions – Christianity and Islam. The weakest link in our humanism is its almost inexhaustible endurance in the face of conquest, colonization and exploitation. But its strengths can best be revealed when we define and redefine it, not with reference to the other religions but in its own right.

African literature and its visual and performing arts sum up everything we could say about the traditional humanism of the continent, and its fortunes and misfortunes in its encounter with the new economics, politics, modes of social reordering and theologies.

Chinua Achebe's *Things Fall Apart* is a dramatization of one such encounter. Okonkwo may be said to have failed in coming to terms with missionary Christianity, thus becoming the agent of his own downfall. But we should also see him as a casualty of colonialism, the church being the only medium through which it could speak to the African's heart. It found a humanism, the essence of which was the art of being. A humanism that was not equipped to resist the physical and spiritual violence of the colonial incursion with a new religion as its vanguard. I feel compelled to interpret the *chi* principle as a pillar of Igbo humanism, which has equivalents and parallels in several other parts of Africa. The *chi* tells me that as long as there is a balance of power between me and itself, life is wholesome. It is like the Hindu *dharma*, which is no more nor less than one's character, and is equal to one's personality. It is also akin to the Buddhist idea of the wholeness of every individual's being, and the human search for one's own true nature. Fighting for one's own god would largely have been unthinkable. Which is what an old man remarks when Okonkwo cuts down the British administrator's messenger, sent to disperse a protest rally. For Okonkwo the meeting was to precipitate a war to defend the Ibo deity against the Christian missionaries. Kofi Awoonor, the Ghanaian poet, has this to say about the *chi* and, by extension, the battle between Okonkwo and his own *chi*.

> *The emphasis is on the individualism of man as expressed by his chi. Chi assumes a ubiquity in the daily life and life cycle of man. The proverb: 'Where one falls, there his chi pushes him' illustrates this overwhelming bond between man and his chi. This stresses further the point of chi's capacity to turn against its owner. Donatus Nwoga, writing on the same subject, suggests that the personal chi is only a refraction of the universal force, a personification of its allotted role in the universal motion toward the ultimate. Each person has a good or bad chi, according to whether that person's role enhances or diminishes his position in the scale of values, which are consonant with his society's ultimate goal. (Awonoor 1975)*

Awoonor further quotes from Donatus Nwoga's essay, *The Chi, Individualism and Igbo Religion*: A person exerted himself to achieve the promise of his good *chi*. If he did all in his power and yet made no progress, he could take consolation in being resigned to his own *chi*. And there is no contractual relationship between a person and his *chi*.

Kofi Awoonor, himself a lyricist par excellence and one of the greatest in the English language, while deriving the best lyrical qualities from his native Ewe, writes poetry that expresses the beauty of community. His poetry is not a conversation with himself, through the medium of a persona. It is resonant with people's voices, heard and unheard, present, past and future, his own prophetic-sounding incantations inspired by Ewe communal ritual and that of the continent at large. He stands right at the crossroads of African Humanism and Western culture, but is fully in charge of the synthesis.

This brings me, finally, to the questions we are constrained to ask ourselves as we stop in our tracks and take stock. Are we taking charge of the synthesis between the best and enduring values from both sides of the cultural encounter, or are we merely drifting and leaving it to fate? I am encouraged by the cumulative wisdom of our people, from the oral tradition through generations of written literature, both imaginative and expository, and by the analyses of African history, sociology, politics, economics and so on that are being conducted by indigenous scholars of the continent. The institutionalisation of our ideas in the form of pan-African organizations is also a source of inspiration. The Islamic north across the Sahara and the Horn of Africa must necessarily be part of the pan-African community, such as we have in the Organisation of African Unity. I think we can do still more: create forums of communication and problem-solving discussions wherever we may find ourselves based and find it possible to congregate. Our universities can do more to create links at another level across the continent. I am sure we can count on universities and other institutions of the world interested in Africa to serve as facilitating centres.

The Fabric of African Culture and Religious Beliefs[1] – 1971

Synopsis by Ndavhe Ramakuela

This article is what one would consider Mphahlele's in-depth exposition of African Humanism and how it differs from other forms of humanism in the world. He discusses where the concept comes from, its use and how it can be used in future.

Mphahlele touches on his distaste for organised religions like Christianity, which he sees as a form of coercion that incites fear in its adherents. In general, though, he perceives religion as but another form of literature; he goes so far as to say of the biblical stories that they are Jewish fables.

Other religions are compared and contrasted with the African religion, which is nature-centred, not restricted to space, and in which humanity and the Supreme Being are neither physically and geographically separated, nor intellectually and emotionally alienated from each other. The parallel between communal and individualistic religion is brought into the discussion here. Land, nature and ancestors are all connected in a complete, communal life.

Being is a vital part of African life; possession is less important. This, Mphahlele indicates, is reflected even in the ways people greet one another in African languages.

After this Mphahlele goes back to show how other aspects of African religion are linked to other religions of the world. Despite differences, Mphahlele calls for open-mindedness in dealing with other people and their religions and beliefs; he calls, more broadly, for peaceful mutual existence.

Forest, desert and sea were formidable barriers to the spread of written culture in Africa until modern times. What we said or did in antiquity was, if it was memorable, passed on from person to person, community to community, and from one generation to the next by word of mouth. We sang our stories and poetry on appropriate occasions.

---

1 I use the term African when I intend to indicate a cultural distinction. Black is unsatisfactory for this purpose as it says nothing that describes a culture. It is as bankrupt a word in this context as it is in the grotesque phrase "black languages". An African in a cultural sense is one who shares the indigenous cultures of Africa that predate the arrival of Europeans. Those popularly referred to as blacks today in official jargon and in the language of mass media, I shall always call Africans. When I use blacks, I include Africans in the above cultural sense, Asians (excluding Japanese, Chinese, Koreans and others who enjoy a special status) and the so-called 'coloureds', sometimes called 'brown people'. In a greater South Africa, the term African will still be a name we can all live with to include all, black and white, who share a majority culture as a spiritual commitment to the African continent.

The poet or storyteller was always the person gifted with speech, with powerful language, and was well known for this. Although we associate 'literature' with what is written, today we speak of 'oral literature', which is spoken. When we speak or write language in a *special* way, so that it expresses deep-felt emotions in well-chosen beautiful words loaded with meaning; when we use language in this fashion to express what a lively imagination is creating – then we say we are producing literature, written or oral.

Traditional societies in black Africa, i.e. roughly south of the Sahara, often communicated in symbols drawn on tree trunks or on sand. It was only with the arrival of Arab and Berber traders, and scholars from the Sudanic belt and East Africa – and with them the Arabic script – that black Africans began to read and write. From the 11th century AD, Muslim missionaries came up the Nile and along the west coast. The hot wet forests of the equatorial belt had to wait for Christian missionaries to bring the Latin script before the native languages could be written.

African myths, legends, stories, proverbs and poetry have been written down and translated by Europeans and Americans, and now more and more Africans are collecting oral literature. In this, as in the arts and crafts of Africa, in her dance and song, can be traced the wisdom and beliefs of black Africa.

The Creator

Most, if not all, African peoples believe in the Supreme Being, the creator of all things, and have done so long before Christians and Muslims brought their religions to the continent. The names of the Supreme Being vary widely: Mulungu (East Africa), Modimo, Tixo, Nkulunkulu (South Africa) and variations of Nyambe from Botswana to Zaire; West Africa has Ngewo, Mawu, Amma, Olorun (Yoruba) and Chukwu (Igbo). There are lesser spirits: gods of storm, forest, earth, water and so on. In West Africa there are temples or shrines or wooden carvings for these deities (gods or spirits). Southern and East Africa generally do not have temples. The spirits of the dead – i.e. the ancestors – are present everywhere.

The Supreme Being or Creator may seem, in the presence of these spirits, to be far away, especially as the worship of him is not as rigidly structured and reduced to a weekly or daily church routine as it is in western religion. African sages will say that God is too great to be contained in a house (church).

In African myths, the Supreme Being is mentioned in a personal manner as if he were flesh, often with a wife and family. But many proverbs still speak of him in the abstract, as an idea, the cause or originator. He is also a personal god or spirit. The Igbos of Nigeria think of the personal god as one's conscience, a guiding spirit, who is bigger than the owner – his *chi*. The Supreme Being is benevolent and does not drive fear into people.

He is a vital force, which dwells in people and things, activating them, causing life to reproduce life, and making the stars, planets and other bodies to move to a definite pattern. He is all-knowing, all-seeing. He is accessible to the lowliest and poorest. He has no form; he encompasses everything and so is the connection between man, animal, earth, sky, bodies of outer space and the elements. He cannot be analysed as the only 'absolute' reality.

There are several 'creation' myths in Africa – as the Adam and Eve story is a Hebrew myth. The Fulani of Mali say that the world was created from a huge drop of milk; Doondari came and created the stone, then stone created iron, iron created fire, fire produced water, water produced air. Doondari came a second time and out of these five elements he formed man.

Then man was too proud. So Doondari created blindness and this defeated man. Blindness became too proud, and Doondari made sleep, which defeated blindness. Worry was created to defeat proud sleep. Then death came on the scene and defeated proud worry. When death became too proud Doondari came down a third time – but as Gueno, the eternal one. Gueno – eternity – defeated death.

According to the Kono of Guinea, there was nothing but darkness at the beginning. Death, called Sa, lived here with his wife and only daughter. Sa had to live somewhere, so he created an immense sea of mud by a magical trick. One day Alatangana, the God, came and visited Sa. Appalled at the dirt Sa was living in, he scolded the latter fiercely for creating such an inhabitable place that had no plant or animal or human life. Alatangana set about solidifying the dirt, thus creating earth. To put life into the globe he made vegetation and animals. Alatangana then eloped with Sa's daughter, whom the father had refused to give away in marriage. They married and bore seven boys and seven girls – four white boys and girls, and three black boys and girls. They each spoke a strange and incomprehensible language. They intermarried and scattered over the face of the earth, becoming a variety of races with diverse colours.

The Lozi of Zambia tell of Nyambe – God – who lived with his wife on earth in ancient times. He made the animals, fishes and birds; he also made Kamunu and his wife. Kamunu was an exceptional species of animal. When Nyambe carved a piece of wood, Kamunu did likewise. Nyambe carved a wooden cup, and Kamunu did the same for himself. Iron was forged. Nyambe began to fear man. The man forged himself a spear and killed the male child of the big antelope. He killed other animals to eat. Displeased with the killer instinct in man, Nyambe chased Kamunu away, but he returned after a year. Since then, God and man have continued to differ on the merits and demerits of killing.

A Karanga (Zimbabwe) story has it that God made a man he called Moon. Moon first lived at the bottom of the sea, but decided he wanted to live on the earth. God cautioned him against the hardships of the world. Moon went on to live on the earth all the same. When Moon wept, owing to the desolate conditions he had to put up with, God offered

Morning Star in marriage to Moon, for the two to stay together for only two years. Morning Star gave birth to trees, grass, and other plants, which all grew until they touched the sky. This caused rain to fall. Moon wept when the period was up.

Then God gave him Evening Star this time, with whom he would have to die. She gave birth to birds and antelopes and boys and girls. Moon was prevented from sleeping with Evening Star on the fourth day because the time for him to die had come. Moon disobeyed, and Evening Star gave birth to leopards, lions, snakes and scorpions. Moon married his beautiful daughters and ruled over a large kingdom. Out of jealousy, Evening Star sent snake to bite Moon. When he became ill he was dumped back into the ocean, but Moon rose from the deep and can still be seen pursuing Morning Star across the sky, his very first love who had given him a happy life.

There are numerous other creation myths. Some even depict revolts against God. From those myths we can justly conclude that basically the Supreme Being, or God, is the product of a poetic state of mind, what man creates out of a poetic imagination to confirm or disprove his beliefs. We seem to create God in our own image, i.e. according to our wants, needs, desires, aspirations and ideals, and the role we see him playing helps us withstand despair, failure, humiliation and so on.

The Khoisan people, who are hunters and rove over vast distances, think of the wind as a carrier of ancestral spirits – unlike more settled communities who want to live and die where their ancestors are buried. The wind thus meets a need in the Khoisan to be assured of a divine presence in their hazardous life. We also tend to create gods, whom we need to legitimise our ideologies, theologies and petty beliefs. We plan for society and then invoke gods, whom we instruct to sign their approval. These gods may often stand for what outrages the loving Supreme Being, but we cling to them dearly all the same. This we can observe in societies that find it easy to draw the line between piety and moral good on the one side and, on the other, political and economic life. Western man has deliberately separated the two areas and wishes to keep his God in the skies, out of his political world where dog eats dog.

The existence of such a variety of creation myths should teach us that no creation myth contains the Ultimate Truth about the origins of humankind. Nor does the scientific theory about the origins of humans in East Africa necessarily make creation myths irrelevant. But then we must acknowledge that poetry and science hold different promises. The scientific theory catches humankind at the stage where he evolves from the ape. It does not explain who made the ape or his original ancestor. We should remember again that creation myths are the product of a poetic mind, a mind creating a poem in an attempt to penetrate the essence of humankind and the universe. Like all other creation myths, the Adam and Eve story was invented by a poet who was trying to understand man's weaknesses and failures – how they all began, whom he is accountable to, and what Almighty Power can save humanity.

Thus the myth deserves no more or less credibility than an African or Indian or Persian or Inca myth as a poetic creation.

The African's religion is omnipresent – it is everywhere. It is centred in nature rather than in fear of a church authority. Nature is an expression of the divine, and thus includes humankind. The African takes a total view of the universe: man is connected with external nature – e.g. mountains, rivers, plant and animal life, the sky and the bodies of outer space. Ancestral spirits are with us as a living force to whom we go in meditation as a link with the Supreme Force. The Supreme Being is a vital force that is the source of life's energy.

When a doctor is faced with a patient he first ascertains what the latter's relationship is with other members of the family and community. Has the patient quarrelled with someone? Is there constant strife in the family involving the patient? And so on. The doctor knows that it is no use trying to heal the body if the spirit is not at ease. He takes a total view of the crisis. The medicines he dispenses are organic substances: they contain life.

Another kind of therapy is indicated in an anecdote cited by Basil Davidson in *The African Genius*. He calls it 'suggestive therapy'. A young husband goes to see a traditional doctor to find a cure for his impotence. The doctor tells him that his sister is a witch; she has removed his testicles. The witch is called to account for her deed. She admits her guilt and explains that she has hidden the testicles in an anthill. In order to keep them safe from ants, she says, she put them in an empty cigarette tin. The doctor goes and digs in the anthill and turns up the tin. It is empty. The patient accepts that his testicles are back and is grateful. Within a year his wife gives birth to his son. Traditional doctors use this type of suggestive therapy, and it works. Dr. Adeoye Lambo, a psychiatrist who was in charge of a mental hospital in Nigeria until he became Vice-Chancellor of Ibadan University, has confirmed that many of the methods traditional healers use to deal with anxiety are successful. Dr. Lambo introduced a now famous system of dealing with mental patients. They live in nearby villages near the hospital, rather than in it, and only come to the clinic for treatment. Village life gives the patients protection and a communal life they are accustomed to. Therapy thus occurs in natural circumstances, by a natural process.

The African's strong sense of community helps contain anxiety and social conflicts. Moral wrong is not, for the African, explained as a 'sin' against some authority, but rather as a violation of social relationships – a wrong against someone or against the family or community. The breakdown in social relationships leads to serious troubles.

Christianity has its origins in the Middle East and was not originally a Western concept. The Western world responded to and assimilated Christianity in ways that characterized the Western mind. The Western mind was shaped right from the start by ancient Greek philosophy as we see it in Socrates, Aristotle and Plato. The early

Christians of Rome were great believers in Aristotle and Plato. The individual personality is all-important. This idea developed into the concept of individual freedom, then free enterprise and capitalism.

This philosophy found much in Christianity that was in harmony with it. Save the individual; let the individual develop his/her capacities to the fullest extent. The African begins with the community and then determines what the individual's place and role should be in relation to the community. These are features of African humanism. It is a communal concept, and there are no individual heroes within the world it encompasses. Man finds fulfilment not as a separate individual but within family and community. No one is made a saint because he was a great humanist.

Land is a source of food and holds the dead. The soil is a gift of the ancestors. The beginning of the ploughing season, harvesting time – these are occasions that the ancestors are called upon to bless. The Mau Mau uprising was a result of a sense of outrage among the Kenyan peasants, who felt that the white man's seizure of their land when the British settled the country had brought incalculable grief to the ancestors. The peasants also felt they had themselves to blame for having let it happen. Only if they regained the land would they be reinstated in the ancestors' favour.

In this country, Africans who are moved in whole communities and settled elsewhere, far from the soil where their dead lie – the sanctuary of their ancestors – are put through a traumatic experience of horrendous proportions. Imagine a woman in her fifties being wrenched from her ancestral base. She used to walk the path to a neighbour that her bare feet had become accustomed to. Her feet knew the warm and the cold feel of the earth, its contours, the furrows they had to cross, the texture of the soil. Her body responded appropriately to the angle of the sun, the direction of the breezes and winds. It changed postures according to the breeze and shape of the landscape. She sat with her neighbours and conversed with them over a tin of snuff or beer or some other beverage.

Suddenly she finds herself on alien ground. Body and mind are completely disoriented. The elements hit her from unfamiliar and irritating angles. Those old landmarks that once gave her a sense of security and belonging are absent. She is far from the graves of her beloved ones. Her neighbours are not the same as those that once afforded a glorious companionship. The landscape is so alien that she is now scared of venturing out of her homestead, a place that is itself in total disharmony with her mind and emotions. She resents this whole experience, and the last days of her life offer no comfort or joy. The wrench has indeed been traumatic. Incalculable harm has been done to the human spirit. The community's culture has been shaken and disrupted and something of great value has been irretrievably lost.

Being, in African tradition, is more important than having. To be is to possess power and vitality. Being has force and direction. There are a few variations in the form used for greeting, one of them being:

Sotho: *Dumelang!* (Greetings!)
       Agee!
       Le kae! (Where are you [in being]?)
       Re gona (or *re bano*). (We are here [we are alive; we are in a
       good state of being].)
Zulu: *Siya nibona!* (We see you [in a state of being].)
       Yebo!
       Ninjani? (How are you? [in what state of being are you?])
       Sikhona. (We are here [in a good state of being].)

The plural form is used even when one person is being addressed. There is a suggestion of force, vitality in the words. There is continuity in life – from earthly existence to the spirit world.

There is a sense of wholeness in the African's perception. The complaint by some white people that Africans do not give a direct and immediate answer when a proposition is put before them is a silly one. It is assumed that when Africans say they still need to talk the matter over, it must be due to 'slow thinking'. This misses the whole idea of the African's sense of community and the wholeness of events, as one thing depends on others which also deserve attention. These features of the African's way of life: *vitality of being, humanism* (man as the centre of life's concern, i.e. community), *continuity and wholeness* (the total view), all converge in health. Health is more than physical being. It implies *healing*, which in turn involves harmony between the individual and the surroundings, right human relationships and harmony with the whole environment.

Religion is not mechanical faith, but a *spiritual experience*. It is all-pervading because at every stage in man's life, in every single activity from entertainment to work, the relationship between man and ancestral spirits and the Supreme Being is contemplated. The divine in man is forever being activated, being set in motion. Religion is a *celebration* of that which we possess or experience. Festivals, feasts, dances, music, artistic expression, recreation of myths – they all celebrate and strengthen the community against evil influences. Indeed, no distinct line is drawn between entertainment or celebration and the functional purpose or utility motive. Song, dance and art entertain and celebrate even as they are expected to strengthen the human spirit in relation to the communal spirit. The divine in man is creative, but it only gains significance when it affects the community, when it lends vitality to it.

African Humanism, because it is based on communal relationships and focuses on the betterment of human existence, is not exclusive; it is inclusive. Compassion is one of its pillars. It has been able to absorb other creeds and systems, often because these were imposed upon it by colonialism. But now that most of Africa is independent, where the people can now make choices for their cultural direction, the openness of African Humanism is turning out to be a tremendous and positive virtue.

Five Main Streams of Humanism

The words *humanist* and (from it) *humanism* first come into prominence in reference to the Renaissance (AD 1300-AD 1600). The humanists led the movement that was to be called a 'rebirth'. The Renaissance began in northern Italy. The age before the Renaissance – the Middle Ages, medieval times – was dominated by the Roman Catholic Church in Europe, and presided over by the pope in Rome. Church authority was fierce, almost absolute. The teachings of the Church were sacred and woe to any who challenged their 'truth'.

The Middle Ages was characterized by superstition and other forms of fear, including the practice of witchcraft. The church itself used tokens, emblems, and other symbolic objects that were supposed to protect the believer against evil, or unite one with supernatural forces. Thus the Church reinforced superstitious beliefs. God was responsible for all man's ills, misfortunes, joys, failures and triumphs.

The literature and sculpture of ancient Greece and Rome were rediscovered by hundreds of Italian scholars. Greek and Roman literature and arts are referred to as 'the classics'. They were full of beauty that astonished Italy. Latin and Greek was translated into Italian. Even monks, nuns and priests devoured the classics with great relish. Italians began to gain a better and stronger sense of self as a creative force. The mind began to expand and become aware of so much that existed outside the church or convent or monastery – the beauty in man and in nature.

Dangerous voyages were made to the East and over the Alps to buy goods that were unknown to Europe, to be sold at high prices on returning. Money flowed plentifully among traders and upper-class people.

The men who were so crazy about scholarship in Italy called the study of classic culture *umanita*, and the scholars *umanisti* (humanists). *Umanita* – the humanities, otherwise called human studies or letters as distinct from the pure or mechanical sciences. The proper study of mankind was now to be humans in all the beauty of the body and all it is capable of performing, through the pain and joy perceived by the senses. Human reason was to be allowed free rein so that it could become aware of its own strengths and weaknesses. Reason and physical beauty and faculties were amply portrayed in the classical literature and art of Greece and Rome. The study of all this, plus belief – the attitude of mind that affirms the value of man as the centre of life's concerns – finds its focus in what is called humanism.

Greek philosophers like Aristotle and Plato were well known in the Middle Ages, especially in the 13th century, but Greek poetry lay neglected in monastery and cathedral libraries. Italian poets and prose writers unearthed the poetry of ancient Greece. It was easy for people of the Renaissance period to appreciate Greek and Roman classics because these ancient writers and philosophers were constantly emphasizing what they saw as distinguishing the human from the animal and from the divine.

The superstitious fears of medieval man, made worse by fear of Church authority, began to break down or to be calmed when new scientific discoveries were made during the Renaissance. Nicolaus Copernicus (1473-1543), a Polish astronomer and a mathematics teacher at the University of Rome and elsewhere in Italy, established a theory that the earth revolved round the sun and the moon round the earth. The Church's teaching was that the sun moved round the earth. If the biblical character of Joshua, the religious authorities argued, was said to have made the sun stand still, then it must have been moving.

The Italian mathematician, astronomer and physicist, Galileo Galilei (1564-1642) was another product of the Renaissance. He was the first man to use the telescope to study the skies. He thus collected conclusive evidence that the earth revolves around the sun and is not the centre of the universe – the popular idea of the times. Galileo thus confirmed and developed to its fullest extent the earlier theory of Copernicus.

Leonardo da Vinci (1452-1519), a painter, sculptor and scientist of Florence (Italy) was one of the most famous Renaissance figures. So was painter and sculptor Michelangelo (1475-1564), also of Italy.

William Caxton (c1422-1491), the first English printer, became one of the fore-most representatives of the English Renaissance. Printing itself, as Western civilization knew it, originated about the middle of the 15th century (1440) in Germany, and showed the inventiveness of the Renaissance mind (Johann Gutenberg is usually credited with the invention). As the Renaissance was a great age for the reading and translation of ancient manuscripts, printing and mass production of books advanced humanism. Through the help of the printing machine, masterpieces of literature from Rome and Greece could circulate all over Europe. Great men of letters in England who shared the spirit of the Renaissance wrote poetry, drama and prose using material that men had read in books from the continent. Chaucer, Shakespeare, Christopher Marlowe and later Milton and so on: these were some of the great figures of the English Renaissance.

The above narrative describes the emergence of humanism, a profound awareness of self. The second main stream of humanism is what some people call 'Christian humanism'. By this they are referring to the salvation of the individual person; how-ever lowly he or she may be, no matter what tyranny, what suppression, what torture, what police terror the individual may be exposed to, he or she is expected, according to Christian humanism, to be saved. Christian humanism is based on abundant and irrepressible idealism pointing the way to some 'promised land'.

The third branch of humanism includes those who invest their faith in the evolu-tion of man from his origins. Man evolved, according to scientific humanism, and was not moulded out of clay. Humanists holding this belief will claim that humans hold their destiny in their own hands, and that religious authority or conscience is some-thing imposed by institutions, outside of the human self. The extreme examples of the individual's destiny which excludes divine help or interference are Hitler (Germany), Mussolini (Italy), Salazar (Portugal), Franco (Spain), Stalin (Russia) and several other fascists and slave masters before and after them.

The fourth stream of humanism lies at the other extreme, in the anti-God land-scapes of atheists and agnostics.

The fifth is African humanism. It will be quite clear from the foregoing account of African humanism that it could never be a godless way of life. The African is a believer in the Supreme Being, whom the human being represents. When you commit a wrong against others you are hurting *yourself, your own soul*. This is more crucial and real than if the person has disobeyed authority or some moral law for which he/she has to be punished. The soul is one's spiritual life, and it is this that the person violates within himself/herself – the divine in themselves. Life is held sacred, and this makes the African a religious person. Here African humanism parts ways with Western humanism as the latter has developed today, which distrusts belief in supernatural forces. Areas we share with Western humanists amount to the value and love of life which we cherish; open-ness of mind; love of self which refuses to be shackled in stifling, suffocating codes of conduct laid down by some authority who commands obedience; and a conscience that emerges from one's own character as a social being responsible to the community, rather than a conscience that is built on the fear of authority: 'humanistic' versus 'authoritarian', as Eric Fromm puts it. We are here talking about Western humanists who believe in a common creed without venturing out to win over supporters. We are not referring to the loose world of so-called humanists who are kept together only because they share the spoils of economic production and industrial progress, which began as a development of individual initiative and free enterprise.

This latter kind of humanist has actually deviated from true humanism. Western civilization has long come to realize that it has glorified personal wealth and advance-ment for too long, and the good of the community has been sacrificed. When this is attended to, the social remedies that are planned merely end up being amoral, i.e. without a morality. Their purpose is temporary relief, and the planners who eventually dispense social services are themselves part of an economic class that has no communal morality.

The aforementioned Eric Fromm, a renowned Swiss psychiatrist, saw clearly the sickness that had already started with the industrial system in the 18th century. What Europe had thought was the 'Great Promise' of happiness for industrial man failed to deliver fulfilment. According to Western man, who relied heavily on industrial progress, (a) the aim of life is maximum pleasure in which any desire or personal need must be satisfied; (b) selfishness and greed – self-love – are essential for the industrial system to function, and lead to harmony and peace.

Fromm insists that a good deal of evidence exists that will show that this pursuit of happiness does not contribute to well-being. He remarks: 'we are a society of notoriously unhappy people: lonely, anxious, depressed, destructive, dependent people who are glad when we have killed time we are trying so hard to save.' (1976)

Egoism has not produced wellbeing either, Fromm states. To be an egotist is to want and hoard everything for oneself: to possess and refuse to share. This (extending into greed) and peace do not go together. Fromm dates the catastrophe from 18th-century capitalism, which underwent a radical change: economic behaviour detached itself from moral values. Whether workers suffered or small businesses were swallowed up by larger corporations did not matter: that was inevitably how an economic system had to function. It was natural law. 'What is good for man?' ceased to be a question; 'what is good for the growth of the system?' became paramount. Industrialists had to rationalize the reversal this way: what was good for the growth of the system (for a single corporation even) was also good for the people.

Corliss Lamont sums up 20th-century humanism thus:

> ...a philosophy of joyous service for the greater good of all humanity in this natural world and advocating the methods of reason, science and democracy... Though it looks upon reason as the final arbiter of what is true and good and beautiful, it insists that reason should fully recognize the emotional side of man. Indeed, one of humanism's main functions is to set free the emotions from cramping and irrational restrictions. (1965)

Western humanism, as a philosophy held by large numbers of people, bears the following features as identified by Lamont:

1. Humanism regards nature as the totality of being.
2. Man is an evolutionary product of nature, of which he is part. Mind and body are an inseparable unity, and so man can have no conscious survival after death.
3. Humanism has ultimate faith in man: it believes that human beings are endowed with the power or potentiality to solve their own problems through reliance upon reason and scientific method applied with courage and vision.
4. Humanism is opposed to all theories of determinism, fatalism, authoritarianism or predestination. Human beings, while conditioned by the past, should possess real freedom of choice and action – within certain objective limits. They are masters of their own destiny.
5. Ethics and moral values are, in the philosophy of humanism, grounded in experiences on this earth; man's highest goals are happiness, freedom, and progress of all mankind, irrespective of nation, race or religion.
6. A harmonization is needed between personal desires, satisfactions and continuous self-development with significant activities that contribute to the welfare of the community.
7. The widest possible development of art and the awareness of beauty, for the entertainment and education of others and *the artist's own self-fulfilment*, is encouraged.

8. Social programmes should be established for the establishment of peace, demo-
    cracy and the advancement of man's economic, political and cultural welfare.
    Reason and scientific method are ways and means by which such programmes can
    begin and be managed. Reason and scientific method presuppose the use of demo-
    cratic procedures, including full freedom of expression and civil liberties.
9. There should be freedom to challenge or question any of the basic assumptions
    and convictions that underlie all philosophies, including humanism itself.
    Whether one talks of scientific or democratic humanism, depending on the
    emphasis one wishes to lay, humanism holds that man has but one life to lead and
    should make the most of it in relation to his own creative work and happiness; that
    human happiness is its own justification. This means it does not need to be justi-
    fied by future rewards.

These are tenets of Western humanism that would readily find acceptance in black
Africa, including Africans in this country. However, Western humanism is not at ease
with the religious belief in the supernatural and dismisses it as 'myth'. It follows that
it cannot entertain any idea of conscious survival after death. Africans come from
traditions where 'myth' and reality, life and death, the natural and the supernatural are
not separate realms. 'Supernatural' is a European term that we could not have conceived for the spirit world, the life of the ancestors and so on. Reason and emotion are
not separate either. What Western man calls vision embraces spiritual forces as well
as intuition, faith, and sense of wonder. The African knows what constitutes the forces
of good and of evil. Today there are far too many people who attribute their misfortunes, including natural disasters like lightning, to someone else's mischief wrought
through magic. I am sure this is a sign of despair. A humanistic education that forti-
fies man's confidence in himself will be necessary to counter this general mood of
despair. Poverty, dispossession, lack of security of tenure where the black man
lives, and several other factors contribute to a new kind of despair. Traditional African
Humanism provides its own ways, including ritual and other forms of communal
involvement, of alleviating despair and anxiety. Because these rituals are available only
in areas *removed* from the concourse of town and country folks – the very region
where despair and anxiety most prevail – the individual finds himself alone, too weak
to resolve his condition. Perhaps new rituals will emerge to answer to new anxieties.

The humanist Julian Huxley has confirmed Lamont's formulation of present day
humanistic theory in the following terms: that it is an idea system based on our understanding of man and his relation with his environment; it must be focused on man as
an organism, though one with unique properties; it must be organized around the fact
and ideas of evolution, taking account of the discovery that man is part of a comprehensive evolutionary process and cannot avoid playing a decisive role in it. Such
humanism affirms the unity of all mankind. It will have nothing to do with absolute

authority, but insists that we can find standards to which our actions and our aims can properly be related. It affirms that knowledge and understanding can be increased, that conduct and social organization can be improved, and that more desirable directions for individual and social development can be found.

Much of this fits in with traditional African Humanism – although we may not go so far as to claim that preliterate societies in Africa or anywhere else systematically figured out the implications of evolution as it involved them.

Perhaps most important of all, African beliefs do not entertain punishment or reward in the after-life. When you die, you end up in the happy land of the ancestors, and no one is favoured over others as one of the elect. Life should be lived here on earth, and rewards and punishments due must be enjoyed or suffered here on earth. In traditional Africa, moral conduct is based on the faculty by which we know life: it is not made up of purposeless and discontinuous fragments. This moral sense of man not only gives him the power to see that the self has a continuity in time, but it also enables him to see that he is not true when he is restricted to his own self.

It is often argued that African belief used to be shared by the white man when he was largely pastoral, i.e. before the 18th century; that industrialization has stripped him of much of his humanism, and it has left him a lonely person. The implication in this argument is that when Africans become industrialized, they will also lose their humanism. So to push the argument to its logical conclusion: what the African believes in and practices is not uniquely his. He is merely a pre-industrial person.

Whether or not the African will change is not important, even though it is possible. But we need to acknowledge that African Humanism was originally a religious state of mind producing moral action; attachment to the soil; social relationships; the art of healing; the sense of community and its welfare; and a sense of organic unity or oneness in the universe in which man is the principal participant, and which is a process permeated by the Supreme Being. All these and other qualities are basically religion at work. So they are firmly rooted in the personality and determine the extent to which adoption of or adaptation to Western ways can go. The Afro-Americans lived in slavery for two hundred and forty years and they later experienced the industrial revolution in America – still later they became full participants in American industrialization. They adopted white American culture in African ways. They constantly emphasize that they are American but at the same time African or black. There are several African survivals in black American ethnic culture. This is due to the collective memory of their pre-slavery life-ways. Apart from the brutal harshness of plantation life, the slave could manage the work competently, because he already knew how to organize work in the settled and advanced societies he had lived in back in Africa.

Likewise the survivals of tradition we see in urban African life came from a religious state of mind which determined moral conduct. The African will continue to adapt to the Western way of life according to the dictates of collective memory, of surviving tradition.

The earliest Western humanists (of the Renaissance) were devout Christians, but of itself the interest in the classics was not religiously inspired. The Western mind was later to draw a line between the intellect and God. Hence humanism became the supreme reason for intellectual freedom and free enterprise, only making allowances for man's emotions. African Humanism still has a religious base.

Western civilization is a process conducted with a cold intellect, separating politics and economics from religious practice and piety. The proper meeting point between this and African Humanism, with its spiritual and moral features, may yet happen in a climate of political freedom, when there will be freedom of association and the African can hold his cultural destiny in his own hands.

The following extract from an essay by Thomas Wolfe, *God's Lonely Man*, is a clear example of how lonely Western man can be – a state that is quite foreign to African Humanism, at any rate at present, let alone in the past:

My life more than that of anyone I know, has been spent in solitude and wandering. Why this is true or how it happened, I cannot say; yet it is so. From my fifteenth year – save for a single interval – I have lived about as solitary a life as a modern man can have. I mean by this that the number of hours, days, months, and years that I have spent alone has been immense and extraordinary. I propose, therefore, to describe the experience of human loneliness exactly as I have known it.

The reason that impels me to do this is not that I think my knowledge of loneliness different in kind from that of other men. Quite the contrary. The whole conviction of my life now rests upon the belief that loneliness, far from being a rare and curious phenomenon, peculiar to myself and to a few other solitary men, is the central and inevitable fact of human existence. When we examine the moments, acts, and statements of all kinds of people, not only the grief and ecstasy of the greatest poets, but also the huge unhappiness of the average soul, as evidenced by the innumerable strident words of abuse, hatred, contempt, mistrust, and scorn that forever grate upon our ears as the man swarm passes us in the streets – we find, I think, that they are also suffering from the same thing. The final cause of their complaint is loneliness.

But if my experience of loneliness has not been different in kind from that of other men, I suspect is has been sharper in intensity. This gives me the best authority in the world to write of this, our general complaint, for I believe I know more about it than anyone of my generation. In saying this, I am merely stating a fact as I see it, though I realize that it may sound like arrogance or vanity. But before anyone jumps to that con-clusion, let him consider how strange it would be to meet with arrogance in one who has lived alone as much as I. The surest cure for vanity is loneliness. For, more than other men, we who dwell in the art of solitude are always the victims of self-doubt, forever and forever in our loneliness, shameful feelings of inferiority will rise up suddenly to over-whelm us in a poisonous flood of horror, disbelief, and desolation, to sicken and corrupt our health and confidence, to spread pollution at the very foot of strong, exultant joy. And the eternal paradox of it is that when a man is to know the triumphant labour of creation, he must for long periods resign himself to loneliness, and suffer loneliness, to rob him of the health, the confidence, the belief and joy which are essential to creative work.

To live alone as I have lived, a man should have the confidence of God, the tranquil faith of a monastic saint, the stern impregnability of Gibraltar. Lacking these, there are times when anything, everything, all or nothing, the most trivial incidents, the most casual words, can in an instant strip me of my armour, palsy my hand, constrict my heart with frozen horror, and fill my bowels with the grey substance of shuddering impotence. Sometimes it is nothing but a shadow passing on the sun; sometimes nothing but the torrid milky light of August, or the naked, sprawling ugliness and squalid decencies of streets in Brooklyn fading in the weary vistas of that milky light and evoking the intoler-able misery of countless drab and nameless lives. Sometimes it is just the barren horror of raw concrete, or the heat blazing on a million beetles of machinery darting through the torrid streets, or the cindered weariness of parking spaces, or the slamming smash and racket of the El or the driven man swarm of the earth, thrusting on forever in exacer-bated fury, going nowhere in a hurry.

Your History Demands Your Heartbeat: Historical Survey of the Encounter Between Africans and African Americans – 1998

Synopsis by Sam Raditlhalo

Academics have recently had the opportunity to re-appraise the intercon-nectedness between the two black worlds of Africa and the United States of America. This article by Es'kia Mphahlele articulates this terrain from a personal vantage point of having lived in parts of Africa and the United States, and having been a witness to the polarities and points of creative convergence between the two societies. Mphahlele explores this aspect of the relationship between the black communities by focusing on historical trends and the effects of cross-pollination of ideas and cultural influences, something which does not decrease with the passage of time. Starting in the period just prior to World War Two, Mphahlele paints a broad picture, showing how the multi-farious media (cinema, radio programmes, newspapers, magazines, and music) brought into the squalor of our lives images and moods of an African American community that was out there, doing and achieving things that black South Africans could not even begin to do, but which later played a significant role in the evolving cultural life of black South Africans. In exile, Mphahlele had a fruitful academic life through which he came into contact with luminaries such as Houston Baker Jr, and began a serious study of African American litera-ture and cultural concerns. He draws our attention to the polarities that exist between artists in terms of the politics of integration, nationalism and the aesthetic pursuit of art. At the same time, he recognises the lacunae in the South African writers' community, which has never had serious debates on what aesthetic best suits our times of (nebulous) reconciliation and nation building.

'Your history demands your heartbeat...' So said poet Sonia Sanchez in a most heart-warming letter on the eve of our departure to South Africa, August 1977 – the day that ended our exile of twenty years. We had had Sonia and her two sons over for supper in our home in Wayne, Pennsylvania.

In another volume of her poems, Sonia Sanchez's protagonist implores woman to:

> *Come ride my birth, earth mother*
> *Tell me how I have become, became*
> *this woman with razor blades between her teeth.*
> *sing me my history O earth mother*
> *about tongues multiplying memories*
> *about breaths contained in straw…*

The African continent has generally a heightened consciousness of history. The colonial experience and that of racism and apartheid must have a lot to do with it. We do not talk of history as an abstraction, as if we were merely engaged in a philosophical contemplation of events, or a general discourse on the human condition. We *feel* its pulse, the place that contains it, as it happens to us and as we ourselves happen to time and place and circumstance. If it flows like a river, then we ride it, swim its waters, try to keep afloat; we feel it wash past and over us, often leaving us holding its debris in our hands. In other words, history is a concrete experience; we seek to comprehend it as cause, effect, aftermath and sets of resonances.

We, the disadvantaged and impoverished in South Africa, and African Americans share this view. Our consciousness of history has peaks and lowlands, agitated moments and relatively sedate periods. This kind of consciousness that involves questions about who you are and where you've come from surfaces and abates in cycles. It was no accident that Steve Biko here sounded the clarion of Black Consciousness in the late 1960s, when it had just been through its most excruciating, turbulent period in the United States. At that time it seemed that the belated public outcry against the Vietnam War (at the time of My Lai) and other issues such as white American feminism and conflicts around class were going to drown black voices indicting white America's racial injustices.

West Indian novelist George Lamming says incisively that literature is 'a history of feeling'. How much more so are those forms of expression that are more socially available, such as the performing and, in some cases, visual arts. Indeed we are close, energetic history watchers even when, as we so constantly do, we give account of thought and emotion set off by moment-by-moment experience whose pain and ecstasy beat against the bone. It's not just the simple stimulus of pain or joy itself so much as the resonance of the experience. The late Hoyt W Fuller brings the literary word even closer to the felt pain and joy when he says of the new Black Arts: 'The Negro revolt is as palpable in letters as it is in the streets.'

It is all the more understandable, then, that black South Africans should have first made acquaintance with the blacks across the Atlantic through the medium of the arts, the written word, religious nationalism and educational institutions. We saw them on the movie screen, heard their music on the gramophone and electronic media and read about them in the press, long before we even began to read about captivity into slavery and the Middle Passage. My age group was still too small in the 1920s and 1930s to know the African American's attitude towards Africa. Indeed, only in the years of World War Two, when we sang 'Negro spirituals', and their lyrics began to register a message more profound than the facile otherworldly promises we had read into them; and when black American representatives of the African Methodist Episcopal Church (AME) told us of grim racial experiences back home; only then, as we were coming of age, did some of those hidden meanings begin to open up for us. Those black Americans who were coming to work for the church felt a genuine attachment to Africa. There were no signs that any large number of their American compatriots shared their enthusiasms, or even the blind old-fashioned desire to 'save' their African brethren.

Time: early 1930s. Place: Royal Cinema, a movie house in the Asiatic quarter of Pretoria. The air is close. Noisy, as teenagers can be at a matinee. When the main feature of the day comes on, after the action-packed serial orchestrated by loud teenage guffaws and gasps and foot-stamping, the noise is subdued somewhat. Enough for one to hear the dialogue. The movie: *Sanders of the River* with Paul Robeson. So this is the famous black singer! I'm thinking, pride swelling within me. I know my playmates share this. I can feel the electric effects of this pride shooting up along the spinal cord to the nape of the neck.

No matter that the adult consciousness later intuited the arrogance of the European colonists depicted in the story, in their reduction of the indigenous ruler to 'chief' (another term for functionary). No matter the internal rivalries for the chieftainship – we just love Robeson. We are overwhelmed by his powerful bass voice, his formidable presence on the screen and his aura of authority. Every so often a boy will be heard in our avenue singing aloud snatches from Robeson's *Canoe Song*. Girls cleaning their classrooms will be heard humming together *Congo Lullaby*, sung by Lilongo in the movie.

This was my introduction to the American Negro, as American blacks were known. Shortly afterwards we see Paul Robeson in *Showboat*. That *Ole Man River* has since returned many times to echo in my mind; Paul Robeson's stalwart presence has continued to prod my memory. Of course *Showboat* was a veritable feast of song around a sliver of contrived plot. But it was solid fun for us impressionable teenagers. Whenever we chanced upon news of a black American celebrity – in music, sports, politics or education – in old newspapers and magazines that we collected from homes that bought them in town (we had no newsstands in the locations) it was cause for great excitement.

With hindsight, I tend to think that our instant response to images of African-American celebrities was an escape for us from a life of abject poverty and low achievement. Here were black folks – black like us – who, in our thinking, were free to achieve, to have, to advance way beyond our own limits. The grim political realities of black life in America – which we were later to discover in our adult years – did not filter through to us in South Africa. When we learned the history and geography of North America we were only told about its colonization by the British; about George Washington, the Boston Tea Party, the Civil War; the prairies, the Rockies, southern cotton and sugar, the cities of iron and steel and so on. America's human face did not feature in the least. So the positive heroic images we slowly accumulated remained unassailable. We were looking for heroes at a time when those from our past history could not suffice.

In contrast to Robeson's serious roles, those of tap-dancer Bill Robinson, clownish Step 'n Fetchit, asked less of us by way of critical responses – such as they were. We appreciated Bojangles' tap dancing moves all right. No wonder we leapt out of our seats when we saw the Nicholas Brothers on the movie screen a decade later.

African American boxers were yet another emotional link with black America. Especially Jack Johnson, Joe Louis, Archie Moore, John Henry Lewis – to mention but a few of those earlier kings of the ring. Whenever Joe Louis was going to fight, whether in a big heavyweight match or in the bum-a-month series, the boxing fans among us huddled round some Indian storekeeper's radio, even if it meant that we would have to stand out front and spill onto the sidewalk to listen in. Some movie house or other filled us in with its newsreel reports.

We were home on school vacation in the mid-winter of 1938. Since the previous year, when the Brown Bomber did us proud by snatching the world heavyweight crown from James J Braddock in Chicago, we had been waiting impatiently for what we called the 'revenge' for the 1936 knockout inflicted by Germany's Max Schmeling on Louis in round twelve. We felt someone owed us something.

The fact that Hitler had sent Schmeling a message of goodwill didn't mean a thing to us then. We knew very little about Hitler in those days, outside snatches we got from borrowed newspapers. A story even went around in Pretoria locations that Hitler was the John Dilinger of Europe! He kept countless arsenals of machine guns in every country and was a dangerous hoodlum on the run, wanted by every big bank in the world. But those of us who knew a little better were deeply and contemptuously offended when, in 1936, Hitler walked away from the Olympic pavilion in Berlin when winner Jesse Owens and other blacks were receiving their medals. Newsreels at the movies showed a very sour-looking and furious führer. This morning of 24 June, 1938, we yelled in jubilation as we grouped round a newspaper being read aloud by a fellow fan in downtown Pretoria. Louis had walloped the German. The title was to stay with Louis until he retired in 1949.

Those of us in boxing clubs could not allow ourselves to lose track of the later heroes of the ring such as Sugar Ray Robinson, Floyd Patterson, Muhammad Ali, George Forman, Mike Tyson, Fraser and so on. *The Ring* magazine had been a staple reading diet since the 1930s.

Tennis stars such as Althea Gibson and, much later, Arthur Ashe could certainly not escape the proud attention of a black world tuned into the media for news about those of their kind who were achievers – the glory of which no one could prevent us sharing.

Equally important in this silent dialogue between two black worlds across the Atlantic were African American musicians, film actors and actresses: just too many for us to mention them all. Suffice it to say that after the short-lived movie appearances of Robeson, he continued to charm us with his bass on record – all 78s.

London, 1959. A memorable moment presented itself when I was able to go backstage and shake hands with Paul Robeson after his awe-inspiring performance of *Othello*. He was head of the Council for African Affairs and his eyes lit up when I told him I was a South African in exile. Even in that short space of time, I felt the presence of this giant tower over my small frame, so that (I imagined) my speech was less than coherent. A man whose image we had only fashioned after our own perceptions of his appearances on the screen; an image of bigness combined with the richness of voice and song. Now here I was meeting him in the flesh some twenty-five years later.

By this time Marian Anderson's voice had also become a valuable addition to our collection of gramophone music from America. *Ebony* magazine, which was already selling in South Africa by the 1950s, brought us thrilling news about outstanding African Americans of all professions. What more could we have wanted to reinforce the already vivid notion, true or bloated, of the black American's conquest of racial disadvantages? Indeed, this was the overall message that leapt out of every page of *Ebony*: achievements of the black race. Something to celebrate. And oh, how badly *we* needed that in our corner of Africa. Come Sunday afternoon, you heard from a good few homes in any ghetto township the sound of jazz records. In some cases young men, eighteen and over, would be gathered in a house or out in the yard to enjoy their music. It was most often Dixieland, swing, bop and the native *kwela* sound that dominated the idiom of the 1950s.

The most famous local bands then, Peter Rezant's Merry Blackbirds, Harlem Swingsters and Jazz Maniacs, matured in the 1940s and into the early 1950s – the high time of swing and bop. Band musicians latched on to swing. Duke Ellington, Count Basie, Cab Calloway, Satchmo, Nat King Cole, Ella Fitzgerald and Lena Horne were among those whose collective spirit flowed into the Blackbirds' music. Rezant's band was not anything like the size of Duke's or Count's, nor did it have their professionalism. Still, his popularity among dance hall patrons consolidated one strand of the cultural lifeline we had had with black America since the turn of the century.

In the 1950s, bop and blues were more popular among the disc music buffs. To my untutored but loving ear for jazz, the elements of conversation or dialogue and interludes for instrumental virtuosity so characteristic of bop draw from the listener an exhilarating commitment. And what better setting for it than in a group, huddled in a house or corner of the yard, where listening is a more intimately shared experience? Social conversation, except between albums, can easily amount to blasphemy in such situations. So Charlie Parker, Coltrane, Sonny Rollins, Miles Davis, Monk, Gillespie, Oscar Peterson and so on were regular fare during our soirees.

We responded the same way to blues. Bessie Smith, Billy Holiday, John Lee Hooker, Lena Horne and Dinah Washington, for instance; Leadbelly, T-Bone Walker and Muddy Waters had a good few imitators in Johannesburg and Pretoria. Cut professionalism; imitation is another form of flattery and admiration. Over the years our collections included singers with mixed repertoires such as Ella Fitzgerald, Sarah Vaughn, Dionne Warwick, Melba Moore, Roberta Flack, Billy Ekstine and Johnny Mathis, to mention but a few.

Because of its intimate terms of expression and virtuosity, only very few musicians in this country ever tried to emulate bop at its high point in America. But we have international names among our black musicians – such as Hugh Masekela, Abdullah Ibrahim, Jonas Gwangwa and Caiphus Semenya – who have continuously experimented with a fusion between traditional and modern styles.

We were so absorbed in the performances that legitimised our lofty myth about the African American that it would not have occurred to us to grapple with questions about origins, tradition, identity, diaspora and so on. What precisely could have intrigued us so much, more than this longing to attain the levels of artistic and intellectual performance that were decidedly superior to ours? Superior even to that of whites – who flaunted their supremacy on both sides of the Atlantic. Of course we can only talk of art forms in which we can fairly compare like with like. Our native idioms have been superbly adequate to our respective communities. And we know *our* highly competent performers only too well. The competitive spirit never compromised communal pride, esteem and enjoyment. To answer the rhetorical question, we must return to that search for heroes. Our own heroes had became martyrs before we were able to acknowledge them. We found several among African Americans and defined them on our own terms.

The black movie character that created a positive image among us was not the dramatic actor. There were not many to be seen beside Paul Robeson, Ethel Waters and so on. It was rather the musicians, the tap dancers such as Bojangles and the Nicholas Brothers, whom the cinema screen brought to us. Most likely cinemas on both sides of the Atlantic conducted a sinister kind of censorship that allowed us only so much viewing and no more. We laughed aloud to watch the buffoonery of Step n' Fetchit and others, who were always depicted with large round eyes that rolled and shone in the dark. But as we grew up we learned better. Those foot-shuffling clowns were not only boring; they offended us. We perceived them to be diminishing people whom we looked up to. No black South African ever appeared in a leading or minor role on the screen until Lionel Ngakane in the role of the Reverend Kumalo's son in *Cry, the Beloved Country* – based on Alan Paton's novel. In the 1950s only commercials and cheap dramatizations portraying Africans appeared on the movie screen – always as clowns chasing each other all over the place.

More recently the bigger actors have begun to assert their presence on the silver screen, among them Sidney Poitier, James Earl Jones, Ruby Dee and Ossie Davis; Morgan Freeman, Sammy Davis Jr., Bill Cosby, Danny Glover, Alfred Woodard, Bea Richards, Cecily Tyson, Harry Belafonte, Louis Gosset Jr., Denzel Washington, Al Freeman and Blair Underwood.

We wanted more. More spectacle, more *something* for our lives. What in particular, we did not know. With hindsight, one can only divine that we wanted to go beyond the high-profile image of other blacks outside our own borders. Something such as John Keats refers to in his *Ode on a Grecian Urn*. Contemplating the mute but busy music players and deities engraved on the urn, he 'hears' things: 'Heard melodies are sweet, but those unheard sweeter'. But let them play on, Keats urges, even if two figures in the picture about to kiss will never attain their dreamed-of bliss. For the unheard melodies one could, in our case, substitute 'unheard story'. And when we did read the story years later, especially as told by the artists, historians and literary men and women – as we pieced together strands and chunks of history we discovered on our own – it turned out to be an epic too huge, too compelling and painful, too multi-dimensional for the mind to contain.

But such is the inexorable drive of nature towards the universal, as Bengali poet and humanist Rabindranath Tagore indicates, that (to paraphrase him) while a bucket of water may be heavy on a person's head, if you enter the sea carrying the bucket, it is almost weightless. The burden and ecstasy of being black ceases to be unbearable for those who are tuned into the interconnectedness of phenomena of life. On the local plane, the enlightened share with their compatriots the latter's intensive, if more confined, concerns.

The Ethiopian movement – the breaking away of Africans from white established churches, including their segregated black congregations – signalled the rise of religious nationalism. This found fertile ground in the South African racist climate. Mangena Mokone, a Wesleyan preacher, defected from the white-controlled church in 1892 because the missionaries discriminated against their black clergy. They maintained separate places of worship for separate congregations. Mokone called his new congregation the Ethiopian Church. Ethiopia was, in those days – as it was among the African Americans in the 1920s – a symbol of religious nationalism and independence. It had no colonizing missionaries. 'Ethiopia shall stretch out her hands unto God' was the biblical line, which was interpreted as prophecy.

Through Charlotte Maxeke (née Manya), who had gone to study at Wilberforce in the United States, Mokone corresponded with the African Methodist Episcopal. Soon, in 1896, these pioneers formed a unity between the two communities under the name African Methodist Episcopal Church. Today the American linkage remains, but in a modified ritualistic form. For decades it was practice for resident AME Bishops to come from the US.

In 1898, the AME in the US sent its senior bishop, Henry McNeal Turner, to South Africa to assist in the Ethiopian venture. He was more than a spiritual leader, spreading also the message of racial equality where he was stationed in the old Transkei territory. A 'departure' that incurred the wrath of the central authorities in no small measure. Turner and other churches also sent young Africans to the US to study at African American universities.

One of these students was John Chilembwe of Nyasaland (Malawi). He was inspired to think of himself as a rebel after the style of the American John Brown. Chilembwe came under the influence of Scottish missionary James Booth, who had come to work in Southern Africa. After his return from a two-year study at Virginia Theological Seminary, the Malawian returned home in 1900. In 1915 he led a revolt against British colonial rule, but it aborted, and Chilembwe was killed. Leaders of the Ethiopian movement in Southern Africa and in black America would have known about these events that promoted the solidarity of the black world. The Pan-African movement spearheaded by W E B Du Bois and contemporary African leaders provided an added impetus.

An essay by African American Benjamin T Tanner, *An Apology for African Methodism* (1867), endorses the black man's religious nationalism, which was an expression of a desire for self-reliance and intellectual independence. Tanner wrote:

> *The giant crime committed by the Founders of the African Methodist Episcopal Church, against the prejudiced white American, and the timid black – the crime which seems unpardonable – was that they dared to organize a Church of men, men to think for themselves, men to talk for themselves, men to act for themselves. A Church of men who support from their own substance, however scanty, the ministration of the Word which they receive; men who spurn to have their churches built for them, and their pastors supported from the coffers of some charitable organization; men who prefer to live by the sweat of their own brow and be free...*

Words like these could not but fire South African blacks who felt the brunt of white racism and stir them to create their own institutions. In the Harlem of the 1920s, names such as 'Ethiopian' and 'African' were pretty common for institutions and places of entertainment and business. The people of the former Ciskei (now part of Eastern Cape province) in South Africa hoped and prayed that Marcus Garvey might come to their salvation in the struggle against white rule and dispossession.

The 1958 special number of *Présence Africaine,* published by the African Society of Culture in Paris and Dakar, was devoted entirely to the theme 'Africa from the Point of View of American Negro Scholars'. One of the contributors, Rayford W Logan, observed that African Americans who grew up in the early 1900s would probably have heard of Africa for the first time at church. The minister or missionary would then be soliciting collections for the missions in Africa.

The missionaries themselves conveyed distorted images of Africa, its life, ways, thoughts and beliefs. Logan remembers reports about the African woman's 'immorality' and 'half-naked body.' The overall impression the preacher left was that Western (Christian) civilization was superior and African life-ways barbaric and at best 'primitive'. Today there are missionaries who have a relatively enlightened view of the continent. But few of them have been able to deal with the present-day political consciousness of Africa – often heroic and volatile, often prostituted by new economic entanglements that it cannot manage.

Logan views Marcus Garvey as 'this Jamaican-born demagogue (who) exploited the disillusionment of American Negroes in the promise that World War One held out to improve their lot.' Yet it is also true to say that Garvey must have symbolized that spiritual part of the African American's consciousness that cherished a dream to restore his pre-slavery strength, dignity and self-reliance. And that dream was never to let go, reappearing in cycles, finding self-expression in the political idiom of any particular time in varying degrees of passionate intensity. Indeed Garvey's back-to-Africa movement was a resurgence of the spirit of the Free Africa Society of Philadelphia, the society that tried to promote a return in 1788.

When the National Council for the Advancement of Colored People was initiated in 1909, and its organ *The Crisis* was published in 1910, the black intellectual's mind was set against the return-to-Africa campaign. On the white man's terms, this would appear to be a process of regression, a retreat from 'civilization'. Because the NAACP was preoccupied with the advancement of the American blacks, it left coverage of Pan-African affairs to *The Crisis*. But it supported the four Pan-African congresses of 1919-1927, in which DuBois played such a major role. As early as 1919, DuBois proposed an *Encyclopaedia Africana*. It was not until after 1957, when DuBois immigrated to Ghana, that the project got off the ground with President Nkrumah's support. The NAACP also involved itself in the League of Nations' Peace Conference following World War One, in questions of postcolonial reconstruction in Africa and elsewhere. Undoubtedly DuBois, together with the West Indian George Padmore, played the most important role in the rise of Pan-Africanism, which in turn helped reaffirm African nationalism. This would not have been possible, naturally, without the leadership of men like Dr Edward Blyden (Liberia), Nkrumah, Azikiwe of Nigeria, Nyerere of Tanzania and other political and intellectual giants.

According to Rayford, Dr Carter G Woodson 'popularised interest in Africa among American Negroes more than did DuBois or Garvey.' Woodson was in touch with scholars and other intellectuals and the larger public to a greater degree than were the other two international names. His Association for the Study of Negro Life and History, which he founded in 1915, attracted interest through its annual Negro

History Week (instituted in 1926). African history naturally became a focal point of study and discussion among blacks.

West African leaders such as Nnamdi Azikiwe and Kwame Nkrumah also attracted black American intellectuals to their respective countries and to the continent in general. Along with Wilberforce and the AME, Howard University and Lincoln University (established 1856) are the oldest historically black tertiary institutions to have contributed to the intellectual and political upliftment of African leaders. Nkrumah, Azikiwe, South Africans, Liberians and Sierra Leonians all went to Lincoln at one time or another. Lincoln symbolized freedom and nationalism throughout Africa.

In a special edition of *Présence Africaine*, famous educationist Horace Mann Bond writes as President Honorarius of Lincoln:

> *Lincoln University African students met the American Negro at work.... in the church, that institution of paramount importance in the social and political organization of the Negro masses...* (259)

The influence of Lincoln in Africa, Bond asserts, was part of the original design of the institution. Its admission of Africans dates back to 1896.

Sociologist E Franklin Frazier features among the array of scholars expressing their views about Africa in *Présence Africaine*. Discussing what the African American could contribute to the social development of Africa, he remarked: 'The Negroes of the United States are poor. They do not occupy positions of influence in the financial institutions, which could supply the capital Africa needs... Upon examination it turns out that the claim that Negroes are economically well-off, or have accumulated wealth, is a myth cherished by Negroes and fostered as part of the propaganda designed to show that Negroes have not fared badly in the United States.' The new black middle class, Frazier went on to say, was composed almost wholly of 'professional and technical workers who are self-employed or salaried, white-collar workers, and the more highly paid skilled workers.'

This is still the situation with us South African blacks. But we are worse off still because we have no technicians or artisans to speak of who could set up on their own, outside white employment. Poverty among blacks in America has grown more massive on a horizontal plane than in Frazier's day. Again, the African American no longer thinks of advancing the African's 'development' in the same terms as he used to, especially from the 1950s through the 1970s. This is no longer the missionary stance of the late 19th century through to the first half of the 20th. The black American's interest in the Africa of the second half of the century seems to have had its origins in the desire to know Africa intimately and redress the poverty of the American school and college curricula, from which he felt disinherited by not studying the continent of his forebears. In addition, white American scholars have for too long been more favoured by foundations and corporations than blacks with funding for research in African life and affairs. A further refinement and consolidation of this involvement with Africa is manifest in historically black universities that want to establish working linkages with corresponding tertiary institutions in South Africa.

Among the prominent African American organizations and personalities who have shown active interest in Africa in the last fifty years have been Paul Robeson, W E B DuBois, the American Society of African Culture (AMSAC), the African American Institute, Transafrica, Randall Robinson, Dr John A Davis, Dr St Clair Drake, Dr Mercer Cook, Samuel Allen, Dr Martin Kilson, Lorenzo D Turner, James A Porter, Horace Mann Bond, Dorothy B Porter, Langston Hughes and so many others – all scholars, educators, writers, politicians, social reformers and observers.

The civil rights activities of the 1950s through to the late 1960s pushed into prominence more politicians and writers who took a profound interest in African affairs, such as Reverend Jesse Jackson. Some leaders such as Malcolm X approached Africa via the Maghreb and Mecca. Malcolm X refined Islam for African Americans after its raw, fundamentalist beginnings under Elijah Muhammad's guardianship.

The Caribbean influence cannot be ignored. For it was men like Dr Edward Blyden, West Indian-turned-Liberian, whose concept of the 'African Personality' towards the close of the 19th century suggested for the black world an African heritage which we all shared on both sides of the Atlantic.

Blyden warned Europe's Christian colonizers and missionaries against undermining traditional African religions in order to impose what they perceived as the superiority of their own. He held Islam in greater esteem for its benign and appreciative entry into Africa. Islamic teachers used indigenous religion, its style of worship and high priests, marabouts and rulers. Islam could thus spread, not as an incursion or invasion (which Christianity was, in reality) but an enriching fusion. The manner and organic quality of the fusion between Islam and the indigenous religion went much deeper in the African's psyche than did the contract between Christianity and Africa. Union with Islam endured even beyond the savagery of the jihads when Islam took to the sword, African against African.

By the time Senegal's Léopold Sédar Senghor and Birago Diop and West Indians Aimé Césaire and Léon Damas became enthralled by the rhythms of African American poetry and prose in the 1920s and 1930s, Blyden had sown the seed for a new consciousness to develop. The francophone elite witnessed a resurgence among themselves of African self-pride, reverence for the ancestors, the tom-toms, shrines, dance and music and the savanna landscape of Western Sudan. Negritude (a word coined by Césaire) came to signify the essence of African Humanism, the sum of African values: humanism anchored in social relationships, the love of life for itself, the evocation of ancestral presences, respect for elders. Back in the 1960s, when African Americans were searching for an anchor in their collective memory – a collective unconscious –

they found part of it in their new-found knowledge of the ancient African empires and kingdoms, jungle and open skies, the whole pristine sense of being.

The dominant image in the early Harlem poets was ancient Egypt, the Nile civilizations, and the pyramids – some dimly intuited world of African origins. Much more boldly, poets of the 1960s and 1970s such as Askia Muhammad Toure confront the era of the Islamic kingdoms – evocation of which produces in his work an exciting blend of the romantic-lyrical and the epic. Others of the same period, such as Charles Thomas and Larry Neal, stop at Shango, Ogun and the orishas – deities that are still valid today for vast sections of Nigeria. It seems that, having negotiated in themselves the terms of being American descended from Africa, they need now to look at Africa as a reality, with all its beauty and crudity, benignity and savagery, and so many other opposites that make up the human condition. The realism extends to the inspiration so many African Americans derive from Nelson Mandela's heroism.

Whatever opportunities or benefits have come our way as South African blacks because of these cross-continental ideas, affiliations and associations, and whatever institutions the black world established around them along the way, it has been largely our refugees and exiles who have exploited them in positive ways. Only in the few cases when a South African institution – such as the Educational Opportunities Council and the locally-based British Council – sponsored selected students to study abroad, did the apartheid government issue passports. It was ostensibly in the interests of human rights that American institutions and organizations, sometimes through the agency of visiting scholars in free Africa, sponsored our exiles for study abroad. The students have undoubtedly been enriched by this experience and come to their own conclusions about their encounter with people of their own colour in the United States.

Scholarship conceptualises and analyses; poetry dreams and feels. With his characteristic elegance of prose style, Alain Locke brings clarity to the black poet's attitudes to Africa as he interprets the 'New Negro' of the 1920s. He calls the collective mood of the time 'the most sophisticated' racial attitude: 'the conscious and deliberate threading back of the historic sense of a group tradition to the cultural backgrounds of Africa.'

Locke sees this act as a defensive stance and imitative at the initial level, growing more and more positive year by year:

> *Africa is naturally romantic. It is poetic capital of the first order, even apart from the current mode of idealizing the primitive and turning toward it in the reaction from the boredom of ultra-sophistication. There is some of this Caucasian strain in the Negro poet's attitude toward Africa at the present time.* (Black Voices, 536)

But Locke does not see this attitude as the dominant factor with the black poet. He also contrasts Countee Cullen with what he calls 'the minor poetical talents' who are inclined to the 'rhetorical and melodramatically romantic.' He appreciates Cullen's potential 'paganism' that, the poet says, he must reconcile with his Christian upbringing. 'For him the African mood comes atavistically, and with something of a sense of pursuing Furies. He often eulogizes the ancestral spirits in order to placate them' – as in the poem *Heritage*:

> *So I lie, who find no peace*
> *Night and day, no slight release*
> *From the unbitten beat*
> *Made by cruel padded feet*
> *Walking through my body's street,*
> *Up and down they go, and back,*
> *Beating out a jungle track.* (Black Voices, 537)

Houston Baker writes in his monograph on Countee Cullen: 'Cullen was interested in a blatant contrast between the benign and unsmiling deities of the new land and the thoroughly initiated gods of the old.' (*A Many Coloured Coat*, 34). Africa serves to symbolize the African American's (in Cullen's terms) self-abandon; the free spirit in him.

Locke concludes this section of his thesis:

> *But if there is to be any lasting restatement of the African tradition, it cannot be merely*
> *retrospective. That is why even this point of view must merge into a transposition of the*
> *old elemental values to modern modes of insight. This is just on the horizon edge in Negro*
> *poetry and art, and is one of the goals of racialism in the new aesthetic of Negro life.*
> (Black Voices, 537)

MacCowdery's lines are to Locke an 'advance statement' on the heritage theme:

> *I will take from the hearts*
> *Of black men – Prayers their lips*
> *Are 'fraid to utter*
> *And turn their coarseness*
> *Into a beauty of the jungle*
> *Whence they came.* (Black Voices, 537)

It seems, though, that if you are not *living* the life of Africa in every sense of the verb, you can but project your mind. MacCowdery's lines are still the script you write for one who wants to go and create with somebody else's materials, his dreams and prayers, because you think he is inarticulate. The illusion here is that the native is waiting for someone to refine jungle life for him.

There is a common thread that runs through the body of verse before the 1960s that alludes to Africa but still does not come to grips with the living continent. Much of it is indeed dreamlike in tone; often it is oblique and sometimes too well textured and poetical to draw us into its movement, emotion and purpose. With the lesser poets, Africa merely provided a 'poetic theme' rather than a deeply felt 'spiritual espousal' of Africa as a human reality.

Ama Bontemps always crafted his poetry with too much clinical care, I think, to convey the passion one divines must have been the initial impulse behind a particular piece. His poem *Return*, about rain, darkness, jungle, sky, vines, river, drum beats and birds, is one such well measured, skilfully crafted product. It builds up an atmosphere of the continent with trite visual effects, and still the essence of Africa eludes us.

Resonances of Africa as the poets of the 1960s replay them bring us closer to what they sought after: a point of identity with its people, beliefs, deities and so on. Clearly the African American was searching for a new basis for the transatlantic connection, black brotherhood beyond the mere catalogue of sensuous effects, the romantic image. But whatever other ways the black American may discover of advancing his African consciousness, he will still feel the compulsive need to give an account of it through the modes of expressive culture.

Novelist Peter Abrahams, born in South Africa but living in Jamaica, was a contemporary of mine in junior high school in 1935, at St Peter's Secondary in Johannesburg. He relates in his autobiography *Tell Freedom* (1954) how he discovered Paul Robeson and soon after was initiated into the 'American Negro's' life through W E B DuBois's *The Souls of Black Folk*. He pulled this out of the shelves of a small pedestrian library of an African community centre in downtown Johannesburg, sponsored by American missionaries. 'For this much all men know,' Abrahams quotes, 'despite compromise, war, struggle, the Negro is not free.' Then he picked up Booker T Washington, James Weldon Johnson and Alain Locke's *The New Negro* anthology. 'Something burst deep inside me,' Abrahams records. 'The world could never again belong to white people only! Never again!'

Peter was way ahead of us at high school where knowledge was concerned, which one could only pick up from wider reading than the syllabus encompassed – especially imaginative literature. Somehow he never seemed to fit into the school's human environment. He was a 'coloured' boy, to use the official term of the day – still current today. Government then was determined that all 'non-European' communities should be classified and named, distinguishable not only from the 'Europeans' but from one another, e.g. Natives, Indians, coloureds. Not that Abrahams was uncomfortable with his 'Native' milieu at St Peter's. He had, after all, come from a suburb where black Africans, Indians and coloureds lived together in harmony. There was no such mix where the majority of students had come from – 'Native locations', as urban reservations were officially known. Abrahams was just generally a restless person in a conventional academic setting.

He had that faraway dreamy look on his face, in his eyes – like that of a person searching for something far away on the horizon. Our presence seemed to have no relevance to his search. He spoke to us, with soft-spoken passion in his expression, about the 'American Negro' he had read about at the social centre. He talked a lot about Marcus Garvey's return-to-Africa consciousness campaign. All very strange talk to us – both his enthusiasm and the story he had to tell us about these discoveries. He had the sharp nose for literary treasures that we others had not yet developed. With hindsight, I realize that ours was a life we lived without any armour to fight off or insulate us against the cruelties of our ghetto life. Its pain consumed all our attention.

Abrahams's first book of short stories and sketches, *Dark Testament* (1942), is clear testimony to the influence African American writing had on him. He was the first African writer, black or white, to cut loose from the leisurely 'correct' and ornate line we were all nurtured on at the time, trying hard to imitate the English Romantics and Victorians and some of their prolixities. All of us in mission schools had teachers who had recently been recruited from England. The literary texts prescribed by the education system took us from Shakespeare, Marlowe, Robert Herrick, Robert Burns, Joseph Addison, Richard Steele, Washington Irving through Wordsworth, Coleridge, Keats, Shelley and so on; through Dickens, Walter Scott, Austen, the Brontës and Quiller Couch. With this kind of diet, who needed plain homegrown corn such as William Plomer, Van der Post, Roy Campbell, William Scully, Percy Fitzgerald and others?

In Abrahams you have a concrete, imagistic style that is generally American but has its own special African American tension and breathless urgency. What Houston Baker Jr says of the post-war black poets, in a preface to his anthology *Black Literature in America*, is true of what happened to South African prose in the hands of Peter Abrahams and his inheritors: 'The new poets tended to work more in imagistic terms, stressing a concreteness of detail and a sparseness of language.' His style was to reach maturity and refinement with the novels *Song of the City* (1945) and *Tell Freedom*.

Indeed it would be impossible to treat yourself to heavy servings of Jean Toomer's and Claude McKay's fiction; James Weldon Johnson and Langston Hughes's prose, and then go back to the orthodox English style.

Who are Peter Abrahams's inheritors? All the authors who wrote for Johannesburg's *Drum* magazine as of 1950: Can Themba, Bloke Modisane, Arthur Maimane, Lewis Nkosi and myself. *Drum*, styled back then in layout after *Life*, was owned by Jim Bailey and published for the black urban proletariat. The 1950s ran its full course before the Government's inferior system of education took effect among the African population. The standard of proficiency in prose among students, teachers and the general public began its downward trend, especially after the mid-1960s. Likewise, the standard of prose in *Drum* dropped dismally. The early 1970s saw the emergence of poetry among blacks (i.e. Africans, Indians and coloureds).

Most of the *Drum* writers of the 1950s had no college education. But they had a sophisticated spirit of adventure, surrounding themselves with American cultural creations. And yet, like the writers of the Harlem Renaissance, we evolved and developed individual styles independently, untrammelled by any particular canon. We had found a voice; that was all that mattered.

The first time I visited the United States was as an exile in 1960. I had been invited from Nigeria to attend a United Nations conference. The next year Dr Mercer Cook, an authority on African literature of French expression, asked me to succeed him as director of African Programmes for the International Congress for Cultural Freedom in Paris. Then I returned to the US for a two-month lecture stint at MIT, Cambridge, Massachussetts. On neither occasion was I able to form an opinion about my meetings with African Americans – few as such meetings were, and confined to intellectuals.

In 1966-68 I was a teaching fellow reading for a Ph.D. at the University of Denver, Colorado. Again, owing to the relatively tiny number of blacks in Denver and its environs, I relied heavily for my information on television magazine programmes, the press, literary products and a couple of black scholars on faculty to provide a composite picture of African-American life.

As I taught Afro-American literature as well as African and Caribbean, I probed further the layers of the black encounter and our interaction. After four more years as a full-time lecturer at Denver, I joined the English faculty at the University of Pennsylvania in 1974. I made the acquaintance of and developed a friendship with Professor Houston Baker Jr. It was also to be a most rewarding intellectual companionship. Sometimes we conducted a joint course in black American literature; at other times he invited me to be a contributor in one of his seminars on the Afro-American Studies programme.

To read and converse with a man of Baker's bright, diamond-edged intellect and drive was an enduring enrichment for me. In an incisive statement about Richard Wright in his *Singers of Daybreak* (studies in black American literature), Houston Baker makes a comment that has a bearing on the South African educational system as well as the American. He takes his cue from Wright's comment on the 'blindness of the white characters' in *Native Son*. The one thing that would have quickly explained the murder of the white woman, Wright pointed out, would have been an 'acknowledgement of Bigger Thomas's humanity by one, or all, of the white investigators.' Baker asserts that Wright's statement 'helps to solve the "mystery" of the missing black American literature in the writings and on the syllabi of white American scholars.'

South African white scholars as a cultural establishment too, have, until very recently, generally failed to acknowledge the black man's humanity. They have lacked the 'intellectual curiosity, a desire to analyse and understand the unique aspects of his culture and to study the answers he has offered to the timeless problems of the universe.' White South African scholars footnote one another, have colonized the research territory, and are endowed with bags of funding from the white cultural and financial establishments.

My systematic study of African American literature, thought and history actually began in 1955 – before my exile. All self-motivated, the kind of activity you undertake out of a burning curiosity to know. Instinctive, too, in the sense that the mind is always pushing outward, reaching out across the frontiers of reference, seeking to know where it stands in relation to this or that. The act of knowing, the ways of consciousness, seem to me to be at the centre of human survival.

In 1948 I read Richard Wright's volume of short stories, *Uncle Tom's Children* (1943) and *12,000,000 Black Voices*. As happened to Peter Abrahams earlier when he read Alain Locke, Countee Cullen and Langston Hughes, Wright blew my mind. My consciousness was heightened, and my writing 'style' – what there was of it – made a sharp turn away from its grammar-book orientation and dead-end track. *Native Son* and *Black Boy* confirmed me in my quest for that territory we could call self-realization, but which is so hard to define.

Langston Hughes's *Weary Blues* (poems) and a volume of short stories, his *Simple* stories, had me hunting for more knowledge about the Afro-American world. He had actually sent me the book of poems and volume of stories, both autographed. A short story from me appearing in a New York anthology of world short fiction in 1955 had caught Hughes' attention. A friendship began, reinforced by occasional meetings across continents and oceans, and his death in 1967 touched me profoundly. His letters to me radiated the kind of warmth I had come to regard as his special characteristic.

His Harlem home on 125th Street expressed the lifestyle of a man who was at ease with himself. As in my brief London encounter with Paul Robeson, I was in awe at that first meeting with Langston two years later, in spite of our five years' acquaintance by correspondence. But in no time Langston's informality and gentle humour set me at ease.

In 1962 I invited Hughes and Saunders Redding (whom I had first met at Lincoln University) to the first-ever conference of African writers on the continent, in Kampala, Uganda. I had organized the event under the auspices of my Paris employers. I shall always remember Langston carrying his books in his armpits, to market them and read to audiences whenever the opportunity presented itself.

He was an intriguing blend of the genteel tradition of manners and down-to-earth, no-frills mien. The lyricism of his poetry is most casual, deceptively transparent.

Among the most enlightening theses that probe the African American consciousness, I found Harold Cruse's *The Crisis of the Negro Intellectual* (1967) a most compelling essay. From what I had read of the Harlem Renaissance of the 1920s, it was obvious that attitudes towards Africa then were spread pretty thin, and tentative. Cruse depicts historian John Henrik Clarke as a chronicler of the consciousness of black America. I met this distinguished scholar (Clarke) in his Harlem home in 1970. Cruse narrates with profound empathy Clarke's shift from the nationalist who did not accommodate any communism or integrationist ideas to a 'peculiar brand of left-wing Africanist integrationism.' The radical Left of 1960, he tells us, encouraged Clarke's transformation 'ushered in by the Cuban Revolution.'

It was Clarke who introduced me to *Freedomways* journal, even though he was not of the communist Left. According to Cruse, Clarke pointed out in 1961 what was different about African nationalism: African intellectuals on the continent were the mouthpiece for its nationalism. Not so in the case of nationalism in the US, nor even the Garvey movement long before. 'Naturally, Clarke could not explain.... in *Freedomways* why it was that his intellectual friends (Robeson, John O Killens, Lorraine Hansberry, Ossie Davis, Ruby Dee, Julian Mayfield, Shirley Graham DuBois, Esther Jackson, Alpheus Hunton et al) supported not Afro-American nationalism but faraway African nationalism, i.e. the 'African Personality'. (340)

When we met subsequently in Columbia (1992) he had lost his eyesight. I had always been impressed by his simplicity and bright, engaging intellect. There was calmness about John Henrik Clarke that told me that whatever resolution of the ancient feuds he had arrived at, he was at ease with himself. Nothing was ever going to ruffle him again.

Harold Cruse highlights, among other things, the tensions between communism in Harlem and Garvey's nationalism in the 1920s and, in the 1960s, communism and Muslim-driven nationalism. Ever since communism was imported into Africa, this has been the tug-of-war. In South Africa tensions were toned down by the Party's role in the liberation struggle, the black nationalist majority led by the African National Congress, and the dual membership that was possible – in the Party and in the ANC, and then within the umbrella Congress Alliance.

This alliance of black and white resistance movements, containing also Asians and coloureds, led to the breakaway in 1959 of what came to be the Pan-Africanist Congress (PAC). The leadership of the PAC, the late Robert Sobukwe, made it known that the radical whites were in reality the leaders of the alliance. They perceived this to be a factor that sapped the energy of African nationalism in order to neutralize it. There are clear correspondences here between black South Africa and black America. Always the Communist Party wielded financial resources their African, coloured and Indian partners could not boast. Now that political freedom has been won, if little else, the tensions between communist dogmatism and the now hardly recognizable residual nationalism have begun to surface again. The CP may well be grateful for this. For now at least they no longer have the rhetoric of nationalism to respond to – which always unsettled them in the past.

What Cruse says about the intellectual poverty of Harlem blacks in the 1920s has been a truism in South Africa till this day. Economic and political domination by the white mainstream has enabled it to marginalize the intellectual activities of blacks (African, coloured and Asian). There can be no comparison between the superior volume and quality of African American scholarship and that of South Africa.

Another informative fact in the understanding of these two black worlds is that the 1950s was a turbulent decade in South Africa. The African National Congress was becoming a mass movement to reckon with. Accordingly, white paranoia reached white heat. The Government passed more vicious anti-black legislation than ever before. After all but the South African Indian Congress had been banned at the start of the 1960s, a lull followed. Likewise, the 1950s were for the Americans generally a traumatic time, in the context of McCarthyist anti-communist paranoia. At the same time, the black civil rights movement was beginning to gather the momentum that would attain a high voltage in the sixties. Black consciousness, the concept of black power, also took shape then, along with the Nation of Islam.

Malcolm X came through Nairobi on his way back from the Hadj. Two African American friends of ours brought him to our home. He seemed extremely subdued both in speech and carriage, like a person who has come out of an elevating, intensive moment of spiritual revelation. Days after that visit, something told me I had sensed a mysterious radiance flash across his face once or twice, ever so subtle. Nothing about his gestures revealed the fiery orator in a hurry to deliver a message, a prophetic statement *now*; even granted that the circumstances of our meeting were social. And when we subsequently witnessed the event of his assassination through the media, we could only conclude that he was a victim of internal betrayal among fellow Muslims.

Malcolm X left us with scant impression of what he really thought of black nationalism, of integrationism, of whites, interracialism, economics, political parties, violence, revolution and so on. Harold Cruse quotes a few lines from an interview held on Malcolm's return from Africa in early 1965, but printed after his death. Malcolm X relates how an Algerian ambassador he met in Ghana, who was as light-skinned as a white, wanted to know from him where Algerians of his complexion fitted in, if African Americans wanted victory for black nationalism. And what about Egyptians, Moroccans, Iraqis, Mauritanians who were white as well, but 'true revolutionaries...?' These questions had begun to plague Malcolm X, as the interview reflects. Did black nationalism hold the answer to the black man's problems? He indicated that he needed time to reappraise black nationalism. 'And if you notice, I haven't been using the phrase for several months.' (Cruse 408-9)

Black nationalism, otherwise called African nationalism, or Black Consciousness, are not dead issues in South Africa, contrary to appearances and riddled though they are with massive ambivalence among us. Yet the black intellectual in South Africa is pathetically absent from the debate on nationalism and integrationism. Nor is he offering any guidance as a basis for understanding or exploring the issues among the populace. White intellectuals, on the other hand, are too nervous, lest they be misunderstood to be advocating the status quo before democratic government. To complicate matters even further are concepts such as 'reconciliation', 'forgiveness', 'non-racialism' and 'socialism', which are being bandied about. All well intended, but also facile, comforting terms that serve to postpone indefinitely issues concerned with identity – being African beyond geographic location, reconciliation between nationalism, socialism and non-racialism, integration and so on.

Our intellectuals used to be fearful of arrest and detention without trial if they spoke out or produced militant literature. Today they are fearful of offending the Government of National Unity if they were to pronounce a warning against mindless, hasty integration, or against irresponsible cultural assimilation of white values. The intellectual still bows his head in the face of the tyranny of the text, afraid of radically criticizing what he reads.

We are also still scared of openly questioning among ourselves the received notions concerning 'committed' art or *la literature engagée;* 'aesthetic standards' of the Western world; the relation between private and public art and so on. To quote Cruse once more about the American scene, which has a bearing on the South African dilemma:

> *The Negro writer has progressively lost his ability to deal with Negro reality. He has been hemmed in by the protest tradition and inhibited against writing objectively because he is afraid of his own truths; tongue-tied about the social implications of middle-class values in Negro life and his own relation to such values. But the root of the problem here is that the Negro dramatist has no theatre institutions that he is bound to defend, and no cultured middle class to defend them. These are the bitter fruits of racial integration on the cultural plane.* (Cruse 412)

The general correspondences suggested here between the two black worlds revolve around black consciousness (lower case 'c'). We in South Africa lost our ability to deal with our reality beyond white savagery, protest and the mounting institutional violence that resulted. We have been afraid of our own truths, hiding behind the stark and visible fact of white tyranny. Understandably, preoccupations with mass rallies and guerrilla activism sapped our energies and left us little which could elevate our arts above the 'freedom agenda', a programme that would seek to send our bleeding words into the battlefield several times over. It wasn't racial integration, as Cruse says of the African American context. Rather, it was the opposite with us: stark naked apartheid. For this we needed to have 'razors between our teeth'. With the removal of at least formal statutory apartheid, we have now entered an era of institutional integration and assimilation. Because we lost our traditional myths with their poetic resonances and prophecy in the deepest sense of that word, we have forfeited the very heritage that would have offered us an anchor.

And so we composed bitter high-voltage lyrics laced with the apocalyptic line, very much in the tradition of the 1960s in black America. We told ourselves we were committed militants and invested every gram of our emotional energy, all the muscle we could build into the written word, in whatever we produced. We believed – without expressing it – that by some mystical chemistry the rhetoric could secure our emotional and spiritual survival. Because our integrity as a people was at stake. And now, alas, the target of our fighting talk has shifted. We can already foresee a manifestation of the fact that capitalism, graft and political dishonesty have no race or colour...

This brings with it its own contradictions. We could easily rationalize ourselves out of the dilemma. We could say we were producing populist lyrics, that no canon says today's verse should work for tomorrow; that populist verse and drama will emerge from time to time, minted out of the socio-political conditions and perceptions of any particular time. But this would still not free us from the responsibility of exploring the deeper and more enduring realities of our lives: our Africanity and Africanism, that sense of ourselves whose traditional value systems are still alive, if we can only tap the collective memory and unconscious and re-evaluate them; the erosion of our own humanity by internecine violence; our resilience, our triumphs...

A considerable part of African American literature that came out of the furnaces and off the anvil of the 1960s and 1970s has informed successive levels of consciousness and literary intelligence that both writer and reader share. I'm sure that, although writers may feel driven by the urgency and significance of what they are saying – or by the agony of the instant – they are happy if years later their work remains influential, whatever we may mean when we talk about a writer's or artist's 'influence'.

The dramatists of that era do not seem to have fared well down the decades because the genre demands an immediate, visual response, as well as speaking to events of immediate relevance.

The fiction and the poetry have come through all right when they probe deeper levels of meaning. Besides, the worlds of poetry and fiction – often overlapping – do not have to be squeezed into the framework of theatre and all that goes with it. To pick only a few poets whose voices have become inseparable from the literary register of the second half of the 20th century, the following have continued to echo through the years: Gwendolyn Brooks, Margaret Walker, Man Evans, Sonia Sanchez, Dudley Randall, Audre Lorde, Lance Jaffers, Amiri Baraka, Margaret Danner, James A Emmanuel, Conrad Kent Rivers, Lucille Clifton, Maya Angelou, Etheridge Knight, Larry Neal, Carolyn Rodgers, Eugene Redmond, Julia Fields, David Henderson, Nikki Giovanni, Shirley Williams, Sherley Anne Williams, Michael Harper, Quincy Troupe, Askia Muhammad Toure, Samuel Allen, David Henderson, Charles Patterson, Sterling Plumpp. Among the pillars of the bridge between the pre-1960s and this side of the line are Allen, Brooks, Walker, Randall – again picking only few. The poets of every decade before the 1960s are still holding their own, especially in Afro-American studies.

It was Gwendolyn Brooks who said in the foreword to *New Negro Poets USA,* edited by Langston Hughes: 'At the present time, poets who happen also to be Negroes are twice tried. They have to write poetry, and they have to remember that they are Negroes. Often they wish that they could solve the Negro question once and for all, and go on from such success to the composition of textured sonnets or buoyant villanelles about the transience of a raindrop. The raindrop may seem to them to represent racial tears – and those might seem, indeed, other than transient. The golden sun might remind them that they are burning.' (Hughes, 13)

It has been my own experience that one cannot sustain indefinitely in one's writing a tug-of-war of oppositionist tensions. Something must give. History has a free ride on time and isn't going to hesitate to climb on and move. I used to pour out all the gall I had into my writing in the 1950s. Exile rescued me, or maybe history would have eventually anyway. So I share fully Brooks's sentiments. Could her 1964 comment have been a precursor of the socio-aesthetic developments of the latter half of the 1970s and thereafter?

Houston Baker Jr assures us of this transformation. 'The distinctive cultural circumstances' of Afro-American life, he tells us, and the economics generated by slavery were factors that led the spokesmen for the Black Aesthetic to regard them as the root of a distinctively 'black folk consciousness.' To translate this profound awareness into forms of expressive culture is also to appreciate the intimate relationship between them and folkways, and thus to establish authenticity. The theoreticians of the Black Aesthetic came to formulate the statement 'culture determines consciousness'. (*Blues Ideology*, 84).

Baker contemplates the late Larry Neal's essay, *The Black Contribution to American Letters: The Writer as Activist –1960 and After* as a critique of the nationalism that started the African American's intellectual quest for his African past and folk origins. It is necessary for nationalism, according to Neal, that it justifies itself by heeding the voice of history. Especially so when oppression is aided by the destruction of the underdog's traditional culture and suppression of the latter's 'intellectual achievements'. The champions of the Black Aesthetic, says Baker, thus responded to the fear of such destruction 'in racial terms' by shouting its protest (and apocalyptic message) against the enemy.

Neal's turnabout at this point occurred when he began to see things in a new light: he now saw nationalist protest in the Black Aesthetic as a distorted 'Marxist literary theory in which the concept of race is substituted for the Marxist idea of class. Neal saw the black man's political struggle as a severely limiting (often even stultifying and distorting) force in its influence on black literature. 'Unlike black music,' black literature 'has rarely been allowed to exist on its own terms, but rather [has] been utilized as a means of public relations in the struggle for human rights.' (*Blues Ideology*, 85)

One wonders if arguments such as Neal's, and those of his supporters, had the desired persuasive effect on writers. Some of us have said similar things in South Africa in the late 1960s and throughout the 1970s and 1980s, when black writers were banned and tortured by the security police. Black Consciousness as an ideology expressing itself through self-help community programmes inspired by Steve Biko and his comrades lived but a decade (1967-1977), ending abruptly with Steve Biko's murder in police cells and the subsequent banning of the programmes. But several young poets are still writing under the impulse of that message, inspired by the search for identity, for the essence of being black and the values we must assert through black leadership.

Judging by the tentative suggestions of a stance approaching an integrationist plea that we observe in a few poems of the 1990s, e.g. Mongane Serote's long poem, *Third World Express*, it will be interesting to see what is happening to the impetus Black Consciousness has sustained for at least two decades. Serote was in the forefront of the Black Consciousness movement from its beginnings until he went into exile in the 1970s. Clearly membership in the African National Congress, the latter's multi-racial composition and policy of non-racialism developed since the early 1950s will have exerted some influence on him and some of his contemporaries.

Another common strain running in the literature of the two black worlds is what I like to call poetry-turned-theatre. Just as black Americans were producing fiery verse in the 1960s to be recited on stage to the accompaniment of the long drums, so in South Africa too our verse writers listened to their own imperious muse. They listened and obeyed. And they still do. Some of our performances work, many more don't. In the latter case the reasons are that spoken verse often serves as a substitute for the more arduous crafting of a poem that will read well, plus speak eloquently; that as a result we write shoddy diction because we'll orchestrate the recitation with loud percussion and wind instruments, and it won't matter that the audience do not hear. They will greet you and thank you with thunderous applause. The general mood is the thing, not words or phrases and their full import and resonance.

Those who speak their verse in a vernacular are in a better position to improve their performance. So dislocated is our cultural heritage that we tend to ignore the fact that in the oral tradition the village poet chose his idiom with artistic acumen. Similarly we discredit ourselves as performing poets if we do not rehearse with something near professionalism. The overriding deficiency in our life is lack of theatre houses in the ghettos that we can control, where we can experiment with form and idiom. The number of black performances I attended in the United States, some of which can be heard on commercial disc and tape, had a lot going for them.

There is no parallel in South Africa to the intensive debate that has raged within the African American fellowship of artists and writers, and on the public platform. Talk of 'revolutionary', 'committed', 'relevant' art – we have heard plenty of that, especially over the last two decades. It is almost as if the militant posture itself were an act of rebellion. When life is no longer programmed for us by the white race, when we can wield material resources so that we become more enterprising and proactive, when we can take the initiative in most of the planning that goes into education and cultural activity and so on, when we can learn from the experience of African Americans in the establishment and administration of black institutions of learning and cultural life, then there will be hope for racial integration that will benefit us.

In spite of the absence of any discourse about aesthetics among South African blacks, their poetry has its distinctive themes, and what Stephen Henderson calls in his most instructive book, *Understanding the New Black Poetry* (1973), structure and saturation. It is distinctive, especially in relation to writing by South African whites. It is a distinctiveness that only begins to emerge with poetry inspired by Black Consciousness. Hitherto, our poetry was in *British* English. Since then it does not, like white writing, consciously or by the simple fact of history, become an organic part of the Anglo-Saxon literary mainstream. Diction, rhythm, figurative language, the 'communication of blackness' and fidelity to the observed and intuited truth of the 'Black Experience' separate it from white verse.

Always, however, 'your history demands your heartbeat,' as Sonia Sanchez will constantly remind us. This will indicate that often what distinguishes black writing is, to borrow from Stephen Henderson's vocabulary, the historical saturation in a literary piece. In some poets a theme such as history makes for the surface quality; in others theme *is* style and idiom and movement. South African black poets such as Sipho Sepamla, Mongane Serote, Mazisi Kunene, Keorapetse Kgositsile, Dennis Brutus, Don Mattera, Achmat Dangor, Christopher Van Wyk, Essop Patel, Shabbir Banoobhai, Mafika Gwala and Mandlenkosi Langa offer good examples of the organic unity between theme and style in varying degrees – even within the constraints of conventional English.

The African Americans I have listed offer corresponding examples of that organic unity. There is a considerable degree of intervention by our vernacular languages, however, and the philosophical contemplation (for lack of a better phrase) intrinsic in them. In other words, there is a more direct connection between author and subject in African American poetry, as English is its native language. In South African poetry, the less derivative the style from native English, the greater the degree of distinctiveness. By implication, the African American can kick English idiom around wilfully to subvert its own conventions for what he wants to express. To distinguish South African black poetry, the reader has to examine the intimacy between subject and writer, tone and feeling. Style and speech rhythms are an added dimension that distinguishes black American poetry. But this does not necessarily invalidate poems that are less racially distinguishable, so I'm not making a value judgment or a pre-scriptive statement.

Houston Baker's evaluation of the Black Aesthetic generation finally corresponds to Larry Neal's and Stephen Henderson's most recent revised view. It implies that to cage literary activity in the Black Aesthetic, so that only those who are immersed in the black man's concrete and spiritual reality are qualified to critique African American expressive culture, is to limit its growth. Black poetry, Henderson insists, 'can and should be judged by the same standards that any other poetry is judged by – by those standards which validly arise out of a culture.' Baker further observes that not all Black Aesthetic advocates revised their canon. But it ran out of gas because the ideology of Black Power and the nation it had hoped to shape did not materialize.

Addison Gayle Jr, another protagonist of the Black Aesthetic, admits in his anthology of essays *The Black Aesthetic* (1971) that not all the contributors hold his views about the critical canon. I have no way of knowing where he stands today. In the absence of any exclusively black canon in South Africa that has become public debate, not even in the indigenous languages, we have continued along empirical lines. All the same the cultural origins of a work have become a more intimate and conscious concern to the writer. Recently there has been a call for writers not to be enslaved by convention. This implies the dominant English-language canon. Yet not all practitioners would hold what I consider the commonsense view – that *people* and *not poems* march, crusade, go to battle; that revolution does not wait for a writer to create militant poems, plays or novels or short stories; that you earn your place in a revolution by being among other men and women. Much in our country is going to develop according to the success or failure of this freedom time and its nation-building effort. Most of this effort has to do with economic advancement, the scourge of poverty, ignorance, homelessness, unemployment and so on.

I have noted points of contact, emotional, intellectual and physical, between African Americans and Africans continent-wide. I have done this in an effort to clear my own mind about what my American experience has done for me over the years. I have kept asking myself: what it is we expect from each side of the Atlantic? Those early acquaintances between us were at once tentative and functional. They were not merely informed by a soul brotherhood. In a rather mystical way, though, we South Africans clung to the image of a people who, in spite of their two hundred and fifty years in captivity, yet symbolized for us a beacon of hope in our life of darkness. Without knowing the history of slavery fully, nor the details of the African American struggle, we simply believed that pictures we saw of white prosperity and the African American music we enjoyed were intertwined. Blacks have *got* to be doing well, we concluded. Blues? Well, we always regarded that as the expression of a private grief, a sense of loss, a thing apart from the public image we cherished.

Whenever I went to Lincoln, Wilberforce, Howard, Atlanta, Dillard or Houston on lecture visits from my base in Denver or Philadelphia, I felt I was walking the campus pathways that were once the stomping ground of great men and women from my country. Men and women who, like Dr John Dube, Charlotte Maxeke and many others, came back to found institutions and organizations that recalled and in some ways reconstructed some of their American experience. The invisible footprints took on an awesome, near-sacred historical meaning for me.

How I would have loved to record the intellectual and aesthetic experiences that have enriched my life since 1948, when I began to read African American literature: the inexhaustible literary treasure troves that it has been my privilege to 'plunder'. I have not even mentioned the bulk of these novelists and dramatists and essayists. But I would have had to sacrifice a lot in the process of the encounter; maybe even come out with an essay of a doubtful pedigree. Still more, I would prefer to leave exhaustive literary comments to those better equipped for the task.

SOCIAL
CONSCIOUSNESS

Community Development for Self-Knowledge, Self-Realization and Collective Empowerment – 1992

Synopsis by Peter Thuynsma

Several of the essays collected in this section on Social Consciousness revolve around Mphahlele's championing of the moral principles and practicalities of a unifying, respectful system of African philosophy. Notes Towards an Introduction to African Humanism – A Personal Enquiry *(see Part 2: African Humanism) and* Education for Community Development *(see Part 1: Education) are prime examples that deserve time from the reader; in some ways these discussions are companion pieces – certainly the three could be read consecutively. This essay, however, delivered as it was to a keen audience of people who are and had been fully committed to community education under severe circumstances for several years – the occasion is the celebration of the Council for Black Education and Research (CBER) Cape Town Branch – is a bold development upon the notions expressed in its complementary discussions. Here Mphahlele addresses, head on, the stark educational realities of an impending democracy. Nevertheless, as in so many of his works, this discussion is also an intimate casual conversation.*

Here Mphahlele is deeply concerned with the apparent decline in African family values and, consequently, the erosion of community cohesiveness as a direct response to apartheid's political tyranny. He develops his thesis around the need to strengthen the family as the most elementary unit in a community, and proposes nine strategies for recharging and invigorating values. Thus he moves towards developing a viable and sustainable ethos for South Africa's imminent democracy – for both urban and rural dwellers. Poised on such a precipice, Mphahlele declares that community development will require a new awareness: one that will demand proactive development rather than the previous reactions to political claustrophobia. Why?

'…what if the state has abdicated its responsibility? What guarantees do we have that future governments will want to build most of the schools we want? Furthermore, I would not entrust a people's welfare and education wholly to State-run institutions. Let governments give community projects money, yes, but leave us to manage them. Governments have made a mess of things by monitoring welfare, health and educational services to stagna-

tion. It is in these institutions where the educator, social worker and health worker can give community enterprise a human dimension. It is here that self-help initiatives can train us to speak for ourselves, experiment with and develop our own ideas, instead of always responding to government policy.'

E veryone who is fifty and over must have observed the rapid decline in the quality of family life among our African people since World War Two. Of course, African family life has undergone systematic destruction ever since the discovery of gold and diamonds, and mining and city industries called for increasingly intensive but cheaply acquired labour. Because so much land had been stolen from us, and we had been pushed into the Reserves that could no longer carry a fast-growing rural population, migrant labour was easy for the new capitalism to obtain. Migrant labour was to become an acceptable institution in both mining and government circles. To hell with the devastating toll it had on family life!

We came to the towns and cities and mines. We saw. But unlike the ancient Romans, we conquered nothing. Instead, we came as a conquered people. The family tried courageously to hold together in spite of these forces that were tearing it apart. When I was a herd boy in the Northern Transvaal, I gathered from conversation among the age group that had been to cities such as Pretoria and Johannesburg to work as messengers, domestics and miners, that they were proud of their mining experiences. They had been initiated into the white man's world, and this status gave them a sense of self-importance, even superiority over those they had left behind. After circumcision, this was the next big initiation into adulthood for them.

Only in later years did it occur to me what a misplaced, yet quite logical, sense of achievement it was that motivated able-bodied young men to go out and hire themselves out to the white world, simply because of landlessness and diminishing chances of eking out a living on what was left. In the process the age-old foundations of family life were being violently shaken up; at the same time the to-and-fro movement of males between home and single-sex compounds were undermining our cherished family values. As the pass laws and their offshoot, influx control, became more and more savage, the family suffered severer stresses. Its members, wherever they were, found other groups that could give them a sense of identity. The sentimental attachment to 'home' in the rural areas tried to hold out, until there was little or nothing there to be sentimental about except one's relations, now quite elderly. Only the collective memory remained. Ironically and subconsciously, it still monitors the conduct of those who had more than just a taste of a rural upbringing.

Political tyranny, which included summary arrests, detention without trial and long jail terms, caused several thousands to flee into exile – all in a matter of some thirty years, since the latter part of the 1950s. And blistering tensions increased within families, some to breaking point. For all those who have been released from prison, and for the former exiles, too, family life can never be the same again. All will now be trying to piece together the broken strands of a life disorganized by long absences from home, by years of longing and frustration and loss of community.

Such is the enduring strength of traditional African humanism, however – with its emphasis on social relationships – the family ties undergo constant cycles of renewal, even while some family members try consciously to cut loose. Physical contact with family will never be the same as in traditional communities, but events that call for ritual always bring the family, local or extended, together. Marriage, death, celebration or veneration of ancestral ties and protection are occasions for this kind of renewal. In an almost miraculous way, word travels to the extended family members, no matter how far-flung, across provincial boundaries, and lines of communication are kept alive.

The family now finds itself harassed by a sense of insecurity – economic and political. This lack of stability filters through to the family from the tremors we feel in most of our communities today, some external, some internalised: the violence, the dead-end politics of our time, the fraud, theft and embezzlement in high government circles. Rocketing prices of consumer goods and homelessness also generate some of these tremors.

What is it that we would most love to see happen to establish the social context in which family life can be re-ordered, even restructured, for the happiest interests of its members and community? Let's remind ourselves of the qualities of an ideal family, some of which are venerated by tradition, some of which refer to the newer kind of family. Such a family is one:

1. whose members are accountable to one another;
2. whose members are either at school or are working, if they are not invalids or physically disabled or pensioned;
3. where both parents or a single parent, or the older children – when parents are either temporarily or permanently absent – assume leadership in the home;
4. where the members empower themselves to provide general education for the whole family, especially in the cases where parents are not literate enough to monitor the children's school work;
5. where harmony prevails; where conflicts, emotional outbursts are contained and amicably resolved;
6. where the members take some appreciative interest in one another's work and pastimes;
7. where from time to time the members sit together and list their collective strengths. In the process the family considers what strengths they can develop still further;

187

8. where from time to time they do things or visit together;
9. where every member feels disposed and free to share experiences, so that the home can be seen as an extra educational resource for the enlargement of the family's understanding of itself and of its own community, immediate and extended.

We, the motivators of services that embrace family life, among other things, can amplify these nine points by way of an in-depth investigation of ourselves as communities.

I have begun this address by discussing the family, the latter being an elementary unit of the community, next after the individual. We might consider community organization as the immediate forerunner to community development, both of which are central to my talk. The Council for Black Education and Research (CBER), both here (Western Cape) and in Johannesburg – and as it was in Pretoria under the leadership of the late Mrs Dora Nkamane – is a community development project. Our target groups are adults, youth, and those preparing for adulthood.

You organize a project, for instance, enlisting the support of some members of the community who share your interests and vision. I find it necessary to emphasize the origins of an idea that eventually becomes the property of the community at large. Out of sheer obsession with democracy as an idea – an abstraction – some self-appointed political faction will often insist that a group of persons who want to translate an individual's idea into a concrete programme first seek its permission to do so. The faction's purpose is undoubtedly to assert its own political supremacy, real or imagined.

And yet the natural path is actually for a project first to take root, driven by a small group of persons who then solicit further ideas from those members of the community whose real strengths are known at a practical level, rather than conferred by 'democratic' elections. It is not difficult to imagine that a committee may be democratically elected but still turn out to be a mix of crooked, indolent, self-seeking but highly articulate, popular figures who happen to be politically 'correct'. A time may come when a project deems it proper, because it has developed strong legs, so to speak, to exercise controlled democracy in selecting its board of management. The most important prerequisite is that its goals be inspired by the highest ideals that we have come to associate with community development. There may be similar, diverse projects in the community, even variations of a particular one. Collectively all these cultivate an awareness among the members of the community of, shall we say, Gugulethu or Langa or Nyanga; an awareness of their own needs and capacity (or lack of it) to deal with their immediate socio-economic problems. Still collectively, the projects stimulate self-help, self-realization and can even lead to the creation of a community chest.

Now, brutal realities exist in our townships that cripple many self-help ventures and excellent ideas for community development at birth. These realities are related to sectional political divisions. It becomes immediately imperative for us to consider the first item on the agenda for community organization as 'community organization towards a unified vision of the road ahead.' Here we could discuss concrete practical strategies for the resolution of sectarian political conflicts. We may even devote several meetings to such a topic. Even if we find the constitution of the group to be one-sided, the agenda must go on. We must simply appreciate that we have to go through a process of evolution, discussion and interaction being part of it.

Some of the major difficulties in African urban community organization in South Africa are: the fact of political strife among blacks, self-generated or incited by a third force; poverty and/or survival consumer economics; and the overarching fact that we are strangers in urban life, even though several of us may be third-generation inhabitants. There is also that part of urban life that does not express us in the fullest sense of the phrase. I mean that we did not choose to live in these ghettos, but were dumped here. Had we created our own urban environment in the first place we would be proud and ready to mobilize our human resources, in spite of our underdeveloped economics, because our commitment to such an environment would be above reproach.

The cosmopolitan nature of our urban townships is forever changing, as new inhabitants enter and shantytowns, which may sooner or later become permanent, spring up. We are generally slow to volunteer services in welfare and educational work. It may be argued that volunteering community service is a typically middle-class way of extending oneself, for people who have surplus time and a relatively comfortable income. That may be. But must this mean, then, that such development has to wait until a middle-class evolves?

In the rural areas communities are more homogeneous, and people are still good listeners and will hear you out if you have a proposition for community organization and development. But you have to be a 'native' son or daughter, or something close to that, in a manner of speaking. They don't easily take to perceived 'outsiders' initiating a project, although we must admit that rejection is not absolute: one simply has to work harder to be accepted. I am optimistic, too, that this is a passing phase, inasmuch as the whole rural landscape is rapidly changing.

May I make the following remarks concerning the origins of community awareness:

1. Both in urban and rural areas there will be individuals who have an extraordinarily heightened and passionate concern for people; they identify problems, and a problem-solving cause is relatively easier to get across to one's audience than a mere brain-wave that brings people together purely for the sake of fellowship. It is to the credit of our women that they have initiated self-help projects in their communities, and are still serving in positions of leadership and as the general membership of other establishments.

2. Initiators or pioneers of community projects display an instinct for priorities in any catalogue of social causes: they also display a restlessness born of the idea that fired their imagination in the first place.
3. They are knowledgeable about contacts with civics, educational agencies, funding establishments and mass media. I'm talking here mostly about natural leaders, among them teachers, nurses, doctors, lawyers, social workers, trade unionists, artisans and so on. Generally, people who are sensitised about human concerns because their occupations bring them close to the people.
4. There is a need for us to form study groups in our communities that can be a resource for initiators of projects intended to serve them.
5. We should harness the energies of survival support groups, such as burial and benefit societies, so as to cultivate among them a social conscience and consciousness that go beyond basic survival. They could use the interest on their group savings for worthy causes.

I am always deeply moved by rural and semi-rural village communities that collect money from their lean savings to build a school. By contrast I have heard urbanites, among them highly placed political activists who should know better, say they are not going to involve themselves with non-governmental organizations engaged in providing alternative and non-formal education. The reason they give is that this is a State responsibility.

I do not deny this. But what if the State has abdicated its responsibility? What guarantees do we have that future governments will want to build most of the schools we want? Furthermore, I would not entrust a people's welfare and education wholly to State-run institutions. Let governments give community projects money, yes; but leave us to manage them. Governments have made a mess of things by monitoring welfare, health and educational services to stagnation. It is in these institutions where the educator, social worker and health worker can give community enterprise a human dimension. It is here that self-help initiatives can train us to speak for ourselves, and experiment with and develop our own ideas, instead of always responding to government policy. It is here that we, as CBER, work towards the development of the whole personality, and not only skills and assimilation of social, political and economic theories. It is here that we create a learning environment of our own, where we have a fighting chance to promote the humanistic qualities of education: free of official commands, threats, blackmail, free of examination-driven curricula and the psychological stresses these generate.

A community is often what we make of it. It realizes its status as such through the alignment of individual and group interests, concerns, anxieties, aspirations and goals, into a unified purpose. Let me cite Soweto here as the most difficult place to organize for community development that I have ever worked in, because of a variety of incompatible interest groups. Its political divisions are too stark and fierce for community organizers to comprehend, let alone to reconcile. Soweto sways any way the majority political influence propels it, because it is advertised as such. It is a city that can easily be manipulated by those who have a high media profile. An announcement in a newspaper by a highly visible political constituency carries the weight of the ancient voice of prophecy. Soweto communities are accordingly shaped and delimited by the politics each one embraces. The communities are mobilized not according to the individual's sense of civic responsibility in response to creative ideas, but rather his or her perceived loyalty to an activist cause, in the firm belief that it must always be logically right because it is morally just.

There is no doubt that most of this is the heritage of generations of local non-government. During all these decades, advisory boards, followed by community councils and administration boards delegated by central government, did little more than exercise control with the aid of the pass law and police. The result has been that civic associations are still marching to the beat of activist drums. That we still have viable community services directed by dedicated pockets of leadership in such a fragmented urban life is yet another record of our resilience.

A community can also be nothing more than a state of mind – something vague but expressing a wishful sentiment. The result is the delusion that fancies a community project to be a product of a whole number of interest groups right from the word go. Purely as a state of mind, a community does little or nothing to define its institutions, because it is a delusion. It should be sufficient that a community-based project:

1. stands within the boundaries of a certain township or village, and has been initiated by one or more of its members.
2. is steered by a management board drawn from its community context.
3. does not inherit any credibility but acquires it, earns it, grows up with it. There is little or no credibility in a project based outside the community it purports to serve, with most of its leadership predominantly white, in some cases attached to a white university, so that members of the community must go out there to use it. The sum of (1) and (2) contributes in the first instance to its credibility, but the degree of involvement of community members, however few, must be extensive and intensive.

I am certain that CBER leadership is keenly aware of the social-political-economic tensions they have to deal with. There are forces tugging away in different directions that often frustrate a project's goals, such as those we cherish. But for the benefit of our community and in the interests of greater clarity – and so that we constantly remind ourselves of what we are dealing with – I would like to list a few of these agents of tension:

1. Poverty that dogs our people all the time.
2. Unfulfilled political and economic expectations; the long history of our hostage condition on this peninsula, where community initiative either fails to take off or barely survives.
3. The education crisis, which has assumed the nature of a disaster area, and thereby almost a separate life of its own.
4. The silence that is so common among our people, whether we be rural or urban communities. I mean the silence that defies questions such as: what do 'the people' think? How do 'the people' respond to so much corruption at all levels of local, provincial and central government, in the schools, in business and commerce, in the sports arena, and so on? How can 'the people' watch open corruption and continue to be so silent, except when they take to the streets or stage sit-ins, where individual voices can be comfortably subdued, safe in their anonymity?
5. The weak links in our sense of identification with our respective communities, so far away from the traditional roots that enriched rural societies, and yet so peripheral to the white man's towns and cities. I can say this without underplaying the survival strategies I mentioned earlier, nor exaggerating their present-day significance.

This is where community ventures, both rural and urban, can buttress individual strengths, while at the same time seeking to liberate them. When such strengths are liberated, they expand and win more and more territory, and increase our moral and intellectual resources, our sense of selfhood. May CBER's mission continue to enlarge its vision, at a time when we are surrounded by so many enemies of progress, so many demons that work against the human spirit, from without and within our communities; and at a time when a considerable number of public and private sectors tend to fund NGOs that work within formal traditional structures, because they are 'safe'. Those that truly reflect the native creative energy, drive and initiative of community life are not given priority. And the nagging question remains: what are they afraid of, if not the possibility that we could succeed so well that we would no longer be dependent on the white man's leadership, trusteeship and ideas? CBER is this kind of project, that will move on the momentum of its own vision; for this we must be grateful.

My Friend, Gerard Sekoto[1] – 1990

Master of Ceremonies, distinguished guests and fellow art lovers, I am delighted to be here for yet another opening of a Gerard Sekoto exhibition – especially after I enjoyed the opportunity of opening the Johannesburg event last October.

What has been to me always extraordinary about Gerard is his resilience. While World War Two was raging in Europe and North Africa, he was teaching and painting. We can observe clearly from the work of the 1940s how successfully he has tamed his environment, its ugly and distressing immediacy; how he has subdued the disorganized world around him: the world of poverty, poor housing and struggle, broken up by only a few shafts of daylight we can identify as cheerful moments. In a sense, as in the case of all art, Gerard was fleeing from the coarseness of raw reality into the protective, if often painful, embrace of art. For even while there is exhilarating, delectable contentment in having mastered materials and the use of line and light, you are held to ransom by a goddess that says: 'You're free to go if you like, but I know you wouldn't dare... for your own inner freedom...'

It is precisely here, as we can perceive, that the analogy of escape into one's art gives way to another irony. For here the artist must live in perpetual restlessness, perpetual hunger after an ideal; he must live and endure for a purpose he can only partially fathom.

It is one of the mysteries of aesthetics, isn't it, that we can respond to good art with intensity of feeling and sharp awareness that somehow compensate – during those moments of passionate perception – for the chaos around us, the drudgery and banality of our lives? The aesthetic experience in no way resolves the violence that is even at this moment stalking our lives, leaving behind smouldering ruins and bodies. But art reminds us repeatedly that even while storms rage around us, children are being born, we still fall in love, make love, a woman still sits on the roadside suckling a baby, humanity still needs abundant compassion. We are increased and revitalized by the sedate, even spare, colours of Gerard Sekoto that have a cumulative intensity.

Again, we live truncated lives in which our experiences become routine, fragmented responses to our living conditions. We therefore need pauses of this kind to contemplate art that speaks to us in Sekoto's language, to re-establish in ourselves a sense of continuity, of perpetuity. It is a sense of continuity that clarifies our experiences for ourselves. Sekoto's work itself brings home to us, through its phases marked

1 The original title of this essay was: 'Addess To Open The Exhibition Of Paintings By Gerard Sekoto At The Art Museum, Pietermaritzburg'.

by his changes in residence, personal development and style, a sense of logical sequence, of organic existence.

There are the figures and scenes that mark his beginnings on home ground; then a transition period during which he is exposed to the Parisian environment – at once seductive, coquettish and impossible to possess. He could possess the freedom of the boulevards, the bistros, the parks and the banks of the River Seine. But he could not conquer the art galleries, the art schools and the inner circles of French intellectual life. Always the European-African encounter has posed questions only the latter must resolve, and which the European as host can afford to ignore. But Sekoto kept an even temper most of the time.

Then there is the phase in Sekoto's work that demonstrates a painful struggle to reach back to Africa. In the two years, 1961-63, during which he, Breyten Breytenbach and my family lived close to each other on the Left Bank in Paris and in affectionate companionship, we tried to motivate Gerard to visit Africa for a protracted stay. His colours were greying, taking on a metallic coldness. It seemed thirteen years of exile were beginning to tell on him. He was sending out his works to galleries outside Paris, even to New York and Johannesburg. A one-man Paris show seemed forever out of his reach.

He looked disarmingly apprehensive when we suggested he might return home or go to Ethiopia, wherever, where he could work with other artists and refuel, so to speak. Gerard settled for Senegal. His Senegalese period yielded work that was a complete departure from the Sekoto known to those of us who had seen him perform in the 1940s. We see tall, slender figures that seem to derive definition and life from the haze of the harmattan, from atmosphere: Senegalese attire and poise.

I had known Gerard slightly when I was a teenager in Marabastad, Pretoria, and he was a teacher in Eastwood, Pretoria, and just outside Pietersburg. We have not seen him these past twenty years since our Paris-based companionship and subsequent occasional visits to Europe. His letters still exude the warmth, gentility, gentleness and abundant sense of being that have always characterized him.

Exile for black people on this continent is a recently motivated experience. A few Africans have found themselves in Europe as products of the slave era, and later as descendants of some line of wealthy families. Sekoto was one of the South African pioneers, after the novelist Peter Abrahams, who left these shores in 1939, and the sculptor Mancobe. I do not imagine that there is a condition of exile anywhere that is without its own peculiar pain. This is the case when one takes a leap out of one culture into another where the individual has already become alienated by industrialization; perhaps even by one's pursuit of a career such as art, that is not accommodated by the white cultural establishment for financial support.

One is thrown upon one's ego, pressing upon it to an excruciating degree. This is the suffering of the exile. Miguel de Unamuno says in *The Tragic Sense of Life*:

Suffering is the path of consciousness, and by it living beings arrive at the possession of self-consciousness. For to possess consciousness of oneself, to possess personality is to know oneself and to feel oneself distinct from other beings, and this feeling of distinction is only reached through an act of collision, through suffering more or less severe, through the sense of one's own limits. Consciousness of oneself is simply consciousness of one's own limitation. I feel myself when I feel that I am not others; to know and to feel the extent of my being is to know at what point I cease to be, the point beyond which I no longer am.

It follows from this that through suffering, exile makes you constantly aware of your being, your own limits, and at what point you begin to be one of others.

I know Sekoto suffered immensely through the rest of the 1940s and the whole of the 1950s, before he could come to terms with his condition. He was an outsider who could enjoy only partial acceptance by Paris, alongside other African immigrants and students. Other exiles in other parts of the world have not been as hardy as Sekoto. He seldom quarrelled with his condition. He took it in his stride. His work is evidence of that acceptance, which at the same time reorganizes the order of things as he found them: Albert Camus' idea of art as rebellion. Indeed it was response to the question posed by exile that Sekoto was perpetually reaffirming being and life. Nihilism would have no place in his scheme of things.

A most immediately stabilizing influence on Gerard Sekoto in the late 1950s and into the 1960s was his association with *Présence Africaine*. This is a journal of literature and the arts of the black world, founded in 1947 by the Society of African Culture. It is based in Paris and Dakar. He found companionship among students and immigrant intellectuals from the French colonies in Africa, the Caribbean, Madagascar and Mauritius. The dominant ideology for cultural nationalism was negritude, the essence and importance of being African, of being a member of *le monde noir* – the Negro world. Negritude came to refer to the amalgam of traditional African values, even for those blacks who were descendants of slaves in the West and East Indies. Negritude's intention was to inspire Africans to return to their roots – largely an emotional and intellectual journey. As long as Negritude did not try to programme African arts, its message carried a profound meaning for the cultural renaissance of Negro peoples. Gerard needed this kind of stabilization in the 1960s. It protected him from irredeemable assimilation into French culture, while it also helped him to monitor the synthesis that must happen in the African if he is to emerge as an integrated personality. From such an artist we can expect a splendidly controlled vision.

How I wish Gerard were here with us to see himself home again in one composite exhibition: home again after several items have been collected from owners across the country, home again on his native soil surrounded by admirers, friends, and well-wishers; home again and out of the rain where he has stood for so long.

No work of art can stop a bullet, or panga or axe. But as a humanist, I cannot but believe that knowledge deriving from free inquiry breeds more knowledge and ideas, even if they may not be genetically predetermined. 'The great adventure of the mind,' as Albert Camus rightly refers to the process. Art, through education, and as process as well as products for the gallery, can constantly remind us that violence to a fellow human is violence to one's own self, a process of dying within the perpetrator, a negation of life and being in direct opposition to what we see around us here this evening. Such knowledge is chastening; it can purge us of the demons that colonize every piece of territory where they find ignorance and insensitivity.

From Dependence to Interdependence:
Towards Nation Building – 1990

Synopsis by James Ogude

This article is about the challenges of nation building facing black South Africans after decades of colonialism and apartheid oppression, which has led to massive dependence on whites. Mphahlele traces the roots of dependency syndrome – described as a condition of relying on someone else – to that moment when colonialism seized the initiative away from black owners of the land, grabbed wide tracts of the African soil, captured its spiritual being and established its authority over the populace through sheer brutal force and political duplicity. And yet the article's compelling tone and tenor of argument directs attention away from the debilitating feeling – that condition of perpetual paralysis – that dependency syndrome often creates among the colonized subject. Instead, the article calls for an awareness of the enduring problems rooted in the apartheid legacy – not so as to weigh us down, but rather to inspire a greater sense of responsibility and duty, and imaginative and creative ways of dealing with what is undoubtedly a dreadful past that is threatening to explode the dreams of a new society.

Written before the 1994 democratic elections, this article warns the oppressed blacks that although the major pillars of the apartheid regime have been brought down, the struggle for genuine nation formation is likely to be a protracted one. The article argues that white supremacy and apartheid structures are likely to hold sway in spite of the political rhetoric that tends to create an illusion of a radical rupture with the past. The search for answers – true decolonisation – Mphahlele insists, must begin with us blacks. The restoration of social agency to the oppressed blacks is at the heart of Mphahlele's message, and introspection would have to underpin the project of restoration.

The article spells out two major areas that need urgent re-engineering. It draws attention to the poverty of vision that has characterized black struggles here in South Africa, even when all signs in our past history of struggle scream out in desperation for alternative structures that would serve as the basis for reconstructing a new and free society. The black student movements, like SASO, signalled the necessity for alternative vision when they broke ranks with the National Union of South African Students. This alternative vision was eloquently articulated, among others, by Steve Biko, who maintained that blacks would have to create their own alternative institutions to survive. The article also draws attention to another related point, namely the black people's total dependence on whites for moral guidance and intellectual resources, among other things. The point made is that so long as blacks continue to be beggars of ideas and moral authority, so long will they continue to remain in servitude. The challenge lies in re-conceptualising the idea of struggle beyond the grand resistance that has tended to define it over the years, to seeing it as a complex process, often driven by keen negotiation and shifting of strategies which may involve weighing of options open to us at every turn. These often require learning how to speak to power/authority, and learning to create small but alternative structures away from officialdom. Indeed, Mphahlele reminds us that if there is anything to learn from the African American experience, it is that a sustainable liberation project is built by creating pressure groups and institutions of civil society that are likely to carry black people's emancipation in South Africa beyond mass rallies.

Finally, the article makes a compelling case for a critical re-assessment of the principles upon which the educational system in South Africa rests, and specifically calls for the disengagement of the education debate from the political forum that has tended to detract from its pedagogical role. It is only by divesting our educational system of political baggage that we will be able to transform it into an instrument of critical pedagogy, rather than a propaganda machine where sectarian interests hold sway and slogans are a substitute for a genuine pursuit of knowledge. The article also calls for the restoration of the voice of authority to teachers; for them to be re-instated on the centre-stage of learning as the ultimate custodians of learnership. To this end, a teachers' centre in which a three-way dialogue between university lecturers and primary and high school teachers could take place is suggested, to harness and stimulate knowledge of and about blacks. When we start to do all these, Mphahlele argues, then true decolonisation will have begun.

T he tensions that have been building up in this country since 1948 are loosening. Now we must be ready for others: the tensions of reconstruction. For let us not forget we are children of the storm – of a long drawn-out political war we always feared might explode into a gruelling, blood-spilling holocaust.

F W de Klerk's removal of a number of apartheid laws and his release of several political prisoners, not least among them those who were in for life or on death row, has created an atmosphere of ecstasy. Yesterday a portion of the world was shouting abuse against South Africa from international forums. Today, congratulations are streaming in from various corners. Even some of our leaders have cast a halo around De Klerk's head for having done what no Afrikaner ever dared to do. If De Klerk is correct in telling the rest of the world that ninety-five per cent of apartheid legislation has been repealed, it can only mean that it needed only the remaining five percent to control blacks and maintain white supremacy in the first place. White supremacy still stands; all other laws are a stockpile of amendments granting the government and its police and army powers to deal with black political opponents. We are not impressed. All the same, it is sad to observe that we are not sure anymore whether we are ululating the leaders just released, or De Klerk and his Cabinet who made it possible.

De Klerk has certainly pulled the carpet from under our feet. He has set political activists in this country rushing about to find new ground on which to stand. His decree to erase some of the worst garbage from the Statute Book finds us, alas, without a strategy. Activists here and abroad have grown up in resistance politics. Political tyranny from the State has been ruthless, engaged in hot pursuit after the young and the old. All our energies have been totally obsessed with surviving the barbarism of the white man's rule. Consequently, we have never paused to conceptualise in detail what alternative society we want – beyond what slogans, charters and manifestos indicate. We have spoken vaguely about the following: socialism, capitalism, a unitary state – i.e. free of the appendages called Bantustans and so-called self-governing territories. We have spoken about sell-outs, irrelevant writers and artists, racism, education, economics, capital and several other issues. Yet we do not have a single manifesto that spells out in detail what kind of new society we visualize and have been planning for. What curricula? What philosophy of education? What social theory? What welfare programmes?

Even while we are banging on the gates of privilege, we should be going to the State with strategies for a new education: revolutionized content, new local administration of schools, a permanent system of career guidance, and so on. I am saying that we should go to the State with blueprints for an education system that expresses us. Obviously, we should have been working on alternative structures and strategies at least since the historic time that saw the breakaway of the South African Students' Organization (SASO) from the National Union of South African Students. On that occasion students, including such fiery personalities as Onkgopotse Tiro and Steve Biko, came to the full realization that we were on our own; that we would have to create our own alternative institutions. The banning in 1977 of those community development projects by the notorious police chief Jimmy Kruger, the murder of Steve Biko under police custody, and the assassination of Tiro, are a clear indication of how pathologically scared the white Establishment was. The ruling class was out to kill the spirit of self-reliance SASO had generated at grassroots level.

We have never recovered from that catastrophe. For now, we observe, we have backtracked to the days of white guidance, white money for self-help community projects, white publicity media. The white Establishment programs our responses to State policies. The white media have been behaving as if Nelson Mandela belongs to them, and are not concealing what they expect to hear him say. They run ahead of him, almost programming him to say the things that please them. But just *almost*, for he maintains his integrity and dignity. And yet that 'almost' is worrisome enough...

In what ways are *we* programmed in our responses to government policies? De Klerk announces the release of his prisoners; he unbans our organizations; removes a whole lot of restrictions; and continues to monitor our responses to these events by urging from time to time that the leaders enter into negotiations without preconditions. If he is serious, why not dissolve parliament and its two walkie-talkie chambers for coloureds and Asians? Why not, jointly with blacks, set up a caretaker government of National Coalition to draft a new constitution? Why does he not call off his police dogs that keep shooting up street demonstrators?

It is our dependence on white moral guidance, education, technological and managerial expertise, intellectual resources and so on that concerns me deeply. I use the word 'dependence' to refer to a condition or fact of relying on someone. It goes with influence, control. Dependence or dependency can be short-lived and we may control or end it. It is a healthy state of affairs when dependence can be subjected to certain limits. Dependency, at another level, is like an addiction to alcohol, drugs and so on: a condition we appear not to control, without which our world is unsteady.

The white man came, saw and conquered. His military conquest in South Africa was complete. Then followed his political and economic conquests. He can move us from A to Z without any moral qualms. He controls one hundred per cent of the landmass of the country, for even the thirteen per cent theoretically allocated to us is totally under his control. He plans the economy, the political life of the whole country, the education and so on. He is the modern sophisticated colonialist who governs on the very land he has appropriated. He is in charge of every aspect of our lives, except, in some respects, our spiritual existence. Even so, once the white man had slapped water on the foreheads of our great-grandfathers and their immediate descendants, our souls were branded with a cross. The myth that we are born sinners was going to haunt us forever. And forever we were going to depend on the European's God and Christ for our salvation. Even African preachers came out of the Christian-Judaic training with a mind that still had a long journey to travel before it could domesticate the inherited faith.

I am saying that the dependency syndrome has its roots in colonialism and conversion to the Christian-Judaic faith. Barring the psychological aberration that sometimes reveals itself in the Zionist and messianic sects, I have a sneaking admiration for the latter. They have tried to carve out a corner for themselves where they could independently create a simple kind of worship, free of the tyranny of theology and other intellectual trappings.

We have waited until the white man gave or did things for us. We raved and railed with clenched fists and toyi-toyied and stood on our heads in an effort to make ourselves ungovernable. He jailed us for it. But he knew – and we knew – that power remained with him to give and to do. In time we developed an attitude that the system owes us everything. True enough, because we are a majority being ruled by a minority that stole the land from us, dispossessed us. But we also began to believe that we could wear the white man out; that because majority rule was a non-negotiable right, we need not establish pressure groups on specific issues. This is the way the African-Americans developed pressure-group techniques – something to admire immensely. For, in the process, they created their own institutions, with only a small reliance on white finance and leadership and some State subsidies. They had to, being free from that majority population complex we suffer from which says we must have all or nothing; that only after the revolution and liberation can we begin to create institutions of our own.

And so we keep going back to speak to people in power. We feel contented after-wards that we *told* them: *Re ba boditse*. We were a strong delegation... The Minister simply had to listen to us. The result: if the State refuses to effect changes, to accede to our demands *now*, we don't exert pressure in limited areas where we stand a chance of winning. Even when we want to take up issue with the government in a particular area such as education, we first call a mass rally, or organize mass marches, in the hope that we can demoralize the targeted department.

'*Re ba boditse*', we keep saying, '*Re ba bolelletse rona...*' It is our traditional belief that the spoken word has mystical power: it can change the listener's attitudes or point of view. We may often be aware that such power does not work in the face of naked tyranny, racism, and foxy manoeuvres that come from another culture altogether. As Africans we know only too well that '*O ka se kgone go loya motho yo a sa dumeleng boloing*' (You cannot succeed in trying to bewitch a person who doesn't believe in witchcraft).

Yes, we may tell a cabinet minister that we are entitled to the national resources he is in charge of. But over and above this, we must wean ourselves from the dependency syndrome by creating our own alternative structures and systems to serve as our power base. We should develop them into pressure groups all over the country. We must have something of our own whose effectiveness we can be proud of. Then we shall not need to take to the State representative our naked, miserable selves. All he does is recite well-rehearsed answers we already know – often the same lies, all over again.

It would be stupid to ignore the extent to which politics have found fertile breed-ing ground in education. This has been so ever since Verwoerd's ideology vomited over the whole schooling system from the ground floor up. But we are going to have to disengage the education debate from the political forum, where activists seek popularity and to further a sectarian ideology. We must restore to teachers and educationists the territory in which curricula, syllabi, textbook reviews, and school management and organization belong. A teacher is an educator, a classroom practitioner. An educationist is a student of education and analyses its methods, principles, philosophy, direction and so on.

If politically motivated bodies such as the National Education Crisis Committee (NECC) are honest in their concern for better education, they must formally cede to teachers the opportunity to carry on with the tasks referred to above. The NECC and other similar political groups must then create an atmosphere that will promote the empowerment of teachers across sectarian politics to deal with schooling and educational matters. The underlying principle here will be to restore the teacher's self-esteem. As long as the political forum holds on ideologically to initiatives intended to resolve the crisis, so long are school children going to despise their teachers. For it has become more respectable in the eyes of pupils to seem to move with the political times, even at the expense of the learning-teaching process. Thus organizations such as the Pan-African Students Organization, South African National Students Congress, NECC, Azanian Students Movement and so on can act as facilitators behind the scenes in our efforts to mend the rifts between parents and teachers and pupils/students. But let the educationists handle the rest, primarily concerned with the establishment of a healthy learning environment where there will be freedom of speech, of association, of co-existence among diverse political affiliations, of school organization and the content of educational programmes.

Teachers' centres are the proper place in our South African context for us to regroup and do the thorough work of becoming educationists. For the State has done everything in its power to reduce teachers to abject, grovelling civil servants whose unions are equally ineffectual. This has been done by intimidation, expulsions, suspensions, demotions and coercion to teach self-demeaning texts. Now we hear that Inkatha is forcing teachers in schools under the territorial government's authority to become its members. Teachers' centres are places where our energies should be invested, whence the New Education can evolve. This is another alternative institution that should not wait for liberation or a so-called 'normal society'. For generations after that divine event, we shall still be grappling with problems inherited from this era.

What should be the university's role in our critical times? While academic staff from universities should rightly discuss education at their level, we should narrow the gap between themselves and teachers at the lower levels. The teachers' centre in any region should be the common meeting ground for primary school, secondary school, university and college teachers. The university departments should elect representatives to the local teachers' centre committee, but all should be entitled to visit the centre for subject seminars, integrated studies and informal discussion. We have been programmed over the years to maintain a separation between teachers at one level of school and others. To wrench ourselves free from this classification we require an alternative structure.

The University's Black Staff Association should create a standing Commission on Education to research new trends in the science, methods, principles and sociology of education. This should perforce be an interdisciplinary commission, although individual subject committees or societies may be directly involved in research projects based on their specialized studies. The commission should contain students in their junior degree studies, Honours and postgraduate programmes, and staff. As they pass through, the students should elect others. The staff members of the commission will ensure continuity of programmes and research momentum.

A standing Commission on Education will be the custodian of documentation from local sources and other territories, researched papers, and so on. Twice a year the commission will assemble to review the previous six months of work. The commission should be ready to analyse crises such as matriculation failures and retrenchment of teaching staff. It should also keep statistics relating to staff and schools, universities and colleges all over the country, independent and State-controlled. If possible such a commission should be housed on each campus, each branch working out its own strategies and its research programmes according to the needs and nature of its human environment. There should be a paid coordinator on each campus. The university should be obligated to fund the commission with only minimal monitoring of its activities. But, although administratively independent, the commission should avoid being bogged down in bureaucratic inanities and constitutional quibbling. If a campus location and a university-paid coordinator are not possible, funding should be raised to finance such an office in a nearby location where a house can be rented.

A coordinator's work includes the inter-linking of all the campus commissions, and the liasing of their local commission with the nearest teachers' centre. It is vital that the regional teachers' centre work hand in hand with a campus commission. The Funda Centre would be happy to co-operate with a teacher's centre near you and provide information as a preliminary step towards co-operation.

At the end of 1989, the Council for Black Education and Research in Johannesburg offered research fellowships – tenable as of February 1990. There are three senior fellowships. Persons who hold at least an Honours degree and have worked for three years, or possess an MA or Ph.D. and have worked for two years in their disciplines are eligible. The grant is worth R4,800 per month for nine months, full-time. Requirements: writing up a project based on research already completed, or starting a research project. Then there are four junior fellowships available at R5,200 per annum. These are for students registered for a higher degree, after Honours, with a black or 'open' university of long standing. Residence in the PWV (now Gauteng Province) area is essential for the duration of the grant. The tenure in this case is twelve months. The fellowship will be repeated in 1991.

It saddens me to say that we have not received more than one single application from black universities; one has come from the University of the North. There is a disheartening tendency for students to undertake 'soft' research areas – such as the history of this, a history of that: mere narratives of secondary sources without any analysis or any critical approach. This is how programmed we are, even in matters of research.

I mention the Council for Black Education and Research because throughout the twelve and a half years I have been back in this country, I have spoken and urged at various black teachers and community groups/unions, until my tongue hung out, that we work out a philosophy and principles of education that express *us* and not the Master Race. We have enough scholars to constitute a team to do this. I have urged that teachers should scrutinize critically the texts they have to use in the classrooms to sift the chaff from the true gems.

Only in alternative structures can we institutionalise our ideas, and create programmes that will express *us*. To wait for the State to provide is to wait to be accommodated in State structures that already stand discredited. It is alternative structures that will show our great-great-grandchildren that we once tried to beat the system, to project a splendid vision into their times. Because we have to wean ourselves from the dependency I spoke of earlier, we shouldn't care a single cocktail sausage whether or not our alternative structures influence the State or not. *We are not building for the State but for ourselves.* When we have a black majority government, we know our alternative structures will be incorporated into the mainstream system.

And by the way, for the next three generations at least our descendants will still be grappling with the fact of dependency, of decolonisation of the mind. If we do not start today, we shall forever regret it.

In Search of an African Middle Class:
The Case of South Africa – 1993

Synopsis by Ndavhe Ramakuela

In this piece Es'kia Mphahlele attempts to understand how class is defined among black South Africans after most of the apartheid laws have been repealed. The article begins with the story of three black executives, KG, FM and TRB, who have recently found lavish jobs in formerly white companies. Entering into the new world, they all go into their new lives and join the middle class, with expensive cars, houses and multiracial schools, but seem to lack independence or are not rooted firmly in any theory or thinking.

Central to this is the lack of sustainable identities. There is that attraction of white privilege in the suburbs on the one hand, and the rejection by blacks on the other. Worse, the new breed of black middle class does not seem to possess any independence or a sense of values that can be collectively defined. Mphahlele goes back to traditional societies to see what distinguished African from European society, and how each of them saw class differently. To Africans, class was accorded mainly because of one's age, rather than wealth.

In the midst of this apparent confusion, Mphahlele tells stories of other successful black people like Reuel Khoza, Aggrey Klaaste, Nomavenda Mathiane, Peter Vundla and others who have established themselves as independent entrepreneurs in their fields. What is interesting about this breed of the black middle class is the level of independence they have maintained, and that they seem rooted in their communities.

This article looks into what makes the middle class interesting today by showing that most blacks haven't established a collective will to redefine themselves in their own terms. The question still remains: 'Can a new black middle class evolve a set of values for itself based on that collective memory?'

We seek it here, we seek it there, we seek it everywhere. Is it coming, is it real, the damned elusive middle class?

KG works for an advertising consultancy. White-owned. He is quite a big nob as their black[1] advisor-in-residence. The firm pays KG a gross salary of ten thousand

---

1 In this article 'black' is the inclusive term for those traditionally called 'African', officially 'coloured' and variously 'Indian' or 'Asian'. The focal point here is the South African community we traditionally refer to as African, as distinct from usage in official documents and general media, where 'black' refers to this community.

rand per month. FM is a copywriter for another advertiser and takes home a heart-warming cheque of fifteen thousand rand less tax. KG owns a brand-new BMW and FM a Mercedes Benz.

They begin to feel that the ceilings of their four-roomed municipal houses – in Diepkloof, part of Greater Soweto, Alexandra, Daveyton, wherever – are too low for their new status in middle management. A metaphor for frustrated, newly found aspirations and dreams. So, off to white suburbia.

For the first time they run headlong into the economics of real estate, suburban or otherwise: service rates; domestic help that no longer comes cheap, owing to its newly unionised status; general maintenance of the house; new and more furniture and curtains for a much bigger house than they have ever possessed; a larger area to provide security for; strange neighbours, and so on.

TRB is a top dog in industrial relations. He had previously been a mere personnel manager or some equivalent. Now employers have to be more vigilant and astute in the face of a labour force that has for decades generally been discontented. From the newly established right to strike or go slow more discontent is surging, this time more definitive in its targets. So now employers need a black guru in industrial relations who will also serve as a shock absorber. They are prepared to pay plenty to retain him – often fifteen to twenty thousand rand per month.

TRB is now in the money, you think. Rightly so. He reckons that he's ready to join the big league in home ownership: if he earns big, he must think and dream big. Rightly so. Maybe for all the six years his focus was on personnel, he endured a township existence, only getting to own a small, second-hand car. He heaves himself up for the big pole-vault act – house, car and all. Reckons it's time to shake off the smell, muck, dust and cockroaches of his ghetto beginnings. Our friend, together with his peers in the African middle management community all over, may have speculated on the distance they were prepared to travel away from their township life. Amply deserved, too, we reckon; we paid our dues, too, having been so long in the cold weather, so to speak.

The irony is that in all these jobs we are being rewarded for just this role; the unwritten footnote to our job description is: *your job is also to be black*. Good for our public relations, is the implication. We all would like to think that those of us who make the big leap have calculated the financial and social implications of our actions before we move on up. The consequences of miscalculation when we are still such a fragile class can be devastating. Yet if we have to move from here to there, where life may be kinder to us and increase our sense of selfhood and self-esteem, maybe *some* people have got to dare.

It is not difficult to imagine the anguish for the new arrival when, as is already happening, there's no backup yet in adequate savings, and he begins to choke on the economics of his new lifestyle. Maybe he loses his job, this being still a game played by the white man's rules, whose culture he has evolved for himself through the generations. There are no laws yet against racist discrimination, and victimisation at the upper levels of the job market is still rampant. Hence the fragility of this class structure; hence, paradoxically, the greater mobility between jobs, because the new arrival reckons that he has more options than in the days when he was compelled to stick with the same job through thick and thin.

How humiliating when he has to retreat, maybe back to the ghetto! It might just turn out that wiser judgment prevailed among those of his peers who stuck it out in the ghetto, refurbishing their homes or buying a new house on the township fringes. They could give themselves more time and ease to study the currents of change before moving out, if ever.

Financial independence, like any other kind, does not come cheap. Brave and resourceful are those who struck out on their own to establish themselves as consultants in business and commerce, finance, education, social welfare and so on. They had enough credibility to secure loans for the capital outlay from banks and other areas of the private sector. All that remained to be done was convince providers of capital that they could bring the risks down to the bare minimum.

Without articulating it in so many words, members of the emergent class argue self-assuredly. That's the difference between an educated person who has special skills and the less educated, less skilled. We have more options than a lot of other blacks. We have something to market: skills. We might add, without saying it: 'And our blackness, too ...'

Are these new arrivals really part of the emergent black middle class? To what extent, if any, can we say it is distinctively *black* or *African*? Is it like a club you join, but from whose insular culture you can maintain a sane distance? Or are we pushing our way into a white milieu, *the* mainstream of a built-in class structure whose values and rituals we want to assimilate? Is it purely economics that has thrown us into this, to sink or swim, or be content merely with the conspicuous trappings of the new, yet old class: house, car, expensive interracial schools, white suburbia that looks like the ultimate in non-pastoral tranquillity?

You don't get far when you ask career politicians and activists what they think of the emergent middle class. The Marxists among them are pretty confused. They tend to tie themselves up in knots with the rhetoric of historical Marxism, 'enlightened' or 'scientific' or 'revisionist' Marxism, 'liberal socialism' and so on. Much of this is ideological claptrap and comes nowhere near clarifying the realities of our life: our yearnings, dreams, desire to own property, confused priorities regarding book learning as compared to technical education, empowerment to create our own employment as compared to being constantly in the white man's employ, and so on.

Politicians generally gloss over issues and, in an odd journalistic fashion, rush to define, categorize and select aspects of a topic that endorse their own beliefs. They are constantly under pressure from their followers and want to impress on the interviewer that they have not moved away from 'the masses'. Nor can they conceive how they could ever be considered to belong to a separate class, above the lower sector of, say, industrial and farm workers or villagers – when these make up the majority of people who are the central concern of political activism. True enough. In the earlier days of political resistance, movements were led mostly by the elite: among them church leaders, teachers and newspaper editors. It is only since the mid-1950s that trade unionists and their members shared leadership with the 'educated class'. Then, and in the years of exile beginning in 1960, military cadres and administrative functionaries took over some leadership positions. Most of the latter had not gone beyond junior high school, if that.

But at this point the career politician begins to show unwillingness to answer questions such as: having yourself come from the lower sector, and having become more knowledgeable, more analytical, how do you feel about this very kind of intellectual sophistication and growth you have attained in relation to that of 'the masses'? You stopped schooling at Standard 8, and through wider reading and in-depth discussion of issues, you attained this level of mental growth and organizational skills. If your income shot up to the point where you decided to move to a better house – still in the ghetto – and buy a car, and could afford the things that correspond to such tokens of comfort, would you consider yourself middle class? In other words, do you reckon that economic standing counts for more than a certificated educational level? Or do you even think that a black middle class is in the process of becoming? Is such a class desirable? Inevitable? Or even a necessary evil? Apartheid has levelled us all to a ghetto or landless villager's existence, whatever our educational achievements have been. Now that there is a measure of upward mobility, with its own financial rewards and demands, should we feel guilty about it? What do you consider are our gains and losses from this new process of stratification?

Questions, and more stubborn questions. Whether we feel alienated from those we were part of only yesterday; whether we think we need to adapt to the historical class structures of the West, while acknowledging at the same time that the West is also experiencing modifications to the classical pattern – lower, middle, upper, going up the vertical scale – for the simple reason that the middle classes are more flexible and fluid today than in the years of Europe's industrial revolution.

Although South Africa is still far from the class of what world-acclaimed liberal economist J K Galbraith refers to as the 'advanced industrial countries', what is happening out there seems to be spilling over here in the rise of multinational investment. Galbraith reminds us that, once, 'all economic and social thought turned on a bilateral economic and social structure':

There were capital and labour, the capitalist and the worker. There were also a landed and a peasant population – the landed often serving in government as the surrogate of the capitalist class; the peasants scattered and politically irrelevant. Capital and labour, capital versus labour.

The economist explains that this is no longer the case in those countries.

In place of the capitalist is the great corporate bureaucracy. Not capitalists but managers. The new class structure embraces, on the one hand, the comfortably situated who have replaced the once dominant capitalist and, on the other, a large number of less affluent or often impoverished who do the work and render the services that make life pleasant, even tolerable... for the culture of contentment.

These shifts are not dramatic over on this side, but one feels their subtle waves, which also seem to whisper to us news of things to come. Certain trade unions here still have to be the 'strongly combative force on behalf of the denied and deprived'. One can say this without denying that the middle class zone has now become one with unpegged boundaries, taking in achievers and chancers.

Whatever British Premier John Major may say to the contrary, his urge to the English to 'return to the basics' must have been touched off by the series of sex scandals erupting among his Conservative top colleagues. The British public may stand outraged by this erosion of morals ailing its middle class, especially because the Conservatives have been traditionally accepted as vigilant custodians of public morality, alongside the Church. Again, because our social, economic and political structures are so derivative in this country, we may very well find that there is no end to the shifting of moral goals among the middle class even here, and that we may be expected to evolve a new code.

The route from the lowest to the upper levels is pretty transparent in the emerging structure. Some education, formal and informal, up to a level that enables you to provide for yourself and your home, to function creatively, and which equips you for social mobility. A tertiary level of formal education used to be a prerequisite. Today other attributes – one's inner strengths and drive – come into play in gaining admission into the circles of the intelligentsia, even as substitutes of tertiary education. A combination of all these factors and the rise in one's financial status, without necessarily owning a business or an industry, gains one a place among a property-owning middle class.

In the Western world people take this line of progression for granted as a natural order. In time, the middle class, Western style, developed an informal set of values or code of ethics, as well as the notion of natural entitlement to the best centres of education. Acquisition of freehold property and/or farmland was also a given among the middle class. Mobility could only be upward or horizontal, never downhill. Educational attainment has come to mean more things today than simply going to school or college.

Blacks come in at this time when the established middle class is experiencing shifting allegiances, a restructuring of values in relation to their sense of social responsibility within their ranks. Out there in the outside world, race and colour have not been legislated as has been the case in this country: new elements – African Americans, white Americans, Asians, Caribbeans, the English – have been undermining the classical terms which created and serviced the middle class. They are constantly redefining these terms, not theoretically but in their lifestyles.

In traditional times, African communities were loosely divided into the ruling family, with the nobility close to it, and the common citizenry. What social differences there might be in modern terms were blurred by the sense of community and moral interdependence that pervaded society. All had common cultural interests, ideals and values. All enjoyed the same music and dance; the village poet spoke a public language. The idea of 'high culture' would have been foreign to everybody. Indeed, the wealthy could barely be said to have constituted a class, in the sense that they would share a perceived morality different from that of the rest of a community; that they would share music and the other arts as an audience apart from the rest, and so on. Yes, wealth might confer on the wealthy some position of political power. Still, one's age group was more important in the ordering of social relationships than the family's economic means, even though abject poverty was a self-demeaning stigma, an affront to oneself and the ancestors. You became an elder in the ruler's court according to age and the esteem you enjoyed among your own kin and clan. Accordingly, they felt increased by your elevated status.

The multinational corporations, which are giant structures of affluent collectivism, may very well have prospered on the strength of education and money among those who operate them. But there is an upper level that requires more organizing and managing acumen than a conventional higher education can equip one with, even though the initial entry may not demand specialist credentials.

The African still needs to show credentials of higher education for that initial entry. It will be so for a majority of blacks for a long time. Except that, because of the relaxation of the erstwhile fierce legal and racial restrictions on entry and upward mobility, it has become possible for Africans to become entrepreneurs. For those who have the natural ability to organize and manage other people with expertise as, say, consultants in industrial and personnel relations, advertising, real estate, trade unions and so on, the gates are now open. They now have a fighting chance in the world of opportunity. The price for that potential is competition: the real world, whether or not we are welcome there!

Perhaps the best way to understand what is happening with the emergent African middle class is to consider if and how it ties in with the terms of definition offered by Roger Scruton in his *A Dictionary of Political Thought* (1982). He points out two interpretations of *bourgeoisie*. (a) The Marxist: owners of private property in the means of

capitalist production; a class that has come into its wealth by establishing a dominant position in production relations and therefore in government. This means that
even before the class came to own such wealth, they could earn the name 'bourgeoisie'
simply by virtue of their being a community of urban traders who possess power. (b)
The bourgeoisie as a class between the level of workers and the old agrarian land-
owning aristocracy.

Without any reference to means of production, the bourgeoisie is often associated
with a culture that is based on its perception of stable family relations and values; on
thoughts and feelings as yet undefined, but making for communal stability; a sense of
individual self-worth. An ideology has come to characterize such a culture. This view
of its own values can look absurd when one ponders that these same values exist
among the working class and peasantry, although there is no cult around them.

Finally, Scruton states: 'A major difficulty is that there are two rival ways of
identifying and theorizing classes. According to one way (class position in production
relations) classes cannot rise; according to the other (class lifestyle, kinship relations,
and ethic), they can.' (1982: 44)

We have already suggested that if we are to understand our emergent class, the
latter of the above two connotations fits the case of such a class taking shape among
Africans.

Class stratification has become a more complex condition in Africa today than the
relatively simple notion of upper, lower and middle. It is especially so in countries
where coloniser became settler and created industrial wealth for himself – e.g. South
Africa and Zimbabwe – with the cheaply-purchased labour of the black man. We
witness complexities, too, in those cities where European colonists have left relics of
administrative and economic structures that visibly display something to aspire to
beyond a pastoral existence: a status of respectability deriving from an education
rooted in Western metropolitan centres; sources and methods of production in food
and raw materials; and political systems to invest united states with the power to rule
and also deal with forces of opposition within the body politic.

As ours is a society in transition, a nation-in-the-making, until we find a name for
it, we shall use the term 'middle class' for professionals and other educated people
– whether they be mere functionaries or not. It can only be a temporary usage, as we
have no upper class. We clearly need a new interim terminology to define the two
major classes in African society: the class that either has some elementary formal book
learning or is illiterate, but derives its income from selling its labour where only
minimal or no education is required. Then there is the class that has something
bigger to sell: an education that has either earned them a career or equips them for
higher levels of employment than the 'working class' can manage.

Members of this latter group are the 'higher ones', the 'upper stratum', to use the
vocabulary of sociologist Thomas E Nyquist in his research essay, *African Middle Class*

Elite (1983). His reference is to the African locations of the country town of Grahamstown, Eastern Cape. 'Upper stratum' comes from common Xhosa usage, *abaphakamileyo*, a Sotho equivalent being *ba phagamileng* or *ba maemo* – higher ones, elevated ones. *Ba maemo* means 'those with status' or of standing; people of importance. Even the vagueness of this indigenous terminology must indicate how alien the Western concept of class is to Africans.

When there was viable untrammelled indigenous rule in pre-colonial days, around which a nobility arose, there was only one other, lower class: the citizenry. Peasants grew their own food and were answerable only to themselves for the work they executed. The educated and enlightened ones (in the Western sense) have now replaced the nobility. Nyquist indicates that in country towns and villages, communities rate the attainments of the higher ones in the following order: education; income or standard of living; a house; position or occupation (shop-owner, school inspector, school principal, teacher, nurse, minister of religion, organisation leader). In the same area, Nyquist shows the ranking of different occupations in the community members' perception of importance as follows, in descending order: doctor, lawyer, school inspector, school principal, chief (local), court interpreter, radio announcer, social worker, minister of religion, senior school teacher, nurse. Although Grahamstown is the case study here, it is typical of African rural and semi-rural communities in South Africa.

In the urban townships, especially since the early 1970s, black communities have been shaken up by political upheavals and the State's tyranny that attended every act of protest and overt revolt. The traditional determinants of public esteem Nyquist documents will not hold in the urban townships. There has been a considerable degree of levelling down of teacher, principal, school inspector – generally, a rejection of all symbols of government authority. But each professional person now has to merit his or her individual rank in the public's esteem by participating in community development, including non-municipal civic duties and national politics at a local level. However, those who deliver services that are perceived to promote human survival in immediate terms rank higher: doctor, lawyer, social worker, leader of a political body or of a labour union, nurse, radio announcer – who is now constantly in the spotlight and therefore highly visible.

Whether this upper stratum in urban life sees itself, as Nyquist says of Grahamstown, as bound together by 'bonds of association' and having a 'binding network of personal relationships'; whether it is held together by common attitudes that 'tend to distinguish them from the (rest) of the community,' is not very clear. These are hard questions *because* this is a fluid society, not collectively in charge of the formulation of its own its aspirations, values, and their synthesis with those of the mainstream white world. New laws may regulate; but a public morality will be long in coming, so far made impossible by the basic fact of inequalities. What is a crime to the other man is often not one to me.

So we inherited from Western civilization a system of social classification that we are not yet at ease with. 'Middle class' and 'bourgeoisie' are used interchangeably, most often carelessly, as terms of abuse or ridicule not only among the working classes, but also by those who feel that they are being swept up by the consuming yearning for education and material comfort – forces that are irresistible. They are ill at ease because they are in 'danger' of qualifying for middle-class status: a reasonably respectable occupation and the public esteem this confers on them. A sense of guilt sets in. The fact of being a small number amid so much poverty, hunger, poor wages, and disgraceful employment practices – this fear overshadows for a while our individual and communal strengths, which have allowed us to overcome these self-same conditions to get where we are.

This is typical of the 'Third World' or 'developing nations' – even without racism – which are largely consumers rather than producers and controllers of capital. It doesn't matter to the underclass that the term 'bourgeoisie' refers to a socio-economic class that is no longer the talk of the town in industrially developed countries who take their class structures for granted, e.g. the United States, Britain and the countries of Western Europe. Neither political writers nor politicians use the word any longer, except to refer to the manner in which people behave and the art they produce. A man may be perceived to be middle class by occupation, sometimes but not always by education, by the circles he moves in, his relatively expensive residence – and still not be bourgeois in his mentality and outlook.

And yet Karl Marx's associate, Friedrich Engels, realized long ago that in an industrial environment classes evolve. They do not remain, as Marx conceived them, absolutely distinct from one another, with a predetermined conflict of interests and aspirations: upper, middle (bourgeois) and proletariat or working class. If there is evolution of class there must also be overlapping or grey areas between one category and another, and within each one. Add to this the fact that among South African Asians there is a merchant class, some of whose members may not have been educated further than junior secondary school.

Religious sentiments also modify the differences. There are many coloureds and black Africans who, person for person, have a higher level of post-primary education than many whites and yet do not, because of racial prejudice and the politics of race, possess much in the nature of material welfare – including a decent shelter.

What are we to say about those blacks who have afforded houses on the fringes of the greater ghetto, made possible by an estate-development mortgage – e.g. in Soweto? These houses are visibly bigger and better serviced, with more and better facilities than, say, the average Soweto municipal 'box'. Many of these people will not have been in school for more than seven primary years. Are they middle class? We do not even have the measuring scale to determine the criteria for classification because our lifestyles are derivative, and only self-generated or self-directed according to the survival book each one writes for himself or herself. Take the customary criteria and consider what marks we score: (a) occupation and level of formal education; (b) income bracket that affords you a relatively high standard of living, and that enables you to choose to own movable or immovable property or both; (c) opportunity to choose and afford the school you want for your children (within the constraints of segregated schooling); (d) power to influence, as part of a middle-class collective, local and central government; (e) a life-style that affords you time for leisure and/or for participating in self-help projects in the community. As most Africans who have a post-matriculation education live on low incomes, (b), (c) and (d) become irrelevant criteria. Education remains the most visible mark of class identity in rural life, even though one's dwelling may be as modest as every one else's, and there is no estate development that sets the educated class apart. It is the way a house is furnished that will distinguish one. But in ghetto life – which sums up the urban experience for blacks – apparent contradictions become the norm.

The estate developers on the fringes of the ghetto sell to the professional class and anyone else who can obtain a housing subsidy or outright loan from an employer or a bank. The residents of such an estate are an interesting mix: teachers and other civil servants, business representatives, advertisers, clerks, nurses, medical doctors and so on. At long last it pays off to have the kind of education that can earn you a job with such fringe benefits. Twenty years ago, education only earned you social status, with less material benefits than the truck or bus driver and others of the labourer class. Today there is hardly the same deference paid to the teacher, for instance, than then. At the same time, unionisation across the labour landscape has been winning urban workers a few extra rands – no more than relative financial relief.

Then comes the crunch: when a person loses his job, and with it the housing subsidy from his employers, and his unemployed condition lasts too long for him to manage mortgage payments. That's how tentative and fragile this segment of the class structure is, almost as if we were amateurish cubs trying for the professional league.

When major cities and their satellite ghetto townships merge, as they must in a new South Africa, more blacks will certainly spill over from the overcrowded slums into affordable downtown apartments. An inner-city life will take root in the place of the typical South African town or city that drains out after working hours and on weekends – whites running to suburban comfort and blacks returning home to their dormitories, box-like brick houses and tin shacks. White suburbia will most probably become more expensive to buy into, thus keeping out most blacks. Maybe the informal mixture of labourers and higher-ranking people will continue the ghetto pattern, as more and more take advantage of the abolition of influx-control measures interfering with the mobility of labour from rural to urban areas.

Will the black intelligentsia sort themselves out into a distinctive class, i.e. once there is freer and more affordable mobility?

Maybe new developments in social mobility will trample over those old identifying markings on the middle-class chart; or at least make some of them relatively irrelevant. Whatever happens, there is an ever-growing class of teachers, social workers, nurses, medical doctors, ministers of religion, trade union leaders, civil servants and other administrators, middle-management personnel in business and industry and techni- cians, who – wave after wave – are going to speak with a new-found united voice and demand attention.

Traditionally the teachers, ministers of religion and trade unionists have been the ones to create political awareness and mobilize the masses for political education, awareness and protest; to interpret the laws made by the white government; to read and interpret the newspapers to their constituencies. The swelling numbers of pro- fessional blacks, and the larger range of career options possible when affirmative action has been set in motion, must create at this level a new sense of cohesion and unity of interests. Poor wages, ghetto survival (both urban and rural), an educational system that was never conceived to express the real aspirations of black people, and the collective psyche across the apartheid lines of racial population groupings – these have constantly conspired to keep the putative middle class down and to reduce it to a subsistence level for each individual.

Successive white governments co-opted some of the educated class into advisory councils, with a myopic view to moulding a class that would distance itself from a mass consciousness threatening to revolt. Even these policy makers soon realized that they were creating a clan of midgets who were never going to be of any use to them. People couldn't be duped by councils that had no statutory powers, or revenue even to remove garbage and clean the township's streets.

Except for the tiny business class and the substantial number of self-employed vendors on streets, in front of white and Asian storefronts and on open unpaved mar- kets, most black Africans have to sell their labour to white and Asian employers. But these vendors and their extension – owners of small businesses – are still an under- class, along with the labourer, in relation to the professional class.

Perhaps our equivalent to the middle class can best be defined in negative terms: those who are not 'working class', with only their skills or muscle or both to sell to employers and no book education. Nor does the class we're looking for control the means of production. They are not upper class either. Even with the term 'working class' we are on slippery ground, as it does not define a monolithic structure. As a result of the black people's exclusion from the mainstream of the economy for at least two centuries – except as an unskilled or semi-skilled work force – we are most of us still in that class.

As a work force, the professional class – or petit bourgeoisie – derive what power its members possess from the status of the employer or hiring institution. By virtue of the low esteem people generally have for the systems of local and central government, for instance, civil servants have no power or influence in their communities that derives from their occupation. Observe, as examples, the post office clerk, the police officer, the municipal clerk and so on. The social worker must earn the community's deference not by the government job she holds, but by her active involvement in the people's concerns.

Mr Reuel Khoza, one of the small rising class of self-employed Africans running consultancies in marketing, human resources and education, believes that the Marxist interpretation is too simplistic to define the South African situation, because race is the dominant dividing line. One's skin counts more than one's education. The whites have developed their own class structure, where the middle class contains the highly educated and those whose skin colour has compensated for a low level of education. Yet they occupy better jobs, with better pay than blacks. 'On the black side of the tracks,' says Khoza, 'race determines upward mobility. The ceiling is low for the majority. Class lines cannot fit into Marx's definitions.'

The intelligentsia – the African equivalent of the white middle class – do they support the political status quo? Do they really benefit from it, simply because it has always been the white man's dream that the 'making', the sponsorship, of a black bourgeoisie can delay, even confuse, political aspirations and action at the lower levels? Are they, because they dress and eat a little better, ripe for co-option by the government to do its dirty job; by big business and liberal institutions in the interests of tokenism? Khoza won't buy this popular jibe against the intelligentsia. Like some other analysts, Khoza points out that, in any case, co-option into statutory bodies cannot breathe life into the dead-end laws that created them. This class is more aware of its racial identity than would appear on the surface, enough to prevent unqualified co-option. Mr Khoza is still optimistic about the future role of the 'higher-ups'. Just as they have been at the vanguard of the liberation struggle as activists and opinion-makers, he argues, 'they'll want to see it yield enduring results for the good of the people.'

Their numbers have increased since before the 1970s, when it was easy to swallow them whole into the system without promising them anything more than respectability. From the rising political consciousness of the masses, the statutory structures that the earlier and small wave of the elite served came under heavy attack. The people boycotted them; their employees couldn't hold their heads high any longer. The newcomers, who may once have believed that they could snuggle under the wings of State protection, have snapped out of their daze in the last decade and a half. And those who once dreamed that their professional associations could stay clear of active politics have had to revise their 'mission statements' radically.

There are two major constituencies of the new and younger arrivals in the 'higher-up' league. There are those who come from or still live and work in a rural milieu. For them, African traditions still mean a lot. They are spiritually in contact with them, Christianity notwithstanding. Then there are those who think and behave with the momentum of the fugitive urban, painfully fragmented in its consciousness though it may be – and often a shoddy imitation of the lifestyle of its shopping town. The other side of the coin will show that, for their own spiritual survival, these ghetto communities have been destabilizing big-town pursuits, creating a distinctive sub-culture, urban in its own way. It invents its own styles while operating Western technology: transport, eating habits, communication media, dress and so on. African elements keep surfacing almost imperceptibly in this culture, which one can only write down to the collective unconscious.

Questions: the powerful urge to pursue the neon lights of urban life, the money and the challenge; to make it to the sirens sounding their seductive melody for all to come to the towns and cities – this urge, is it not going to push us to a scramble for whatever new jobs a 'new South Africa' may yield? Are we not going to be sucked into a race whose rules the white man has determined and lived over several generations, either directly or by heritage? Then what? Can a new black middle class evolve a set of values for itself based on that collective memory?

Khoza's response is that if we see ourselves as part of the larger continent, then 'reliance' on that Africanist essence I believe still resides in us will sustain us. It will buoy us up so we're not dragged down into the mire – whatever the negative forces of the scramble may be.

Are the higher ones doomed as a class? Can they promote change in South Africa? What about the intelligentsia who have led the political struggle and labour unions since their creation? Has it all been for nothing? Will they be sucked into the white middle class as and when their numbers increase, each succeeding generation of achievers attaining higher levels of education than the previous one?

In organizations, it seems, the higher ones will yet make an impact far beyond their dreams, rather than when they act as individuals. Khoza offers examples such as the National Association of Federated Chambers of Commerce and the Black Management Forum, and the unions and associations of teachers, educationalists, social workers, medical doctors, nurses and auxiliary health workers. By its very nature the Black Lawyers Association never cherished apolitical dreams: the formation of a number of professional groups was a political statement to begin with.

'The ruling class in South Africa,' he observes, 'made it impossible for blacks, especially Africans – educated or not – to own capital, let alone invest it in the country's economy. 'We are an educated class without the economic gains to show for it, except what goes back into white capital as we amass consumer goods; no civic or political rights, nor the ability to run civic affairs, even when we have multiracial civil administrations.' Khoza emphasizes the point that the middle class in other parts of the world is proud to consider its status a personal achievement. We blacks resent the notion that we are such a class, because we might be regarded by the underprivileged as stuck-up, snobbish and aloof from their struggles against poverty. Then we begin to feel guilty.

The doers among the new higher class who blaze new trails to make themselves marketable in territory that is traditionally the white man's preserve, especially in the corporate world, have little time to sit and brood over their relatively privileged position. An example is Herdbuoys, a group of five young men who have set up a marketing and advertising consultancy in Johannesburg. They have brought to the fledgling company experience they acquired working for white agencies. Their spirit of adventure is expressed in the words of the young Managing Director, Peter Vundla: 'Herdbuoys is about black people being in control. Running our own lives without running to high management to report. We are our own people, and we don't owe an explanation to anybody but ourselves…'

So why the guilt? Why the rejection of the possible implications of a rupture that higher status may bring about between us and the people we associate with our lowly beginnings in the ghetto or rural village?

'We must have a middle class,' declares Mr Aggrey Klaaste, editor-in-chief of *Sowetan*, 'or whatever we choose to call it in our special context and historical circumstances.' Klaaste is a veteran journalist – more than thirty years on this beat. He has worked his way up from the dusty-street and rough-and-tumble reporting of township life – from the Sophiatown of the 1950s, and Soweto. He has lived amidst the muck and smell of township life, the smut of its alleys and low and high lives.

His beginnings were vastly different from Reuel Khoza's. Although both their fathers were teachers, Khoza's childhood was rooted in a rural-agrarian and therefore traditional culture – in north-eastern Transvaal. 'My father taught without having acquired a teacher's certificate,' he relates. 'I'm the first-born in my family and according to Shangana-Tsonga custom, such a child must be brought up by his grandparents.' From here on it was rural schooling, and then boarding secondary school in Afrikaans under missionaries: from rural discipline under African mentors, who were nevertheless role models for him, to missionary discipline where survival was the name of the game.

> We were spiritually and intellectually distant from the mission-school education fed to us by Afrikaners. We were even hostile to it, because it was not learner-friendly. Well, I felt the brunt of poverty in those years, which convinced me that to be poor was sinful in a more profound and broader sense than the Christian concept. I had only one off-white shirt to change into, just to meet the requirements of a school uniform.

Khoza senior wanted his son to be a medical doctor, but he knew this was not for him. University followed – the University of the North, the cradle of Black Consciousness as of 1968, an affront to white supremacy; by the same token, the university became a centre of ideological control, as it was dominated by Boers on the academic and administrative staff. He inevitably became embroiled in student politics. Later, when he taught psychology at the same institution, he was fired for not complying with the Boer conventions imposed on the black college.

> I was denied entry into the white but so-called 'open' University of the Witwatersrand to study for the Master's in Industrial Psychology. By government decree, I had no right to enter a white university if I could pursue the subject of my study in an African college, and not just any black college – Indian or coloured. Studies in marketing management followed at Lancaster, UK; Lausanne, Switzerland; and Harvard Business School. Then I held jobs in marketing management for companies. My studies were mostly sponsored through scholarships from companies.

And then there is Khoza's own consultancy company in business and public affairs, of which he is Managing Director. Mr Khoza has left the ghetto for a semi-rural semi-urban dwelling outside Johannesburg, where he grows some food. He still maintains close ties with his folks in the villages. Klaaste does not want to leave his house on the fringes of Greater Soweto, where a homeowners' area has developed with white capital, and where there are bigger and better dwellings than municipal housing in Soweto. He reckons that as an editor of a paper read by over a million and a half Africans, most of them in Soweto, he needs to be where the hub of life is. It's also a psychological necessity for his own sanity.

Klaaste's father taught in the urban areas. But he was fiercely proud of his African traditional origins. Like so many of his generation – from the first decade of this century through the end of the 1940s – Klaaste's father picked up the spirit of Ethiopianism, a religious nationalism. Parallel with the African American experience during the Harlem Renaissance – from the early 1920s through the 1930s – Africans looked to Ethiopia to reinforce their love of and identity with Africa, because Ethiopia was the only country on the continent that stood out as an independent and uncolonised nation. It also boasted a passionate religious nationalism, deriving its form of Christianity from no European missionary incursion.

Much of this rubbed off on the son, in spite of the crush and urgency of urbanisation; the same, older and pristine Africanism that influenced Khoza. Young Aggrey had hoped to become an academic after his Arts degree at the University of the Witwatersrand in the 1960s, but the journalist bug got to him. By this time his family had moved from the diamond town of Kimberley to a Johannesburg mine compound. Then it was Sophiatown. When that was levelled by apartheid's bulldozers, the family moved to Meadowlands, Greater Soweto.

'Let's appreciate,' Klaaste points out, 'that generations of social engineering by whites has placed us where we are. What middle class does evolve among us to a self-confident status can at best be a visionary thing for now. After a pause, 'I mean you, me and others who fall in this category must pull our intellectual resources together.'

Klaaste speaks from experience, as he himself conceived of 'nation building' a few years ago as a rallying cry for reconstruction for unity and self-reliance and self-help. Through and around the *Sowetan*, he called for people with vision to devise programmes for social change. African Humanism – *Botho* (Sesotho) and *Ubuntu* (Nguni) – lies at the base of the concept. 'See, we've got to work out how to caution against a mindless rush into what appears on the surface to be a new kind of sophistication, surrounded by all that white prosperity seems to promise. I see it as a leadership matter...'

Opportunity, success, instruments of control: aren't these the stuff middle classes are made of? 'Take care,' Klaaste still warns. 'In a multiparty democracy, the governing party may easily reserve the best for its loyal followers, efficient or not. You think we've arrived at a level of education where equitable distribution of resources is possible? No, decidedly *no*! That's a culture that requires its own kind of education and experience, and we've still got a number of cycles of democratic practice to go to attain it.'

The major plague in African politics continent-wide is ethnicity. Thanks to Hendrik Verwoerd's creation of African tribal enclaves, we've joined the continent's league on that. The African National Congress and the other political movements that came later on the scene – coupled with industrial development where a diversity of language groups converged – had all but brought us out of our ethnic seclusion. What have we the higher-ups to say about this? 'That's the point I'm making,' Aggrey cuts in. 'I mean concerning our responsibilities and capabilities. After all, the rest are looking up to us to be the opinion-makers, the planners and the interpreters – I mean us, the higher-ups.'

It would have to be a conscious programme – inside and outside school, wherever we can find a platform, just as the political movements did. 'This class,' Klaaste stresses, 'provides personnel who can think clearly and search for truths, for answers to the numerous questions we know people are all asking, e.g. about the continuing violence, sectarian politics, the education crisis, the destabilizing of schools, colleges and university campuses, and so on.

Both Khoza and Klaaste believe that we shall evolve a new social structure that may be characterized by any combination of factors that shaped the historical middle class, minus, maybe, possession of property. 'I think we should become a socialist state,' Klaaste says, almost thinking aloud. But apartheid and capitalism have fed into each other for so long that education, economics and the bureaucracy are all set to create a class stratification that is anything but equitable. To this, Khoza's response is: 'The bottom line is for us to deal with the problem we *actually* have, rather than with a hypothesis.'

'There are painful contradictions in this whole debate,' Klaaste remarks. 'To my manager on the *Sowetan* – he's white – success is everything, the ultimate ambition, i.e. personal success. But why not? It's good for my paper.'

At what cost? People often become vicious in the effort to succeed, to achieve. So how do we balance intellectual independence against the collective will?

Khoza urges that we conceive a political vision shorn of its 'frills and embroidery', and see the absolute minimum the middle class would claim on behalf of all the deprived: black majority rule unadulterated by organized or sporadic violence or by the Marxist vision of the class struggle, because ours is largely a race struggle.

The current political clamour for a non-racial society, however, towards which its proponents can only conceive multiracial structures – political, economic and social – may plunge the middle-class-in-the making into a crisis of conscience never before experienced in the years of its becoming. But then, the very status our education has set us up for since our humble beginnings has been predetermined by opportunities that are a mixture of success by standards operating in the white world, and self-motivated effort on our part.

Where might the conflict lie? Political analysts and economics may well, on the face of it, find it easy to predict a common cause between white and black workforces under a non-racial regime. Does such a scenario allow for the imponderables: the possible disillusionment among the mostly black underclass, amid the huge backlog of services in health and housing, economic welfare, education and so on; amid forces tugging towards federalism as against unitary rule? Will history complete its vicious circle in which the white middle class will, as in earlier times, support the status quo – this time reinforced by the black middle class of some later generation – and find itself faced with workers' strikes, mass protests, boycotts, and so on? Will the rules of success or achievement change as employment ethics and practices become aligned with international labour codes?

Questions, questions! Always, the answers must come round and find weight and validity along the them-and-us axis. As always, we seem doomed to define ourselves *with reference* to the white man – at least for a long time to come. As Klaaste warns, the middle class that won freedom must still deal with the question of success and its rating in the equation of racial ethics and affirmative action. And Klaaste and Khoza are agreed that, politically, we (blacks) first need to be in charge, *truly* in charge, and not objects of white trusteeship. Then we must, from a position of strength, sway whites to our thinking on a number of vital cultural issues, even while we use their structures and technology. We should compel them to realize that their survival lies in thinking African, no longer in their perception of themselves as an outpost of Western civilization. We have got to inject our own thinking into the edu-cational system, establish new values through what we teach our children in and out of school, open up the curriculum and give it a new direction. One of the responsi-bilities of the middle class is to go beyond privilege, to project a vision; to under-stand what has been happening to our minds in the process of acculturation on the one hand and, on the other, through the social engineering whites have rammed into us in order to contain rebellion; to understand what is happening in the rush into new jobs.

'Maybe we're trying to arrest a passing wind,' says Nomavenda Mathiane, half flippantly. She is a journalist who has covered some of the most dangerous events of the most troubled epochs in our history: the time of the schools revolt in 1976-78, and 1984-86. A time infested with police informers in the black townships, a time of bannings and detention without trial, arson and mayhem, security police and military patrols in township streets, tanks tearing across the country like rabid hounds.

Nomavenda Mathiane explains:

> *Our society is fluid, especially since the removal of restrictions on our people's movements from rural to urban areas. One day you think you're in the midst of middle-class Africans, yet we conduct ourselves in a casual ghetto manner; another time we mix easily with folks who would not readily start a conversation on a topic such as the one we're at now. We slaughter a beast for the ancestors, brag good-humouredly about our extended families and sisters and nephews and nieces we are taking care of, whose school fees, clothes and books we have to buy.*

You scan Mathiane's face and something there tells you the topic is a challenging one for her, that her mind is working to find the appropriate language for her thoughts. From one newspaper and journal to another, she has had to fight her way through clusters of male chauvinists – white superiors and black co-subordinates – and through the racism of white males and females.

> *I bet you very few of us ever stop to ask ourselves where we're going. What does urban and rural development mean to us? Sometimes we manipulate Western values, at other times it's the other way round.*

Mathiane declares that she does not care if people call her 'bourgeois' just because she has achieved a status above the working class:

> *I'm not going feel guilty or ashamed of working for material prosperity. After all, I'm not living on handouts; me in partnership with opportunity that I grabbed while the white man wasn't looking, we earned what I possess. Sure, being a child from an educated family – father a Salvation Army captain and all that, who sent the children to school – that helped. But out there in the world of racism and sexism you're on your own, you fight every inch of the way… You go to school because it's the thing to do…Asking why wouldn't even occur to the mind to dare.*

You want to ask: which way do we go from here, then? Nomavenda bristles all over with that characteristic enthusiasm as she says:

I cannot help feeling that this is all tied up with culture in general and education in particular. We have to cultivate pride in ourselves as black people, in our role models. Our heroes have been demeaned for too long…Let our teachers set an example for our children, I mean an example of the moves we'd like to see renewed. Let our writers reaffirm the positive values we cherish …Let's start talking about ourselves, who we are, where are we coming from…Where are we heading?

She pauses, her mind almost visibly minting her words: 'You know, there was a spectacular breakthrough in this process of self-searching, self-affirmation, self-reliance, self-pride when the Black Consciousness movement was born.' And what happened to it?

The arrest of Steve Biko and the South African Students Organization, who were its backbone…the banning of the community projects the leaders had set up… Biko's murder. If only BC had stayed a movement, instead of an organization with all the trappings of partisan leadership and its hierarchy, constitution and stuff like that… it would have penetrated the awareness of many more of us. I think we'd better be able to understand what class is all about. It has everything to do with consciousness, right?

And what has all this to do with the price of potatoes?

Look at it this way: this class that's in the making – ever since the earliest missionary schools in the 19th century it has been building up, proportionate to the slow growth in the number of schools and post-secondary institutions. A trickle at a time, yes, but building up all the same, until we see university graduates emerging. Still too small for a large black population like ours.

She tells the doleful story of how the new class of barely literate and untutored youth find book learning irrelevant to their aspirations. You see them hanging out in front of shops in townships and villages. What are we left with? Borrowed dress styles, borrowed hopes, borrowed neuroses, borrowed everything. Hence she emphasizes the imperative on our side to create our own definition of class distinctions – our own concept of a middle class – in accordance with the new education we want to and must structure.

In other words, co-option must give way to partnership, assimilation to adaptation, to a synthesis between the best in our African consciousness that we can restore and recreate, and the best we can identify in modern technology, science and life skills. Obviously, every one of the new elite will tell you that the motivation that can still be found among our children derives from the age-old passion in black parents to see them obtain an

education: 'Go to school, my son, and come and get a job and lift us out of this poverty…
You have the opportunity we never enjoyed because our own parents had nothing to offer
us but love and the basic things.

Nothing to offer, indeed. Thousands of us have had to hang in there while struggling with school and college studies, because we knew only too well that our parents had stripped themselves of their hand-to-mouth earnings to pay our way. Even those parents who had an education – usually teachers and nurses (the latter only since World War Two) – did not earn much. Still, we all regarded schooling as the open sesame to a life out there which seemed to promise better things. A mindless idealism, but the antithesis of that was something we all must have dreaded: admission of defeat.

Eslin Shuenyane is the wife of a business representative who has an executive portfolio, directing his company's programmes of social responsibility. She has the degree of Master of Arts in public health and the degree of Master of Education. Shuenyane's family lived on a mining compound near Johannesburg, the father being nothing more than a functionary in the compound administration, even lower than a clerk. He was literate enough to read the Bible in Xhosa. There were no other books in the tiny hovel the family lived in. Mother did white folks' laundry; the ten-year-old Eslin had to make several trips to suburban homes to fetch and deliver laundry. She was up and about by four in the morning on washing days, so as to be at school several hours later, by eight. She recounts:

Mother gave me the handkerchiefs to wash. They were full of dry mucus which turned into
nauseating slime in water. I resented it. I cried, until an aunt of mine advised me to pour
salt in the water first. The mucus would then come off and I could wash the handkerchiefs
in fresh water.

'Now listen, child,' Mother would say, 'if you want to be free from all these jobs when
you're grown up, and not have to travel the same road your Tata and me are travelling,
go to school, uyeva – you hear? Go to school, hear me tell you.' Well, things did lighten
up for myself and family when I qualified in social work and began to earn some money,
even pay for my senior siblings' schooling. The rest of my academic [career] – well, that's
the road we Africans travel: self-motivated university studies, on our own steam.'

Shuenyane, after her MA in public health obtained in North Carolina, USA, took another master's degree, but in education. She felt she needed this, as she lectures in community health at the University of the Witwatersrand's medical school – but not before the Johannesburg City Council rejected her application for a job in its department of public health. She was 'overqualified', they told her!

> *Most of us start with no privilege or money, both of which are easily available to most whites moving up to higher levels… except of course when they just don't have it in them to achieve anything.*

What are the categories that determine status for the African? Those who neither have an education nor a trade but must sell their manual labour to employers – mostly white; those with a primary-school level of literacy and numeracy who acquire a retail business, and for whom this is a terminal status; and those who stay in school long enough to obtain a profession, e.g. medicine, law, teaching, nursing, social work, religious ministry (to the extent that this is no longer simply a calling), business or any other consultancy, advertising.

Before World War Two, the only jobs above manual work that existed countrywide for blacks were, in descending order of volume and prominence: 1. teaching, 2. low-level clerical (including insurance agency), 3. religious ministry, 4. medicine. From the 1940s on: the same for 1, 2, 3, followed by 4. nursing, 5. law, 6. medicine. From the 1950s on: the same for 1, 2, 3, 4, followed by 5. social work, 6. political leadership, 7. law, 8. medicine. From the 1970s on: the same, followed by business and commercial representatives (including marketing, personnel, industrial and public relations, consultancy, industrial chemistry, various kinds of research, engineering, laboratory assistance, accountancy), which took precedence over law and medicine, and then the informal sector of business (trading in shops, open markets, running taxis and chauffeuring for private persons). Since the mid-1970s the last mentioned business sector – especially taxi transport – has increased in volume to take a position above law and medicine. Still, the people doing these jobs have continued to live cheek by jowl in the ghettos until the mid-1980s, when a tiny number of blacks began to move to the historically white suburbs if they could afford this new lifestyle.

Most owners of retail stores operate on a subsistence level, and so competition in their ranks is minimal. Those with a trade – e.g. plumbing, cabinet making, electrical mechanics – mostly pick it up in the white man's service rather than through formal apprenticeship, which is still a rarity for black industrial workers. The present technical colleges, which are miserably few, produce low-level 'technicians' who can only function when they are instructed by the white man. Meantime, the white employer is blissfully unaware that a break must come about one day, when his labourer will strike out on his own in his ghetto yard, after gaining some more knowledge and experience on the job. This is an amorphous freak class living from hand to mouth on the fringes of the larger economy. But with a programme of continuing education it could become a viable class with a distinctive sense of status, as African townships lack the basic services the trades could immediately provide. Black local governments have themselves never possessed the capability for sponsoring training for such essential, readily consumable services.

Among the smaller, but lately most vocal, higher sector – the professional class – there is beginning to emerge some competition for top positions. With this goes the usual jostling for jobs put aside for pals and other favourites. Most of the men and women in this class work in white-controlled institutions and are outnumbered by white staff. As a minority class, they see no alternative but to assimilate the work ethic by the rules they find: the system of promotions and competition; comportment and other demonstrable personality traits and quirks peculiar to business management; ambition – the whole culture of achievement and success.

'I often find myself in awkward circumstances,' Aggrey Klaaste reports with a good laugh. 'I mean in top management meetings.' He doesn't know the code, he admits, and senses that his white colleagues become restless when he behaves with the self-confidence of one who can afford to skip the code. Klaaste says his white manager is ambitious to achieve. But at the same time his drive is good for *Sowetan,* 'and it's fine for me as far as that goes,' he remarks with a chuckle.

The extremely long history during which the white man tried to run the country single-handed left no room for the African to develop self-reliance, except on the political and guerilla fronts. The sour legacy from this is evident in a deep-rooted dependence syndrome among us. Even in the professions – where collectives could emerge among associates, strengthen individual morale and wean us from dependence on whites, who must assert their own standards and ethic.

'In spite of my level of education and the social status I've moved into as a result of it, I don't feel removed from my roots ... the lowly community that socialized me in the Hammanskraal semi-rural area – some forty-eight kilometres north of Pretoria.' So Ms Matshilo Motsei tells us – a former nursing tutor and currently a research officer at the University of the Witwatersrand. She became dissatisfied with the regimented tutoring and archaic administration in the nursing college of Baragwanath Hospital, Johannesburg, the largest institution of its kind in the southern hemisphere. Motsei is a product of the 1976 schools revolt, during which she was in high school in Soweto. The major motivation in that revolt was the youth's resentment of the authorities and their repressive political and educational policies.

One of the humiliating experiences the higher-ups share is the stone wall its members run into on the job where things are controlled by the State. Equally unbearable is the situation where whites are in control – whites who immediately feel threatened by the arrival of a black person, especially a woman, who is highly qualified. 'Overqualified' here would therefore imply 'more qualified than us'. Colour and race are at the centre of the white person's fears. So it boils down to something deeper than a simple two-way competition. You are a much bigger threat to whites than to fellow black strugglers. Among the latter, all you have to be content with for a while is the fact of relative achievement. Few promotions in middle-management – e.g. in personnel relations, public relations, sales management, social responsibility and advertising – are more than token. You still have a white superior to be accountable to, and it is a long, gruelling haul to an executive position.

Lack of affirmative action also means that white staff and executive management will be slamming doors and windows shut to prevent or slow down the African's upward mobility. Their jobs have built-in benefits and guarantees, which may not be easily revised. We are a long way from establishing worker-employer relationships of the quality and level we observe in highly developed democracies. This is because of the dimensions of racism and racialism that define South African labour affairs. When leaders of a trade union table demands to management, the grievances go far beyond the conventional items concerning wages, working conditions, plain strikes, solidarity strikes and so on. Matters are thrown in that concern poor housing, poor water supply, poor health care and social welfare or lack of them, lack of educational services, and several other areas that directly concern the State, provincial and city governments.

The spectre of apartheid continues to haunt boardrooms where recognition agreements, notices to strike, overtime and so on are discussed. Too many members of the higher rank occupy the status of the old Western petit bourgeoisie – they sell their services that derive from their education and professions to the white person or agency that offers the best salary. This class still finds it well nigh impossible to support their perceived standing in society.

Not more than twenty-five years ago, teachers, matriculated clerks, nurses and other health workers lower than doctors, and other Africans with an equivalent standard of education received less money than a bus driver. This is rare today, and the professions are doing much better. Yet the disparities are still too stark for those in the professions to have developed a distinctive class with common concerns when union or association matters and the camaraderie they generate have been reckoned with. Survival by trade union solidarity is still the order of the day.

Reverend Lebamang Sebidi, director of the Trust for Educational Advancement, further demonstrates that the Marxist theory about class will not hold in South Africa. Sebidi is a theologian and Catholic priest by training. He came up from nothing: a rugged and somewhat casual upbringing in the pastoral life of Lesotho, during which the father handed the boy over to close relatives to raise, a common practice among Africans which no child ever questions aloud. Young Lebamang was shunted to another relative living in the then Orange Free State; another move took him to a sister in Soweto. A Catholic priest took him under his care, and saw to it that he attended school regularly. After matriculating from high school, the priest sent him to Rome to study for the priesthood. He obtained the Master's degree in theology. After his return to South Africa as a practising clerk, Sebidi read for the Master's in education.

He became involved in committees trying to stabilize Soweto civic life in the turbulent 1970s, when police terror and countless cases of detention without trial and banning orders were the regular fare for blacks throughout the country, but most savage in the black townships. In his work Sebidi got to know intimately the pain and travails of a people living virtually in a state of siege, on borrowed time, during the 1976 schools revolt and its aftermath.

Among blacks the higher-ranking class is far outnumbered by the 'working class'. Again, because of racial barriers, several members of the educated class find themselves reduced to doing jobs just a few notches above the labourer. Consequently, to possess a post-matriculation education and be black, and in addition be female, compels one to constantly regard the white man as a usurper. 'We're a footnote,' Sebidi comments, referring to the putative black middle class.

Sebidi cites Nico Poulantzas in the distinction he makes between class determination and class position. 'You can claim to be in a class even if circumstances might deny you its traditional benefits,' the Reverend reiterates. 'A predetermined capitalist may take up a position actively sympathetic towards workers... Just as it was the educated class that founded and led the nationalist movements in Africa.' Indeed, the educated elite, followed by its offshoots in later years, too, created the African National Congress – for it was the intelligentsia who were sensitive to the political issues of their day.

Contradictions: will this class become insignificant if it is shoved aside by new and younger activists, whom history has hoisted from the ranks of the less privileged and undereducated? 'Insignificant per se,' is Sebidi's reply. 'But with the aid of enlightened followers the class will survive – e.g. within a labour movement which sells its labour as a collective.'

Still more contradictions: while the educated class is powerless in the context of the national economy, it manages to keep an even keel in maintaining a rented municipal home and a family. This is because, on the one hand, it is so dependent on employment by both the public and private sectors and, on the other, the culture of poverty from which this class has just emerged has conditioned them to the ethic of thrift.

On the surface it might appear that the new arrivals have their sights set on role models in the white middle class who form the bulk of the employer sector, and among the petit bourgeoisie in government service. 'But it's not as simple as that,' Sebidi argues. 'Look at the teachers' defiance against government. Any day they can go into a chalk-down act and refuse to teach as a national union. So too with the health and allied workers, who have been picketing hospitals and bringing them to a standstill. Employers today think many times before they can apply the ancient rule of "no work, no pay".'

'Even when a new democratic government has been set up?' I ask.

'Even then,' the cleric replies, 'workers are not going to wax chummy-chummy with government just because blacks have now become the majority ruling class.'

Are the faint signs of an emerging class of black entrepreneurs for real, or a mirage? It's still too small a class for us to predict its short-term future. For now, it is a case of 'arise and stake your claim and grab!' But this does not rule out the possibility of co-option into the white class that controls corporate finance and operates its own work ethic. Consider also the fact that Shuenyane, Klaaste, Mathiane and all the other people interviewed emphasized that their children, when they are on their own, are not voluntarily going to settle for anything less than the social and family environments that conditioned their mental and emotional lives. They feel their social class is all cut out for them. Nor can their parents possibly negate what they themselves invested, materially and emotionally, in their children's education. But it is not without a twinge of guilt and apprehension that they contemplate the increased social distance between the achievers among their children and the large masses of people who are never going to attain their level. This distance is greater than that between parents who have moved into suburbia and their own immediate beginnings. So there are bigger challenges ahead for the educated class in general.

Challenges? We are caught up in the process of climbing up, perhaps even moving from one cultural milieu to another. In a white-dominated world that sets the rules for us, we can dream of days when we can sit back a little, and contemplate what we can become beyond the sheer grinding effort to survive; how we can begin to happen to events rather than the other way round, as it has been for centuries. We have to admit that most of us are burnt out by the time we reach the limit of our capacity to achieve, because of that protracted and grinding effort to survive. And so we take it easy, which we are not good at either, alas!

For all these reasons, we have unconsciously pushed to the back of our minds those constant exhortations by school, church and civic authorities, and guest speakers (black and white) at the schools we attended. Those exhortations were mostly loaded with biblical and martial proverbs and parables: 'Do not hide your talent under a bushel ... Be a beacon to your people. Go out and fight the forces of ignorance and superstition among your people, armed with the good education your teachers have given you at this school'. Some African speakers even reached cautiously into their store of political lore: 'Lead our people out of bondage like Moses who cried out, "Let my people go!" Take a leaf from Booker T Washington's book, *Up From Slavery* ... Let us draw inspiration from men like Dr James K Aggrey, who so loved education and became a scholar of international renown ...'

Of course some of the images that were held up to us, drawn from South African life, signalled little more than elitist comfort and self-congratulation. But they were defined by values that were external to us, evolved from the limited vision of our mentors. However, the central message remained unimpeachable: the utilitarian principle underlying education rather than enlightenment for its own sake. By the same token, the responsibility remains that we translate that principle in modern terms.

Henry Louis Gates Jr, the W E B DuBois Professor of the Humanities at Harvard University and one of the leading scholars in African American history and culture, has brought that message back to us in an article entitled *Two nations...both black* (Forbes Journal, 14 September 1992). Gates goes back to remind us that W E B DuBois, 'black America's greatest intellectual', wrote in 1903 that the Negro masses could be uplifted in no quicker way than 'by the effort and example of [their own] aristocracy of talent and character'; that 'the history of human progress' shows that the biggest mistake that ever hindered that progress was the notion 'that no more could ever rise save the few already risen... and that it would better the unrisen to pull the risen down.'

The Harvard professor draws a picture of the African American condition that is pretty close to the bone in our own black experience here. DuBois, he recounts, wrote in those early decades (1910-1932) that to be an entertainer or athlete was fine and good. But the disciplines that were going to count in achievement ratings were law, medicine, education and scholarship – the elevating stuff of the 'Talented Tenth'.

True enough, the black middle class in America has a longer history than our fragmented intelligentsia and is a much more firmly established institution. The African Americans have a long and heroic history of self-help educational institutions pioneered and administered by their own elite, offering tertiary and technical studies and sponsored by churches and such organizations as the Negro College Fund. You only need to think of institutions of higher learning such as Wilberforce, Fisk, Howard, Dillard, Hampton, Lincoln and Tuskegee (which inspired Dr John L Dube to establish Ohlange). And then there are the blacks who go to well-endowed historically white universities and colleges. But one can see a parallel history unfolding here. Gates cites two historic events on his side of the Atlantic: 1954, the schools desegregation law and the 1965 Voting Rights Act. Things were not going to be the same after that, notwithstanding the racism and poverty that still dog the black Americans.

In all this, Gates sees a process of class mobility over the decades which gathered rapidity and volume in the last thirty years or so. In the light of this development, he considers that the black Americans 'do great harm to the truth when we pretend the problems confronting the black underclass are identical to those confronting the black middle class.' He can even talk of an 'upper' middle class – heirs of the Talented Tenth. They are isolated from the black underclass and yet still subject to racial insults from waitresses, shop assistants and taxi drivers, and discrimination by banks, on the job and on historically white college campuses.

The emergence of an African intelligentsia in this country was slow and scattered, except when nationalism brought them together as leaders of the African National Congress, All-African Convention, Pan Africanist Congress and so on. Otherwise they did not, as African Americans do, have either the means or the sponsorship to neutralize the geographical and social distances between their respective localities, to allow them to feel that they were part of an *intellectual movement*. Such a movement would have felt committed to the corporate will to undertake scholarship while systematically and constructively debating social issues. Whites have always been at the helm of that ship; we, on our side, are simply and uncritically footnotes, extracts from their texts, even when these derive from research on 'Native life' and are based on European and American social and philosophical theories. Today the quality of our scholarship, such as it is, is not significantly higher than it was thirty years ago, and so cannot fully represent the deeper levels of our cultural being – where we are coming from and what we may really hope to be. We need not recite here, all over again, the litany of our woes that racial oppression and a fiercely legislated life have wrought.

But we are not entirely blameless for our lot. We can take a few hints from Professor Gates' catalogue of things that his people may need to face up to the obligations implicit in their class structure. Relatively freer social and physical mobility affords them the time and motivation to take charge of some of the dynamics of class consciousness. First, he says, it is time for the black middle class 'to stop feeling guilty about its own success while fellow blacks languish in the inner city of despair.' He stresses that black prosperity is not born of black poverty. Success has come about for some because their communities and families '*prepared* them to be successful.'

Second, 'we don't have to fail in order to be black. Surveys,' Gates adds, 'have recorded far too many black youths saying that success is white.' ('Bourgeois' is our idiom here which, by derivation, they equate with white.) So is aspiring and entertaining dreams. Relevant to our own case here, where the youth have made a cult of failure, the Harvard academic suggests that it was unthinkable in earlier times, when the Talented Tenth was in the making, for any one to deride success. 'We need *more* success individually and collectively, not less.'

Third, 'we don't have to pretend any longer that thirty million [African-Americans] can ever possibly be members of the same social class.'

Finally, also relevant to the South African blacks, Henry Gates points out that poverty stems *both* from the conditions that structures of racism and neglectful government have created for us, and from the behaviour of blacks themselves (my paraphrase).

Sociologists, he reminds us, have tended to emphasize the economic and political structures as the arch-enemies of blacks. Consequently, they (the scholars) have rejected the notion of any such thing as the 'culture of poverty'. Yet African-Americans would do well to acknowledge such a concept. For, in spite of the economic and political ills that compound themselves to create the larger pattern, poverty creates its own culture. Human behaviour – the human will – must come into full play at this point. How could there not be a culture of poverty? How could we imagine that culture *matters*, Gates proceeds with his telling statement, and refuse to acknowledge that 'in general, a household made up of a sixteen-year-old mother, a thirty-two-year-old grandmother, and a forty-eight-year-old great-grandmother is not a site for hope and optimism. It's also true that not everyone in any society wants to work, that not all people are equally motivated.'

By now we should have come to realize that we of the elevated class – whatever term will best describe the level between the labourer and anything higher than the manufacturer, the exporter and importer, the civil servant, and other professional personnel – can no longer leave matters to evolution. We have the same responsibilities that Dr DuBois formulated towards those less privileged than ourselves: the 'masses'.

There is very little participation in community development by those whose inner drive has led them to recognize and exploit opportunity and achieve. This involvement, in whatever professional capacity, in existing structures and/or those we ourselves initiate, is one important way in which we can come to terms with the ethics of our higher status. Without doing this, our talented few don't stand the slightest chance of remaining accessible to those levels of the community that opportunity, education and training have removed us from – whether we like it or not. We can thus translate education as *process* into community development.

Portrait of a Man in a Glasshouse (1976)

Synopsis by Sam Raditlhalo

In its tone and philosophical self-examination, this article takes us into the mind of a man as he mulls over the viability of returning to apartheid South Africa after an absence of nineteen years. Unlike other exiled South Africans, the Mphahleles were gainfully employed and secure. Such seemingly enviable middle-class stability could not even begin to compare to the uncertainties of eking out an existence in South Africa, where black professionals were by law assigned second-class roles to their white counterparts. Yet it is not really 'autopathography', since the writer seeks to reintegrate in a society that tyrannically holds him to itself. The tyranny of place is something to which he submits. The article is measured in its chronicling of a mature life in progress, without necessarily descending into navel gazing. His ever-critical mind could not allow him to rest, to attempt to reconcile the tyranny of place with the condition of exile, of placelessness and displacement.

**The gods help us: how can a man teach among people whose
cultural goals he cannot share?**

E very so often you hit a certain age when you pause on the road of this life to take stock. I remember I did it when I hit twenty-one. A muddle-headed pause it was, I'll tell you – like when you drive into a bay off the road marked out for a scenic view. Another bay was thirty, then forty-two, now fifty-five. Odd intervals, I'll say, because I've come to measure my life in decades. *Me and myself.* Although, really, I can't say for sure at any time who of the two is observer-commentator, who is the driver. I live in a glasshouse, the one I ran into seventeen years ago. It's roomy but borrowed. I can live in it as long as I pay the rent and as long as I don't start kicking things about or scratching or staining the walls, I'm told. I can see the change of seasons, light, tints, patterns of shade clearly when the rain is gone – in a way I could never have done in the painful South. I go down in the cellar often to sharpen the arsenal of my brain, oil and grease it and generally train the panzer division of my mind.

I'm here not because I was invisible. Sometimes it's cold in here, sometimes warm, sometimes full of light, sometimes shadows come down upon me. There are no ultra-bright light bulbs, not one, not one thousand three hundred and sixty-nine of expensive filament type. I hear ghetto blues, too, and so I know what I've done to feel so black and blue. I'm not invisible, I say, have never been. How could I be? For every one of *them* there are four of me in that southern corner of Africa. That's why I ran. Always I hear a river. So often it has become part of *me* and *myself*. For hours I can stop and listen to it, feel it rub against the sides of this glasshouse sometimes, right under my basement. Sets wild things quivering and grating like pebbles back of my skull, sending clues to my ego centre about the togetherness of happenings even while I hear a war cry, voices from the whirlwind prophesying chaos and doom like I think not even that dome-crazy reefer-stricken Kubla Khan would have dreamed in the splendour of his sacred river …

Not yet time for him to stand and stare out the window, stare at nothing special, just stare, fingers interlocked behind him or twitching with arthritic messages or arms folded across the chest. Just staring, rain or shine. Not yet time for him to scratch his armpit self-indulgently, mop wet eyes with heel of the hand. Not yet time to act grandfather: that can wait, he says, until he's a drooling old fart, too old to care when children climb on his lap or tug at his sleeve. Brought up five of his own children and says *ho lekane ho lekane* – enough is enough! That was steep and rough enough in the ghetto shanty for him not to want to mess with the dumb things now, *whoever* their parents may be. Never had a babysitter for mine, he says. Says why should these young folks have babies and not want to look after them without conning grandpas and grandmas with chocolate candy or tobacco to baby-sit? If I had to do it all over again I'd still have five at the age we were. We'd still look after them. I'd still come to this point where a day with small kids – well, that's the day I resign. Now look at this mess around us... Look... These people hang on to their children with hoops of steel man, won't let them go live their own lives until there's a crisis... See them go, and then Pa and Ma are after them again with hoops of steel. Parents drive them around to keep their dates, lend them cars for their dates no matter how erratic each new friendship. See them almost kill their children with protection and entertainment; see them project their own neurotic anxieties into their kids and dogs and cats; see the children try to run from them as they grow up and Ma and Pa still after them with hoops of steel. Hear the kids talk to their parents or about them and the parents follow the book that tells them to give children free scope and speech. See them resent parenthood, drag it into the mud. And Pa and Ma out again after them with hoops of steel. Funny how a culture helps people contain its own mess, its own miscarriages and abortions and monstrosities. Same all over. Cultures of Africa will do it with theatre, ritual, poetry. Give me small kids in small doses; mix every dose with Scotch every time. The day the African allows his children to devour him – that'll be the day the grief of the gods will strangle Time, mutilate it, leave us wandering mindlessly without day without night.

I could, if I chose to renew my lease indefinitely on this glasshouse, quite forget, write off my past, take my chances on new territory... I shall not. Because I'm a helpless captive of place, and to come to terms with the tyranny of place is to have something to live for, to save me from stagnation, anonymity. It's not fame you want, it's having your shadow noticed, it's the comfort that you can show control over your life, that you can function. Comforting also is to feel you can coil around the ego centre, feel and hear the juices flow within and when the time is ripe, uncoil, stretch out and feel and hear the spiral motion of body and mind interwoven with other lives at a specific time and place. The place is not here, alas, so the moment must wait for renewal time. Something else: I could seek to enlist for the black American cause. But I'm still a captive of the place I fled. The common pangs and joys, the crossroads and fork-ways of blackness? Yes. Time enough to learn and feel them. That is all, that is all that's possible. To fight a cause you've got to feel its history and its future in your blood and bones and dreams. Outsider... Always on the outside... In this ghetto of the soul, what need have I for rats and cockroaches of the Western hemisphere, its gun-toting cops, when all my life in the painful South they crawled all over me and nibbled on the marrow of my being – what need have I? Time enough time enough to feel and learn time enough...

Not yet time for him to fart like a horse and dangle on an elongated burp without care who's around. Nor time yet for him to gargle with words and syllables and sighs and saliva and spit them out together. Nor yet time to flip over on his side before he carries his partner to the hilltop, flip over and wheeze in long irresponsible bars, the heart panting like it's just turned back on the edge of a precipice, now scared of what could have happened, partner looking at the ceiling and thinking madly, 'super-annuated cock!' or else, 'well, we're not getting any younger dear, don't fret on it.' No, not yet time: he can hold his own, still at the peak of manhood. He's past the age for any new regrets to bother him. They can wait. The old ones have mellowed. They don't affront him, stick their tongues out at him, or stab him between the ribs with needles. They plod like oxen inside him, resigned, enduring, sure of surviving many more ploughing seasons or of getting their freight to its destination, noble in their patience. New regrets can kick about, buck like an untamed donkey, head down, ears pointing back at a mean angle, tail swishing and fanning off one anal explosion after another. He has learned to wait, dead certain he'll wear off the young bucking regrets.

Teaching, writing, writing, teaching – the same interminable cycle in the long, long quest for a metaphor, for the right word, lucid, fresh like water straight out of rock, or like city lights on a clear night that I have viewed from the foothills – reassuring, promising, seeming to breathe like the life that is stirring down there. If only, if only – ah, these days the 'if onlies' seem to come from unexpected corners, in numbers, in broken ranks like bedbugs: if only I could teach in my own native land or continent! Here among strangers, where the young grind the aged under with steamrollers, here where to be forty is an affront to youth, I can't help but say under my breath as I stand before undergraduates: You're going to listen to me, you dumb clattering tin cans and cymbals, you bouncing bundles of tender cartilage, because you want to gather credits like ripe mangoes, because you're on your way up to the middle-class totem pole that you spit upon, because you crave the respectability you pretend to scorn, because to shake off Papa's subsidy you've got to earn your independence, because among your stampeding herd are those who'll take to other hills, other pastures, other streams for their own survival. I know that left to yourselves you'd kill me, kill all the fifty-year-olds because they stand for the stability you still have to earn... But you're going to listen, aren't you? Yes? I thought so... The gods help us: how can a man teach among people whose cultural goals he cannot share?

A little while longer, you keep saying to numb the pain: just a while longer, the lease must hold, stretch it out a little longer, just to function like they'd never let you do in the painful South. So inch along, there's ample margin for your classroom style to stretch, expand its muscle. The solid core of students – ten or eight or six – will still be there to join you at the crossroads where minds must meet and mate. For I'll concede this much, as one of many, many dissenters: there's something rotten in the state of middle-class values: certain notions of success, the way parents want to devour their offspring, the where-did-we-go-wrong refrain, the phoney sanctity of marriage and notions of man-wife fidelity and Christian morality. I choke with anger at the elders who declare wars recklessly for no love of country that is threatened, and push young bloods to the battlefront, and outlaw them if they refuse to die. And then my river whispers *it's none of your business here, none, you hear!* Anger splutters and settles down to a smoulder which is called indignation. The glass around me registers again on my senses, reminds me that I have been looking at the landscape outside so hard the glass dissolved, merged into the light out there.

Social Work and the Politics of Dispossession – 1987

Synopsis by Peter Thuynsma

Although this is a public address to a gathering of professional social workers, Es'kia Mphahlele wades rather boldly into their arena to address not only kinship and welfare – the very stuff of social work as a discipline – but also to advocate African Humanism through a use of scholarly chronicle and through examples of lyrical poetry!

He recognizes kinship as a kingpin in the fabric of social relationships and organization that has economic and political significance as well as social. He further asserts that inheritance and succession are of economic importance because these and other factors make the family an economic unit. Once again, the overriding interest is in the cohesiveness and sustainability of the African family.

Fully cognizant of the dynamics of communities, he champions the traditional mindset without regarding such persons (largely rural dwellers) as unrealistic or innocent. Mphahlele prefers, instead, the assertion that:

'…in traditional society, all institutions and individuals co-operate within a unified social unit to help give society a member it can be proud of. The child is surrounded by several models of good conduct and not only by his immediate family. The whole community takes an interest in his growth and welfare.'

And he concludes:

'The value of the individual life and communal life is thus heightened in our consciousness: the essence of African humanism.'

Education is basically a social service – from circumcision schools to formal tertiary education. The more you learn, the more you earn; the more you contribute to your community. It is from this perspective that the essay gets its thrust.

L et us try to trace the history of human development on this continent since the Stone Age. Although there are regional cultures in Africa, the existence of *Africanity* cannot escape us. By this we are referring to the common cultural experiences we share on the continent – the whole landscape of culture. We are talking about culture as a concept that defines what we as humans do and make to cope with the material realities of life. On the other hand, it also defines the body of knowledge, ideas, morals, beliefs, religion, the arts and language that make up the sum total of our being. It will be appreciated that economic, political and social systems embrace our intellectual creations, material advancements and expressive culture such as the arts. All should be seen as aspects of culture.

Africa has long been recognized as the original home of the human species. Dr Louis Leakey, the leading Kenya-born scientist who did most of his archaeological research in East Africa, wrote:

> *The many new discoveries that have been made during the past eleven years make it possible to state without doubt that man himself – as well as his 'cousins', the living great apes – evolved in Africa. Not only can we now be certain that Africa was the continent that witnessed human evolution; we can even pinpoint the most important regions where this took place. (1971)*

Leakey explains that some twenty to twenty-five million years ago, man's ancestors split from the ancestors of the great apes in the evolutionary line. East African fossils show themselves to be the remains of three families: the hominids (humankind), the giant apes (gorilla, chimpanzee and orangutan), and the quick-footed gibbon with long arms. It is most likely, Louis Leakey concludes, that the single ancestor of the three branches is to be found in the fossils discovered in Egypt, west of the Nile, dating to thirty-five million years ago.

As the original home of humans, Africa must also be the cradle of human culture. Tools and weapons of stone are the earliest signs of African culture. The earliest period to which remains of these tools can be traced is called the Stone Age. According to scientists, this period can be divided into three: the Old Stone Age, the Middle Stone Age and the New Stone Age. To make certain tools out of stone required skills first developed in the Old Stone Age; the Middle is associated with the art of pottery; and the earliest farming and the taming of animals for home use matches with the New Stone Age.

The cultures of the Stone Age were practised over the last million years BC. The Ice Age in other parts of the globe coincided with the African Stone Age. Although Africa never experienced the moving giant glaciers of the Ice Age, certain of its regions were affected by them – e.g. the Great Rift Valley that runs through Kenya, and the Red Sea. The Ice Age effects also left behind the beautiful scenery of East Africa, and a warm region: Africans could be comfortably spared the cold of the glaciers here.

The Stone Age nurtured a tool-making culture, which became its trademark. The Africans used and developed the hand axe for skinning and chopping up game, defending himself and carving crude wooden tools. More developed blades, scrapers and choppers for hunting and self-defence surfaced in the very late Old Stone Age, mostly in the savannahs. When vegetables became scarce over long periods of drought, humans became meat eaters.

Culture has often been said to be a product of the mind. The human being had to sit down and mentally design the appropriate tool for a specific occasion. He had to project his mind at least into the near future. Tool-making distinguishes humans from apes. Pebble tools have been dug up at many sites in South Africa, and at Olduvai and other sites in East Africa. Hundreds of these tools have also been discovered in several parts of Western Europe and in south India.

Some one hundred to three hundred thousand years ago, the use of fire was discovered. The handled, or two-piece, tool was invented. Navigation began; fishing became a profitable occupation. Populations grew as a result of these historic events of civilization, leading to farming and stock rearing in the New Stone Age.

Obviously the tool makers were hunters first, before agriculture and stock rearing evolved. Throughout the eras of hunter-gathering and early farming, people lived in closely knit family units. Later, villages developed. Pastoral nomads, however, continued to roam the continent. Family units held them together. The larger extended family – the clan – became an added dimension of the need for safety and responsibility to one another. As long as individuals felt this responsibility, human life was secure. The custom of inheritance and succession worked smoothly. People cared for each other, provided for each other. Need, whether caused by sickness or old age or other misfortune, did not haunt a person day and night as is the case today.

When hunters, herders and food growers were so closely connected by blood or occupation or both, mutual care was pure. There was no ulterior motive behind it, because there were no possessions and no property that was not shared in common. The same applied in village life. Groups cared about the welfare of their members, be they tribal or ethnic or age groups, or regiments. Where urban life has not inflicted much damage, directly or indirectly, on traditional mores, beliefs and customs, the ancient order prevails even today. I shall therefore use the present tense in the rest of my narrative.

Kinship is crucial in the fabric of social relationships and organization. It has economic, political as well as social significance. Inheritance and succession are of economic importance. This and other factors make the family an economic unit. Inheritance is by descent within the family – a unity that is at the centre of the community. Inheritance of wealth or rank is matrilineal, i.e. son from maternal uncle, rather than from his own father. Son inherits from father or paternal uncle in a patriarchal society. Most societies are patriarchal, women serving as agents of power.

The systems of polygamy and the extended family make it possible for kinship groups to be self-sufficient and take care of one another's welfare. Whether in the nuclear (also called elementary) or extended family, every member enjoys rights and acknowledges obligations and responsibilities towards other members. No one need starve or stay neglected if infirm or disabled.

Orphanages are hardly known in traditional life, nor are old age homes. The extended family takes care of the elderly and orphans. The mentally handicapped, like the physically disabled, are provided for. In present-day conditions, where economics make it imperative for every adult to contribute to the home income, it becomes evident that handicapped members are overprotected. The few opportunities that exist for their training are not exploited by the family. They do not want to appear to be abdicating their responsibility by isolating their next-of-kin for others to take care of. Taking care of someone is a concept as old as the humanism of Africa and has survived into modern times, when we are compelled to find a new meaning and function for it.

Care is taken to balance individual rights with communal rights. Collective labour is common: cultivating someone else's field or building his house. So is sharing of food in times of scarcity and where one is unable to fend for the family through no fault of one's own. Land is held in trust by the ruler, to allocate to his or her people. There is no individual ownership. But if someone is too lazy to work his field, it is taken away from him. Grazing land is used by all who keep livestock.

When subsistence farming was the prevailing custom, it did not matter whether a man inherited his father's or maternal uncle's rank or wealth. But when cash-crop farming replaced the subsistence mode, i.e. just enough to feed the family and save for drought periods, the property to be inherited had added value. It thus became necessary for a son to inherit property from his own father, so as to keep it close within the immediate family.

Land is a gift from the ancestors. It is an outrage against their protection of you to neglect the land. So is it an outrage when it is taken from you by force. What actually made the Mau Mau in Kenya rise against the British colonists in 1952 was this sense of indignation. They were angry against themselves for having had their land taken away by the settlers. They felt they had betrayed their ancestors. Hence the oath that every man who joined Mau Mau in the forests had to take. They believed they were waging a religious war against the British.

Cattle are another vital commodity for economic exchange and contracts. Marriage, the bride prize, succession and inheritance, residence, erection of a place of abode, ancestral rituals related to the fertility of the soil and woman – all these and other activities are part of the rhythm of life. It is a rhythm controlled by the Life Force or Vital Force that has established a chain linking all beings: humans, plants, animals, rivers, mountains, soil, rocks, seas, lakes, the elements and so on. The Vital Force is the Supreme Being. We do not worship the ancestors. They are our mediators, intercessors with the Supreme Being.

What has all this to do with welfare? I have tried to indicate a social order in which life is still together, has a unified purpose. The dictionary meaning of 'welfare' reads: 'the state of being or doing well; condition of health, happiness and comfort; well-being; prosperity; those government agencies concerned with granting aid to those suffering from poverty, unemployment, etc.' The meaning listed last – granting aid to those suffering from poverty, unemployment, etc. – represents what welfare initially and essentially has been until today. Indeed, the organized effort of modern times often detracts from the earlier essential meanings.

For in trying to aid, to alleviate, we may very well be damaging a person or community's well-being, state of being, happiness and so on. But I should not here trespass into an expert's area.

Welfare in a traditional society is more humanistic than it is today, when it is a battery of agencies that try to measure suffering by statistics. The former, on the contrary, is between a person or persons who 'give' welfare as a way of life; as a pristine culture, an expression of a state of mind that comes out of a natural humanitarian desire to help a fellow being. A desire that is as old as human life itself. If I am happy and comfortable, while my next-of-kin at the elementary level and fellow human at the communal level is not, my cultural instinct tells me to reach out and help. Culture is an acquired, learned and compulsive act. We learn from our mothers, who pass on to us what is called mother wit. This cultural instinct worked magnificently when social conscience still came naturally to us. Our social needs were relatively simple; our humanism was still readily available.

There are still communities in Africa where these practices and qualities can be found in a slightly or largely modified form. In such a society status comes with age and experience (a less complicated term for education). Your position in the family determines your role. You have goals set by tradition. The way in which you became part of society and act the part according to norms you know very well by example, in other words your socialization, is determined by those goals.

Virginia van der Vliet has written in an essay *Growing Up In Traditional Society*:

> *Traditional society was relieved of the problem of different socializing agents pursuing conflicting goals. In Western society, home, school, church and peer group may all have very different ideas about what constitutes suitable behaviour.* (cited in Hammond-Tooke 1974: 24)

Brothers and sisters look after each other in the absence of their parents. Let me paraphrase what the author proceeds to say, if only to reinforce the picture I have been trying to sketch for you. She states that in traditional society, all institutions and individuals co-operate within a unified social unit to help give society a member it can be proud of. The child is surrounded by several models of good conduct and not only by his immediate family. The whole community takes an interest in his growth and welfare.

241

It would be a mistake to think little of what appears to be a very simple system of welfare, merely because life in traditional society is not as complex as it is today. At the base of welfare, care for one's fellow human is religion. Not a church-going religious practice, nor one that we observe in temples, synagogues and mosques. Religion in traditional Africa permeates all life. What the Western world derisively calls 'superstition' in traditional practices is but a fragment of profound African religious thought and belief.

If the Supreme Being resides in every being – animal, plant, human, inanimate nature, ancestral spirits, the elements, the universe – and breathes its vitality into them, it stands to reason that as humans we are all linked to nature by a force that commands our reverence, our sense of wonder. There is continuity in these interrelationships that is self-fulfilling for humans. We love life. We believe in the sanctity of life and carry in us a strong sense of community. We gravitate towards one another rather than pull away from each other. We are a singing, talking people. There is communal solidarity in our traditional political and economic activities and in our social services, although these are not styled after Western patterns.

The value of the individual life and communal life is thus heightened in our consciousness: the essence of African humanism. This is not to ignore the violence we have often committed against the values we attach to humanism. War, witchcraft, ritual murder, the killing of twins in certain African communities – all these have been and are still part of our lives. But the majority of us acknowledge such crimes as the monstrosities, the aberrations of our society. To acknowledge them and to condemn them unequivocally is to assert the positive elements of our ancient civilization, particularly our humanism.

Our social and personal interrelationships can be seen to lean towards a strong social conscience. According to our humanism, wronging another human, neglecting our duty by the things and values we hold sacred such as the soil, and desecrating ancestral ground such as graves are acts we must atone for. Always a third party must act as mediator. We must go to the person we have wronged, and only through a mediator ask to be forgiven. Another person we go to with the deepest secrets of our soul is the doctor. He or she is the custodian of our customs, all the ancient ways of the community. This immediately rules out the ghetto quack and the self-styled diviners who are mere slimy money-mongers. Yet another is any highly respected elder in the community, who is a symbol of ancient wisdom.

Hundreds of proverbs and other oral literature express our social conscience that stands at the centre of social welfare. You do not drive away a stranger at your door. He who travels alone will be eaten by a lion: everyone needs his or her kin. Deaf-to-advice stayed on a rock and wanted to build with grass and sticks, but it collapsed. Laugh while you still have your teeth: enjoy life while it lasts. If you have something on your mind, say it; let it grow and it will kill you. The real medicine that brings happiness is to be at peace with everybody. (This clearly indicates a homogeneous community where enemies are not particularly dangerous.) We do not listen to a loner: he has no witnesses. The heart of a person is a sea: it is like a sea where all the rivers empty themselves without ever filling it. People are mealies: take care of human beings with kindness, as you would take care of mealies in the granaries, or don't allow weeds to choke them in the fields. To help is to store for yourself. The head of a man is a secret storage place. The heart of a man is like an intricately woven net. The fool would say this world is a virgin, the wise man knows the world is old. Where is the protection by those who praised you? Today they carry you to the place of burial. (In this saying is the bitter and ironic reality of our love for community.) Faults are like a hill: you stand on your own and talk about those of other people. If you do not allow a friend to get a nine, you yourself will never get a ten.

In long-settled communities, interdependence between members was reinforced and legitimised by religious beliefs such as I have outlined under the concept of African humanism. Among groups that lacked a central authority, and perhaps even lacked a single ancestor, there tended to evolve a belief that certain people were invested with extraordinary powers. People so endowed are able to produce more and more food when natural forces can be attracted to collaborate.

The Tiv in Nigeria are such a community. The extraordinary capability is called a person's tsav: a personal potency. Some have greater *tsav* than others. It is also believed that such people with high potency, known as *mbatsav*, can exercise power on natural forces themselves – e.g. they can cause rain to fall. One's *tsav* is believed to be a positive, creative force, promoting welfare, reinforcing the forces of nature, giving life to the soil. This could be one of the oldest forms of what we call charisma.

The case of the *tsav* among the Tiv is a clear example of how myth in countless communities can be so potent that it compensates for a lot of weak links in a culture. A people's welfare is thus ensured. A myth is a fictitious idea we believe in collectively for the power it inspires in us. We do not have to prove that a myth has any truth in fact. It is enough that it lends a passionate purpose to life.

Traditional societies are admirably integrated. They also see life as an integrated, organic process reflecting the interconnectedness of phenomena, ideas, events, people and the cosmos. They are self-sufficient communities. There is no need to have dis-advantaged people in them, except those who are physically and mentally handi-capped – nothing like today's communities of displaced and alienated persons with serious psychological problems.

The following poem makes it quite clear where the public stands in its attitude to poverty. Soul-battering poverty is quite disgusting, demeaning, and devastating to one's self-esteem. In other words, there should be no reason for poverty that is beyond the *subject's* control. The poem is a translation from the Swahili, in the oral tradition:

The Poor Man

The poor man knows not how to eat with the rich man.
When they eat fish, he eats the head.

Invite a poor man and he rushes in
licking his lips and upsetting the plates.

The poor man has no manners,
he comes along with the blood of lice under his nails.

The face of the poor man is lined
from the hunger and thirst in his belly.

Poverty is no state for any mortal man.
It makes him a beast to be fed on grass.

Poverty is unjust. If it befalls a man,
though he is nobly born, he has no power with God.

God here must be equated with the highest and most beautiful qualities in the person. Poverty violates them.

The next piece represents a poet who is at ease with himself. It is also a traditional poem, translated from the language of Kuba in Zaire. Death is nothing to fear. Instead, it is a moment of triumph, cause for celebration of a life that must continue beyond the grave. In the societies we see around us today death is something to be dreaded. It comes in many more, and different ways than in the olden days: chronic and short-lived illnesses, physical violence, a sudden and unpredictable event, murder and so on. People rush about trying to prepare for the unknown by forming themselves into burial societies. Eventually we find ourselves fretting over the dying more than we do over the living who are crying out for help at this very moment. In this poem, however, death poses no threat:

Death

There is no needle without piercing point.
There is no razor without trenchant blade.
Death comes to us in many forms.
With our feet we walk the goat's earth.
With our hands we touch God's sky.

Some future day in the heat of noon,
I shall be carried shoulder high
through the village of the dead.
When I die, don't bury me under forest trees,
I fear their thorns.
When I die, don't bury me under forest trees,
I fear their thorns.
I fear the dripping water.
Bury me under the great shade trees in the market,
I want to hear the drums beating
I want to feel the dancers' feet.

Education is basically a social service. Even the traditional circumcision school, where there is formal instruction about the rights and responsibilities of adulthood, is a social service although it is not rationalized as such. By and large education in traditional societies is informal, except in those communities where Western social systems have overtaken the old ways.

In pastoral and agrarian communities you grow up tending livestock. For the whole day you are receiving messages from surrounding nature. You become its pupil. You learn to judge distances and develop an acute sense of direction and body balance. Your senses of smell, taste, touch, sight and hearing are constantly activated. Your animals teach you responsibility. You get to know what to do when a cow or goat has given birth. You have to carry the kids home, even though they may be triplets. You become sharply aware of the rhythm of the seasons, of day and night. You develop a sense of wonder. You grow up also to learn by example from the older people what your expected role is in the community. If you want to marry, you have to build a house. When your children are born, you pass on to them what you learned as a boy or girl.

Except for the mentally or physically handicapped, there are no dropouts. Promotion is by age and therefore automatic. Every person acquires arts and crafts without any notion of specialization. Both man and woman will perform several other duties according to a division of labour, even when they are artists.

Members of all ancient communities collectively became aware at one time or another that humans almost regularly experience a surplus of time and energy. When harvesting time is over and cattle are at the cattle post, it becomes time for people to weave mats, create art such as carving, decorate walls with coloured patterns, do woodwork, repair thatched roofs and so on. The performing arts go on perennially.

A person who brings this kind of mental, physical and spiritual equipment to urban life is going to be doubly enriched. He or she will soon realize that it will take time to bring their rural social education to good account in the new environment.

They start at a disadvantage because urbanites look down upon them as rustics. They may sooner or later begin to despise themselves, and want desperately to acquire urban township or location habits and thus some imagined 'sophistication'.

At this point urbanization has begun, for better or for worse. But apart from this phase in the lives of certain people, the largely un-programmed education in traditional society builds up that sense of well-being, of self in relation to community that I have been talking about. This is welfare as a state of being, free from the intervention of social work.

Before people become urbanized they go through a period of transition, especially migrant labourers. They bring to the urban area sets of mores learned in rural life. Rural relationships survive for a while, until they do not matter any longer. Whereas the newcomer in urban life at first allows no outsiders into his network of relationships deriving from his rural life, he gradually outgrows these and reconciles himself to a new network. Eventually he acknowledges unconsciously that this is how urban life is going to be. It is such networks that constantly surface when communities regroup in urban areas. They compensate for what is lacking in welfare services, or they supplement what is there in small doses. They do it in a way that expresses *their own selves*, and not the welfare agencies

Even rural life has changed and continues to change in South Africa, to the extent that we have come a long way from the traditions I have been describing. The rise of urban centres, along with the spread of the industrial revolution, has now brought us complications education has hardly equipped us to deal with – thanks to race politics. More than this, we are in charge of no process in the realms of economics and politics that matters. I repeat: we are in charge of nothing that matters!

Towards a Definition of Nation Building – 1996

Synopsis by James Ogude

This paper, written after South Africa's democratic political dispensation, confronts the vexed problem of nation-building by drawing attention to the fact that nation-building as desire and process has to be inclusive and tolerant of the divergent, plural groups that constitute any normal society for it to succeed. Rooted in South Africa's history of the last few decades, the paper argues that South Africa has always been plagued by authoritarian nationalisms that sought to impose their ideologies on others and worked to undermine the genuine nationalisms of the conquered communities. What was encouraged was a negative form of ethnic consciousness whose sole aim was to fragment traditional African communities. Indeed, even within urban centres where new forms of affiliations and networks were beginning to be forged successfully, apartheid nationalist ideology worked through legislation and physical force to divide the Africans. Ethnic groups, Mphahlele argues, became conditioned to their separate entities and ethnic cocoons, a condition that was further com-pounded by the spirit of consumerism that modernity had imposed on the emerging African elite. This middle class status, instead of reinforcing national engineering, became its nemesis. But although apartheid worked to undermine nation formation that is inclusive, African nationalism managed to rally the people around the struggle for freedom.

The challenge in the new dispensation, Mphahlele believes, is how to translate the ideals and rhetoric of nationalism into nation building beyond the battle cry. The danger of some subcultures seeking to dominate others remains real if we cannot translate vague notions, such as reconciliation, into bold political acts beyond moral platitudes. The retrogressive subcultures, whether they are rooted in ancient nationalisms like tribalism or fascist ideologies akin to Afrikaner nationalism, can only work to undermine the project of nation building. The paper conclusively suggests that for nation building to succeed, it will have to be underpinned by the principle of fairness and a bold recognition of South Africa's diverse ethnic and racial community, to produce, in the words of Mphahlele, 'a mosaic we can all be proud of.'

T he concept of 'nation' assumes the following cardinal premises:

1. A sovereign state with political authority.
2. Containment within a fixed territory.
3. Sharing of a common language or dialects of it or, in the South African case, a group of languages whose speakers perceive themselves to share a common identity and destiny.
4. Upholding of a common legal system that supports the legitimacy of a state.

We assume that these elements must form an organic unified whole, partly by an unwritten contract, partly by pragmatic recognition of need for such an organic unity. In time we expect, ideally or otherwise, a sense of national identity among a people who enter into patterns of free association.

Early in our history we had a multiplicity of communities that called themselves something approximating 'nations'. Each nation conceived itself as unified by language or dialects, with one political authority vested in a monarch. Tribal units, chiefdoms, were smaller entities within a nation. But conquest of the weaker by the stronger determined, in an arbitrary manner, who would constitute a nation.

Came the European colonists who reduced kings to 'paramount chiefs' and other menial functionaries. With the permission of the white authority they alienated vast stretches of arable land, and left us hanging on to feeble lines of authority or living as labour tenants on white farms.

Boer nationalism emerged, asserting itself against what the Boers saw as their enemies: British rule and the indigenous black majority they believed were going to exterminate them. British colonialism had set out to anglicise the Boer and neutralize him. On this premise the Boers saw themselves as a nation that had to survive the African nations plus the British. They regarded their triumph, especially the ballot victory of 1948, as a vindication of their mission of God-sanctified 'leadership' and 'trusteeship'. Nation building for the Afrikaners became a rationalization of their policy of apartheid. They knew they had liquidated the political authority of the English-speaking people, many of whom readily subscribed to the new laws.

When the South African Native Congress (parent of the ANC) emerged in 1912, the first political ideology on its agenda was the unification of our ethnic groups. It would have to happen across several major potential constituencies: the rural communities still occupying their traditional habitats; the ethnic mix living close to urban centres – the white man's residential preserve; those on mine compounds; and the labour tenants who, because of the harsh nature of master-servant controls, were inaccessible to political organizers.

But the nation-building ideology was otherwise pervasive in urban locations. Intermarriages became very common. The rural enclaves were to become history's gift to the architects of 'separate development' as the human infrastructure for the balkanisation.

It was no accident that the African National Congress became a predominantly urban phenomenon, even though many of the elite leadership had strong rural roots. The fact of inter-ethnic cohesion in the urban areas galvanized several rural communities into action. The late 1940s and 1950s demonstrated the strengths of a real mass movement in the making.

The dark side of this picture is that rural activism was painfully fragmented, because of the very nature of undeveloped rural terrain. Thus the apartheid regime swiftly dispatched such pockets of ad hoc resistance as tried to counteract the evils of the Bantu Authorities Act and the extension of the system of passes to women.

Apartheid systematically undermined the socio-political process towards inter-ethnic unity and therefore nation building. Ethnic groups became conditioned to their separate entities, which were confined to enclaves. The notorious systems of influx control and the then government's ways of manipulating the labour force any way it desired are still too close to us in time to need further analysis. We became ambivalent in our attitudes towards the enclaves we were confined to. While we looked back to the years between 1912 and 1960 with nostalgia, we were clutching at anything for individual and group survival. We had long begun to view co-option into the white man's life ways, including consumerism, as a way of enhancing our own self-esteem. Because if we lived and thought like those who had all the power to be in charge of all our lives, if we could own the visible things *they* possessed, it would psychologically buoy us up while moving in the shadow of that power. We hoped these manufactured goods would help ease the pain of deprivation and political tyranny.

Secondly, to wrest political power from whites – a time-honoured struggle – would be as much as we could ever want. The fact that whites were not necessarily morally superior, that we had our ancient moral codes and symbols, was not in the forefront of our consciousness. To be politically right was to be morally right. Ironically, we became psychologically over-dependent on the white man.

Another psychological dilemma is that of class. Because of the legacy of deprivation and want, we are not yet reconciled to the very status we are relentlessly aspiring to by attending school and pursuing higher studies: the middle class. Historically, the middle class was largely a merchant class. An intelligentsia came into being in the Western world and reinforced the moneyed class. In the developing countries, however, there are huge classes of people with at least a certificated education who are not worth much in money terms.

Like the African American, most of us believe that poverty or poor financial resources are a culture that is peculiar to us – our trademark. We have created a folklore that is built into the state of poverty. So if some of us attain a middle class status, we are denying our beginnings – betraying the culture we think is our monopoly.

Usually we do not expect ethnicity to respect class or vice versa. It cuts across class divisions. But because history has shaped notions about class as a concept so tied up with white values, the nation-building mission to minimize or neutralize ethnicity and racial separateness will have to redefine class. Again, even while we struggle to reconcile our racial and ethnic groupings, we must monitor closely our aspirations to prosperity and well-being, as racial (though not ethnic) behaviour influences them. We only need to observe the radically transformed bargaining and work ethics that have been developing in the black sector of the labour movement. History has seen to it that whites generally do not see strikes, lock-ups, negotiations, affirmative action and the ethics that define them in the same way as black workers do. But thanks to the new Labour Relations Law, both races can rationalize their attitudes and the law will set the parameters for this projected alignment.

The two traditional nationalisms – African and Afrikaner – will evolve their respective redefinitions in time as racial feeling diminishes. They may respectively seek a new anchor, a new basis and rationale, a new meaning within the framework of ethnic interaction and, therefore, new modes of cultural expression. Nation building may very well persuade us all to realize that we have to deal with disparate ethnic cultural forms rather than the historically heightened and emotionally charged nationalisms.

African nationalism has accomplished its mission of unifying ethnic groups to win the struggle for freedom. We have now acknowledged the need to elevate nationalism beyond the battle cry. Then only can we give it a more refined holistic South African focus or meaning. It amounts ultimately to a shift in a consciousness so that it becomes national rather than sectional. National and communal institutions perpetuate a culture. We can no longer, for the sake of nation building, tolerate as before subcultures that want to dominate in any of these institutions.

Reconciliation is a political act on the one hand and a moral one on the other. Some of us, this writer included, would be disinclined to bring in the moral aspect. For this comes with a whole baggage of Christian and Islamic theologies – the former tinted with church morality. The more pragmatic approach would be to think of reconciliation for nation building as a political act. In this, we can more clearly see the benefits of letting go of the recent past, provided that we allow ourselves to learn from that part of our history.

Having achieved the monumental task of creating the Constitution, we have space to develop our diverse modes of cultural expression and produce a mosaic we can all be proud of, with no one having justifiable cause to feel threatened. Happily, culture is least of all a museum repository of past traditions. It is like a living organism, i.e. it evolves.

Conclusion

There are forces that continually reappear from time to time, threatening to undermine the nation-building ideal and process. Ancient nationalisms that, in the present phase of our history, amount to tribalism or ethnicity. They refuse to die and keep reappearing in various guises. Most recently, tribalism has put on the guise of patriotism that is passionately pushing for a federation of provinces/states. All over Africa, ethnicity has attained power in the higher echelons of government, from which height they apply ethnic preferences in the distribution of jobs. Somalia and Tanzania, which are largely monolingual (Somali or Swahili), are for the most part free of tribalism. All over, language decides ethnic identities. Thus the dominant language represents an ethnic group in high profile.

We have thus observed a pattern actually unfold in which nationalism won the people's independence from colonialism by appealing to the idealism that envisaged a nation free of tribal sectionalism. This idealism, which all Africa shared – including Africans here – began to wear off just when the nation-building process was beginning. Now it is quite evident that tribalism did not die. When the leadership elite began to fight over the spoils of neo-colonialism – European and American investments – the big ethnic wars swept through the continent, leaving devastation, famine and genocide in their wake. It is a tale of horrors that still has to be told with a true understanding of what is happening to us. We can only hope that we can yet save South Africa from this tragedy.

There is a danger that the present leadership, which is glaringly weighted on the Nguni side in its constitution, will continue to entrench itself. There are clear signs that tribalism is with us. This does not augur well for nation building. Indeed we often overlook semantics in the present euphoria of freedom. For instance, 'enthicity' is a state or condition – a neutral word. It refers to a situation in which we observe facts of social organisation. In this there exist ethnic groups. But 'tribalism' indicates attitudes towards one another as people of various ethnic groups. When such attitudes cause the practise of exclusion by the numerically dominant group – Ngunis – against non-Ngunis as less worthy, they amount to tribalism.

What's New in The New South Africa? *and*
Face the Truth About the Spectre of Tribalism – 1996

Synopsis by Marcus Ramogale

Mphahlele, in addition to being an accomplished writer, teacher and critic, is also a well-known social commentator. Over several decades, he has articulated his social views both orally (as a public speaker) and through print (as an author and social critic). Newspapers have played an important role in this, for they have provided him with a platform for his timely social interventions. This is perhaps not surprising because he was once a journalist.

Prophecy and censure are two important themes in Mphahlele's writing. In these two articles published in City Press in 1996 and 1997 respectively, he speaks out against tribalism in post-apartheid South Africa. He reminds us of the need for national unity, which is a political aspiration that was cherished by the founding fathers of African nationalism in South Africa. He argues that post-apartheid South Africa, as during the years of exile, is witnessing the evil of tribalism in parastatals and in government at both provincial and national levels. The ANC leadership ought to promote national unity rather than use the electorate as 'voting cattle'. Tribalism, he reminds us, is a social evil that has destroyed a large part of Africa. His angry, reproachful tone is that of the prophet and seeker of salvation for his people. African humanism and a pan-African sensibility provide him with the ideological and spiritual resources for this social intervention.

What's New in the New South Africa?

P at Matosa, former African National Congress (ANC) leader in the Free State, claimed that Patrick Lekota's supporters in that province's Mickey Mouse drama were demanding that he (Matosa) go back to the Transkei.

Your editorial of 10 November 1996 comments that the ANC regards tribalism as 'anathema' – so it should not allow any of its provincial administrations to be divided by tribal differences. A most worthy comment. In practice, however, the record looks dismal.

Most of us who supported the ANC in the 1950s did so because its founders of 1912 and their successors set out to unify the ethnic groups into a strong nationalist base. In the early part of this century, political protest was localised: in raw spots such as Pretoria, the then Orange Free State, and Natal acts of defiance against segregation, the pass system and land and labour laws were ruthlessly suppressed. The 1946 miners' strike that the late J B Marks organized stands out as the first major landmark of mass militancy. African nationalism had indeed taken root. The turbulent 1950s saw the ANC truly becoming a mass movement.

Historical events too complex for a brief analysis compelled Z K Matthews to propose a Congress of People. His dream was a charter for a democratic and just society, which would be the final consolidation of people's demands from all the branches of the ANC. Towards this end, the movement forged its tentative alliance with the Coloured People's Organization, the Congress of Democrats (white), and the Communist Party (white and black). 'Tentative' because these constituent units continued as independent bodies. The Unity Movement – based in the then Cape Province – saw itself as the genuine union of black and white. This alliance offended the leadership that was to create the Pan-Africanist Congress (PAC) in 1958 and break away in 1959. The late Robert Sobukwe, Zeph Mothopeng and their comrades in arms fanned the flame that Anton Lembede and Peter Mda had earlier kindled. They believed that the ANC had betrayed the cause of African Nationalism by allowing itself to be led by the Communist Party (predominantly white) and the Congress of Democrats (all white). Indeed, the Freedom Charter, endorsed at the Kliptown Congress of the People in 1955, bears the fingerprints of the two white bodies. But the ANC leadership declared itself supreme partner in the alliance.

The saddest irony is that the ANC and, less visibly, the PAC should have developed open tribalistic practices within their own ranks when they were in exile. We saw tribalism play itself out to the full out there – intensified by the disruptive agony of exile. Leadership positions, the administering of international funds for bursaries, scholarships, armed struggle, general maintenance of the liberation front – in all these the predominantly Nguni-speaking elite corps practised tribal preferences. Both organizations had lost the vision of the old stalwarts, from Dr Pixley Ka Isaka Seme to Sobukwe, Mothopeng and Philip Kgosana. It is something that would have shocked those who stayed at home, either inside or outside the prison walls, on the island or the mainland. For did not the Boer government create petty chiefdoms, Bantu advisory boards, and ethnic schools for the very reason that African nationalism and inter-ethnic marriages and other intimacies had united us to such an alarming extent? Who among us would have been happy to see the foundations of ethnic unity undermined by the leadership in exile? At the same time the question must be asked: how did this kind of tribalism come to claim affiliates, even from the ex-islanders who had shared the alienation of prison life?

In the present cabinet and lower levels of national government, and in parastatals, the top dogs are predominantly Nguni-speaking; the Indians are highly and dispro-portionately visible at the higher and lower levels. You have to lower your eyes to see Tsonga, Venda, coloured and Sotho/Tswana figures, thinly spread as they are. And yet the Northern Province (now Limpopo Province) gave the ANC more than ninety per cent of the votes in 1994. Does the leadership see these men and women as merely voting cattle? That the provincial administration represents the ethnic mix or the dominant language group of the region is a socio-historical circumstance that we had no political power to design for. There is no virtue in the inevitable, is there?

Look at SABC television. Nguni languages and English are dominant, where Afrikaans and English formerly ruled the roost. Tsonga, Venda and Sotho-Tswana come struggling behind, often looking pathetic when the presenters sit uselessly side by side to announce a programme. Slogans are loudly English and Nguni; even Afrikaans often pushes out Tsonga, Venda and Sotho-Tswana. Who is the SABC try-ing to fool? Or are we seeing government's 'democratic' interference that we cannot yet decode? I fear that if the right wing's awful rattle about 'Afrikaner cultural rights' gets noisier, Pretoria may make even more concessions to the language.

This is clearly the season for lollipops: people receiving awards for what they did for the liberation movement – and their ethnic origins. Let us in the dizzy moments of celebration forgive white murderers and assassins, but dismiss Holomisa and demote Lekota; let us overlook the *Sarafina* scandal and speak contemptuously of our martyrs (such as Sobukwe). We can then smack our lips over our lollipops, content-ment oozing from our pores. And the celebration float can keep rolling, on and on up to the front porch of the year 2000.

Who knows – the 1999 elections may yet become an arena for ethnic jostling and feuding rather than for national aspirations. On the job market Sotho/Tswana-speaking officials will sponsor Sotho/Tswana-speaking candidates, Zulu will look out for Zulu, and so on. This is the story of the African continent, alas.

So what's new in the new South Africa?

Face the Truth About the Spectre of Tribalism

An editorial in *City Press* earlier this month (1997) should leave those of us concerned about tribalism with sobering thoughts. One hopes that the ANC is listening too. But I do think that the argument by Benison Makele deserves comment. It was merely another interpretation of history in relation to the painful present. My plea to Makele and those who think like him is for us not to reduce a matter like this to the status of 'tribalistic trivia'. It is the burden of all Africans to resolve our history, rather than – as the editor puts it – to 'wish it away'. Ask West, East and Central Africa to tell you their horror stories about tribalism. Yes, the people south of the Orange bore the brunt of the initial wave of colonialism. But, after the trekboers left the peninsula in 1834, they travelled across a vast human landscape, pillaging and plundering all the way to the Limpopo. Shepstone, that rascal of British Natal, created hell for King Sekhukhune in the eastern part of the then Transvaal Republic – thanks to the support he enjoyed of thousands of Boer and Swazi troops, as well as Sekhukhune's half-brother. On the other front, the Boers failed to flush the Pedi, under Makgoba, out of their vast forest near Makgoba's Kloof (adulterated in Afrikaans as 'Magoebaskloof'). They rallied six thousand Swazis to enter and slaughter hundreds of Makgoba's soldiers and civilians, decapitating him as proof of their success (1894).

The inhabitants of the whole area from the Orange to the Limpopo, from the Botswana border to the Indian Ocean, did not just sit and welcome the British and the Boers. Only the celebrated traitor Moroka of the Free State (1795 to 1880) befriended the Boers, aiding them against Mzilikazi. Later he had a running battle with King Moshoeshoe to please the Boers.

In his letters to a cousin in Holland, Van Riebeeck showed that to him the killing of a 'Hottie' or 'savage' – as he called the natives – was nothing. He ordered the killing of some San people in order to stuff them for his museum at the Cape. In the hinterland the whites were trying to exterminate the Khoisan. But what has the ANC ever done to educate (at least) its followers about the plight of the Khoi and San, the first people to be enslaved by the Dutch and to feel the muscle of colonial policy? But then history is only a storehouse of memory. If used unwisely it can reinforce a dangerously false image of ourselves. Its positive side inspires us and elevates the best image of ourselves. One thing it does not naturally do is predetermine or sanction present-day social or political forces. If it inspired nationalism, for instance, it cannot have predicted the styles of its expression at a future time.

The future generation has the option to cherish and actively use the unchanging truths that lie at the core of movements that shape, for example, nationalism, socialism, or humanism. By the same token, we can dismiss elements of history that lock us up in tribal compartments. What the ANC is doing is trying to govern by ethnic exclusion. This is immoral, for a diversity of ethnic groups have – with equal heroism – absorbed the white man's bullets. And we all put you in charge. So we say to our leaders: 'Lollipops are not forever…'

LITERARY
APPRECIATION

A Dreamer in a Continent of Tongues:
In Search of the Continent in Himself – 2000

Synopsis by Peter Thuynsma

Es'kia Mphahlele is best known for his autobiography, Down Second Avenue, *yet this is the first title of a trilogy of autobiographical studies. The sequel was the novel,* The Wanderers, *and that was succeeded by the memoir* Afrika My Music. *More than merely a narrative of self, these works are searches for self, and together they form an intricate cycle from Marabastad into exile and back to Lebowakgomo.*

This particular essay, A Dreamer in a Continent of Tongues, *again couches Es'kia Mphahlele's trend of plumbing his being for meaning, and this October 2000 text may well provide a possible answer to this pervasive preoccupation. Here, in brisk prose, an almost impatient voice sprints along a path in search of self. 'A search for myself', it proclaims, and a quest to understand the African continent whose history, society and life are intrinsic parts of Mphahlele's very fibre. The essay is also a quest to know where Mphahlele fits with everything that is Africa: its botany, its sociology. He separates himself from his SA tutors in order to get to know his continent.*

He says:

'If I seem to be engaged in a dialogue with myself, so be it – but we, we get to glance over our shoulder, always.'

The dialogue begins as a synoptic gallop across his personal history and then uniquely fuses the personal pathways with a broader perspective – superimposing himself against a historical canvas. Deftly, the journey accounts for political and literary luminaries, and also discusses his work in the contentious Congress for Cultural Freedom (1961-62). On display are his thoughts on Negritude, African socialism, Pan-africanism, moral tensions, etc.; here is a veritable bicycle ride through contending philosophies.

Le mots que la langue française m'a prêtés, je les rends avec intérêt. Cet intérêt,
ce sont les mots de ma poésie. Des mots plus francophones que français. Proches du
français, mais plus proches encore de mon créole natal.
Edouard Maunick, Sepia Editions No 15, 1994 [1]

R|ight from the start it was a journey towards a quest, a search for myself. Wanting to teach in Nigeria grew also into an overwhelming desire to understand Africa outside the Southern African enclave. Such is the tragedy of life in this country that, being black – and by derivation white – has also meant growing up pathetically ignorant about each other, not to mention greater Africa, which gives it its physical existence. The human geography of Africa, its histories, botany, sociology, ecology across racial barriers – these are for the most part lost to us. Yes, colonial boundaries have kept us apart; a condition that found its own kind of brutal manifestation in legislated apartheid.

All our lives, we here were too busy trying to survive each other – black and white. And only when you came physically away from South African politics did you realize just how miserably petty these preoccupations were in relation to the vast landscape of being that revealed itself to you. Yet, in the clearer perspective afforded by the West African experience, you understood better the savagery you left behind.

Paris became the starting point. The metropolitan centres of the colonial powers were always the gateway to their respective colonies. The Colonial Office and its equivalents expected missionaries, scholars, traders and sea merchants, explorers, hunters, colonial administrators and their apprentices and entourage – all these, and other Europeans, to enter Africa through the colonial capitals. Right down from the governors and commandants to the menial functionaries, it became clear to any informed observer that they were coming to Africa each in search of his/her own soul, whatever their means of livelihood.

In the early months of 1960, when Senegal and other French colonies attained independence outside or within the French Community, Léopold Sédar Senghor was to remark that the spirit of nationalism was slow in developing the expected *prise de conscience,* i.e. realization, moral awakening and sense of commitment. The intelligentsia were still locked into French institutions. He could have said the same of the countries of English, Portuguese, Italian, German or Belgian influence. 'We lack a moral tension,' he would say, in place of the 'vast indifference'. He was obviously

---

1 The words that I borrow from the French language I deliver back with interest. This interest becomes the language of my poetry. Words more francophone than French (that is, more as they are spoken by a non-French tongue than a native). Close to French, yet still closer to my native Creole.

struggling with his own concept of Negritude, seeking relevance for it, especially to rural development. In other words, the relevance of ideology to the hard realities of economic activity and security, to the need to shake off dependency and inferiority.

As I began to learn the ways in which ideology can manipulate its adherents' thinking and activity, it came home to me how painful it must become for an ideology's protagonist to admit the perceived need to sustain its momentum, as well as its relevance, even in the face of changing socio-political circumstances and new imperatives. There is also the pain of its self-manipulation and fear of self-betrayal if the ideology is abandoned or modified.

Against Negritude as an ideology for the arts – a conceptual programme for Africa – was the cultural baggage, such as it was, that I came carrying with me out of South Africa: a tangle of strands of racial struggle and political oppression as physical and psychological realities; the clash between rural and semi-urban sensibilities deriving from apartheid.

I began to learn French in Paris in 1960 in a State audio-visual laboratory. At the same time, I was helping establish cultural programmes for African countries, when-ever and wherever they invited the international organization I was working for: Congrès pour la Liberté de la Culture, later to become the International Congress for Cultural Freedom.

It was elevating for me to have the privilege of meeting and discussing Africa with cultural activists such as Alioune Diop of the journal *Présence Africaine*. Its Rue des Ecoles offices were a vibrant venue for African intellectuals: my countryman and painter Gerard Sekoto, then a Parisian since his emigration in 1948; poet and elder statesman Aimé Césaire from Martinique, West Indies; French Guiana's poet Léon Damas; poet Edouard Maunick from Mauritius, still very young and full of beans – I mean bounce – from Senegal; Senghor himself; poet Birago Diop; novelist and film-maker Sembene Ousmane; novelist Cheik Hamidou Kane; scholar Cheik Anta Diop; Congo's poet Tchicaya UTam'si; Cameroon's Professor Bernard Fonlon; novelist Ferdinand Oyono; novelist Mongo Beti; poet Mbella Sonne Dipoko; Côte d'Ivoire's poet-novelist Bernard Dadié; Madagascar's poet Jacques Rabemananjara; Mali's scholar Amadou Hampate Ba; Burkina Faso's scholar Joseph Ki-Zerbo; Benin's Paulin Joachim. If this reads like an honours list, then so be it.

The Congress sent me to tour West, Central and East Africa in 1962. I was to investigate and identify existing cultural programmes and ascertain, on the evidence of what the leaders perceived as their cultural priorities, what material assistance they wanted from the Congress. The most popular projects turned out to be writers' and artists' clubs, and educational and media conferences (always the print media).

In 1963, we organized two conferences of writers and educators from tertiary institu-tions – one in Freetown, Sierra Leone and the next the following week in Dakar, Senegal. The theme was: 'The rightful place for African Literature in University

Curricula'. In the following decade things began to open up in West African universities for the teaching of African literary works.

These activities can be regarded as a landmark in the development of the new African self: an awareness among the intelligentsia of the proper role of the university in the cultural life of the nation. Terms such as 'self-awareness', 'self-improvement', 'intervention', and others used by an interpreter of Senghor – 'the invention of a meaning so that the world can be seen with fresh eyes, and turned inside out by men working to improve it and themselves' – such terms went a long way towards defining the elite's perception of Negritude and its related project. Furthermore, we realize today that; *prise de conscience* (realization of the African's being), the new awareness 'killing the old negro', 'African socialism', 'Pan-Africanism', 'moral awakening' and 'moral tension' point to cultural projects that are far from being resolved.

The reality did not dawn on me until almost a decade later, when I was teaching and helping organize cultural activities in East Africa. The valiant efforts by the two foremost thinkers in black Africa to bridge the gaps between the concepts of public and individual morality, the conduct of governance, community development and political competition, began to distinguish them from the rest of black African leadership. These were Léopold Sédar Senghor and Julius Nyerere, men of high calibre. Their fervour in this direction was never to be seen again in any other leader south of the Sahara. Senegal's Cheikh Hamidou Kane, in his colonial novel *L'Aventure ambigue* (translated into English as *Ambiguous Adventure*) portrays a woman who counsels her son to go and attend the white man's school, where he can learn to govern without being right. What we see more and more occurring is the widening of the distance between different branches of ethics.

The homage I paid Senghor (see pp 291–294, this volume), when he turned seventy a little over twenty years ago, says a lot about the cross-currents of self-awareness as a process of my own growth. His poetry reveals a master of the grand gesture, of the grand resonance, of the Grand Ideal and the passion it inspires.

In any setting that was once colonized, we bring to the common meeting ground – political or literary or social – our respective brands of vanity, each formatted by the particular colonial cultural style. It continues to puzzle me that we act out these funny theatrics on each other, while our less educated publics remain at ease with themselves!

If I seem to be engaged in a dialogue with myself, so be it. Because I am trying to trace the changes or regressions in our many-patterned African consciousness, I feel it makes more sense to reach for one landmark after another. Take Sierra Leone's poet and fiction writer, the late Abioseh Nicol (aka Davidson Nicol):

The Meaning of Africa

Africa, you were once just a name to me
But now you lie before me with sombre green challenge
To that loud faith for freedom (life more abundant)
Which we once professed shouting
Into the silent listening microphone
Or on an alien platform to a sea
Of white perplexed faces troubled
With secret Imperial guilt; shouting
Of you with a vision euphemistic
As you always appear
To your lonely sons on distant shores.

We look across a vast continent
And blindly call it ours.
You are not a country, Africa,
You are a concept,
Fashioned in our minds, each to each,
To hide our separate fears,
To dream our separate dreams.
Only those within you who know
Their circumscribed plot,
And till it well with steady plough
Can from that harvest then look up
To the vast blue inside
Of the enamelled bowl of sky
Which covers you and say
'This is my Africa' meaning
'I am content and happy.
I am fulfilled, within,
Without and roundabout...'

Whether or not we are aware of it – sometimes or always – we are exiles inside our own countries, in the greater Africa, or overseas. One might even say exile is but another aspect of the human condition, in some more abrasive than in others. After writers such as Césaire, Senghor and Damas before him, all looking through different island and mainland windows, Edouard Maunick has more recently stated: *'J'ai vecu pendant vingt-neuf ans dans la pluralite d'etre.'* The plurality of being. Yet, from the African mainland, writers have for centuries had to deal with more rigorous, often soul-battering, particularities. Especially where you were never allowed to forget that you are black and dangerous in a white-dominated society. Also, the black man's exile was seldom voluntary.

And the pendulum of social circumstance – historical time – settles down to the measure of one's being. As the subject refuses to be erased from journalists' or commentators' minds, the question came from an interviewer, to whom Maunick gave an eloquent reply:

> *Personne n'est un poète de la négritude. La négritude est un phénomène à la fois biologique et culturel. Il fut essentiel à un certain moment qu'on prit compte du fait nègre et des être noirs pout pouvoir sortir d'un certain ghetto – l'aventure, la mauvaise aventure n'est pas complètement terminée aujourd'hui, même si on a fait un bon bout de chemin. Mais on n'est jamais poète de ceci ou de cela. La poésie est en soi universelle. Comme la parole. La parole habite l'air, l'air n'a pas de limités.*[1]

African literature of French expression has not always lived at the philosophical level. A great number of novels and short stories have portrayed the colonial scene and contemporary life in the tradition of social realism and continue to do so. As in its counterparts in the other European languages, the lyrical alternates with the dramatic.

Cameroon's Ferdinand Oyono's novels *Une Vie de Boy* (*Houseboy*) and *Le Vieux Nègre et la Médaille* (*The Old Man and the Medal*) portray the savagery and insensitivity of French colonial administrators. Senegal's Sembene Ousmane uses the method of the chronicle in his fiction, which abandons several of the orthodox strategies in the making of a novel, bringing to mind the griot's narrative. *Les bouts de bois de Dieu* (*God's Bits of Wood*) is a highly impressive narrative of the epic railway strike of 1947, in which he traces the experiences of a number of people all the way down the railway tracks to the sea. He paints vivid scenes of black-white conflict and of the white man's hatred.

As in the case of its counterparts, francophone literature in Africa and on the islands has been through one phase after another: oral, anti-colonial (mostly written) inspired by nationalism, post-independence and neo-colonial. We are now no longer addressing ourselves to the Western world, but learning to speak to one another. We are on common ground, all African countries, because independence went wrong over most of the continent. Military coups, dictatorships and their constant companions – corruption in high circles, poverty, disease, and illiteracy – these are with us at all times. South Africa is teetering on the edge – free of the dictatorship that is sanctioned and sustained by sectional politics, but sharing the other weaknesses.

---

1 Nobody is a negritude poet... Negritude is a phenomenon at once biological and cultural. It was essential at a certain moment to give an account of the fact of blackness and for black souls to be able to get out of a particular ghetto. The adventure, the horrible adventure, is not quite over today, even though we have gone a fair stretch of the road. But one is never a poet of this or that (ideology). Poetry is in itself universal. Like speech. Speech exists in the air, and the air has no limits.

One day, I hope our communication systems among African nations will reach maturity so that we may get to know one another better by direct lines. One of my major dreams is that, in search of the long-elusive African identity we can succeed in transforming our curricula, right from primary school through to tertiary programmes – especially in the human or social sciences and humanities. A strong African content must take the place of the present Eurocentric education – as with Kenyan novelist Ngugi wa Thiong'o's scheme to abolish the department of English at the University of Nairobi, and create in its place a department of literature. It would include indigenous languages as well as literatures of several European languages and diasporas.

African Literature:
A Dialogue of Two Selves and the Voice of Prophecy – 1975

Synopsis by Sam Raditlhalo

African literature as a creative act and a discipline is the subject of this article. It is a literature that started as a voice of protest against the injustices of colonization, oppression, alienation and dehumanisation. This is largely where written African-American literature has its roots, and Mphahlele handles the two traditions as parallel streams of consciousness. If both began as a way of addressing the oppressor, they subsequently outgrew this role equally and moved on to address the concerns of the people in an idiom that they could understand.

While African American and Caribbean literatures display a profound sense of alienation and displacement, even while they affirm the right to be citizens of the 'new world' they find themselves in, Africans draw inspiration from the continent, can come back to it and revitalize themselves in a setting they understand. In both streams Mphahlele finds a continuous dialogue, reflected in the artists' compulsion to speak out even as they grapple with the past and present.

At every turn of interrogating an existence that has changed so radically, there is a need to re-invent communal concerns and aspirations, for it seems that 'after every awkward fall / We are at the starting point'. It is here that the voice of prophecy in African literature becomes apparent, for the artist must of necessity become the lightning rod of the community. It is also true that, while Africa has made significant strides in de-colonization in the last fifty-odd years, it has stagnated significantly in key areas of economic development, of instituting a human rights culture, in areas of education for all, and in overall human upliftment. We are always at the 'starting point' that Lenrie Peters writes about, with the new or revived aspirations and explorations that it calls for. These streams of literature will therefore continue their dialogue amongst themselves, as well as between themselves and their socio-political and economic realities.

W E B DuBois said that in black people there is always a two-ness in the personality. One ever feels this two-ness, like the American and the black. Two souls; two thoughts; a seemingly irreconcilable striving. It is a continuous process. There is convergence and divergence at different points.

Some of the poetry I particularly like in the Bible lies in the Proverbs and the Psalms. And one Psalm that strikes me forcefully is Psalm 137, because it reflects very much a parallel to the black condition. I often call it the 'Zion Blues' because it is charged with the blues mood:

'By the rivers of Babylon we sat down and wept when we remembered Zion. There on the willow-trees we hung our harps, for there those who carried us off demanded music and singing, and our captors called us to be merry: "Sing us one of the songs of Zion!" How could we sing the Lord's song in a foreign land? If I forget you O Jerusalem let my right hand wither away; let my tongue cling to the roof of my mouth...'

It's the wailing of exiles everywhere in the world. And whenever you are an exile, or have been colonized, you always have to entertain the masters. They want you to pick up your guitar and sing. 'Sing us a song, sing us one of your black songs, man.' Your colonizers are so barren themselves and will always want to jump out of themselves and get fun from the people they have colonized. You have left your home ground way back there, but you don't want to forget it. If I forget you, cut off my tongue or let my tongue cling to the roof of my mouth... And we're with the black condition still. 'I will go back to darkness and to peace,' said Claude McKay, African American poet:

But the great western world holds me in fee,
And I may never hope for full release
While to its alien gods I bend my knee.
Something in me is lost, forever lost,
Some vital thing has gone out of my heart,
And I must walk the way of life a ghost
Among the sons of earth, a thing apart.
For I was born, far from my native clime,
Under the white man's menace, out of time.

'The one world holds me when I want to go away', said Langston Hughes, another African American:

I, too, sing America
I am the darker brother.
They send me to eat in the kitchen

when company comes,
but I laugh, and eat well, and grow strong.

And tomorrow he will sit at the table and nobody will send him to the kitchen because they will see how beautiful life is. 'I, too, am America.'

Langston Hughes had a patron. A white patron who wanted him to write 'primitive' stuff. There was the urge among the 'Rhythm Boys' of the Harlem Renaissance to sound the African beat, and this woman was always telling him to write in the 'primitive style.' 'Tom-tom-tom. Wah-wah-wah.' Things like that. Hughes replied that he was not going to do anything like that because he was Chicago, Lenox Avenue and Harlem. The dialogue of two selves continued. Hear again what Hughes writes:

I've known rivers:
I've known rivers ancient as the world
and older than the flow of human blood in human veins.

My soul has grown deep like the rivers.

I bathed in the Euphrates when dawns were young.
I built my hut near the Congo and it lulled me to sleep.
I looked upon the Nile and raised the pyramids above it.
I heard the singing of the Mississippi when Abe Lincoln went down to
New Orleans, and I've seen its muddy bosom turn all golden in the sunset ...

To the extent that the black man had to adapt to a new setting, having by force of historical circumstances been separated from Africa, he had to psychologically grow away from the continent. We know now that when a group wants to merge with a dominant one, it has to cut itself off from its roots. But when it is rejected it looks back into itself to rediscover itself and to re-evaluate its own characteristics. And this is what has happened throughout the colonial world.

The advantage we have in Africa is that we are still rooted in our African soil, except where one had to leave one's homeland in flight; exile becomes a kind of abstract, mental or spiritual thing that you can snap out of if you put your mind to it. If you find yourself lonely and disoriented in Paris, you can go back to your people in Africa. You don't have to sit out there in Europe, cooped up in cold, dilapidated and disintegrating buildings. You go back home. Just go back into the stream of your beginnings. It is simply that so often our people don't even want to make that decision because they are terrified of it somehow. The alienation in the Caribbean and the Afro-American is, to me, so real. So real and so agonizing. On African soil it is something that you can deal with in very physical terms, if you want to and have set your mind on it, as I said. But then, I also know that I may be projecting my own bias into trans-Atlantic black situations. It is conceivable that later generations have no longing for an Africa they only read about and have never seen. Yet still, something must barely remain in the collective symbolic memory, cruising up and down the trans-Atlantic highways and byways.

Sometimes the two voices in the dialogue speak as if they were one. But you know that the dialogue is going on. Sometimes, when you have one here and the other out there, they speak in two different poets. For instance, Bob Kaufman, the African-American poet, writes of Ray Charles:

> Ray Charles is the Black wind of Kilimanjaro
> Screaming up and down blues,
> Moaning happy on all the elevators of my time
> Smiling into the camera, with an African symphony
> Hidden in his throat, and (I Got a Woman) wails, too
> He burst from Bessie's crushed Black skull
> One cold night outside of Nashville, shouting,
> And growing bluer from memory,
> Glowing bluer still.

'And you have another side' – this idea is repeated by Julia Fields, who writes:

> Take my share of Soul Food -
> I do not wish
> To taste of pig of either gut
> Or grunt
> From bowel
> Of jowl
>
> I want caviar
> Shrimp soufflé
> Sherry
> Champagne
> And not because
> These are the
> White's domain
> But just because
> I'm entitled -
>
> For I've been V.D.-ed enough

Another side of the dialogue. And somewhere you have got to find an equilibrium.

Kofi Awonoor, the Ghanaian poet, writes about these two selves in the poem, *Rediscovery*. He says that we shall always do things together, celebrate our oneness. The music we hear now is 'the new chorus of our forgotten comrades / and the hallelujahs of our second selves'.

Another Ghanaian poet, Francis Parkes, sees the coming of the white man as a holocaust. And he cries out:

Let us build new homesteads
New dreams to decorate these ruins
Let us weave fresh rafters from rescued stalks
Let us start all over again

The past is a pitiless dream
A dread nightmare, you may remember …

Kwesi Brew of Ghana sees us still shuffling our feet in an African dance; still leading the sheep or the goat to the sacrifice. With a tone of reassurance Brew tells us that the ancestors observe this and must say to themselves: 'they have not changed.'

If you really feel alienated as an African just go back to your continent, because there the present and the past live side by side. The traditional past is also the present. You can commute between the European stream and the indigenous. You can make reference to the one while you are in the other. The indigenous consciousness is there. It is solid. It is changing physically, yes. People are growing apart. Families are breaking up, yes. And yet age-old custom has survived, and this is why the dialogue continues between the old and the new.

The late Abioseh Nicol of Sierra Leone wrote: 'you are not a country, Africa, you are a concept fashioned in our minds, each to hide our separate fears and to dream our separate dreams.' The theme of the homecoming is very common in African poetry. People who were educated abroad and lived there a number of years come back to find that the landscape has changed, to find that the people are not the same any more or else the observer himself has changed. Lenrie Peters, the Gambian poet, sees his homecoming as a decent by parachute:

Parachute men say
The first jump
Takes the breath away
Feet in the air disturbs
Till you get used to it.

Solid ground
Is not where you left it
As you plunge down
Perhaps head first
As you listen to
Your arteries talking
You learn to sustain hope

.....

Jumping across worlds
In condensed time
After the awkward fall
We are always at the starting point.

The dialogue continues. And then, suddenly, we hear a voice of prophecy. I am using the idea of prophet not in the restrictive sense in which we talk about the man who predicts the future. I am talking about the man who sings. The prophet sings, and in what he sings he repeats a number of things. And again, I am using the word 'sing' in the widest possible sense. When you sing you repeat a number of notes. One note echoes what you said before. Just like blues. As you sing, it echoes and it goes forward and then back over what you said before. A prophet does that. Now before you become a prophet, you have got to be discontented. No person gets up in the morning one day and decides that he is going to prophesy, just like that, without feeling a kind of ecstasy or rage – without a sense of compulsion. You've got to be driven by an inner compulsion. You've got to be indignant or ecstatic about some Vision Splendid you are striving towards. And if you are going to sing, then you are going to have to distil the anger into your song. As Chinua Achebe says, African writers have assumed the role, or want to assume the role, of priesthood. And this is when the writer is very close to the community and is not out there playing around with images and symbols just for the jive. Because if you purport to be speaking on behalf of a people, you take on the voice of prophecy.

There are three ways in which the voice comes through: in the novel, and in two kinds of poetry. The voice may be heard in the poet's sense of loss, and it may issue forth as an expression of the communal public voice – especially in situations of political and social upheaval. When that happens the poet comes up and shouts and yells and speaks in a tone of certitude: he is sure he is right. He knows where the people should go, what they should believe in and what they should try to get back of what they've lost. Here, the prophetic voice becomes strident.

In one of his plays, *Kongi's Harvest* (1967), Wole Soyinka gives a portrayal of this kind of social upheaval. Kongi decides that he is going to take over the powers of the

Oba. Now, the Oba has political as well as spiritual functions. Kongi, the modern political leader, decides to take over both the political and spiritual powers. In the process, he also undermines the purpose of the Yam feast, where the Oba has to eat the king yam before the harvest. He also surrounds himself with a number of young men who call themselves the enlightened Owerri. They are a caricature, unlike the elders who in traditional custom surround the Oba. It is almost as if overnight a volcano has erupted in independent Africa. Communal life is shaken up. The poet's voice becomes strident. Wole Soyinka became a prisoner of the federal government for twenty-seven months during the Nigerian civil war. He writes about his small prison cell. He feels political authority has laid siege to humanity, and truth is suppressed. And his poetic vision foresees greater catastrophes:

> *Where*
> *Are all the flowers gone?*
> *I cannot tell*
> *The gardens here are furrowed still and bare.*
>
> *Death alike*
> *We sow. Each novel horror*
> *Whets inhuman appetites*
> *I do not*
> *Dare to think these bones will bloom tomorrow...*
>
> *The voice is harsh, the diction metallic, the rhythm grave:*
>
> *Come, let us*
> *With that mangled kind*
> *Makẹ pact, no less*
> *Against the lesser*
> *Leagues of death, and mutilators of the mind.*
>
> *Take Justice*
>
> *In your hands who can*
> *Or dare. Insensate sword*
> *Of power*
> *Outherods Herod and the law's outlawed ...*

The new politician must be thrilled to hear 'the Muse's constipated groan.'

Christopher Okigbo prophesies the Nigerian civil war in verse under the title *Path of Thunder*. He talks about eagles now being in sight, about shadows on the horizon:

The robbers are back in black hidden steps of detonators
For beyond the blare of sirened afternoons, beyond the motorcades;
Beyond the voices and days, the echoing highways; beyond the latescence
Of our dissonant airs; through our curtained eyeballs, through our shuttered sleep,
Onto our forgotten selves, onto our broken images; beyond the barricades
Commandments and edicts, beyond the iron tables, beyond the elephant's
Legendary patience, beyond his inviolable bronze bust; beyond our crumbling towers
Beyond the iron path careering along the same beaten track
The glimpse of a dream lies smouldering in a cave, together with the mortally
  wounded birds.

Go down to the deep south of the continent and there are no dreams, no nostalgia. Here people do not brood over the past. Because the cruel present is with them always. Police come storm-trooping up and down the pavement. And they come and kick your doors open and flash their lights throughout the house, upset mattresses and blankets; get you out of your bed searching for anything. That haunting poem by Sterling A Brown, *Old Lem*, keeps sounding in my mind when I think of the Southern African blacks:

They got the law
They don't come by ones
They got the sheriffs
They got the deputies
They don't come by twos
They got the shotguns
They got the rope
We fit the justice in the end
And they come by tens.

They got the manhood. They got the courage
They don't come by twos. We got to slink around,
Hang tailed hounds.
They burn us when we dogs
They burn us when we men
They come by tens ...

Brown's refrain speaks tons of terror:

> They don't come by ones
> They don't come by twos
> But they come by tens.

Says Dennis Brutus:

> The sounds begin again;
> the siren in the night
> the thunder at the door
> the shriek of nerves in pain.
> Then the keening crescendo of faces split by pain.

There is no relief, Brutus says: the sounds always come back, on the pavements, against the door when the boot kicks it open or a fist bangs on it – always the sirens. In spite of all this, we survive. Tenderness and affection between oppressed and oppressed will outlive these cruel times.

Another South African exile, Mazisi Kunene, warns the white killer in a prophetic tone:

> If your species multiply
> And all men derive from your image
> We shall open our doors
> Watching them sharpening their swords with the morning star
> And spreading their blades covered with blood.
> They shall obstruct our passage in our travels
> And cut our heads because we were of alien clan,
> Believing that our blood is desirable.
> But the growing of the powerful buds
> Will not let them triumph;
> They will haunt them with talons of weeds
> Piercing them in their dreams.

A poet's voice hardens in situations of political and social upheaval. It becomes apocalyptic, prophesying doom and disaster for those on the opposite side.

'My name is Africa,' says Keorapetse Kgositsile, who lives in exile in New York:

> So will the day of the stench of oppression
> Leaving nothing but the lingering

Taste of particles of hatred
Woven around the tropical sun
While in the belly of the night
Drums roll and peal a monumental song...
To every birth its blood
All things come to pass
When they do
We are the gods of our day and us
Panthers with claws of fire

At other times, the dialogue is simply a song about the exile of a people because physically they have been thrown apart and they are trying to re-assemble somewhere. They may have left the graves of their ancestors far behind and their houses may be in ruins. Those graves, those ancestral graves and shrines: can you restore them? Your religion is determined by your place, by your locale, by your landscape, by your needs and by everything around you that sustains you. For instance, San and the pygmy wandered about a lot. They have always had to leave their dead behind. So where do they reconnect with their ancestors? They devise an image of the wind. The wind is the carrier of the ancestors' message because the wind is everywhere you go. And you don't have to feel lost; it's always bringing the ancestor's voices to you.

Often this lyricism strives toward prophecy in African poetry. The lyric in the hands of Léopold Sédar Senghor, Kofi Awonoor or Christopher Okigbo is a good example of this. One might say the poet came from A, is now at B, and is in search of a metaphor that will best express the dialogue between the A consciousness and the B consciousness, a process that also suggests a synthesis. The poet projects his vision to some point we could think of as C. The degree of intensity, of his ecstasy, tells us something of the quality of his prophetic assertion. To be a prophet you have to assume that there are certain things that *must never change*. Certain areas of A must not be destroyed. Thus, from B you must decide how to move towards C – that point which can best be conceived through a variety of lenses, all prospecting for the ideal metaphor or image as it were. Ghana's Kofi Awonoor is always urging us to go back and restore the ancestral shrines, to return for purification. He says that he is not only talking to the elite, but also to the man in the street who may be tempted to aspire to elitism. In the poem *Night of my Blood* he says:

Did they whisper to us the miracle of time
Telling us over the dark waters
Where we come from? Did they
Call us unto themselves
With the story of time and beginning?
We sat in the shadow of our ancient trees

275

> While the waters of the land washed
> Washed against our hearts,
> Cleansing, cleansing.
> The purifier sat among us
> In sackcloth and ashes,
> Bearing on himself the burdens
> of these people

He pleads:

> Sew the old days for me, my fathers, sew them that I may
> wear them for the feast that is coming, the feast: of the
> new season that is coming.

Finally, the novel. How does the voice of prophecy express itself in fiction? Here one must think of the novelist who sings. The novelist whose song keeps re-echoing in our ears. And one sees this cycle in Chinua Achebe's works. This is the best example I can give because there is a singing quality throughout his fiction. It is a song that is woven through the fabric of his people's language, through the fabric of his people's allegory, their metaphor. This is how the song works. One metaphor keeps re-echoing what he said before. And as the people talk, you hear a song issuing from deep down there, like a prophecy that sets up vibrations in one response mechanism.

The resonance, the things that keep vibrating when you've left the novel behind, that's what I am talking about. In *Arrow of God*, Ezeulu, the high priest, is in trouble. He has lost count of the number of yams that he has eaten and of those that remain for him to eat before he can pronounce the time to begin harvesting. This, because he is in jail. He cannot order the people to go and harvest their yam crop because there is one yam left to be eaten.

When he arrives back home the people are in a hostile mood. But this is merely the climax of a crisis that has been building up as a result of Ezeulu's notion of himself as God's arrow, God's instrument of retribution. He is a stubborn, strong-willed man.

Ezeulu's loneliness echoes that of Okonkwo in Achebe's *Things Fall Apart*. The rendering of Igbo idiom echoes and re-echoes throughout this fiction. In the character's language we hear a communal voice.

And then again, in the interplay of what the individual says and what the people say, various distances occur that reflect the never-ending tensions between the individual and society. This resonance, this recital, this 'song' takes on the character of prophecy. It seems that prophecy is the ultimate point to which the dialogue between two selves in African literature strives.

Exile, the Tyranny of Place
and the Literary Compromise – 1973

Synopsis by Ndavhe Ramakuela

This piece reflects on what writing is and how location influences the act of writing and the literary artefact. Mphahlele argues that, despite some of its advantages, exile was not the greatest moment of his experience; it deprived him of his desired contact with home – which was, for him, the creative hub for the writer. The home environment presents familiar things – for example, the symbolic significance of smell, acceptance of the rot, the sounds and noises. These are the things he misses when he is in exile.

The second part of the piece deals largely with the art of writing and its consequences. It tells that writing issues from experiences of contentment and its opposite, in both turbulent times and periods of calm. Continued happiness, or 'the unbroken song', is what the writer needs.

Mphahlele also makes an argument for African literature at high schools and reading for enjoyment. The pain of exile was that what the writer wrote could not reach his primary audience in South Africa because of the hostile environment created by the South African government. There was always this feeling that it could possibly be pointless to write if there was no one listening. Here, again, he draws our attention to his attachment to place, and the urge to return to the home ground.

'My very return is a compromise between the outsider who did not have to be bullied by place and yet wanted it badly, and the insider who has an irrepressible attachment to ancestral place, anywhere from a rural to an urban setting.'

S ome African poets, particularly those of French expression, can say sweet things about night. Night as a symbol of blackness. Night 'teeming with rainbows', as Aimé Césaire would say. Night of ourselves. Black souls communing with night and listening to its mysteries; night defining black souls and their pride. Night is no longer to represent the ugly, the mysterious, the sinister, and the darkness of the spirit.

After the terrors of pastoral life, my nights in the slum were orchestrated only by screams, moans, police whistles and the screech of tyres of police squad-cars. Life became a myriad burning fuses radiating out, each to its own dump of explosives. Explosives that seem to renew themselves by their own rubble and ashes, creating always their own fuses in the process. Daytime is what we perpetually seek in the African townships. Come the night of machine guns and fire and water, we have still less reason to contemplate nights of beauty.

The tyranny of time. The tyranny of place. The muck, the smell of it, the fever and the fight, the cycles of decay and survival. And 'the sounds begin again'; I want daytime, I want place, I want a sense of history. Even though place will never be the same again for me – because its lights and shadows may change – I want to be there when it happens.

Back to 1941 when, at twenty-one, I took up my first job as a teacher of the blind in an adult institution, in Roodepoort. Fresh from teacher training and the protection of boarding-school life, and utterly confused. I made up my mind to finish high school by private study and proceed by the same route up through tertiary education. I lived in another slum, fifty miles from my place of birth, and it could have been the Pretoria slum transplanted. Night screams; the barking of half-starved mongrels; the rattle of wagons loaded with human manure collected from lavatory buckets; the smell of night; the throb of a life seeking at once some violent release, some affectionate contact, and a corner to deal with the terrors of night and take stock of the hurts, the buffetings, the braveries of daytime.

Something strange happened to me as I studied by candlelight, listening at intervals to the throb of night out there. I found myself writing a short story. During my primary school days, I had rooted everywhere for newsprint to read – any old scrap of paper. Our ghetto had no newspaper deliveries, no school libraries (forty years later we still don't have them). There was a small one-room tin shack the municipality had the sense of humour to call a 'reading room', on the western edge of Marabastad. It was stacked with dilapidated books and journals junked by bored ladies from the suburbs – anything from cookery books through boys' and girls' adventures to dream interpretations and astrology. Mostly useless, needless to say. Still, I went through the whole lot indiscriminately, like a termite, just elated with a sense of discovery and of recognition of the printed word mostly connected with the mere skill of reading. But one day I dug out of the pile Cervantes's *Don Quixote*. Cervantes was to stand out in my mind forever.

My imagination was also fired by the silent movies of the 1930s. Put Don Quixote and Sancho Panza together with Laurel and Hardy, with Harold Lloyd, with Buster Keaton, with all those heroes of American cowboy folklore – Hoot Gibson, Tim McCoy, Buck Jones and so on. Put *Don Quixote* next to *Tarzan the Ape* or *Tarzan the Tiger*: a crazy world. And yet, unwittingly, we wanted just this kind of entertainment to help us cope with the muck and the smell and the demands for gut responses of everyday life. As we read the subtitles aloud amid the yells and feet-stamping and bouncing on chairs to the rhythm of the action, amid the fierce clanking of the piano near the stage of the movie house, 'fantastical' ideas were whipping around in my mind. I was intrigued, captivated by the age-old technique of storytelling. All we saw in the movies, all we read in those journals and books was about faraway lands, not our own sordid setting. It was an exciting release, although we were mindless of the reasons for it. The tyranny of place ... the tyranny of time...

This was some of the equipment I brought to the adventure I found myself embarked upon even before I knew it. I had not read any short stories before – not of the artful kind we compose today. Lots of tales, yes. So I had no genuine models. I simply stacked them up without any hope of publishing any of them, as it would have been unthinkable for a white magazine even to consider them: not even a white-owned newspaper circulating among Africans. Looking back on the stories now, they read hopelessly like the kind of thing that aspires to be a novel and so fails to make the incisive point it set out to make – except to suggest the aura of tragedy that surrounds black life. I wrote simply to depict the situation and the human beings who act it out, without the technique by which dramatic and rhetorical con-nections are made between real-life suffering, the socio-political system and art. Focus was always on the drama of life as lived in the ghetto. I saw 'white' life as merely peripheral.

The exercise in literary compromise had begun for me, something even more pro-found than what is often referred to as 'writing yourself out of a situation'. And the sounds begin again. Outside there, from inside this tin shack in Roodepoort location, I can hear a wedding song. The singers will stop at our corner, I'm sure, to dance. The moon is out. Its light will be trying to bounce off the corrugated iron roofs, but rust will resist being dragged into that moon game. Maybe I'll step out for a little diversion when the group comes round the corner. The tyranny of place ...

Four and a half years later, having finished my senior high school course, I was eligible for high school teaching. But I would have to continue with private study. I went to Orlando in 1945. And the sounds begin again: the gang wars, the police squad cars, the political rallies, the baton charges and cops shooting. High school teaching and further self-education. A new phase for me: teaching English in a ghetto.

I rediscovered Dickens in my studies, the classics. I discovered Gorky, Dostoevsky and Chekhov in my preparation for my classes. Somewhere along the line, my high school students and I discovered each other. I was constantly asking myself questions relating to the value of poetry for me and my students, and for the township culture we were sharing – a culture that was very much an assertion of the human spirit fight-ing for survival against forces that threatened to fragment or break it. Of what use was poetry in a social climate that generated so much physical violence? In a life that

resisted any individual creative efforts, a social climate that made the study of literature – particularly in a foreign but official language like English – look like playing a
harmonica or Jewish harp in the midst of sirens and power drills and fire-brigade
bells? It was the full recognition of these factors by student and teacher that conditioned the love we developed for literature. A love that had to be self-generated, given
all the hostile external factors. The element of escapism also helped sustain that
interest. For me, as one who was then writing short stories, the whole literary adventure was a compromise between several desperate drives and urges.

The function of literature became tied up with the motivation to master English at
the grassroots level of practical usage. English, which was not our mother tongue,
gave us power, power to master the external world which came to us through it: the
movies, household furniture and other domestic equipment, styles of dress and
cuisine, advertising printed forms that regulated some of the mechanics of living and
dying and so on. It was a key to job opportunities in that part of the private sector of
industry where white labour unions had little to lose if they let us in. We had
embarked on an adventure. This sense of adventure explains the enthusiasm, the
energy and the drive with which Africa confronts the imperatives of learning.

It was during this period of self-education, of teaching and trying to understand
what my students wanted, that I made three interrelated discoveries. Things that were
to change my whole outlook, my whole stance and, consequently, my literary style. I
became sharply aware of the realism of Dickens, of Gorky, Chekhov, Hemingway and
Faulkner. I became aware of the incisive qualities of the Scottish and English ballads
and saw in them an exciting affinity with the way the short story works: the single
situation rather than a developmental series of events; a concentration of the present
moment or circumstance; action, vivid and dramatic; singleness and intensity of emotion, generated by the often terrifying and intense focus on a situation; the plotted and
episodic nature of the narrative; the way in which character, instead of developing
fully, is bounced off; the lack, or paucity, of information about what has gone before
and about the characters, or the 'telescoping' of where the characters come from and
where they are at present; the intensive moment of discovery or illumination; the tension; the 'leaping and lingering' technique in which the ballad passes from scene to
scene in the narrative without having to fill in gaps, leaping over time and space and
lingering on those scenes that are colourful and dramatic; the resonances. I have
never, since, ceased to be moved by those ballads. They are so close to our own folk
tales that depict violence and the supernatural. With so much death and violence
around you in the ghetto, you seemed to be reliving those old days when life was so
insecure, nature was both kind and cruel, and whatever force presided over human
affairs had abandoned us to our own predatory instincts.

That ballad about the two ravens, for instance, talking about their dinner.
Cynically speculating on how they are going to deal with a dead man lying nearby, the

ravens tell us what the skeleton will look like. Over those bare white bones, they say, the wind will blow for evermore. Then there is the ballad of the two sisters, the power in the telling of that story. It may, on the surface, appear to be nothing more than a child's folk tale about a girl who pushes her younger sister into the sea to drown. Nothing more said between them than a plea from one and a wilful desire to kill from the other. Beyond the structure of the ballad and its economy of fact and diction, the impersonal or detached mood gripped me. I could not myself afford to be objective about the violence around me, but the poetry portrayed a life from the past with all its primitive ferocity and desperate urge just to survive: the same life we had been reduced to. Cut the supernatural and romance, and you have left the startling revelation of a tragic event, the resonance that comes from the combination of this and character.

The third discovery, and the one most directly related to my style and point of view, was a chance discovery in the late 1940s of Richard Wright's short stories, *Uncle Tom's Children* (1936). He was an Afro-American novelist who died in exile in Paris in 1960. I smelled our own poverty in his southern setting; the long, searing, black song of Wright's people sounds like ours. The agony told me how to use the short story as a way of dealing with my anger and indignation. It was the ideal medium. I fed on the fury and poured more and more vitriol into my words until I could almost taste them. I came back from work, waited for the time my family would be asleep, did my studies, and returned to my short-story writing. I went out onto the porch for a break; from this part of Orlando I had a clear view of the distant lights of Northcliff, thirty kilometres or so away. And more and more they took on a symbolic meaning for me – those lights – because between them and me was the dense, palpable dark. And ever since I returned from the rural north as a boy, electric lights had never ceased to enchant me. They reminded me, as they still do, of the unfriendly darkness and riotous floods of moonlight in the rural north. Seen at a distance, the lights taunted me, ridiculed me, tantalized me, reassured me, set off in me an urge sometimes to possess them, sometimes to spray them with black paint, to kill their blinking fun.

The tyranny of place, the tyranny of time. Grassroots. The muck, the smell, the fortitude, despair, endurance. Always the sounds begin again. Experience and the place that contains it… the tyranny of it… the politics of education, the campaigning, the voices of protest. As reporter and fiction editor of *Drum* magazine in the mid-1950s, I was to find myself striving towards a sense of balance – actually compromise – between writing as self-expression and as objective reporting of the social scene.

September 1957: Nigeria, first stop on my route into exile. For four years I looked for the smell and feel of place. It was there all right: the smell of Lagos, the smell of Ibadan; the harmattan scouring the savannahs of the north – harmattan, that dry desert wind. The abundance of humanity in Nigeria and its theatrical style… a glorious sense of freedom and daytime, after the South African nightmare. You wanted to do anything, everything, to slow down the palpitations and shake off the cold sweat with which the nightmare spat you out into the full glare of Nigerian daytime. You must stop clawing around you in search of opposition, of insult. But you seem to hear, still, the distant proclamations of law and order across the Congo and Zambezi and Limpopo, down in the painful south of the South. Your anger was still sediment in the pit of your stomach, waiting for time's purgative or agitation. The harmattan was nothing like the fierce August winds of the South. Down in the South you learned to lie to the white man in order to survive; you were made to think that anger and bitterness, running and fighting and running and fighting, were vital compulsions. In Nigeria, or in Ghana, you had to stop running or else you'd plunge into the Niger or bolt into the Sahara and would not live to learn a lesson. Then you knew that the immigrant's journey is a long, long, heavy road. He tunnels back again, beneath pounding footsteps of thirty-seven years of South African living bearing down from ground level.

When you could have been ready to enter into a commitment to a permanent place in Nigeria, you ran into another and different set of colonial educational politics. You thrived in freedom, you were well received – generously even – but you were always an outsider, a pebble in a mouthful of rice. You had to leave, even though voluntarily.

France. No sense of place, no commitment, no desire to be sucked into French intellectual life, especially at the peak of the Franco-Algerian troubles (1961-63). Still straining at the tether that tied you to the centre of the South African experience. The tyranny of place, of time, was taking on a symbolic meaning, i.e. the inner compulsion to hold on to the smells and texture of southern life.

Kenya, 1963-66; Denver, Colorado, 1966-68; Zambia, 1968-70; back to Denver; then Philadelphia, Pennsylvania, 1974-77. Still accumulating experience, knowledge, but also hoping to strike anchor – a commitment not merely to that vague and general community called the Black World. At the level of banners and militant talk, anyone of black ancestry can qualify for membership. And you can coast along, easy, unimpeachable. Not commitment in the sense in which we speak of affiliation to a cause. That comes naturally. It is given to a South African, whether it is dramatized or not. Exile politics turns one into a professional exile, and I would have none of it. You want a commitment to a place, an attachment in which you are prepared to invest your emotions and intellect and socializing energy. And only South Africa had this, for all the agony one is forever trying to survive.

Several of us South Africans improved our academic qualifications so as to be able to compete on the world market, so to speak. It paid off. The stimulating academic life of the United States and its academic freedom gave us a sense of purpose. We could not have traded it for anything. After you had equipped yourself with international experience and training, then what? Towards the end of our nine years stay in the United States, I became painfully aware that I was not contributing meaningfully –

i.e. meaningfully to myself – to American education and cultural goals, in spite of the stimulating intellectual environment. Indeed, but for periods of students' unrest, you can cuddle up in an American university atmosphere, become engrossed in your intellectual pursuits, and simply insulate yourself against the sound of human concerns out there. But my wife felt, as a social worker, that she needed a cultural context if her work was to be fulfilling. We found American culture, to the extent that one can call it 'American', too fragmented. I could not see my teaching contributing to unified cultural goals – much as we were both appreciated in our respective social and academic circles. I could not capture the smell and texture of American life. I switched to writing literary criticism. For fiction writing, I would need to enter one of the cultural units. The nearest would be an ethnic segment, like that of the blacks.

But Afro-American political and intellectual concerns were too formidable for me to pretend that I could adopt them in a way that would contribute substantially to black aspirations. To do this, one has to feel a people's history in one's blood and marrow, down to one's genitals. I was getting too old to identify more than intellectually and emotionally. I must have place, with its tyranny and all. Poetry can overlook diversities, or try to unify them if one wants to produce public poetry – because the poetic sensibility strives to put things together, explores the quality of that interconnectedness, the quality of relationships. Fiction, as a process, thrives on conflict even though the final product demonstrates a single, total focus. For conflict and diversity, you need to be intimately familiar with particulars. I did not have these, and could not fake them even if I wanted to. Some people say that they can write novels in which place does not matter, in which place and time do not need physical and temporal qualities. They can create a theatre in the mind. This kind of experiment goes against everything I hold sacred in the composition of fiction; the tyranny of place is something I submit to. In the final count, it is a tyranny I would rather try to understand and deal with so that I learn how to reconcile its imperatives, its diversities, in relation to that 'far-off divine event'. Or is it that far away?

I looked at the Rocky Mountains, thirty miles to the west of Denver, Colorado. I don't like such high mountains. Nor could I join the crowds that seemed to experience an orgasm in their contact with those high mountains. (I could not be ecstatic about snow either.) The mountains of my youth and the flat lands still haunted my dreams, and I remembered the dark nights when I often had to sleep in them. Still, I could conquer them with my imagination.

The tyranny of place. When we returned to Denver in 1970, after two years in Zambia, we bought a house whose owner decided to leave a piano in the basement, because it would cost the equivalent of fifty-two rand to have it carried out. He flatly refused to acknowledge the responsibility of having it removed. I started to hack it down with an axe. I threw the iron frame down on the concrete floor and the damn thing was shattered. Some friends and others who heard of it were horrified, because the instrument was still in good working condition. That was a moment of glory for me! My wife and I did not see why we should inherit someone else's junk. You love your own junk because it has a smell that expresses you. We needed more room for our four children: if they wanted to learn to play the piano, they could work and buy their own when the time was ripe. I resented being drawn into a piano-ornamented culture.

This mood of rejection, of revolt against the brittle elegance of suburbia, its rectangular, well-ordered, antiseptic manners carried over to another object – the crab-apple tree. This highly fertile thing grew in front of our yard. We spent the first summer sweeping away fruit that had fallen and was decaying in the water on the sidewalk. By the next summer I had got someone to dig out the damn thing. Again some of our tree-infected friends expressed horror. Kill such a lovely tree, ecology and all! You could have made jam with all that fruit; you should see the blossoms in the spring, they said. But my next-door and opposite neighbours were happy, annoyed as most of suburbia is by highly fertile things and humans. Having been raised in the country, where you have all the wild nature you want and more, and in an urban slum where we swept the yard every day, I couldn't be excited over the tending of a lawn.

I seemed to be doing everything to alternately court and diminish the tyranny of place. A tyranny that gives me the base to write; the very reason to write. And yet only seldom does an exile get to live on his own terms. You look at the Rockies. They seem to say to you: 'You've been moving fifteen years. Here's where you stop.' Try climbing over and you stop dead at the Pacific. You're not Cortez, you know. Even if I can't return to Africa, I must still have place. I must know whom I'm speaking to. Not a place in the theatre of the mind, but a place whose real life I can feel in my blood and bones. There's the rub. I must stay with the South African reality. A reality so deeply rooted in my life that I could never lose it, dare not lose it. That is its tyranny and its value as the root of commitment to its culture.

Most black South African writers living in exile are banned for their native readership. They must continue writing for that vaguely defined or non-existent 'world intelligence'. They can never know what the people – whose concerns they share in South Africa, who make the material for their writing – think of them. They may be applauded or discredited by people whose critical standards they don't care for. They are indeed like disembodied voices that echo from hill to hill: Dennis Brutus, Mazisi Kunene, Alex la Guma, Arthur Maimane, Keorapetse Kgositsile, Lewis Nkosi, Cosmo Pietersen and Bloke Modisane. There are also five mounds of permanent exile, alas, from which only silence will ever be heard.

I can hear even now in their poetry of exile that muted longing that is born of the mystical attachment to the tyranny of place, the tyranny of time. It is a poetry haunted by 'silences', 'fear', 'cries', 'sirens' and 'distance'. As he goes about his daily business, the 'wanderer', the 'troubadour' – as one exile, Dennis Brutus, calls himself – is haunted:

> *wailings fill the chambers of my heart and in my head*
> *behind my quiet eyes*
> *I hear the cries and sirens.*

Another poet, Authur Nortjé, calls exile:

> *a gutted*
> *warehouse at the back of pleasure streets:*
> *the waterfront of limbo stretches panoramically – night the beautifier lets the lights*
> *   dance across the wharf.*

Nortjé concludes:

> *You yourself have vacated the violent arena for a northern life of semi-snow under the*
> *Distant Early Warning System:*
> *I suffer the radiation burns of silence.*
> *It is not cosmic immensity or catastrophe that terrifies me:*
>
> *it is solitude that mutilates,*
> *the night bulb that reveals ash on my sleeve.*

In a piece entitled *To Mother*, Keorapetse Kgositsile writes:

> *What of the act my eye demands*
> *past any pretentious power of any word I've known? My days have fallen*
> *into nightmarish despair. I know*
> *no days that move on toward laughter, except in memory stale as our glory.*
> *The anguished twists of our crippled day will calm my voice. Woman dancer-of-steel,*
> *did you ever know that the articulate silence of your eye possessed my breath for long*
> *days? Yet still I know no dance but the slow death of a dazed continent.*

There is another dimension of exile that, at any rate in its artistic expression, emphasizes intellectual and spiritual alienation, such as we do not observe immediately in the South African poetry of exile. The poetry of intellectual alienation has its roots in the French colonial policy of assimilation. Africans and West Indians who came from French colonies to study in Paris in the 1930s eventually felt uprooted, stripped of their African identity, spiritually removed from their ancestral shrines. A sense of spiritual exile or alienation informed Negritude poetry, but it was at the same time a reassertion of African values. Since H I E Dhlomo's famous poem, *The Valley of a Thousand Hills* (1941), South African poetry written by blacks has never paused to contemplate intellectual alienation. The present has become increasingly abrasive and we fight for permanence in industrial life. At least half a decade earlier, the black poets of Harlem, USA, had already begun to ask questions about Africa, the land of their ancestors – e.g. Langston Hughes, Countee Cullen and Anna Bontemps. Senghor and Césaire read them in French translation and were startled by new images. The black American and the Caribbean knew very well that their condition of exile would have to be resolved where they were, and not back in Africa. They were being alienated by European racism, the roots of which had to be traced back to slavery. References to Africa in the black American poetry of the time – late 1920s and early 1930s – were mostly an intellectual and emotional escape: a response to their condition of loss and deprivation in a white man's world.

Although Claude McKay wrote outside of the Harlem Renaissance in the 1920s and resisted its poetic style, he could not help but be influenced by its mood. He expresses the black American's exile in the following terms:

> *Although she feeds me bread of bitterness,*
> *And sinks into my throat her tiger's tooth,*
> *Stealing my breath of life, I will confess*
> *I love this cultured hell that tests my youth*
> *Her vigour flows like tides into my blood,*
> *Giving me strength erect against her hate.*

The West Indian could not return to Africa, nor could the Afro-American. Africa was only an idea to them. But the Africans could return. Senghor tells himself in another poem that it is time to leave. Or else he may be tempted to sink his roots deeper into the alien ground in Europe; tempted by the glitter of hotel suites or the screaming solitudes of city life. Time to go. He can already hear the termites boring through his bones and tearing down the youthfulness in his limbs. He eventually comes to regard himself as a prodigal. So back to the shrines; this time in flesh. Even as he is about to leave again for France, as an appointed deputy in the French House of Deputies, the poet prays to his ancestors and blesses them for their lack of coarseness that comes of hatred. Because, he says, he has made friends with Europeans: 'those champions of the intellect, obsessed with form...'

Exile, return; the literary compromise. This dimension of exile makes another story – for next time. Except this: that without necessarily supporting Negritude as an aesthetic programme, as more style than theme, as Senghor will have it, I can identify with his longing to return to the ancient shrines – even though his lifestyle is completely European. What do I really mean by the literary compromise? Throughout our twenty years' exile I have been sustained partly by this compromise. Even as I mumble thus to myself, I am aware that writers do not make political revolutions;

they wield no power that immediately counts in the struggle for political and economic power. In spite of the existing Afrikaner cohesion at the time when Celliers, Leipoldt and Totius wrote poetry, it cannot sincerely be said that their literature moved anyone to political action. And yet without them where would *die Tweede Taalbeweging* (Second Language Movement) be?

Creators of serious imaginative literature, engaged in a middle-class occupation, can only be read by the educated, who can move beyond the supermarket thriller. It does not matter if we write about the concerns of the common man, sometimes or always. We are not read by him. He reads us only when we over-simplify experience or give him a ride on the wings of fantasy. The politicians and financiers run our world, not people who play with images and symbols. Politicians and financiers run the Third World even though they may not live there. Yet we keep writing, because we are obeying a compulsion. We are historians of feeling. I might go insane if I did not write. The obsession to do so is a therapy for us, and it is no use deceiving ourselves that the world will be saved by poetry or fiction or the arts in general. But we must produce literature because it is a cultural act, a cultural imperative. I can only see its cumulative impact in the context of a national culture, a culture that has a definite geographic place and integrated objectives.

I am looking forward to a day when a writer will stand in front of a judge or magistrate and a prosecutor, charged with writing bad verse rather than with inciting people to violence through his poetry. Well-written poetry incites no one to violence – not even Biblical poetry on the tongue of a gifted preacher. Its magic arrests action and draws tears, and what have revivalist tears to do with the price of potatoes? A court that realizes this will to my mind have demonstrated that at last culture, refinement, enlightenment have been vindicated. At last!

The writer must know that imaginative literature is, in public terms, at best a compromise – an investment in the cultural well-being of his people, a way of keeping a language alive, of increasing us, something that may mature, that may be relevant today and irrelevant in the future, and again relevant at another time. And even when it is relevant in terms of enduring moral values, such as what the Shakespeares, the Tolstoys, the Dostoevskys, the Balzacs, the Prousts, the Goethes and others had to offer, it is only spoken about by us academics within university and school walls.

I see the literary compromise at the social level and the aesthetic level. The writer may decide to make a compromise between the inner compulsion to create and the pressure to enter social action. The two are not mutually exclusive, but one has to fix one's priorities and decide which one of the two realities, if at all, has to feed into the other, according to one's capacity and temperament. Andre Brink's recent statement in this respect seems to be evading compromise. And he begs some questions. He has quite clearly decided what to do and what not to do. But, although he makes us think that if you decide to do the one you may not do the other, I suspect that there is a lot more happening inside him that can be regarded as a compromise, but which does not find a precise language in what he says:

> *I had for a long time the same agonies as Breyten (Breytenbach) both as an Afrikaner and as a writer. I had to work my way through this to resolve the question: Is it sufficient to write or must one be a man of action? My decision has been to function through my writing and I have accepted that writing means opting for a non-active role... My attitude is that politicians fight it out on a practical level in the domain of the possible and the expedient. It is a writer's task to find out essentially what it is all about, to weigh the human values...*

Andre Brink also gives us the impression that an active role must necessarily be Breytenbach's. As a teacher and writer, I feel quite at home in integrating various cultural activities at the communal level with my writing, even when political obstacles stand in the way of cultural activism. And I see no intrinsic polarization between being a writer and peacefully demonstrating a love of human justice.

At the aesthetic level we can best conceive compromise through the German transcendental idealism of the 19th century. Schelling saw the artistic product as the meeting point between the subjective, conscious 'I am' and objective, unconscious, external nature. This artistic product in turn becomes an unconscious phenomenon, which epitomizes infinity. A comforting thought, and I am not being ironical. Aren't we, after all, happy and gratified by an awareness of some mystical presence in a work of art that we comprehend and that moves us – all of us who go to art galleries and theatre, and who read books in order to feel increased? This is another compromise I identify with.

There is yet another that should not be ruled out. We shall always experience the age-old interplay between literature as a historical item on the one hand – here today, there tomorrow, as the Hungarian critic, Georg Lukács – saw it, and on the other as a transcendental phenomenon. Lukács sought to strip us of idealistic notions of art as a static thing, supra-temporal, eternal, transcendental and so on. I do not see anyone ever theorizing out of the way this interplay between the historical and the transcendental in literature; the realism and idealism that brought me back home.

I have returned after twenty years of exile and live in a town in Lebowa, seven miles from where from ages five to twelve I herded goats and cattle, forty-five years after I left it. In the last year I have been re-acquainting myself with the smell and texture of the place. It is a changed human landscape in many ways, one that is still changing but essentially still real to me. Pockets of African urban life have broken into the idyllic natural scenery, but not violently. Boys do not herd cattle and goats any longer: instead, they attend school regularly. Women still carry water on their heads for long distances, just as they used to forty and more years ago. Land cultivation has diminished considerably owing to the migrant labour system and lack of good land. Those who come back to live here go into commercial ventures, or professional and administrative jobs.

Yes, a changing human landscape, but still essentially rural. Unlike in those early days of my childhood, Mirage aircraft from the military bases farther north come whizzing overhead every so often. From the southern urban complex echoes of another turbulence and pain come to my ears, like the sound of ocean breakers staking a claim on the shore. The imagination strains for a meaning of these phenomena: supertensed birds of steel here, the painful south and its turbulence down there and, between them, this pastoral serenity and I – who have in the last twenty years become thoroughly suburban. So suburban, because I could live anywhere I liked if I could afford it, that I could not live in a slum again, and have to regard this enforced retreat as an unhappy arrangement. A poem is straining to be born, even as I labour the theme of compromise, social and aesthetic, which I would not trade for any other of the same order. It was Vinoba Bhave, the Indian mystic, who said: 'Though action rages without, the heart can be tuned to produce unbroken music...' Super-tensed jets, political noises, the power drills of the south and its tremors; the wanderer returned to look for a physical base, for social and cultural commitment. My very return is a compromise between the outsider who did not have to be bullied by place and yet wanted it badly, and the insider who has an irrepressible attachment to ancestral place, anywhere from a rural to an urban setting.

The teacher and the writer in me made a deal: that as we both want place, you to teach among our people and regain a sense of relevance, I to create a metaphor out of physical place and its human environment, we should return to the country of our birth. Just don't you breathe down my neck, teacher, and tell me how to write. Because you're an almost irresistible pedagogue, and soon I shall be dragged before a tribunal accused of writing bad verse and worse fiction. Just stick to the classroom and let me take care of the metaphors, understand?

Es'kia in 1941

Homage to Léopold Sédar Senghor – 1980

Synopsis by Marcus Ramogale

Léopold Sédar Senghor (1906-2001), the Senegalese poet, statesman, and champion of Negritude, was born in the coastal town of Joal, Senegal. In Homage to L S Senghor, published in Présence Africaine in 1976, when Senghor turned seventy, Mphahlele pays tribute to this great son of Africa. Senghor was educated at mission schools in Senegal and later at the Sorbonne. From 1946 to 1958, he was Senegalese deputy to the French National Assembly. The Senegalese Progressive Union, of which he was founder, took Senegal to independence in 1960 – when he was elected the first president of Senegal. He held this position until 1980. During this period, he became the most influential statesman in francophone West Africa. Within literary and intellectual circles, Senghor is best known as a poet and advocate of negritude.

Mphahlele pays his tribute to Senghor in the manner of a praise singer. Here the African praise song does not have just a celebratory function, but also serves as a historical narrative in its recounting of its subject's experiences and achievements, struggles and honourable accomplishments. As he describes some of Senghor's achievements, Mphahlele brings in some aspects of his own life experience and also tells, in passing, of the impact of Senghor's writing and thoughts on his own intellectual and political development. He brings together biographical and autobiographical elements for purposes of comparison and contrast. In a sense, therefore, this piece – which has poetic resonance in some places – is about both Senghor and Mphahlele. One writer pays tribute to another and, in the process, the homage itself inspires creative self-writing.

I greet you, fellow-African, on your seventieth birthday. It has been a long haul since Joal. For so long, too, you've stomped up and down *le chemin de l'Europe, chemin de l'ambassade.* Maybe longer than you care to remember. I greet you. You had a country to come back to. And you returned to lead a people that needed you, wanted you. They wrenched you from your moorings, you and your fellow-men, I mean those Frenchies. But they did not let you wander aimlessly on the seascape. They took you in hand. They gave you a language, you grabbed it and used it like a master. With it you made rhythms on the *balafon* of your soul, its *kora*, its drums. You, master of the grand gesture; of the grand resonance; of the grand Idea inflated with so many moments of feeling; sometimes emotion dripping schmaltz from the lush and grand Idea. Like in the *New York* poem. It was somewhere else I found the power of your music, the real longings of your heart, the pain of your ecstasy, the ecstasy of your pain.

I myself have long since learned that word is rhythm, word is meaning, rhythm and word and meaning and being are one. But I see only too well your dedication to poetry; am reminded always where we are with it when I read your lines:

> Ah! mourir à l'enfance, que meure le poéme, se désintègre
> la syntaxe, que s'abîment tous les mots qui ne
> sont pas essentiels.
> Le poids du rythme suffit, pas besoin de mots-ciment
> pour bâtir sur le roc la Cité de demain.[1]

And so you must yourself feel the irony that lies in our love for the word, us children of black Africa, the poetry that rolls from the tongue with it all the time.

I greet you, Senghor, I greet you !

I met you first in *Chants d'Ombre*, nineteen years ago when I was still wondering how my mate and I had survived thirty-seven years of white tyranny. A regime that had come to work by sheer police and military muscle and terror. I had come from a life which an artist could only discern in concrete minute-by-minute, day-by-day responses – responses that could best be captured though a racy, breathless, pressured diction. And here you came with the long musical line, with the grand aristocratic gesture. How could I but be either entranced or knocked off balance? First, I tripped and fell, and then I was enchanted. And then again, when I heard that music in your lines, the voice of self-assurance, the measured pace of feeling rightly placed and pouring out in volumes, I became impatient, impatient because I loved my anger, loved my hatred. But always I learned what two different sets of white political values had done to you and me.

No matter. I had already accepted the meeting point, the merging of the West and Africa in me down there in the painful, temperate south. Yet, the things that I saw around me and read and listened to in the new Nigeria-Ghana terrain – your voice among them – did something to steady me, to measure the energy of Africa in me, the thing we had taken for granted in ghettos where you could never efface your blackness, where you've got to feel the tyranny of place and time. Even now I have not yet

---

1   Ah! Die to childhood, let the poem die the syntax fall apart,
     let all the essential words be swallowed up
     The weight of the rhythm is enough, no need of word-cement
     To build on the rock, the city of tomorrow.
                         Reed & Wake p91, *Elegy of the Circumcised*

tamed the anger in me that never ceased to be touched off by the whirlwinds around me. Nor do I want to tame the bastard, lest I forget...

> Ecoutons la voix des anciens d'Elissa. Comme nous exilés
> Ils n'ont pas voulu mourir, que se perdit par les sables
> leur torrent séminal.[2]

That is it, you see. I've come full circle into the age-old theme of exile. Nineteen, even ten, years ago I still hoped for asylum in Africa; I did not yet perceive the poetry of exile. Reading you again it seems I'm hearing you for the first time.

I listen also to another singer, Kofi Awonoor's lines about lost souls, lost souls who must return for purification. And something inside me leaps into a flame and tells me to be on the go again – this time, back to the tyranny of place and time. Only that will fortify the enclave of my identity wherein sanity is secure.

> C'est le temps de partir, que je n'enfonce plus avant
> mes racines de focus dans cette terre grasse et molle.
> J'entends le bruit picotant des termites qui vident
> mes jambes de leur jeunesse.[3]

Jeunesse? Ah, that's anywhere along the rugged road of commitment – till it pitches you over the cliff when it has no longer use of you.

I have been back these last few weeks, for twenty-one days there in the painful South. The brief moment when the hounds at the gate were called off. In the wake of their power exercise that grounded so many children, you saw the hounds sniffing around all over. You motored up and down the cold, cold killing ground of Soweto; you could almost smell the smoke from the guns. I saw the graves of my folks south and north, having known all along my ancestors had blessed the return journey of a native son. I had known it.

Think of me standing in the valley of my childhood in the north, fixed at the foot of the mountain where I had known the terrors of the dark – even when on summer nights it was jubilee for myriad fireflies.

---

2   Listen to the voice of the ancients of Elissa. Exile like us
They have never wanted to die, to let the torrent of their seed be
lost in the sands.
                            Reed & Wake p5, *Nuit de Sine*

3   It is time to go, before I sink my fig-tree roots still deeper in this
rich soft soil
I hear the picking of the termites eating the youth out of my limbs.
                            Reed & Wake p20, *Time to go*

Think of me standing in the schoolhouse where I had learned to read and speak, while, as it once was with your own return:

> *au loin monte, houleuse de senteurs fortes*
> *et chaudes, la rumeur classique de cent troupeaux.*[4]

I greet you, Senghor, I greet you !
Once you heard the doors of your soul bang in the wind while you felt unanchored from yourself, from your mother's language, from the wisdom of your ancestors, from the music of your primal being. This time on the earth of my own ancestors, which I scooped up to feel the warmth of it bathe my hands, I secured my door with a strand of wire to stop it banging about in the wind – it had been banging so long I'd ceased to care until, like now, I wanted calm so I could listen. Yet I know the wind will come again and start the rumpus with my door, and I will let it so I don't forget... Which is why for now I still cannot say to my ancestors:

> *Soyez bénis, qui n'avez pas permis que la haine gravelât*
> *ce cœur d'homme.*[5]

Because even this day my ancestors walk on the killing ground, on the farming lands assigned to white folks by decree that drove away my people by the hundreds of thousands. 'Desecration here and desecration everywhere – who will atone?' I hear the ancestors cry.

You and I and all should know by now the poetry of a prodigal imagination – take comfort that we've got to kill it lest it cover more ground and choke the native crop like those insatiable weeds...

I know that you can, with the power and means at your command, aid the young towards the greater freedom of the mind, the nursery of the truest poetry.

I greet you, Senghor, I greet you, and hope that you'll accept my humble tribute; my apologies for replaying your music.

---

4   ... in the distance arises surging with strong warm smells, the classic
murmur of a hundred heads.
                     Reed & Wake p30, *On the Appeal From the Race of Sheba*

5   Bless you, you who have never let hatred gravel this heart of man
                     Reed & Wake p23, *The Return of the Prodigal Son*

Landmarks of Literary History in South Africa: A Black Perspective – 1980

Synopsis by Marcus Ramogale

Mphahlele presented this paper at the University of the Witwatersrand in 1980 as part of the University's Senate Special Lectures. A revised edition of the paper appeared in an anthology of critical writing published by Ad Donker in 1992. In this paper, Mphahlele surveys the development of black South African writing from the 19th century, when a written literary tradition emerged, to the 1970s – when the so-called Soweto or New Black Poets were active. The paper's approach is sociological, for it attempts to situate black literature within its wider socio-political context. It shows Mphahlele's extensive knowledge of black South African literature and his appreciation of the tense and discordant relationship between black writing and white power in pre-1994 South Africa.

As Mphahlele shows, black writing was started by mission-educated Africans and was used as an extension of the missionary evangelical endeavour. Black political consciousness, which later became a characteristic feature of black writing, emerged as a consequence of blacks' disillusionment with white-directed 'progress' and the 'many shams' created by white people. Political consciousness in black writing was, as Mphahlele shows, a weapon in the broad struggle against white oppression. It energized black writing and gave it a distinctive character. Africa's oral traditions have also vitalized the writing. Some black writers, such as Herbert Dhlomo and Sol Plaatje, used the oral tradition as a 'source of inspiration' and creative strength to domesticate and enrich the alien cultural practice that writing was.

This paper, because of its succinct yet extensive survey of black literary developments from the 19th century to the 1970s, is a useful starting point for anyone looking for a digestible introduction to black South African literature in English.

Humankind gave a thing a name and it took on life. Humankind gave the hero of the country a name and immortalized him. To tame the territory around them in order to control it and arrest its essences, humans imposed upon it a metaphor. They were stricken with a sense of wonder and admiration, and even awe. As lightning flashed before their eyes and thunder rumbled above them, they came to know the Supreme Being. They created a three-dimensional metaphor – a piece of sculpture – to celebrate their sense of organic unity in the universe, of which they are part and about which they learned from the ancestors. This organic unity is itself the Supreme Being, the Vital Force.

And so poetry was born. It illuminated God for humankind, just as the three-dimensional metaphor does. And in turn the sense of awe and majesty in the universe – the beginning of religion – illuminated poetry. And poetry can most clearly be seen to have been a way of perceiving, in those days when humanity could truly feel the presence of the Supreme Being in all phenomena.

Hence the common habit of mind to create metaphor out of the stuff of sensory perception. The calabash, or gourd, as a symbol of womanhood: smooth on the outside, fragile, container of good things that give nourishment, the inside suggesting the shape of the womb, the receptacle of a new life. The earthen pot as a symbol of the womb, so that a woman who has had a miscarriage is said to have broken the pot. The kola nut as a symbol of hospitality; death as a journey to be made on a ferry, rowed by someone of significant social standing. Death is in the leg; it is the body's locomotion. Behold the praying mantis shaking in the wind, so fragile that you wouldn't dare kill it: that is the Khoikhoi god – a creation of their poetry. The king is like the rising moon whose appearance scatters the scourge of famine.

Then came the 'Red Strangers'. 1885, the Berlin Convention. The continent of Africa lay there on the gigantic international dinner table, ready for the carving. Britain, France, Belgium, Germany, Portugal, Spain and Italy had all come in for a chunk. But two centuries and three decades before this the 'Red Strangers' had already established a presence in what came to be known as South Africa. The traders, the missionaries and the army had all ganged up to impose a new order. The missionaries, while busy winning new souls for the Almighty, while taming what they considered a savage landscape, were arranging treaties with the African rulers in the Eastern Cape to prepare the way for the British administration to exercise control. Dr John Philip and other missionaries were vying for prominence in the 'pacification of the native tribes.' The Moravian Brothers were working on the Khoikhoi, and Dr Johannes Theodisius van der Kemp (1747-1811) was busy on the Africans east of the Great Fish River. Later, in 1880, Van der Kemp moved into Ngqika's domain in the Tyumie Valley. Reverend Joseph William followed, and was himself succeeded by John Brownlee in 1820 – the year of the British Settlers.

And so Lovedale Mission Station was born. In the midst of this turbulence in the Eastern Cape, its frontier wars and cattle thieving and yet more reprisals, Ntsikana emerged: the first African on the subcontinent to compose Christian hymns. Not a voice crying in the wilderness, but a self-avowed prophet singled out from Van der Kemp's flock. He and his followers sang and danced to the beat of drums.

Dr Philip turned a deaf ear to the Africans who hoped he would be a true mediator between themselves and the colony and redress the wrongs they suffered during each raid. All the same, Ntsikana stuck to his new-found god. By contrast, his rival 'prophet', Makanna (also called Nxele), taught a separatist kind of Christianity. This was his way of demonstrating his distrust of the British.

Ntsikana renounced the traditions of his people, as his chronicler John Knox Bokwe (1855-1922) reports with partisan fervour, 'never to return to red clay and heathenism' (1904). To quote from the critic A C Jordan, the hymns were 'the first literary composition ever to be assigned to individual formulation – therefore constituting a bridge between traditional and the post-traditional period.' Jordan also finds in a specific hymn 'the idioms, style and technique of the traditional lyric' adapted to 'new conceptions' (1973).

Church, school and printing press became the three-sided infrastructure of missionary endeavour in South Africa. The Lovedale of 1826 was this kind of base for the Church of Scotland. Journalism in the Xhosa language began. Tiyo Soga (c1829-71) grew up in this kind of environment. After training for the ministry in Glasgow, he returned to face a famine-stricken people just come out of the disastrous cattle-killing event of 1857 inspired by Nongqause. As a missionary himself, Soga was also a self-appointed go-between and interpreter for the African and the colonist.

As an authentic reporter, Soga was to write in 1865:

> The missionary to Kreli will have most difficulties. He must be a man of prudence, good judgement, and tact. Kreli looks upon the missionary as a political agent, who may influence the Government of his country for good or evil. (in Chalmers, 1877)

In 1866 Soga wrote to Dr Somerville:

> In my opinion, the Gcalekas will now, more than ever, resist the introduction of the Gospel. They may not prevent the establishment of mission stations, but they will oppose the progress of the Gospel among the people. The prevalent opinion in that tribe is that missionaries are the emissaries of the Government to act upon the minds and feeling of the people with an instrument which they call 'the Word' and that those who have become affected by the Word, and exchange Kafir customs for those of the white men, become subjects of the English Government. (ibid)

After Xhosa journalism had all but ceased, Tiyo Soga restored it in 1862. First there was the paper *Ikwezi*, followed by *Isitunywa Senyanga,* then the magazine *Indaba,* in which Soga contributed articles rooted in Christian morality. He wrote hymns and translated the first part of *Pilgrim's Progress.* The second part was translated by his son, John Henderson, in 1929.

Tim Couzens sums up Tiyo Soga's role in his doctoral study, *The New African*, as follows:

> *The missionaries and Soga attacked heathendom and wanted to replace it. They gave various reasons for it characteristic of the arguments of the time. It was not only per se un-Godly, anti-Christ, but also it was an ideology which was backward, allowed for no ambition, produced people capable of none of the 'higher' intellectual pursuit and catered only for 'bodily wants' – 'dark minds in dark bodies …' (1985:88)*

Soga sang praises to the Europeans in *Indaba* (June 1863). According to him the European had brought things that were a 'blessing and a boon', such as woollen blankets, trousers, and jackets to replace karosses made of skins; hats, methods of cultivation, iron tools, knowledge, wisdom and skills. More than anything else, the white man had brought the Bible and knowledge of God, Jesus and heaven.

Indaba disappeared and other journals followed. One of these was the *Christian Express* (later called the *South African Outlook*) and another *Isigidimi sama Xhosa* – the latter edited by John Tengo Jabavu. Later, William Gqoba edited *Isigidimi* in 1884 and wrote for it. He contributed historical narratives, collected Xhosa proverbs, and published *Discussion between the Christian and the Pagan* – an allegory – and *Great Discussion on Education*. Christianity was spreading like bushfire when John Ntsiko, a blind catechist and hymn writer at St John's Mission in Umtata, expressed his sense of disillusionment in the new creed in a poem published in *Isigidimi* (1884) under the pen-name Uhadi Wase-Luhlangeni ('The Harp of the Nation'):

> *Some thoughts till now never spoken*
> *Make shreds of my innermost being;*
> *And the cares and fortunes of my kin*
> *Still journey with me to the grave.*
>
> *I turn my back on the many shams*
> *That I see from day to day;*
> *It seems we march to our very grave*
> *Encircled by a smiling Gospel.*
>
> *For what is this Gospel?*
> *And what salvation?*
> *The shade of a fabulous ghost*
> *That we try to embrace in vain.*

The African had found a voice. Xhosa literature was flourishing. Political comment, history, hymns and poetry were the main forms of expression in Xhosa and English.

At least one poet in *Isigidimi* (I W W Citashe) exhorted his fellowmen to 'turn to the pen, Take paper and ink. For that is your shield ...'(in Couzens and Patel, 1982:6).

Lovedale Institution was the hub of African intellectual life, represented in the activities of two societies – the Lovedale Training Society and the Lovedale Literary Society – which were mainly discussion groups. In the 1870s the *Christian Express*, *Isigidimi*, and *The Lovedale Press* were the journals most closely associated with these societies. As war raged – the frontier wars in 1877, 1879 and the Gun War of 1880-1881, in which Xhosa, Zulu and Basotho were the prime actors opposite the whites – the intelligentsia were becoming more and more discontented. A C Jordan observes that the rapid changes taking place were undermining 'the African's manhood in all walks of life, and the writers (were) concerned with this rather than with entertainment.' Hence the depressing nature of the few short stories that were published at the time. The same writer of the poem quoted above had complained bitterly in *Isigidimi* of April 2, 1883 that 'the true nationality of *Isigidimi* was in doubt'; that the paper silenced attacks on the white administration made by Africans but gave prominence to articles that were favourable to the whites. Why, for instance, he asked, could not a poet emerge from among Basotho who could sing in the following vein:

> *Arise, ye sons of Thaba Bosiu,*
> *The hyena howls, the white hyena,*
> *All ravenous for the bones of Moshoeshoe,*
> *Of Moshoeshoe who sleeps high up on the mountains.*
> *Its belly hangs heavy and drags on the ground,*
> *All gorged with the bones of warrior-kings;*
> *Its mouth is red with the blood of Sandile.*
> *Awake, rock-rabbits of Thaba Bosiu ...*

John Tengo Jabavu (1859-1921) was succeeded by Gqoba as editor of *Isigidimi* in 1884. Its life came to an end with Gqoba's death. Jabavu produced the first number of the bilingual weekly *Imvo Zabantsundu* (a paper that is still alive today) on 3 November 1884 in Kingwilliamstown. The desperate faith in and desire for formal education, the growing distrust of the missionary liberal, an atmosphere of anything but peace – into these conditions *Imvo* was born. Jabavu was joined by John Knox Bokwe, a hymn writer who later entered the Presbyterian ministry. There is a similarity here between the creation of an African educated class and the Afro-American's counterpart in the days of Booker T Washington (1856-1915) and W E DuBois (1868-1963). The men of letters were also a political elite those days. 'Dipping the bucket where you are and not disdaining facilities within your grasp' became a common imperative shared across the Atlantic. The only weapon of protest was the delegation that could solicit an audience with the government authority concerned.

In 1909, Jabavu and Walter B Rubusana (1858-1916) were delegated for talks in Britain, intended to influence that country against the entrenchment of the colour bar in the Union's constitution. These writers were also faithful to their traditional poetry and lore. Rubusana himself collected proverbs and praise poems and wrote political articles for *Izwi Labantu* (founded 1897). He wrote a *History of South Africa from the Native Standpoint* and became one of the founders of the Native Congress.

There were other events that conditioned and redefined the culture of the African people in the 19th and early 20th centuries, and to which the writers responded. They were right in the concourse of violent cross currents of history: frontier wars; vehement missionary evangelisation; the establishment of church schools, teacher-training institutions, and presses; the upsurge of journalistic writing; the entrenchment of the white man's political supremacy and apparent negation of the Christian faith as the new converts understood it; the conflict between Christian and traditional values at a time when the missionary had established in the minds of the convert the idea that to be Christian was to be civilized and vice versa; the dramatization of self by the newly-converted Christians; the formation of Union; the Native Labour Regulation Act of 1911 and the Natives Land Act of 1913; the founding of Fort Hare College in 1916 and of the South African Native National Congress in 1912; all following closely upon – and responding to – the end of the Boer War and the formation of Union. There was also the impact of John Bunyan's *Pilgrim's Progress* as an allegory for the writer of the African's travails, and so on.

The visits of men like J D K Aggrey from the Gold Coast (1921) and the contact between African and Afro-American students in the United States also left their imprint on the intelligentsia throughout South Africa. Later, when the African Methodist Episcopal movement was seen as a symbol of black religious independence, a long-lasting association between the two black worlds was clinched. As was the case all over Africa, white people had conceived the grand Christian design for the taming of the African landscape, both human and physical. Through this very design, operating through church and school, the African came to perceive white people's political motives for what they were.

We observe the persistent pursuit of folkloric materials, including praise poetry, in other writers like Samuel Mqhayi (1875-1945). Together with Rubusana, he wrote for *Izwi Labantu* and later co-edited it and *Imvo*. Mqhayi's first sustained prose work was *Ityala Iama-wele* ('The Lawsuit of the Twins') published in 1914. It was followed by a utopian allegory *U-Don Jadu* (1929) which weirdly previsions present-day Transkei as an 'independent state.' Mqhayi, known as *imbongi yesizwe* ('national poet') and dubbed by Vilakazi 'the father of Xhosa poetry', was a participant in the Conference of Bantu Authors at Florida, Transvaal, in 1936 – called by R H W Shepherd of Lovedale Press. Shepherd was later to become editor of *South African Outlook* – successor to the *Christian Express* – in 1922. Mqhayi published a volume of eight cantos on Hintza, one of the rulers of Eastern Cape, and yet another collection of poems, *Inzuzo* (1942). He was able to bridge the distance between traditional and modern idioms. In mock heroic lines Mqhayi praises the Prince of Wales (later Duke of Windsor) on the latter's visit to South Africa in 1925:

> *Here comes the Prince of Britain!*
> *Offspring of the female buffalo, Victoria! –*
> *Young woman who is a god in the land of the blacks.*
> *Spirit-like, priest of war, wizard,*
> *Here comes the boy son of George V;*
> *Of the Royal House, a boy coming to men.*
> *Dung-coloured one whose eye flashes lightning.*
> *If it so much as touches you with a glance, it will blind you.*
> *The dung-coloured one, who is a – it's impossible to tell by looking at him –*
> *His eyes are like living creatures when they look at you.* (1925)

Great Britain is hailed 'land of the endless sunshine' that has conquered the oceans. She has drained the rivers dry, conquered the skies; she sent the preacher, the Bible, but also brandy. She preaches truth but denies us the truth. She talks of life but deprives us of it, brings light but keeps us in the dark, 'shivering, benighted in the bright noonday sun.'

Lesotho was not to be spared missionary penetration. But in her case, it was on King Moshoeshoe's terms that the *Société des Missions Evangéliques de Paris* (Paris Evangelical Missionary Society, PEMS) set up house at Thaba Bosiu in 1833. On the contrary, the Moravians, London Missionary Society, Glasgow Missionary Society and so on became themselves tools of whatever government was in power during their time. By the same token, political writing produced by Beersheba and, later, Morija Press was not one of confrontation with authority. PEMS came in the wake of *difaqane* (wars that attended the expansion of Shaka's kingdom, 1818-1830). The paper *Leselinyana la Lesotho* was established in 1862, the printing press having been first introduced in 1841. As a written language, Sesotho first went into print in 1872, when the Reverend Mabille finished translating Bunyan's *Pilgrim's Progress* – *Leeto la Mokreste*. *Leselinyana* became the first to publish Sotho writing by an African, Chere Monyoloza. In 1889 he published articles on traditional divination, which, after five issues, the editor stopped unceremoniously. The writings of Azariele Sekese (1849-1930) first appeared in *Leselinyana*. He translated Sotho heroic poetry for the paper. The new editor, Edouard Jacottet, encouraged this and Sesotho lore. *Lentswe la Batho* was set up to oppose *Leselinyana* in 1899. But Morija remained the main publishing centre.

Sekese published in book form his *Mekhoa ea Basotho* (a book of customs and proverbs) in 1893. His major book is an animal satire, *Pitso ea Linonyana* (1928), about a conference of birds personified in order to illuminate Sotho law. The conference is intended to try the hawk for its greed, cruelty and injustice. Vulture is presiding. The hawk is acquitted, as the members of the court are both corrupt and powerful.

Of the same generation as Mqhayi was Thomas Mofolo (1876-1948), whose novel *Moeti oa Bochabela* was first serialized in *Leselinyana* (1906), and brought out as a book in 1907. Once more we witness the dramatization of what the African has become after the encounter with the white man, although Mofolo's bias is Christian. Mofolo was subject to missionary censorship, so that the Christian characters of his fiction are strictly programmed to avoid offence to the reader. He began by identifying Europeans with Christian morality. In *Pitseng* (1910) he portrays the conflict between the Christian ideal and naturalistic human conduct. In Mofolo's formidable novel *Chaka* (1925) about the Zulu emperor, the hero is portrayed as a man larger than life-size, a tragic figure. Mofolo brings together here forces in conflict – his own conception of Christian morality and the lust for power. Completed in 1910, the novel was not published until fifteen years later. It was suppressed by the missionaries because Mofolo invested his hero with human qualities denied him by historians, missionaries and administrators – who saw in Shaka only the unmitigated savagery of a beast.

When Mofolo's former teacher Everitt Lechesa Segoete (1858-1923) published his *Monono ke Moholi, ke Mouoane* (1910), he demonstrated a theme that was to be repeated in Mopeli-Paulus's *Blanket Boy's Moon* (1953) and Peter Abrahams's *Mine Boy* (1946). Segoete's is a heavily didactic book, whose title says that riches dissipate like mist, like vapour. A clergyman, Segoete published several religious works. He also could not resist dipping into his traditional oral literature, as shown in his *Raphepheng*. Zakea Mangoaela (1883-1963) and Edward Motsamai (1870-1959) were also producing religious works, although Mangoaela also published praise poetry for Lesotho kings and co-authored a Sotho grammar textbook.

The emergence of Isaiah Shembe, born in the late 1860s in Natal, resembles that of Ntsikana of Ngqika's country. But Ntsikana was too much the missionary's spiritual child. Shembe, on the other hand, abandoned orthodox Christianity that did not observe Saturday as the Holy Sabbath. His church was thus part of the Ethiopic-Zionist movement that was inspired by religious nationalism. Shembe became the Zulu Messiah and created his own hymns.

In 1920 the Mariannhill Catholic Mission (in existence since 1882) became the venue for stage plays. These were largely sketches with a quick succession of scenes, and were popular. A period of decline in hymn composition followed, a genre that had been inspired partly by the American Board of Missions. To explain this decline, Dr B W Vilakazi stated in his essay *The Conception and Development of Poetry in Zulu*:

> *Even when most of the Zulus had gone through some appreciable standard education, those who have studied the system of Native Education up to about 1930 in Natal and Zululand will agree with me that students were not introduced to the spirit of poetry. The only poetry, which they could recite like parrots, was English ... The result was disastrous because we cultivated a dislike for poetry in general ... Such a system of education, I presume, is largely responsible for the lack of continuation of the work begun by Gumede and Luthuli, who themselves may have even forgotten what they did for the beginning of a new era of poetry ... Not until lately, when the educational standard was raised, did the Zulus feel the responsibility they had for their culture. They began to look back to the isibongo. This looking back was also greatly influenced by Stuart's Zulu books ... (1938)*

Prose writing in Zulu only began in 1922, as historical narrative, characterized by nationalistic sentiments. John L Dube (1870-1949) founded Ohlange Industrial School (1901), inspired by the example of Dr Booker T Washington's Tuskegee and Dr John Hope of Atlanta University. He was of the generation of Mofolo, Mqhayi and Sol T Plaatje (1876-1932). He founded the first African newspaper in Natal, *Ilanga laseNatal* (1907). He led the Natal Native Congress, which opposed the African National Congress, and was led regionally by George Champion. Dube typifies the group of enlightened Africans of the 19th and early 20th centuries who were Christian writers and also public figures. He passionately believed in Ohlange's place as an institution that would turn out first class Christian agriculturists. To him culture change could only be valid if it was directed by Christianity. Dube's first book contained beliefs he had assimilated from Booker T Washington and was published in 1922. The theme, as suggested in the title, *Isitha Somuntu nguye uqobo lwakhe*, was to demonstrate that black people are their own greatest enemy. Always, it seems, the African writer in those early years felt impelled to give an account of himself in relation to traditional mores and beliefs. Hence Dube's novel in his own mother tongue, *Insila ka Shaka* (1930), was the first to be published in Zulu and was his only fictional work.

In a preface to his novel *Mhudi* (written 1917-1920 but published in 1930), Sol Plaatje tells us the two motives for writing it:

> *to interpret to the reading public one phase of 'the back of the Native mind' and...*
> *...with the reader's money to collect and print (for Bantu schools) Sechuana folk tales, which with the spread of European ideas, are fast being forgotten. It is hoped to arrest this process by cultivating a love for art and literature in the Vernacular. (1978)*

In *Mhudi* Plaatje is trying to re-interpret history from an African's point of view. The use of English was a way of appealing to a large number of African readers. He had already published in 1916 *Sechuana Proverbs with Literal Translations and their European Equivalents.*

Plaatje expressed a high esteem for the missionary Robert Moffat's success in devising a Tswana orthography for the purposes of writing the language, which he himself was to use extensively in translating Shakespeare's plays. Much has been documented to give us the background to Plaatje's creative energy and writings. I need only refer you to Tim Couzens's introduction to the latest Heinemann publication of *Mhudi*, and articles elsewhere based on his painstaking inquiry into primary sources, and Stephen Gray's essay on Shakespearean sources in the novel (1977). Plaatje, Couzens points out, 'was the inheritor of the oral history of his family.' Plaatje's sources here were his grandmother, daughter-in-law of his great-grandfather, and her brother. Folk tales are woven into the novel, and once again we can appreciate how those early writers exploited indigenous thought and belief. Couzens also discusses the epic qualities of *Mhudi,* a love story orchestrated by the bloody clashes between Mzilikazi and the Barolong, and then the Boers.

Music men like Caluza, Griffith Motsieloa, Peter Rezant, 'King Force' Silgee; intellectuals like Benedict W Vilakazi, Z K Matthews, D D T Jabavu, A B Xuma, Jacob Nhlapo, Paul Mosaka; politicians and trade unionists like Champion, Msimang, Clements Kadalie, Selope Thema, Matseke, Makgatho, Mweli Skota; debating societies; self-improvement societies; institutions like Adams College, Ohlange, Kilnerton, Mariannhill, Grace Dieu, St Peter's Secondary School, Wilberforce, Healdtown, Lovedale, Fort Hare, and others; popular musical forms, from four-part choral compositions to ragtime, marabi, swing, jitterbug, boogie-woogie and bop; mass media like the *Bantu World, Umteteli wa Bantu, Ilanga, Inkundla, Abantu Batho* and others; a changing rural landscape – due to legislation that regulated land, labour and urban life; migrant labour and land shrinkage; increased migration into urban areas and the growth of slums. This, in sum, was the world that moulded our writers before the 1950s.

Whether in indigenous languages or in English, their literature had a largely pastoral setting; the action was concerned with historical events. It was in effect a dialogue of two selves, the dramatization of a dual personality – the traditional and the Christian. When urban life was portrayed, it was with reference to rural life. The ideas that whipped about in the writer's world of those early years included formal education as an imperative, and ideas about educational and religious organization that came with those who returned from study tours in the United States, where they had attended Afro-American institutions. Ideas centred on liberalism in the tradition of Ray Phillips, Professor Hoernlé and Edgar Brookes, and so on; ideas of nationalism as perceived by the Congress; of civil disobedience as a weapon of protest that was to be used effectively by Makgatho of the Transvaal branch of Congress in Pretoria trains and on pavements.

In a sense, Rolfes Dhlomo's novella, *An African Tragedy* (1928), and its presentation of city life as evil – together with Herbert Dhlomo's long poem *The Valley of a*

Thousand Hills (1940) – create a whole picture of Africans as disoriented people, of their landscape as wasteland. Rolfes depicts the wickedness in city life; Herbert cries out with a sense of outrage over lost innocence and corrosion of pastoral humanism. Both brothers wrote a lot for the newspapers, especially *Bantu World* and *Ilanga*. As R Roamer esq., Rolfes satirized urban life in *Bantu World*. Four years before the *Valley* poem, Herbert had launched into historical drama with *Nongqause*, or *The Girl who Killed to Save* (1936). This was followed by *Ntsikana, Cetshwayo, Moshoeshoe, Shaka* and *Dingane*.

Herbert Dhlomo went back in history in order consciously to come to terms with the African's traditional past that was still alive in his time, whatever damage had already been done. He also believed that African dramatic forms should be used as a source of inspiration. He understood – as his published comments show – the way traditional African drama works: that it is religious ritual, expressed in song and dance; that there is no clear line between audience and actors; that the audience are also participants. He also appreciated the African's 'greatly developed powers of speech', whereas the European has to be trained in elocution. He was, on the other hand, also a universalist, believing that Hamlet, Job, Joan of Arc and Nongqause were common to all races. He also believed that African drama could not grow wholly out of its indigenous roots, but needed support from Western modes. Dhlomo insisted that the past could serve African art only when the latter had grasped the present. African drama would have to deal with present-day concerns and activities – school, church, the slum, the car, commerce, and so on. He observed also that the African predicament – birth and progress – affords a rich store of material for drama. He wanted playwrights to dramatize and proclaim African philosophy and history, to dramatize oppression, emancipation and evolution.

In 1939 Dhlomo differed radically with Dr Benedict W Vilakazi (1906-1947) when the academic and poet declared that Zulu poetry needed to adopt Western techniques – e.g. rhyme and rhythm (metre) – while using the African experience for its content. Vilakazi clearly saw a literary piece in which there was a perceptible line of distinction between 'form' and 'spirit'. Dhlomo, on the other hand, saw a traditional literary piece as an esoteric item that defied academic analysis; which was for that matter a distorted form of the original 'primitive, tribal, dramatic pieces.' Dhlomo felt his notion of how to graft traditional idioms – e.g. dance and praise poetry – onto modern works (such as his play *Shaka*) to be corrective to Vilakazi's notion that poetry can best develop and improve when it assimilates Western idioms. To Dhlomo, rhyme was a 'cold tyrant', a preoccupation with technique that made poetry a self-conscious composition. He enlists the anthropologist's support to point to the African's universe as an organic unity between people and natural phenomena. Dhlomo's statement, 'rhythm is essentially African', is akin to the Negritude of Senghor and Césaire and their contemporaries, a concept they began to formulate in the 1930s in Paris. In other words, African poetry had nothing to learn from European rhyme and rhythm. Poetry and dance in African society were inseparable.

Benedict Wallet Vilakazi, who became a lecturer in African Languages at the University of the Witwatersrand and held the post until his death in October 1947, did for poetry and scholarship in Zulu what his contemporaries B M Khaketla (born 1933), Sophonia Mofokeng (died 1957), K E Ntsane, S M Guma and, lately, Daniel Kunene have done for Southern Sotho language and literature, and Guybon B Sinxo, James J R Jolobe and A C Jordan for Xhosa language and literature. Although he wrote a novel, Vilakazi is best remembered for his poetry in Zulu and for his scholarship. The poetry covered a wide range of subjects. Jolobe was as industrious a writer in Xhosa as he was in English, into which he translated some of his poems – notably *Thuthula* (1936). This is a brief epic poem about the Ndlambe Ngquka confrontation. But it was the publication of *Ingqumbo yeminyanya* ('The Wrath of the Ancestors') by Archibald C Jordan in 1940 (Lovedale Press) that would be the highest point in the development of the Xhosa novel, just as Mofolo's *Chaka* had been in Sotho. Jordan takes a detached view in the dramatization of the conflict between traditional and Christian beliefs.

It is one of our tragedies as a conquered people that what began as a vigorous literary movement in African languages, with an adult appeal, has in the last thirty years degenerated into writing that is published only for school children and is not particularly elevating. As Afrikaans publishing has captured the largest share of the school market in African areas, and as the education system for blacks was designed for us in the interests of the ruling class, scores of manuscripts in African languages are entirely prevented from reaching the school readership and the general public. Each language group has a semi-official 'Bureau', whose members are supposed to be highly knowledgeable in the particular language it monitors. Publishers send manuscripts to the Bureau for its opinion. Manuscripts that have an adult appeal and/or are highly political in content are suppressed. The stock argument is that Africans generally do not read their own languages outside school. Publishers who took the general readership seriously would lose money. But surely if elevating literature were published for school in the first place, good taste and interest would be developed to a sufficiently high degree at that level for children to be able to sustain enthusiasm for it into adult life. So publishing for an adult readership would find ready patronage. Today only independent indigenous presses such as those in Lesotho can be relied on to continue the rich tradition I have outlined.

The lean volume of prescribed literature in the African language departments of our universities is a mockery of tertiary education. At the same time, Afrikaans literature continues to enjoy political and economic patronage at all levels of education. I studied Totius, Leipoldt, Celliers, A G Visser, Eugene Marais and so on in high school and later taught them. If poetry of the same political passion as we find in these writers were in African languages, and were today suggested for high-school reading, the educational authorities would reject it. More than this, the authoritarian system of education that we are operating in schools resists the introduction of African literature in English. This is partly to monitor our cultural awareness in relation to the continent, and partly to hold onto the monopoly in educational publishing.

Mofolo, Sekese, the Dhlomo brothers and Jordan paved the way to realism in African writing on the sub-continent. Although Herbert's *Valley* poem uses much of the predictable lofty machinery of Romantic poetry, he is a realist when it comes to literary theory. It is in part this realism that our institutions resist. A thoroughgoing realism, however, really burst into full blossom for us when Peter Abrahams published *Dark Testament* (1940) – a volume of stories and sketches – about two years after he had arrived in England. Abrahams acknowledged the influence of Afro-American writing – e.g. Countee Cullen, Langston Hughes, Claude Mackay, and so on – on his own. *Dark Testament*, *Tell Freedom*, *Path of Thunder* and *Song of the City* particularly demonstrate this influence. Abrahams's novels were to provide an inspiration for later fiction, that of the next decade.

In 1950, *Drum* magazine entered the cultural scene. Through literary contests it attracted new talent, especially for journalistic and fiction writing. The late Henry Nxumalo attained the peak of his journalistic career in *Drum*, through his exposé of the Bethal farm prison labour and of jail life. Can Themba later took over *Drum's* investigative reporting, and 'Mr Drum' went to church in search of a white god and black souls that might have blundered into the company of white worshippers. Like Themba, the other fiction writers were also journalists: Arthur Maimane (now in London), Lewis Nkosi (now in London), Bloke Modisane (Rome), Todd Matshikiza and Casey Motsisi (both deceased, the former in exile), and the present writer. Nat Nakasa, who died in exile, was later to join the team. The Cape Town trio, Richard Rive, Alex la Guma and James Matthews published short stories in *Fighting Talk* and *New Age* (both long since banned), as well as in *Drum*. So did Alfred Hutchinson, who later died in Nigeria.

Before *Drum* – and the lesser picture magazines that shot up in the 1950s like *Zonk!*, *Afrika* and *Bona* – blacks could not publish in papers meant for a predominantly white readership. The only white journal that ever published any of my fiction was *Standpunte* – the story entitled *The Woman*.

I became Fiction Editor of *Drum* in 1955. Our writers did a number of exciting things to and with the English language in *Drum*. Then, in 1957, the proprietor decreed that fiction was not a hardsell; we had to stay exclusively with crime, sex, heartbreak stories, sport and chit-chat features on the social and political scenes. This coincided with my decision to pack up and quit the country. Several other writers followed. What had begun as a vibrant literary renaissance came to a sad close. In his story *Crepuscule*, Themba captures the temper of the times:

> We drank, joked, conversed, sang and horse-played. It was a night of the Sophiatown of my time, before the government destroyed it.
>
> It was the best of times, it was the worst of times; it was the age of wisdom, it was the age of foolishness; it was the season of Light, it was the season of Darkness; it was the spring of hope, it was the winter of despair; we had everything before us, we had nothing before us; we were all going direct to Heaven, we were all going direct the other way – in short, the period was so far like the present period, that some of its noisiest authorities insisted on its being received, for good or for evil, in the superlative degree of comparison only.
>
> Sometimes I think, for his sense of contrast and his sharp awareness of the pungent flavours of life, only Charles Dickens – or, perhaps, Victor Hugo – could have understood Sophiatown. The government has razed Sophiatown to the ground, rebuilt it, and resettled it with whites. And with appropriate cheek, they called it Triomf. (1985:19)

The 1950s was a period of political ferment, as the mass organizations were relatively free to protest on the open platform. The Suppression of Communism Act broke upon us in 1950, and it precipitated riots and the first bannings. The Eiselen Commission published its report in 1951, which was meant to be a blueprint for so-called Bantu Education. The teachers who campaigned against it were fired and prevented from ever teaching in the country. The Defiance Campaign followed in 1952, the leaders of which – black and white – were subsequently tried under the Suppression of Communism Act. They all came out with suspended sentences. The Bantu Education Act followed as sure as night follows day in 1953. About the same time, the removal of Sophiatown was afoot. Teachers and pupils boycotted schools and tried to organize independent institutions. More arrests and bannings. In 1955, the black and white organizations held the Conference of the People at Kliptown, attended by people from far and wide. It was here the Freedom Charter was adopted. The Treason Trial followed in 1956, which involved 156 leaders and dragged on for four years. Then Sharpeville in 1960, and the acquittal of all the accused at the Treason Trial.

Amidst all this, *Drum* was publishing stuff that appealed to a black proletarian readership. The writers used an English style that was well understood by the township reader. The imaginative writing courted no political confrontation: it spoke of the drama of black life, its triumphs and defeats, survival, its culture and sub-cultures, the police terror and legislated restrictions it was subjected to. The black writer was asserting his sense of permanence in an urban ghetto life where he was being told he was a mere migrant worker with no hope for security of tenure in his municipal box-house. The writers helped fashion a township culture and gave it literary expression: the music and dance that had a distinctive flavour and beat, the rituals of birth and death and marriage and church activity, the pass laws, the violence and shebeen life which became such a cult that, long after prohibition has gone – since 1960 – it still survives. To the extent that black politics was dramatized and indeed displayed a theatrical style, the masses developed an awareness. They had found a political language suited to their own time. Similarly, the writer had found his tongue – a language – and relative freedom of expression that matched the political expression of the decade.

The literary style of the 1950s was racy, agitated and impressionistic; it quivered with a nervous energy, a caustic wit. Impressionistic, because our writers feel life at the basic levels of sheer survival, because blacks are so close to physical pain: hunger; overcrowded public transport in which bodies chafe and push and pull; over-crowded housing, and the accompanying choking smell and taste of coal smoke; the smell of garbage, of sewage, of street litter, of wet clothes and body heat in over-crowded houses on rainy days; baton charges at political rallies; detention and solitary confinement; torture in the cells; violence between black and black. The writer attempted all the time to record minute-to-minute experience – unlike his counterpart in the former British and French colonies, who has the time and physical mobility and ease that allow him philosophical contemplation, a leisurely pace of dic-tion. Poetry was almost entirely absent in the 1950s. Narrative prose and essays became the most handy and accessible modes of expression to deal with one's own anger and sense of urgency. Our writers displayed a greater mastery of English prose and sheer verbal felicity than we can observe today.

After Sharpeville, anti-black legislation piled up. Political protest was all but muf-fled. In addition to the laws that drove several blacks into exile, censorship has been cracking its own whip since 1963. The authoritarian had begun to stifle the human-istic conscience. Those who went into exile began to produce full-length books for the first time, except for Alex la Guma, who wrote his novel *A Walk in the Night* (1962) when he was under house arrest in Cape Town. There is Todd Matshikiza's *Chocolates for my Wife*; Alfred Hutchinson's *Road to Ghana*; Bloke Modisane's *Blame Me on History*; La Guma's *And a Threefold Cord*, *The Stone Country*, and *In the Fog of the Seasons' End*; Lewis Nkosi's *Home and Exile* and *The Transplanted Heart* (both collections of essays); and this writer's *Down Second Avenue* and other works. Nat Nakasa's reportage was later to be assembled in a volume. Significantly, six of the above publications are autobiographical.

These writers were later joined in exile in the 1960s by Dennis Brutus, Keorapetse Kgositsile, Mazisi Kunene and the late Arthur Nortje – all poets who have since produced single-author books of poetry. For the first time in South African literary history we have a volume of literature written out of the condition of exile. But because of censorship, South Africans will not hear its voices. The poetry from these exiles speaks of 'days that have fallen into nightmarish despair'; of the mutilated soul; of memories of 'uniforms of iron and buttons of steel' standing in front of 'faces filed against a prison wall'; of silences. It is a poetry haunted by 'nightmares of sealed walls', although it can still continue to hear 'cries and sirens'. The poetry speaks of silences, of exile as 'driftwood on an Algerian beach' amid the din and bustle of happy bathers, seabirds, sea rollers. For one poet, exile is a ghetto of the mind; for another, the isolation of exile is 'a gutted warehouse at the back of pleasure streets.' There is also the exile who speculates on dying in exile, in the absence of human voices, away from ancestral ground, in the midst of stony faces...

Towards the end of the 1960s, poetry emerged from among young students who, as members of the South African Students' Organization (SASO), were hauled before the court to answer to charges of inciting people to violence through their verse. One African academic gave evidence to the effect that poetry, unless it was utterly bad verse, could not incite anybody to violence. Then one would have to give it – that is, the bad verse – another name and not 'poetry'. There were more immediately felt human compulsions that caused violence, the academic explained. This was, to the best of my knowledge, the first time in South African history that imaginative literature stood trial in a court of law.

Poetry has, since the turbulent days of the late 1960s, become a popular medium. Prose fiction is only now catching up. Several young people read their verse at public meetings. Typical of this way of reaching an audience, which has long been practised in Russia and the United States (especially, in the latter country, among black poets), public readings have turned poetry into theatre. And what the writer in turn produces often becomes poetry turned theatre. It is an attempt to restore poetry to its original social setting: that of ritual enacted in public. Among the most prominent poets who emerged in the late 1960s, when SASO became active, are Oswald Mtshali, Mongane Serote, Sipho Sepamla, Mafika Gwala and Njabulo Ndebele. Serote, Sepamla and Gwala are the most innovative and adventurous of the lot in their styles and way of perceiving. There is a subtle interplay in the poetic styles between what is intended to be spoken aloud and what should survive in print. One can say this without implying that all the poets of the 1970s and 1980s write exclusively for oral performance. But theirs is by and large the language of public rather than privately contemplative poetry.

Most of the writers discussed, up to and including the Dhlomos, sought to elevate tradition through their works and strove towards African nationalism. The conflicts they dealt with were a way of comprehending the new world they lived in. Somewhere in their works is a myth, one that has been undergoing a process of erosion because of industrialization, education designed for other people's purpose rather than our own, and the political strife – all of which have denied us our history. This is not a uniquely South African phenomenon, except where politics are concerned. Industrialization and migrant labour – which the law has sanctified – have played havoc on traditional values. Other parts of Africa have been spared the more excruciating forms of deprivation and displacement that we are experiencing in this country.

Literature in African languages having degenerated to heavily censored reading for schools, it is not likely that the myth hinted at will be restored by the verbal arts in our languages. The myth concerns traditional self-pride that evokes the source, the beginnings of a specific consciousness. The source of that consciousness is African Humanism, rooted in our people's strong sense of community even while it has accommodated and assimilated other cultures. It is a humanism that has absorbed and reacted to external pressures coming from political authority. It is a humanism for which we have paid heavily, as prisoners on Robben Island and other islands on the mainland, as exiles, as occupants of other cells, six feet deep, screaming our own eternal silences.

Political styles demand a redefinition of a people's culture from time to time, and we have been too busy surviving. Our literature in the last thirty years reflects this. We have lost sight of the myth that could stabilize our spiritual and mental life, and save it from the religion of the desperate, the poor, the helpless and the downtrodden. The missionaries left us hanging while a pretty noisy and powerful segment of the Western world was asserting a completely different set of claims for Christ from those that we had been hoodwinked into believing.

As present-day writers, we need to go out in search of the myth and redefine it. In order to do this we need to know our literary heritage. We shall never attain such education at school, unlike the Afrikaans-speaking child, who is brought up on the writers of his race. Those who are in charge of our education have made sure that we should never know, still less be inspired by, our heroes – political, literary, or educational – so they stuffed us with the history of heroes who conquered us, whose ideas we are supposed to honour. Present day black writers will simply have to go to libraries to consult books that will inform them about their literary heritage. Those 19th-century and early 20th-century writers, and later writers like Plaatje, Abrahams, the Dhlomo brothers, the *Drum* writers, writers from other parts of Africa – all these can be the self-education writers need to help them reconstruct the myth. Reconstructing the myth is also a process of reassembling the fragments of Africa into a whole and single consciousness. Our writers need to go beyond the stimulus-reaction level. They need to take the readers beyond the physical, emotional and intellectual experiences that they grasp so well in real life. As readers we want to be increased, to be elevated beyond the present pain. This is what a myth can do for our writing – give it an extra, cultural context. Because myth implies resonances, the long unbroken song.

Literature: A Necessity or a Public Nuisance?
An African View – 1983

Synopsis by Peter Thuynsma

This is an address given at the then homeland University of Boputhatswana on 9 September, 1983. The occasion is the novelist Sol Plaatje's anniversary, a significant event on a relatively quiet campus with a fairly minimal academic industry other than the production of credentials.

This was a time when the homelands, under the mock authority of homeland leaders who were appointed by the apartheid government, established international airports, large stadiums and universities as semblances of a real national sovereignty. If the ethnic populations were trapped in this macabre game, the students at the universities were held hostage by these structures. Their teachers, however, were often serious about the business of an academy and battled for respect through research and through populating their campuses with African events and personalities in their respective fields. Sol Plaatje, an extraordinary pioneering novelist, diarist, journalist and political analyst and commentator, provided the occasion for this address.

Events immediately preceding this address might be significant. Five years earlier, in 1977, Mphahlele had returned from exile. A year later, in 1978, his attempts to secure an appointment as the Chair of English at the University of the North were thwarted by the government, and he was obliged to accept a position as an inspector of schools in Lebowakgomo, the then 'capital' of his assigned ethnic homeland of Lebowa. In 1979 the University of the Witwatersrand appointed him a Senior Research Fellow in its African Studies Institute, from which he progressed to Professor of African Literature. He established the first instance of African Literature being read as a fully-fledged academic discipline in South Africa.

Further extraordinary professional successes came as he joined a number of writers to found the African Writer's Association and, in 1982, published both his second novel, Chirundu *(arguably his finest prose to date), and* The Unbroken Song: Selected Writings of Es'kia Mphahlele.

Disappointment and literary success mixed to find an outlet in the Sol Plaatje address, and only very few punches are pulled. Here a vibrant voice extols the values of literary exploration and expression, and addresses remarks quite directly to prospective writers. There are also some splenetic wallops tossed at political authorities.

F rom time immemorial, ever since mankind found a spoken language, people
have delighted in telling stories, singing praises. When mankind began to conceive the presence of the Supreme Being, the Vital Force residing in rivers, mountains,
in savannah and jungle, in animal life, in every thing and being; when people became
conscious that they were weaker than the natural forces around them and the mysteries of their own natural life were beyond them, they discovered they needed a religion.
A religion that would help humans contain the abundant ravages and goodness of
nature. Humans merged with their environment in a way Western man was never able
to do centuries later. Religion did this for him, because then the human being was one
with the rivers, the mountains; with the vegetable and animal kingdoms.

Religion required ritual. Ritual required poetry. Which is how the idea of God
comes from the poetic imagination. The poet in every language conceived a creation
myth. The Hebrew poet created the Adam and Eve myth about the meaning of evil
and the fall of man. There are hundreds of creation myths in Africa, and tales
about evil and good. Images of God are also numerous. No one has any right to
think that his or her God is superior to that of other people. To think so is unforgiv-
able arrogance.

Why does ritual require poetry? Briefly, poetry compresses meaning into a few
words, phrases or sentences. It says more than one thing at one time. Image – i.e. word
picture – can make this possible. Images are also contained in metaphor or figurative
speech. The symbols such as we have in sculpture and drama used in ritual also contain several meanings. All these are a kind of poetry. Even mime is a form of poetry.
When we want to express joy, a sense of awe and reverence, praise for the hero, sorrow or the sense of loss that accompanies death or other disasters – in all these situations and moods, we need poetry or some other form of art.

Literature is thus a way of life; it is a compulsive cultural act. We need it for survival; we need it to maintain our sanity. We need it for revitalizing language and keeping it alive.

Consider the following metaphors or proverbs in our languages concerning the
human heart. There are several variations of these from language to language:

It is a sea.
It works ceaselessly like a bee: never in the air for long, always seeking someone to love.
Like a baby, it is not easily comforted.
It is like deep water concealing plenty of things, plenty of life.
As the eye is never dry, so the heart is forever filled with emotions
The heart cannot be borrowed, will brook no substitute. No one can carry its load

except the owner.
You cannot feel my hurt nor I yours.
Even a cough will betray what the heart thinks.
The unfeeling person is like a hole in a tree without honey.
Love that is not returned can kill the heart.
The day he opened his heart to confess his guilt it was like the sea vomiting.
It is the one who loves who is vulnerable, who must hurt.

The sages contemplate the meaning of things, of time and space, of life and death, their essences, and then they make utterances like the above. These utterances, in the form of proverbs, then enter communal speech. An utterance of the essence of any-thing makes poetry.

The Khoi poet creates a myth in an attempt to comprehend the way of the ances-tors. How can he, wandering man, invoke the ancestors when he is forever travelling away from his burial ground? So the poet invents a metaphor: the wind that traverses vast spaces must be the carrier of ancestral spirits. In the passing wind are the souls that wander.

Who but the poet could, like the Khoi, conceive such an exquisite representation of God in the frail and fragile praying mantis? Who but the poet could, like the San, create the image of the moon as a sign of man's immortality? For the moon is said to have sent a message to the San that, just as he disappears and returns, so will man also die and return. Praying to the moon, the San poet says:

Take my face and give me yours. Take my face, my unhappy face. Give me your face,
with which you return when you have died, when you have vanished from sight. You lie
down and return. Let me reassemble you; because you have joy, you return evermore
alive, after you have vanished from sight. Did you not promise us once that we too should
return, and be happy again after death?

Listen to this beautiful song from the Tewa, an indigenous North American people:

Song of The Sky Loom

O our Mother the Earth, O our Father the Sky,
Your children are we, and with tired backs
We bring you the gifts you love.
Then weave for us a garment of brightness;
May the warp be the white light of morning,
May the weft be the red light of evening,
May the fringes be the falling rain,

May the border be the standing rainbow.
Thus weave for us a garment of brightness,
That we may walk fittingly where birds sing,
That we may walk fittingly where grass is green,
O our Mother the Earth, 0 our Father the Sky.

Confronted with death you lament. If you have the gift of speech, e.g. a poet, you sing a dirge. This is a personal lament. The Ghanaian poet Awoonor has translated several of the dirges of his people: the Ewe of south-eastern Ghana. They have an extraordinary dirge tradition. Awoonor, himself a superb lyricist, explains that the man who developed the tradition of the dirge was Vinoko Akpalu. He was ninety years old when Awoonor, his translator, published his book *The Breast of the Earth* (1975). The dirge 'opens with a statement about the mourner's condition or predicament, then moves into a general lamentation, and ends with a message, supplication or prayer to those gone ahead into the spirit world.' The following is one of Akpalu's dirges:

Soon I would be dead and gone from amongst you.
This branch will break off.
The sons of men have gathered in counsel
debating how they will deal with Akpalu.
Death is within my homestead.
My mother's children, soon I shall be gone from amongst you.
This branch will fall.
Someone find me tears to shed.
Vinoko says he wished he had some tears to shed;
a mother-in-law may get back a thing, but not one's tears.
I say I wish I had some tears to shed.
Some people write
to deny the blood that binds us,
that Akpalu should be severely dealt with,
that Agoha's ring should cease.
The sons of men are in counsel,
debating just how to deal with Akpalu.
The singer's death is not from any distant place.
Death is within my homestead.
Children of my mother, soon I would be dead and gone
from amongst you.
This branch will break off.

I have started my talk with a statement about the oral beginnings, because speech and drama (the two main elements of ritual and any oral performance) are closest to poetry as a state of mind. It is thus a vital part of the life process, in our waking hours and in our dreams and visions.

When Thomas Mofolo published *Chaka* (completed 1910, printed 1925) and Sol Plaatje his *Mhudi* (completed about 1917, printed 1930), they embarrassed the missionaries and other whites who were the chief publishers of the time – and other circles where the novels were known – because they invested their African heroes with nobility. Whites generally did not credit Shaka the man with any qualities higher than savagery and barbarism. The hero and the heroine of Plaatje's novel, like Shaka, were makers of history – whereas it was generally believed that the European alone made history and the African merely reacted to it. Like the savannah, the jungle and the mountains, he was to be tamed. Plaatje had gone even further by narrating the factual story of the African's displacement and deprivation in his *Native Life in South Africa* (1915).

Before Mofolo and Plaatje, in the early days of publishing at Lovedale, Morija, Botswana, men like Tiyo Soga, William W Gqoba, Azariel Sekese and, later, Mqhayi, Jolobe and Mangoaela were writing in order to redefine the African under the onslaught of frontier wars, of British imperialism and of Christian arrogance. They were beginning to distinguish Christianity from Western civilization – which the Europeans were touting as synonymous.

And thus began the tradition of African writing in Southern Africa: what one can call the quest of self, towards self-definition. The African had to redefine himself as an act of self-knowledge, embattled as he was by forces that were ranged to destroy him, deprive him of his identity, of his heritage – material and spiritual.

From the historical perspective established by Mofolo and Plaatje, we move into social realism with Peter Abrahams and H I E Dhlomo, who were ushered in by World War Two in the early 1940s. These two are a watershed in our literary history, as are the lesser versifiers who were publishing in papers like *Umteteli wa Bantu* and the *Bantu World* at the same time.

Peter Abrahams's *Wild Conquest* is an exception because here he follows in Plaatje's footsteps to pursue a historical theme. Social realism includes an account of the immediate predicament of blacks: urban and rural poverty and insecurity, landlessness, urban violence, the dirt and stench of urban ghettos, the struggle for survival, police terror, the black-white encounter, political tyranny, migrant labour and so on. Abrahams's novels like *Song of the City*, *Path of Thunder*, *Mine Boy*, and his autobiography, *Tell Freedom*, provide abundant detail of black reality. H I E Dhlomo's long poem *The Valley of a Thousand Hills* cries out against the white man's greed that destroyed the pastoral beauty of the Valley and scattered its spiritual togetherness.

Then the turbulent 1950s – a decade filled with the voices of Alex la Guma, Richard Rive, James Matthews, Bloke Modisane, Todd Matshikiza, Arthur Maimane,

Can Themba, Henry Nxumalo, Lewis Nkosi and this speaker. That was the decade of prose. Not only the prose that came from the writers I have mentioned, but also oratory from the political platform: orchestrating mass rallies, the Defiance Campaign (1952), the Congress of the People and its Freedom Charter (1955), Bantu Education and the Bantu Authorities, school boycotts, resistance against the removal of Sophiatown, the Treason Trial of 1956-1960.

Then Sharpeville broke upon us on 20 March 1960, followed by the Rivonia Trial and the banning of open political activity. Robben Island and other mainland prisons rose into prominence in the country's consciousness. The 'underground railroad' was laid for those who were forced into exile.

Towards the end of the 1960s and early 1970s, the voice of poetry trumpeted defiance, self-assertion and reaffirmation of blackness from among university students and writers like Sipho Sepamla, Mongane Serote, Oswald Mtshali, Mafika Gwala, and several others.

Today, poets, prose writers and playwrights like Mothobi Mutloatse, Miriam Tlali, Jaki Seroke, Nape a Motana, Mtutuzeli Matshoba, Matsemela Manaka, Julius Mtsaka, Ntambeleni Palanndwa and several others have joined the chorus.

All these writers have his or her own style of grappling with our social realities. There was a typically urban sense of urgency in the 1950s. Today it is of another order. Today some writers charge into the arena with a more passionate intensity, hot steam shooting out of the nostrils. The voice speaks directly to an audience to shake it up. Some of the writers speak with a subdued tone, while at the same time we can still hear the rumble of anger, indignation and defiance underneath the surface. Others give it to us red and raw and bleeding. Others again write for public readings, the devil take the hindmost, so that they may 'tell it like it is'.

The censorship board takes the trouble of reading literature because it is aware its practitioners take themselves seriously. We take ourselves seriously because writing is for us a desperate necessity. For the black person it is the cry of a soul in torment. If governments anywhere take the trouble to ban or drive authors into exile, as happens in much of Africa and Eastern Europe, it is because they take us seriously. It speaks volumes against a government and the touchy, wretched sections of the public when they read the ugliness and sordidness writers portray, and then proceed against them as if a gall bladder had been emptied into their plate of succulent steaks and *boere-wors*. Such action says that the enraged reader is feeling insecure or lacks confidence in his judgment or policies.

Literature is necessary because it is powerful words expressing powerful feelings; it revitalizes the imagination and the language it is written in; it is an act of culture, an act of self-knowledge. It presents a picture of society as it was, is and hopes to become. It strengthens a people morally, it gathers together and explains some of the inner mysteries of our lives.

For a long time African writers have been retelling history, explicating culture, and thereby redefining Africa through literature. It is not only a necessary activity, but also something we cannot help doing. Literature is to the mind and spirit what the biological processes are to the body – e.g. breathing, blood circulation, the pumping of the heart, and excretion through the various openings in the body.

But it is not enough to say that literature is a compulsive act. The writer's purpose or intention, and his readers, are as important for our consideration as the product of his imagination. Otherwise we may just as well say that because we cannot prevent a child being born unless we kill the foetus, let it grow up aimlessly, casually. My counsel to young writers is this: literature expresses powerful feelings and thoughts with powerful words. But remember this is not enough. Powerful words are not ready-made. You have to breathe your power, your energy into words. Their power is also their beauty. This is what our forefathers did when, as poets, they composed praise songs, heroic songs and incantations for ritual. They did not use shoddy or clumsy language when they recited their poetry. What gives words power and beauty is your own energy and something else. This something else is what we call perspective. Perspective is a way of seeing a person or a thing or an event in relation to the world around it: the immediate environment and the larger and still larger. This perspective creates what I would call resonance. Think of resonance as you might the vibrations of sound that comes from a bell that has been struck.

Perspective helps to suggest meaning. If you merely record that people are hungry and live a dog's life under tyranny, and then climb the public platform to recite, you are doing nothing useful. You may as well turn a jet stream from your hosepipe onto the audience, which merely reminds them that life is rough and that they are suffering. Doesn't it occur to you that if you stood there for twelve hours reciting without a pause one event of misery and agony after another, you could not possibly make your words a substitute for the people's real-life suffering?

You need rather to create a perspective for the experience you are relating: place it in history, or in the context of present-day ideas, of our beliefs, traditions, communal hopes and myths, or of economics and so on. The aim of doing this is to lead your audience to explore the meaning of their suffering, its significance. This is perspective; this is what produces resonance. It helps us to go beyond the pain of the instant. It leaves the experience vibrating in our being.

When one listens to black poets and playwrights of this era as a chorus rather than as individual voices, one is struck by the passionate intensity of the tone I am talking about. The young poet and dramatist must make his/her own choice – to be part of an undefined chorus held together only by common suffering and historic time, or to create his or her own diction, project his or her own personal vision and wisdom, drawn from a distinctive quality of the imagination. If you rush through a composition simply to be one of those who said something as a chorus, i.e. if you are avoiding the loneliness and painful ecstasy of individual effort that are part of the writer's adventure, then you have begun to die. You are a river emptying its life into desert wastes. You are cheapening your imagination. Work hard at your composition first, so that you take genuine grain to the chorus and not chaff, so that you become worthy of the chorus. Of course if the chorus is already singing and dancing off-key, or out of the mere compulsion dictated by a befuddled brain as in a beer garden, you join it simply to lose yourself in the crowd. Another form of death. There are many such choruses that do not revitalize language, nor elevate anybody.

A last word to those in authority, any authority – political, religious, any person or institution that is in charge of something and controls the lives of people. The writer is the sensitive antenna of the community or of society. Because of this, he is constantly probing the health of society – particularly its moral health. He is sensitive to corruption in high and in low places, among the haves and have-nots. As people in authority are highly visible, the writer often comes down heavily upon them. During high political times, when sectional interests and power are most intensively dramatized, public morals lose their equilibrium. The hotter the competition the lower our morality sinks. Dictatorship and political tyranny is as much a product of a people's weakness and wretched helplessness as it is of a leader's lust for power.

In varying degrees, national leaders all over the world are touchy when criticized. Writers are often in the frontline of the critics' campaign against authority. Especially when authority retaliates harshly, e.g. by detention without trial, often referred to as 'preventive detention'.

The more cultured a leader, the more tolerant he can be about criticism. It seems to me then that he should devote more energy and time to the enrichment and liberalization of his people's formal and informal education than to glossy, glib, official propaganda. A good humanistic education (as distinct from the authoritarian) can help people to discriminate between truth and half-truth and lies – between what is elevating and what is trash – in what they read. A cultured leader can distinguish between criticism against his own person and against the institution or system he is operating, i.e. the whole ruling class or government. He will not take all criticism personally. He understands which writers share his own culture and who do not, and the consequences of this fact.

The cultured leader appreciates that there is a wide range of attitudes towards audiences among different writers at different periods of history. There is, for instance, the poem that is apocalyptic in tone, i.e. that threatens the fire next time, or predicts doom for any institution the writer dislikes. There is the poem that satirizes or caricatures authority or a system; the poem that redefines Africa in a process of change, desirable or not; the one that speaks with the voice of history; the love poem; the nature poem; the private and the public poem; the poem that is the cry of a soul in torment, and other kinds.

Drama in Africa today is author (through his actors) speaking straight to the audience, delivering a message rather than agonizing over 'the human condition'. The novel, on the other hand – because it can exploit the wide range of human drama, dialogue, symbolism, allegory, characterization, setting – makes the direct message impossible.

The cultured leader will appreciate that there is no easy one-to-one relationship between literature and life. This means that if the hero in my novel is a seducer of women, the reader will not necessarily want to imitate him; or if my hero leads a successful strike, the working-class reader is not going to incite people to strike because of such reading. People do not wait for the writer to compose a poem or play or novel before they know that they have no political rights – that they are poor and live in tents.

Again, I have not come across any generation of writers sustaining anger and bitterness indefinitely. If they tried, they would soon discover that anger and bitterness poison the writer's system if prolonged unduly, just for the sake of keeping on the heat. We must let up somewhere. And if we have the potential makings of 'long distance runners' as writers, and want to grow, we shall find other, more elevating and enriching ways of using words and the raw material of life experience.

Prodigals, Exiles and Homecomings – 1976

Synopsis by Ndavhe Ramakuela

The author here will have us appreciate that certain individuals may decide to avoid alienation by returning to their own communities, either physically or spiritually. Mphahlele talks about the rediscovery of cultures after, among other factors, processes of urbanization have led to partial or wholesale undermining of or disregard for some elements of African cultures. Through his travels, he discovered that African culture, because of its humanism, is still strong and can be sustained. He observes in the writing of most Africans a sense of exile, of being outside their own environment – physically or spiritually. But such writers have managed to make a comeback by either rooting themselves in their communities once more or drawing on images and metaphors from those communities.

Mphahlele further shows examples of how African Humanism remains strong in the face of adversity. He sees this against the backdrop of African Americans, who have recreated a black culture even while participating in the wider culture. He concludes by indicating that, although he enjoyed some of the privileges of the West during his stay in exile, that experience has not done anything to take away what he feels about his culture. Interestingly, though, towards the end he acknowledges and celebrates some of the benefits that his experience of the synthesis of cultures in exile afforded him.

I

One seldom re-examines one's culture unless one is confronted either by another that displays stability and self-assurance, or by a culture that is shaky and whose direction is fragmented and manifold. The former makes one ask oneself: 'I wonder where we lost these elements – or did we ever have them?' The insecure culture compels one to ponder and savour the strength of one's own roots.

When I began to teach in Nigeria in September, 1957, it was my privilege to work within formidable and ancient cultures, such as those of the Yoruba, the Ibo and the the Hausa. British colonialism had always been ambivalent towards other people's indigenous cultures, although generally the British like museum pieces that preserve ethnic cultures. What the Christian missionaries did to scatter or destroy the African shrines, outrageous though this was, turned out to be relatively unimportant, as so much African life defied – and still continues to defy – assimilation or destruction. And yet African cultures have the capacity to contain diversity, to accommodate alien cultures, to adapt. These great cultures made me rethink my own cultural origins. I had been a product of both rural and urban African cultures. I realized how much the white man's civilization had wrenched us from the moorings of our tradition, while at the same time it denied us the essential facilities for fully owning its benefits.

Thanks to my four-year stay in Nigeria and to further visits and tours to other formidable African cultures, I began my spiritual journey back to my origins. I realized that, without being aware of it, many of us Africans in this country had lived through so many cycles in urban areas that we had become psychologically capable of dealing with that life; that the rural landscape had undergone a change – mostly owing to the back-and-forth movement of migrant labourers and farm workers. I realized that although there had been a number of losses along the way, given the chance – to determine our own culture as a single African people, to define for ourselves our cultural imperatives, to decide for ourselves how to be the mental and spiritual arbiters of our destiny, while sharing ideas and instruments of human welfare with the rest of the world – left free to do all these things, we could make a go of it. Yes we could! Because we have essentially not lost the collective unconscious where the deeper springs of African humanism lie. All over this continent, and over the centuries, other cultures have sought to abuse this humanism, to satisfy their own greed for wealth and lust for conquest. It has survived. It is true that the largest portion of independent Africa has not yet settled down in the last fifteen years of self-determination to the point where African humanism can give a good account of itself in the reshaping of political, economic and educational systems. Yes, there have been many catastrophes; some strategic strands are gone forever. This is the age of mistrust for Africa today: there is a wide area of mistrust between government and the enlightened. Educated men and women are continually under official surveillance, and are victimized in one way or another, whether under military or civilian rule. But at the same time African humanism has a long arm; its solid core will remain a shrine for us to return to for wise counsel when they are ready for it.

During the last eight years of teaching in the United States, I have become aware of how culturally shaky and insecure the Afro-American is. But there is widespread disagreement among them on this. Considerable as the achievements are that he has made – as an integral part of the country's economy, and in the areas of education and entertainment; considerable as his political and physical mobility is – the black American remains in a state of siege. As a minority, he can go only as far as the dominant race will allow him, depending on how much of a threat he may or may not be. He shares much of Western culture with the dominant group, but at the deeper spiritual levels he remains black. This is the part of him that echoes his African ancestry and early American beginnings. But this African side of him has no geographical territory that can, as it does for the South African black, provide constant nourishment. Because of this, because South African blacks outnumber the custodians of Western civilization, there is no way the African in them can be totally sucked into white culture. Apartheid has seen to that, too. The black American continues to ask: who are we? What are we? Where is our ancestral home? The South, with all the humiliation and hostility the name conjures up, or the Africa of glorious ancient kingdoms?

And so I have been searching deeper into my cultural origins all these nineteen years. Fourteen years ago (five years after I had left South Africa), I thought in desperation: 'The white man has Westernised me, he'd better go the whole hog!' By which I meant he had dragged and pushed my people into his history, so he cannot morally deny us the fullest benefits of technology, of labour organization, of education, etc. If I had meant that he should make me, culturally, a white man – i.e. to exorcise my traditional humanism – it would have been dishonest of me. Other African cultures confirmed me in this belief. Scratch but the surface of an African, and beneath the trappings of Western civilization is his own personality that has come from centuries of civilization, a civilization built upon the firm foundations of behavioural patterns, social relationships and spiritual values. We have arrived at a point of synthesis between the two.

II

The literature of a people – its poetry, fiction, drama, serious journalism – is for the reader an exploration of its imagination. The imagination probes and captures through the writer's vision and sensibility a people's collective consciousness – its myths, its yearnings, its failures and triumphs. In our literature we can see ourselves as we are and as we can or might be. It is an impressive record of our traditional values, our encounter with the white man, our conflicts, rejection and acceptance of each other as black and white, our fortitude and survival, the fortunes and misfortunes of the African personality, the return to the traditional wisdom of our people; it is a record of physical or psychological exile, of homecomings.

First, the wisdom of Africa as we find it in some of our traditional oral literatures. Among the Ewe people of Ghana and Togo, mourners shoot and sing and drum over the dead person. The idea is that the deceased takes all this merriment with him on his journey to the land of the ancestors:

> *Sing me a song of the dead,*
> *That I may take it with me.*
> *A song of the underworld sing me,*
> *That I may take it with me*
> *And travel to the underworld.*

> The underworld says,
> Says the underworld:
> It is beautiful in the grave.
> Beautiful is the underworld
> But there is no wine to drink there.
> So I will take it with me
> And travel to the underworld
>
> And travel to the underworld... (in Trask 1966:49)

And here is *Mugala's Song*, sung while hoeing in the fields by Busumbwa in Tanzania:

> We were born under an evil star, we poets,
> When the jackal howls!
> We were given a thankless trade.
> They who are marked with python's excrement,
> They are born lucky,
> They are the rich.
> God created me ill. I had a desire.
> I do not know, but if I had stayed
> In my mother's belly, it would be over and done with.
> Crafts are dealt out.
> I was sound asleep,
> I woke – someone calls me:
> 'You're asleep, Mugala! Come out here and see
> How the ground is ringing.' (ibid: 92)

Notice the way Africans will say what would be literally translated as 'Let me see how it rings' or 'Do you hear how it tastes?' or 'Hear how it smells.' It is worth noting also that a song defining the role of poets is sung in fieldwork conditions. Poets are after all ordinary people when it comes to working for a livelihood and fulfilling other social roles.

It should no longer be necessary for us – now that we ought to know better – to vindicate the beauty and power of the oral poetry of the Khoikhoi and San. So I merely present the following Khoikhoi song – *Song for the Sun That Disappeared Behind the Rain Clouds* – without comment:

> The fire darkens, the wood turns black.
> The flame extinguishes, misfortune upon us.
> God sets out in search of the sun.

The rainbow sparkles in his hand.
The bow of the divine hunter.
He has heard the lamentations of his children.
He walks along the milky way, he collects the stars.
With quick arms he piles them into a basket,
piles them up with quick arms like a woman who collects lizards
and piles them into her pot,
piles them up until the pot overflows with lizards
until the basket overflows with light. (Beier 1971:22)

Ritual strengthens people. Every culture has ritual and poetry, as a vehicle of ritual, is one of the features of a rich and old culture. Heroic poetry, in the form of praise or war songs, is a component ritual. Professor Daniel Kunene quotes a war song recorded by A M Sekese in *Leselinyana la Basotho* of 1 February, 1891. Sekese observes in his introduction that the song is 'one that strengthens the warriors; when it is sung, they shower themselves with tears.'

... Stop hovering up there vulture –
we're burying a man.' The carrier of spears is not buried at home;
The victim of spears will lie in the mountains, his grave is the tall
seboku grass.

We men we're oxen
to be fed to vultures; men are always courting death; they'll call it
when they brandish spears, some young brave,
his mother's going to mourn.
The young girl cried, she cried when the sun went down.
'When they said you should stay you said you'd go.'
'Leave me alone vulture,
let me go and see the homesteads.'

Don't tell yourself your man's alive, woman,
once again tomorrow we must go.
'Woman, give me food I go to war,
I'll spend the whole night on my knee!'

There they go: qu! qu! qu! qu!
There the cattle men are coming.
Belt the song
all you men

> *why so sullen*
> *man-eaters that you are? There's no accord*
> *you give it grudgingly.* (Kunene 1971:6)

We have lost and gained since we were shanghaied into the history of the West. We can say this without approving colonization and slavery. Some of us became enchanted with the ideas of the West, its technology and its 'urban' lifestyles; others remained in the traditional stream of African thought and belief. But even they had to modify some of the traditions or throw them out because they could not cope with modern economics. Because we were a conquered people in so much of Africa, the white man determined government, economics and other areas. So we had to go to school and master the white man's language, his system of knowledge if we were to 'succeed' or survive in such conditions. In the process, we lost ourselves in the sheer effort of obtaining an education; we became intrigued with the history of Europe, with the libertarian ideas contained in 19th-century Western philosophy and the verbal arts. We even selected our own heroes and earmarked them, so to speak. The French tried to suck us into their culture and assimilate us; the British, who were segregationist at heart, were quite content to let us be, as long as we obeyed the African political head whom they appointed to rule on their behalf. The Portuguese tried to be at once integrationist and segregationist; the whites in Rhodesia and South Africa did everything to us at the same time, and fixed the ceiling beyond which we could not grow.

Some of us, especially those in French-speaking Africa, broke loose and began a psychic trip back to their African roots. As Léopold Sédar Senghor puts it, they realized that they had become prodigals. Not because they had squandered their heritage, but because they had sought to bury it. The dominant theme in much of Senghor's poetry brings together the figures of exile and prodigal. He urges in one poem that the woman light the lamp and let the children talk about their ancestors – 'Listen to the voice of the ancients...' Because, exiled like us, the ancestors 'have never wanted to die, to let the torrent of their seed be lost in the sands' (Senghor, 1964:5). It was out of a sense of exile that Senghor (Senegal), and his friends and colleagues Aimé Césaire (Martinique) and Léon Damas (Guiana) conspired in the Paris of the 1930s to restore the dignity of Africa in their literature, to assert a faith and pride in themselves.

After sixteen years in France, Senghor returns home for a visit. He visits, among other places, his father's grave. In the poem, *The Return of the Prodigal Son*, he writes:

> *And my heart once more on the steps of the high dwelling, I prostrate myself at your feet,*
> *in the dust of my respect. At your feet, Ancestors, still present, who rule in pride the great*
> *hall of your masks defying Time Faithful servant of my childhood, see my feet where the*

mud of Civilization sticks. Clean water for my feet, servant, and only their white soles on the mats of silence. Peace, peace and peace, my Fathers, upon the brow of the Prodigal Son. (ibid: 22)

In addition to the spiritual torment Césaire and Damas's poetry records, these poets could not, as Caribbeans, return to Africa in the hope of making a home there. For Senghor and his African colleagues, exile was only spiritual. The role of Senghor in World War Two, together with his fellow Africans as members of the French army, is one of those painful ironies of colonialism that are not new to Africans anywhere. However unreal the terms of the return often sound in the poetry inspired by this sense of loss, Senghor's sense of exile and his frank recognition of himself as the product of the colonial dilemma make beautiful, moving poetry. Especially when he is not trying to be mystical. It is time to return home, he says:

It is time to go, before I sink my fig-tree roots
still deeper in this rich soft soil.
I hear the picking of the termites eating the
youth out of my limbs... (ibid: 20)

Kofi Awoonor of Ghana sees his people, who also represent Africa, as exiles who left their traditional shrines. Having regained their awareness, they pray that the moon shine on their way:

Shine bright for us to go home.
The return is tedious
And the exiled souls gather on the beach
Arguing and deciding their future
Should they return home
And face the fences the termites had eaten
And see the dunghill that has mounted on their – birthplace?
He hears the exiles
... shuffle their feet in agonies of birth
Lost souls, lost souls that are still at the gate. (Awonoor, 1971:23)

Having been forced into the white man's history, we need to locate a point of equilibrium. Awoonor is always urging us to return for purification, to revive our ancient shrines and song – 'sew the old days for me,' he asks his ancestors. And yet he does not try to make the return appear easy. Indeed, it can only be a qualified return, because of the equipment we bring back with us, because of the new socio-economic demands we have to meet. He knows very well that culture is not static, that it is the death of a people from the day they ever decide that their culture is adequately defined and neatly packaged for all time, available any time at OK Bazaars. Prodigals, exiles, 'the chorus of our forgotten comrades,' as Awoonor says; 'the hallelujahs of our second selves' – the indigenous consciousness and the superimposed styles of Western culture.

No, the rediscovery of our African self is not an easy return. The equipment we bring is symbolized in a poem by Lenrie Peters of Gambia – *Parachute Men*. He sees his own return to his country after years of study and work in England as a descent by parachute. You reach the earth with a jolt and then lug your gear across the field. You have absorbed the ideas and lifestyle of the country that gave you shelter and room to develop, and your reaction to the changes in your country will be coloured by this cultural equipment you've brought with you.

In another poem, *We Have Come Home*, Peters tells how we have come home 'from the bloodless wars / with sunken hearts.' Bloodless wars, because out there in the world of strangers there is a constant war with the environment for the maintenance of our sanity. It is a silent war. We have to survive and so must adapt:

> *We have come home*
> *From the bloodless wars*
> *With sunken hearts*
> *Our boots full of pride*
> *From the true massacre of the soul*
> *When we have asked*
> *'What does it cost*
>
> *To be loved and left alone.'*
> *We have come home*
> *Bringing the pledge*
> *Which is written in rainbow colours*
> *Across the sky – for burial*
> *But it is not the time*
> *To lay wreaths*
> *For yesterday's crimes...* (Peters 1967: 31)

Prodigals, exiles, homecomings... The late Christopher Okigbo, Nigerian poet, often spoke of himself as a prodigal. To the extent that he was always watching his spiritual growth very closely, always measuring the distances and limits of his being, he was being too harsh on himself in the use of 'prodigal'. In his poetry he continually revisits his shrines and the spirits of his universe:

Thundering drums and cannons in palm grove:
the spirit is in ascent.
I have visited, the prodigal...
In palm grove. long-drums and cannons:
the spirit in the ascent. (Okgibo 1971:16)

And when the time for worship comes, he pleads:

softly sing the bells of exile,
the angelus,
softly sings my guardian angel. (ibid: 17)

He is peeved by the thought that he does not wear the ancestral mask but his own. Which represents the Christian faith. So he invokes the help of his mother Anna:

protect me
from them fucking angels; protect me
my sandhouse and bones. (ibid: 3)

Another time, he returns to Idoto, one of his people's river goddesses, 'naked,' as he puts it, before your water presence: 'a prodigal'. (ibid:3)

On the other hand, he may very well have been profitably prodigal with time and energy in the pursuit of a metaphor from the traditions of English, French and classical literatures; prodigal in the excessive facility and glee with which he moved in and out of classical allusions. (Okigbo *had* majored in Classics for his first degree, and distinguished himself.) Thank goodness for the open and powerful poetry Okigbo wrote just before his death.

This particular kind of prodigal mind can be extended to cover all writers who either wholly glorify Africa or wholly portray her as excessively violent. Yambo Ouologuem's *Bound to Violence* is an illustration of the latter. Another instance of the prodigal imagination that quite obviously derives from an excessive admiration of certain European models of fiction, certain areas of European thought, is the violence and the unbearable existential loneliness we experience in Ayi Kwei Armah's *Why Are We So Blest?* There is only one thing a prodigal can do to redeem his writing: like Okigbo, go back and listen to the rhetoric and concerns of his people, to the music and drama of his native landscape. He should not expect a fat bullock to be slaughtered to celebrate his return. The return per se is sufficient reward.

African literature in English, French and Portuguese is an abundant and rich dramatization of the above experience. Ousmane Sembene's novel *God's Bits of Wood* (1960) is a fine epic of the 1948 railway strike that surprised the French colonial administration and business in Senegal. In Ferdinand Oyono's *Houseboy* (1956) and *The Old Man and The Medal* (1956) we have vivid dramatizations of the African as the helpless victim of European brutality. But in the end the victims begin to understand what they are, or have been, up against.

Sometimes the long journey into European enlightenment turns out to be an adventure into the night. Diallo, the young character in Cheikh Hamidou Kane's *Ambiguous Adventure* (1961), is advised to go to the white man's school, to learn 'the art of conquering without being right.' The school bewitches the soul and makes conquest permanent. But you must take your chances. When Diallo is in France, moving in the European corridors of learning and observing the life of the European, his Islamic sensibilities are outraged. When he is back home, still shaken by his experience abroad, he is killed by the village fool who thinks Diallo has abandoned the ways of his Islamic upbringing. It has been a long journey into the night. It is a serious business when the African undertakes the adventure into the realms of Western education. It becomes a burlesque when it is the other way round – when the European is cast out of his society and seeks to serve an African king. In other words, to identify with African culture. Such a man is Clarence in Camara Laye's *The Radiance of the King* (1954). The white man ends up with a number of 'illegitimate' children of various shades and colour. His Christian sense of guilt becomes silly in the face of the African's zest and reverence for life – life for its own sake. A moment of revelation for Clarence. Sometimes the journey leads to a point of equilibrium between Western enlightenment and African humanism.

Ngugi wa Thiong'o's *The River Between* (1965) is a lyrical portrayal of innocence. A village teacher realizes, before he is mature enough for the problem, that the unity between a Christian village and a traditional one is far less important – because it is too idealistic – than the unity that works towards the overthrow of colonial rule. In *A Grain of Wheat* (1966), Ngugi goes right into the fabric of rebellion as represented by Mau Mau. There is direct confrontation; but more prominent in dramatic terms is the element of betrayal among the detainees and those who escape detention.

Of all the African novelists, the one who is most preoccupied with the spiritual values of his characters is Chinua Achebe of Nigeria. European rule and religion figure mostly in the background, but exert considerable influence on the chief dramatis personae, who are African. The European presence often generates conflict among the Africans, like the proverbial soft voice of the serpent. In his *Arrow of God* (1964), Achebe describes and dramatizes the grief of the old high priest who is detained in a jail because he refuses to be chief of his villages, in the manner in which the British often appointed one in the absence of a traditional ruler. Disaster follows – the collapse of the protagonist and his deity.

Confrontation, victims, heroes, the adventure of Western civilization... Yesterday the writers in the now independent Africa probed the mysteries of their own cultures.

They are mostly products of university education. They stopped somewhere in the early days of independence, or on the eve of it, to reconsider their condition – the condition of a man who has been intellectually thrown out of his community by the very nature of Western education. They had to rediscover, relocate, and redefine their cultural position in relation to communal goals – real or imagined – and examine the African personality, each with his own individual vision.

Today, almost twenty years since Ghana became independent, twelve years since Zambia and Malawi became free from British rule, Africa is re-examining itself through its writers. There have been military coups, people have been and are still being jailed without trial and executed in public. Africa, Europe and the Americas have become a vast concourse of refugees and exiles who have fled one kind of political tyranny or another. *A Man of the People* (1966) by Achebe deals satirically with corruption in high places. The climax is a riot. In *The Beautyful Ones Are Not Yet Born* (1971), Ayi Kwei Armah of Ghana has fictionalised the fall of Nkrumah. Again corruption in government becomes the focal point. The play *Kongi's Harvest* (1967), by Wole Soyinka of Nigeria, is a sharp-edged satire on Nkrumah's fall. The new political head is described by his sycophant as: 'Uneasy Head ... A Saint at Twilight ... The Face of Benevolence... The Giver of Life'. Much the same way Nkrumah's sycophants showered praises on the President.

In his play *The Swamp Dwellers* (1963), Soyinka records with lyrical beauty the beggar's description of the coming and going of drought and rain in his home village:

> *The rains came when we wanted it. And the sun shone and the seeds began to ripen. Nothing could keep us from the farms from the moment that the shoots came through the surface, and all through the months of waiting. We went round the plantains and rubbed our skins against them, lightly, so that the tenderest bud could not be hurt. This was the closest that we had ever felt to one another. This was the moment that the village became a clan, and the clan a household, and even that was taken by Allah in one of his large hands and kneaded together with the clay of the earth. We loved the sound of man's passing footsteps as if the rustle of his breath it was that gave life to the sprouting wonder...*
> (Soyinka, 1963:181-2)

In *Kongi's Harvest* the king, whose authority has been usurped by Kongi, the new political head, speaks to his heir:

Danlola: *Did he not promise a reprieve for the condemned men, in return. For the final act of my humiliation? Well, did he not?*

Daodu: *Yes, and I know our man will remind him of it.*

Danlola: Then perhaps you have not heard
             What the wooden box announced
             As I returned to palace. Such a welcoming
             I've never known. Did not one
             Of the dying enemies of Kongi
             Seize suddenly on life by jumping
             Through the prison walls?

Daodu: I heard about it.

Danlola: And the radio has put out a price
             Upon his head. A life pension
             For his body, dead or alive. That
             Dear child, is a new way to grant
             Reprieves Alive, the radio blared,
             If possible; and if not – DEAD!
             I didn't say it, the radio did
             In my primitive youth, that would be called
             A plain incitement to murder. (Soyinka 62-63)

Something sinister is afoot here, and one can feel the tension in the diction. Danlola eventually flees Kongi's wrath, into exile.

In one decade the lyricism of several African poets has shifted from the celebration of 'arrival' (of independence) or the innocent and leisurely quest for the inner mysteries of tradition, the ways of birth and dying, the way to the gods and so on, to a hard impatient tone. The elegy is about loss of another order. J P Clark (Nigeria) wrote:

Another flood is finished to a fall
Finished, finished with a roar and rush
And you and I two reeds on the bank
Go dipping hungry blades in her wash. (Clark, 1965:11)

He wrote this in a volume concerned with the recent Nigerian civil strife:

Caucuses at night, caucuses by day,
With envoys, alien and local,
Coming and going, in and out
Of the strong room. What brief
In their cases? The state,
Like a snake severed of its head,
Lies threshing in blood, and

Unless a graft at once is found,
The bird will flee the tree. (Clark, 1970:7)

The late Christopher Okigbo wrote:

The stars have departed,
the sky in monocle
surveys the world under.

The stars have departed,
and I – where am I?

Stretch, stretch, O antennae,
to clutch at this hour,
fulfilling each moment in a
broken monody. (Okigbo, 1962:13)

Already in 1965, Okigbo was invoking the talking drums to 'hide us; deliver us from our nakedness...'

Come; limber our raw hides of antelopes...
Thunder of tanks of giant iron steps of detonators,
Fail safe from the clearing, we implore you:
We are tuned for a feast-of-seven souls. (Okgibo, 1965:45)

The drums should now sound a message of warning, of collective effort against political power gone insane. He would be killed in the Nigerian civil war, 1967.

Kofi Awoonor, another fine lyricist, could sing a few years ago in a manner that vividly and poignantly captured the grief of his people caught between anvil and hammer, but always enduring:

Caught between the anvil and the hammer
In the forging house of a new life,
Transforming the pangs that delivered me
Into the joys of new songs
The trappings of the past, tender and tenuous
Woven with the fiber of sisal and
Washed in the blood of the goat in the fetish hut
Are laced with flimsy glories of paved streets. (Awonoor, 1971:29)

Today he smells blood in the air, amid all the political rhetoric and gestures:

> At the central Committee today a vote was taken on democratic centralism it will
> be written next week
> Into the Constitution everything comes from God...
>
> Left, right, left, right
> the weak ones fall out
> For their feet are tired... (ibid: 87)

At the time of writing Awoonor is under detention, having been taken three months after he had arrived back in Ghana, where he planned to live and work. The military government is charging him with subversion and with harbouring a suspected political criminal.

It has been a short-lived phase of lyricism, of almost innocence. The language is harsh now, the imagery evokes anguish and cruelty. Okot p'Bitek of Uganda records the plaint of his political prisoner (*Son of a Prisoner*, 1971) in these words:

> The dark silence
> Urinates fire
> Into my wounds,
> The hollow laughs
> Of my uniformed Brothers
> Fan the fire,
> I am engulfed
> By a red whirlwind
> Of pains
> Hotter than the pangs
> Of childbirth,
> More deadly than
> The venom
>
> Of the black mamba.... (p'Bitek, 1971:47)

III

The beginnings of the novel in Bantu languages, as we know, are to be found in the genius of Thomas Mofolo (born 1876) and Samuel Mqhayi (born 1875). Mofolo's Christian orientation was quite intense, as we can judge by his lofty moral purpose in *Moeti wa Bochabela* (1907), first serialized in *Leselinyana* in 1906. The hero of the book leaves home, disgusted with the drunkenness, feuds and sexual looseness of his folk. In his novel *Chaka* (1925), Mofolo conceives his hero from a Christian sensibility. But we can say this without implying that moral conflict per se is exclusively a Christian concept. It is enough to point out that Shaka in history was, as most Africans have been, a religious person. Religious in the sense that they believed in the constant contact with the ancestors, who are always present. They are intercessors between man and the higher supernatural forces. Chaka's excesses were an outrage against the traditional love of and reverence for life. Christianity was not the first religion in Africa, and the African has his own notion of good and evil that sometimes merges with the Christian idea and sometimes stands opposed to it – without being necessarily inferior to it.

Mqhayi's first prose work was *Ityala lama-Wele*, published in 1914 although finished earlier. The author's purpose was to entertain and at the same time comment critically on African law and justice in order, in turn, to plead its validity. African law was being diminished by the imposition of district courts. Azariele Sekese of Lesotho (born 1849) had, before Nqhayi, attacked the corrupt legal system of his people in his *Pitso ea Linonyana*, in a folkloric manner. But Sotho law was not harassed by any European legal system.

The father of written Xhosa poetry is Ntsikana (born 1783), who lived in Ngqika's territory, although his poetry was in the oral tradition. Ntsikana's poetry came out of a Christian spiritual experience. Mqhayi, better known for his poetry than for his fiction, also adapted the oral tradition to a modern style. The late Professor A C Jordan translated for us the now famous Mqhayi praise poem, written on the occasion of the visit of the Prince of Wales (later Edward III and still later Duke of Windsor) to South Africa in 1925.

> *Ah Britain Great Britain Great Britain of the endless sunshine*
> *You sent us the truth, denied us the truth;*
> *You sent us the life, deprived us of life,*
> *You sent us the light, we sit in the dark,*
> *Shivering, benighted in the bright noonday sun.*

Sotho literature flourished in prose to begin with, and the first volume of poetry appeared in 1931, written by Theko Bereng. This was also in the oral tradition, being praises to King Moshoeshoe:

> *…When the Ruler of Lesotho was buried*
> *We saw frightening scenes*
> *Because wolves and people walked together,*
> *Snakes moved away from the bush,*
> *When people buried the Chief*
> *With the war son of men echoing afar.*

Like Ntsikana, Isaiah Shembe of Natal (born late 1860s) was a leader of a messianic and nationalistic Christian sect – much less orthodox than Ntsikana's. Shembe's hymns were put together with his son's in a book in 1940, entitled *Izihlabelelo za Nazarethe* ('Hymns of the Nazarites'), although some were first sung in 1910. After the hymns of Reverend P J Gumede and Ngazane Luthuli (editor of *Ilanga lase*, Natal 1938), there was a decline in Zulu poetry. The late Dr B W Vilakazi made some perceptive comments in 1945 on the poor manner in which poetry was taught in Natal until about 1930. The pupils were not introduced to the spirit of poetry, and the only poetry they learned was English, which they reeled off by rote. This, he concluded, 'cultivated a dislike for poetry.'

I have sketched the beginnings of the literature written in our languages so as to remind myself about our roots, and that, as W E B DuBois wrote in another context in the early 1920s: 'You and I have been breasting hills.' Those early writers began under the impulse of the Christian faith. After all, it was the church that brought the school; it was the mission press that published the writers. They were thus fervently didactic in the representation of their own reality. That reality is still with us, but to the extent that these are high political times, our didacticism today is political. We are not irreligious by and large, but the Christian church cannot any longer assume that its god is also ours. The African writer is empirical in his approach to social reality. The cruelty of the times dictates this, whether we write in the vernacular or English or Afrikaans. No monolithic Christian or Muslim authority can be trusted any longer.

Prodigals, exiles, homecomings, victims, heroes... In the 1930s we saw more and more people come to the cities to seek work. Rural land had shrunken tremendously and was deteriorating. The mines were also draining the land of manpower. We could have considered ourselves exiles then, coming as we were into a land of strangers. Writers like R R R Dhlomo (born 1901) reacted strongly to what they considered to be corroding influences of city life. In his novelette, *An African Tragedy* (1923), he tells a story of a teacher who falls foul of city ways. There is on the other side of the coin nostalgia for traditional custom, from which the African was supposed to have been seduced by city sinners. There is a more profound and noble sense of nostalgia in H I E Dhlomo's *The Valley of a Thousand Hills* (1941). With a lush and lofty diction, Dhlomo recalls the grandeur and beauty that the Valley had for Africans, before the white man's greed set in: 'The song and pace now widen out into / A flooded stream all dark and fierce with wrongs.'

But the movement between urban and rural lives has gone through so many cycles now that we have ceased to be exiles – that is, in our esteem of ourselves. We claimed permanence while the government was insisting that we were 'guests'.

Sol Plaatje's historical novel *Mhudi* (1930) was actually completed by 1920. Plaatje seemed to feel the need to look back at the epic phase of our history – the heroic era. He captures this in the account of the clash between Mzilikazi and the whites, and the involvement of Barolong and Griquas. As a political organizer who cycled from place to place, he saw enough to give him a historical perspective and an understanding of what was happening at 'the back of the Native mind'. He saw enough landlessness to reinforce his understanding of displacement. Wanderers, exiles...We were exiles but knew only a fraction of it. When we came to know it all, we were no longer exiles. We were fighting for survival, for a sense of place. Segregation was never going to let us forget that we are black. So we couldn't possibly be spiritually alienated. We regrouped in the city – across ethnic divisions – and our traditional sense of community reasserted itself and sustained us. There was no possible way of escaping the fact of our blackness. Those who tried to play white or superior became a subject for jokes. That Jim-comes-to-Jo'burg image won't work any more as a subject for literature, because it's not real any longer. The *bafundisi* of *Cry, the Beloved Country* won't impress anybody either – if they ever did.

Realism in English writing burst into full blossom for us with Peter Abraham's *Dark Testament* stories in 1940. He carried it further in his later fiction, to be joined by others like Alex la Guma, Peter Matthews, Richard Rive, Lewis Nkosi and so on – all of whom dramatize the dark and excruciating side of black life. Alex la Guma, in particular, exploits to the farthest extreme the physical and social setting of District Six.

The entrance of *Drum* magazine in 1950 marks another phase in African writing in English. Can Themba, Arthur Maimane, Bloke Modisane, Todd Matshikiza, Casey Motsisi, Lewis Nkosi, Nat Nakasa, to name only those who produced imaginative writing, stand out in our memory.

Heroes, victims, the cruelty of the times.... The 1960s and 1970s have ushered in another wave of prose writers like Dugmore Boetie (*Familiarity is the Kingdom of the Lost*), D M Zwelonke (*Robben Island*) and Enver Carim (*The Golden City*). Then there are poets who are still on home ground and are adopting a more conversational tone – a let-me-tell-you-one-thing manner – to contain the urgency of their theme. There is a parallel to this in Afro-American poetry of today, although we must not forget that the latter poets are writing for an audience who speak English every day. Of their 'I do not know wealth, nor poverty,' Mongane Wally Serote writes:

> *I know a want, a ravaging hunger like a rage.*
> *To the end of that far horizon, I have like a bird*
> *Flown in delight. To the sky of friendship, came down*
> *Sat and hatched eggs.*
> *But do I look to him like he to me?*

In *The Actual Dialogue* Serote puts his finger on the blame, and in telling lines concludes:

Do not fear Baas,
My heart is vast as the sea
And your mind as the earth.
It's awright baas,
Do not fear.

Casey Motsisi tells us with acid irony how parents responded to their little girl who declared: 'I'm going to be just like Dan the Drunk':

'God Almighty, save our little Sally.'
God heard their prayer.
He saved their Sally.
Prayer. It can work miracles.
Sally grew up to become a nanny. (in Royston, 1973:10)

We need, as writers, to listen to our own gripes and fears and doubts and certitudes, but at the same time we must listen to the music and drama of our people – quite apart from dramatic politics. We laugh and cry, dance and die, love and hate, kill and bury, grow up and surrender, betray each other, and so on, amid the rhetoric of hookers or other participants. We need to explore this drama, replay it – as Njabulo Ndebele does in his poem, *The Man of Smoke*. The persona in the poem is a small boy strapped to his aunt's back. There is warmth there under the blanket. She takes him with her to a meeting of a religious sect. As the members dance to the drumbeat and the boy stands in a corner, the bizarre quality of the atmosphere registers on his mind. He is afraid. To accentuate the sense of threat there is a carving of a man 'with teeth as big as fingers' emitting smoke from its mouth. Everything is huge in the boy's eyes: the dancers have legs like 'massive pillars':

All are mad here,
They kneel before the face of smoke
they cry, they shriek, they breathe in gasps
they say a wind must enter them.
they are quite mad.... (ibid:35-36)

There is, of course, always the 'dark world, where thousands of men pine and are forgotten.' Another version of that world, Stanley Mogoba implies, is an enclosure of cement, in which both air and human flesh are cold. Inside there, your imagination is set in motion, punctuated by introspective moments. Imagination and introspection:

Stretch themselves painfully over
The reluctant minutes of the marathon day. (ibid:50-51)

In Psalm 137, the children of Israel tell of their Babylonian captors who demand of them merrymaking music –

> *How could we sing the Lord's song*
> *in a foreign land?*
> *If I forget you, 0 Jerusalem,*
> *Let my right hand whither away;*
> *Let my tongue cling to the roof of my mouth …*

We may well tell ourselves the same thing today – as we grapple with questions of cultural conflict, reconciliation, truce and spiritual exile. In this, one may eventually surrender his soul and adopt the idiom, images and symbols of the dominant political culture, even when they are used against him. It should not take a South African black, who has been drilled into a culturally self-reliant state of mind, long to snap out of the trance. This would be a return to his people's idiom, with which he could redefine the symbols and terminology. 'Black consciousness' is too journalistic and facile a term to define the ideal state of mind to return to in the South African context where, I repeat, segregation has taught us never to forget we are black. I use the term guardedly, because there *are* certain things that have seeped into our consciousness from Western culture that we need to sort out. Our Jerusalem should be the African humanism I began to talk about. Stanley Motjuwadi's poem sounds like a signal for the return from exile:

> *But for Heaven's sake God, just let me be.*
> *Under cover of my darkness let me crusade.*
> *On a canvas stretching from here to Dallas, Memphis, Belsen, Golgotha, I'll daub a*
> *white devil.*
> *Let me teach black truth.*
> *That dark clouds aren't a sign of doom, but hope. Rain. Life.*
> *Let me unleash a volty bolt of black,*
> *so all around may know black right.* (Royston, 1973:12)

It is interesting how, like Keorapetse Kgositsile, Mafika Pascal Gwala has adopted the tone and rhythm of Afro-American poetry. In his poem *Gumba, Gumba* he writes:

> *Struggle is when*
> *You have to lower your eyes*
> *And steer time*
> *With your bent voice*
> *When you drag along -*
> *Mechanically.*
> *Your shoulders refusing;*

> *Refusing like a young bull*
> *Not wanting to dive*
> *Into the dipping tank.*
> *Struggle is keying your tune*
> *To harmonize with your inside.* (ibid: 55)

The message sinks deep here, because it is presented so casually. 'What am I?' asks Oswald Mtshali. 'Am I just a minute beetle hiding under a clod of sand / ready to be squashed by a white beach stroller's foot?' He feels his body in the coils of a python. Mtshali often gives us a close-up picture of people and scenes, always with an aristocratic sense of irony, as in the poem *An Old Man in Church*:

> *I know an old man*
> *who during the week is a machine working at full throttle:*
> *productivity would stall, spoil the master's high profit estimate if on Sunday he*
> *did not go to church to recharge his spiritual batteries.* (Mtshali 1971:21)

The punch line comes at the end of another poem, *The Washerwoman's Prayer*, when a preacher says: 'Blessed are the meek for they shall inherit the earth.'

Prodigals, exiles, homecomings... When you have been politically and therefore physically compelled to move from your country, exile is still a ghetto of the soul. You have to stay out there, hang in there, and wait for sunny days back home: scared to borrow the commitments of your new base, which is your asylum, because you dare not forget the original commitment, and because you want to conserve your energy for some future time as a native son. Also, if you've come out already as an adult, you won't have the capacity to know the full story of your new human environment sufficiently to justify affiliation – to know if you are accepted or not and to know if you can become relevant. For a writer there is something about geographical place, which, however brutal, will never let you go. The very memory of it gives you identity, which you need to maintain because you can't opt for anonymity in your new milieu.

In Southern Africa, you get to know the real agony of exile, not just at the philosophical level at which you are preoccupied with the dangers of cultural assimilation. You've always been locked up in your ethnic enclave, and you are too busy trying to invent ways of keeping alive and fulfilling yourself to worry about anything else. Rather, you get to know exile in a very physical sense.

In exile, one poet contemplates the purpose of it all:

> *My days have fallen into nightmarish despair. I know no days that move on toward*
> *laughter, except in memory stale as our glory. I see no touch of determined desire,*
> *past the impotence of militant rhetoric.*

He refers here to the impotence of exile politics: 'I know no dance but the slow death of a dazed continent.' Another poet dreams of waking up and calling: 'We have come home…' But what is it *like* at home?

> *There were those shadows that were human*
> *Others followed the long outline of knives*
> *And uniforms of iron and buttons of steel*
> *And faces filed against a prison wall.*

A man in exile will continually be haunted by 'nightmares of sealed walls', although he can still speculate on 'rich tomorrows.' Another poet who wrote about the sounds of ghetto life when he was still in South Africa – sirens, knuckles, boots – now in exile, says:

> *gentle I am, and calm*
> *and with abstracted pace*
> *absorbed in planning*
> *courteous to servility*
>
> *but wailings fill the chambers of my heart*
> *and in my head behind my quiet eyes*
> *I hear the cries and sirens*

He sees himself as driftwood on an Algerian beach, amid the din and bustle of happy bathers, seabirds and sea rollers. Always he is driftwood.

Arthur Nortjé, who died at Oxford recently, refers to 'the isolation of exile' as 'a gutted warehouse at the back of pleasure streets.' And:

> *Origins trouble the voyager much, those roots that have sipped the waters of another*
> *continent. Africa is gigantic, one cannot begin to know even the strange behaviour*
> *furthest south in my xenophobic department…*

For my part, and as a concluding statement in this essay, I quote from a poem I recently published. In it I contemplate the ugly possibility of growing old in America, if no African country cares to claim me. There is always the chance that one may end up in a nursing home for the aged – that miserable institution where the concentrated smell of old age clings to the walls, the furniture, everywhere. Again, old people are today having their apartments broken into, and being robbed, raped and harassed in other ways:

black
white and beige,
where youth will trample down the old and rock and roll
jive away
or leave them shaking in their holes grounded by the pack
that now are breathing scratching on the door, then
drip
drop
drip
something trickles from your ego centre sinister
like water dripping
from a pipe within a wall
out of reach ...

We blacks in South Africa have often taken our blackness for granted, for reasons already stated. We do not need to launch into the elitist fantasies of Negritude at its worst. But we need to keep reminding ourselves that there is a living African tradition that should interact with the demands of modern life. Through the Institute of Black Studies we can harmonize all the idioms of our people and now consciously forge a reconciliation between our traditions and the best of Western values. This cannot be done without *institutionalizing* our projects. At every stage in the history of Afrikanerdom institutions have been set up to consolidate its culture, to give it a concrete presence and continuity.

Es'kia in 1960

Prometheus in Chains:
The Fate of English in South Africa – 1984

Synopsis by Ndavhe Ramakuela

Mphahlele enters the language debate from a rather interesting perspective, arguing that since English has been freed from its colonial assumptions and representations, it can now be used effectively by writers to articulate their newly found freedom. To illustrate his point, he draws on the Greek myth of Prometheus and how his release from Zeus' torment reflects partial liberation of humanity from bondage. This is extended through some commentary on Shakespeare's The Tempest, *especially on how Prospero teaches Caliban his language, which the latter will later use to curse the master for taking his land. So is the case with English; it has been released to serve humanity freely.*

Language, the argument holds, is primarily influenced and shaped by the use to which writers and other practitioners put it. Mphahlele draws further examples from African writers who have taken English and moulded it to serve them and their communities and how, in this sense, English can reasonably be said to have become a unifying force.

But Mphahlele's concern remains – namely that the present-day teaching of English does not have liberating potential. He finds in the teaching a rather mechanical approach that appears to be informed by utilitarian concerns. He also traces examples of how some South Africans have been able to use English to their advantage: for example, he speaks with pride about the writers of the 1950s, who made great contributions through their journalistic writing. Sadly, modern-day students and their teachers do not appear to have the inclination to reach the height of academic competency exhibited by their predecessors.

I

By way of refreshing your memory… the *Oxford Classical Dictionary* tells us that 'Prometheus' is derived from the Greek word meaning 'the fore-thinker'.

Prometheus

According to ancient Greek myths, Prometheus was one of the group of gods called

'Titans'. Originally, he was imagined to have no moral scruples. Sometimes he challenged Zeus (Jupiter), the supreme god, and outwitted him.

One tale told about Prometheus is that he stole fire that Zeus had hidden away from man, and returned it to earth. To punish mankind Zeus – the myth goes – is to have created woman as a constant source of confusion. Pandora was the first woman, so-called because she had 'all gifts' from the gods. But this image of woman as supreme tempter is a side issue with which Prometheus is not connected. What concerns us here is the other tale about Zeus's wrath against Prometheus for restoring fire to mankind. He chained this rebel to a boulder and sent an eagle to feed on his liver. As it was a god's liver, it was replaced overnight just as soon as the eagle had savaged it during the day. Prometheus was thus tormented, until Heracles (Hercules) released him.

Greek playwright Aeschylus (born 525 or 524 BC) was witness to the end of tyranny in Athens as a youth. He lived through the reign of democracy that followed and lasted after his death in 456 BC. His play, *Prometheus*, shows the author's sympathy and sense of outrage against Zeus the tyrant and tormentor. He has Prometheus finally making a deal with Zeus for his release. When Percy Bysshe Shelley (1792-1822) picked up the myth for his own play ('lyrical drama' as he called it), *Prometheus Unbound* (1820), it was to express his own position against tyranny. His Prometheus is also a champion of mankind. Jupiter is driven from his throne, and Hercules, representing strength, releases Prometheus. A time of love and peace follows. Shelley's hero symbolizes humanity. His release is that of humanity.

Prospero and Caliban

Shakespeare's Prospero and Caliban (*The Tempest*, written about 1611 and printed 1623) have come to represent the main actors in the story of colonization. Prospero the master; Caliban the slave. The trans-oceanic slave traffic and exploration during Shakespeare's time can be regarded as Europe's rehearsal for colonization. The shipwreck incident is taken from the reports of an actual one – Sir G Somers's on Bermuda Island (West Indies) in 1609.

Prospero, the Duke of Milan, has been deposed as ruler by his brother Antonio. He is exiled with his daughter Miranda. They are shipwrecked on an island formerly inhabited by the witch Sycorax, now in banishment. With his knowledge of magic, Prospero has released a number of spirits (including Ariel, his new agent and messenger) who were imprisoned by Sycorax the witch. Another slave Prospero appropriates is the witch's son Caliban, a deformed monster; he is the only being on the island. Prospero teaches Caliban his language. It is in this language that the native curses and rails at the master for having taken his island away from him.

II

First there was slavery, then colonial conquest followed. Prospero taught us his language. But he administered the knowledge in small doses, never sure about the limits of his own magical power, sometimes startled by his Caliban's growing impertinence and hidden native strength. The colonial master appears in various guises. For instance, he may have fled responsibilities and competition among his people back home, like Shakespeare's Prospero; he may simply have been fired by a lust for adventure; he may have been inspired by a sense of mission, to bring the fruits of Western civilization to Africa. There may have been a bit of each of these in one and the same white man. Whatever the dominant overall motive, such as commercial and expansionist interests, the colonial administrator came to be the centre of power and authority, the use of which fascinated Shakespeare when he created Prospero. Again, Shakespeare contemplates the colonist's constant fear that the native desires his wife or daughter.

Without so much as a hint of what was going to happen three centuries later – the colonial enterprise – Shakespeare dramatized in *The Tempest* race relations that were to be part of a pattern from 19th-century colonialism onwards. The first stage is indicated by O Mannoni in his *Prospero and Caliban* as the subject's implicit dependence on the colonist – in this case the Malagassy's dependence on the French – because his traditional authority had been shattered. The second stage is Caliban's revolt, while on the other hand Prospero demands gratitude from both Ariel and Caliban.

Caliban reminds Prospero that the master took his island away from him:

> *When thou cam'st first,*
> *Thou strok'dst me and mad'st much of me ...*
> *and then I lov'd thee*
> *And showed thee all the qualities of the isle ...*
> *Cursed be I that do so! ...*
>
> *For I am all the subjects that you have*
> *Which first was my own kind; and here you sty me*
> *In this hard rock, while you do keep from me*
> *The rest o' th' island.*

Prospero destroys any possibility of a third stage, when calm and progress must prevail after crisis:

> *Abhorred slave.*
> *I pitied thee,*
> *Took pains to make thee speak, taught thee each hour ...*
> *but thy vile race,*

Though thou didst learn, had that in't which good natures
Could not abide to be with; therefore wast thou
Deservedly confined into this rock ... (ibid: 31)

Caliban's reply has since become famous because of its relevance to the uses of the colonial language.

It is at this point where my image of the African Prometheus takes over. The fire he stole to bring to us, against the will of the gods, gave us in Africa a weapon of protest and a means of extending Caliban's nationalism towards political indepen-dence and later pan-African unity. That weapon was language – be it English, French, Portuguese or Spanish. I say 'stole' both as a mythological and a historical fact – because no one owns a language to the extent that they can limit or control or monitor the direction it will take on the lips of other users beyond its national bound-aries. We appropriated these colonial languages, domesticated them in order to express an African sensibility – traditional, modern, rural or urban, political or religious – the ultimate phase of emancipation. Even in the days of slavery, these European languages became the rallying point for Africans who found themselves thrown together on the plantations of the West Indies and of the Americas. The lang-uages, learned from the plantation masters, were also domesticated. In the process a new native identity was consolidated, fashioned by the place and experience that contained the respective languages. When the African Americans began to sing the blues, they were asserting an American identity – after two hundred years of slavery – even while their collective consciousness was African. Even while the educated Africans of Brazil and other Latin American countries – and those of the West Indies – spoke Portuguese, French, Spanish and English, the masses were hammering out Creole and some other patois, which was a mixture of a European language and words and images taken from what the memory could salvage from an African past.

Phillis Wheatley, who was in her teens in the 1760s, published poetry as broad-sides and in Boston and Philadelphia magazines. She was a domestic slave of a liberal Boston family who brought her up, educated her and sent her to England to enhance her accomplishments as a poet. Her first published poem appeared in a Rhode Island paper on 21 December, 1767. A biographer of Phillis Wheatley's wrote in 1930 that her first volume of poetry had seen fifty-three reprintings to date.

Wheatley wrote in the only tradition available to her – the Anglo-Saxon tradition as expressed by 18th-century Britain. There is in the following extract the genteel and grand neo-classic line:

Should you, my lord, while you peruse my song,
Wonder from whence my love of Freedom sprung,
Whence flow these wishes for the common good,

> *By feeling hearts alone best understood,*
> *I, young in life; by seeming cruel fate*
> *Was snatch'd from Africa's fancy'd happy seat*
> *What pangs excruciating must molest,*
> *What sorrows labour in my parent's breast?* (in Robinson, 1975:41)

This is from a poem entitled *To the Right Honourable William, Earl of Dartmouth, His Majesty's Principal Secretary of State of North America, etc.*

I have not seen published anywhere a collection of letters from the pen of an African writer since Ignatius Sancho's, which appeared in the 1780s in England. They went into several editions. He kept a small shop near Richmond, where he lived with his wife and large family. Among Sancho's correspondents were members of the aristocracy whose protégé he had been and whose children he loved. Letter No 84, written in 1782 to a Mr G, reads as follows – displaying also the genteel gesture, the classical clarity and 18th-century conceits:

> *Sir,*
>
> *The very handsome manner in which you have apologized for your late lapse of behaviour does you credit. Contrition, the child of conviction, serves to prove the goodness of your heart – the man of levity often errs, but it is the man of sense alone who can gracefully acknowledge it. I accept your apology, and if in the manly heat of wordy contest aught escaped my lips tinged with undue asperity, I ask your pardon, and hope you will mutually exchange forgiveness with I Sancho.* (in Brown, 1973:21)

A number of American slaves wrote narratives about their experiences of bondage. This literature was used by abolitionists on both sides of the Atlantic, particularly at public meetings, during the campaign against slavery. The most outstanding autobiography in this category was Frederick Douglass's (1817-1895). He was born into slavery and later escaped as a young man. By then he had been taught to read and write English by the mistress of the house where he worked. From then on it was self-education for Douglass. Not only does his magnificent charisma come through in his autobiography, exquisitely blended with humility, but he also displays a remarkable mastery of the English language. The art of oratory found memorable refinement and expression in Douglass. The resonance of his diction is something an actor would thrill at; the chance of lending his voice to the long rolling lines we are accustomed to reading in 19th-century English prose, especially from writers like John Ruskin, are all here – with the pace well suited to the spoken medium.

Here is a sample from a speech delivered at the dedication of the pavilion exhibiting artefacts from the republic of Haiti. (Chicago, 1 January 1983):

> *Much has been said of the savage ferocity and sanguinary character of the warfare waged by the Haitians against their masters and against the invaders sent from France by Bonaparte with the purpose to re-enslave them, but impartial history records the fact that every act of blood and torture committed by the Haitians during that war was more than duplicated by the French. The revolutionists did only what was essential to success in gaining their freedom and independence, and what any other people assailed by such an enemy for such a purpose would have done.*
>
> *They met deception with deception, ambuscade with ambuscade, arms with arms, harassing warfare with harassing warfare, fire with fire, blood with blood, and they never would have gained their freedom and independence if they had not thus matched the French at all extremes, ends and opposites.*
>
> *History will be searched in vain for a warrior more humane, more free from the spirit of revenge, more disposed to protect his enemies, and less disposed to practice retaliation for acts of cruelty than was Toussaint L'Ouverture. His motto from the beginning of the war to the end of his participation in it was protection to the white colonists and no retaliation of injuries. No man in the island had been more loyal to France, to the French republic and to Bonaparte; but when he was compelled to believe by overwhelming evidence that Bonaparte was fitting out a large fleet and was about to send a large and powerful army to Haiti to conquer and reduce his people to slavery, he, like a true patriot, and a true man, determined to defeat this infernal intention by preparing for effective defence.*

To return briefly to that Prospero-Caliban image. George Lamming, the West Indian novelist, has pointed out in an essay that Caliban has been absorbed into Prospero's 'civilization' after being 'colonized by language, and excluded by language.' Only through language can Caliban be of service to Prospero. It is his survival kit, in other words. Prospero is separated from Caliban to an extent the former can gauge by instructing the slave in a 'civilized' tongue (Lamming, 1967:15, 110).

Frantz Fanon of Algeria has told us that the use of language 'means above all to assume a culture, to support the weight of a civilization.' Again, the colonized person is 'elevated above his jungle status in proportion to his adoption of the mother country's cultural standards' (Fanon, 1967:17-8). We must, of course, contemplate the relative distances the peoples colonized by the French, the English, the Portuguese and the Belgians respectively experience in relation to the metropolitan culture.

Confrontation and clamour for emancipation is the immediate result of the mastery of the colonist's language. The Promethean gift can only begin to give a good account of itself when the ex-colonial strives towards a synthesis, a point of equilibrium. This is an exciting, if often excruciating, experience. Agonizing when you become ambivalent towards the language you have appropriated and its culture; when you seek to redefine your people's identity in relation to an alien but dominant culture all of Africa has to come to terms with. Exciting when you try to hammer out an idiom that will do justice both to English and to allegory, metaphor and symbolism inherent in your native being; when you compose or replay an African song in English that brings with it its lyrical and dramatic qualities. The Afro-American scholar Mercer Cook says that this is:

> Taking the white man's language, dislocating his syntax, recharging his words with new strength and sometimes with new meaning before hurling them back in his teeth, while upsetting his self-righteous complacency and clichés... poets rehabilitate such terms as Africa and blackness, beauty and peace. (in Cook and Henderson, 1969:52)

A West Indian scholar, Lloyd Brown, offers interesting and persuasive insights into the thought processes that have gone into Chinua Achebe's novels, *Things Fall Apart* and *No Longer at Ease*. By quoting from Yeats's *The Second Coming* at the opening of *Things Fall Apart*, Achebe means to draw a parallel between the cycles in the Irishman's mythology and Africa's history. The 'first coming' ends the pre-Christian era, which in turn must be succeeded by a terrifying and unknown cycle – the new 'cradle', the new 'Bethlehem'. Achebe's world falls apart when Europe intrudes for the first time, and who knows what era will follow?

Brown puts it this way:

> ... in evoking Yeats's themes, Achebe implies that the sense of history and tradition, the burdens of cultural continuity, decay, and rebirth, have all been the African's lot as well as the Westerner's. And in the process the novelist has exploited the European's cultural criteria – his literature and historiography – in order to reverse the white man's exclusivist definitions of history and culture.

Achebe's *No Longer at Ease* recalls T S Eliot's *The Journey of the Magi*. The birth of Christ is supposed to end the 'pagan' life. His dying is supposed to be the beginning of a new morality or civilization. In following the star the Magi learn new things, new ways, observe a new dispensation of faith, challenging to the old world they have come from. The protagonist in the novel, Obi, returns to Nigeria from university study in England. A new cycle begins for him. But he comes back a confused man, unable to make up his mind about the relative merits of tradition and the new intellectual dispensation. He ends up an alienated person, crushed between the burden of tradition and the burden of his education. Achebe has thus used Eliot's sense of history to illustrate the cycles of African history. But at the same time he refutes Eliot (and thereby Western concepts) by showing the beauty and strengths of his own world – Nigeria.

We have all as African writers been influenced by British and American literatures of one kind and another, from Shakespeare to Hemingway and Richard Wright. We drew from the models of this Anglo-Saxon tradition. But in time we have learned with varying degrees of success to apply our lessons to the African reality or actuality in the context of our histories, and to our quest for self-knowledge.

Translations from mother tongue into English and the reverse have also been a way of re-interpreting ourselves. The act of translating is also a way of criticizing the original, of exploring its moral content afresh and in depth. Ghana's poet, Kofi Awoonor, Nigeria's Gabriel Okara and South Africa's Mazisi Kunene write in their respective native languages and translate into English. Our Tiyo Soga's translations of parts of the English Bible into Xhosa, Sol Plaatje's of Shakespeare into Tswana, Daniel Kunene's of Thomas Mofolo's *Chaka*, and A C Jordan and his wife's translation of his *Ingqumbo Yeminyanya* also served to increase the capacity of their own languages to absorb new ideas, new literary structures, new metaphors and symbolism.

If it had not been English it could have been French or Portuguese or Hindi or Japanese – anything – depending on the colonizer's language. But there was something about the *laissez faire* approach of the English to cultures outside their own that made it possible for their literature to take root in Africa only when the natives could use it to further their own education and creativity. This kind of live-and-let-live attitude towards culture persists till this day, even in the English diaspora. But it is loaded with ironies. The English could be saying: 'Let the natives remain where they want to'; or: 'Don't pressure the natives, they're slow on the uptake'; or again: 'If I were you I should push them up so far and no further, their capacity is severely limited...' But more of this later.

In his book, *The Discovery of India*, Pandit Jawaharlal Nehru notes the contradictions of early British rule in India. The British Government in Calcutta and in London, he tells us, set out to check progressive changes, especially the acceleration of education – for fear that the Indian people might be strengthened and ultimately weaken the colonizers' hold on the country. When changes did come, they were a British translation of the impact of the West. Nehru, writing a graceful and sedate prose, gives an illuminating account of Indian life from 1780 onwards in the three centres of the new enlightenment – Calcutta, Madras and Bombay. The first Indian-owned newspaper was published in English in 1818, Englishmen having printed several since 1780. The central figure in this history of the press in India was philosopher, educationalist and reformer Ram Mohan Roy. English became a vehicle of what Nehru calls a renaissance in Bengal, to which Rabindranath Tagore contributed immensely. Ram Mohan Roy had learned English privately, as there were no English schools or colleges outside Calcutta, and the government persistently stood against the teaching of English to Indians. Nehru writes:

> *English education brought a widening of the Indian horizon, an admiration for English literature and institutions, a revolt against some customs and aspects of Indian life, and a growing demand for political reform... English-educated people in the professions and the services formed in effect a new class, which was to grow all over India, a class influenced*

by Western thought and ways and rather cut off from the mass of the population...
(Nehru, 1964:337)

Nehru goes on to describe how radically Bengali society changed. The old agrarian economy broke down, and with it the feudal system. New classes arose. The English-educated classes in the learned professions and subordinate services all looked to British power for advancement and to English liberalism for inspiration; they revolted against rigid conventions and structures of Hindu society. As Muslims rejected English thought and language and the Hindus saw in them a source of inspiration, the 19th century – according to Nehru – produced 'a galaxy of brilliant Hindus in Bengal.' By the same token, there was hardly a single Muslim Bengali leader of any outstanding merit.

A fascinating figure was the Bengali poet and thinker, Rabindranath Tagore, whose speech Nehru quotes to illustrate how the Bengalis came to English, invested a lot of faith in England, and challenged long-established social codes. Tagore's speech was made on his eightieth birthday (May 1941), within a few months of his death. The educated Bengali, according to Tagore, readily took to English because of the strictly limited scope of the life of their day. 'Their days and nights were eloquent with the stately declamations of Burke, with Macaulay's long, rolling sentences; discussions centred upon Shakespeare's drama and Byron's poetry and above all upon the large-hearted liberation of the 19th-century English politics.' (ibid: 339-40)

Tagore came full circle:

> *In place of these set codes of conduct we accepted the ideal of 'civilization' as represented by the English term. In our family this change of spirit was welcomed for the sake of its sheer rational and moral force and its influence was felt in every sphere of our life... I naturally set the English on the throne of my heart. Thus passed the first chapters of my life. Then came the parting of ways, accompanied with a painful feeling of disillusion, when I began increasingly to discover how easily those who accepted the highest truths of civilization disowned them with impunity whenever questions of national self-interest were involved.* (ibid: 341)

Tagore was later to turn out exquisite poetry in English and explore the inner mysteries of Hindu thought and belief, even whilst he declared that his religion was poetry and that we must forever strive towards universal man. He was later to win the Nobel Prize for Literature.

III

Fleet-footed Prometheus the Titan blazed new trails wherever man was in chains, brandishing the fire he had stolen from Zeus. He was the 'fore-thinker', the master craftsman who could make man with clay, plus bits from other animals. After he blazed a trail across the Karoo northwards, he set about teaching us a language through which to emancipate ourselves. By an accident of history English became that language.

As long as the dominant language belonged to the white man and excluded the black man – particularly the African – Zeus and his demi-gods were happy. When Prometheus gave us the fire and taught us to master it and we found a voice, Zeus had to arrest him and order the smithy god to chain the rebel to a rock. There an eagle had to feed on his liver. As the liver was as immortal as the rest of the Titan prisoner, it grew again overnight. And there he must consequently continue to hang.

Aeschylus invests Prometheus with moral dignity, with the passion to help man against the tyranny of Zeus. I take my cue from Aeschylus about some of the qualities of Prometheus but, like Shelley, I repudiate the possibility that Prometheus will agree to be set free on Zeus's terms – Aeschylus's resolution of the Titan's agony – rather than his own. As Shelley says in a preface to his 'lyrical drama', *Prometheus Unbound*, the moral interest of the story is 'sustained by the sufferings and endurance of Prometheus,' whose importance would be shattered if conceived of as 'unsaying his high language and quelling' before his enemy Zeus (1820:225-6). Again, like Shelley, I use Prometheus as a symbol of energy, passion for freedom and toughness of the human spirit. The early Dutch in this country tried to resist the English language. Some of them, in order to survive it, tried to accommodate it. The Great Trek happened partly as a repudiation of a civilization the Dutch feared was going to transform their collective personality. They had a circumscribed notion of civilization and had not experienced the drive towards a new humanism that was straining to be born in Europe when the British settlers arrived.

The Dutch cherished the notion that all the civilization they needed was contained in the Bible and enshrined in the restricted life of family and small community. The later drive for the enthronement of Afrikaans was an act of establishing a conservative base from which to assert a new sense of belonging and propriety unimpaired by any nostalgia for a European past. Afrikaans became thus a *cause célèbre*, a reason to resist the political authority of the English and the civilization it represented.

But the Afrikaner came to realize that English was a door to the larger world, and had to be mastered. This ambivalence is still noticeable today. The fact that so many of the big Afrikaner politicians speak English, albeit with varying degrees of proficiency, is testimony to this ambivalence. Once the first monthly journal in Afrikaans was published (*Die Patriot, 1876*), however, it was going to be war all the way, until in

1925 Afrikaans was recognized as an official language. Even after 1925 the Afrikaans-speaking community felt that until Boer nationalism triumphed and attained political power, Afrikaans would always continue to play second fiddle. That moment came in 1948.

When the gods woke up to the fact that many more Africans spoke English than Afrikaans, and that the former had become the carrier of Prometheus's fire, Zeus gave commands in 1953. The other gods listened and trembled and cried: '*Hoor, hoor!*' The flowers began to droop and to wilt. Mother-tongue instruction was enforced in the primary and secondary schools. Although this process did not last, its run was long enough to inflict considerable damage. The gods had come to realize that they had to limit thought, to immobilize the vital processes of conceptualisation, to prevent the free flow of ideas, blast language from the lips of its users or make it appear incon-sequential – at best a difficult nuisance; it becomes necessary to reduce it to an incoherent stutter. Because to create concepts you recreate language. Concepts like liberalism (with a small 'l'), nationalism, unity, Africanity, 'freedom in our time', oppression, fascism, tyranny, socialism, democracy and so on are only possible when you have a language for them. Likewise, if you have a language you can create new concepts. The mother tongue was not equal to this.

Prometheus's captivity was orchestrated in the same decade by the Suppression of Communism Act, the Bantu Authorities, the Bantu Administration and Bantu Education Acts, the treason trial of 1956-1960 and the abolition of 'native represen-tatives', i.e. whites representing Africans in the two houses of parliament. The pass laws were tightened and the black universities were set up. If Prometheus hoped that some miracle might set him free, he must have thought again.

The 1950s were a decade of prose. You heard it on the political platform; you read it in commercial newspapers and in the periodicals of the radical Left and the Congress Alliance. Political pamphlets proliferated; all the printed media talked in English prose shared by an urban proletariat. Writers of fiction and reportage tuned in to the language of the literate masses and recreated an idiom for them in turn. The journals included *The Bantu World, Drum, Fighting Talk, New Age, Zonk, Inkundla, Bona, Post, Afrika* and *Africa South*. The African journalist had a better command of English than the present-day black writer; he was more adventurous, even more visible. His prose was racy, impressionistic, generally characterized by nervous energy. The writer had found a voice. Largely as a result of the banning of political movements and their mass meetings, and the creeping virus of Bantu Education that was gnawing at the vitals of the English language, prose began to lose its energy, its tension, in the late 1960s. Verse took the floor then, into the 1970s and 1980s. The early crop of poets during the 1970s had just barely survived the virus, and were still full of purpose: Sipho Sepamla, Mafika Gwala, Mongane Serote, Njabulo Ndebele and so on.

Meantime, in the schools and teachers' colleges and in the universities there was a progressive deterioration in English speech and writing. University students began to complain that English was being taught in such a way as to make it appear difficult, in order to frustrate them and cause them to drop out of the discipline. Proportionally, Afrikaans classes were being swelled because the discipline was made highly passable in the examinations. Honours classes in English at one university never had more than five students. Where proficiency in written and spoken English is poor, communication fails; the study of other disciplines must suffer. And Prometheus is still in chains, crying like Shelley's hero: 'Ah me. Alas, pain, pain ever, for ever.' (Shelley, 1820:229).

The things we do to try to compensate for the evil days English has fallen upon are not going to restore its earlier energy and vibrancy, because we are all rushing about looking for things to remedy in English, science and mathematics – the weakest subjects in the black schools. Various groups have moved into the business of trying to provide tuition for students who have asked for it. We are all working independently of one another, all churning out notes and study guides that the students eat up voraciously. We teach them how to waylay the examiner. They keep coming for more, in huge numbers. Weekend after weekend you see schoolchildren flocking at centres that offer some tuition... They are prepared to plug into every station that promises them a learning experience. Everything here is simplified, draws no blood or tears.

Similarly, teachers are permitted to leave their classes to be 'seminared', 'workshopped', 'up- and down-graded', 'in-serviced'. An image is conjured up here of cattle being forced into a dipping tank. They dare not ask searching questions about reasons for this activity, its validity and so on. They tell themselves that if they want a higher certificate and the salary increment that accompanies it, then this is the route to follow. Furthermore, holy water from the Department of Education has been sprinkled on this road. Very few of them undertake in-service studies, because such training can increase a person so that they are able to give more of themselves to their students. We are doing things to teachers and students all the time. Always we and English are happening to *them*, they never happen to us or to English. They are not articulate enough to ask the right questions and we, especially those who run our lives from Pretoria, do not encourage the teachers to ask. This way we don't have to discover better techniques, better structures. No one who matters in the power structure ever asks teachers and students what they themselves would have us do, so that together we may liberate English studies.

With Prometheus in chains, English is also being held in captivity. Especially school English. For, in spite of the twenty years of stringent censorship, and in spite of the unfriendly socio-political climate all round, South African writers, black and white, have been trying to liberate the people. Our fragmented society has always made it impossible for black and white writers to speak to one and the same audience, across the barriers that exist. And there's the rub: despite our relative freedom to shape the word that we want to send out; despite the fact that censorship is now being relaxed under a new chairmanship, we are nevertheless in chains. The life of privilege some of us were born into because of our race counts for little in immediate terms – perhaps even ultimately.

While Afrikaans and, to a lesser extent, the African languages have enjoyed a live contact between their literatures and classroom language teaching, our writings in English have not entered prescribed reading lists in the school system to any appreciable extent. Other parts of Africa, on the other hand, are bringing more of their writers into the classroom, so to speak.

Inanity upon inanity. As we mindlessly entrap teachers and students so that we stuff school English down their throats, especially the kind we fashionably call 'second language', we are at the same time reinforcing the barricades that the whole authoritarian socio-political system has erected. We have this obsession – that we must 'teach' English only within officially hallowed structures, only for the official public examination. All we succeed in doing is ensuring that we remain in sheltered employment. The following vignette will serve to illustrate this inanity. The patient is in the doctor's surgery for consultation.

Doctor: *What seems to be the matter?*

Patient: *I have trouble with my English.*

Doctor: *What's wrong with your English?*

Patient: *Just so many things.*

Doctor: *Let's start with the basics.*
    How are your vowels and diphthongs – is the motion regular?
    I mean like saying 'gel' for 'girl', 'ben' for 'burn', or like those on my side of the tracks who say 'feud' for 'food', ' fuel' for 'fool', 'pork the core' for 'park the car', 'naas' for 'nice', 'waaf' for 'wife' – stuff like that?

Patient: *No, my vowels and er – what did you call them? – they're OK I think.*

Doctor: *What else can you tell me?*

Patient: *I'm having poor syntax and…*

Doctor: *You mean you* have, *not* having *– OK, go on.*

Patient: *It's like this, you see, take the verbs 'smile' and 'beat'. Now you can beat something or someone, right, but you're supposed just to smile. I mean you can't smile anything, right? I spend sleepless nights wondering why I must beat something and cannot smile anything.*

Doctor: *Ah, you're talking about transitive and intransitive verbs.*

Patient: *Is that what they're called?*

Doctor: *Yes. It's the idiom of the language – that's the only reason you can't smile anything and must beat something, see?*

Patient: *I get it.*

Doctor: What about your speech?

Patient: What about my speech, does it sound funny?

Doctor: No, I mean direct and indirect speech.

Patient: Oh, I see. Now that's another rugged patch – gives me piles I can tell you that. You see I was never given any drill in such matters.

Doctor: We'll look at your piles. Do you ever paraphrase or have you ever in your school life paraphrased?

Patient: What's that?

Doctor: I can see you've never… Never mind, we'll prescribe appropriate exercises for you. If you can't rephrase a passage in your own words to simplify it, to explain it for others, your English is going to develop the worst kind of verbosity you can imagine – and it's malignant. It's like what we call, in medical language, précis – you know, you condense a speech or written matter to a quarter of its length. If that part of your English is not taken care of, it's going to tie you up in knots as you grow older and circumlocution's going to strangle you and even that won't startle your audience out of their boredom.

Patient: What are you going to do for me, Doc?

Doctor: Let my receptionist give you an appointment pretty soon and we'll run tests to ascertain any leaks and frayed parts and hardened or immobile sections of your English. You need a crash course of about six months, the way I see you now – it could have been worse. Cheer up, we'll straighten you up in no time.

And so the ritual of remedial English continues, while we pump drugs into teachers and students who have no say in the matter. We stay fenced in. We accept our condition. We fail to summon up courage to cut loose from existing structures so as to liberate English studies, for fear that we should lose our so-called credibility – on which hinges our sense of security. The furies that torment Prometheus are upon us too – those 'ministers of pain, fear, and disappointment, and mistrust', to use Shelley's language.

A personal experience at this point may throw some light on some aspects of English teaching. Those of us who learned English before the new order set in were taught by dedicated teachers in missionary institutions. That dedication and the open learning environment we enjoyed served to inspire us to read widely and expose ourselves to the ring of words good literature brought to our sensibilities. Yes, we ploughed through some very dull 18th-century stuff and through the tangled thickets of Victorian diction. It was nevertheless an exciting adventure.

The sound of English had a fascination for us. In addition, English was a functional study, without which we could not enter the other thoroughfares of learning, i.e. the other disciplines. We needed this key to education – Oh, how desperately we needed and wanted it! The effort beefed up our determination to overcome the difficulties, which were numerous. I came to dislike Milton and his stodgy Christianity that felt like balls of steel chained to my ankles. I ceased to care which paradise was lost and which was regained. But we kept going. When we went on to higher studies we appreciated the options before us and could dump the English authors who failed to interest us. That sense of adventure is no more in our present-day schools, alas.

We were put through exercises in paraphrase and précis, in sentence construction, which today's teacher usually ducks. Of course, there are certain methods our teachers applied which I would not want to emulate today. I have an experiment going at present in the teaching of 'senior' English in Soweto. Without following any official syllabus, I am endeavouring to restore paraphrase, précis and sentence construction. Also, I am exposing an assortment of thirty students to various uses of English prose: reportage (in newspapers and periodicals), oratory and business language – e.g. memoranda, correspondence – literary English and the language of advertising. I try to engage the students in a pleasurable learning experience where English fits in as a living language. I know it will be argued that, given a core syllabus in the school system, a good qualified teacher can do all this. The truth is that it is not being done, and there is a general attitude that resists this learning process. I am beginning to observe signs of enthusiasm and the joy of adventure among the participants in my class.

The English-speaking people of South Africa have, since the 1820 settlers, been complacent about the official status of English. When the British wielded political power, there was no need to 'stand up' for their language.

Meantime the Boers were setting up Afrikaans in opposition to English. The first and second language 'waves' (to suggest a loose translation of the Afrikaans 'taalbeweging') saw feverish efforts to establish the language as a written and spoken medium in the 19th century. Even after 1925, the Afrikaner did not fold his arms in contentment. His brand of nationalism had to attain a level of self-fulfilment first if the language was to maintain Afrikaner supremacy. The English-speaking community still felt confident that God was in the heavens and everything was all right, unaware – or unwilling – to admit that the days of their political supremacy were numbered. There was no equivalent English organization to the Federasie van Afrikaanse Kultuurverenigings. Founded by the Broederbond on 18 December, 1929, the Federasie was, according to a Dr N J van der Merwe, born of strife, a product of a conflict of soul, a search for a united front against 'hostile forces which divide him and smother his soul...' It was also his view that 'an enslaved people can only bring to light a slave culture.'

It was one of the aims of Afrikaner Christian National Education to teach in the medium of Afrikaans right through a child's school career through to university, relegating English to the status of a 'foreign language'. This educational ideology was a product of the Institute for Christian Education that had been established to counter dual-medium instruction. The English continued in their complacency when Afrikaner stalwarts like J G Strijdom assured them in 1953 that no one wanted to deprive them of their rights, including their language. This attitude is reminiscent of the 19th century, when English enjoyed undisputed dominance in African colonies. The extreme examples of this dominance were to be found among the Creoles of Freetown, Sierra Leone and the coastal Liberians – all of them former slaves returned to Africa by British and American ships in the days of Emancipation. Both these communities declared that a thorough knowledge of English was to be the standard by which a civilized person could be identified.

The gods eventually caught Prometheus in their net and nailed him. When the English lost political power, some of them fell easy prey to the Afrikaner's flattering invitation for them to prove their commitment to white supremacy. They allowed themselves to be co-opted. Others relinquished the teaching profession and took up other careers. Not having felt the need for an ideology with language as its *cause célèbre*, or having been too comfortable to fear any threat to their language, or having never been weaned from the traditional empiricism of the British and unwilling to dirty their own hands with ideology, the English had no practical answer for the arrest and torture of Prometheus. Today they are still as bashful in the face of this ideological outrage against English as they seem to be fearful of losing more than their initial power base. Like a eunuch who is being goaded into fighting over a woman to possess her and is thrown into a conflict, he is not yet sure that his manhood will never rise again.

I make bold to suggest that the black man here has vested interests in English as a unifying force. Through it the continent of Africa can be restored to him. Together with French, English provides a pan-African forum; it widens his constituency. English is therefore tied up with the black man's efforts to liberate himself. Through his literature the language is entrenched in the deeper recesses of his consciousness – his sense of other self – in his redefinition of the indigenous self. I am suggesting that he will be the Hercules conceived by Shelley as the liberator of Prometheus.

Shelley's romantic vision and the constraints of his dramatic form, plus those of Greek mythology, may create the illusion that the saving of Prometheus by Hercules is one heroic, miraculous event engineered by a condescending god who is never around to give us support when we suffer and endure an analogy of what was possible in 19th century Europe. But I am sure Shelley knew that liberation is a process, that the chain-busting act is but a climax of an ongoing movement – not the 'last syllable of recorded time', so to speak. And even with this a new cycle has begun to be followed by still more and more. The literature of the English-speaking people in South Africa, as the literature of blacks, is testimony to the workings of Prometheus's fire. The white writers have no cause to say, like Shelley's terror-stricken Fourth Voice, of Zeus's tyranny:

> *And we shrank back... for dreams of ruin*
> *To frozen caves our flight pursuing*
> *Made us keep silence...*
> *Though silence is as hell to us.* (Shelley, 1820:231)

At any rate they have not succumbed to the threat of censorship, even when some of their books have been banned.

These writers are speaking up in their own respective idioms. Alliances are formed and collapse, and the cumulative process of struggle, orchestrated by the writers' voices, may yet move forward and attain the intensity of that Herculean moment. Yet Shelley's passionate projection does not fail to intrigue me: it is a beautiful dream. Prometheus must be unchained.

I suggest that the English Academy, the 1820 Foundation, the South African Council for English Education and operators of other English-language projects wake up to the fact that preparing teachers and students to fit into official structures is going to retard rather than promote the cumulative struggle I have referred to. They must disengage from the oppressive, unimaginative official structures they are serving and jointly create English syllabuses and massive language and literature programmes. These must allow for abundant creativity and freedom of the intellect and spirit, while at the same time working towards proficiency. Such freedom will permit the literatures of the English-speaking world at large to become part of the emancipating enterprise. Prometheus must be unchained ...

South African Literature Versus the Political Morality – 1983

Synopsis by Ndavhe Ramakuela

This is one of Mphahlele's contributions to the debate on the value of literature. This debate became prominent during the days of apartheid in South Africa, and asked whether literature should serve a political cause. Mphahlele's argument is that literature should be seen 'as a compulsive cultural act, an act of self-knowledge, an act of language'. He differentiates between two types of literatures, one meant to satirise and the other to attack overtly its opponent. He uses a number of examples of writers from the African continent – each of whom have taken different routes in their creative writing endeavours – in order to elucidate the difference between the two forms of writing.

At this point Mphahlele seeks to differentiate between various forms of literature and the purposes to which writers put them. There is that central aspect of literature as a cultural event in a process – the act of self-knowledge, of language – that he emphasizes time and time again.

Another argument that Mphahlele makes here is that we can read certain aspects of history in literature, those that portray the African experience both negatively and positively.

'Perhaps a day will come when black and white writers in South Africa will find themselves waging a concentrated assault on the political morality of the times. Perhaps that day we shall be equally aware that as historians of feeling we shall be making cultural or intellectual history'.

Yet the central theme holds all the way through this essay: the political morality of the establishment. Against it is ranged revolutionary literature by black and white. Different voices, disparate music, but all with a unity of purpose: to expose the moral self-debilitation of the ruling class and its wretched bunch of rulers.

For the purpose of our discussion I propose that we think of literature as a compulsive cultural act – an act of self-knowledge, an act of language. Against such a proposition we can best see how intimately literature can monitor intellectual and emotional growth and contribute to its refinement at the personal and social levels. While literature is itself an extension of culture, as culture's expression it can step outside the rough-and-tumble of human concerns and activity and monitor, record and refine them.

This contemplation of human concerns and activities naturally involves moral values. If as a writer you could not ever step outside your culture every so often, you would find yourself a full participant in its monstrosities, abortions, miscarriages and other abominations. Every culture has its own abominations and crudities but, if it is developed, we expect it to display awareness to these and institutionalise efforts to purge itself. To the extent that the writer is a historian of feeling (to quote George Lamming), he or she at once expresses, monitors and refines what society feels and thinks about events that involve everybody – including him or herself. Professor N C Manganyi's essay is relevant here, in which he states:

> When we write, paint, sing and dance primarily to conserve culture, we kill something – communication and clarification. The hodgepodge that is education in our country today is not futuristic enough. It is so intimately tied up with our outmoded ideas about race and our conservationist approach to culture and identity that it hardly is a preparation for the kind of South Africa that is emerging... (1981:70-1)

Good writers are always challenging old moral and political assumptions and the myths of their cultures. The assault on these is not a mere fun game. Something in the writer has been touched off by the social evils that are sanctioned by the old beliefs. He is outraged by the defensive ideology of his people; by the cultural in-breeding and the stagnation that it has led them to; by the corruption, pettiness, tyranny and racism that may characterize his culture.

We observe two main literary approaches to these social evils. One is ridicule through satire: either the nihilistic kind that will not even stoop to plead alternatives, or the kind that blends subtly with comedy and acknowledges man's frailties even while the author laughs at the foolishness of humans. The other approach is a more direct and passionate show of resentment intended to incite the readership. Apocalyptic rhetoric abounds here, threatening the 'fire next time'. The distinction between the two satirical modes can be illustrated by Ayi Kwei Armah's novel *The Beautyful Ones Are Not Yet Born* (the nihilist does not care much for people), and Chinua Achebe's *A Man of the People* (the comic in which indignation is toned down by a love for people).

The apocalyptic tone finds freer and sustained expression especially in the literatures of the communist world, the black world – e.g. African, Afro-American and Caribbean – and the rest of the Third World, e.g. Latin America and parts of Asia. Because of the very nature of the novel as distinct from poetry, the latter's apocalyptic tone is more direct, incisive and passionate than what the prose narrative can achieve without losing its fictional quality.

Alex la Guma's fiction illustrates the Marxist emphasis on setting. He documents the setting in all its sordid and oppressive detail to show how human character can be held hostage, ravaged, or even exiled by the political and economic structures determined by a ruling class. There is an implied apocalyptic message here directed at the ruling class: its power is bound to collapse. The direct message is for the oppressed: his awareness needs to be sharpened if he is to rise against the oppressor. This awareness shapes and defines the dialectic: I am thus because of that, which in turn flows from something else.

The apocalyptic message is quite explicit in the following extracts from Afro-American and African writing. Amiri Baraka (African-American) writes:

> Poems are bullshit unless they are teeth or trees or lemons piled on a step. Or black lady's sing of men leaving nickel hearts beating them down. Fuck poems and they are useful, and they shoot come at you, love what you are, breathe like wrestlers or shudder strangely after pissing. We want live words of the hip world live flesh & coursing blood. Hearts Brains Souls splintering fire.
> We want 'poems that kill'. Assassin poems. Poems that shoot guns. Poems that wrestle cops into alleys and take their weapons leaving them dead with tongues pulled out and sent to Ireland. (in Henderson, 1973:213)

Christopher Okigbo, who himself was to be killed in action during the Nigerian civil war of the late 1960s, prophesied it in this poem, *Come Thunder*:

> Now that the triumphant march has entered the last street corners,
> Remember, O dancers, the thunder among the clouds
> Now that laughter, broken in two, hangs tremulous between the teeth,
> Remember, O dancers, the lightning beyond the earth
> The smell of blood already floats in the lavender-mist of the afternoon.
> The death sentence lies in ambush along the corridors of power;
> And a great fearful thing already tugs at the cables of the open air,
> A nebula immense and immeasurable, a night of deep waters –
> An iron dream unnamed and unprintable, a path of stone.
>
> The drowsy heads of the pods in barren farmland witness it,
> The homesteads abandoned in this country's brush fires witness it:
> The myriad eyes of deserted corn cobs in burning barns witness it:
> Magic birds with the miracle of lightning flash on their feathers
>
> The arrows of God tremble at the gates of light,
> The drums of curfew pander to a dance of death;
> And the secret thing in its heaving

Threatens with iron mask
The last lighted torch of the century. (1971:66)

Okot p'Bitek, Ugandan poet, who died last year (1982) had lived through the tyranny of Milton Obote's regime and that of Idi Amin's. The speaker in p'Bitek's long poem, *Song of a Prisoner*, describes his fury at the thought that the chief who flaunts a Mercedes-Benz is sleeping with his wife on his (the prisoner's) bed:

Big chief
Is dancing my wife
And cracking
My sacred rock!

Do you plead
Guilty
Or
Not guilty?

I plead
Guilty
To hatred,
My anger explodes
And destroys like a hurricane,
My jealousy darker
Than the coming storm
And madder than thunder...

Cut off this rope,
Free my hands and feet,
I want to chase
The thief,
I will smell him out
And smear the road
With his brain
I want to drink
Human blood
To cool my heart,
I want to eat
Human liver

> *To quench my boiling thirst,*
> *I want to smear*
> *Human fat on my belly*
> *And on my forehead.* (1971:66-8)

At the symbolic level, the revenge here is directed at the political system that must keep its radical opponents in jail while it abuses the nation, particularly its defence-less members. Mazisi Kunene, a South African in exile, has this to say to 'the killer':

> *If your species multiply*
> *And all men derive from your image,*
> *We shall open our doors*
> *Watching them sharpening their swords with the morning star*
> *And spreading their blades covered with blood.*
> *They shall obstruct our passage in our travels*
> *And cut our heads because we were of alien clan,*
> *Believing that our blood is desirable.*
> *But the growing of the powerful buds*
> *Will not let them triumph;*
> *They will haunt them with talons of weeds*
> *Piercing them in their dreams.* (1970:48)

Another South African exile, Keorapetse Kgositsile, writes with overwhelming despair about the condition of exile. Memory, love, justice, are but a process of compromise – an 'affirmation of conflicting interests' (1974:24). The exile is surrounded by silences, only skeletons 'rattle between the yellowing pages' (ibid), and he is haunted by a sense of failure and cowardice. As the exile walks the streets alone, he tells him-self to snap out of his despair:

> *If you are not an artefact dead as any curios.*
> *Then, like my sister said, sick of your loud mouth:*
> *If you are the soldier they shout you are Shoot!*
> *Shoot then... shoot buckshot in their hearts.*
> *Let them know that heaven is a hole in the air and hell needs its teeth kicked out,*
> *here and now!* (ibid: 25)

The title itself of the relevant volume of poems by Kgositsile is ominous: *The Present is a Dangerous Place to Live.*

In a poem with an equally ominous title, *Time Has Run Out*, Mongane Serote recalls the grief that sums up the African's life. In his characteristic style that always seems to reel off an interminable row of threaded beads in a variety of startling colours and sizes, Serote presents a pressurized series of images that all reinforce the sense of urgency suggested by the title of the poem. 'You cannot kill children like cattle and then hope that guns are a monopoly' (in Mutloatse, 1981), Serote says, reaffirming the history of a bloody struggle: 'we know when it is too late or, to put it another way, when there is nothing any longer to lose... we can now say, while we claim our land and die in the process: our history is a culture of resistance...' (ibid). Finally the poet says:

> ... my countrymen, can someone, who understands that it is now too late,
> who knows that exploitation and oppression are brains which, being insane,
> only know how to make violence;
> can someone teach us how to mount the wound and fight ... (ibid: 222-8)

Sipho Sepamla prays that the spirits breathe life into this time of suffering:

> spew here and now the shine of your gold
> that we may live in times glittering singing:
> igoli igoli igoli. (in Chapman & Dangor, 1982:126-8)

Again, something new must emerge from the ashes after blood and death. Mafika Gwala believes that the 'children of Nonti' (suggesting an ancestor-father) die; but many will survive, because truth unites them:

> They shall fight with tightened grip of a cornered pard ...
> Then there shall be Freedom in that stand by the children of Nonti.
> (in Chapman & Dangor, ibid:131-3)

He wants to 'get off the bus ride' which is the deadly repetitive run of an African's life:

> Black is when you get off the ride
> Black is the point of self-realization
> Black is the point of new reason
>
> And then a voice from somewhere warns:
> I'm the Voice that moves with the Black Thunder
> I'm the Wrath of the Moment
> I strike swift and sure. (ibid: 134-9)

In his dramatic vignette, *Dark Voices Ring*, Zakes Mda has a man saying to a woman whose daughter died in a fire started by rebellious prison-farm labourers:

> *We have done away with crying, ma. We are finished with weeping. Black people don't*
> *cry, ma. They don't weep.* (1980:43)

The woman is defending her husband, now a paralysed old man who used to be a
'boss boy' on the farm, and whom the man is accusing:

> *They always say that (they were doing their duty).*
> *Every one of them ... They are doing their duty, whilst they mow down peaceful children*
> *marching down the streets ... That is why I am going ... Because now I know that our*
> *salvation lies only in ourselves ... in our guns.* (ibid)

Mtutuzeli Matshoba is one of those black writers of today who wrench the spiked cac-
tus from the ground with bare hands, so to speak, in their attack on the system. He
extracts experience from raw life and does little to impose an aesthetic structure on
the material. And yet in his piece *Seeds of War*, which is part play, part straight commentary, he writes a refined narrative prose while he pushes ideas and their words into
his characters' mouths in the dramatized portions. The dialogue – such as it is – is the
only feature of the piece that aspires to dramatic movement, without arriving there at
all. It does not pretend to speak the way the characters should, and it is marred by
expository intention. Writers like Mtutuzeli Matshoba feel called upon to range their
words against the oppressor. They resist that intrinsic tendency for words to weave
themselves into metaphor and allegory to express high seriousness in memorable diction, and prefer a prose that goes straight to the visible target. Maybe they know no
other way. The writing displays the spontaneity of oral expression, unrefined, which
is closer to the heart – to a state of mind – than the written word, which has had to
earn its candidacy. In Matshoba's piece, a young man leaves his village in anger to go
and join freedom fighters when his people are forcibly removed from their land.
While the family are waiting for the white officials to move the community, the head
of the family says: 'I will either kill one of them or never see tomorrow myself.' (1981)
   The old man commits suicide. When his son is asked to stay for the funeral he
protests: 'You want to make it impossible for me one day to mete out just retribution
to those who have killed my father... I shall return to weed his grave and put a stone
on it, but only after I have followed my destiny to its logical end.' (ibid.)
   Pleading, resisting, asserting, prophesying retribution and doom on the one hand
and regeneration on the other; writer as priest and prophet; poetry turned theatre,
wrapped in an atmosphere of ritual: these are the commonest and most prominent
features of most of the literature from blacks that began to emerge in the late 1960s.
It is at once a response to the immediate – to the instant – and a direct, urgent confrontation with the dominant political morality. The dramatization of a message is the
major concern. The intention to *make* literature is either ignored or subdued. I mean

literature in the sense in which we speak of a process of tradition and refinement, a memorable act of language with transcendental possibilities. Literature as a compulsive cultural act, an act of self-knowledge, claims most of the writer's energy. Self-knowledge is a process that seeks to affirm an identity. The older writers of the group that emerged in the late 1960s, namely Sepamla, Gwala and Serote, work harder at their language, their imagery, and have reconciled the three elements of the proposition with which I began this paper. In other words, when you extend your cultural being and seek to know yourself, you have to express powerful feelings in powerful words (*powerful* also meaning *beautiful*), explore and establish perspective.

It is safe to say that the Anglo-Saxon tradition in particular, and the European in general, has consciously negotiated the delicate balance between passionate intensity and understatement, and developed satire to the finest degree. It consciously seeks to vibrate with resonances other than those calling a selected audience to pay immediate attention. The writer who stands squarely in this tradition tends to orchestrate indignation, resentment and general criticism – whenever these elements constitute the dominant melody – with other material. This orchestration lends the work more colour, volume, complexity and, it is hoped, a total richness peculiar to the poetry and drama of life. And yet there was a time when the same tradition was dominated by the didactic habit of mind, when almost everything, every event, could be transformed into an allegorical representation of man's spiritual decline or ascendancy.

African writers generally began by documenting their cultural milieu and showing the real-life conflicts between indigenous and Western values. In the process they gave a lyrical expression to the rediscovered myths and inner mysteries of traditional life that still dominated the landscape. Some writers created a lyrical representation of a world coming apart, of abandoned shrines graced only by sacrificial oil that has gone mouldy. Other writers again celebrated the nationalist sentiment, the coming into consciousness that was to win political independence.

After the mid 1960s, that lyrical expression began to give way to a hardened, edgy, dramatic diction to comment on the turbulent politics of a changing time. The colonial villain gave way to the African tyrant. The writer began to take an intensive inward look. He saw a new monstrosity being born in the form of political tyranny, followed by one coup after another – generating even more tyranny and more deaths and driving thousands into exile. Writers of this generation, like Kofi Awoonor (Ghana), Lenrie Peters (Gambia), the Nigerians Wole Soyinka, J P Clark and Chinua Achebe, and Kenya's Ngugi wa Thiong'o – to mention only a few – have lived through these swift changes and registered them in their work, its tone changing from the lyrical to the dramatic and apocalyptic.

The South African scene presents a partly different picture. It seems that a whole new generation of Afrikaans-speaking writers had to come on the scene to replace the immediate inheritors of poets like Totius, Celliers, Leipoldt and Visser, who were extolled by their own community as the authentic voice of Afrikanerdom and Boer nationalism. Those early Afrikaans writers set their audience at ease, flattering their pioneering sentiments and self-love. Our contemporaries, like Andre Brink, Etienne Le Roux, Breyten Breytenbach and Elsa Joubert, have come to jolt their audience out of their sense of political triumph, upset their self-satisfaction and lofty notions of their God-ordained mission; to ridicule their rituals.

By the same token, it was to be expected that the African's literary history on this subcontinent should reflect right at the start a growing resentment and indignation against white power and destructive religious zeal. In various ways, this is expressed by Tiyo Soga, William Wellington Gqoba, Samuel Mqhayi, Azariele Sekese, Sol Plaatje, H I E Dhlomo and Peter Abrahams – writers of the 1950s through to those of the 1980s. After all this, our political gains have been negligible. We observe how differentiated the white reading public is, correlated with the different ways of perceiving social reality among white orthodoxy, liberals and radicals. The black readership, on the other hand, is generally held together by a common predicament.

In 1908, already observing the consolidation of the white man's exclusive politics in South Africa, Olive Schreiner wrote as follows in *The Native Question*: 'I believe that an attempt to base our national life on distinctions of race and colour, as such, will after the lapse of many years, prove fatal to us… For the dark man is with us to stay… not only can we not exterminate him, we cannot even transport him – because we want him.' (in Krige, 1968.) But why did Olive Schreiner want Africans to stay? 'To labour in our mines, to build our railways, to work in our fields, to perform our domestic labours, and to buy our goods. We desire to import more of him when we can.' (ibid.) She would appear to be subverting the political morality that saw the white man in South Africa as the sole arbiter of race problems – and yet this morality is precisely what she is out to endorse. The naive utilitarian view of the African as a marketable commodity has typified the person of European ancestry for generations; Schreiner's liberal thinking was at once limited, vague and misplaced. She went out of her way to coax the Boers into acceptance of a unified country. She argued a distinctive trait in the Boer, being that he was 'devoid of all passion for conflict'. This argument was expected to appease the British.

There is something sinister about white liberalism in this country that feels constrained to operate from a Christian base. Furthermore, the liberal – being himself white – must believe that the white fascist or tyrant is capable of attaining grace and thus of ruling with a human wisdom. To believe otherwise would look like writing off one's own kind as unfit for Christian redemption – hence historical liberalism's abhorrence of violence and preference for gradualism in the liberating process. The liberal tries to allow for a variety of human foibles that can result in misrule and tyranny. The underdog's 'backwardness' or 'primitivism' makes the liberal's heart bleed, and so he ends up praying for both the oppressor and the oppressed in one breath: may they both find grace and acknowledge each his own moral shortcomings and love each other. White liberalism constantly pleads that the law be obeyed, and that the political morality of the rulers can only be subverted when the same rulers experience a change of heart. Failure to change, Alan Paton warns, must result in unspeakable tragedy. Jarvis, in *Cry, the Beloved Country*, pleads in this vein. We must acknowledge that activist liberalism (as distinct from garden party or paternalistic liberalism) has moved a few paces forward since 1948, on questions like the franchise and rate of political change, and seems unequivocally against the ideology of separate development. And yet the constraints it set for itself in the manner of resistance remain: extra-parliamentary mass resistance is out of the question.

That earlier stock of British settlers, including Thomas Pringle and William Scully, were, at best, curious observers; at worst, inheritors of 19th century thought with its notion of the 'noble savage'. To quote a line from Conrad:

> *In the cruel serenity of the sky, under the merciless brilliance of the sun, the dazzled eye misses the delicate detail, sees only the strong outlines, while the colours, in the steady light, seem crude and without shadow.*

And because the early writers observed only the 'strong outlines' they were inclined, by turns, to the melodramatic and the maudlin.

At a time when the Christian missionaries believed passionately in their 'civilising role', William Plomer was to unsettle whites generally by insinuating uneasy, even brutal, questions about 'Christian civilisation'. Plomer was himself not totally free of the notion of the noble savage, whom he regretted was destroyed by Christianity. But Plomer's sense of awe and wonder in response to the African landscape, his humility, personal warmth and sensitivity which affected me so deeply during our friendship of two decades before his death prevent me from classifying him with descendants of arrogant Victorian gentry.

The indigenous humanity of Africa is something that will always be a mystery to the white writer. When he is privileged to touch the warmth or coldness of a black person's hand he is struck with a sense of wonder. The point is that *Turbott Wolfe* challenged the political morality of its time by portraying unorthodox black-white relationships. There is no such mystery about the white girl behind the shop counter, the high official behind the glossy desk, the sheltered low official behind the iron grid, the man behind the badge, the farmer, the bank clerk, the academic and his secretary. All represent prosaic power in the eyes of the black writer: a ferocious demonstrative power that pathologically denies its own mystery, its own poetry. Power must speak in everyday prose and with action, for fear it may be misinterpreted. Of course, the seasoned black writer must pause to ask what may possibly lie behind that shrieking voice and swinging baton and the Saracen tanks. The truth may come for him in flashes, but that will be all that is possible for now. For my part I've long given up the pursuit. I am but human; idealism has given place to cynicism: this is South Africa.

Another questioning writer is Laurens van der Post. The white protagonist in his novel, *In a Province*, asks questions that are crucial to the accepted political morality of his time:

> *We don't allow the black people to enter into the system of living for which our justice was obviously devised. By refusing to do so we imply that they are psychologically and racially in a different class. Yet we proceed very logically to inflict our system of justice upon them as if they were like ourselves.* (1953)

Quite clearly Van der Post is tentative and does not himself have a straight answer. The magistrate who speaks the above words may be implying a choice for white authority: either accept Africans into your system and apply your justice to all alike, or keep them out and apply *their* legal system to their situation. In other words, white trustee-ship in the context of 'separate development' – which is at the centre of South Africa's political morality – is not being seriously challenged here.

The political morality of white South Africa assumes that the white man should continue to be the sole arbiter of everyone's fate, because he is superior in intellect and is a highly developed and organised creature; he represents an advanced civilisation. It assumes that for there to be peace, white and black should live apart and administer their own affairs separately; but with blacks having to submit to white tutelage, trustee-ship and employment, content with the crumbs that fall from the master's table. This has been the white man's 'historic mission'. No matter what modifications the state may make in the constitution, the eternal assumption is that white tutelage and trusteeship and political and economic supremacy must be considered fundamental to the white man's political ethic, to his survival. He tells us these are 'non-negotiables'.

Thomas Mofolo's *Chaka* (completed 1910, published 1925) and Sol Plaatje's *Mhudi* (completed in 1920, published 1930) challenged church morality as represented by the white missionaries, who in turn influenced publishing policy and the political authority's religious stance. In a review in *South African Outlook* LXII, John Tengo Jabavu wrote of Chaka:

> *[It] gives a new impression of the redoubtable Tshaka in that instead of the hero of history who is rendered repulsive by his unbridled, unjustifiable and insatiable thirst for murder, we get a human being we can sympathize with for falling, through no fault of his, under the baneful influence of a sorcerer during his tender years that followed a miserable child-hood in which he was treated with heart-rending harshness.*
> (Loveday, 1932)

Morija missionaries resisted this portrayal of Shaka for fifteen years. Other publishing circles resisted Plaatje's novel until Lovedale Press issued it. Plaatje was re-interpreting South African history from his own vantage point as an African. In both *Chaka* and *Mhudi* the African is a maker of history and a full-blooded actor in the theatre of that history. This perspective displeased the white cultural establishment, the unified sensibility of which took in political, religious and commercial authority. The Native Land Act of 1913 comes under heavy attack from Plaatje's pen in *Native Life in South Africa* (1916).

Plaatje, Mofolo, Everitt Segoete – like the Lovedale group including Soga, Mqhayi and Gqoba – were all Christians and products of missionary teaching. But they were all grappling in their writings with the contradictions between the white man's Christianity and the 'civilisation' that had always been presented to Africa as synonymous with it. They certainly began to realise that to be a Christian was not necessarily to be civilised and vice versa. Again they perceived that, given the brutal history of South Africa, the real African hero was not John Bunyan's Christian; that the real-life pilgrim's progress was not a poetic fancy touting a hazardous bus ride to paradise for the humble and meek, but a brutal historical reality that cannot wait for the afterlife to be resolved.

R V Selope-Thenia (later first editor of *Bantu World* at its inception in 1932) wrote in the weekly *Umteteli wa Bantu*:

> *The duty of Bantu writers and journalists, as that of other writers and journalists of other races, is to call attention of the leaders to the things that are detrimental to the interest and welfare of the people. A writer who does not criticise and correct the mistakes of his people does not fulfil the purpose for which God endowed him with the power of the pen. A writer is a prophet, and his duty is not only to prophesy but also to rebuke, when necessary, the people for wrong going; to criticise, when occasion demands it, the conduct and methods of the leaders of his race, and to point out the way to salvation.*

Like Plomer's *Turbott Wolfe*, this statement takes on a deeper meaning when juxtaposed with the literature that supported the white political morality of the time. This latter literature was obviously circumscribed and fashioned by the white man's obsession with survival.

The emergence of Peter Abrahams and H I E Dhlomo, at the beginning of World War Two, is a watershed. Their work shows a greater degree of intimate involvement between author and subject, a greater sense of urgency, an impressionistic replay of reality. This style was to be developed further by black writers of later decades. As my fellow student at St Peter's Secondary School in Johannesburg, Abrahams was constantly reading to us passages from the Harlem Renaissance writers of the 1920s, and from Marcus Garvey's speeches extolling blackness and attacking the political morality of their America.

Abrahams's style in *Dark Testament* (1942) and *Song of the City* (1944) – just as the style of Richard Rive and Alex la Guma's early fiction and that of the *Drum* writers, including this author, was to emerge in the 1950s – came from a reading of Afro-American literature. There is a sense in which a revolt against a social order, even if it be merely a documentation of suffering, is often waged in a literary or artistic style that is itself a renunciation of traditional norms. The converse is not necessarily true. The Imagists did not begin with a revolt against the social order before they developed a style that was a break with the genteel, complacent manner and prolixities of the Victorians and their immediate successors. Eliot, Pound and William Carlos Williams can, however, be said to represent the maturest and, for much of the time, finest ful-filment of the Imagists' sensibility and mode of perceiving.

Although Dhlomo's style in *The Valley of a Thousand Hills* is highly mannered and derivative, he challenges with a passionate intensity the morality that wrought ruin upon the beautiful valley; a morality founded on greed and political power. Dhlomo's prose is but a product of his times, of his schooling that emphasized the grand line, the grand phrase. South Africa's political morality must surround itself with an ample, vigilant and loyal police force and defence force, because it asserts itself on otherwise impossible terms. Impossible because it goes against natural law and morality, against common decency, and stands opposed to humanistic existence. It is a morality based on power. The predicament in which the sensitive white man who questions the morality and the power predictably finds himself is naturally acute. The love affair between a white woman and a coloured man in Abrahams's *Path of Thunder* ends in a tragedy. Paton's protagonist in *Too Late the Phalarope* is doomed right from the begin-ning of his affair with the black woman. Andre Brink's Ben du Toit involves himself in an African's fate and that of his son when they fall foul of violence in police custody. The white man realises in time the painful truth of what a journalist tells him: 'there aren't many ordinary people around nowadays... very few people seem prepared to be simply human – and to take the responsibility for it.'

In each of these novels someone goes against the moral, quasi-religious sanctions of his tribe and his destruction is sewn up and ready for him to pick up at the end of the line. The limits are set for the development of character, and there remains but a narrow margin for an error of judgement to be played out fully. What has the protag-onist really challenged or affirmed that will carry over in the novel's resonances once we have closed the book at the end? The odds are just as loaded against the author's attempt to subvert public morality as they are against his protagonist. In comparison with Abrahams and Brink, Paton's Biblical resonances strive towards the lyrical, rather than the dramatic mode which is dominant in the others.

There is a sense in which the South African situation is a most suitable context for a genre or mode akin to ancient Greek drama. The social parameters are set; the ceiling is fixed; the landscape is pegged. Human drama within this context can only be created when a person, black or white, moves outward to realize himself fully, to realize the freedom nature calls upon him to claim. Other things happen; the person pushes his energy until he hits the high-voltage fence or clears it. Either way he is going to leave us for good. He may quail before it and retreat and have to deal with the psychological consequences.

There is a brooding fate dogging our movements everywhere; land mines are all over. And then the catastrophe. In the social milieu that the law has assigned me to, I consciously document that life to explore its drama. It is a drama of survival. I am consciously trying to answer the question: what of this ghetto life can process itself, independent of or in spite of the malicious gods that waylay it, regardless of this brooding fate that they represent? I am never allowed to forget the high-voltage fences, so I have to create my own myth about survival, about the collective memory that orchestrates the human drama here. I must then regard the fences as a given and go on with the drama.

This is not a fantasy because ghetto life, urban and rural, *does* move as if it were independent of the fences, of the booby traps, of the brooding fate. The myth I endeavour to establish is that this part of our South African humanity will yet outlast at least some of the malicious gods, even when these have been replaced by another pantheon. This life justifies itself, affirms itself, and is *itself* a challenge against the forces of alienation and destruction ranged against it, sanctified by law, supported by a mean police force and the military, which are in turn kept alive and together by the impulse for ritual killing. They call it 'patriotism'.

In the process, I may or may not explicitly be subverting the dominant political morality. But I tell myself that I retreat into my racial milieu also because of the moral courage I draw from a sense of community. It provides me with a richer life to draw from. I feel safe in it because I do not know the family and class rituals of 'white' life. I meet whites only as adults or as young students. A large portion of their life is closed to me. Whites will continue to be shadowy figures or ready-made portraits in my fiction and poetry. Or they will represent that brooding presence that Moses in Doris Lessing's *The Grass is Singing* does. But that is surely not the most painful poetic justice white people can suffer! It is simply that I have ceased to care how whites appear in my writings, short of falsifying their real-life behaviour or attitudes. I call this desperate retreat elsewhere the 'ethnic imperative'. Desperate as it is, it is not an exclusive imperative, not even an ideology. I am not like that rabbit that has run into a hole and waits for the bloodthirsty breathing of the hounds to recede from the vicinity. No, it is a creative act that must take care of business while we wait for and move towards the richer resonances only possible in an integrated South Africa.

I have said that I *consciously* retreat into my milieu. Before I left South Africa in September 1957, I was not consciously burrowing into my racial community. We almost took for granted our separate existences and wrote about one another –

Africans, whites, coloureds and Indians. Africans mixed freely with whites in township and suburbia and with the other black communities. Today the boundaries have been frozen and we share little or nothing as equals among the four groups. Anger, bitterness, a sense of urgency to define oneself and one's milieu and be heard – that is what propelled one. Writing was a way of dealing with one's anger. Now I am older, I can contain that sense of urgency, that anger and bitterness, and deal with them. I am now conscious of the moral deprivations on both sides of the colour line and across the ethnic boundaries defining those of us who are not white.

I can now spend more time to orchestrate the single melody of struggle and endeavour, to assemble resonances from the larger life – for what the effort may be worth. I still function out of a sense of compulsion, but I have the time and the will to monitor my reflexes which, in my younger days, worked overtime and which I indulged. I did this as a compensation for always being expected to account for myself to the white man, no matter what his status was. Now I can consciously work out the profit and loss of my ethnic imperative against the moral deprivation in each area of this painfully fragmented country, where one group is kept together by privilege and the other by the desire to destroy the social order that entrenches that privilege.

The subversion of the political morality is not necessarily a literary confrontation, in which the imagination, prophecy, revelation and impact of message explicitly tries to diminish the workings of such morality in the hope of laughing or cursing it out of town. One feels compelled also to demolish conventional imagery and symbolism that are the expression of traditional morality. New imagery, new symbols – or a rearrangement of old ones – are an ancient preoccupation of the artist. The question arises: does the demolition of a social order in a poem, a novel, a play and so on eventually erode or subvert in any way that order in real life? The evangelists whose ritual it is to meet and decide what reading material to ban or not to ban think literature *can* do harm or shake up a social order, to say the least. The relation between aesthetic taste and incitement to political action – between that taste and the collapse of a church morality that masquerades as a spiritual exercise – is too complex to go into now. What has become quite clear is that censors tend to extract 'objectionable' or 'obscene' passages or words from a work and ban it on the strength of their interpretation. Reading a literary work like this shows lack of basic comprehension skills and the readers would obviously fail a contextual question in a language test. On the other hand, it may merely suggest (a) that the official reader believes that literature has a one-to-one relationship with life; (b) that he is subverting his own humanistic sensibilities; or, related to this, (c) that he loves power and in some puritanical or ascetic way is brutalizing his own person for king and country, becoming ironically the first victim of the authoritarian conscience invested in him by his schoolmasters and his superiors.

If a person writes a poem, a play, or fiction in the language of a manifesto or any other sociological text, this negates the inherent intention of any of these genres.

People do not wait for a writer to juggle with images and symbols and language and produce a poem or play, let alone a novel, before they go on strike or out into the streets to demonstrate, which points to the complexities of metaphor and the conditional *if* that underlies a work of art. In a perverse way, the censors seem to be telling us that a poem or story is so bad or crude that it can easily incite readers to public action and so the country's morals should be protected from such literature (shades of Pope's territory in *The Dunciad*). But it would be crediting these custodians of the country's morals with an insight not typical of officialdom.

Generally, the censorship department of the pantheon wants to uphold traditional mores ordained by the political and religious authority. That department does not like to see its standards of desirability, acceptability and moral taste flouted. The writer who is true to his craft will constantly attack those mores, explicitly or in a code language. It is but an act of faith that has little or no immediate visible effect on tyranny. Nor will it mobilize people for social action. The writer's perception of his audience has to be considered, too: whose emotions in particular does he want to re-order or revitalize? Maybe writers will have to be content with that part of their function that says literature is an act of culture, of self-knowledge; that it revitalizes language and keeps it alive; that it increases the reader by expanding his capacity to feel and think.

In the absence of a national literature that is defined by common ideals, sentiments and major concerns, South African writers find themselves speaking, recording and replaying from separate cubicles, talking to minute constituencies. Nadine Gordimer keeps battering on the accepted code of white suburbia; J M Coetzee strips western civilisation down to its essential barbarism that seeks to exterminate the Khoisan communities, regarded as just another form of wild life; Elsa Joubert brings into bold relief the travails of that class of black worker that is a mere object to be tossed hither and thither by the pass laws; Guy Butler will reveal to us the vibrant darkness of the African, his simple life-perpetuating activities refined and enshrined in the poetry of ritual. Breyten Breytenbach presses an urgent point when he writes in *A Season in Paradise*:

> *Does it ever occur to us that our country is attached, irrevocably, to Africa? Is it not amazing that the golden age of the Sixties, that time of harvesting our nice fat prizes and of wanting to fight to the bitter end about who should get the Hertzog Prize, that it co-incided with a period when more and more unread, and therefore non-existent, books by fellow South African authors were being banned? Does your mouth too, have that insipid taste of shame? ... I contend that our literature, no matter how clever sometimes, is largely a product of our stagnation and our alienation... Do we have alternatives? Are we nothing, then, as writers, but the shock absorbers of this white establishment, its watchdogs?* (1980:157-8)

In one way or another all the writers I have mentioned in this paper have attacked traditional political assumptions, while at the same time some of them consciously and seriously want to 'create literature', to contribute to a literary tradition in which they belong. On the other side of the tracks, however, there has been a shift from the writing before the end of World War Two – which was consciously 'a thing made' – to the conversational mode that is expressionistic in purpose, has an immediate black audience in mind and has directness of impact. It will not matter to present day black writers that Bantu Education has slowed down the rate of literacy, that they are therefore accessible to a very few readers who share their concerns intimately. These writers will steam ahead with a sense of purpose, of urgency – to teach their readership by sharpening its awareness.

The use of English, French and Portuguese in all of Africa is a political statement. These languages unify a diversity of language groups and are thus vehicles of nationalism. In South Africa, where the political establishment has been undermining English for the last thirty years and relegating it to the position of a mere 'second language' for some twenty-five million blacks, black writers – more than whites – use it not only as a political statement but also as an act of faith: that there is someone out there who is constantly tuning in to their literary creations; an audience clearly or vaguely defined.

Because black writers have been shut off from the voices of their predecessors who were silenced by the political authority, they have experienced a dissociation from the Africa-wide tradition of letters. So the white South African writer has a greater sense of literary tradition and sense of belonging in the civilization in which that tradition is enshrined. His education and lifestyle perpetuate this outlook. Hence his commitment to the idea of *making* literature, in addition to addressing the South African condition. He is consequently more conscious of the cumulative impact literature has over generations.

It is because of this lack of a common tradition and common imperatives that the climate is not ready for the growth of a South African PEN (International Association of Poets, Playwrights, Editors, Essayists, and Novelists) club. The effort to form and maintain one a few years ago was bound to abort. Not only do we not share a common tradition as literary practitioners; not only have blacks as well as whites been denied by their education any link with the rest of African literature, but published black writers have had to bring along with them to PEN a considerable number of people who were either still apprentices or wanted assistance in starting. PEN, on the other hand, was always conceived by whites as a forum for published writers, who were not fishing for writing techniques. Also, several of the beginners were coming for the ritual of poetry-reading performances.

Perhaps a day will come when black and white writers in South Africa will find themselves waging a concerted assault on the political morality of the times. Perhaps that day we shall be equally aware that, as historians of feeling, we shall be making cultural or intellectual history. Somewhere along the line there is an interplay in our consciousness between literature as historical process – recording, commenting on, replaying life – and on the other as a transcendental force capable of shaping the human spirit in ways we can never articulate or define in precise terms. Bad political morality is going to be with us forever, even though its interests, obsessions and neuroses may change from age to age. Its roots lie in the very fact of being. Censorship of one kind or another will also stay alongside the political morality. This keeps writers in business as men and women engaged in a compulsive act of culture, culture that recognises its own abortions, miscarriages and monsters.

The African Critic – 1975

Synopsis by James Ogude

In this essay, Mphahlele outlines his conception of aesthetics in African arts. He argues that discussions of aesthetics in Africa are informed by theories initiated and systemized in Europe. Because of this European heritage, the African continent appropriates a cultural system that separates the critic from the artist and audience, thus creating monstrous problems in the literary and graphic arts, as well as in sculpture.

Traditionally, the African critics of, say, performance arts were also their audience and sometimes even practitioners. Mphahlele argues that both white and African critics trained in Western theories and methodologies, which lacked knowledge of how African readers felt about books written by Africans, unfairly judged African literature. But the African writer, by producing replicas of European literature, was also implicated in this European-oriented reading of African texts. Although a few white critics worked hard to inform themselves about the indigenous culture and heritage that informed African aesthetics, still these critics relied on European standards of excellence. Consequently, Mphahlele argues, the African critic evolved concepts such as the 'functional' nature of African literature to counteract European ideas.

To Mphahlele, another feature of the European influence on African aesthetics is the relative importance of the literary artist. He argues for a situation where the artist and critic listen to one each other. Mphahlele opposes the idea of artist being treated as a special personality. Critics should be sensitive to the shortcomings of the artist, because literature as a modern institution is still in its formative stage in Africa. They should capture the tension between individual and collective sensibilities and realities. Mphahlele is also concerned about the significance of meaning and its accessibility in art: art need not be difficult and obscure. The African writer should produce work for the general reading public in Africa, and evolve another kind of narrative by domesticating the novel. Finally, Mphahlele insists that aesthetics should not be 'imposed from above', but should rather evolve from the interaction of all sectors of society. This will produce an aesthetic that will answer today's questions.

Let me make a brief statement concerning aesthetics. I shall make use of passages from my essay *The Function of Literature at the Present Time: The Ethnic Imperative,* published in *Transition* No.45 (abridged) and *The Denver Quarterly*. This essay is really an extension of the piece on 'function'.

Fortunately or unfortunately, we begin all this talk about aesthetics not on the basis of theories we as Africans initiated and systematized: we begin with a European heritage. We have moved into and even appropriated for our continent a cultural system in which the critic, the artist and the audience are three independent factors – in any case, a problem of terrifying immensity for us as Africans. It is in literary, graphic arts and sculpture that our problems are acute – as distinct from the performance arts like music, theatre and film, where the audience as critic is paramount. The orthodox critic will still be required for the performance arts – to explicate the ethnic cultures that surround and nourish the performances, to continue the ritual of the performance by further sharpening the awareness of the audiences, etc.

Consider the kind of schooling people of my grandparent's age, down to my generation – now in our fifties – were born into and that is still being conducted in Africa. Consider the fact that we began to be published and reviewed by Europeans; the fact that our parents, with the noblest of intentions, were always ready to forgo their own comforts in order to pay for our schooling, even though they knew the terrible moment would come when they would lose us to the bigger world out there, and die a bit in the process. And consider the reason they had to do this: they thought of us as an extension of themselves into a world created by the white man that *they* could not deal with at the level where an education is of vital importance. Our audience as writers will be only those who travelled this road before us, our peers and those following after us. All of whom, like us, were educated to deal with a world created by European man, who had become the main point of reference even in the world created by African man. How, then, can there not be the same dissociation between artist, critic and audience? Our parents' world has got its own poetry, its own idiom, and its own narrative. Indeed, it is only now that writers are *beginning* to talk about audience.

It is no use talking in the abstract about an African worldview based on traditional values, if at the same time we are content to live in a physical and human landscape created or determined by a European worldview – what we were educated to deal with in the first place, the reason we felt the impulse to write. An aesthetic begins with the very dust you kick around, the shit you smell, the houses you look at that make your environment and that you live in, the quality of life around you. In other words, with place and all the benevolence and tyranny you get from it. *You* have to be responsible for its shape, its texture; but while you dissolve in it, it dissolves in you.

This dissociation that we have inherited with European educational styles is illustrated in an open letter by the American film actor Tom Laughlin, published in *The New York Times*, 18 May 1975. He is angry with critics who tried to bury *Billy Jack* and its sequel *The Trial of Billy Jack*, in both of which box office successes he plays the title role. Laughlin asks:

> *Why is it that editors continue to employ critics who are totally out of touch with the audiences they are paid to review for? Why is it that critics almost consistently condemn the very pictures that their readers want to see the most? Why is it that critics invariably look down their noses at the 'mediocrity' of certain films when their readers have over-whelmingly voted them the most popular...?*

He charges that the only people who really pay attention to the critics are other critics and the bosses in the film industry, and that critics are out of touch with the American audiences for whom the industry is supposed to be making films. Critics, he concludes, have no impact whatever on what films audiences will go to see.

Although this is sales talk, the letter definitely indicates the world we have come into. On a much smaller but significant scale, we have had a similar situation with African writing. The white critics, except those who were involved with African indigenous theatre – like Ulli Beier – hadn't the faintest idea how African readers felt about the books they were making judgments about. Nor did we Africans who came in later do better, taught, as we had been, critical approaches by disciples of Leavis, Eliot, I A Richards and Bradley, and by francophone disciples of Appollinaire, Sartre, Breton, Levi-Strauss, etc. If our writers were judged by European standards, it was often because we produced replicas of European literature, especially the novel (a particularly bourgeois genre that requires a leisured class with enough money and time at its disposal), and poetry that was too clever and erudite to be understood by readers outside British and French cultures. A few white critics worked harder to inform themselves about the indigenous culture, in which poetry was born that contained the thought and beliefs inherent in that culture. But generally these critics, as well as many of us Africans, had a notion of excellence which had nothing to do with, because it was above, 'the popular'; Cyprian Ekwensi was often spoken of as a 'popular writer', and therefore not counted among the 'classics' by European standards of excellence. Didacticism was also embarrassing to critics of this breed, because it suggested 'popular.' Some of our own critics even gratuitously set up straw men in the form of stale concepts like 'art for art's sake', as if there were a one-to-one correspondence between African writing and that of 19th-century British aesthetes. We heard people talk of African literature being 'functional', as the antithesis of the concept of 'art for art's sake'. Some people even thought Africa had a mission to save Western civilization, by showing how far they had adopted the transcendental attitudes of Europe. At the same time we were writing criticism for other critics, for scholars.

There is another feature we have inherited, which concerns the relative importance of the artist, especially the literary artist: 'the roar and boom of the traffic, the
roar and clanging of machines, the marching orders of political authority, the politician's lies, the incantations of racism' – these, I say in the *Transition* article referred to,
'make up the prosaic beat of our lives.' Our own lives in Africa have, like those of the
Western world, become fragmented, differentiated, even within the large area of the
'African consciousness.' Political and economic styles, including systems of land ownership and the technology that we inherited, have brought us to this point.

And so we have to make the journey back. Not just psychologically, but also
collectively in the way in which we reorganize land ownership and agriculture, town
and village structures, housing projects, labour and so on. We must create a situation
in which the writer, the critic, the artist and the teacher at all levels will listen to one
another and take one another seriously. Apart from the fact that the artist is the
sensitive point of a society – its cultural conscience – he is nothing special, and we
must stop talking about artists as if they were a bunch of bearded barefoot messiahs
who have drunk the milk of paradise. If I am furious over the fact that bookstores in
Africa do not stock enough titles by African writers, I am equally furious that there is
little else that is suited to the thirst and capacity of the non-school-going public. If our
educational systems become also institutions of culture, this dissociation will be
remedied, and the artist and the critic will realize that they are merely part of the
educational machinery.

There is also a danger that as critics we may become, like the majority of Western
critics who are a kingdom unto themselves and therefore answerable to no one else,
so hardened and void of compassion (among ourselves as Africans) that every literary
lapse will seem like the beginning of doom for a society, a symptom of a disease in the
individual artist that will contaminate society.

Because whatever we find fault with in an artist, particularly at this formative stage
for literature as a modern institution, is still an African reality, not necessarily a
monstrosity. In the 18th century, British arbiters of taste and wit viewed what they
regarded as poor literary products this way – as if the whole of British morality
depended on literature. I can very well see that this view must stem from the passion
to return to the times when a society was homogeneous, so that the functions of the
sculptor, the singer, the poet, the doctor, and so on were integrated and the work of
one affected the rest of the community. African reality, as Wole Soyinka so often
reminds us, takes in both the individual and collective sensibility and vision. I venture to say that we have not heard the last about the tensions between these two. I am
implying that an aesthetic that simplistically glosses over such tensions or ignores
them in the interests of the collective is bound to stagnate. And we know full well
that aesthetics leads to the general principles and problems with which the critic
works. Thus aesthetes examine what *is*, the *actual* features and tendencies of art

that recur; they correlate, connect cause and effect, and observe human behaviour in response to art.

Aesthetes need, then, to come up with a body of knowledge concerning techniques and the nature of art so that the critic may use such knowledge with an educated and perceptive mind. Otherwise aesthetics will amount to a mere doctrinaire prescriptive posturing. Some people may feel that at this time in Africa's history we need an ideology. I am not sure about this, although I am aware that there are certain ideological principles writers are agreed on. On the other hand, these must be tested against everything that goes into the African experience, even if we are only talking about a phenomenon contained in national boundaries. So far what we are agreed on has only moved in our circles, the intelligentsia, and we have been our own audience as writers. We are now acquainted with that ideology that emphasizes material prosperity, and which sacrifices something vital in the human personality that dictates what kind of art it will create, what quality and direction of response it will make to works of art. We are also familiar with the ideology that emphasizes free enterprise: material must be attained by hook or by crook, even if a large segment of the society has to be enslaved. The artist here has become entrapped by his own sense of freedom. Both these camps have their own rebels, some vocal, some not.

If we must evolve an ideology, it will have to come out of the interaction of all functions of society. An ideology builds fences around an aesthetic, whether we like it or not. Do we want this? Shall we be able to cope with it? These are relevant questions, because our views of a work of art change according to socio-economic demands and imperatives from time to time.

Some critics urge that writers strive towards 'surface meaning' that is accessible. This is a just demand. Difficulty for its own sake is undesirable. For a long time American poetry has been a long way ahead of British poetry in transparency of texture, because the latter tended to use a knotted diction, exasperating allusions and so on. Hence the legacy of obscurity we find in some African poetry that falls neatly in the tradition of 20th-century British poetry, a legacy that has led to the importation of imagery and postures that are alien to traditional life and our new ideological drives: Latinisms, classical names, chalices, crucifixes, halos and so on. The caution is sound. Indeed, my idea of a healthy English syllabus for high school is that we begin with African oral poetry, then move to written African poetry (without the pretentious erudition) and Afro-American and Caribbean poetry. (A new anthology of the poetry of the third area will have to be devised so as to exclude the more difficult poetry, which can be introduced in the higher grades.)

Problems arise here that theories of value cannot afford to dismiss or minimize with any prescription: 1) imagery that truly derives from the poet's Christian, Muslim or some other belief; 2) difficulty that is organic to the mental processes dealing with certain subjects. Although I am neither a Christian nor Muslim, I still would not dismiss a poem or novel that came out of a genuine Christian or Muslim sensibility. Owing to some quirk of history, Africa became a dumping ground for ideas and creeds from outside, which we were utterly unequipped to evaluate. And they came to us raw, unprocessed. Yet I'm also aware that there are millions of Africans who find self-fulfilment in these creeds. They have become an African reality. I would certainly reject a poem or play or novel (like Alan Paton's *Cry, the Beloved Country*) which makes a pitch for Christian benevolence and forgiveness. Or, indeed, any work of art for which our responses have to be preconditioned, a work in which the images run into a cul-de-sac because they are predetermined by the religious message laid on pretty thick, that falsifies life and demeans human dignity.

We shall have to make up our minds whether a poet's tone (i.e. his attitude to his audience, his mood) is false or facile as a result of one image or another that derives from the Christian, Muslim or ancient African religion. It is relatively simple to recognize a tone of ridicule or hostility against a particular religion, as in Okot p'Bitek's *Song of Lawino*. Let us not forget also that the tone of a poem can be just so much bluff when the writer imports imagery from an ancient African religion or mythology for mere resonance, or a touch of authenticity that he does not feel in his blood and bones; nor can he project his or her mind fully into its spirit. But what is the tone in the following samples? Are the poets writing from inside the Judaeo-Christian or Muslim traditions?

> *a flutter, where the birds once sang,*
> *and the chatter of damsels where the daughter of Sion fell. For now the drum-beats*
> *hug their darkened maidens, ten firm fingers rap on stretched drum-skins.*
> ('The New Jerusalem' by M C Echeruo)

The poet's note says the 'New Jerusalem ... is in the new world – a conjunction of Africa anew, the chatter of damsels and the drum of West Africa ...'

> *They are singing obscene songs in the streets today Bud played his eyes closed*
> *in the little club cords of sorrow, of hyssop soaked in rags for the saviour to drink*
> *upon a Cross.*
>
> *He drank it, for the Lord did not*
> *let the cup pass away I will drink it, My God gave it to me, this calabash; I will drink it....*
> ('Hymn to my Dumb Earth' by Kofi Awoonor, 1971)

> *slowly downward in remote subterranean shaft a diamond tipped drill-point crept closer*
> *to residual chaos to rare artesian hatred that once squirted warm blood in God's face con-*
> *firming His first disappointment in Eden.*
> ('1966' by Chinua Achebe)

Achebe recalls here the days immediately preceding the outbreak of the Nigerian civil war: people seemed to be absent-mindedly and idly playing with the controls of government machinery, when the ancient hates erupted from deep down there.

In the title poem of Achebe's volume, he depicts with tenderness the manger tableau set up by the nuns. This, to highlight the abject real-life picture of a worshipper at the manger, whose feeble child lies 'flat like a dead lizard / on her shoulder ...' In another poem he says: 'We are men of soul ...'

> *We have*
> *come to know from surfeit of suffering*
> *that even the Cross need not be*
> *a dead end nor total loss*
> *if we should go to it striding*
> *the dirge of the soulful abia drums*

Achebe thus accepts the possibility of a merger between Christian and traditional African symbols. So they must be more than just literary devices.

> *Our God is great*
> *Who dare deny it?*
> *Our God is great*
> *Powerful and dark*
> *Peering through the ages*
> *Healing, Killing, guiding along*
>
> *Our God is black*
> *And like any goddamned god*
> *Guiding when loving*
> *Killing when angered ...*
> ('Blackman's God' by Kobina F Parkes)

Does Parkes accept such a black God? What makes him so sure of the reasons why God will kill (if he does) and what mood he'll be in? The line: 'Who dare deny it?' is a clue to the tone of the poem and tell us where Parkes stands.

> *Holy Mary, full of Grace*
> *myriad times knock against the trunk*
> *Of my being if there ever shall*
> *In this rapturous storm stand in silhouette,*
> *Or faintly smear on the façade human holiness*

> *That seems so far from the Holy Gate*
> ('Holy Mary' by Jared Angira)

Incidentally, I have borrowed here a critical technique from the Western tradition. The examination of tone works for me, because tone relates very closely to audience. So, of course, do the poets' feeling and intention.

As far as difficulty is concerned, there are those who will argue that a reader must take his chances and drill through rock if he wants the treasures down below. By the same token, the writer who spares himself the painful effort of going through his work to find alternatives for gratuitously difficult lines and phrases and words is also taking his chances. He will lose a considerable part of his audience. Short of employing nursery rhyme diction that cannot carry the burden of certain patterns of thought and feeling, I can only remind writers (including myself) that we have an unwritten contract with our readers. Even in the work of art that is accessible, there can be difficulty deep beneath the transparent membrane, which is the prose meaning (surface meaning if you like). Sometimes it makes for a culture gap between the work and the observer. We cannot ignore these barriers. But once in, the reader is on the ground floor. He has to listen to the sounds from the upper floors, the attic, from under the ground, from the yard, the toilet, the kitchen and so on. These are cultural resonances that, if one patiently goes about decoding them with the help of documentary material, can become available. The fear some people who refuse to take time to achieve lucidity often express – that they don't want to write down to the audience – is an idle one.

Millions of people would rather read sex thrillers, autobiography, adventure or factual literature in simple prose, than the kind of novel critics tout as masterpieces or classics. It is a good thing for people to be able to choose such literature, if trying to plough through Shakespeare or Dickens or Melville or Ellison spoils their taste for reading.

This should be a lesson for Africa. We must not delude ourselves that the novel as we have inherited it from the white world is the ideal genre in its present form. It will be read in school and university but it is too long, too involved and too expensive for the larger literate segment of society in Africa, a segment that consists of people who have had either secondary schooling or part of it and are out there on the labour market. We need to produce pamphlet fiction, novellas and pamphlet poetry that is well written and goes beyond the Onitsha chapbooks in the sense that they will *increase* the reader's personality, which is what I always mean when I speak of writing as 'elevating'. We also need to evolve another kind of narrative by way of domesticating the novel, without necessarily telling people to stop writing the novel in its present form. Also, autobiography should be encouraged. Epic forms should be revived. We should be able to sell literature in the marketplace, on newsstands, in supermarkets. We shall also need to produce books by a cheap offset printing process. We must campaign for sizeable supplements in Sunday newspapers, which will contain short stories, poetry and book commentaries. It gives great pleasure to a working man to be able to read and finish a book or complete work, so the length is most important.

We should campaign for frequent book shows in local bookstores; we must concede that a huge and diverse continent like Africa must produce literature covering a wide range of themes. The degree of complexity in technique (which includes structure), even when one has reworked the diction to the most satisfying and satisfactory degree of effectiveness, depends in the final analysis on the theme. Out of the interaction between writer, audience and critic, the writer – if he is worth his mettle – should be able to hit upon a style that suits his personality best and communicates effectively.

Private themes need not lead to difficulty or inaccessibility. The fact that to our greatest relief Christopher Okigbo, for instance, moved from difficult poetry, much of which *happened* to be private, to much more accessible poetry – which happened to adopt a public stance – should not lead us to think that private themes are necessarily taboo. Although the public stance helps loosen diction, there is a way in which poetry, however private, can reflect an individual vision of life as lived by *people,* including the poet himself. By a (to me) mysterious process – because poetry puts things together, interconnects them in organic wholes (as distinct from the novel, and from drama that does not come out of the very bowels of ritual, where conflict is the central ingredient) – the best private poem rises to the level of a communal consciousness. A useful poet should be able to let us enter his private world and make us feel it is ours.

That poet whose intention is to sound public responses and articulate them on our behalf is not guaranteed a passport to successful art – art that necessarily increases the observer. Likewise, the main character and events in a novel may be atypical, unusual – and yet, through other things that the novel does, the writer may persuade us to accept the character and events, even on the basis of the conditional *if...* I am thinking here of novels like Camara Laye's symbolic work, *Le Regard du Roi* (in English, *The Radiance of the King*) and Ayi Kwei Armah's *The Beautyful Ones Are Not Yet Born.* I am saying here that the individual vision and private concerns have a place in our lives, unless there is an utterly monstrous falsification of life through and through. The African sage, elder, doctor, high priest and so many other people in traditional life took time to be alone in order to contemplate experience. It is like the sick kind of loneliness we do not yet share with the Western world.

In the *Transition/Denver Quarterly* essay referred to earlier, I draw a metaphor for literature from the shape of the tortoise. That is, literature as a whole body of works of the imagination, not individual works. By literature's (the tortoise's) awkwardness and sometimes plain refusal when it is ordered to meet immediate social purpose or action, I do not mean inaccessibility of language. If we share a public language, accessibility is no problem. I mean something more complex than that. Simply that there are uses of literature for which the tortoise need not be opened up or pick-axed. One way or another we can tune in when we need to, and we shall find it whenever we want it.

Historical and socio-economic conditions may create a situation in which males may generally adore their mothers but treat their wives and fiancées with much less love and respect. You could expose such a society to lots of poetry, fiction and drama that glorifies woman or invests her with dignity or captures her portrait in tender loving words. The males I am thinking of are not necessarily going to change, even if they may be moved by the literature. So often it is just enough that such literature has been created. This is partly why we have to do the thing right: articulate our reality in memorable language, take pains in fashioning powerful words so that years from now they will still be beautiful, so that people will still be moved even though the socio-economic conditions may be different. I say we can tune in when we need to, when we want to, because after all we don't wake up reciting poetry or talk literature at table every day. We have other functions as human beings.

I insist that aesthetics should not be imposed from above. They should evolve from the interaction of all the sectors of society: writer, critic, audience, programmed media, other disciplines and other social functions. This way we can get out of the situation we are in today, where the writer is generally peripheral to our lives – even expendable. The politics and economics of the Western world have shaped a dominant aesthetic for the West. But even in this camp there are rebels, because the features of art and taste are variable in part, constant in part, and cannot be boiled down to immutable formulas.

Our aesthetics should describe both the constant and the variable. If we need an ideology, within national or pan-African boundaries, to help us arrive at an aesthetic, we shall have to be careful not to trap ourselves in a corner. Just as an ideology is a *historical* moment, so are art products also *historical* items – i.e. fashioned by historical moments. Today we need this kind; tomorrow we need another; the next day we may return to today's source of moral guidance. To try to sound transcendental about our aesthetics, about literature itself; to try to pretend that today's answers will be tomorrow's, is to be romantic. But, while we live, let's work toward an aesthetic that will answer today's vital questions.

Es'kia in 1988

The Art of the Writer and his Function / Letter to a Beginner – 2000/1991

Synopsis by Peter Thuynsma

> **For some of us must**
> **storm the castles**
> **some define the**
> **happening.**

These lines by poet Arthur Nortjé capture the very essence of – and most likely precipitated – this exploration. It is a serious essay intended, primarily, for the beginning writer and it comes with a companion piece, 'A Letter to a Beginner' (which follows this discussion). The intention behind combining the two pieces is 'to suggest to the beginner that while he/she is grappling with a literary genre of their choice, it is imperative that they should be knowledgeable about the arts in general.'

The title suggests a daunting task, and when many of us approach such an academic discussion it is with a seriousness of purpose and even some trepidation. The author admits a possibility that the experience could also be as entertaining as it is enriching or polemic. This essay is a surprise. Here Mphahlele trips through a minefield of contending critical opinions, including those of John Dewey, Albert Camus and Christopher Caudwell, in remarkably accessible prose simply because he asks himself 'what art does and how it does it for society.' And, lest we forget, the concern comes from a writer and an academic who very neatly dovetails his interest in aesthetic theory with the craft of the writer. In Mphahlele's words: 'Works of the imagination, alas, have various levels of meaning that obey no law.' He extends this point into: 'Art is at once an instrument and a thing whose viewing we enjoy. It is at once a process and product, i.e. the doing it and the thing produced.'

It is a good place for Mphahlele to echo his favorite adage of what art is (especially poetry): vigorous words expressing vigorous feelings 'in a way that either searches for or states or affirms the meaning of whatever its subject may be.'

In 'Letter to a Beginner', Mphahlele the creative artist gets to work by simulating a dialogue with a novice in order to impart some time-tempered guidance. This is a lighthearted romp through some tough territory, in which the key advice is wrapped up in statements like:

'You have to explore the life that pulls you into itself. This is largely the desire that pushes you into this writing adventure ... you should be committed to ideas, to life, as a man or woman among men and women, as a social being.'

These two articles are imperative readings for any budding writer and could be an enormously useful reference to the practiced writer – both works talk through such classic dilemmas for the artist/writer as ordering disorder, and the predicament of narrating an event with the license to embellish, detract or even distort. It is the texture and scope of a writer's freedom to create that interest Mphahlele; he addresses what the writer does with the disorder that surrounds him or her, and the repressible compulsion to write about that disorder.

Note: Argument is the essence of this paper. It says nothing that is new. In it I try to bring together strands of exposition from a few authorities on education and the arts in an attempt to give the argument focus. 'Letter to the Beginner', attached hereto, can be regarded as a personal word of advice. It gets away from the argument but is driven by the same conviction that informs the focus of the longer exposition. The primary aim in combining the two items is to suggest to the beginner that while he or she is grappling with a literary genre of their choice, it is imperative that they should be knowledgeable about the arts in general. This provides a context that we can call cultural history. The apprentice does not need to wait for this cultural history to be accessible before he or she embarks on the learning process in his or her genre. Read and digest small chunks at a time.

T he Marxist interpretation of art and its function is concerned with showing how art is related to society. It concerns itself with what art does and how it does it for society. I'm quite aware that the lines are somewhat blurred between capitalism and Marxism with respect to the origins of art in social relations and community; and as social relations have no limit in either time or scope, the line of continuity leads from the origins of art through the present day, into the future.

Social being determines consciousness. In other words, the individual becomes aware of self and of its own environment as a result of its relations to other humans. It follows that what an artist produces is consciously or unconsciously shaped by his or her social relationships and role in society. Related to this view of consciousness is the Marxist approach to art that sees it as process with reference to which individual, finished items can be discussed.

It is futile to discuss the art and function of the writer outside the context of the arts in general. The art and function of the writer immediately raises the question: what is the function of literature? Or why do people write fiction, poetry, drama and so on? Or what does the writer consider so important as to want to put it down on paper?

I want to talk about writing as both a craft and an art. For just as we need to master a language to be able to write in it, so can it only be useful to the literate. Likewise we have to be knowledgeable (the equivalent of 'literate') about the graphic and plastic arts, music, dance and theatre, for these to make sense to the viewer or listener. By *knowledgeable* I mean having more than a mere nodding acquaintance with the object at hand. Another reason for including the other art forms – besides the mere fact of their unity – is that most of us lack the skills to read, study and discuss our responses to the book, painting, sculpture, dance or play, that we read or view. The fairly or highly literate are equally impoverished in this respect.

We first need to shake off the old notion that artistic products are either useful, i.e. have utility value, or are 'fine arts'. Also, the line that is usually drawn between art and craft oversimplifies their relationship. Art is at once an instrument and a thing whose viewing we enjoy. It is at once a process and product, i.e. the doing it and the thing produced. Thus, as John Dewey (1859-1952), the American philosopher, tells us: art is experience, experience is art. When you separate the art of making something from the thing itself, experience ceases to be art and then the experience of art is faulty; the meaning of experience and art is thus obscured, corrupted.

'Arts that are merely useful are not art but routines,' says Dewey. By *useful* Dewey is referring to material use, e.g. for money or for manipulation as a tool, an instrument in the literal sense. And arts that are merely finished products are not arts 'but passive amusements and distractions.' They only differ from other frivolous, wasteful amusements in that we need to bring with us some measure of refinement to these finished products. Dewey also states that an object of art that is not also instrumental 'turns in time to dust and ashes of boredom.' (Dewey, cited in Richter, 1967:424-425). By *instrumental* Dewey does not necessarily refer to art that incites people to social or political action, or is an item of domestic use. He refers to art that is a continual source of enjoyment, inspiration and education, that 'refreshes and enlarges the spirit instrumental to the production of new objects... in turn productive of further refinements...'

Likewise, artistic objects or acts are often treated by religious and political moralists as excellent or virtuous and as the final answer to questions about good or evil, slavery or liberation. Those who only seek beauty and perfection in the arts, art that will provide happiness for its own sake, go to the other extreme. We should see art as both artistic objects and as acts, a process towards greater meanings and as a source of immediate satisfaction.

'Either art is a continuation,' Dewey states, 'by means of intelligent selection and arrangement, of natural tendencies of natural events; or art is something dwelling exclusively within the breast of man, whatever name be given to the latter' (ibid: 425). In the former case, appreciating art is a life experience, an education that is provided by nature. It is an experience that deepens, intensifies and extends our satisfactions. New meanings, which increase us, arise from it. But if art has nothing to do with our activities and products, then it has nothing to do with life experiences, our social being. It has sprung from some supernatural circumstances that make of the artist a unique character. We would not even have a language to describe such art. Dewey continues to argue against those critics who would continue to isolate art from its human environment. They will say art is 'the expression of the emotions.' Thus, for them, subject matter is merely a vehicle for such emotions (Richter 426). Implied in this view is also the notion that emotion is sitting somewhere in the individual, waiting for a form of art to express it. On the contrary, if we believe that art springs from life or experience, then we must see emotion as a thing of daily life:

> For emotion in its ordinary sense is something called out by objects, physical and personal; it is response to an objective situation, in a more or less excited way, in some scene of nature or life... It is intelligible that the artist himself is one capable of sustaining these emotions, under whose temper and spirit he performs his compositions of objective materials. (ibid: 426)

In the use of materials from his environment to compose, the artist can exercise strict economy by being acutely selective, while heightening the emotional response from viewers or readers.

John Dewey builds up a theory of aesthetics. This is the study of how we perceive and interpret works of art and their social significance, how they are composed or performed, and the underlying motivation of a composition. He begins with everyday human experiences rather than with works of art. For without such experiences art would not exist. To him the experience of art continues with other experiences. He argues that once a work of art has been declared a classic (that is, the best of its kind or class), 'it somehow becomes isolated from the human conditions under which it was brought into being' (ibid: 427). Thus a wall is built around it. One might even say that it is placed in a glass cage, separated from the materials that constitute everlasting human effort, experience and achievement.

We only need to observe how students of literature in colleges and universities treat classics – e.g. the plays of Shakespeare, the poetry of John Milton, the novels of Charles Dickens, and so on. They quote chunks of critical prose to support or to substitute their own independent responses to the literature. Year after year both lecturer and student discuss the text in the work to death, until the book becomes an abstraction; until we think of it as an item that has its own life, separate from the social and other concerns of the environment that gave birth to the book, and from contemporary life.

Let us turn to Albert Camus (1913-960), the Algerian-born Frenchman. He believed that art is rebellion in its purest form. Art should, therefore, give us a clue to the nature of rebellion. Camus observed that all revolutionary reformers denounced art – including Tolstoy (a Russian novelist) and Karl Marx (a German political and economic theoretician). 'The revolution movement of modern times,' Camus wrote, 'coincides with an artistic process that is not yet completed.' The French Revolution, he remarked, produced no artists; the only prose writer fled to London. A little later 'socially useful art' and 'art for progress' became common slogans of the revolution.

The Russians turned their backs on art. According to Marx, art expressed the values of the privileged ruling classes. Thus the only true form of art expressed revolutionary aspirations dedicated to overthrow the ruling classes. Beauty was considered a distraction, leading people away from rationality – the use of reason. History itself was to be transformed into 'absolute beauty'. The beauty created by ancient Greeks, Marx insisted, was the expression of the 'naive childhood of this world'. The reason people still appreciated this beauty was the nostalgia it evoked for this childhood.

Marx once said that the Russian shoemaker who was conscious of his revolutionary role was the real creator of ultimate beauty. And Camus comments: 'We notice in fact that in the contest between Shakespeare and the shoemaker it is not the shoemaker who maligns Shakespeare or beauty, but on the contrary, the man who continues to read Shakespeare and who does not choose to make shoes – which he could never make, if it comes to that'. (Camus, cited in Richter 1967: 439)

We must already sense a contradiction between Marx and the refined theories of art developed by the Marxist tradition in more recent times, as indicated at the beginning of this paper. In likening art to rebellion, Camus argues that they both try to reorganize reality, which they both rejected at the beginning. Reorganizing involves rearranging the elements, most often unlike one another, of reality to create a harmonious whole. When I write a novel or short story, for instance, I restructure rather than present its features raw. Even features that conflict I reorganize into a form that expresses a kind of unity. In other words, I impose an order where there was none, put together conflicting elements so that I present a unified picture without falsifying their differencs. The artist rejects certain features of the world, but also accepts others and gives them a high status. For the artist, Camus believes, is never a complete nihilist – i.e. one who totally rejects the world and all its beliefs, religion and morals, thus reducing it in his mind to nothingness. Whenever we rebel, something in us compels us to sense disorder and seek unity as a substitute.

An example. Here are notes for a poem I wrote not so long ago. The scene:

Delmas on the East Rand. Delmas: name of small farm in France belonging to the grandfather of a French settler who came to South Africa... settler ordered Delmas to be surveyed for use... Political trials... treason, sabotage, subversion terrorism, etc. Judges: how often do they feel compelled to pass harsh sentences, even death, how often do they themselves seek revenge on behalf of government and society they serve? Delmas, town surrounded by potato and cereal farms, one of fertile gardens of Transvaal... property of white farmers... weeping mothers, other next-of-kin of the condemned, and so on.

The conflicting aspects of Delmas apparently peaceful but carrying the system. Town apparently without a blindfolded woman with scales and death-in-life cannot escape me: small quiet town, full weight of the South African judicial conscience. Blinkered judges symbolized justice in front of her presiding over life.

I am rebelling against this disorder and seek through the poem to present a unified picture of Delmas, made up of features that do not rhyme as it were, do not fit into one another in real life. I want to reconstruct a place according to my understanding of it.

I am a craftsman carving a figure of some shape with words. My language will seldom be direct. So don't wait for us, my people, to tell you to storm the castles, occupy the trenches, march through Delmas – wherever – to protest. We know you wouldn't – couldn't – wait anyhow. For, as artists, writers have to select words, a language, that is memorable and at the same time probe the meanings of torment, death, terror: a judge's sentence passed with the arrogant sermon of a man speaking from within the safety and comfort of the fortress that is guarded day and night. And so many other events.

All artists find themselves in a world they feel is disorderly, in which they are uncomfortable in varying degrees. They are haunted by a sense of some predicament, some crisis. Then, through their art, they try to reconstruct a substitute world symbolized by the novel, poem, play and so on. Some are also activists and throw themselves into the arena of public affairs together with the rest. Agostinho Neto, the former President of Angola, and Amilcar Cabral, the former President of Guinea-Bissau, both of whom are now no longer with us; Léopold Sédar Senghor, the former President of Senegal, and Aimé Césaire of Martinique (West Indies) were among such poet activists. All these have lived in colonial times and written out of that experience. Their sense of disorder around them and restlessness impelled them to write.

Camus quotes the Dutch painter Vincent van Gogh (1853-1890), who writes: 'I believe more and more that God must not be judged on this earth. It is one of His sketches that has turned out badly.' Camus comments further:

Every artist tries to reconstruct this kind of sketch and to give it the style it lacks. The greatest and most ambitious of all the arts, sculpture, is bent on capturing in three dimensions the fugitive figure of man, and on restoring the unity of great style to the general disorder of gestures. Sculpture does not reject resemblance, of which, indeed, it has need.

> *But resemblance is not its first aim. What it is looking for, in its periods of greatness, is the gesture, the expression, or the empty stare which will sum up all the gestures and all the stares in the world.* (ibid: 440)

Camus would assert that if I am an artist, my rebellion against reality, for which fire-eating revolutionaries might condemn me, 'contains the same affirmation as the spontaneous rebellion of the oppressed' (ibid: 441). I cannot survive, as an artist/writer, on continuous total denial:

> *Man can allow himself to denounce the total injustice of the world and then demand a total justice that he alone will create. But he cannot affirm the total hideousness of the world. To create beauty, he must simultaneously reject reality and exalt certain aspects of it. Art disputes reality, but does not hide from it. (ibid: 442)*

The writer in my title includes the journalist, even the orator; especially the investigative reporter, the feature writer and the columnist. The feature writer may not necessarily be doing a sustained series of articles that have come out of his or her investigation. Writers in serious journalism, such as the late Henry Nxumalo, Harry Mashabela, Aggrey Klaaste and the late Sam Mabe, are examples. In his report *A People On the Boil* (1987), Harry Mashabela writes a vivid eyewitness account of the Soweto uprising of 1976. He highlights graphically the march of the students on the fateful day of 16 June. He follows it from street to street, school to school, as it picks up momentum, volume, fury and seriousness of purpose, even while the students are chanting. Mashabela selects from the enormous volume of details, material that he can reorganize into a narrative to express both his own agony and that of the chief actors on our side of the law. His own detention and permanent bodily injury are reported with economy of events and language.

Even more than we can say of Henry Nxumalo's good and courageous investigative reporting in *Drum* magazine, Mashabela's falls into a class that has come to be described as 'literary journalism'. Here the writer presents an intensely personal and impassioned account of events, whose chief actors take on a life that is almost fictional in its intensity. What is important here is to observe that even the serious journalist has to reorganize disordered reality and impose order on it. The writing itself becomes a kind of activist occupation if it is not divorced from real-life experience, environment and the time that makes it possible. Simply because a writer may not have it in himself or herself to join the march or throw a hand grenade does not make the writing irrelevant. And though the writing does not directly incite revolutionary action, we would be dimwitted to dismiss it as irrelevant. This kind of activist acts on fellow beings through a process of education. Education results when the reader contemplates, i.e. views experience mentally and ponders with a purpose.

The Russian Marxist philosopher, sociologist and historian, G V Plekhanov (1856-

1918) tells us that art has a social function both in its educational value and in the enjoyment it gives. He insists that in its broadest sense, what we call the utility value of an activity – i.e. the practical use we can put it to – can lie in its good for both the individual and the society. In the latter sense, it is a social organizer in bringing together whole communities for education or celebration, or both. Here it is that the individual sense of identity, i.e. belonging, is reinforced. This is a source of joy. Thus the writer does not have to, and cannot in most cases, throw his readers into social action, into a labour strike or into a street march, or get them to throw missiles at the agents of authority. For this we need a manifesto, a charter or action flyer or poster: media whose text we do not consider to be art. Indeed the essence of art lies in its indirectness of impact, in its cumulative force. It uses symbols, metaphors, things to represent other things or ideas. At its best, a piece of literature as art is vigorously selective in the language it uses. This gives it power and effectiveness that, in turn, we call beauty. I have said elsewhere that good writing is vigorous words expressing vigorous feelings in a way that either searches for or states or affirms the meaning of whatever its subject may be.

In his *Studies in a Dying Culture* Christopher Caudwell, another Marxist, says art is more than a deepening of consciousness: it reorganizes (by imposing order on disorder) emotions according to the demands and shape of the real world. 'The value of art to society is that by it an emotional adaptation is possible' (Caudwell 1958: 53-54).

Our instincts are pressed in art against the changed shape of reality (achieved by the artist). We thus reorganize our emotions stirred by the artist, so that we acquire a new attitude. This is the result of adaptation to reality given back to us by the artist in a new form. Caudwell sees the human being's inner freedom as a product of society:

> It is the most refined product society achieves in its search for freedom. Social consciousness flowers out of social effort. Learning how to accomplish this, we learn something about the nature of reality and how to master it. This wisdom modifies the nature of our desires, which become more conscious, more full of accurate images of reality. (ibid: 216-217)

The human being, interacting with outer reality, becomes free. The more we know the more we want, and so we are driven to become freer. But action must go along with knowing, i.e. with contemplating.

During the turbulent days of the American movement for civil rights in the 1960s, African-American writers clamoured for the arts to make revolutionary statements. They believed passionately that literature, along with the other arts, could make revolution desirable, even possible. Public reading of poetry – and a theatre that was largely designed to shock audiences – was the order of the day. Indeed, the language of verse itself was theatrical. (We have seen a similar development in the 1970s here, especially when the journal *Staffrider* entered the literary arena in 1978.)

The following statements made by African-American poets about themselves and other writers sum up the mood of rebellion in the explosive 1960s. The civil rights movement had pushed matters to their ultimate limits on the Black Panthers front, arming themselves for war. On other fronts there were sit-ins in restaurants and buses and teach-ins in schools. Activists in universities, colleges and high schools insisted on studies in African-American life, thought and history.

These statements can also be read as one declaration of faith: the belief that literature can, like the spoken word, inspire faith in the hearts of the oppressed; it can fire their awareness and spur them to self-liberating thought and deed. I shall leave the reader to puzzle out how the poets perceive literature can achieve these lofty objectives.

It is a declaration that vibrates through our own blood and bones. For a while we feel reassured of greater days to come. This is the myth that enriches so much of the fighting poetry and drama of the African American. A myth is a fictitious person, thing or idea we popularly hold dear and passionately believe in as a possibility, independent of any logic. A myth takes us beyond the pain of the present; it makes music, as it were, between the lines, woven into the very structure and content of the poetic statement. This is the myth one misses so much in the fighting poetry of black South Africans. Some of the drama succeeds in myth making:

> *Black art is created from black forces that live within the body... Direct and meaningful contact with black people will act as energizers for the black forces.* (Don L Lee)

> *I am black because I am black; everything I write, poems and stories, will be black without any artificial strain.* (Charles F Gordon)

> *Black words do not exist in this country apart from the minds and voices of black people. The function of our poetry parallels the function of our music (extensions of the voice); both give motion back to the people... the difference between black music and black poetry seems to be that black music is a product of the creative faculties of a black individual who reorganizes all of his perceptions to express himself, while black poetry depends on the predicament of black people living here. The music utilizes all perception, black poetry only the perceptions that directly and collectively relate to the mass of black people...*
>
> *The purpose of black poetry is to evoke response in its audience, the black masses, since ideally it is the mass of black people who are speaking. The response evoked must lead to change whether that change be immediate or proceeding over an undetermined period of time... I hope to wake up one morning in a land where I can write anything I want to, for part of the creative process is choosing what one wants to create rather than creating what one has to.* (Quentin Hill)

> *In the future, the only relevant literature will be that which has gone directly to the heart of blackness... The black experience seems the most intense experience in the modern world. It is better that black people write it ourselves rather than have it written for us exploitatively.* (Julia Fields)

> *We are an oppressed people. What is therefore needed is a revolution. A revolution is self, family, society, nation, values, culture. The black writer must necessarily aid in the liberation struggle. He must help black people. In the process of directing his work toward black people, he is creating a new man, a new humanism.* (S E Anderson)

> *Essentially art is relevant when it makes you stronger. That is, the only thing that is fundamental to good art is its ritual quality. And the function of ritual is to reinforce the group's operable myths, ideas, and values. The oldest, most important art has always made their practitioners stronger. Here I refer to the Black Arts: ju-ju, voodoo and the Holy Ghost of the Black Church. The Black Arts are among the earliest examples of mixed media. They combine ritualistic drama, music, the poetry of incantation, and the visual arts. The intent was to communicate with the Spirit. The ritual act served to make the participants stronger...* (Larry Neal)

> *We are calling for all black people to come to terms with their minds. We do not want a black Santa Claus or a black Peter Pan. We want change, not a white society painted black.* (Elton Hill-Abu Ishak)

> *Poetry is the most precise use of words because it is most particular, intense and brief. Poetry is the way I think and the way I remember and the way I understand or the way I express my confusion, bitterness and love... Poetry challenges the apparent respectability of abstractions by offering a completely particular statement of a completely particular event, whether the event is a human being or the response of one human being to poverty, for example.* (June Meyer)

The late Richard Rive, teacher, novelist and critic, reminded his audience in a lecture at Funda Centre (1988) of Arthur Nortjé's words:

> *For some of us must*
> *storm the castles*
> *some define the*
> *happening.*

Rive was reaffirming that writing and fighting, although they might happen at the same time, were two distinctive activities performed by different people or by a single person. Each has its own rules, its own way of achieving its own purpose.

If Camus and Caudwell are right – and I am deeply persuaded by what they say – that the writer is a rebel, then true writers are also activists. Only, writing often works indirectly and through a process of education. It acts upon the individual before its impact is felt by the community. All social reformers and revolutionaries are driven by a fierce idealism. This is often a passing phase, giving way to cold, bare reason and realism, sometimes swinging back to the original expressions of romantic enthusiasm. Likewise, if Dewey is right (I find him most persuasive) – if appreciating art is an educational experience – then communities deserve free access to works of art. We require to be educated in order to read, know and gain more education. I do not necessarily mean education for high academic achievement. Caudwell's notion of the education of the emotions through literature reaffirms this fact.

I have sketched the art and function of art, especially the verbal and visual arts; I have sketched the way a writer composes, the way we respond to a work of art, and the way it works on us the audience. Art is life; art is for life. We should regard the writer simply as a rebel who has the gift of language, as one who has extraordinary powers of observation, as one who is not especially equipped to make revolution. We must understand that the writer is an educator, the sensitive antenna through which society becomes aware of itself, its dreams, yearnings, abortions and miscarriages; its past, present and what it would like to be in the future. We should therefore cease to think of writers and artists as people who are enjoying themselves while towns, cities and rural settlements are exploding, burning. The other side of the coin is the image of artists as people waiting to be ordered to make specific kinds of poetry, fiction and plays. We are also just as likely to insult them by thinking of them as special, as people engaged in art forms that we hope will compensate for our political failures and frustrations; for resolutions we have failed dismally to fulfil.

I have not said anything about art and ideology. Much has been written on the subject. Suffice it to say that while an artist should not dismiss ideology, he should also avoid choking on it. He should not be bullied by it; he should rather tame it if it is a positive belief or set of beliefs. An ideology can either enrich a work of art or undermine it.

I conclude with a quotation that sums up what there is to be said about the artist as leader of a revolution: 'The artist's revolution is an ongoing process, not an ad hoc historical event. He is engaged in a revolution of mind and feeling. He is a teacher, an interpreter, a historian of feeling. (George Lamming, Caribbean novelist, in *Tribute* magazine, May 1988:144.) He also revitalizes language and rescues it from possible death or unbearable banality.

Letter to a Beginner:
On the Art and Craft of Writing as a Product of the Imagination

17 November 2000

Dear Fellow Dreamer,

I first wrote this letter at the request of the Guardian newspaper in London, in the United Kingdom, which published it some time in 1990. Apart from the additional bit about journalism, a few updated facts and other minor changes, the letter expresses what I still believe. I urge you, if you find it echoes your own ambitions, to read it several times over, maybe even refer to it from time to time. For at least it will stimulate you to check your experience against those of my statements that call for it, and vice versa. Works of the imagination, alas, have various levels of meaning that obey no law.

Let me say a few things about journalism, to begin with. A young man came to me the other day wanting advice on where to go to ask for a scholarship. What do you want to study? I wanted to know. 'Journalism,' he told me.

My reply was, 'Not likely – you don't find such a thing. Moreover, you don't need a full-time course in journalism as a beginner. You attend short courses when you're in it already. Not because it's easy to become a journalist, get me? It's simply because it is an art and craft that wants you out there among the people and their doings. Journalism is itself a way of life, even while it translates real life into print as information. Are you with me, young man?

'Let me tell you a true story: Sol Plaatje, one of the first major investigative reporters (1876-1932) – he'd been a Post Office messenger in Kimberley before he became serious about writing. Secretary of the African National Congress, he cycled miles and miles of territory investigating the forced removals triggered by the Land Act of 1913. He was deeply moved when he witnessed long dusty lines of Africans and their livestock carrying their belongings, leaving their ancestral lands behind them. And the result of his journeys? His famous book, *Native Life in South Africa,* published in 1916.

'Right. There have been volumes and volumes of journalism in the press circulating among Africans since the pioneering years of *Isigidimi Sama-Xhosa* (founded 1870), *Imvo Zabantsundu* (founded 1884), *Ilanga Lase Natal* (1903) and so on. Then their successors, *The Bantu World* (1932), *Umteteli* (1921), *Abantu-Batho* (1930) and *Inkundla ya Bantu* – founded in 1944 by one of the most remarkable enterprising journalists, the late Jordan Ngubane.

'You listening, young man? Well, there was a line-up of fine thinkers who wrote for those papers I can tell you – simply remarkable considering that they had not been to university at all. I knew most of them personally – no brag, just facts! Men like Herbert and R R Dhlomo, Selope Thema, T B Mweli Skota, John Mancoe, Walter Nhlapo, Peter Abrahams – the man who broke clean with the earlier style of prose fiction. It caught fire in the hands of the *Drum* and *Golden City Post* reporters in the 1950s, with us going to dip into the same fountain Abrahams had discovered: the African American (Harlem) Renaissance of two decades before. The 1950s also had a passion for African American jazz and we were creating new modes. Just as the 1920s was also the jazz age. Are we still together, young man? Fine.

'We wrote a style that spoke to the urban condition of the masses and went straight to its target, to hell with upright antiseptic English. Black Consciousness gave birth to a new crop of writers in the 1970s who built upon the style of the 1950s, and gave it a national dimension in both verse and prose. We still breathe the spirit of Black Consciousness in our style today – a carry-over of the 1950s in its directness of impact and a life that you can smell, touch, taste, feel and tune into. Read the writing for yourself and savour it.

'The 1970s and 1980s exploded into our faces – what a regime of raving mad men whose Secret Service was everywhere with us, like dogs with rabies salivating poison throughout the land! You know the devastating results, even for those serving on the white-white media. Meanwhile the forebears of the newspaper the *Sowetan* were evolving into what it is today, all minted out of a fire of a million flames.

'Now, you tell me, young man, do you think all these journalists had any 'school of journalism' to go to, with or without a scholarship? You made yourself or you didn't, full stop.

'All you need to do is read, read, read, till you feel you can't take in anymore. The pain is sweet, uplifting, cleansing, hear me tell you. You're now launched, so go up like a rocket. Books, newspapers, magazines, the lot. Write articles in which you record events around you, personalities, your human environment and so on. Keep sending them out to editors; get a sense of the kind of stuff each publishes. Bug the pebbles out of them with your writing, be aggressive. Work towards being a stringer at least to begin with, in order to make them aware you exist. I take it for granted that you will be holding a full-time job for your daily chow while you go through this kind of initiation. It's a long story I've been telling you, but nothing near the full story. Find *that* out for yourself. When you're a practicing journalist already, you need to attend workshops, often an in-house activity, to strengthen your position. This is not the same thing as attending a formal course.'

Even before I asked him, I just knew I had lost the young man. 'Do you make any sense of what I'm saying?' I asked anyway. The look he gave me told me volumes. Thinks I've wasted his time, for sure; I'm a letdown, and who knows what else! O, *dependence*, your name is the colour *black*!

So much for journalism. Let's get on with our main topic. So you want to be a writer? Poetry or drama? Expository prose – e.g. essays, public addresses? Make up your mind. *Now.* It is not easy to try more than one while you are learning. You need to be committed to the one you like best, and which speaks to your nature and ability.

Whichever genre you decide to move into requires your commitment. In other words, you unconsciously make a pledge to yourself to write verse or fiction or drama or whatever, and explore what it is about life or a piece of it that excites you. A genre is a class of composition whose form and style distinguishes it from other compositions. It is easy to observe such distinctions in novels, poetry, drama and so on. Binding yourself to a genre or form saves you wandering all over the place trying to decide what you can really be good at; finally, what you're best at.

When you have slaved productively enough for some years in your favourite medium, maybe even in a second favourite, a fancy may take you to explore a form outside your first choice or choices. Actually, I'm oversimplifying the process. Rather than a fancy or whim, it is that experience, dramatic or emotional or both, that vibrates in your blood and bones and nervous system: *that* is what will tell you to make a poem or play or fiction out of it, to explore it. You don't go about saying: 'I want an experience I can write a poem about.' For the writing of it is itself part of the experience. Which is why authors will tell you that it is not so much that you *find* a theme to explore, as that it is the theme that finds you.

You should have a fairly clear idea about the form of the novel, short story or drama that has been passed on to us from earlier times. This will suggest that each of these forms, as in all the other arts, has a *tradition*. So has the language in which a particular piece of writing is written. In other words, Sesotho or Setswana or Zulu or Tsonga or English writing demands that we get to know its tradition: where it has come from; what forms and styles it used; what concerns formed its subject matter.

To emphasize, we use words such as 'poem' and 'novel', with reference to what we have actually experienced by reading. You should read, read, read in your chosen genre and others: items that are satisfying and those that are not. Learn to rely on your own judgements. But any judgement that you arrive at, on why something you read is satisfying or not, should follow after extensive reading and sufficient consideration. This way you develop the habit of independent inquiry or investigation. Remember you are learning *how* to write, to translate real-life experience into a writing experience. This requires learning other skills related to books and other texts.

Right here I should say something about diction – the choice of words. You know, friend, the ancient people's poet was honoured by the community for her or his gift of the spoken word. Those poets were seldom sloppy in their speech. They showed this in their oral performances. They even seemed to taste their words on the palate! So why should we today imagine that self-expression is all we need worry about? Anyone who tells you the content or subject matter is more important than your style of writing is naive and misleads. It's much like what a misinformed teacher tells his or her learners – that a particular essay should be given high marks because it expresses the right ideas, even if it is badly written. You will learn in time that what you say in your writing shapes, and is shaped by, the manner of expression – style. You can't speak nonsense in beautiful language. Not really.

Work hard at your diction, among other things. After you've been writing and reading for a number of months, and you've reached a certain level of ease with language as a means of self-expression, certain themes or subjects will appeal to you more than others. Hold on to one that you feel *passionately* about. Writing about things without *feeling* anything, as we do in school where some of the most dreadful methods of teaching exist, takes you nowhere. Be patient: subjects – the ones that draw you in to their concerns, and the ones that are like sawdust, too lifeless to be fit writing materials – will sort themselves out for you.

The fitting diction you create makes characters, things, events and places come alive. Likewise, if you are in verse or drama, breathe into the piece of writing your own zest, your own enthusiasm. With longer and still longer training, your instincts will tell you which subject calls for a novel or poem or drama or short story or essay. Observe that W H Auden (1907-1973), British-born poet, once said that poetry is 'memorable speech'. Indeed, this is what distinguishes good works of the imagination from exposition – a medium through which information comes to us. Exposition is, as you know, a text that explains and must therefore analyse factual situations, things, real people.

Early in your writing career, diction (i.e. the words you choose to use) and other features slip into your work that come from your reading, things that you've a strong liking for. So be it. Hack your way through the bushes, so to speak, till you discover your own style – the one that expresses the real *you*. There is such a thing as a literary plot or tragedy or comedy, or character. We produce this when we borrow the emotions that we have picked up from what we read by other writers, e.g. anxieties, grief, humour, hate, love and so on.

There are also literary habits or customs we often pick up: figures of speech, for example, such as 'busy as a bee'; 'half a loaf is better than none'; 'a square peg in a round hole'; 'his announcement sent shockwaves through the gathering in front of him'. And thousands of others that have been chewed up dry and lack tension – like a donkey that has been ridden so many years that its back is hollow, almost spineless. We must work at creating our own figures of speech or expressions out of the situations and characters we are portraying, the vivid impact they make on us, which in turn we want to draw our readers into. Yes, we must keep composing our own expressions: not for mere ornament, but in order to highlight a point. We have to *compel* attention to an image. When you come to your writing without enthusiasm, you begin to suck your thumb and your images become unconvincing. It is refreshing to come upon a simile such as I heard from a radio short story: that someone ran away like a lizard out of a burning bush…

Of course, you're not going to wait until you have exhausted the reading list you have made up – from your own knowledge and what other people suggest. It serves as a guide. When you have some idea of a novel, a short story, a poem, a play (they are all represented here) you get down to the business of writing. In prose fiction, several people find it better to begin with the short story, writing several before attempting a novel. It works, both for your own development and because a publisher is often impressed by a bunch of stories you've published in journals, magazines and so on; they urge him or her to read your longer manuscript – the novel you want published. They realise that you've at least gone beyond the first steps in the art of telling a story. Those who write verse and drama most often simply plunge into their medium. In such a case, a short piece of prose is merely an option that interests them.

Write about five hundred words a day, at least: maybe a narrative, a descriptive piece or dialogue; perhaps a poem of twenty to thirty lines. This is to develop the basic ease you need with written language.

You've probably read some of the verse that came out of the decades of bitter struggle – the 1970s into the early 1990s. Most of that stuff was mere information: here today, gone tomorrow; talkative verse, I like to call it. Their sense of urgency drove them to recite it in public, to the roaring applause of the audience. They called it 'being relevant' or 'committed'.

What most people thought in this connection was commitment to the 'struggle' – portraying it with a tone of protest, prophesying doom for the rulers. It is not too soon to realise this, friend: that we are still up against racism and the brutality that often goes with it, State blunders, misuse of power at all levels of life and so on; that you're always tempted, as a writer, to use your art and craft to kindle the spirit of revolt among your readers. There are clumsy, often ignorant, ways of doing this, so that your writing ceases to be art, to move the reader. There are creative and good ways that do the opposite: your writing then interests people: memorable words expressing vigorous, memorable thoughts and feeling.

The latter is a long road that leads through thorny bush and prickly grass and up-slopes and ditches, so to speak. Keep to it with a sense of commitment, adventure, and exploration; with courage and persistence. For, you see, you cannot send your poems, fiction, and drama into the battlefield to speak and act for you. It is a battle-field where we toss ideas about, argue, explain, sort out facts, classify them, make statements about them and so on. In such a case you go in there yourself as a man or woman, not as a storyteller or writer of lyrics. These latter are the creators of *imaginative literature* that, on the other hand, deals with emotions, character, events and places. Its aim is to throw light on them in order to *reveal* various sides of experience and human behaviour; whatever else lies beneath the outside, visible surface.

You have to explore the life that pulls you into itself. This is largely the desire that pushes you into this writing adventure. In other words, you rightly do not want to rely solely on the information the journalist writes. You want to explore deeper truths beneath the information. Thanks to the lessons of time, a goodly number of poets know better today. They now recognize the enduring values and truths of life in its many dimensions. Political freedom has meant freedom to respond to this larger life.

Likewise, I'd say you should be committed to ideas, to life, as a man or woman among men and women, as a social being. March and demand and boycott and picket as a political animal. Not 'political' in the sense in which we speak of elections, parties and government, but political in the sense of the previous two sentences. When you come to writing, your commitment is first and foremost to yourself, to the rest of humanity, your subject, your style of expressing it, the point you want to make, the value of life and other values. For we all write to reveal something, to make a point. Not to preach or draw moral conclusions to convert our readers.

Say this to yourself: friend, that you can train yourself to carry your curiosity forward to sharpen your powers of observation, and the desire to know more about people. Listen attentively when people talk, laugh, cry, and when someone tells you an anecdote – that brief account people like giving of an interesting thing or event. Make notes about those that your instinct tells you have a social meaning and importance. The same for newspaper reports: incidents can suggest a story behind their bare visible happening. There are thousands of themes in these news reports, as there are in your daily life.

Stories and poems build up in my own mind. I let them turn around inside as I replay the themes in my mind, making notes to remind myself. This can last a year or more before I put them down on paper. Most of what I do, once I've got started, is to *try to get the thing right:* tell it right, breathe life into it. When you have been reading for months, you will realize that there is something that we call the 'story line'. This is like the single melody in music. Around it are the notes that the orchestra or band provides: the orchestration. It creates resonance: those sounds (meanings and their suggestions) that remain vibrating in our minds and bodies after hearing them, much like echoes; the images, the scenes you relate, the physical surroundings, the lives of other people connected to your theme. They all come together to create the orchestration. It enriches the performance – the experience of the music – while at the same time the music becomes memorable, just as a piece of writing becomes memorable. Its resonance makes it possible for us to continue to hear and think about it long after we have read it.

Writing can be a painful business. But the 'pain', as I've indicated, is chastening, pleasurable. Because you, the writer, are obeying an inner compulsion to come to grips with the search for the meanings of what life's experience offers: the feelings and thoughts and action.

Not to obey it is to kill a longing inside, a longing to imagine things happening and express them to relieve your soul. It is also gratifying when you see your work in print. You see yourself renewing experience, your own self and your emotions, knowing yourself better; giving language a fresh ring and in turn continuing to increase us, your readers.

So much for the other part of my story, friend. You'll notice that I repeat myself in different ways along the way, re-emphasize, rephrase. I can afford to do it, *you* can't; the function of this letter being a thing apart from what you're setting out to do.

Go to it, then, and happy hunting, happy writing!

The Function of Literature at the Present Time – 1996

Synopsis by James Ogude

Addressing itself to the English department at the University of Fort Hare, this paper begins by drawing attention to the deplorable state of literary criticism. In Mphahlele's view, current trends in literary criticism have reduced literature to a lifeless academic exercise in which what he calls 'a history of feeling', the affective principle that has traditionally separated literature from other disciplines, has been deleted. Literature, the paper argues, is fundamentally about the subjective zones of society and humanity. It should direct attention to the inner states of people and being. And, although the paper eloquently demonstrates that there are two major functions of literature that could be reduced to the personal and the social, it privileges the personal function. The paper insists that the primary function of literature is the elevation of the individual through emotional and intellectual participation in a work of art. It is only through literature's ability to deal with the individual engagement with the story, through personal impressions and attitudes, that the 'social necessity' of literature can be realized, as a vehicle for unifying the community in its organic social function. The sterile and mechanical approaches which characterize our institutional programmes tend to dismember literature, and deprive it of its inner being by privileging theory and voices external to the text. What is often undermined is the significant role literature ought to play in helping us to make contact with human beings and their passions in art. The other thing that detracts from the social role of art is the tendency to see art as a mobilizing tool. This tendency, born of a certain strand of Marxist thinking, Mphahlele argues, is arrogant and misguided; it places the intellectual in charge of a social process that he cannot engineer. Mphahlele is drawn to Lukács's view that literature should be seen as an object rooted in historical reality, with its production and function subject to time and place. Looked at in this way, it is possible to see why literature compels us to see it through reality, on which it feeds; and why it is defined by tension, because there are several conflicting voices out there that literature recalls and addresses itself to. Literature can only become a meaningful form of knowledge when we register these tensions and acknowledge that as writers, as a people, we carry with us the tensions and ambiguities of our time and place. Finally, the paper asserts, literature as an act of culture and of language will invariably draw the attention of readers towards character,

humanity and situation, beyond the arena where only intellectual analysis, rhetoric, exposition and academic hardware apply.

I n the economically advanced parts of the world life is so differentiated, teeming with so many specialists, theories and their constituencies, and analysts, that one is hardly ever sure about audiences: what they want in relation to books and authors and literature as a whole. At the lower levels of such societies – the majority – it is evident that readers crave simple thrills when they buy books and magazines; that is, when they want a break from the monotony of watching television and listening to the radio. So they go for picture magazines, science and detective fiction and love stories, some of which portray explicit and steamy sex. At the higher levels, literary works have been largely analysed to shreds – so that they are no longer an exciting adventure to read again. Some of the analysts have even raised their arguments, otherwise called 'literary theory', to the level of philosophy. I cannot help feeling that they are bored with questions about the value and purpose of art. The 'haves' of the world, generally, find it difficult to deal with profound or simple but genuine emotions. They tend to rationalize genuine feeling when they look at works of art. They are no longer in touch with themselves.

My lecture will stay with that part of the world where all colonial and neo-colonial societies – be they black, Latin American or Asian – commonly share the same concerns, real or imagined, about the function of literature. The writer in these parts constantly hears vigorous rhetoric whipping about around concepts such as social relevance, commitment, protest and so on. In the developed democracies of the Western world we hardly hear these terms except in Leftist circles. The literatures of this latter world have long come to terms with these concepts and have been taking them for granted for generations. They lie at disparate levels somewhere beneath the human largeness and resonances of a good novel or poem or essay. Long before we Africans, known for our mimicry of other people's cultures, realized it, European Marxism and capitalism had shaken hands of friendship in financial houses and ventures, and left us hanging on to the disembodied rhetoric of the Left and the Right.

I have excluded oral literatures. The poetry we find in the shrine ritual, the epic, the praise song, the folktale, myth, proverb and so on was cut out for these modes of expression. The griots, praise poets, healers and others could and did improvise and choose their own diction, but always within specific traditional forms. There could not have been any argument about function: to inform, entertain and elevate the individual poet and listener; to celebrate the spiritual forces that keep us together, and preserve the communal order and harmony.

What sets oral poetry and narrative apart from the written literary forms is that the former is a statement-making genre, in which the performer utters truths already discovered and established as possessions of the community. The speaker renders in vivid language a combination of revelations inherited and learned over centuries of communal experience. The stuff we write, on the contrary, most often takes the form of an exploration of experience, aimed at arriving at an understanding of meaning, or illuminating the way to an as yet unresolved meaning. The straightforward, deadpan interjection of the proverb or aphorism in oral poetry rather irritates in modern literary art because it pre-empts the process of revelation.

The fighting talk we find in resistance poetry in tense political times is also a statement-making verse, for the same reason that oral poetry is. For the verse-maker-turned-performer is declaiming sentiments he is sure his listeners share. He turns his declamations into ritual, ostensibly to inspire and strengthen the oppressed. In the process his utterance becomes verse turned theatre. The theatrical dimension, if well executed either on the printed page or public platform or both, makes the audience visualize the conflict, recognize the protagonists.

I shall talk mostly about poetry, a little about drama, and exclude the full-length novel. As they more closely approximate song or ballad and everyday speech, poetry and drama declare function and intention for us more openly and much sooner than the full-length novel can do – especially since the novel developed its own tricks and moved away from the simple narrative, trying to outdo in complexity even the life it tries to portray. A few African writers have begun to write fiction in the manner of responding to an audience's request: 'Please tell us a story, son (or daughter) of the soil...' We can say roughly the same thing about the short story as about poetry and drama in relation to function. I consider the short story a short cut to prose meaning: in a few broad strokes, without having to portray characters going through a long process of development in a single story, the writer can make his or her point.

It seems that, for all the diversity of functions the world at large may define – each constituency for itself – we may safely state in general hypothetical terms what we perceive as an overarching idea of function we globally subscribe to. It is that literature, as I see it, is an act of knowledge, an act of language, and a compulsive act of culture. This happens in context and thus gains perspective. Perspective compels us to appreciate the relationships between things, people, events, ideas and the cosmos. As an act of language it heightens experience, with vigorous words expressing vigorous thoughts and feelings. It thus goes through a conscious process of renewal. Yet it is not enough to say that literature (and all the other fine arts) is a compulsive act, something we cannot help making and experiencing. The author's intention or purpose helps him to be selective in what he explores or declaims, so that he may move his or her audience.

Let us view function not only as academics and students but, more importantly, as readers actively involved in the interpretation of a literary item – in other words, participating in its form, content, and search for meaning, revelation or affirmation of some truth. This inevitably implies entering into the available emotion of a work and its intellectual thrust. The danger is always that we can let go of our ideally enjoyable role as intelligent readers and fly into the rarefied atmosphere of literary and critical theory. At this level, literature has become an academic discipline, routine rather than process; not a 'history of feeling', to use novelist George Lamming's telling phrase. Although the imagination is a single writer's crafting and shaping spirit, it should ideally reflect a people's collective consciousness, dreams and struggle to become. I don't think we have any use for the alienated human desperately trying to chew up his or her own intestines.

But at the same time, let us not fool ourselves into thinking that we can easily write for the masses, apart from literacy publications and news stories. The masses have their own literature, largely oral. It is spoken, acted or sung, and has its own kind of spontaneity, its instant satisfaction. Then again, we would have to come to a common understanding of the term 'the masses'. For this purpose we might accept that there are levels of 'masses' that are above basic literacy. The kind of prose fiction that Mbulelo Mzamane writes fits conveniently into this class of reader. We can say this without implying that anyone above this level will find the fiction unengaging. This kind of reader is a fluent and sophisticated person who at the same time can deal with the life issues represented in a text that triggers physical, emotional and intellectual responses. The average reader easily relates to the psychology of Mzamane's characters and situations. There is an unconscious ease with which his characters move and speak, whether they find themselves in comic or sad circumstances.

One of the most difficult things is to write a script based on a play fashioned out of people's experience in a workshop situation – because one is then freezing on paper the dialogue, a living idiom that has blood and bones and marrow and heart. Turning a scripted play into a stage experience by using materials that the masses provide is quite a different matter: it has always been done. There are worthy efforts being made today by publishers who are printing literature for a general readership in the eleven ethnic languages available in this country. As people become literate, they will share in both worlds: the oral and the written.

And so to our central theme I turn. I deal with function at two levels that seem to me to be obvious: function at the personal level and function at the social level. It seems that at the personal level we can be reasonably certain about what literature does. But at the social level our doubts and fears begin to loom large. Naturally so, since societies are not homogeneous anymore, as they were in pre-literate times, when art, religion, magic, medicine, modes of production, education and so on served a unified social function. We seem to be generally agreed that the individual contemplator of a serious work of art feels his consciousness of the world sharpened and deepened by it if it is accessible to him; that he can be compelled by it to reorganize his emotions, and form or modify emotional and intellectual attitudes towards the experiences that make the work or serve as a point of reference. We are agreed that the individual is moved, entertained, possibly elevated by his emotional and intellectual participation in the work of art.

Marxists often speak of the 'social necessity' of literature, because they never lose sight of function as the root of literature. But they do not think of 'necessity' merely as deriving from what Wellek and Warren call literature's 'fidelity to its own nature'. They take the idea of 'social necessity' from the origins of art in ancient times, when it unified the community in organic social function.

Do we feel this 'necessity' today? Maybe, but it must manifest itself differently. Audiences are too differentiated to give us more than just a superficial quality of collective consciousness in art galleries and salons, at poetry readings, in public libraries and bookshops. The only people who perpetuate the study of literature as a collective occupation are cranks like us in schools and colleges. Even then, we work out a programme because we are paid for it. Of course, *sometimes* we are inspired; we enjoy hearing ourselves talk about these works of literature. Furthermore, we enjoy our sheltered employment. But year after year we replay our literary repertoire to our students, ask them to replay the stuff for us, eat up footnotes and references voraciously and get sick or choke on the stuff. Often both tutor and student just feel that the original text is for the birds – we can do with study notes. Through them we know the bare bones of the story, the prose sense of a poem and its interpretation, so we need only (we reckon) to read sections of the larger text to illustrate what the author of the notes tells us. Herein lies the mockery of our 'literary studies'.

Let goats eat morula fruit that has fallen on the ground. Overnight in the kraal they chew the cud and cough out the stones of the fruit. Shell them and you can feast on the delectable nuts. Would that our literary studies could yield such nuts (no pun intended). Our students know what they are getting. But I don't know of any students anywhere else in the world who are confident or knowledgeable enough to question the validity or otherwise of prescribed texts. Nor would it be healthy to produce the ideal tailor-made syllabus. We would expect students to read broadly enough to establish for themselves a richer and wider context against which they can judge prescribed texts.

We faintly hope that when we have come through the education pipeline, we can break loose from the inevitable cylindrical mould of the pipe. We should then be free to answer the questions this lecture should raise in our minds. The critical canon we are raised on at university seldom makes reference to these questions. Only after my formal studies did I realize that we had been made to chew sawdust, and convince ourselves that we were studying literature for life as well as for the exam. If students regard these recitals of prescribed texts as an initiation ceremony for some unknown future life, that will be the beginning of wisdom.

I shudder to even think of the kind of students we ourselves shall bring out as future teachers. All I see around me in the school system are men and women who are dying every minute intellectually because they failed or neglected to re-educate themselves when they left university or teachers' college. All too many chose the easy way of handling texts: by reading printed study notes, alas, and prescribing them for their classes.

Amid this fragmented audience, amid the din of industry, of crime, of war, of the politician's shrieks and crack of his whip; amid the howls and roar of racism, the rhetoric of political opposition in high-profile TV suits, amid the extravagant claims of some shimmering shadow called 'counter culture' – amid all these, where lies the collective consciousness that must determine the 'necessity' for literature?

British Marxist critic Christopher Caudwell has some perceptive things to say about the origins of poetry in his *Illusion and Reality* (1935). But when he says that '... [art] tells us what we really want – it projects our desires on reality and shows us that, as we desire, we can alter the world to the measure of our needs,' I feel he is really telling us what he *hopes* art (including literature) will yet do, what it *should* be doing. He tends always to transfer the personal responses into the communal realm, as if the latter were the only next step to go; as if a group attitude were necessarily the sum of so many personal attitudes, which it is not. He goes further than attitude even, and proposes *collective action*, when he says that 'in making eternal reality glow with our expression, art tells us about ourselves.' Caudwell is more convincing: we are back to the personal response. He sees an educational process in the uniqueness of the individual's emotions in the response to art. That is also convincing. When he sees in art an emotional guide to *action* – collective drive for economic welfare – he loses me. When some Marxists say that literature can help the working class in determining the specific goals of revolution and moving towards that end, we know they are romanticizing the worker. Those we conveniently call the working class – all who fall outside the category we conveniently label 'professional people' – spend their leisure time in ways that do not include literature at the level where we analyse it. They have their own poetry, their own spiritual pursuits. I don't see how we as writers can play around with symbols and images and fantasies and mirrors and representations at a level that does not correspond to that of the working class, and yet ask of its members to decode our verbal messages for use in the class struggle, wherever this may be found. Do we then, after the hypothetical revolution, call them back to a peaceful order with different symbols and images and fantasies and verbal gymnastics and fireworks? I think this is romanticism carried to the point of arrogance. We place the intellectual in charge of a social process that he cannot engineer, because we think he is superior.

I am still groping for a point of entry into literature that may suggest social use. Even if we look at literature as another view of reality – the imaginative view that tries to explore other realities that lie beyond the reach of scientific quest – we can still not escape the fact that reality is essentially historical. In this regard, I take my cue from another Marxist – the Hungarian critic and philosopher, Georg Lukács, who died in June 1971. Reality, essentially historical, is always changing and developing, especially because 'literary reality' comes to us through a verbal act. A verbal act is a social thing, and society has a history. Lukács entertains the old-fashioned idea of art as a copy of reality. Without being aware of a contradiction, he goes on to say content and form are inseparable.

What Lukács's historical view, which I am readily drawn to, does is to strip a work of art of all the idealistic notions about it as a static thing, supra-temporal, eternal, a unique and mysterious kind of knowledge, transcendental, and so on. For him, a work of art has in itself what he calls the historical here and now, subject to the time and place where it occurs.

Lukács also stresses *evocation* as the end of art, unlike that of religion and magic, which have ulterior ends. He implies that whatever practical effects may incidentally flow – or be intended to flow – from a work of art do not necessarily translate themselves immediately into social acts. 'The real strength and depth of artistic evocation is directed above all to the inner side of men.' He further says, in *The Historical Novel* (1962): 'A man can know himself only in so far as he has the power to know the world which surrounds him as it really is.' There is a pull between the 'world as it is' and the tendency in works of art to outlive that world.

There is also a way in which the intellectual sees not single works of art, but a succession of works through the centuries that collectively constitute a history of ideas, a thrust of the imagination, in any given culture. This is a process in the contemplator's mind that seems to overwhelm him with awe and a sense of mystery; a state of mind that in turn creates a comforting illusion of infinity. That is, until he hears the roar of the traffic; the explosions of war; the sounds of AK47 artillery in, say, the midlands of KwaZulu-Natal; the fire and fury unleashed by the Malanite generals and their mindless messengers upon the families of Kwamakhutha; the din of an electronic age; until he becomes aware of racial or ethnic imperatives. We end this illusion of the infinity of works of art, or suspend it temporarily, when man's animal brutality takes charge.

In his essay, *The Dehumanization of Art* (1925), Spanish philosopher and humanist José Ortega y Gasset (1883-1955) characterizes modern art as a mode of expression that presupposes 'an aristocracy of instinct'. An instinct that precludes the traditional involvement of 'the people' or 'the masses'. He asks: what do the majority of people call aesthetic pleasure? His answer is that people like a work that 'succeeds in involving them in the human destinies it propounds. The loves, hates, grief and joys of the characters touch their hearts'. They say a work is 'good' when it manages to produce the degree of illusion required to make characters look like real-life people. 'In poetry, they will look for the loves and grief of the person behind the poet. In painting, they will be attracted only by those pictures where they find men and women who would be interesting to know.' Human beings and their passions are what they want to make contact with in art.

Modern art leaves these people without any chance of participation. Ortega y Gasset maintains that this involvement with human destinies, which a work of art may represent, is a different thing from 'true artistic enjoyment'. Indeed such concern with the human element of the work is strictly incompatible with aesthetic gratification. 'Modern art,' he states, 'is an artistic art, because it is moving toward the ideal of "art for the artists",' not for the masses. This will be achieved when it has eventually dispensed with the *too* human elements typical of romantic and naturalistic works of art. He claims that our enjoyment of romantic and naturalistic art, for which we do not need 'artistic sensitivity', is in opposition to the approach of this kind of 'pure art'; all we need is to possess 'humanity'.

Ortega y Gasset characterizes the contemplation of humanistic art with the way we look at a garden through a glass window. We get so involved in the garden that we hardly think of the glass we are looking through. The glass corresponds to a work of art. Let us replace the garden with two women across the street. We are witnessing a drama in which the two are vigorously shaking fingers at each other, waving heads this way and that; arms akimbo, arms which from time to time fly in the air to reinforce a statement as threatening as the thickness of the arms. Lips are moving fast; one woman turns as if to go, but returns to her aggressive stance, spitting as she does so. Mutual contempt is quite clear from the contortions on their faces.

When our eyes return to the glass itself, we merely perceive the drama as a confusion of movement, which seems to stick to the glass. From this metaphor we could conclude that to see the drama and to see the windowpane are two incompatible operations: the one excludes the other and they each require a different focus.

Some modern theorists would of course find no contradiction between the glass and the drama. The critic among them would shift his focus back and forth and arrive at a total view, while at the same time being aware of the 'moments' that the work of art is made up of. It is quite clear that Ortega y Gasset views this 'dehumanisation of art' as a healthy development. It helps establish the role he thinks art should play – 'as play and nothing else,' as something that 'makes no spiritual or transcendental claims whatsoever.' He speculates on the day when the modern artist will have triumphed over the human. Because, he argues, 'life is one thing, poetry is another... The poet begins where the man stops. The latter has to live out his human destiny; the mission of the former is to invent what does not exist. In this way the function of poetry is justified.' That is, to augment existing reality with a dimension of unreality.

Ortega y Gasset goes on to make a still more astonishing claim: that metaphor is 'the most radical instrument of dehumanisation,' although not the only one. Metaphor, he says, is one way to escape from reality, from the human, by palming off one object in the guise of another. He has the old-fashioned notion of metaphor as an act of flight instead of a quest for, or even an arrival at, a meaning of human realities.

Without trying to lay the ghost of 'art for art's sake', we can establish how remote this view is from African arts – visual and performing – and its unconscious pre-occupation with human actions, beliefs, desires, concerns and so on. Especially as we are constrained to examine his philosophy in the context of his own social milieu and segment of the art world – the Western world. There is, in African art, constant dialogue between artist, the creation and its process and the human environment that helps shape a work of art. This environment is at once form and content of the art.

If I seem to have been thinking aloud this far, it is only because this essay is meant to be exploratory. I have paced up and down the corridors of theory trying to find the door marked 'social function'. I hear a number of voices beckoning me to follow one trail after another. Always I go back to the area of individual response, personal impressions or attitudes in relation to works of art. 'Give us some words of wisdom,' you request of literature. 'Tell us about life.' 'What life?' literature asks in turn. 'I have my own, you have yours.' 'But you eat the same food we do, drink the same thing, I mean figuratively.' 'Yes, but I mind my own business.'

Elsewhere, I have used the metaphor of a tortoise to describe literature. In one of those desperate moments when you need reassurances from this strange thing called literature, the animal draws its head in for self-protection. You can kick it around, throw it over on its back. Inside there is another system of life with its own rules, covered with an impenetrable shell that yields no answers. You will have to smash the damn thing with a huge rock or pickaxe if you are really desperate to know. But that will be the death of the creature. On the other hand, as long as it is alive, it will feed on the very reality against which it compels us to evaluate it.

Always we are aware of this paradox that is literature. The tensions can never be completely resolved, if ever at all. Tensions such as those between the human habit of asking the tortoise to answer questions about life – beyond the ring and resonance of rhetoric – and the refusal of literature to yield; between the view of a whole work as a metaphor, and the peculiar rules operating within a literary work; between a literary work as an expression, as cultural history, and as a thing made, autonomous in itself; between the illusion and the reality; between the writer's tendencies to overcome old myths and to create new ones; between the individual vision and voice, and public experience and voice; between subjective and objective truths; between language as a social act and literature as the clumsy, all-knowing tortoise at one time and, at another, as the prostitute who is ready to be had the way you want her, when you want her. These are some of the most obvious tensions in a literary work.

And the roar and boom of the traffic, the roar and clanging of machines, ambulances and police sirens, the marching orders of political authority, a politician's lies, another's repetitive jargon, the incantations of racism – these and other elements make up the prosaic beat of our lives. The 20th-century fragmentation of life must be carried to its logical conclusion, yielding pockets of consciousness labelled 'Protestant', 'Catholic', 'Jewish', 'Anglo-Saxon', 'black', 'bohemians', 'feminists', 'gender activists', and so on: some well-defined, some ill. And then there are larger areas of consciousness that are clearly distinguishable, falling into religious categories, e.g. Hindus, Muslims, Buddhists and so on. There are those who view Africa as a diversity of ethnic communities and those who see Africa as an idea. Those who never fully shared Western culture have tended, in the face of its fragmentation, to find it easier to reinforce their own fences. The degree of anger and sense of a disinherited mind among Africans, African Americans and some of the Caribbean communities is a measure of the intensive Westernisation they have experienced. These communities feel trapped in the vicious tangle of an ethnic/national condition, which has to come to terms with changing times and perspectives. Again, there are the rich and the poor of the world.

The elite of each group naturally want to determine who their audience will be, what the audience shall be educated to read and interpret, how they shall interpret, what bearing their assessment of literature will have on cultural development. They define their group; they go out to tell their audience not to listen anymore to the lies that the dominant group has been telling over the centuries. Independent Africa had its years of political struggle, and now writers want to set the record straight and carry on the process of decolonising the mind. Back in the 1960s, black Americans sought to pull out of the mainstream, which always determined that white Anglo-Saxon Protestants set the literary canon as well as educational content.

The voices of that decade sounded fierce, giving the impression of a state of emergency. Although the fires are still smouldering, African Americans have settled down to the affirmation of a duality of personality, sharing some of the values of white culture but insisting that 'we are American but we are also African,' that there are values they must cherish that have their origin in African thought and history. Among other socio-environmental factors, these influence African-American literature, its point of view and thrust.

The African and the Caribbean are still defining their societies. When white rule still held centre stage in Southern Africa, black writing here displayed a sense of desperate urgency, very much like African-American letters in tone. As a result of Bantu Education, which consciously lowered the standard of English in schools over an effective period of at least twenty-five years, writers took to writing verse. Prose suffered immensely, as it requires a mastery of syntax and vocabulary to sustain meaning for the three thousand words of a short story or the sixty to seventy thousand words of a novel, with the novella falling between.

Verse became the readiest and most convenient tool, as it can dispense with the full sentence, using imagistic language, however clumsily. By the same token, much verse easily lapsed into a talkative, finger-wagging tone. Beginners wrote such verse expressly for it to be spoken before live audiences. It was largely resistance verse containing, as one would expect, an apocalyptic tone: the oppressor had to be told that doom awaited him, 'the fire next time'. This verse is still very much the vehicle of apprentices and enjoys a particular class of listening enthusiasts whose frenzied applause would be the joy of any performer.

Mzwake Mbuli is of a class slightly higher than the common run of performer, enjoying the same popularity. Unfortunately his is no longer the robust resonant statement that held the audience's attention in the 1980s. Today his popularity is merely a matter of habit, of ritual, 'full of sound and fury', boosted by special effects such as the accompaniment of a band and dance group.

There was a time in the 1980s, too, when the eloquence of Ingoapele Madingoane's spoken poetry was due to the power and beauty of diction and social significance. He has been silent in the last few years. At the same time, superior writing was coming out – from the pen of poets such as Sipho Sepamla, Don Mattera, Mongane Serote, Mafika Gwala, Keorapetse Kgositsile, Essop Patel, Achmat Dangor, Christopher van Wyk and so on; their poetry has its roots in the Black Consciousness movement and dates back to the early 1970s. And yet their writing does not necessarily flaunt the Black Consciousness banner.

Poets such as Dennis Brutus, the late Arthur Nortjé, Mazisi Kunene, Sepamla, Mattera, Musaemura Zimunya (Zimbabwe), Lance Nawa, Achmat Dangor, Patel, Shabbir Banoobhai and several others have given us poetry with a subdued rather than a desperate, shrill tone of urgency. Latter-day practitioners – e.g. Morakabe Seakhoa, Lance Nawa, Baleka Kgositsile, Nthambeleni Phalandwa and several of their contemporaries – write in a resistance mode, but the pace is not breathless. Nor is it the talkative verse so many of their unrefined contemporaries produce, where metaphors often clash, epithets fly off the handle, and the writer-performer goes on talking at high pitch.

The classic sequence of events in African history, each period with its poet-commentators, has run as follows: white rule; independence; indigenous African rule with the nationalist leaders taking charge immediately; military coups and dictator-ship alternating with elected civilian government; political arrests and detention; sporadic resistance; exile.

Hastings Banda began his despotic rule almost immediately after 1964, never pretending that he liked democratic elections, even if he were to face the firing squad as an alternative. For three decades he ruled with an iron fist and all unsanctioned arts in Malawi ceased. Twenty years after Malawi's independence the poet Innocent Banda was to describe the likes of the dictator thus: 'They lacerate our land with the steel /

hair of their fly whisks,' even while Banda's party women clad in red sing national hallelujahs. '[W]here is the fruit of this land you promised,' is the poet's rhetorical question, 'when you said, "the good things are to come"?' This last line echoes the refrain in a poem by Kofi Awoonor of Ghana: 'All things come from God,' he repeats as he mocks the dictator's promises. Innocent Banda states that '[t]error has wedded horror' in the villages.

Still fourteen years later, from exile Frank Chipasula mourns the fate of Malawi:

> I have nothing to give you, but my anger
> And the filaments of my hatred reach across the border
> You, you have sold many to exile
> Now shorn of precious minds…
> ('When My Brothers Come Home')

For the people, this is an aesthetic that firmly denies a place for 'universal value', which they see as a dissipation of energy that must consequently fail to focus on racial realities.

Here are some of the outstanding pressing necessities the African American perceives to be calling out for action:

> Black Poets here are practically and magically involved in collective efforts to trigger real social change, correction throughout the zones of this republic. We are mirrors here and we know that anybody who has ultimate faith in the system is our enemy… Our weapons are cultural…our poems exist primarily for and go directly to our central human needs, the people, our strong desire.
> (Clarence Major, 1969)

> My poems be talkin bout blk people and the kind of tickology the devil done devised for us. My poems be chant / moans of blk alone. My poems be talkin bout what can be. And will be if we stop jiven.
> (Sonia Sanchez, 1970)

> For Black Poets belong to Black People.
> Are the Flutes of Black lovers. Are
> The organs of Black sorrows. Are
> The Trumpets of Black warriors.
> Let all Black Poets die as trumpets,
> And be buried in the dust of marching feet.
> (Etheridge Knight, 1972)

> *Poems should breathe like wrestlers, or shudder strangely after pissing. We want live*
> *Words of the hip world live flesh & coursing blood. Hearts Brains Souls splintering like*
> *fire. We want poems like fists beating niggers out of Jocks or dagger poems... Assassin*
> *poems. Poems that shoot guns...*
> (LeRoi Jones, alias Amiri Baraka, 1965-66.)

Most of the advocates for the quest for an African American aesthetic are themselves literary practitioners. The language of their expositions shows all too clearly what a tricky and obstinate creature that figurative tortoise can be.

In the 1960s some writers like Gwendolyn Brooks, Nikki Giovanni and others expressed a regret that the black man should, because of what and who he is, have to push his language to such excruciating limits. They hoped that one day it would be possible for them to write about other things their instincts might dictate. Again, some of the spokespersons merely apply the Western aesthetic to their ethnic content and idiom. Yet again there are several blacks who are content to be makers, practitioners of a craft, interpreting their ethnic realities that evoke a whole range of responses related to poverty, personal loss, family love and loyalty, betrayal, survival, the individual's thoughts and feelings in situations of racial upheaval, music and so on. Often black pride and survival were celebrated. Apocalyptic pronouncements were wrought through a freewheeling verse in which the violation of traditional form was obviously an expression of revolt against all the cultural norms of the dominant group.

Form is also a matter of some concern for black Americans. To the extent that they are infusing their poetry with the speech idioms and rhythms of the race, capturing the spirit and pathos of blues music, jazz, gospel singing; to the extent that they are liberating the English language, these writers are moving toward a distinctive ethnic expression.

It won't matter to many African Americans that the idiom and rhythm of street and market talk can be imposed on only a limited number of subjects – e.g. description that evokes sensory perception, narrative. Nor will it matter that the contemplative lyric may refuse to yield to these rhythms and demand its own, whether or not the substance of their verse will survive them – although it must be said that there is a good deal of ambivalence here. Those who want poetry and prose to survive them or serve as ritual cannot but have their sights on posterity. Some poets will want to write stuff that is meant for contemplation, for exploration of self and society, and stuff that is meant to be sent out into the arena of social conflict to fortify the revolutionary heart, to consolidate group aspirations and to recreate their myths and symbols. The writer in Southern Africa has portrayed white tyranny and the suffering it generated among Africans, leading to death or imprisonment or exile.

The Boers have continually declared their own priorities. Their literature was shaped by perverse Calvinism, the fear of black revolt, of miscegenation and biological extinction. Theirs was in the main a frontier literature within a time frame between 1652 and the 1970s. The writers then displayed nothing but contempt for black people. They also regarded themselves as the vanguard of the passionately vocal campaign to have Afrikaans made an official language, side by side with English. The Afrikaner attained this official status in 1925. Its advocates came to regard Afrikaans writers such as Andre Brink, Elsa Joubert and Breyten Breytenbach as marginal, because these and a few others rejected racial supremacy and all its attendant evils.

English-speaking writers of Southern Africa, most of them relatively progressive, by and large saw themselves as African representatives of the Anglo-Saxon tradition of English letters and therefore contributing to it. They were not consumed by the racial conflict as the indigenous African writers have been, always on the offensive against white despotism. But the English-speaking writer did not evade the theme of race. He or she, educated as they were in white schools, had absorbed European approaches to art. To try sending it out to the battlefield would, for them, be debasing it. So, although they were partisan towards the liberation movement, they wove their stories and poems and dramas around racial themes in such a way that dramatic action and emotional content would demonstrate, rather than explain, the evils of injustice. The general idea would be for a writer to unobtrusively persuade rather than seize the microphone and pound on the podium with rhetoric and exposition. Among the prominent English-speaking writers in the above-mentioned class are William Plomer, Laurens van der Post, Nadine Gordimer, David Livingstone, Athol Fugard, Guy Butler and Don Maclennan. To paraphrase Nadine Gordimer, she said recently that black African literature has been recording the history of the political struggle. We now need to wrap up this record as a transient, if compelling, activity and move on to the enduring values of society.

In South Africa in particular, black poetry, fiction and drama are a record of deprivation, loss, death and the agony of being black. The belligerent, apocalyptic tone is unavoidable. Here, too, it is a pressing priority that the dominant function of literature be linear self-expression – damn art as a thing crafted, that we value mostly for layers of meaning and resonance! Expression of anger is a way of defining yourself when your dignity is being undermined.

In Southern Africa (including Malawi) the writer's major difficulty today, if he rates himself highly, is that of having to walk the thin line between, on the one side, bull-horn statement-making talk and, on the other, the artistic crafting of a work that gives memorable language to thought, feeling, and historical reality. The weight is all too often tilted on the side of the former. I have mentioned the writers who survived the conflict and gave us works that contain at once social-historical reality and the language of art, which includes resonance that derives from layers of meaning.

South Africans in particular, especially since apartheid was written into the laws of the land, have seen themselves as messengers to relay felt historical truths and carry the torch of knowledge; to mobilize the crowds, hoping to galvanize them into action. Today, writers in the former colonies are saying, in the message contained in their poetry and drama, that there needs to be a shift in focus. The focus is now on social manners, the betrayal of the nation by corrupt black dictators, the individual's relationship to political and economic power, the neo-colonial subversion of national goals, and so on.

The banning of thousands of publications and films and stage plays from the outside world since 1963 was based on the 'undesirability' of any lines that even smelled of sedition and anti-government talk. In several cases they did not amount to art at all. When they did show some merit at all it was by and large beyond those honourable dimwits, the censors. The inanity in the selection of material they censored was an insult to the nation's intelligence. It made one suspect that few, if any, of the Censorship Board members would ever have stopped to ponder the complexity of art in relation to society and the overall function of literature in particular.

We can sum up the arts of the economically underdeveloped world as evidence of a heightened response to the unabating call of history. There is something excruciating about the way in which the artist seldom lets up in the felt need to record his responses; almost as if he were afraid history would pass him by or slip through the fingers. On the once rare occasions when African writers of the post-Negritude era have expressed themselves on the purpose of their art, it has been mostly in relation to their perceived audiences. Also, they have insisted that Africa rid itself of colonial rule. Kenya's Ngugi wa Thiong'o writes in his essay, *The Writer in a Changing Society*: 'A writer responds, with his total personality, to a social environment, which changes all the time.' (1972: 47.) History has been the paramount agent of change in Africa this far. Ngugi urges a decolonisation of the mind. He considers one of the hallmarks of change to be our use of indigenous languages in our literature to capture most faithfully our cultural being and to make our writing accessible to our people, as do Soyinka, Achebe and others. Ngugi confronts in his plays and fiction corruption among the governing elites, and the greed for material wealth.

Chinua Achebe, the well-known Nigerian novelist, denies emphatically the claim that Africans *have* to address themselves to an extra-African audience – a claim that derives from the low level of literacy in Africa. He insists that a novelist should be a teacher. One deduces from the examples he gives that he considers literature primarily as knowledge. It should inform people, but in an imaginative manner; in this way art engages physical responses, the mind and emotions. Achebe said at another time in an interview that his role (anti-colonial) had been changing. After independence, he said, he realized that he and the politician were on different sides, because the latter had broken faith with the nation. Even in that part of West Africa that still maintains at least a sense of historical Negritude – consciousness of the essence of being black and self-assertive African pride – Achebe characterizes much African thinking today when he says: 'Let's not waste too much time explaining what we were and pleading with some people and telling them we are also human… Let us map out what we are going to be tomorrow.'

African writers generally are impatient of critics who interpret their works by Western standards. They see themselves as serving an African function within nation states. While we have internationally known novelists and other fiction authors writing in English and French – like Achebe, Soyinka, Sembene Ousmane, Ayi Kwei Armah, Ngugi wa Thiong'o, Alex la Guma, Richard Rive, Bessie Head, Mongo Beti and so on – there are several others whose works would appeal only to Africans. They emphasize character and situation, bypassing, or not paying much attention to, other novelistic techniques the West would consider equally important. They dislike literary formulae, or any dogma that threatens to programme their writing. They want to arrive at African critical standards, not as a matter of urgency but as the result of experience, of a process of reconciliation between the cultural streams that inform their art and their African selves.

In trying to define themselves, locate themselves and their communities in the cultural tradition into which they were dragged, they realize that at this stage in African history new sets of socio-economic and political demands are needed. These in turn must make changing demands on art in general and literature in particular. The function of literature as knowledge, as an act of culture and of language – whether or not these are perpetually at the forefront of their consciousness – goes a long way in drawing the attention of readers towards character, humanity and situation. The sense of urgency in this quest for a metaphor to define their communities in transition arises only in times of political and social upheaval, including civil war. Writers have to remember that they are part of the society they are criticizing. Because art is a way of perceiving, literary demands must needs vary from country to country – one social situation to another.

The realization that national goals have been betrayed or subverted or deflected comes as a violent shock to the writer. Overnight he may find himself an exile or refugee – like the South African – at the crossroads of a variety of African cultures. Where it concerns what one says and to whom in an atmosphere of relative political calm, what drives our literature continent-wide shares little or nothing with Western demands. When it comes to the 'how' of literary expression, we and the Western world share a public medium, a public vehicle of distribution of cultural products. We draw the line when we give attention to grassroots communities and must cultivate literacy, general life skills and knowledge. We have also begun to share the same political and economic concerns with the West, varying in complexity from one to the other. Africans generally do not have the reflexes of the developed Western democracies around concerns such as the fact of dictatorship. We do not as yet readily pick up cudgels in an effort to rid ourselves of the tyrant in our midst. In some developing countries, black or white, there is even an attempt to rationalize a dictatorship. The people see it as somehow not so objectionable nor urgent if it is accompanied by a kind of paternal attitude in the 'father figure'. In Africa dictatorship gets entangled with traditional cultures that revere king, queen or chief, whose role is also tied up with religious authority, real or imagined.

Academic and intellectual freedoms are also concepts that tend to stay at the abstract level – until an authoritarian government raids an educational and/or cultural institution and makes a few arrests. The populace hesitates in its response, the writer also wavers out of fear, maybe even consternation, and often we rationalize ourselves out of the situation. More and more, however, the intelligentsia – mostly writers and teachers at the levels below tertiary – are finding their voice and the courage to speak up and mobilize in protest.

In one decade, the focus of several African poets has shifted from the celebration of 'arrival', i.e. independence, or the innocent and lyrical, unhurried affirmation of the inner mysteries of tradition, the ways of birth and dying, the way to the ancestors and so on, to a hard, metallic, impatient tone. The elegy today is about loss of another order – that arising from social and political turmoil and instability.

Nigerian poet J P Clark wrote this in a volume concerned with Nigerian civil strife that erupted in 1967 and continued, leaving unspeakable famine, disease and dead bodies in its trail, especially in the breakaway eastern region of Biafra:

> caucuses at night, caucuses by day,
> With envoys, alien and local,
> Coming and going, in and out
> Of the strongroom. What briefs
> In their cases? The state,
> Like a snake severed of its head,
> Lies threshing in blood, and
> Unless a graft at once is found,
> The bird will flee the tree.
> ('The Usurpation' by Clark, 1970: 56)

His compatriot and poet Christopher Okigbo died in action for Biafra in that war. He had invoked the talking drums to 'hide us; deliver us from our nakedness...' The drums should sound a message of warning, he urged, of collective effort against political power gone insane.

Nigerian poet and playwright Wole Soyinka celebrated life and the inner mysteries of Yoruba thought and belief in his earlier lyrics. During and after imprisonment (1968 and beyond) for speaking out against the warlords who plunged the country into civil war, Soyinka's lyrics take on an elegiac tone. He mourns the replacement of Nigeria's beauty by the 'flowers that fill the garden of decay.'

> From a distant
> Shore they cry, Where
> Are all the flowers gone?
> I cannot tell
> The gardens here are furrowed still and bare.
> Death alike
> We sow. Each novel horror
> Whets inhuman appetites
> I do not
> Dare to think these bones will bloom tomorrow
> ('Flowers for my Land' by Kofi Awonoor, in Soyinka, 1972: 62.)

Ghana's Kofi Awoonor, one of the most accomplished lyricists, could in the past poignantly record the ordeal of being:

> Caught between the anvil and the hammer
> In the forging house of a new life,
> Transforming the pangs that delivered me
> Into the joys of new songs.
> ('The Anvil and the Hammer')

He has realized that the 'trappings of the past, tender and tenuous... are laced with flimsy glories of paved streets.' In the Ghana of today, as in the rest of self-ruled Africa, Awoonor smells blood in the air, amid all the political rhetoric and posturing:

> At the central committee today
> A vote was taken on democratic centralism
> It will be written next week
> Into the constitution
> Everything comes from God...
> Many more hymns shall we sing
> To the Pentecostal spirit,
> To the Paraclete,
> To grind our knives of war
> Ready for his coming,
> The war of the new season that is coming...
> ('Hymn to my Dumb Earth')

For the most part, African writers sing with a public voice: they speak with the voice of a high priest, of prophecy, and feel it in the blood and bones that their public is with them. What is functional to the African must of necessity speak to 'social concerns'; the poet sees the human and the aesthetic as indivisible. We want to live the ecstasy of the spoken word, the spoken metaphor. All the better when it is elevating as well. And there are people today who write to entertain, to inspire, to play games. Then again, when the times demand it, the poetry projects the voice of prophecy. In such a role, it does not analyse or 'explore' in the common usage of the term, because it is so close to the ancient shout, or wail, or sense of wonder or cautionary speech that first found expression in figurative signs.

We are back to the image of the tortoise. Earlier I said that ethnic demands tend to ignore the many tensions that operate in a literary work. Especially when such demands set themselves against others, such as we see in the African-American world. If the tortoise created by the literary establishment won't yield what people want for an immediate social purpose, then they will try to create another thing. Yet those who would try to turn their words into bullets are asking language to do something on impossible terms. The African American Don L Lee warns in a poem of his that he 'ain't seen no poems stop a .38... no stanzas break a honkie's head... no metaphors stop a tank.' Until his similes can protect him from the police, he concludes: 'I guess I'll keep my razor I & buy me some more bullets.'

If you want to say what is on your mind in order to move people to action, you speak the prose they use every day. Poetry is no such language. Even when the tortoise itself forages on social reality, like the speech rhythms of common man, you have created something in the tortoise that will remind you the imagination works in non-prosaic ways. A lot more goes into the making of a novel, poem, and prose drama than the writer may have intended. He creates a metaphor that must by its very nature be loaded with layers of meaning. That crowd waiting to be galvanized into action has neither the capacity nor the inclination for this game. You may not have intended to invest the creature with a shell, but it grew anyhow!

Among the writers who imply these tensions in their prose statements is Ghanaian poet, Kofi Awoonor. The poet unites sensibilities, he says: 'I insist upon technical competence because anybody can say anything, but how well you say it is contingent upon your understanding of both worlds and therefore of yourself as an artist.' The clause 'how well you say it' is important to note, lest one jump to the conclusion that Awoonor is invoking Western techniques. South Africa's Dennis Brutus is another: 'I have tried not to preach about racism or to make political speeches about racism in my poetry because I really believe that there is a thing called artistic integrity.'

Am I saying that ethnic/racial priorities count for nothing in the long run, because the tortoise won't yield to group demands, i.e. beyond the intellectual ritual? They *do* count for something, because as a social reality they help us comprehend and validate the cultural revolt of a group. If literature is going to be written at all, then a group has the right to determine what language it is going to restore and exercise a propriety over, seeing that the dominant culture fashioned a language (in both figurative and literal senses) that is meant to maintain its supremacy, to express aspirations that often stand in opposition to those of the group it colonized. The dominant culture has control of the mass media, most of the publishing, school curricula in educational institutions and so much else, even when the initial stage of democracy has been won.

The pressing literary necessities count for nothing if they mean to lift literature into the transcendental realm where it can pretend that those tensions between the tortoise and its creator do not exist. On the other hand, let us bear in mind that the tortoise cannot forever pretend that it can jive with the man-in-the-street, without ever tipping over helplessly on its back, feet up. The tortoise will listen to a few readers meeting together to consult him, if they want more than the ritual that literature can be as language revitalized, more than just a mirror of themselves. He will move them according to their individual capacities. If you want him to participate in human quarrels, if you want to send poems out into the battlefield, you have to make him differently. But because you are using figurative language to say more than just one thing at one time, you cannot expect him always to speak plainly. You may find him too clumsy for your purpose. Some of your audience may even feel there are more important things to do 'beyond all this fiddle', as American poet, Marianne Moore, puts it. You fight revolutions and other political and social issues in the arena where they happen; you do it as a man or woman among other men and women. In your private corner you work out a literary composition, giving your full attention to the crafting of it so that it comes out as a work of art. For this latter you require tools that do not work in the arena where intellectual analysis, rhetoric, exposition and hardware apply.

Literature need not wait for conscription or the draft to become a vehicle of revolutionary passion either, although it may sensitize us to the need for it. We need constant control of language, and always we want literature to help us gain this. To the extent that it portrays human endeavour, human possibilities and frailties, and is a thrust of the imagination, a renewal of language, and a source of knowledge, it must always be revolutionary. The ideal that sees sectional goals based on racial or ethnic demands (in the broadest sense of 'ethnic') being collectively realized out of individual sensibilities shows a tremendous, if desperate, act of faith that cuts across the intrinsic tensions. For life out there operates by other rules. It is the politician and manipulators of the economy who determine our welfare and make or trigger actual revolutions, whether sane or otherwise. They regulate our lives at vital levels. The politician can order us to be shot and institute a commission of inquiry afterwards to establish how and why we died. He may even offer to confess his guilt before a truth commission in order to buy a reconciliation certificate and amnesty. On the economist's counsel or without, a political authority can order us to go to war. Indeed, writers should be grateful that they can be read by *some constituency*. They can slot in at some point up and down the vertical range and across a wide spectrum of interests, according to the individual writer's accessibility and meaningful content for the reader.

On the other hand, if you, the writer or the audience, do not regard the tortoise (i.e. literature) as 'necessary', keep out of its way. But would you *dare? Would you* really?

It is evident that for the part of the world whose material resources are still vastly underdeveloped, questions literature will always ask will include: after the deluge, then what? What more should and can we say? When we have done flinging missiles at political, religious or other authorities, maybe even subdued or suppressed them, do we go back to the forge to make us more and other weapons for confronting the new order? How can literature, being a compulsive cultural act, survive the mass media, e.g. television, and the boomcha-boomcha and gumba-gumba of stereo music whose sounds are all-pervasive in town and country, night and day? What about the rumour – valid – that not far off in the future the written word will become redundant in the face of the electronically-recorded word side by side with the visual image? What will become, then, of the power and resonance of the written word? What will happen to the book library and all the other printed media? In the face of all these, how can we prevent speech deteriorating to monosyllables and meaningless exclamations such as 'Terrific!' 'Stunning!' 'Super!' 'Simply hilarious!' and so on?

My Destiny is Tied to Africa – 1973

Synopsis by Ndavhe Ramakuela

Perhaps more than in any other article that Mphahlele has written, this response to criticism by Prof Addison Gayle Jr shows us a man who, though compassionate and humble, is nevertheless firm and will not be pushed around; a man who stands his ground, particularly when it concerns his identification with Africa or when his sense of dignity is challenged.

The charge made against him in the review of Voices in the Whirlwind *is, among others, that the book leans too much to the West, a point that Mphahlele does not take kindly to. He asserts his Africanness, without necessarily showing his indebtedness to Africa during the journeys he made while in exile, and reminds his critic that even his teachings were based on African experiences and literature. In all the wanderings, Mphahlele attests, his heart and actions have always been rooted in Africa. Besides being a rebuttal, this essay stands alone as one man's explicit and hard-nosed defence of a bond established between him and his community.*

'What I am primarily concerned with in my book is the level at which the imagination is shaped, cultural imperatives are determined, language is appropriated and released, and so on.'

Mphahlele reaffirms that his connection with the West may only have served to strengthen his already existing love and respect for humanity. He argues a case for the interconnectedness of cultures and indulges his view that no one culture can claim superiority over the other; cultures enrich and complement one another in different and complex ways, and to be familiar with other cultures need not be read as a betrayal of, or alienation from, one's own.

I find Prof. Addison Gayle's review of my book, *Voices in the Whirlwind and Other Essays*, the most damaging indictment I have ever received. After reading it several times over, I wonder what it is in the book he finds 'moving'. He has constructed an image of me as a kind of Afro-Saxon or Euro-African who can't be trusted to speak for Africa, and is still less fitted to penetrate black American writing. In the light of this, whatever complimentary remarks he makes about me make less and less sense to me.

Why? Why the attack? Has communication broken down? Mr Gayle swiftly assesses my analysis of black poetry and cultures with a few complimentary words and then launches into answers to questions *he himself* raises, leaving my text way behind, because he imagines I am too much in love with the West to look that far ahead. And yet he read the book twice, he says. I want to put the record straight, as I feel my integrity is in question.

There are two levels of approach to Western culture by any people that has once been colonized by it: what I may call the utility level and the philosophical. My book explores the encounter between Western and African cultures and the poetry of the black world in situations of political conflict. I make a number of observations along the way of the areas in which Africa is absorbing elements of Western culture at the utility level, as a historical necessity. For me, literature as a product of the imagination, and the dynamics of culture in general, offer ample opportunity for empirical enquiry and to understand what makes a people do one thing and not another. The choices they make help shape their response to the philosophical assumptions of the West.

There is plenty of corruption in the West, but we must eat, dress, go to school, trade with the technicians and technology and so on. Which is all I mean when I say: 'It is perhaps the Western elements of these cultures that will yet be the unifying force as a common medium.' Prof. Gayle must surely know that this is what is happening in Africa. But he climbs on the philosophical level, ignores what I say at the utility level, and indicts me fiercely on the basis of his own reiterations of what is now acknowledged historical fact: the stink of the West. Where I make open-ended statements because I don't pretend to have the answers, he insinuates conclusions that he wishes I had made, in order to justify his image of me.

It is surely no news to anybody that the West has for a long time been engaged in destruction, acquisitive acts, racism and so on. What I am primarily concerned with in my book is the level at which the imagination is shaped, cultural imperatives are determined, language is appropriated and released and so on. *This* is always new. His parting shot at the end of the review, which clinches the superior pedagogical tone of the whole piece, is: 'One senses from his book that he is both an honest writer and a good man. For one who has been so long involved with the West, this is a remarkable achievement.' Indeed, a tone that is a mixture of accusation, rebuke, caution, harangue, exasperation, embarrassment, doubt as to whether he likes the book or not, grudging admiration and so on.

Prof. Gayle says I have been 'involved with the West.' From the substance of his essay, it is clear that he is using the phrase in the same sense in which we speak of a love affair. If anyone can come to this conclusion after reading this book, then there is nothing I can say that will disabuse him. He cannot mean by 'involved' that I have been arguing and quarrelling and grappling with the furies the West rained over

Africa. Because he would then not need to say that, in spite of it, my book is a 'remarkable achievement.'

I learned English seriously at the age of thirteen, speaking my mother tongue at home and in the streets and English only in the classroom. I write in English as a nuisance I have to put up with. I taught in a ghetto school and worked as a journalist in African communities. Out of the thirty years I have been teaching, I have spent five years to date in the United States, distributed over two periods.

The twenty-five remaining years were spent teaching Africans. Even when I was based in France for two years (1961-1963), my cultural work was done in Africa. The first time I ever had whites in my class was when I came to teach in America in 1966. I have been through all the things Gayle says I have experienced under colonialism. Yes, I went through a Western system of education. My literary models had to be from the Western world. Right from the time I found myself in the centre of educational politics in South Africa, and was by the same token launched into the bitter fight against education for slavery, I knew that I had crossed the Rubicon. In those years – the early 1950s, after we had fallen foul of government banning orders – we were also reading news reports of the black civil rights movement in this country. We had in the late 1940s read Richard Wright, Jean Toomer, Langston Hughes, Rudolph Fisher, Du Bois, Garvey, Baldwin, and so on. We saw our position as Africans in immediate terms, in which we felt the muscle of white power. And always the echoes of the civil rights movement in this country assured us that we were not alone.

After I left South Africa at the age of thirty-seven, I entered another dialogue – the dialogue that had reference to the colonial presence, the European acculturation, which had never been the issue in the politics of racism in my country. The white man's physical presence, his police, his army, big policies of segregation, all these engaged all our faculties. I have said in my introduction to *Down Second Avenue* (Doubleday, 1972) that political struggle defines a culture, 'that you don't jump out of a cultural cocoon, do battle out there, and return to fit snugly back into it'; that culture and political struggle define and feed on each other all the way. That's how it was and still is in Southern Africa.

This other colonial presence in Africa north of Zambezi was something else. In my own intellectual growth, which is recorded all the way through my writing career, I came to recognize the connections between one part of the white world and the others, the unity of purpose in the white world. I felt free in those early days of exile in Nigeria, because for the first time I could *function* and see the fruits of my work, both as a teacher and as a writer. I was literally free of police terror, of physical and emotional tensions.

Prof. Gayle seems to think it is a sin for a man to glory in the freedom of others when he has not enjoyed freedom in his own territory. Because, as he says: 'what after all does freedom mean for the *writer*? It is not, as Mphahlele seems to suggest, some metaphysical thing outside of any reference except the determination of one man to recognize the humanity of another...' And yet he says in the next paragraph that I understand all this, i.e. that freedom 'is a shared experience of all men, which unless it be the experience of all men, is the "experience" of no man.' I repeat, I have the freedom to function when I work in independent Africa. That is when I am allowed to. I find the fulfilment I would not find in the police state that South Africa is. If the book under review suggests for Gayle that freedom is 'some metaphysical thing', or that I am so drunk with the freedom I found in other parts of Africa that I have forgotten the nature of the beast, he should illustrate it with specific examples from the text.

Look again at what I say in the book: 'As writers we (South African exiles) are more like disembodied voices that echo from hill to hill. Our audience is as vaguely constituted as that which T S Eliot conceived of as "intelligent man". And this won't do. It knocks the bottom out of poetry as ritual: And only as ritual can it contain conflict.' How then, I ask, can I – as Gayle puts it – be unaware that wherever I go in the West, I shall be an outsider, an alien, 'never able to sing the songs of (my) fathers'?

Indeed, in paragraph after paragraph of his essay, Prof. Gayle seems bent on registering just this message that I am an outsider, even in relation to that part of the Afro-American world he purports to be speaking for whenever he says 'we'. 'The freedom which he was denied in South Africa,' Prof. Gayle says, 'exists for him nowhere under Western skies, and his assertion that it does makes a mockery of the very term.' He lashes me to a pillar, as in the above statement, and says in effect: *Let's see you get yourself out of that!*

If I say yes, I do have this 'illusion', then I am a sick man. If I say I know some freedom outside South Africa, then I am defending the West, which, in Mr. Gayle's terms, defines the human universe. This is an unfortunate method of reviewing a book. As also when he drives his car through a whole puddle of metaphors past me, so that *some* mud will get me. For instance: the Algerian metaphor; Western skies; the beautiful, diseased woman; what in Western culture makes black men forget those many thousands gone; the rape of Africa by major Western powers; stepchild of the West ...

So, I won't be fenced in or baited. Suffice it to say I know what freedoms I have outside South Africa, and how I can use them; I know what freedoms I don't have – not even under black skies. I also know what a spiritual ghetto exile is. My book should have made this much clear to Prof. Gayle. Not even he can deny that, although he is not altogether free, he is much more so than the African black, let alone his own great-great-grandfathers. He can function better. I wonder why he wants to project his sense of guilt about these freedoms into my situation, as if he were privately grateful to Western man for them. Why does he think that, because I cherish certain freedoms, I glorify the West for it and don't care about the 'thousands gone'?

Which brings me to the point about 'involvement with the West' that I began by querying. My intellectual journey; my involvement with Africa since I was born; the questions I have tried to grapple with in my teaching; the quest for meanings of literature and its function in Africa; my role in the campaign to give African literature prominence or supremacy in African high schools and universities; my role in workshops for creative writing and African theatre; my active participation in the creation of idioms in music, drama, fiction and poetry hammered out of the very substance and essence of Africa. All these and other activities: why does Prof. Gayle write them off and charge me with being 'involved' with the West? I say to myself: maybe because Prof. Gayle knows my ambivalence, which he also calls 'a dualism of spiritual dimensions'; maybe because I have for so long talked about the West I must be in love with it, so strongly that it is remarkable I can express the ideas I do!

I shall not pretend that up until I was thirty, particularly all the time I was studying for a BA degree, I did not glory in my conquest of knowledge: Western literature and science, the history of revolutions in Europe, some of the ideas of the West, and so on. I had to survive my ghetto existence. I had to use my imagination to conquer Western techniques of resistance for the benefit of my people. I was a teacher and I wanted to be a writer. And I am not ashamed that I was intrigued, nor are the millions of Africans I represent. It was only the high-water mark in a process that had begun generations before. The conquest of the written word in grade school fired our imagination. After this period of enchantment, we (i.e., those of my generation) came to realize that our activities would have to be geared towards the restoration of an equilibrium, the creation of African institutions. There would have to be a synthesis, a process Gayle hates so much. But evidently he has been luckier than we in Africa: he can easily dump the whole thing, at any rate intellectually.

I don't know where he was born – whether in an urban or rural setting. Whatever the case may be, he was born in the West, learned English on his mother's lap, went through a Western system of schooling, was surrounded all his life by Western technology, literature, privilege and poverty, arts, and so on. Who has been involved with the West longer and more deeply – he or I? I mean *involved* in the sense of immersion. Everyone who has ever been colonized has two selves and, therefore, is ambivalent. When it is Mphahlele who is ambivalent, beware of him! Gayle, immersed as he is even now in Western life, more deeply than I am in Africa, can be sure exactly what parts of the West he needs to subsist and what he is rejecting; if he can be dead sure that there is no synthesis going on inside his personality, he is a miracle of creation. If he refuses to acknowledge he is already a product of Africa and the West, and no area of indigenous African culture claims him, then, it seems, he has defined himself as a veritable product of the West.

It is easy to be sure about the evil of the West and its immensity; it is obvious in all the ugly events past and present. How can one be sure concerning matters of

432

everyday life: technology, communications, family life and so on? Can Prof. Gayle give me an example of a people on the earth who have assimilated Western technology without adopting some of the cultural assumptions that are organic to it, like the concept of time and organization of family life?

You cannot speak a language, like English, without swallowing the cultural assumptions it expresses. And once the dialogue is set off between selves in a human personality, a synthesis must be arrived at. Either Prof. Gayle thinks I am incapable of arriving at a synthesis, because, according to him, 'the West retains its hypnotic fascination' for me, or synthesis is irrelevant. And what proof does he present for this notion? He finds it in my tentative statement that Africa may be at a disadvantage for its capacity to contain change, if we can say this without justifying the colonial destruction of some African cultures.

Gayle pushes his attack further. I must be madly in love with the West when I say that the bridge between African tradition and urban life may lie in the 'Western elements' of these cultures. By 'elements' I mean technological communications, including formal education and literature. For instance, the railroad and the truck have brought about tremendous mobility in Africa. Market towns have become bigger and more cosmopolitan as a result. Musicians have brought traditional idioms to the towns and, with the guitar, have adapted their ethnic idioms to their urban needs.

We use modern techniques in our productions of African plays – such as sets and other designs. Modern government has brought together in legislative and executive institutions people from diverse ethnic groups, institutions that form the basis for nation building, whether governments be one-party or multi-party or military. Western law has yielded tools not only for the establishment of a collective consciousness, but also the codification of African traditional law and custom. These are some of the 'elements' I am talking about. What's wrong with dualism if you can use it for the advancement of national interests, and if you can, through national institutions, maintain equilibrium? Is Gayle free of any cultural dualism? Why does he think that the use of Western elements means their 'glorification'?

Why should I not, after having been immersed in the writing techniques and a language of the West by historical accident, not be aware of and feel the paradox of standards and audience and tradition? Is Prof. Gayle exasperated by the fact that I do not give clear-cut answers to these questions? Tough luck: I do not have them. I do not have the capacity and wisdom and certainty that he enjoys in defining his own truth.

I am arrogant enough to believe that my views represent a very large segment of Africa in this whole matter of 'dualism', that I am reporting Africa at first hand. We are working at the grassroots level; we are not yet bored with 'progress', wealth, abundance of goods and so on – as so much of the West is – because we do not have them. This will account for the sense of adventure that I hope my book reveals. It is also Africa's sense of adventure. I believe that Africa will evolve its own methods of dealing with the West, of containing it, methods that defy any formula based on a simplistic total rejection – even as I criticize some of its leadership; and I am not alone in this. I am aware of a new scholarship and new methods that are emerging among Africans. They will get there. We are more optimistic than Prof. Gayle is.

Prof. Gayle baffles me when, in search for a 'central thesis' in my collection of essays, he tests what I say about Africa against his own formulations regarding the Black Aesthetic. I am recording African thought and attitudes as the times change and I change too. He understands all this. Because he has got his sights fixed on the Black Aesthetic star, up there, which is all-inclusive, he loses sight of the realities Africa has to come to terms with. He insists on reading into my writing his own condition: he sees me as 'torn by dualism of spiritual dimensions'. He refuses even to believe that I have discarded a considerable part of the West, as indeed Africa is doing all the time. In his insistence that I am in love with the West, he must cast doubt on my rejection of much of its teachings, including Christianity. 'We believe,' he asserts, 'that Mphahlele accepts it (i.e. my dumping of the Christian god) being more true than it actually is; that he still retains little more than "reverence" for his ancestors and their culture.'

He is baiting me. He has the text in front of him. Why does he abandon the more sensible method of examining my text for the dangerous venture of mind reading? His phrase 'little more than "reverence" for his ancestors' indicates that he does not think much of the word 'reverence'. I used the word to mean 'a feeling and act of profound awe and respect and love' that I have for my ancestors. African scholars try to avoid 'worship' because the term does not define accurately our relationship with our ancestors, nor even our connection with the Supreme Force. They are, among my people, intercessors. But enough of this. As one of Chinua Achebe's characters in *Things Fall Apart* says, we do not fight for our gods.

I keep asking myself what specifically in my book leads Prof. Gayle to form an image of me as some kind of survivor from a holocaust, a victim of shell shock, as a man who has come out into the glare of the sun and can't take it, having stayed so long in the dark of the Western world: 'the Western assault on his intellectual sensibilities'; 'South Africa provided him with terrifying experiences'; 'hypnotic fascination' (for the West); 'what does he glorify in the West?' If all this and more has happened to me, he says, 'then the central thesis of *Voices In the Whirlwind* is never stated.'

I don't understand the connection between what he says the West has done to me and the next paragraph about the lack of a 'central thesis'. Then he continues and locks me up in the cage that he assigned in the beginning to Wright and Wheatley. The theme – (and not the 'central thesis', due to the nature of the essays) – is what justifies my having put them together, and what makes the pieces hang together: it is my examination of the literatures and other aspects of culture in the black world. How are language and socio-political styles used in response to aggression from the

Western world and to its political power? I always take the empirical view in such matters. My essays are therefore *exploratory* most of the way. I don't peddle in dogma. Whatever assertions Prof. Gayle may make about a Black Aesthetic, the works of the imagination, through the language they have appropriated, will at least indicate the signposts to, and give us glimpses of, our own reality. So I examine each part of the black world according to the cultures that yield literary works, because that is the reality most accessible to me. I try as much as possible not to apply one single yardstick to all literatures and cultural styles. Certainly I compare and contrast. In the title essay I reproduce poetry to help me penetrate the social forces that produce it and see how its language deals with such forces.

I point out what I see in black American diction that is informed by blues, jazz and speech rhythms. I say I find it most moving. Within the limited scope of the essay – it is only about forty thousand words – I tried to show how, in each of the three theatres of black literature, poets have responded to revolutionary times from one cycle of consciousness to another. I make it clear, even though Prof. Gayle thinks my analyses are 'sketchy', that the new black American poetry seeks to harmonize Afro-American goals, and that it talks about the concerns of both the elite and the masses – unlike the poetry inspired by Negritude in Africa. I make the point that the Negritude movement in francophone West Africa began as an elite concern; its protagonists allowed it to get into the hands of Europeans, who continued to define it for them. Also, although I did not explicitly say so, the francophone elites in Africa – while they communed among themselves about their alienated condition – addressed themselves to Europe in the 1930s, and later turned back to home ground. Prof. Gayle understands all this, and acknowledges it. Yet he has this to say as well: 'There is the impression that, had Mphahlele moved forward in his explication of African-American poetry, he would have applied the same censure to the proponents of the Black Aesthetic.' Why does Gayle keep making wild assumptions like this? How do I move from an analysis of black American poetry as an earthy mode of expression serving the interests of a revolution in black consciousness, to the point where I dismiss the Black Aesthetic 'elite-orientated'?

I ask questions about the Black Aesthetic. But he puts assertions into my mouth. Assertions that suggest that I have already discovered what the Black Aesthetic is: it is 'little more than one to which Western writers have long ago ascribed', 'little more than the stepchild of the West'. That is what, he says, I have arrived at! Evidently what exasperates Gayle is the fact that I use the Western aesthetic as a sounding box: 'Knowing what is being rejected may throw light on what the new product will be.' I don't say anywhere that there is no black uniqueness in aesthetics. I use Christopher Caudwell's *On the Beginnings of Poetry* because, as I indicate in no uncertain terms, he defines for me in the best way I know those origins of poetry that black American writers, as a chorus, are revitalizing for their audience: song, emotive statement that use symbols and metaphor, and so on. And there is nothing Western about these origins: that is how poetry began as a human need – the need to take charge of one's environment and spiritual forces through ritual. I quote I A Richards because he says something about communication that I find relevant in a discussion of poetry as direct speech and as a contemplative statement. The West has no monopoly on the essence of communication. Statements about the Black Aesthetic have so far had reference to the easily recognizable attributes or areas of it, e.g. music, speech patterns, theatre, point of view: aspects one does not have to define in relation to the Western aesthetic. A look at the titles alone of the essays Prof. Gayle edited recently, *The Black Aesthetic,* confirms this. For the literary critic and the practitioner who produces works of the imagination it is only a general philosophical framework or guide – useful as it is for the *social interpretation* of the black experience and as background to the study of literature. There has been no book on the analytical approach to black imaginative literature until this year, when Stephen Henderson published his outstanding and thorough document of critical standards – *Understanding The New Black Poetry* – at least a year after I had finished mine. Henderson devises a system here that we should use in the approach to black American poetry. In a way I could never have done, he uses as his tools the same elements I mention in my book, and which I refer to as the most readily recognizable features of the Black Aesthetic – speech and music. And he arrives at a critical element he calls *saturation:* a very valuable term indeed. But I don't apologize for using some Western elements that I accept as valuable statements for the understanding of the origins of poetry and the writer-audience relationship. If Gayle chooses to regard my selective approach in this respect as a sign of a 'hypnotic fascination' with the West, there is nothing I can do about it. I have never at any time even suggested that the Black Aesthetic is a stepchild of the West.

As Prof. Gayle uses a quote from an essay on African cultures from which to launch his indictment against me for virtually or actually glorifying the West, I feel constrained to ask a few questions. There are areas we can categorically identify in which the West, as a system, has wrought and is still wreaking havoc. Africa does not need to be lectured on this: racism, Sharpeville, Indo-China, the Middle Passage, and so on. Gayle goes further. He cautions that one cannot separate Zola from Napoleon, Goethe from Hitler, Tolstoy from Stalin, Thoreaux from Nixon, the beauties of European art from slavery. Would Prof. Gayle quarrel with Africa for its selective approach to the West, because if we touch one thing we are tainted with the whole system? Are black Americans going to sing or play only black music? Is Leontyne Price not to sing Verdi? Is no black actor to act in plays of the Western world? Should Duke Ellington have performed only black music? Should Paul Robeson have sung only black songs? It burnt me up to see Russian crooks link up with the other crooks of the West, to see them hug one another and take garden strolls and junkets while American bombs rained over Vietnam and Cambodia. But even so we are not surprised. Asians are the victims. And then we see China – now a mighty industrialized giant – linking up with the West. How tainted are the Chinese with the West, how much of its power structure has it resisted? Japan is trading with South Africa in spite of European racism and oppression. Aren't we seeing, in fact, a shift in the centres of power that cuts across ethnic aesthetic values and/or fixes them in the geographical place that contains them? Is Prof. Gayle not in fact idealistic in thinking of a Black Aesthetic as a transcendental, Utopian force that will live above the prosaic imperatives of survival, existence and self-interest? Again these are questions, and Prof. Gayle must not go off again and anticipate my answers, because I don't have any.

We can identify the collective vices: the dog-eat-dog competitive mania, the cannibalism, the persecution not only of blacks but also of whites by whites, and so on. I cannot spend sleepless nights worrying on behalf of the West over these vices. Nor am I, as Gayle implies, about to set out on a mission to save the West from itself. I suggest no such program. Indeed, in my revised edition of *The African Image,* and elsewhere, I emphasize the need for Africa to stop parading itself in the eyes of the world through huge arts festivals presided over by Europeans like Malraux; to stop thinking that we can peg African culture so as to preserve it. We need to begin talking to our own people, exploring with them the inner strengths and weaknesses, the potential of our cultural selves. At the same time we need to confront our poverty, ignorance and diseases.

There are situations involving the West that define at one time its collective guilt and at another time cut across it. This identification of collective guilt has serious implications for the black world, and it will continue to plague us whatever certitudes Gayle may rightly catalogue for us. A statement of the problem will say something about my empirical approach towards certain issues in the cultural encounter between the West and Africa – an approach that works from a base of cultural particulars, symbols and images, up to concepts and generalizations – and about Prof. Gayle's dogmatism and monolithic republic. I gather from Gayle's account of the collective guilt of the West – Zola and Napoleon, Goethe and Hitler, and so on – that he means the stink of Western morality permeates everything they produce, material and aesthetic.

He can't simply mean that to understand Zola we must understand Napoleon, and vice versa. It is collective guilt he is talking about. He must mean that in the Black Aesthetic, life will be so integrated that, if you juxtaposed the names of writers, businessmen, politicians and so on, you would find no disparities because of a collective responsibility of a higher order we have; on the one side, Africa and the Caribbean on the way to self-determination before and after formal independence, and the blacks of the two Americas on the other, besieged but working towards their emancipation. Doing all this while sharing in considerable measure the techniques and language of the

Western world. I appreciate that Prof. Gayle can best speak about his part of the black world, and he must appreciate that I know independent and colonial Africa better.

In a situation of political conflict, it makes plenty of emotional sense to conceive of a monolithic image of the enemy. In Africa and the Caribbean, where blacks have of historical necessity had to use Western technology and systems of education and administration to overthrow colonial rule and develop their countries, we realize that the unity of political and cultural sensibilities that was so necessary in the fighting days cannot any longer be taken for granted. The cultural conditions in which life was integrated do not exist anymore in their original preliterate forms. Political institutions have developed in typical Western style, independently of traditional mores. There has come about a considerable degree of dissociation between politics and public morality. Elite governments can and do exist with or without public censure. Whether we like it or not, we must work towards a synthesis. Walk up and down Africa and the Caribbean and you will see vast areas of synthesis. This is a historical fact. Instead of moaning and bleating like a goat giving birth, we are working on the Africanisation of our institutions. We are beginning to see in independent Africa what has been happening in colonial Africa. But for different reasons that are related to power, writers like Wole Soyinka, the late Christopher Okigbo, Camara Laye and others have already fallen foul of official wrath in their own countries. I do not need to be lectured on the fact that the African leaders whom I censure 'for mistreatment of blacks, and the African middle class that places material values above spiritual ones... have been culturally twisted and dehumanised by white nationalism.' Gayle says I fail to understand this. I actually point out in my book that critics of African establishments have to resolve the dilemma in which they find themselves as members of the same culture as the leaders they censure. Blacks criticize one another in America, from the highest platforms of enlightenment to the playground where pea-shooting passes for literary criticism. Shall we say these critics fail to appreciate what the white man has made of their people?

We have attained a phase in which we realize that because of historical imperatives and the systems we have inherited, politics and economics determine a vital segment of our lives, as they do in the Western world. Presumably in Prof. Gayle's republic this dissociation will disappear: the functions of the writer, the artist, the musician, the intellectual, the politician, the government, the church minister, the lawyer, the teacher, the artisan, the farmer and the doctor will all become integrated in a single-ness of purpose. No wars, no destruction or other evils, all of which I write down to economics, greed and the misuse of power. I regard the dissociation of these elements in a differentiated society as another manifestation of what Prof. Gayle calls white nationalism. 'To move towards the Black Aesthetic is to come like one naked from the womb,' Gayle says, 'having cast aside the old definitions, symbols and metaphors of the West.' My inference about an integrated, all-inclusive black republic is based on 'statements' like this one, on his description of the Western aesthetic in terms of the evils it has perpetrated against all the 'darker peoples', in terms of the collective guilt that connects Zola with Napoleon, and so on. Obviously, we cannot discuss one without the other, the arts independently of history. But how *far* does Mr. Gayle dare to carry his idea of collective guilt? If writers and artists of the West are as guilty as the politicians and businessmen and the army, would he want to apply this formula to black societies, even in Utopia? Where would he place Alexander Dumas, Pushkin? Even were his republic attainable, how could he get away from the unalterable fact that there must *exist* an Establishment, a police force, political campaigns, business interests and other institutions of power? In the event of a foul-up because of conflict or collusion of interests, would he still damn the black writers and artists together with the representatives of these interests? Gayle will answer that in his republic the Black Aesthetic will prevent a dissociation of these interests. I respect his idealism.

He goes for big stakes. As a teacher and a writer I deal with personalities, their potentialities, their collective and socializing energies, and their physical and human environment – elements I can handle because they are the basic realities I am in immediate contact with. My book should be clear evidence of the levels I am operating on. I search for meanings so that I can in turn help my students, the young struggling writers of poetry or fiction or drama who grapple with language as a way of coping with and communicating their social reality.

Prof. Gayle is way beyond me. If he is addressing himself to a black American audience, and if he is expressing its corporate will, then it's not for me to pass judgement. If he wants this also to define African cultural imperatives, he'd better forget it. Even in reference to the black American world, I have my doubts about being able to 'move towards the Black Aesthetic ... like one naked from the womb,' much as I commend in my book the creation of new symbols and metaphors.

I repeat: politicians and businessmen run our lives in Africa, whether we like it or not, because of the dissociation of functions and roles which we have to deal with in various ways. The man in power is never going to be actively moved by a poem or a novel. The author of imaginative literature – the artist in general – is performing a cultural act. He always has to revitalize language and experience in this sense; he is always revolutionary. He does not have to wait for conscription or the draft in times of social and political upheaval. But he must know that as a man of action he has to get out there among the crowds, primarily as a *man*. The crowds out there are busy fighting for survival; they are not waiting to read poems and novels, which is a 'Western bourgeois activity'.

Those crowds already have their own poetry, their own metaphors and symbols. The best the poet or novelist can do is to try to link up with this poetry and its metaphors among the children of the soil. If literature is to be written at all, black people must not lose by default. They must appropriate the language and release it, with the help of what the children of the soil say. I keep making this point in discussing a number of the new black poets. The writer is a two-legged paradox. He is engaged in the necessary cultural activity of keeping language alive and interpreting social realities for us – desperately necessary because, among other things, we want him, through language, to *increase our capacity to perceive and lead.* And yet he is peripheral to the pedestrian beat of our lives, where political and economic survival and thrust have taken control. He is writing a language readers must be educated to read. The novel in particular is for a leisured class, which in turn is a product of economic and land policies. Another dimension of the two-legged paradox is the fact that we writers of imaginative literature are part-time exploiters: we have a way of plundering and foraging for materials provided by the lives of suffering millions while we eat and dress well. We give little or nothing back, except the pulp, which reaches only those who have attained the level of education required to tune into our literature.

We must write, yet this cannot be a substitute for social action. We must reach back to the levels of existence that cannot wait for a Utopia, necessary though this is to remind us of the ultimate destiny we are shaping. If the Black Aesthetic glosses over this paradox at the levels of existence I am thinking of, and fails to help the writer resolve it; if the concept of the Black Aesthetic remains a dialogue for men like Prof. Gayle and me, independent of that control we desperately need over educational and mass media, we are playing games. It is at this pragmatic level where my lifelong concern has lain.

Gayle approvingly quotes Imamu Baraka as saying that 'we are not nationalists or black aestheticians because of the devil; we would be so if no devil existed.' Before the white man entered our history, this will have been so. Today, no people assert their nationalism and aesthetic unless it is threatened. In our history, the West has been a threat. Why else would we want *new* symbols, metaphors, gods? The concern for new symbols and metaphors and gods is common to the black world in general. The cultural manifestations of these concerns differ. And because these questions arise in confrontation with white power, my experience has taught me that the struggle redefines our cultures – whatever the Utopian notions may be – all the way. I don't see the chance or even the desirability of returning to the innocence of the womb. If Gayle thinks it is possible and desirable, he is far ahead of me, and I admire his vision and act of faith, however desperate.

Gayle does well at least to remind us in lofty terms that we need an ideal to live up to, although, alas, throughout his review essay he sets his notion of the Black Aesthetic against that of the West and defines it in relation to it. For my part, I take comfort in the knowledge that Africa is more optimistic than Gayle's circle. Also, in the hope that I have at least exposed Africa to black American poetry which is not read much or studied in that continent. In my revised and updated edition of *The African Image,* to be published next spring, I have reiterated some of these ideas, and tried to explore further the relationship between the black worlds. I have also pushed further my insistence that while we set for ourselves ideals that invoke a pan-Negro consciousness and ties (I use Negro, 'as always, in the healthy sense in which it is used in Africa and the Caribbean'), we must realize that, as Fanon says: 'Every culture is first and foremost national,' inasmuch as the problems which kept Richard Wright or Langston Hughes on the alert were fundamentally different from those which confront Léopold Senghor or Jomo Kenyatta; that, again to quote Fanon:

> The man who wishes to create an authentic work of art must realize that the truths of a nation are in the first place its realities. He must go on until he has found the seething pot out of which the learning of the future will emerge.

It is equally unrealistic for black Americans to hope that Africa can help them fight their cultural and political battles, or to project their own revolutionary goals into the African landscape. Africa, generally, has no psychological need for affiliation with American blacks. Black Americans need to go to Africa to see it as a present-day reality, not as an idea. And even then they are going to have to wait to be acknowledged, in the profoundest sense of the word; to be invited to share in African development. No Utopian rhetoric that conceives the whole black world constructing a common monolithic aesthetic, however noble and elevating the thoughts and feelings that inform that ideal, can afford to ignore the cultural and political specifics in the four main black worlds.

Prof. Gayle has sought to make it clear that I am an outsider where the black American is concerned. I have never pretended to be otherwise. But I understand something of the Afro-American's concern, and some of his literature – which Prof. Gayle says in effect that Mphahlele knows nothing about. The answer we give to his questionings, he actually says, 'cannot comfort either him or those who seek a synthesis between the Western and Black Aesthetics.' (My italics.) In these terms he writes me off. In the process, he writes off my attempts to arrive at the answer through an exploration of the literature before me. There is no reason why, if I am an outsider, I need to be comforted or distressed by any formulation of the Black Aesthetic as Afro-Americans see it for themselves. I know the levels at which, as a black man, I respond to what is being done to other black men outside my own culture, in a way I do not to what whites do to other whites. And yet Prof. Gayle must also know that the literary and cultural imperatives of Africa and the Caribbean will define what to reject from the West, even while we appropriate some of it and Africanise it. I shall continue to probe the Black Aesthetic, beyond the elements in it I have already acknowledged. My thanks, again, to Stephen Henderson's Understanding the New Black Poetry, which provides a unique critical principle.

The Role of the Writer at the Present Time – 1993

Synopsis by James Ogude

In this article, Mphahlele argues that every writer is a product of his or her own history, and that the writer's thoughts and feelings can be shaped by events and moments of world history whose impact registers on people as a world community. Thus South African writers cannot escape the influence of the global systems of communication or avoid the country's historical realities. He believes that younger writers in South Africa do not appreciate that art refines history, which he also calls reality. A good writer, to Mphahlele, is one who does more than merely document reality; he must also invent it. Invention of reality allows the writer to recreate it, which is a process of transcending it or searching for its meaning. At the same time, Mphahlele feels that for one to write competently, one has to read widely and extensively – in addition to continually doing exercises in writing.

On the future of writing in the South Africa, he wishes to see a more enterprising spirit, in which writers experiment with mixed media and languages – such as a mixture of South and North Sesotho and Tswana. He also wishes to see writers challenge publishers on works that are experimental in style and content; and should publishers continue to be prescriptive about what they wish to publish, then Mphahlele suggests that possibilities of setting up a publishing company owned by writers be looked into. Such a venture would make use of cheap material and make available literature, such as pamphlet stories, poetry, novellas, and drama, directed at the general market. Finally, Mphahlele argues a case for efforts to be directed at the creation of a body of translators who can find books in other languages that deserve translating into Sesotho.

You are a writer like any other in the rest of the world. But every writer, as every other artist, is a product of his or her own history – family, ethnic, territorial, and national history. There is also a sense in which a writer's thoughts and feelings are shaped by those events and moments of world history whose impact registers on us as a world community. For instance, we the people of South Africa cannot escape indefinitely the influence of communication systems that connect parts of the globe that are so far apart that such a link-up would have been inconceivable two or three decades ago. Print and electronic media are only a few among several networks that bring us in close touch with world history; the networks are also in themselves – in their very existence – moments of history. It has now become almost a cliché for us to state that the cruelties of our own history will leave their imprint upon our writing for many more generations to come. How could it be otherwise, when we have to consider a history of at least three hundred years?

What I think several of our younger writers do not appreciate, and still have to grapple with, is that art *refines* history – which can also be called, in concrete terms, *reality*. I could go so far as to say that history is a process made possible by reality in motion. Events, people, place, time, the universe – these sum up our reality. When reality moves, develops and breeds sets of realities, we are witnessing history in the making.

The writer works with real-life materials to compose a story, a poem, a play or an essay. But you do more than merely document reality. Journalists do this and there is a professional technique for it. They are writers too, of another kind. Indeed, serious journalism can rise to the level of what is called literary journalism. In this, the reporter elevates his style in a way that will capture real events with a passionate intensity. Let us think here mainly of the other writers – those who invent because they have to recreate reality. We do so because we are trying to search for a meaning of the piece of reality we are dealing with. This is a way of transcending reality. It is not, as happens in much writing, escaping it.

I should like to take it as a given that a writer must read widely and intensively as part of a process of self-education and enrichment; a writer must also write as an exercise even while he or she is waiting or preparing for the sustained period of work on a specific manuscript. This exercise may also serve as an initial activity in the shaping of the manuscript. (Read *Letter to a Beginner* and *The Art of a Writer and his Function* – both included in this book.)

I cannot presume to make projections about the fate of our African languages. But we should be continually asking ourselves if we are enterprising enough to venture into new regions, both in our styles and in the subjects we select. We are doing a disservice to our literary medium, our audience and ourselves if we stay fixed in a rut – or walk the goat path that others have scraped for generations with their hooves. Have we, for instance, ever contemplated writing a story or poem or play in a medium that is a mixture of South and North Sesotho and Setswana? We have, of course, been – and still are – slaves to our publishers, and perhaps even to the language bureaux and individuals they consult about manuscripts that reach them. We should be asking ourselves if we shouldn't become a pressure group within this organization, to persuade publishers and their advisers to entertain works that are experiments in style and content. The publishers are likely to respond that the school market gives them a livelihood and consequently they dare not upset the Education Department's plans as reflected in the syllabi for African languages. If this is the response, should we not be thinking seriously of the possibility of setting up our own publishing company? It could start small. The initial research should be into the use of newsprint instead of the standard paper used for books. This kind of paper is used in other parts of the world for pamphlet literature: stories, novellas, poetry and drama. And in our case, too, pamphlet literature need not be restricted to radically experimental writing. It's good writing, but the chief market is the general readership – without barring school children from obtaining the literature. It means that we could find many more outlets to sell the pamphlets than the conventional booksellers we have today: grocery shops, general dealers, marketplaces and so on.

And we need to consider translations. Are we making any concerted effort to create a body of translators who can find books in other languages that deserve translating into Sesotho? There should be a consensus among members – with the co-operation of people knowledgeable about the original language -- on the acceptance of any item for translation. I include English here.

Why I Teach My Discipline – 1973

Synopsis by James Ogude

In this essay, published as an address to the English faculty at the University of Denver, USA, in 1972, Mphahlele attempts to offer personal reasons why he has continued to teach English ever since 1945. Several historical conditions helped him to make up his mind, but three factors stand out. Coming from a disadvantaged background, English not only equipped him with vocational skills, but it also enabled him to gain access to the external world of knowledge, while literature in particular provided him with relief from the daily burden of oppression and violence inflicted on his people by the apartheid regime. When he was in exile and teaching in Nigeria, he could not help but notice the different ways in which different societies responded to English. Unlike in South Africa, in Nigeria English was a medium of self-realization and an economic weapon among the elite; in South Africa it remained a political and economic tool for the proletariat. It is no wonder that Mphahlele writes of his disappointment with the American students, who most often treated literature chiefly as a source of ideas and a site for contemplation on the deeper issues that afflict humanity. They paid too little attention to diction and other features of formal English. In the broadest sense of language and literature, Mphahlele writes, English helped him to bridge the communication gap across diverse cultural and ethnic boundaries; to discover the African self through a medium that combines an African sensibility with an English mode of expression; and to discover himself through an understanding of the meeting point between imitation and innovation. But more importantly, it helped him to find fulfilment and avoid anonymity in conditions of exile such as in America, where matters of literature and culture are taken lightly. Under such conditions, Mphahlele avers, the teaching of literature is the only way to preserve one's sanity.

It seems unavoidable, indeed most desirable, to think of teaching in close relation to the culture in which one belongs and which shapes one's dreams and reality.

I received my education up to the degree of Master of Arts in a culture I had been born into, a culture that for over three centuries since the coming of the 'Red Stranger' had been grappling with oppression and resistance, with all the conceivable things that make life insecure in a situation of racism, e.g. police terror, ghetto conditions, landlessness, forced residence and mobility, and forced labour.

What made me decide in 1945 to go and teach English in a ghetto school in Johannesburg? For one thing, teaching is my vocation. On my own terms, I do little else as successfully. For another, English was a compulsory component of the syllabus. I had to bring something else to the task: my love for the literature of the English-speaking world. A love every teacher in my schooldays had blissfully and unwittingly tried to murder. Joseph Addison, Richard Steele, Leigh Hunt, Alpha of the Plough, Dryden, Milton, some of Shakespeare's comedies, Dickens, Thackeray, Jane Austen, Walter Scott – try to imagine this forbidding line-up in an African setting. Consider that throughout my junior high-school days, 1935-1937 (let alone before that), and throughout the 1940s, mission schools allowed no one to teach English who was not of English stock. Only public schools were staffed entirely by black teachers, but they were poorly equipped. We had to pass exams; we had to succeed; our parents had little or no education; we had been told education was a key to power, and we wanted that – oh , how desperately we wanted that. So we had to chew on a lot of sawdust.

I came out of that bludgeoning with perhaps a fragment of Dickens, a chunk of undigested Shakespeare. I resisted Milton until I ceased to care which paradise was lost, which was regained – for the simple reason that the concepts of the fall of man and of hell are alien to African traditions. You take the good and the bad on this earth, strive, succeed in maintaining that delicate balance between individual aspirations and the communal will; suffer and endure, thrive, and then end up in the happy land of the ancestors. Yes, we had been virtually blackmailed into a Christian baptism. You might not have a birth certificate – in fact as a black man you couldn't have one – but a baptism certificate was irrefutable proof that you were once born and figuratively reborn, that your father and mother were identifiable, and the minister who patted your forehead with cold water couldn't possibly lie. But beneath the surface, the idea of original sin would always be a big puzzle in Africa...

I continued to read Dickens, Shakespeare and other authors avidly. I did all my university schooling by private study while I was raising a family. I subjected myself to a process of re-education. For the most part I had to find answers to my own questions. I rediscovered the classics that had fossilized in the ivory hands of many a desperate missionary spinster. During these years my love for English literature was reconfirmed. There is a close correlation, I am sure, between one's love for a discipline and the intensity of one's passion to teach it – if one is going to teach at all. Vanity, the urge for self-fulfilment, is an incentive of no mean proportions.

Somewhere along the line my high-school students and I discovered each other. Through the inspiration of my English professor, with whom I corresponded frequently as I could never afford vacation school, I was constantly asking myself questions relating to the value of poetry for me and my students and for the ghetto culture we were sharing – a culture very much an assertion of the human spirit fighting for survival against forces that threatened to fragment or break it. I was constantly asking myself what we could possibly learn from English culture, which was filtering through to us as we assimilated the thought structure and the ideas contained in the language and its literature.

The reasons for learning English were that it was compulsory; it was a key to job opportunities in that part of the private sector where white labour unions had little to lose if they let us enter in one's own community; and it gave us a sense of power to be able to master the external world which came to us in English: the movies, household appliances, styles of dress and cuisine, advertising, and printed forms that regulate some of the mechanics of living and dying. Also, you could carry on your education by private study and general reading if you had a mastery of the language skills. The political climate, the physical violence in the ghetto resisted any individual creative efforts and made the study of literature – particularly in a foreign language like English – look like playing a harmonica in the midst of sirens and power drills and fire brigade bells. It was the full recognition of these factors by student and teacher, I think, that conditioned the love we developed for English. A love that *had* to be self-generated – given all the hostile external factors. The element of escapism helped sustain that interest too. Only in later years did it occur to me that it was one short step to sheer snobbery. And snobbery is the cruellest joke anyone can play on oneself in a ghetto situation.

These were my grassroots beginnings as a teacher. When I went on to teach in Nigeria, the first stop in my exile, I was entering cultures that had not been disturbed much. They were self-sufficient; they were not threatened by political harassment or by racism. And yet the British-style examinations, almost as terrifying as the French baccalaureate that marks the end of the school year, afforded powerful motivation for learning English. In West Africa English could be a key to even bigger things, especially the civil service and the diplomatic service – unlike in South Africa, where these services are a white man's territory. The spirit of intellectual and creative independence, seized in earnest in Nigeria and the rest of West Africa from the beginning of the 1950s, gave rise to an exciting new phase in the production of indigenous poetry, fiction and drama written in English. This would hardly have happened if it had not been activated by the English literary forms the writers had assimilated. They used them to create a fusion with African history, mythology, setting, theatre and the symbolism these elements made available.

The similarities and contrasts between South and West Africa indicate that, where a community governs itself and can determine its destiny – other things being equal – a foreign culture may be assimilated by those who are so disposed or feel compelled by necessity; with the confidence that the native culture will be the richer for it. South

African writing in English by blacks has emerged both in spite of racism and because of it. English here is a political and economic weapon for a burgeoning proletariat. In West Africa it is a medium of self-realization, while serving as an economic weapon among an elite.

I repeat, these were my grassroots beginnings – where we grappled with syntax, semantics, paraphrase, précis, and the processes of comprehension, composition, and language at work as we see it in literature.

I came out of that tradition of education with an ingrained habit of mind, which is to read a text closely even before one contemplates the ideas that inform the litera-ture. We live on the fringe of ideas identified as Western. We therefore do not readily discuss the ideas or the philosophy that form the context of the poem. Since coming to the United States I have discovered how passionately students discuss ideas and the social milieu of a writer, even before they have exposed themselves fully to the language in the text. In Africa, the teacher tends more often to rely on the language and on correspondences between, say, an English situation and an African one – or lack of correspondences. I mean, it will in the final analysis not be important that an African does not know what a daffodil is when one deals with Wordsworth's *I Wandered Lonely as a Cloud*. What is important is what the daffodils do to Wordsworth in a vacant or pensive mood. What will be the all-important thing is the fact that an African would never contemplate nature the way Wordsworth did. In rural life we are surrounded so much by nature that it ceases to be something outside of ourselves. We are part of its rhythm. Its birth is our birth, its death ours; its stagnation or suspen-sion is ours. In the city we are just too happy to have escaped the bleakness of the rural landscape, the cruelties of external nature and its rules of survival, to feel nostalgic about it.

As more and more of us are being uprooted and becoming urbanised, we are becoming less conscious of what enchanted words are worth. If you never had some-thing you can't miss it, but those of us whose hearts are tuned to the unbroken song of poetry – the inner poetry common to us all – such are the ones who will step off the highway to take deep breaths and contemplate the scene around us, and savour it.

When we deal with Browning's poem *My Last Duchess*, the teacher will certainly want to inform himself about the Renaissance. That's his responsibility, not primarily the student's, because we don't have public libraries in the ghetto where the student can fruitfully spend time looking up background information; nor have the schools libraries, except for mission schools. The teacher has to use a white liberal to procure books for him from the city or university library. In independent Africa, library facil-ities, both public and university, are incomparably better. But the habit of mind I have referred to still prevails. So when we have done reading *My Last Duchess*, the teacher looks for contrasts and correspondences: it is common in African tradition to send an emissary to negotiate for a bride. Instead of a dowry, there is a bride price. Painting as an art rather than a communal ritual is a recent arrival in Africa, but the photograph is good enough for reference. So there is the picture of the deceased duchess on the wall. What is the Duke telling the emissary whose lord's daughter he wants to marry? That his late wife smiled too kindly to every man, behaved too graciously to all men, reserving little for the husband. So, as the Duke says, he gave commands and all smiles stopped at once. If his prospective wife does not behave herself, she may suffer the same fate. Certainly, he intends to tame her if she is wild. Killing a woman out of jealousy is a universal passion. Only the circumstances will be different.

You stay with the poem so much longer. Why am I recounting all this? I am thinking aloud, trying to locate the point at which my interest in literature began. Because the reason why I teach hinges on that. I would not teach it if I would rather teach something else. The pleasure principle is important for me.

We produced poetry in the oral tradition in Africa and never analysed it – just as the European ballad lived long before it was recorded and analysed. Formal education and the mental growth it promotes came to us in English to begin with. Our mental growth was promoted in the English language. So we read the classics as a learning process in the basic sense of the phrase, and there is no escape from that. After chewing on everything we were given, the mind would some time later sift and select and distil – if you were not perpetually punch drunk after all those years, or a living corpse. And self-education begins with this sifting process. I can thus proudly say I am one of the survivors, not from a shipwreck, but simply from a historical accident of a momentous nature. Or should we call it historical necessity? We might have been colonized entirely by the Portuguese, who were the first whites to touch the African shore – or by the Germans, alas. But Europe carved up the continent and by historical chance we came under the English, the French and so on. There is no reason that one can explain for liking the colonizer's language. It is a nuisance one learns to put up with because one has to use it in order to get along. You find yourself taken over, your mother tongue given second place. The colonizer's language introduces you to the outside world and even gives you a clue to the inner workings of power manifested in the colonial presence. At some point it seems that the whole process fixes you in a trance. The printed word has that magical effect. I am sure that you can, when you have snapped out of the trance, go back to the language of your people with greater dignity and a more systematic frame of mind: systematic in terms of your new life.

Over and above the utilitarian aspect of learning English – the basic learning process that English is part of – those of us who had a feeling for the arts, whose artistic sensitivity was already active in the creation of and exposure to music, dance, sculpture, drama and poetry, responded readily to the treasures of the English language when they reached us. English literature was merely an extension of our artistic temperaments.

If English is organic to the learning process, and to a certain extent, if not entirely, loses some of the features that marked it as a foreign language in the beginning, then the reason for teaching it at this level is self-explanatory. But a literature is growing in Africa produced in English. At this level I teach for the following reasons: to promote a vehicle of communication among ourselves across diverse cultural and ethnic boundaries; to discover ourselves through a medium that combines an African sensibility with an English mode of expression; to discover ourselves through an understanding of the meeting point between imitation and innovation, and between two cultures, one of which stimulates and releases the creative energies of the other. I have been in the centre of these processes. Studying and teaching literature has been part of that process of expansion from the mastery of reading and writing skills to higher levels of consciousness.

In the United States, I am outside the grassroots situation. I suspect if we tried to tell freshman students here to paraphrase, do précis and comprehension exercises or analyse sentences, it would set off a furore of some kind. Even when students read literature, they resist anything that does not engage them in talk, talk, talk. They call this talk 'ideas', sometimes they call it 'relevancy'. They don't really care how these ideas are expressed in the text. They refuse to read a poem closely, aloud, to hear the ring of words. They skim through a novel and rush to read what the critics say about it. They have little or no regard for things like style in printed prose. I am always asking why there seem to be no radio plays in this country, which are most popular in Africa. Have people indeed lost the ability to listen to the spoken word? Or are they bored with privilege, with prosperity? Of course there is nothing wrong with a discussion of ideas as such. Ideas inform creative writing. But they are not the concepts and definitions the scientist peddles. They are what T S Eliot implied when he talked of 'felt thought.' Although he was talking about poetry, 'felt thought' is inherent in all imaginative literature. What can one do as a teacher to ensure that this recital of ideas about a literary production reach back to the original work, where one can think and feel and listen, so that the ritual revitalizes rather than regimentalises our responses? Or are we contented with this interminable and mindless chewing of gum and popping of bubbles? I warn the listener, however, that I am deliberately exaggerating the picture for effect.

Try asking Huckleberry Finn what he thinks of the frontier mentality of America; ask him if he thinks dedicating himself to helping a runaway slave is an escape from civilization, back to one's beginnings. Questions like these, which some people worry about. Huck is likely to make a bolt for it, back into the novel, for protection. Back into the novel, which is the house Mark Twain built for him. One's fictional children, if they are really his, will always run back to one for protection when they are being molested by the social scientist. Herein lies the beauty of a work of art: every time you try to dissect it, the spirit of the whole keeps reclaiming the parts and the thing comes together again – even though the whole tempts one to want to dissect it.

Nor does the social scientist's language help the serious student of literature. One reads phrases like 'horizontal orientation of agencies'; 'vertical articulation', 'the horizontally oriented permissive community organiser' ... and so the social scientists continue to pass notes under the table, trading new terminology, quoting one another on it, footnoting one another about it. What exasperates one is to discover that they even understand one another! And yet one knows they are themselves in a state of siege, and the proliferation of new terminology is a way of dealing with their own situation. The language will stay, it will find its way into one encyclopaedia or another dealing with one special field or another. All I am saying is that it does not make life easy. Do not imagine we don't have cripples in our family too – literary critics. But I can safely say we are dealing with that malady on that front, because we have critics of critics in our discipline – and writers themselves are watchdogs of their own storehouses.

The question plagues me: am I relevant to American education? I am outside the area where I consciously felt English was an organic part of one's extension beyond local horizons; where I was part of an organic process of cultivating the mind. I cannot pretend that I am part of a corresponding system here, because the cultivation of the mind here operates on other and different assumptions, determined by a pluralistic culture. I have come into a long line of continuity in the American tradition. All I have is that vague and indefinable something a person is supposed to contribute as a member of the world intellectual community. A community that, to a foreigner, has no place, no boundaries, no tangible commitment and no corporate will. Otherwise – in any meaningful way – nothing. So I teach my discipline because (a) if I don't teach I think I'll shrivel up into anonymity. I don't like anonymity. I'm a vain man. I want to extend myself; (b) I find fulfilment in teaching it. I'm entertaining myself, which is also a process of self-education. Of course I want feedback: that is the only way I shall be able to tell if I am enjoying myself. Of course I feel a responsibility toward my students. I said I'm a teacher at heart, and a teacher who does not feel a responsibility toward his students is fit for firewood.

These two are all the reasons I have left. At fifty-two I do not think I can ever make any contribution to a culture – and that is what education is in essence – with which I have only a superficial contact. True, it is the kind of contact that enables me to find circles of human intercourse sufficient to sustain me in exile such as I could find nowhere else in the world, at least at this time, because Americans are all exiles of one kind or another.

There is one thing that I cherish, which ties up with the two reasons I hold on to for dear life: it is the contact I have with students who acknowledge some impact I have made on them, a contact I find in turn elevating. Again, if my contribution lies in another direction – as a writer – teaching my discipline will necessarily give an account of itself in that direction. What *that* legacy is worth is not for me to judge.

Es'kia Mphahlele (1919 – Present)

Prior to 1979 he published as *Ezekiel* Mphahlele. Upon his return, after twenty years in exile, came a name change to *Es'kia* Mphahlele. Although only privately dramatic, this name change underscores an unusually heavy dependence on personal experience, a strong folk-sensitivity and frequent wrestling with the condition of exile.

It is not merely the exile on alien soil that dominates his work, but also the exile from ancestral soil. These are features that characterize his personality and his writing. It is out of this material that he has hewn two autobiographies, three novels, more than twenty-five short stories, two verse plays and a number of poems. Add to these two edited anthologies, essay collections, more than one hundred and sixty single essays and significant public addresses, several awards and a Nobel Prize nomination for literature, and what emerges is to many a dean of African Letters.

As a young reader, Mphahlele seized upon the maxim that a story had to be well told[1]. It became the simple credo that drove his work along – all his work. It is reflected in his critical criteria and the corpus of his creative writing. He prefers to view life as framed experience, ordered and patterned into a story. And if this is not an extraordinary trait in a writer, as Mphahlele's mainstay it is of major critical consequence.

Personal experience, whether fictionalized or not, formed his creative impulse. Both its simplicities and its complexities determine the lives of his characters and become microcosmic of the South African experience on one level, and of the more specific black South African experience on another. His work, both critical and creative, becomes a forum in which he examines himself, feeling experience spinning around him and dancing past. His writing is less successful when he is unable to feel an incident as real or when he cannot identify with its emotional core[2]. He is, in fact, locked in a constant discourse with the experiences of his own life.

Biography

A basic familiarity with Es'kia Mphahlele's background is imperative if one is to respond to the fabric and texture of his writing; to touch the 'felt thought' so characteristic of an African writer. His is a story of a goatherd, office clerk, teacher, acclaimed academic and award-winning writer. Little is private about his life, which has moved from his native South Africa into exile abroad and back home again. His poetry is intensely personal, and his large body of fiction is hardly more than an extension of his own life. Even his criticism betrays his restless consciousness in exile, and this is continued after his return to home soil.

Mphahlele was born in Marabastad, outside of Pretoria, in 1919, but was soon taken to live with his paternal grandmother in the rural Northern Transvaal (now the Limpopo Province) near Pietersburg (Polokwane), in the village of Maupaneng. These were less than happy childhood years under his tyrannical paternal grandmother; his first autobiography, *Down Second Avenue* (1959), records her harshness alongside images of fearful, towering mountains. It is a period of fear and loss, of bewilderment, displacement and, to a minor extent, alienation. But these years also saw the forging of a sense of storytelling and a growing awareness of the need to shape experience:

> *Looking back to those first fifteen years of my life – as much of it as I can remember – I cannot help thinking that it was time wasted. I had nobody to shape them into a definite pattern. Searching through the confused threads of that pattern, a few things keep imposing themselves on my whole judgement.*

> *My grandmother; the mountain; the tropical darkness in which glow-worms seemed to try in vain to*
> *scatter; long black tropical snakes; the brutal Leshoana river... cattle, boulders; world of torrential*
> *rains; the solid shimmering heat beating down on yearning earth; the romantic picture of a woman*
> *with a child on her back and an earthen pot on her head, silhouetted against the mirage. (p.18)[3]*

He learned how to make it through each day; learned how to survive. And it was a lesson excellently learnt, for when the country boy returned to Pretoria a tough ghetto life lay in wait. Some of the early obstacles came at school: in the Fifth Grade he was told he was 'backward':

> *The principal said I was backward. My aunt said I was backward. So said everybody. My mother did*
> *not know. I had no choice but to acknowledge it. (p.47)*

Despite it all, there emerged a boy who ferociously consumed anything he could learn. His determination resulted in a teacher's certificate from Adams College, Natal, in 1940, and matriculation by correspondence studies two years later, while working as a teacher and shorthand typist at the Ezenzeleni Institute for the Blind in Roodepoort, west of the Johannesburg city centre. He went on to teach English and Afrikaans at Orlando High School in what is today Soweto, until he was banned from teaching in 1952 for campaigning against the Bantu Education proposals. The years 1952-53 saw him return to Ezenzeleni as secretary, and in 1954 he entered his first brief exile in what was then Basotholand, as a teacher in Maseru.

Academic honours began when a BA degree was awarded to him in 1949. A BA Honours degree followed in 1955 and a Masters degree, with distinction, in 1957. All three degrees were awarded by the University of South Africa, and studies were conducted via correspondence. The MA was the first cum laude degree to be awarded to a black South African, and it obliged the University of South Africa to arrange an entirely separate graduation ceremony. Mphahlele's Ph.D. was granted in 1968 by the University of Denver, USA, and his first honorary degree of Doctor of Humane Letters was conferred by the University of Pennsylvania in 1982. An equivalent tribute came from the University of Colorado in 1994. Similar honours were accorded him when the University of Natal awarded him their Doctor of Literature in 1983, and Rhodes University followed suit with their highest academic accolade in 1986. In the same year, the French government awarded him the *Ordre des Palmes* medal as recognition of his contribution to French language and culture. In 2000, Nelson Mandela awarded him the Order of the Southern Cross.

Ghetto life in South Africa could hardly anticipate such academic accolades. Among the scant career options available after he was barred from teaching in 1952 was a post as a journalist, and his love for writing was indeed strong enough to make him join the staff of *Drum* magazine in Johannesburg. In his short stay with this groundbreaking magazine he held the posts of political reporter, sub-editor and fiction editor but, discontented with his role as a journalist and deeply disillusioned by the South African situation, he resolved in 1957 to leave for a life in exile. This led him to Nigeria, France and Zambia, and a double sojourn in the USA. Twenty years later, in 1977, he returned to his native South Africa.

Mphahlele's career is in spatial terms a map of both Africa and the world. Yet against such a broad and colourful canvas, his creative involvement with the African experience has been restricted to specific themes. His work shows a keen awareness of the strength of black women, yet he certainly does not develop his women characters as feminist scholars would prefer – although his novel *Chirundu* may well be an exception. He often depicts the ambivalence of the African personality, caught between a rural and urban sensibility, and his human landscape inevitably eclipses physical setting. The white-black encounter stalks his themes. Mphahlele thrives on the communal point of view; always coming to grips with his milieu, with his Pan-African world-view. He is constantly engaged in some form of self-definition – a wrestling that is rooted in cultural imperatives. He is determined to write *about* something and not *of* something as he addresses the African experience.

Autobiography

A splendid introduction to the panorama of Mphahlele's writing is provided by his autobiography *Down Second Avenue*. Begun in South Africa, it was completed in the early days of his twenty-year exile, in Nigeria in 1957. Driven along by its contemplative tempo, *Down Second Avenue* is perhaps more an autobiographical essay than it is a novel, yet its narrative is poetic enough to involve the reader in the world of a novel. Incidents are picked from memory with ease and care, and each is precisely suited to the overall purpose of the work: to articulate an existence and to comb it for meaning.

The work is a poignant record of the development of a personality within the dynamics of African culture, showing how the African is inseparable from his or her past, and how that past is a rehearsal for the future. The narrative delineates a unique reverence for the past. *Down Second Avenue* serves as a theatre in which Mphahlele confirms his identity – a feature common to several other autobiographies by black South Africans. And, coming as it does after Mphahlele's experiments with short stories, it is a logical extension of shorter narratives around a common theme. Basing the work on actual experience makes it an exciting and a realistic venture with credible characterization. The African-American models by James Baldwin and Richard Wright (as well as the early slave narratives) provide similar examples. There are, for instance, remarkable structural similarities with Wright's *Black Boy*, although Mphahlele did not in fact read Wright's autobiography until after *Down Second Avenue* had been published.

Whatever the motivations behind the work, it is clear that Mphahlele enjoyed the romance of reconstructing his life; of shaping it, and the lives of those who helped him grow. So we often find Mphahlele identifying with an incident in the most emotional of terms, and yet with very careful authority over any possible lapses into sentimentality. A device he uses to combat such lapses is the 'Interlude'. At five crucial junctures, Mphahlele feels the need to pause to introspect; he becomes intensely personal and even confessional. Each Interlude needs to happen; it is as if the narrative has actually managed to get under his skin. Each adopts a near stream-of-consciousness mode and works its way through a crisis. The first reflects on poverty and the slums. The second follows lively accounts of a street gang and street wisdom, of Rebone, Ma Lebona and Ma Bottles – each a figure in a raw ghetto world. Their depressing details get the better of him, and in this Interlude he wishes he had the Biblical Moses's luck. Ironically his renegade father's name was also Moses – the father who scalded his mother with steaming curry and who walked out on them. This Interlude has the younger Mphahlele emotionally recounting, feeling, and assessing his youth:

> No use trying to put the pieces together. Pieces of my life. They are a jumble. My father's image keeps coming back only to fade. I can't think of him but as a harsh, brutal, cold person. Like his mother. And that brutal limp of his. The smell of paraffin from the stove and the smell of boiling potatoes and curry. (p.74-75)

Eight chapters later he documents his mother's death and predictably answers the need to step out of the narrative into the third Interlude. Here he also mourns the passing of Marabastad – the ghetto area that was razed under the government's forced removal policies.

Marriage and religion enter. Adulthood and its responsibilities in black South Africa begin to assert a stranglehold, and his career at that point forces him into the fourth Interlude. This marks the six-month-long first exile into Basotholand. The style is crisper, much more controlled; it is more academic. And with this the narrative quality alters dramatically. A severity enters as the adult explores the few options his environment offers. His anti-white sentiment grows; white South Africa begins to suffocate him and gives way to violent protest. Almost aloud, and perhaps to himself, he says:

> The main weakness in South African writers is that they are hyper-conscious of the race problem in their country. They are so obsessed with the subject of race and color that when they set about writing creatively, they imagine that the plot they are going to devise, the characters they are going to create and the setting they are going to exploit must observe an important message or important discovery they think they have made in race relations. (p.195-96)

In the final Interlude he struggles with the decision to leave South Africa for a life of exile. A fully mature mind speaks – depressed, but not in despair.

These five Interludes are invaluable punctuation devices. They reveal much of Mphahlele's own development and provide an ingenious inner frame for the work. They do not, however, reveal the vibrancy of the work itself.

Down Second Avenue is a particularly brilliant catalogue of characters. Like their dialogue (however sparse) they are earthly and colloquial. They speak in the idiom of their ghetto and mother-tongues and most, like the venerable Aunt Dora, are personally trying to come to terms with reality. Others stumble their way through Mphahlele's memory, like the sentimental view we get of an unreachable girlfriend, Rebone. Aunt Dora, much like Mphahlele's mother Eva, dominates the story. Both share the limelight as the most admirably dominating women in the author's life. Both have an inescapable presence: Aunt Dora's presence comes through physical assertion, Eva's through a quiet, more subtle aura. For Aunt Dora:

> ...the past never seemed to hold any romantic memories; she never spoke about the future; simply grappled with the present. (p.107)

And grapple she does. She is volatile and always active. She is protective, loves meat and life, intimidates at least one of Mphahlele's teachers and beats up an Indian shopkeeper. Yet she is implicitly obedient to her passive husband. Eva Mphahlele is the epitome of motherly tenderness – in sharp contrast to his menacing father.

Eva is romantically drawn and even laced with sentimentality. She is also a profound indictment: her son must succeed! She remained a major influence on her son and also became his private symbol for Africa's resilience and tenderness.

Mphahlele emerges as a natural and sensitive hero in *Down Second Avenue*, but this is not repeated in *Afrika My Music* (1984).[4] Within the conventions of the memoir, this later work is a broad and colourful mural of almost all the people who have been part of the author's life. Much less emphasis is given to his own inner self. With bold pen-strokes he sketches a literary history of which he was an integral part. In robust style, he raids his past to rationalize his decisions. But a straightforward memoir this is not. It is a review of a man sparring with his readers' suspected judgements on how he has managed his whirlwind life; he explains to himself and to us why he did what he did. There are no Interludes to grant him respite here; this time authorial commentary is his choice of form.

The formula seems to be: 'My role: how have I represented my people?' He winces as he recounts the placelessness of exile and its tyranny of time. Exile failed to give him a commitment to a locality, and he remembers tugging at the moorings of Nigeria, France, Kenya and Zambia, and twice at those that tied him to American shores.

The narrative structure of *Afrika My Music* is particularly striking. Its opening image is that of a mature man recalling the ironies of the most recent events in his life. Then, in a series of concentric circles, he spreads out internationally and returns to the porch of his Lebowakgomo home (about five kilometres from his childhood village of Maupaneng). We see him on his way back to his new porch (or perch), having gathered mountain flora from nearby mountains for his rockery garden. Ironically, the mountains he went to loot are the same fearsome, towering hills that tormented him in those childhood nights as a goatherd in *Down Second Avenue*.

This book leads everywhere before it returns to the Lebowa porch, and in its course it mirrors a life which is more content and reconciled. He had moved away from his birthright and returned after twenty years. Unlike *Down Second Avenue*, which is remembered for its honest accounts of ghetto life, *Afrika My Music* represents the Mphahlele who has successfully written himself out of the ghetto. But having achieved this, he feels no more free from the tyranny of colour that dominates South African life.

Although a more personal celebration, *Afrika My Music* is indeed an energetic sweep across a human landscape, and its course is only disrupted by such historical sledgehammers as Sharpeville, 1960. Ironies serve to elevate this memoir into an art form, particularly when the narrative excavates the condition of exile. For the first time his wife is unveiled as 'unsinkable Rebecca', and when he touches on their role as parents, one feels their anguish over their elder son's delinquency. Here we get a glimpse into the trepidations that may have led to the father-son sub-theme in his first novel, *The Wanderers*.

The title *Afrika My Music*, although every bit as metaphorical as *Down Second Avenue*, is less easily defined. It is the work's alternative title (the original *Round Trip to Liberty* was dropped), yet it embraces the work without restricting it to itself. Here is a syncopated record which hints at several cathartic and traumatic moments – moments which ground the work to a number of significant halts in its composition, ostensibly because for Mphahlele this was not a mere record of events. Consequently, a certain patchiness betrays the very long journey from Wayne, Pennsylvania where it was begun, to Lebowakgomo in the Northern Province of South Africa. As in *Down Second Avenue*, there is a large measure of the 'I-am-us' formula – so Mphahlele-esque, so utterly humanist.

In the many cameos of fellow exiles, we see how well Mphahlele could listen to another's music and drama – a man who attended to the fibre of another's character, their concerns and interests. In the end we see a man at peace with himself; a man who has reconciled his beliefs and commitments but who remains disturbed by the inequalities in his land. He yearns for human dignity, and success for him means something different from fame: 'It isn't fame you want in my line of work, it is having your shadow noticed – to have a presence.' (p.22)

Fiction

The Wanderers[5] marked Mphahlele's first attempt at novel-length fiction. Completed in 1968, the manuscript was submitted as a dissertation for a Ph.D. degree in the Creative Writing program at the University of Denver, where he also taught. The African Studies Centre at the University of California, Los Angeles, awarded the unpublished novel its first prize, naming it the best African novel for 1968-69. At the same time, Mphahlele was elected to Phi Beta Kappa and nominated for the Nobel Prize for Literature.

In ten years of exile he had become a senior and distinguished academic. Through his work as director of African Programmes with the Paris-based Congress for Cultural Freedom (later renamed the International Association for Cultural Freedom), his activities throughout the continent placed him at the very hub of a burgeoning literature. He organized conferences and workshops on education, writing, the arts and the press. He was directly instrumental in establishing Chemchemi Creative Centre in Kenya and the Mbari Club in Nigeria. He also boldly challenged the emergent romanticism of Negritude in the early 1960s and became its chief dissident.

In full-length fiction, as in autobiography, Mphahlele utilizes his personal experience. He also bears witness to his own conscience. *The Wanderers* leans heavily on the autobiographical as it confronts the thoughts and events Mphahlele lived through. Here is, on one level, the sequel to *Down Second Avenue* and the bridge between it and *Afrika My Music*. Here too we find the unconscious (conscious?) wrestling with the distinction between autobiographical fiction and fictional autobiography.

A variety of narrative devices transform personal experience into fiction. While the main character is hardly less than Mphahlele himself, this is also the story of more than Timi Tabane and his family in South Africa and in exile. The father-son sub-theme certainly reflects the tensions between Mphahlele and his own eldest, Anthony. The relationship between Timi and Felang forms the framework of the plot, which comprises five interrelated sections.

Book One is a thin outline of Mphahlele's early adulthood in *Down Second Avenue*. Timi has been banned from teaching and is forced to become a journalist, without a real liking for his job on *Bongo* magazine. He becomes too deeply and personally involved in investigating the disappearance of a man into a labour-farm system. When the story is eventually published in *Bongo*, it leads to several reforms and Timi emerges a hero. His impersonation of a labourer drives home the frustrations he feels as a black South African. The abduction case only deepens his ambivalence about whether or not to leave South Africa:

> ...to stay and pit my heroism against the machine and bear the consequences if I remained alive; or stay and shrivel up with bitterness; or face up to my cowardice, reason with it and leave. (p.59)

When he does decide to leave, his application for a passport is refused and he crosses the border illegally.

Book Two is narrated by the editor of *Bongo* magazine, Steve Cartwright. He too faces a personal crisis. As a man with a liberal conscience, he cannot escape from his whiteness. He despises the white government and falls in love with Naledi, whose husband's disappearance Timi had investigated. Their circumstances, however, make her remind him that Steven is white. This second book is a drawn-out account of several related events. It is a dense and labored narrative from Cartwright's sickbed.

Book Three has no specific narrator, and jumps ahead by two years into a fictional West Africa where Timi Tabane has a teaching post. His family joins him some time later in Iboyoru. Iboyoru suffers a military coup d'etat and Steven Cartwright, now a journalist in England, comes out to report. He had not only resolved to leave South Africa but had also married Naledi. However, the primary feature of Book Three is Mphahlele's focus on Timi's son Felang. This is a rather unadulterated recounting, and quite likely an examination of Mphahlele's painful relationship with his own eldest son.

Timi resumes his role as character-narrator in Book Four, with the Tabane family resident in Lao-Kiku (the Kenya of Mphahlele's wanderings). The relationship with Felang deteriorates and the boy jettisons his family. Timi's own disillusionment with Iboyoru merely transfers itself to

Lao-Kiku and to Africa itself. The relentlessness of his African exile is merely compounded by Felang's death.

In *Afrika My Music* Mphahlele says of fiction:

> *In fiction, as in drama, you work with diversities, conflict, and you need an intimate familiarity with the world you depict. You need a locale, its smell, its taste, its texture... in the process of composition, you are tied to the place that contains the experience.* (p.168)

This is the extent of his commitment to the lessons gained from his own experience. This is perhaps reason enough for him to weave a rather thin plot into the scope of a novel of such substantial length. Minute details abound, and the experience of the narrative is the very texture of its protest aesthetic.

Despite its sombre, if not morbid, storyline, there are moments of humour that surpass even those of Aunt Dora's fight with Abdool in *Down Second Avenue*. But the humorous instances are almost callously juxtaposed with tragic circumstances. A township funeral is perhaps one of the most appropriate instances to illustrate this sardonic humour. The funeral sequence in the novel goes beyond its apparent absurdity to become an example of African humanism and another illustration of ghetto poverty:

> *'I haven't got the time to go about looking for Kabinde and paying him twenty shillings to say a few words over a corpse when not even its wife cares.' Of course I had some time. But I did not see that the costly coffins, hearses and bus convoys that went down Nadia Street to the cemetery gave a corpse greater dignity than one he had in a crude but acceptable coffin. Once a small group passed, all solemnly rigged up for a funeral. It turned out that the coffin was full of liquor.* (p.46)

(Liquor was contraband in black possession the during apartheid years.) What follows the arrangements Timi makes is a description of himself, his wife Karabo, his mother-in-law, the widow, the not-too-sober driver and the coffin, all the precariously perched on a horse-drawn cart:

> *Karabo and I sat at the back, our legs dangling. The driver stopped several times to greet friends and chat a little.* (p.46)

Timi, a little uneasy about it all, has his embarrassment confirmed when one of his journalist colleagues spots them and comments: 'What's this, a one-man bus boycott?' The irony of the funeral is vested in the abandoning of even traditional rites: the man is buried in a way that only accommodates the financial environment in which he died. This sense of absurdity is a defence that black South African writers (at least!) have adopted to combat the debilitating atmosphere, and to proclaim life over idea. And so they are – Mphahlele in particular – almost Jesuitical in resisting despair.

Another draught from his African exile is evident in his second novel, *Chirundu* (1979)[6]. This is a much more determined venture into fiction, which concerns the bigamy charges filed against a cabinet minister in an independent central African country. It is also a work which marks Mphahlele's dissatisfaction with the limited themes of many younger writers, especially those in South Africa. In *Chirundu* he explores the resonances of African mythology, and in so doing he presents, in part, a fresh variation of a common theme: the confrontation between a traditional African sensibility and a Western one.

Chirundu was born out of the abortive attempt to re-establish African residence in Zambia in 1968, which lasted a mere twenty-one months.

Mphahlele favours revealing much of a story's conclusion early on, and then takes on the challenge of sustaining the reader's interest. *Chirundu* tells us from the outset of the main character's fall from power. The process begins with his demotion from an Interior Affairs portfolio to that of Minister of Transport and Public Works. The downward trend is unsurprising, but of course this is not all. The novel also gives us an intimate view of personal, political and moral corruption in which we are made to examine our own attitudes towards polygamy in Africa, towards African education as part of the colonial inheritance, and also towards missionary-imported religion. Three strains of action are involved: Chimba's relationship with Terenje and Monde; his nephew Moyo's rise within the ranks of organized labour; and a portrait of a group of South African refugees. All three strains are drawn together by complex structural patterning, not at all dissimilar to the expansive episodic structures of oral narratives and panegyric.

Elaborate flashbacks, for example, construct the past and are inextricably bound to the present. They reach back to traditional rural Africa and set it against the chaos of the urban present. Chirundu and Terenje were married under Bemba law, but Chimba also insisted on their marriage being registered under a British colonial ordinance. After independence, Chirundu's power and status invite a mistress. The affair becomes serious and, to head off speculation and rumour, Chirundu decides to marry Monde (his mistress). Terenje, after heart-rending attempts to repair their marriage, feels that she has no alternative but to file bigamy charges in a modern court of law. She does so and wins. Chirundu knows he cannot contest the charges, but wishes to challenge the law by breaking it.

Similarly, gloom and defeat surround the narrative of the refugees. Chimba Chirundu's nephew, Moyo, however, is a symbol of hope. He values the order of the old world and learns that it must be protected. However transparent a symbol he may be, he is the hope set against the disillusionment of new-found power and against the exile of refugees. We see his foundation solidly laid, but without any guarantees for the future. As a faint but glimmering hope, Moyo is perhaps all Mphahlele can muster when he considers independent Africa's dismal political record.

Writings by black South Africans have addressed the dynamics of the present, but are largely consumed by bitterness and anger and have little time to employ indigenous cultural elements beyond diction and idiom. Mphahlele is acutely aware of this absence of resonance, and invests his character Moyo with a substantial cultural foundation. The boy's confidence stems directly from his faith in his ancestors. As the governing motif, Nsato the python, king of reptiles, is another example of Mphahlele reaching for the mythological dimension. The python becomes a versatile and dramatic symbol of power. Mphahlele uses it to illustrate sexual power when Chimba Chirundu embraces Terenje in happier years, and again later as unbridled power when he is Nsato; 'gone mad because he is full of himself.' (p.18.) Ironically, the python gives us a glimpse into the externals of power: 'A real king does not go about picking fights with small creatures like human beings.' (p.17.)

Not only are there very strong parallels with Mphahlele's Zambian sojourn (the bigamy case is in fact based on an actual incident), but there are also several other autobiographical intrusions. Characters both local and refugee are often based on real people, and Mphahlele frequently uses them as his personal mouthpiece. Studs Letanka, for example, longs to return to South Africa to teach – as Mphahlele did. An even more notable instance of Mphahlele speaking directly through a character is in *Chirundu*'s anti-Christian invective, which is seen to make him the victim and symbol of modern Africa's decadence. And so *Chirundu* becomes an uncompromising indictment of the abuse and hypocrisy of new-found power.

Clearly a dramatic departure from the essentially South African-bound setting of his earlier work, *Chirundu* is not without its weaknesses. Here is a vibrant story drawn from a rather mundane situation, and a story that unfolds less organically than either *Down Second Avenue* or *The Wanderers*. But the meticulous attention to characterization, its overall thematic value and its beautifully lyrical prose go a long way towards making up for its flaws. A character like Terenje is warm and unforgettable. She, too, is undoubtedly a symbol of Africa's strength, and another manifestation of Mphahlele's admiration for the power of the black woman. She is compassionate and completely loyal. Sometimes the narrative seems forced; the multiple shifts in time and persona develop a choppiness that reflect the author's condition of exile. He finds himself alienated, rootless; free to be no one; free to be impotent. Exile has made him excessively sensitive and observant, and so he prefers a kaleidoscopic view.

Short Fiction

Mphahlele's consummate strength lies in his short fiction. It launched his career as a writer when at the age of twenty he retold a folktale at Adams College. He maintains that he began writing, and continued to do so, for the sheer joy of it, but also readily admits that reading his early work is somewhat embarrassing, with its 'clumsy, heavy and awkward idiom'[7]. Despite this style, his first collection, *Man Must Live* (1946)[8], carries a thematic title that has developed into a major clarion in his work; Mphahlele regards it as a central statement and as the basis of action: *the individual must survive!* Yet, Mphahlele can be eminently forgiving of the means of survival within the tyranny of place that was the South African arena.

In *Man Must Live*, many vague characters move through weak plots, but then these stories represent Mphahlele's first steps in using literature to come to terms with his own life. It is as if literary exercises were used to confirm for him his responsibilities and his commitments. These stories display the strengths that hostile environments extract to ensure survival. The hero, Zungu, is a portrait of tenacity. Knowing how to live is paramount to a man whose physical size alone makes him superior in crowds of people. But Zungu's brashness and bluster hide a deep uncertainty about himself. He eventually chooses a wife who, along with her children, comes to belittle him constantly. He takes to drinking heavily and slowly begins to disintegrate until his desperation drives him to set his house on fire. By sheer chance he remembers his code that 'man must live', and rushes out aflame. He is taught the true reality of the life he must live.

Stilted language pervades the remaining stories, as does Mphahlele's reliance on personal history. The melodrama of *Tomorrow You Shall Reap* is particularly overbearing, but the use Mphahlele makes of fiction is striking. The mother of the story's narrator kills herself after her husband abandons them. The boy is allowed to explore these circumstances in the face of a love affair of his own. Prophetically, he is allowed to say:

> *Yet, I told myself not to think of it. I must think of a new life at a boarding school. I must not pity myself even if the circumstances seem to justify self-pity. I must try to run away from my conscious self and dope myself with romantic ideas and ambitious so that I should feel the pain of blunt reality.* (p.50)

As early as 1946, Mphahlele had begun to explore the meaning of raw experience in fiction. Whatever the incentive – be it autobiography, hearsay or a newspaper item – he scours an incident for its dramatic quality and associations.

Two major anthologies followed *Man Must Live*. *The Living and the Dead* appeared from Nigeria in 1961. Six years later he issued *In Corner B* from East Africa. Selected contents of both volumes (plus another story) have since been anthologized in *The Unbroken Song* (1981)[9].

The Unbroken Song is a collection that includes a broad spectrum of Mphahlele's short fiction that grew from the South African and Nigerian settings. In many, the exiled self confirms its

461

responsibility to home soil. All his moods are on display here, including his guilt, and each reveals his struggle to find his bearings in exile.

The Living and the Dead gives us Stoffel Visser, a man who is frantically defensive; a character who is suspicious of every black person and distrustful of anyone else around him. Although circumstances in the story challenge his stock attitudes – even to the point of releasing some hidden store of compassion – these are short-circuited, and he only reconfirms his distrust. He reminds himself of his whiteness first, then of his limited humanity. Like Zungu, his code of survival must hold true, and neither he nor Mphahlele's portrayal of Visser as a white character deserves further comment. Here, as in most of his writing, he makes no effort at multidimensional character construction; he is not interested in Visser the man, only in Visser's relation to blacks. Constructing multi-faceted characters need not be the concern of a short story, and so Visser's limitation could be a matter of convention; yet the fact that Mphahlele deliberately casts most, if not all, his white characters in a stereotypical mould also has thematic significance. At its most basic level, the South African racial environment breeds Visser's distrust and Mphahlele's relative ignorance of whites. Consequently, part of the meaning of these stories lies in the limited vision and function that Mphahlele is able to afford these characters.

Man Must Live, *The Living and the Dead*, *The Leaves were Falling* and *Tomorrow You Shall Reap* demonstrate the same aspects of the moral dilemma that the black-white encounter entails. Incidents of actual conflict are inevitable. In *Dinner at Eight*, one is struck by the almost casual tone and quiet relentlessness with which the story develops. The white character, Miss Pringle, is a representative type: an extreme paternalist who loves to have blacks hover around her. It is in her transparent defiance of the system that Mphahlele locates her sexual frustration. The sexual undertones, however, are never realized; instead, after refusing several previous invitations to dinner, Mzondi kills her with his crutch – his symbol of police brutality and the lessening of his manhood. *The Suitcase* is another tale where dreams die. Here the irony is couched in the event. Timi claims an apparently forgotten suitcase which he finds on a bus, and fantasizes about its contents. When policemen arrest him on suspicion of theft he avidly maintains ownership, but when he and the police discover the contents – a dead baby – Timi could not have wished harder to disown the case. Suspense is thoroughly maintained throughout, and this is a fine illustration of Mphahlele's basic theory that purpose determines form. Here, there is a definite ironic point to which he directs his tale and from which he keeps incidental information away. He needs a portrait only of Timi's fantasies concerning an animate object; he does not need to establish Timi's presence as a character, as he would have had to do in his novels.

All the stories in *The Unbroken Song* have appeared elsewhere. All have received positive critical acknowledgement, but few have provoked as much comment as *Mrs Plum*, where people and plot are meticulously patterned in a story whose length approaches that of a novella, but whose techniques are those of an excellent short story. *Mrs Plum* is indeed the craftsman's finest piece. Mrs Plum's paternalism has more substance than Miss Pringle's (*Dinner at Eight*). Mrs Plum's domestic helper, Karabo, has an apparent simplemindedness that provides all the motivation for her employer's concern. She is 'made' to eat food that is quite foreign to her at the family table with a knife and fork. She is treated very well, paid regularly, and yet there is no real attempt made at understanding her. She is no more than a target for Mrs Plum's patronizing intentions. Bewildered at first, Karabo develops in the course of events. She is the narrator, and her learning process is also ours. She is always an intelligent observer, even without the lessons she learns from other domestic servants in the neighborhood. Karabo teaches herself and soon learns that, despite Mrs Plum's liberal gestures, the racial code does not allow either her or Mrs Plum to regard each other as individuals.

This is the testing ground as Mphahlele weaves pertinent complications into the plot: Mrs Plum's daughter Kate falls in love with a black physician. Karabo fancies him too, but blacks who are invited to the Plum residence tend to treat Karabo as inferior to them. Mrs Plum's affection for her dogs, Monty and Malan, borders on the immoral. She hoses down a police raiding-party with Karabo's aid; she refuses to pay the fine and is jailed for fourteen days. As narrator, Karabo, despite her surface simplicity, is sincere, cheerful and consistent – and she demonstrates a firm grasp of situations. Above all she knows her limitations. To her, Mrs Plum is a human being – albeit an eccentric one. The relationship Mrs Plum has with her dogs, Monty and Malan, marks her neurosis and sterility. Nevertheless, if Karabo senses Mrs Plum's concerns for blacks, she also senses abstract codes informing her actions.

Mrs Plum reflects the white liberal's dilemma, and her position is untenable and unenviable. Mphahlele's abhorrence of domestic pets is also fully exploited here, and the implications are thoroughly racial. Ultimately, he demonstrates how seriously he regards his responsibility as a writer: no matter how narrow his vision, how focused, how narrow the South African worldview, he means to explore its dynamics. His need to tell a story is irrepressible. As he has said: 'I write because it is a compulsive act. I believe people write because it is a compulsive cultural act.'[10]

Poetry

In one of his earlier poems, *Exiles in Nigeria 1960*, Mphahlele describes how, after three years in exile, he is stung by guilt. Why was he fortunate enough to bask in Nigeria's freedom? He turns to poetry to explore his ambivalence. What emerges is one of the clearest examples of Mphahlele the artist using the form as vehicle to express the cumulative experiences of his culture. Here he works at finding relevant metaphors and symbols from his background; his imagery captures the reality and the anguish.

> *My claws have poison:*
> *only let me lie down a while,*
> *bide my time,*
> *rub my neck and whiskers,*
> *file my claws and remember.*

He resolves to use his freedom to serve his people that he left behind. This leads to the near-obsessive wrestlings of his twenty-year exile. As he had by this time just completed *Down Second Avenue*, exile begins with the harrowing harmattan that sweeps across northern Nigeria:

> *North wind*
> *all I know*
> *is that you numb and jolt me*
> *lash water off my flesh*
> *and fill me with a sense of insufficiency,*
> *vague longings and forlorn moments*
> *and brittle promises – maddening!*

His poetic imagery refines free verse into visual prosody, allowing ready access to a factual and concrete realism. Cultural images become ideas. Always the associations; always the tug of the South. Sometimes when placelessness threatens more acutely it provokes an angry outburst, but more often he entertains a remote hope:

> somewhere a woman gives the world an artist:
> a child who sings and dances,
> dreams and weaves a poem round the universe
> plunging down the womb.

The cult of youth, as Mphahlele called it, held frightening implications for him as a United States resident. He feared growing old in a culture that he felt could easily shun the elderly, whereas growing old for an African should be noble. This fear compounded the discomfort of exile, and in the latter part of the twenty years he yearned to know his burial place. Thus his declaration in a letter to Guy Butler that he wanted 'to lay my shadow on ancestral soil' is hardly surprising. *Afrika My Music* is confirmation of this.

He acknowledges that he was unable to draw nourishment from the worlds of his exile and is firm in his resolve to begin again, despite the existing odds:

> I've tunneled through
> back again
> beneath the pounding footsteps of five decades
> breaking down on me,
> because I must step forward
> and be counted with the rest
> whose lives derive their meaning from
> the tyranny of place
> here on the killing ground
> here where the ancestors forever
> keep their vigil.

In *A Prayer*, as elsewhere, there is no time for refined metrics. Always the diagrammatic structure, the vibrant vocabulary of protest. He regards it as imperative to register his encounter with history and to do so as realistically as he can, no matter how private it may be.

---

1. 'My Experience as a Writer', *Momentum: On Recent South African Writing*, Edited by M.J. Daymond et al. (Pietermaritzburg: University of Natal Press, 1984), p.75.
2. Ursula A. Barnett, *Ezekiel Mphahlele*, (Boston: Twayne, 1976), p.54.
   This discussion forms an intereseting companion to N C Manganyi's psycho-biography of Mphahlele entitled *Exiles and Homecomings* (Johannesburg; Ravan Press, 1983). Barnett's work was the first extensive biography done on Mphahlele, but was done more via correspondence and so suffers from certain inaccuracies. Nevertheless, I have used Ms Barnett's text quite frequently even though I have not always quoted from it.
3. *Down Second Avenue* (London: Faber & Faber, 1959.) All references are to this edition.
4. *Afrika My Music: An Autobiography 1957-1983* (Johannesburg: Ravan Press, 1984). All references are to this edition.
5. *The Wanderers* (Cape Town: David Philip, 1984). All references are to this edition.
6. *Chirundu* (Johannesburg: Ravan Press, 1979). All references are to this edition.
7. Tim Couzens, *A Conversation with Es'kia Mphahlele*, Johannesburg: Wits University CTV Videotape (1983).
8. *Man Must Live and Other Stories* (Cape Town: The African Bookman, 1946). References are to this edition.
9. *The Unbroken Song: Selected Writings of Es'kia Mphahlele* (Johannesburg: Ravan Press, 1981). All references are to this edition. The USA edition was published by Readers International in 1988 under the title *Renewal Time*.
10. 'South African Fiction and Autobiography', in *Issue*, African Studies Association, University of Texas, Austin, Vol IV, No. 1 (1976), p. 20.

Editors' Biographical Details

James Ogude

James Ogude, Ph.D. Wits, is Associate Professor and Head of the Discipline of African Literature in the School of Literature and Language Studies at the University of the Witwatersrand. He has published numerous articles and reviews. He also co-edited, with Steve Kromberg, *Soho Square: A collection of New Writing from Africa* (1992). He is the author of *Ngugi's Novels and African History: Narrating the Nation* (London: Pluto Press, 1999).

Sam Raditlhalo

Sam Raditlhalo, Ph.D. Groningen, Netherlands, lectures in the Department of English at the University of Venda for Science & Technology, focusing specifically on the areas of Drama and American Literature. His Ph.D. thesis interrogated the construction of 20th-century identity in South African life writings.

Ndavhe Ramakuela

Ndavhe Ramakuela was until recently a tutor in English studies at the University of the North, South Africa. His research interests are in South African Literature, African Drama, Cultural Studies, Writing of the Transition and (auto)biography. He has read a number of papers on these topics and published in national literary journals. His latest entry on Es'kia Mphahlele (done with Prof. Adrian Roscoe and Seitlhamo Motsapi) was published in the *Dictionary of Literary Biography, Number 213, 2000.* He is currently Deputy Director: Multimedia, Marketing and Communications at the University of the North.

Marcus Ramogale

Marcus Ramogale, born near Pietersburg (Now Polokwane), South Africa, was educated in South Africa and in England. He holds a Ph.D. in English Studies from the University of the North, South Africa. He is now Associate Professor of English at the University of Venda, where he is also Head of Department of English and Vice-Dean of the School of Human and Social Sciences. His research interests are in South African and African English Literature, post-colonial studies and stylistics. He writes prose fiction.

Peter N Thuynsma

Peter Thuynsma, Ph.D. Denver, enjoyed Es'kia Mphahlele's tutelage in both Zambia and the USA. He succeeded Mphahlele as Head of the Department of African Literature at the University of the Witwatersrand, Johannesburg before leaving to form the Institute for Human Rights Education – also in Johannesburg. Thuynsma later returned to the University as Special Advisor to the Vice-Chancellor's Office and after three years, in 2002, joined the University's Foundation Staff.

Selected Bibliography

ES'KIA MPHAHLELE

Autobiography
1959 *Down Second Avenue*. London: Faber & Faber.
1983 *Afrika My Music: An Autobiography*.
   Johannesburg: Ravan Press.

Fiction
1971 *The Wanderers*. New York: Macmillan;
   Reprinted Cape Town: David Philip, 1984.
1974 *Chirundu*. Johannesburg: Ravan Press;
   reprinted 1994.
1984 *Father Come Home*. Johannesburg: Ravan Press.

Non-Fiction
1962 *The African Image*. London: Faber & Faber;
   Revised Edition New York: Praeger, 1974.
1972 *Voices In The Whirlwind And Other Essays*. New
   York: Hill & Wang.

Collected Works
1946 *Man Must Live And Other Stories*. Cape Town:
   African Bookman.
1961 *The Living And The Dead And Other Stories*.
   Ibadan, Nigeria: Ministry Of Education.
1967 *In Corner B And Other Stories*. Nairobi: East
   African Publishing House; Reprinted 1972.
1981 *The Unbroken Song*. Johannesburg: Ravan
   Press; Published in the USA as *Renewal Time*.
   Readers International, 1988.

Broadcast and Published Interviews
1962 'Outlook: An African Viewpoint.' An interview
   with Muriel Howlett, *BBC General Overseas
   Service*, 11 & 13 July. (Tape 7 1/2 Tbu 164461.)
1963 'Un Panorama De La Litterature Africaine De
   Langue Anglais: Entretien Avec L'ecrivain Ezekiel
   Mphahlele.' *Afrique* 20.
1964 'Modern African Writers: The Black Writer In
   Exile.' An interview with Lewis Nkosi and
   Richard Rive, *Negro Digest* 14.2. (A transcript of
   Net – a New York Interview.)
1965 'Ezekiel Mphahlele Ou La Hantise De La Vie
   Communautaire.' An interview with Irmelin
   Hossmann, *Afrique* 44.
1979 'A Rebel And His Roots.' An interview with
   Gavin Schreeve, *The Guardian* 7 May.
1981 'Looking In: In Search Of Es'kia Mphahlele.'
   An interview with N C Manganyi, *Looking
   Through The Keyhole*. Johannesburg: Ravan Press.

Drama
1976-77 'The Return Of Motalane.' *Greenfield Review*
   5.3/4.
1979 'Oganda's Journey.' *Staffrider* 2.3. (A dramatisa-
   tion of a story by Grace Ogot.)

Essays and Lectures
1952 'The Syllabus And The Child.' *The Good
   Shepherd*, November.
1955 'African Teachers.' *Fighting Talk*, October.
1956 'The Blackest Magic.' *Drum*, September.
1964 'African City People.' *East Africa Journal* 1.3.
1964 'African Literature.' *The Proceedings Of The First
   International Congress Of Africanists, Accra 11-18
   December, 1962*. Eds. Lalage Bown & Michael
   Crowder. Evanston: Northwestern UP.
1964 'The Fabric Of African Cultures.' *Foreign Affairs*
   42.4; Reprinted in *Voices In The Whirlwind*. New
   York: Hill & Wang, 1972.
1965 'An African Writer Looks At Israel.' *Jewish
   Quarterly* 13.3.
1965 'Negritude: A Phase.' *The New African* 2.5;
   Reprinted with modifications as 'A Reply', in *African
   Literature And The Universities*. Ed. Gerald Moore.
   Ibadan: Ibadan UP.
1966 'African Literature For Beginners.' *Africa Today*
   14.1.
1966 'The Language Of African Literature.' *Harvard
   Educational Review* 34.2.
1966 *A Guide To Creative Writing: A Short Guide To
   Short Story And Novel Writing*. Dar Es Salaam: East
   African Literature Bureau.
1967 'A Disarming Reticence: A Review Of *The Jail
   Diary Of Albie Sachs*.' The New African 7.2.
1967 'African Literature: What Tradition?' *Denver
   Quarterly* 2.2.
1968 'Realism And Romanticism In African Literature.'
   Africa Today 15.4. (This issue guest edited by Es'kia
   Mphahlele.)
1969 'African Literature: A Dialogue Of The Two
   Selves.' *Horizon* 11.10.
1969 'Censorship In South Africa.' *Censorship Today*
   2.4.
1969 'The International Symposium On The Short
   Story, Part Three. South Africa: Ezekiel Mphahlele.'
   The Kenyan Review 4.
1970 'African Literature And Propaganda.' *The Jewel Of
   Africa* 2.3/4.

467

1970 'Introduction.' *Emergency*. Richard Rive. New York: Collier.

1971 'Introduction.' *Night Of My Blood*. Kofi Awoonor. New York: Doubleday.

1972 'Black Literature At The University Of Denver.' *Research In African Literatrures* 3.1.

1972 'Variations On A Theme: Race And Color.' *Présence Africaine* 83.

1973 'From The Black World.' *Okike* 4.

1973 'The Tyranny Of Place.' *New Letters* 40.1.

1973 'The Voice Of Prophecy In African Poetry.' *Umoja* 1.2.

1973 'Why I Teach My Discipline.' *Denver Quarterly* 8.1.

1974 'From The Black World II.' *Okike* 5.

1975 'Notes From The Black World III.' *Okike* 8.

1975 'Notes From The Black World IV: Images Of Africa In Afro-American Literature.' *Okike* 10.

1975 'South African Black Writing 1972-73.' *Ba Shiru* 5.2.

1975 'The Function Of Literature At The Present Time: The Ethnic Imperative.' *Transition* 9.2; Reprinted in *Denver Quarterly* 9.4.

1976 'The African Critic Today: Toward A Definition.' *Reading Black: Essays In The Criticism Of Caribbean, And Black American Literature*. Houston Baker Jr. (Ed). Ithaca: African Studies & Research Centre, Cornell UP.

1976/77 'Tribute To L S Senghor.' *Présence Africaine* 99/100

1977 'Back To Ancestral Ground.' *First World*, May/June.

1977 'South Africa: Two Communities And The Struggle For A Birthright.' *Journal Of African Studies* 4.1.

1977 'Higher Education In South Africa.' *The International Encyclopedia Of Higher Education* 8. San Francisco: Josey Bass.

1977 *Modern Commonwealth Literature: A Library Of Literary Criticism*. Eds. John H. Ferres & Martin Tucker. New York: Frederick Ungar. (Criticism On Aidoo, Awoonor, Brutus, Cope, Krige, Mofolo and Rive.)

1978 *Modern Black Writers*. Ed. Michael Popkin. New York: Frederick Ungar. (Criticism on Aidoo, Awoonor, Baraka, Brutus, Dadié, Kunene and Plaatje.)

1979 'Exile, The Tyranny Of Place And The Literary Compromise.' *Unisa English Studies* 17.1.

1980 'Landmarks Of Literary History In South Africa.' *The Voice Of The Black Writer In Africa*. Johannesburg: Witwatersrand UP.

1980 'Education: Towards A Humanistic Ideology.' *Report On The Conference On Educational Priorities In A Developing State*. Pretoria: De Jager-Haum.

1981 'The Tyranny Of Place And Aesthetics.' *English Academy Review* 1.12; Reprinted in *Race And Literature / Ras En Literatuur*. Ed. Charles Malan. Pinetown: Owen Burgess, 1987.

1982 'Africa In Exile.' *Daedalus* Spring.

1983 'African Literature And The Social Experience In Process.' A typescript of *Inaugural Lecture Given At The University Of The Witwatersrand*, Johannesburg, October 1983.

1983 'Literature: A Necessity Or A Public Nuisance – An African View.' *The Sol Plaatje Memorial Lecture*, University Of Bophuthatswana, 9 September 1983; Reprinted as 'If It's Not From The Soul, You're Dying.' *The Classic* 3.1, 1984.

1983 'South African Literature Versus The Political Morality.' *The Auetsa Papers 1983*; Reprinted in *English Academy Review* 1.

1984 'Prometheus In Chains: The Fate Of English In South Africa.' *English Academy Review* 2. (*The First English Academy Of South Africa Lecture* delivered at the University Of The Witwatersrand).

1986 'Images Of Africa.' *South African Outlook* 117.1383; Reprinted in *The Capricorn Papers* 6.

1986 'Poetry And Humanism: Oral Beginnings.' *22nd Raymond Dart Lecture*, Institute for the Study of Man in Africa, Johannesburg.

1987 'Foreword.' *Echoes Of African Art*. Comp. & Intro. Matsemela Manaka. Johannesburg: Skotaville Press.

Biographical and Critical Studies

1962 Mphahlele, Ezekiel. *The African Image*. London: Faber; 2nd Edition, 1974.

1976 Barnett, Ursula A *Ezekiel Mphahlele*. Boston: Twayne.

1980 Christie, Sarah, Geoffrey Hutchings & Don Maclennan. 'Ezekiel Mphahlele: *Down Second Avenue* (1959).' In *Perspectives On South African Fiction*. Johannesburg: Ad Donker.

1981 Hodge, Norman. 'Dogs, Africans And Liberals: The World Of Mphahlele's 'Mrs Plum'.' *English In Africa* 8.1.

1983 Manganyi, N Chaban. *Exiles And Homecomings: A Biography Of Es'kia Mphahlele*. Johannesburg: Ravan Press.

1986 'The Way I Looked At Life Then: Es'kia Mphahlele's *Man Must Live And Other Stories*.' *English In Africa* 13. (See this issue for other articles on Es'kia Mphahlele.)

1986 'Es'kia Mphahlele: Interviews by Tim Couzens, Norman Hodge and Kate Turkington.' *English Academy Review* 4.'

1989 Thuynsma, Peter N (Ed.). *Footprints Along The Way*. Johannesburg: Justified Press & Skotaville Publishers.

Bibliography
1989 Woeber, Cathrine & John Read. *Es'kia Mphahlele: A Bibliography*. Grahamstown, South Africa: National English Literary Museum.

GENERAL

Abrahams, Peter. 1919. *Dark Testament*. London: G. Allen & Unwin.

Abrahams, Peter. 1952. *Path Of Thunder*. London: Faber & Faber.

Achebe, Chinua. 1958. *Things Fall Apart*. London: Heinemann.

Achebe, Chinua. 1964. *Arrow Of God*. London: Heinemann.

Achebe, Chinua. 1966. *A Man Of The People*. London: Heinemann.

Achebe, Chinua. 1973. '1966' In *Christmas In Biafra And Other Poems*. New York: Doubleday Anchor.

Achebe, Chinua. 1975. *Morning Yet On Creation Day: Essays*. New York: Anchor Press.

Achebe, Chinua. 1986. *No Longer At Ease*. Oxford: Heinemann.

Alexander, S. 1968. *Beauty And Other Forms Of Value*. New York: Thomas Y. Crowell Co., 1968.

Angira, Jared. 1972. *Silent Voices: Poems*. London: Heinemann.

Armah, Ayi K. 1968. *The Beautyful Ones Are Not Yet Born*. Boston: Houghton Mifflin Co.; Published in the African Writers Series London: Heinemann, 1969.

Armah, Ayi K. 1972. *Why Are We So Blest?* New York: Doubleday.

Asante, Molefi K. & Kariamu Welsh Asante (Eds.). 1985. *African Culture; The Rhythms Of Unity*, Westport, Greenwood Press.

Awoonor, Kofi. 1971. *Night Of My Blood*. New York: Doubleday & Co.

Awoonor, Kofi. 1971. *This Earth My Brother*. New York: Doubleday & Co.

Awoonor, Kofi. 1975. *The Breast Of The Earth*, Garden City: Anchor Press/Doubleday.

Baker Jr., Houston A. (Ed.) 1971. *Black Literature In America*. New York: McGraw Hill.

Baker Jr., Houston A. 1974. *Singers Of Daybreak: Studies In Black American Literature*. Washington DC: Howard UP.

Baker Jr., Houston A. 1984. *Blues, Ideology And Afro-American Literature: A Vernacular Theory*. Chicago, London: University of Chicago Press.

Baraka, Amiri. 1973. 'Black Art'. *Understanding The New Black Poetry*. Ed. Stephen Henderson. New York: William Morrow & Co.

Barnett, Ursula A. 1976. *Ezekiel Mphahlele*. Boston: Twayne.

Barnett, Ursula A. 1983. *Vision Of Order: A Study Of Black South African Literature In English (1914-1980)*. Cape Town: Maskew Miller Longman.

Barrett, Leonard. 1974. *Soul Force: African Heritage In Afro-American Religion*. New York: Anchor.

Beier, Ulli (Ed.). 1966. *The Origin Of Life And Death: African Creation Myths*. London: Heinemann.

Beier, Ulli (Ed.). 1967. *Introduction To African Literature*. Illinois: Northwestern UP.

Beier, Ulli (Ed.). 1971. *African Poetry*. Cambridge: Cambridge UP.

Beier, Ulli (Ed.). 1980. *Voices Of Independence: New Black Writing From Papua New Guinea*. Queensland: University Of Queensland Press.

Bell, Bernard W. (Ed.). 1972. *Modern And Contemporary Afro-American Poetry*. New York: Allyn & Bacon.

Berman, Edward H. (Ed.). 1975. *African Reactions To Missionary Education*. London: Teachers' College Press.

Blyden, Edward W. 1887. *Christianity, Islam And The Negro Race*. Edinburgh: UP.

Boetie, Dugmore. 1984. *Familiarity Is The Kingdom Of The Lost*. Ed. Barney Simon. London: Arrow Books.

Booth, Newell S. (Ed.). 1977. *African Religions: A Symposium*. London: Nok Publishers

Breytenbach, Breyten. 1980. *A Season In Paradise*. London: Jonathan Cape.

Brown, Lalage (Ed.). 1973. *Two Centuries Of African English*. London: Heinemann.

Brown, Lloyd. 1976. 'Cultural Norms And Modes Of Perception In Achebe's Fiction.' *Critical Perspectives On Nigerian Literatures*. Ed. Bernth Lindfors. Washington D.C.: Three Continents Press.

Brutus, Dennis. 1968. *Letters To Martha And Other Poems From A South African Prison*. London: Heinemann.

Brutus, Dennis. 1978. *Stubborn Hope: Selected Poems Of South Africa And A Wider World, Including China Poems*. London: Heinemann.

Caccia, Angela (Ed.). 1982 – 84. *The Beat Of Drum*. Johannesburg: Bailey.

Camus, Albert. 1953 [1951]. *The Rebel*. Trans. Anthony Bower. London: Hamish Hamilton.

Camus, Albert. 1974 [1960]. *Resistance, Rebellion, And Death*. Trans. Justin O'Brien. New York: Vintage Books.

Carim, Enver. *The Golden City*. (Publication details could not be located.)

Caudwell, Christopher. 1935. *Illusion And Reality*. London: Macmillan.

Caudwell, Christopher. 1958. *Studies In A Dying Culture*. New York: Dodd Mead.

Chalmers, J. A. 1877. *Tiyo Soga*. Edinburgh: Andrew Elliot.

Chapman, Abrahams (Ed.). 1968. *An Anthology Of Afro-American Literature.* New York, Toronto, London: The New American Library, The New English Library Ltd.

Chapman, Michael (Ed.). 1989. *The Drum Decade: Stories From The 1950s.* Pietermaritzburg: University Of Natal Press.

Clark, J P. 1965. *A Decade Of Tongues.* London: Longman.

Clark, J P. 1965. *A Reed In The Tide.* London: Longman.

Clark, J P. 1970. *Casualties: Poems 1966/68.* New York: Africana Publishing Corp.

Couzens, Tim. 1985. *The New African: A Study Of The Life And Works Of H. I. E. Dhlomo.* Johannesburg: Ravan Press.

Cruse, Harold. 1967. *The Crisis Of The Negro Intellectual From Its Origins To The Present.* New York: William Morrow & Co.

Davidson, Basil. 1969. *The African Genius.* Boston: Little, Brown.

De Unamuro, Miguel. 1962 [1921]. *The Tragic Sense Of Life.* London, Glasgow: Collins.

De Vries, J. Lukas. 1978. *Mission And Colonialism In Namibia.* Johannesburg: Ravan Press.

Dewey, John. 1958 [1934]. *Art As Experience.* New York: Capricorn Books.

Dhlomo, Herbert I E. 1941. *The Valley Of Thousand Hills.* Durban: Knox.

Dhlomo, Herbert I E. 1985. *Collected Works.* Johannesburg: Ravan Press.

Dhlomo, R R R. *The African Tragedy.* (Publication details could not be located.)

Dickinson, Margaret (Ed. & Trans.). 1974. *When Bullets Begin To Flower: Poems Of Resistance From Angola, Mozambique And Guiné.* Nairobi: East African Publishing House.

Diop, Cheik Anta. 1974. *The African Origin Of Civilization: Myth Or Reality.* Trans. Mercer Cook. Chicago, Lawrence Books.

DuBois, William E B. 1969 [1903] *The Souls Of Black Folk.* New York: Signet Classics.

Du Sautoy, Paulo. 1962. *The Organization Of A Community Development Programme.* (Publication details could not be located.)

Ekwensi, Cyprian. 1963 [1961]. *Jagua Nana.* London: Panther Books.

Engle, Shirley H. & Anna S. Ochoa. 1988. *Education For Democratic Citizenship.* New York: Teachers College Press, Columbia University.

Fanon, Franz. 1967. *Black Skin White Masks.* Trans. Charles Lam Markmann. New York. np.

Ferres, John H. & Martin Tucker. 1977. *Modern Commonwealth Literature: A Library Of Literary Criticism.* New York: Frederick Ungar. (Criticism on Aidoo, Awoonor, Brutus, Cope, Krige, Mofolo and Rive.)

Freire, Paulo. 1968. *Pedagogy Of The Oppressed.* np: Seabury.

Fromm, Erich. 1976. *To Have Or To Be?* Ed. Ruth N. Anshen. New York, Hagerstown, San Francisco, London: Harper & Row.

Gayle Jr., Adison. 1971. *The Black Aesthetic.* New York: Macmillan.

George Shepperson & Thomas Price. 1958. *Independent African.* Edinburgh: The Edinburh UP.

Gérard, Albert. 1981. *African Language Literatures.* London: Longman.

Gregory, James M. 1834. *Frederick Douglass, The Orator.* New York: Thomas Y. Crowell Co.

Hammond-Tooke, W. D. (Ed) 1974. *The Bantu-Speaking Peoples Of Southern Africa.* London: Routledge & Paul.

Henderson, Stephen (Ed.). 1973. *Understanding The New Black Poetry.* New York: William Morrow & Co.

Hodge, Norman. 1981. 'Dogs, Africans And Liberals: The World Of Mphahlele's 'Mrs Plum'.' *English In Africa* 8.1.

Hughes, Langston. *New Negro Poets USA.* (Publication details could not be found.).

Hughes, Langston. *Weary Blues.* (Publication details could not be located).

Ilogu, Edmund. 1974. *Christianity And Igbo Culture.* New York: Brill.

Jones, Leroi (alias Amiri Baraka). 1969. *Black Magic: Sabotage, Target Study, Black Art; Collected Poetry, 1961-1967.* Indianapolis: Bobbs Merrill.

Jordan, Archibald C. 1973. *Tales From Southern Africa.* Berkeley, Los Angeles, London: University Of California Press.

Jordan, Archibald C. 1973. *Towards An African Literature: The Emergence Of Literary Form In Xhosa.* Berkeley, Los Angeles, London: University Of California Press.

Jordan, Archibald. 1980 [1940]. *The Wrath Of The Ancestors.* Alice: Loveday Press.

Kalu, Ogbu U. (Ed.). 1978. *African Cultural Development.* Enugu: Four Dimension Publishers.

Kane, Cheikh H. 1972 [1963]. *Ambiguous Adventure.* London: Heinemann.

Kenyatta, Jomo. 1980 [1938] *Facing Mount Kenya.* London: Heinemann.

Kgositsile, Keoprapetse. 1974. *The Present Is A Dangerous Place To Live.* Chicago: Third World Press.

Knight, Etheridge. 1972. *For Black Poets Who Think Of Suicide.* Detroit, Michigan: Broadside Press.

Komey, Ellis A. (Ed.) 1964. *Modern African Stories.* London: Faber & Faber.

Krige, Uys (Ed.). 1968. *Olive Schreiner: A Selection.* Cape Town: Oxford UP.

Kunene, Daniel. 1971. *Heroic Poetry Of The Basotho.* London: Oxford UP.

Kunene, Mazisi. 1970. *Zulu Poems.* New York: Africana Publishing Corp.

Lamming, George. 1967. *The Pleasures Of Exile.* London: Oxford UP.

Lamont, Corliss. 1965 [1949]. *The Philosophy Of Humanism, 5th Edition.* London: Barrie & Rockliff, in association with The Pemberton Publishing Co.

Lanham, Peter & A S. Mopeli-Paulus. 1984 [1953]. *Blanket Boy's Moon.* Cape Town: David Philip.

Laye, Camara. 1959 [1954]. *The Radiance Of The King.* Trans. James Kirkup. London, Glasgow: Fontana Books.

Lee, Don L. 1968. *Black Pride.* Detroit, Michigan: Broadside Press.

Lee, Don L. 1968. *Don't Cry, Scream.* Detroit, Michigan: Broadside Press.

Locke, Alain. *Black Voices.* (Publication details could not be located.)

Lukács, Georg. 1962. *The Historical Novel.* Trans. Hannah and Stanley Mitchell. London: Merlin Press.

Major, Clarence (Ed.). 1970. *The New Black Poetry.* New York: International Publishers.

Manganyi, N. C. 1981. *Looking Through The Keyhole.* Johannesburg: Ravan Press.

Manganyi, N. Chabane. 1983. *Exiles And Homecomings: A Biography Of Es'kia Mphahlele.* Johannesburg: Ravan Press.

Margolies, David N. 1969. *The Function Of Literature: A Study Of Christopher Caudwell's Aesthetics.* New York: International Publishers.

Mashabela, Harry. 1987. *A People On The Boil.* Johannesburg: Skotaville Publishers.

Mason, Phillip. 1962. *Prospero's Magic.* Oxford: Oxford UP.

Matshikiza, Todd. 1982 [1961]. *Chocolates For My Wife.* Cape Town: David Philip.

Matshoba, Mtutuzeli. 1981. *Seeds Of War.* Johannesburg: Ravan Press.

Matthews, James. 1983. *The Park And Other Stories.* Johannesburg: Ravan Press.

Matthews, Z. K. 1983. *Freedom For My People.* Cape Town: David Philip.

Mazrui, Ali. 1986. *The Africans: A Triple Heritage.* Boston: Little, Brown & Co.

Mbiti, John S. 1969. *African Religions And Philosophy.* London: Heinemann.

Mda, Zakes. 1980. *We Shall Sing For The Fatherland And Other Plays.* Johannesburg: Ravan Press.

Modisane, Bloke. 1986 [1963]. *Blame Me On History.* Johannesburg: Ad. Donker.

Mofolo, Thomas. 1907. *Moeti Oa Bochabela.* Morija: Morija Sesuto Book Depot.

Mofolo, Thomas. 1981 [1925]. *Chaka.* London: Heinemann.

Motsisi, Casey. 1973. 'The Efficacy Of Prayer'. *To Whom It May Concern.* Ed. Robert Royston. Johannesburg: Ad. Donker.

Motsisi, Casey. 1978. *Casey And Company: Selected Writings.* Johannesburg: Ravan Press.

Mqhayi, Samuel E K. 1947. *Ityala Lamawele.* Loveday: Loveday Press.

Mtshali, Oswald J. 1971. *Sounds Of A Cowhide Drum.* Johannesburg: Renoster Books.

Murphy, E Jefferson. 1972. *History Of African Civilization.* New York: Dell Publishing Co.

Nakasa, Nat. 1975. *The World Of Nat Nakasa.* Johannesburg: Ravan Press.

Nehru, Pandit Jawaharlal. 1964. *The Discovery Of India.* Bombay: Asia Publishing House.

Newman, John H C. 1922. 'The Idea Of A University.' *Discourse Versus Knowledge For Its Own End.* Ed. C. F. Harrold. New York: Macmillan.

Ngugi, James. 1967. *A Grain Of Wheat.* London: Heinemann.

Nortjé, Arthur. 1973. *Dead Roots.* London: Heinemann.

Noss, John B. 1956. *Man's Religions.* New York, London: Macmillan.

Nyquist, Thomas E. 1983. *African Middle Class Elite.* Occasional Paper No. 28, Institute Of Social & Economic Research, Rhodes University, Grahamstown.

Okigbo, Christopher. 1971. *Labyrinths.* New York: African Publishing Corp, with Mbari Publications.

Ortega y Gasset, José. 1925. *The Dehumanization Of Art.* Princeton: Princeton UP.

Ouologuem, Yambo. nd. *Bound To Violence.* (Publication details could not be located.)

Oyono, Ferdinand. 1956. *The Old Man And The Medal.* Paris: Julliard.

Oyono, Ferdinand. 1966 [1960]. *Houseboy.* Trans. John Reed. London: Heinemann.

p'Bitek, Okot. 1966. *Song Of Lawino.* Nairobi: East African Publishing House.

p'Bitek, Okot. 1971. *Song Of A Prisoner.* New York: The Third Press.

Park, Frank Kobina. 1965. 'Blackman's God.' *Songs From The Wilderness.* London: University Of London Press.

Paton, Alan. 1948. *Cry The Beloved Country: A Story Of Comfort In Desolation.* New York: Scribner's Sons.

Paton, Alan. 1953. *Too Late The Phalarope.* London: Jonathan Cape.

Peters, Lenrie. 1965. *The Second Round.* London: Heinemann.

Peters, Lenrie. 1967. *Satellites.* London: Heinemann.

Peters, Lenrie. 1971. *Katchikali.* London, Ibadan, Nairobi: Heinemann.

Plaatje, Sol. 1978 [1930]. *Mhudi.* London: Heinemann.

Plaatje, Sol. 1982 [1916]. *Native Life In South Africa Before And Since The European War And The Boer Rebellion.* Johannesburg: Ravan Press.

Plomer, William. 1965. *Turbott Wolfe.* London: The Hogarth Press.

Popkin, Michael (Ed.). 1978. *Modern Black Writers.* New York: Frederick Ungar. (Criticism on Aidoo, Awoonor, Baraka, Brutus, Dadié, Kunene and Plaatje.)

Radhakrishnan, Sarvepalli & J H Muirhead (Eds.). 1952. *Contemporary Indian Philosophy.* London: Allen & Unwin.

Radhakrishnan, Sarvepalli. 1961. *A Tagore Reader.* New York: Macmillan.

Richter, Peter E. (Ed.). 1967. *Perspectives In Aesthetics: Plato To Camus.* New York: The Odyssey Press, Inc.

Rive, Richard. 1988 [1964]. *Emergency.* Cape Town: David Philip.

Robinson, William H. 1975. 'Phillis Wheatley.' *The Black Detroit.* Detroit, Michigan: Broadside Press.

Roux, Edward. 1964. *Time Longer Than Rope.* Madison: The University Of Wisconsin Press.

Sanchez, Sonia. 1970. *We A Baddddd People.* Detroit, Michigan: Broadside Press.

Sankange, Stanley. 1966. *On Trial For My Country.* London: Heinemann.

Schadeburg, Jurgen (Ed.). 1987. *The Fifties People Of South Africa.* Johannesburg: J. R. A. Bailey.

Scruton, Roger. 1982. *A Dictionary Of Political Thought.* London: Pan Books, in association with Macmillan Press.

Sembene, Ousmane. 1970. *God's Bits Of Wood.* Trans. Francis Price. London, Ibadan, Nairobi: Heinemann, 1970.

Senghor, Léopold Sedar. 1964. *Selected Poems.* Trans. John Reed & Clive Wake. Oxford: Oxford UP.

Sepamla, Sipho. 1982. 'Song Of Mother And Child' and 'Soweto'. In *Voices From Within.* Ed. Michael Chapman & Achmat Dangor. Johannesburg: Ad. Donker.

Serote, Mongane W. 1975. *No Baby Must Weep.* Johannesburg: Ad. Donker.

Serote, Mongane W. 1982 [1978]. *Poems.* Johannesburg: Ad. Donker.

Serote, Mongane. 1981. 'Time Has Run Out.' In *Reconstruction.* Ed. Mothobi Mutloatse. Johannesburg: Ravan Press.

Shakespeare, William. 1956. *Prospero And Caliban.* London: Methuen & Co. Ltd.

Shakespeare, William. 1976. *The Tempest.* Cape Town: Maskew Miller.

Shelly, Percy Bysshe. nd. 'Prometheus Unbound.' In *John Keats And Percy Bysshe Shelley*: Complete Poetical Works. New York: Random House.

Soyinka, Wole. 1964. *Five Plays.* London: Oxford UP.

Soyinka, Wole. 1967. *Kongi's Harvest.* Oxford: Oxford UP.

Soyinka, Wole. 1969. *The Swamp Dwellers.* London: Oxford UP.

Soyinka, Wole. 1972. 'Flowers For My Land.' *A Shuttle In The Crypt.* London: Collings, Hill & Wang.

Soyinka, Wole. 1972. *The Man Died.* New York, Evanston, San Francisco, London: Harper & Row.

Soyinka, Wole. 1975. *Death And The King's Horseman.* New York: W W Norton & Co.

Spicer, Edward H. (Ed.). 1952. *Human Problems In Technological Change.* New York: Russell Sage Foundation.

Tabori, Paulo. 1972. *The Anatomy Of Exile.* London: Harrap.

Tagore, Rabindranath & L. K. Elmherst. 1961. *Rabindranath Tagore: Pioneer In Education.* London: Murray.

Tagore, Rabindranath. 1913. *Towards Universal Man.* London: Macmillan & Co.

Tagore, Rabindranath. 1929. *The Religion Of Man.* London: Allen & Unwin.

Tagore, Rabindranath. 1964. *Sadhana.* London: Macmillan.

Tagore, Rabindranath. nd. *Essays: The Housewarming And Other Writings.* Ed. Amuja Chakravaty. New York: New American Library.

Themba, Can. 1972. *The Will To Die.* Comp. Roya Harrold & Donald Stuart. London: Heinemann.

Themba, Can. 1985. *The World Of Can Themba.* Johannesburg: Ravan Press.

Thuynsma, Peter N. (Ed.). 1989. *Footprints Along The Way.* Johannesburg: Justified Press & Skotaville Publishers.

Trask, Willard R. (Ed.). 1966. *The Unwritten Song 1.* New York: Macmillan.

Trask, Willard R. (Ed.). 1967. *The Unwritten Song: Poetry Of The Primitive And Traditional Peoples Of The World.* New York, London: Macmillan,. Collier-Macmillan.

Turnbull, Colin. 1976. *Man In Africa.* London: David & Charles.

Van der Post, Laurens. 1953. *In A Province.* London: Hogarth Press.

Washington, Booker T. 1901. *Up From Slavery.* Garden City, New York: Doubleday.

Wa Thiong'o, Ngugi. 1965. *The River Between.* London: Heinemann.

472

Wa Thiong'o, Ngugi. 1972. 'The Writer In A Changing Society.' *Homecoming*. Westport: Lawrence Hill & Co.

Weiss, M. Jerry. 1970. *Man To Himself*. Jersey City: Cummings Publishing Co.

White, Landeg & Tim Couzens (Eds.). 1984. *Literature And Society In South Africa*. Cape Town: Maskew Miller Longman.

Williams, Donovan (Ed.). 1983. *The Journal And Selected Writings Of The Reverend Tiyo Soga*. Cape Town: A A Balkema.

Wright, Richard. 1936. *Uncle Tom's Children*. New York: Harper & Row.

Zwelonke, D. M. 1973. *Robben Island*. London: Heinemann.

Index: General

Index: People